Humanistic Psychotherapies

Humanistic Psychotherapies

Handbook of Research and Practice

David J. Cain, Editor
Julius Seeman, Associate Editor

American Psychological Association
Washington, DC

Published by
American Psychological Association
750 First Street, NE
Washington, DC 20002
www.apa.org

To order
APA Order Department
P.O. Box 92984
Washington, DC 20090-2984
Tel: (800) 374-2721,
    Direct: (202) 336-5510
Fax: (202) 336-5502,
    TDD/TTY: (202) 336-6123
Online: www.apa.org/books/
Email: order@apa.org

In the U.K., Europe, Africa, and the
    Middle East, copies may be ordered
    from
American Psychological Association
3 Henrietta Street
Covent Garden, London
WC2E 8LU England

Typeset in Goudy by World Composition Services, Inc., Sterling, VA

Printer: United Book Press, Inc., Baltimore, MD
Cover designer: NiDesign, Baltimore, MD
Technical/Production Editor: Emily I. Welsh

The opinions and statements published are the responsibility of the authors, and such
opinions and statements do not necessarily represent the policies of the American
Psychological Association.

Library of Congress Cataloging-in-Publication Data
Humanistic psychotherapies : handbook of research and practice / edited by David J.
Cain and Julius Seeman. — 1st ed.
    p. cm.
Includes bibliographical references and index.
ISBN 1-55798-787-4 (alk. paper)
1. Humanistic psychotherapy. I. Cain, David J. II. Seeman, Julius, 1915–
RC480.H83   2001
616.89′14—dc21

2001022916

British Library Cataloguing-in-Publication Data
A CIP record is available from the British Library.

Printed in the United States of America
First Edition

*To Carl Rogers and the Brooklyn Dodgers—both pioneers
in their own way—and to our clients, who taught us that our
humanity and faith in them, not our methods, made the difference*

David J. Cain

*To all of the humanistic psychologists who paved the way
for the enduring human movement reflected in this book*

Julius Seeman

CONTENTS

CONTRIBUTORS

Michael P. Accordino, DEd, CRC, is an assistant professor in the Rehabilitation and Disability Services Department, Springfield College, Springfield, Massachusetts. He is certified as a relationship enhancement (RE) couples therapist and program leader. Dr. Accordino has published articles pertaining to RE training in community mental health and prison settings.

Ted P. Asay, PhD, is a clinical psychologist in private practice and a research associate at the Timberlawn Psychiatric Research Foundation in Dallas, TX. Dr. Asay received his doctoral degree in clinical psychology from Brigham Young University and later completed a postdoctoral fellowship at Timberlawn Psychiatric Hospital. He has written and presented on various topics related to treatment outcome.

Christine Boisvert received her PhD in clinical psychology from the University of Ottawa, Ottawa, Canada, in 1999. During her clinical internship, Dr. Boisvert specialized in working with families and children. She also worked under the supervision of Susan Johnson, doing emotionally focused therapy with couples. Currently, Dr. Boisvert is employed at Children's Mental Health Centre in Ottawa, Canada, where she works with adolescents who have severe emotional and behavioral problems.

Sue Carlton Bratton, PhD, LPC, RPT-S, is an assistant professor in the Counseling Department at the University of North Texas (UNT) and clinical director at the UNT Child and Family Resource Clinic. Dr. Bratton is respected nationally and internationally as a lecturer, consultant, author, and clinician with extensive experience in play therapy and filial/family therapy. Dr. Bratton is president-elect of the International Association for Play Therapy and is coauthor of *The World of Play Therapy Literature*.

Jerold D. Bozarth, PhD, is professor emeritus of the University of Georgia, where his tenure included that of chair of the Department of Counseling and Human Development and Counseling Psychology. He was also director of the Person-Centered Studies Program. He is founder and senior fellow of Person-Centered International, a nonprofit organization that promotes person-centered principles. He is the author of *Person-Centered Therapy: A Revolutionary Paradigm*.

David J. Cain, PhD, ABPP, received his doctorate in clinical and community psychology from the University of Wyoming. He is director of the Counseling Center at United States International University and adjunct faculty in the Department of Psychology at Chapman University. He is the founder of the Association for the Development of the Person-Centered Approach and was the founder and editor of the *Person-Centered Review*. He is a fellow in clinical psychology of the American Board of Professional Psychology, is a member of the National Register of Certified Group Therapists, and serves on the editorial boards of the *Journal of Humanistic Psychology* and the *Humanistic Psychologist*.

Robert Elliott, PhD, is a professor of psychology and director of clinical training at the University of Toledo, where he also directs the Center for the Study of Experiential Psychotherapy. He has served as coeditor of *Psychotherapy Research* and as president of the Society for Psychotherapy Research. He is a fellow of the Division of Humanistic Psychology of the American Psychological Association and serves on the board of the new World Association for Person-Centered and Experiential Psychotherapy and Counseling. He is coauthor of *Facilitating Emotional Change* and *Research Methods for Clinical and Counselling Psychology* and the author or coauthor of more than 70 other publications.

Rhonda Goldman received her PhD in clinical psychology from York University, Toronto, Ontario, Canada, in 1997. She is currently a professor at the Illinois School of Professional Psychology, Meadows Campus. She has written a number of articles and chapters with colleagues on topics such as case formulation in experiential therapy, empathy, and the practice of emotionally focused treatments for depression. She recently completed a research project looking at the effectiveness of two types of humanistic/experiential treatments for depression.

David M. Gonzalez, PhD, is a professor and director of training of counseling psychology at the University of Northern Colorado. He received his doctorate from the University of Colorado, Boulder, and is a licensed psychologist. He coauthored *Helping Relationships:*

Basic Concepts for the Helping Professions with Art Combs and coauthored *The Process of Counseling and Psychotherapy* with I. David Welch.

Leslie S. Greenberg, PhD, is a professor of psychology and director of the psychotherapy research clinic at York University, Toronto, Ontario, Canada. He has published a number of books and research papers on an emotion-focused approach to individual and couple psychotherapy. His practice includes individuals and couples and the training of therapists.

Bernard G. Guerney, Jr., PhD, director of the National Institute of Relationship Enhancement in Bethesda, Maryland, has won several awards from national professional organizations for his work in couples/family enrichment and therapy. Nationally and abroad, he oversees the training, supervision, and certification of Relationship Enhancement® therapists and does workshops and live therapy demonstrations.

Marion N. Hendricks, PhD, is a clinical psychologist in New York City and the director of The Focusing Institute, which received the Charlotte Buhler Award from the Humanistic Division of the American Psychological Association in August 2000. She lectures and presents workshops internationally and supervises the 2-year therapist training programs for the institute. She was a core faculty member for 10 years at the Illinois School for Professional Psychology. She has published articles on focusing-oriented experiential psychotherapy.

Susan Johnson, PhD, is a professor of psychology and psychiatry at the University of Ottawa, Ottawa, Canada. She is also the director of the Ottawa Couple and Family Institute. She is the main proponent of emotionally focused interventions for couples and families and presents internationally on couples therapy, adult attachment, emotion in psychotherapy, and working with traumatized couples. She is the author of *The Practice of Emotionally Focused Marital Therapy: Creating Connection*. She is the recipient of the American Association of Marriage and Family Therapy award for Outstanding Contribution to the Field for the year 2000.

Lorne M. Korman received his PhD in clinical psychology from York University, Toronto, Ontario, Canada. He is a psychologist in supervised practice in the Concurrent Disorders Program at the Centre for Addiction and Mental Health in Toronto and assistant professor of psychiatry at the University of Toronto.

Michael J. Lambert, PhD, is a professor of psychology at Brigham Young University in the Clinical Psychology Graduate Program. He is currently an associate editor of the *Journal of Consulting and Clinical*

Psychology and the editor of *Psychotherapy and Patient Relationships*. He has conducted research on the effects of common factors on therapy outcome and the effects of providing therapists with feedback based on patient response to treatment.

Germain Lietaer, PhD, is a professor at the Department of Psychology, Catholic University of Leuven (Belgium). He teaches client-centered/experiential psychotherapy and process research in psychotherapy and is a staff member of a 3-year part-time postgraduate training program in client-centered/experiential psychotherapy at the same university. He is chief editor (with J. Rombauts and R. Van Balen) of *Client-Centered and Experiential Psychotherapy in the Nineties* and coeditor (with Leslie S. Greenberg and Jeanne C. Watson) of the *Handbook of Experiential Psychotherapy*.

Brian McElwain, MA, is a doctoral student in clinical psychology at Duquesne University. His dissertation research focuses on the meanings of race in the experiences of interracially married couples. In July 2000, he completed his predoctoral internship at Miami University's Student Counseling Service. He is currently a visiting instructor at Miami University, teaching courses on cultural diversity.

Richard C. Page, PhD, is a professor in the Department of Counseling and Human Development Services, University of Georgia. He wrote a book with Daniel N. Berkow titled *Creating Contact, Choosing Relationship: Dynamics of Unstructured Group Therapy*. He has published over 80 articles in refereed, professional journals and published numerous book chapters and other kinds of publications. Dr. Page has research interests in humanistic group therapy, drug abuse counseling, and international comparisons among the cultures of different countries. Dr. Page has done training in many countries in the area of unstructured group therapy.

Sandra C. Paivio received her MEd in counseling from the University of Western Ontario, London, Ontario, Canada, and her PhD in clinical psychology from York University, Toronto, Ontario, Canada. She is currently on the clinical faculty at University of Windsor, Windsor, Ontario, Canada, where she teaches graduate courses in research methods and experiential psychotherapy. Her current research interests are in the areas of psychotherapy process and outcome, emotional processes, and trauma.

Garry Prouty, PhD, is the originator of pretherapy and presymbolic experiencing and the author of *Theoretical Evolutions in Person-Centered/Experiential Therapy: Applications to Schizophrenics and Retarded Psychoses* and coauthor of *Pra-Therapie* (German language).

He has lectured to universities, clinics, and client-centered training organizations and established hospital programs in Europe. Currently, he is an editorial advisor to several European journals and is a fellow of the Chicago Counseling, Psychotherapy and Research Center.

William Watson Purkey, EdD, is a professor of counselor education in the School of Education, University of North Carolina at Greensboro. He is an active writer, lecturer, researcher, and author or coauthor of over 80 professional articles and nine books, including *Invitational Counseling: A Self-Concept Approach to Professional Practices* (with John J. Schmidt). His latest book is *What Students Say to Themselves: Internal Dialogue and School Success*. Dr. Purkey's interest is in inviting people to realize their potential.

Dee Ray, PhD, LPC, NCC, RPT-S, received her doctorate from the University of North Texas with a specialty in child counseling and play therapy. She has published and presented nationally on play therapy and play therapy research. She has also worked in the field as an elementary school counselor and clinical therapist for disturbed children. Dr. Ray is currently assistant professor of counseling at Texas A&M University–Commerce.

David L. Rennie, PhD, is a professor of psychology at York University, Toronto, Ontario, Canada. His research interests are in qualitative research methodology and its application to the study of the experience of psychotherapy. He teaches and practices psychotherapy within a humanistic orientation. He is the author of *Person-Centred Counselling: An Experiential Approach* and is coeditor of *Psychotherapy Process Research: Paradigmatic and Narrative Approaches* and *Qualitative Psychotherapy Research: Methods and Methodology* (forthcoming).

Rainer Sachse, PhD, studied psychology at Ruhr-Universität Bochum, Germany, from 1969 to 1978 and earned his doctorate in 1985. He worked in a psychological institute in Dortmund from 1978 to 1980. Since 1980, he has been an academic assistant at Ruhr-Universität Bochum. In 1989–1990, he held a lectureship at the Reichsuniversität of Gent, Belgium. His postdoctoral qualification was attained in 1991. Since 1997, he has been professor of clinical psychology and psychotherapy at the Psychological Department of Ruhr-Universität Bochum. The focus of his work is on clinical psychology, client-centered psychotherapy, and behavioral therapy.

Julius Seeman received his PhD in counseling in 1948 from the University of Minnesota. His first position was at the University of Chicago Counseling Center, where Carl Rogers was director. He was coordinator of research during the center's first funded study of psychotherapy outcomes. The challenge of deriving theory-based empirical outcome criteria so fascinated him that he devoted most of his subsequent research career at Peabody College to this task. A significant part of his research has focused on developing empirical definitions of the "fully functioning person." Presently he is professor emeritus at Peabody College of Vanderbilt University. He is currently doing consultation and psychotherapy. He is the author of *Personality Integration*.

Paula Helen Stanley, PhD, is an associate professor of counseling and development at Radford University and assistant director of the Radford University Honors Academy. Her areas of specialty include group counseling, internal dialogue of counselor trainees, and counseling with adolescents and young adults. She is a licensed professional counselor and licensed marriage and family therapist in Virginia. She has authored or coauthored two books and over 30 articles in professional publications.

William B. Stiles, PhD, is a professor of psychology at Miami University in Oxford, Ohio. He taught previously at the University of North Carolina at Chapel Hill and held visiting positions at the University of Sheffield and University of Leeds (U.K.), the University of Joensuu (Finland), and Massey University (New Zealand). He is the author of *Describing Talk: A Taxonomy of Verbal Response Modes*, past president of the Society for Psychotherapy Research, and currently North American editor of the journal *Psychotherapy Research*.

Uwe Strümpfel received his PhD in experimental research in cognitive/clinical psychology. His work and publications are in the areas of terminal diseases (AIDS/HIV and multiple sclerosis), crack dependents, and street children in Sao Paulo, Brazil. He founded a research group in the German Association of Gestalt Therapy in 1989 and was psychological director of the Psychosomatic Clinic for Substance Dependents, Center II, Berlin, Germany. He has been in private practice since 1996.

Reinhard Tausch, PhD, is a professor of clinical and educational psychology at the University of Hamburg, Psychological Institute 111, Germany. He and his wife, Anne-Marie Tausch, conducted empirical research on client-centered therapy with 950 patients and also on the effects of the person-centered approach in education. Dr. Tausch has chaired 28 doctoral dissertations and 112 master's theses in these areas.

Russell A. Walsh obtained his PhD in clinical psychology from the University of New Mexico and is currently an associate professor and chair of the Department of Psychology at Duquesne University.

His research used hermeneutic methods to identify client, therapist, and researcher values with respect to psychotherapy processes. He has published several articles addressing the role of interpretation in psychotherapy and psychological research.

Jeanne C. Watson, PhD, is an assistant professor in the Department of Adult Education, Community Development and Counselling Psychology at the University of Toronto, Toronto, Ontario, Canada. She is coauthor (with Eileen Kennedy-Moore) of *Expressing Emotion: Myths, Realities and Therapeutic Strategies* and coeditor (with Leslie S. Greenberg and Germain Lietaer) of the *Handbook of Experiential Psychotherapy*. Dr. Watson has written numerous articles and chapters on psychotherapy process and outcome and has a part-time private practice in Toronto.

James F. Weiss, PhD, received his doctorate in counseling psychology from the Department of Counseling and Human Development Services, the University of Georgia, Athens. He also holds master's degrees in counselor education from Wake Forest University, Winston-Salem, North Carolina, and in theology from Christ the King Seminary, East Aurora, New York.

Fred M. Zimring, PhD (deceased), was professor of psychology and director of clinical training at Case Western Reserve University. He focused on the reasons that changes occur in client-centered therapy, including the investigation of ways that client-centered therapy alters the self phases of clients.

PREFACE

Carl Rogers and other humanistic psychotherapists revolutionized the way psychotherapy was conceptualized and practiced. Rogers taught therapists to listen and demonstrated the profound impact that the therapist's attitudes, personal qualities, and manner of relating have on clients' capacity to tap their resources for constructive change. Laura and Frederick Perls showed that clients' immediate awareness of their experience in the context of an I–thou encounter with the therapist enables them to live authentically in the moment. Existential therapists taught clients to address fundamental life issues such as freedom–choice–responsibility, meaning, death, and isolation and to challenge their manner of living while encouraging them to live full and meaningful lives. Experientially oriented humanistic therapists recognized the profound importance of clients' emotional and bodily lives and pointed the way to help clients to value, attend to, process, and learn from their emotional experiences. In short, some of the most creative and powerful means of engaging in the therapeutic process have been developed by humanistic psychotherapists.

Given the enormous contributions of the humanistic approach to the field of psychotherapy, one would expect that humanistic therapists would be strongly represented among practitioners. Yet this is not the case. We remain a relative minority in the field of psychotherapy. I have been concerned and puzzled for many years that there are relatively few humanistic psychologists and psychotherapists. Roughly 10% of practitioners in the United States identify themselves as humanistic. I wondered why this was, especially because humanistic approaches in psychology and psychotherapy have made an enormous contribution to the well-being of individuals, couples, families, groups, organizations, social causes, and even conflicting countries.

Out of my concern for our minority status in the field of psychotherapy, I gave considerable thought as to what I could do to increase our numbers and impact. Like many other humanistic psychologists, I engaged in a number of activities that I hoped might make a difference. I founded and edited the *Person-Centered Review*, founded the Association for the Development of the Person-Centered Approach, presented papers and workshops at national and international conferences, and edited and wrote articles for publication. I have spent more than 25 years of my professional life teaching and training a variety of mental health practitioners in humanistic theory, research, and practice, only to find that many of the graduate students to whom I taught humanistic approaches eventually became practitioners of other schools of psychotherapy. This scenario was also commonly reported by my humanistic colleagues, many of whose efforts and contributions have been much greater than mine. Although our efforts did make a difference, the impact remained modest. This perplexed me because almost all of the students I trained or supervised in humanistic approaches readily embraced the fundamental importance of the therapeutic relationship and empathy to the client's progress. Humanistic therapy looked like what graduate students imagined therapy should be: a relationship in which a sensitive, understanding, caring, supportive, and authentic person engaged in a personal encounter with the client in a manner that facilitated personal discovery and learning. Yet, many of these graduate students would eventually embrace cognitive or cognitive–behavioral therapy or some of the "brief" or "strategic" approaches emphasizing therapist technique and wizardry.

On reflection, a number of factors accounting for this phenomenon became apparent. First, many students were influenced by the current therapeutic zeitgeist with its emphasis on diagnosis, treatment planning, and rapid remediation of clients' symptoms. Some acknowledged their concern that, with the limited sessions likely to be allotted to them through managed care, they needed to learn more rapid and direct methods than humanistic therapies seemed to offer. And, of course, their other professors made it clear that they needed to master *Diagnostic and Statistical Manual of Mental Disorders* (American Psychiatric Association, 1994)[1] diagnosis and to develop highly specific treatment plans to treat their clients' symptoms. In other words, they were becoming technicians, trained to use a medical model of psychopathology and treatment. In addition, passing departmental written and oral comprehensive exams and state licensing exams essentially required them to demonstrate their competency in using a medical model. Consequently, most students

---

[1] American Psychiatric Association. (1994). Diagnostic and statistical manual of mental disorders (4th ed.). Washington, DC: Author.

pursued a practical course of action that would enable them to become licensed practitioners.

It has also become clear to me that part of the problem is that my humanistic colleagues and I remain underrepresented and outnumbered in our university departments. Graduate students generally choose as their orientation either the prevailing orientation in the department or that of their primary supervisor. Thus, in the few universities with a predominantly humanistic orientation in psychology, graduate students usually became humanistic psychologists and therapists. Unfortunately, humanistic approaches to psychotherapy continue to be underrepresented in university clinical and counseling psychology training programs despite the strong clinical and research evidence supporting its effectiveness. Therefore, it is essential that humanistic psychologists increase their presence in university clinical and counseling training programs. To increase our presence, we need to seek out and attain such teaching and training positions. This has not been easy because humanistic psychology and therapy are not currently in vogue, although there are signs that this is changing. Furthermore, the reputation of humanistic psychologists has been damaged by the questionable practices and antischolarly attitudes during the mid-1960s to mid-1970s of some of those who identified themselves as humanistic. Despite the impeccable ethical and professional practices characteristic of current humanistic therapists, our reputation has not been fully restored in the eyes of mainstream psychology. Our earlier tradition of scholarship and research represented by such giants as Carl Rogers, Abraham Maslow, Gordon Allport, Rollo May, Virginia Satir, Kurt Goldstein, Clark Moustakas, James Bugental, and Authur Combs, to name some of the most prominent contributors, needs to be carried forward.

If we are to move forward, we need to embrace fully our tradition of rigorous scholarship and practice based on sound theory and research. To some degree, we are already doing so, but not in great enough numbers. The best way for humanistic psychologists to make a greater impact on the practice of psychotherapy is to conduct more research that constantly refines its methods and improves its efficacy. The good news is that, over the past 60 years, practitioners and scientists have indeed generated substantial research evidence supporting effectiveness of humanistic therapies. However, much of this research is unknown to university faculty, clinical practitioners, graduate students, clients, or the general public. This situation inspired me to create the present volume, *Humanistic Psychotherapies: Handbook of Research and Practice*. I believe that such a book will raise consciousness among university faculty, including psychotherapy researchers and practitioners, about the substantive contributions of humanistic psychotherapies. Only by increasing our presence and impact in the academic community will we have an opportunity to train the next generations of humanistic therapists.

THE FACTS ARE FRIENDLY

Humanistic psychotherapists have cause for optimism. Sixty years of development in theory, practice, and research have demonstrated that humanistic approaches to psychotherapy are as effective or more effective than other major therapies. Substantive advances in theory and refinements in practice have been taking place over the past 25 years. Unless one is a student of systems of psychotherapy, one is likely to be surprised by the ways in which humanistic therapies have evolved. Significant research results, through both natural and human science efforts, have accumulated in the past few decades that support the effectiveness of all major modalities of humanistic therapies for a wide range of personal problems.

As mentioned earlier, my primary motive for the creation of this handbook is to restore and enhance the presence and impact of humanistic psychotherapy in universities. Toward this end, it was desirable and necessary to gather together in one volume the research on humanistic psychotherapies because there was no such text available. Nor was there a text that provided guidelines for therapeutic practice based on the research. Thus, the present volume is intended to provide state-of-the-art information regarding the current status of research and practice in the major approaches to humanistic psychotherapy.

Second, in this day of eclecticism in the field of psychotherapy, most practitioners select what they find to be the most useful concepts and therapeutic methods from a variety of therapeutic approaches. Although much of humanistic therapeutic practice, especially Carl Rogers's contributions, has been incorporated into the training of therapists with widely different approaches, many of its distinctive strengths are still not fully known or appreciated. These include (a) its strong research evidence confirming the impact of an optimal therapeutic relationship on successful client outcome; (b) the refinement of a variety of empathic response methods; (c) the development of innovative and sophisticated methods to work with an increasingly difficult, diverse, and complex range of individuals, couples, families, and groups; and (d) the substantiation of the profound importance of emotion in human functioning along with groundbreaking methods of working therapeutically with client emotion. The contributions of humanistic therapies to practice are valuable to all therapists and can be integrated into their preferred style of working. The larger goal is to enable all therapists to provide optimally effective treatment for their clients.

Third, there is a trend in the field of clinical psychology that seems desirable yet problematic: the establishment of "empirically supported treatments" set forth by the American Psychological Association's Division 12 Science and Practice Committee. Although efforts at identifying effective treatments for clients experiencing various forms of psychopathology should be applauded, I am concerned about significant limitations in the approach taken by the Division 12 Science and Practice Committee. The criteria used for defining client psychopathology are quite narrow and, consequently, unrepresentative of the typical client who seeks help for a more varied and complex cluster of problems. Treatments provided are manualized; consequently, therapists are constrained in their ability to respond with adaptivity, spontaneity, and variability when clients require it. Furthermore, there appears to be a strong bias toward treatments that embrace a medical model of psychopathology that focuses on remediation of symptoms using means that emphasize therapist technology. The emphasis on therapist technique runs counter to the preponderance of research on psychotherapy that indicates that the quality of the therapeutic relationship is the strongest predictor of successful client outcome. Although humanistic approaches are not ruled out, the criteria used do not favor therapies that are primarily relational, holistic, discovery oriented, and client directed. Another problem with the empirically supported research studies is that they favor natural science research methods over human science methods that are more appropriate in exploring and understanding clients' subjective realities.

Furthermore, there is the horrific possibility that a few defined therapeutic treatments will be identified as the primary ones that practitioners are expected to provide for their clients. Worse yet is the possibility that only these treatments would be reimbursed by health insurance. The strong evidence that the major established forms of psychotherapy are roughly equivalent in their effectiveness seems to be disregarded or ignored in the search for empirically supported treatments. In addition, the possibility of narrowing the training of graduate students in psychology and counseling to a few "valid" therapeutic approaches should be of concern to all in the helping profession. A plethora of texts purporting to articulate what therapeutic treatments work best for specific problems have also been published in recent years. Although such texts and the Division 12 Science and Practice Committee may have as their goal the provision of sound treatments for those in need, they also have the potential to limit freedom of choice in consumers. This dubious situation could occur because many effective therapeutic approaches have not yet been researched sufficiently, if at all, to establish their credibility. Lack of evidence does not mean a treatment is ineffective. It simply means that it has not been proven effective by somewhat narrowly defined research standards. Ideally, all approaches to psychotherapy, including humanistic, will be constantly evaluated and refined, thus providing the consumer a variety of sound options from which to choose. Furthermore, because the practice of psychotherapy is evolving, inevitably many innovative and effective methods of treating a variety of forms of psychological distress have not yet been developed, much less tested. As is well known, creative approaches to psychotherapy are first developed by practitioners "in the trenches," not by researchers. We can ill afford to stifle creativity when there is so much yet to be learned.

A fourth reason for this book is to expose graduate students in clinical and counseling psychology and related fields to a variety of humanistic approaches. In recent decades, there have been relatively few university graduate courses taught in humanistic approaches to psychotherapy. As mentioned earlier, this trend represents the current zeitgeist during which the academy has emphasized cognitive–behavioral therapy and relatively little else. Students are lucky to receive a skeletal introduction to humanistic therapies. A puzzling paradox is that graduate students in the helping professions are often taught empathy and relational skills early on in their training only to abandon or deemphasize those skills to a large degree when they are taught methods that primarily emphasize therapist technique. Because psychotherapy research consistently demonstrates that therapists' relational skills and attitudes are more strongly related to client progress in psychotherapy than are therapists' techniques and methods, it seems desirable that students learn to be more effective relational beings.

Fifth, it is my hope that this handbook will encourage and advance the research tradition initiated by Carl Rogers in the 1940s. Although a substantive amount of research has been generated by humanistic psychotherapists, there is obviously much to be learned about what works and how it works. Many recalcitrant forms of psychopathology exist for which there are not yet effective treatments. In recent years, humanistic researchers have made encouraging strides to treat some of the most difficult and debilitating problems. A related goal of the book is to encourage therapists and researchers to collaborate. Creative therapists often develop promising therapeutic methods that need research evaluation. Conversely, practitioners need to practice in a manner that is informed by sound research evidence. Collaboration between researchers favoring natural science and researchers favoring human science methods in understanding and evaluating psychotherapy is also desirable.

Sixth, but certainly not least in importance, the present volume has a goal of carrying forward the spirit and pioneering efforts of the founders of humanistic therapies who advanced a new view of the person and the bold and radical proposition that the quality of the therapeutic relationship was the most potent factor in facilitating constructive change in the client. The excitement and optimism of these founders is being furthered by creative and dedicated scholars and practitioners all over the world. It is my hope that this book will lend hope and encouragement to those who now share the responsibility for the ongoing development of humanistic psychotherapies.

AN OVERVIEW

A particular strength of this handbook is its cast of authors. Most are leading experts in the field of humanistic research and therapeutic practice. They have done an exceptional job in reviewing relevant research and providing user-friendly guidelines for practice. In Part 1: Historical and Conceptual Foundations (chapter 1), I present an overview of the history, defining characteristics, and evolution of humanistic psychotherapies. Part 2: Overviews of Research provides summaries of basic research findings. Elliott's (chapter 2) meta-analysis of humanistic psychotherapies indicates that humanistic psychotherapies have substantial effect sizes and are equally effective or more effective than other major approaches to psychotherapy. Next, Sachse and Elliott (chapter 3) review the extensive process and outcome literature, including recent and illuminating microanalyses of effective therapeutic processes. This section ends with Rennie's (chapter 4) review of human science research provides a penetrating, provocative, and highly useful view of clients' and therapists' inner experiences of psychotherapy.

Part 3: Major Therapeutic Approaches contains reviews of the major humanistic approaches to psychotherapy. Bozarth, Zimring, and Tausch (chapter 5) review the voluminous literature on client-centered therapy and find clear support for Rogers's "necessary and sufficient conditions" for therapeutic change. The accumulating research on Gestalt therapy reviewed by Strümpfel and Goldman (chapter 6) provides solid evidence for the basic methods of this approach, including two-chair and empty-chair work. In chapter 7, Hendricks reviews the evidence for Gendlin's focusing-oriented experiential psychotherapy, demonstrating that this experiential approach is effective with a wide range of clients and can be readily incorporated into the practice of other humanistic therapies. Walsh and McElwain (chapter 8), in an intriguing discourse on the essence of existential psychotherapy, show that much of the humanistic psychotherapy research is compatible with and supportive of the basic postulates of this approach. Elliott and Greenberg (chapter 9) review the research on process-experiential psychotherapy, which is a synthesis of client-centered, Gestalt, existential, and experiential therapies that strongly emphasize the processing of client emotion.

Part 4: Therapeutic Modalities examines various therapeutic modalities beginning with couples and family therapy, which is reviewed by Johnson and Boisvert (chapter 10), whose emotionally focused therapy with couples and families is beginning to make a strong impact on the field. Humanistic group therapy with clinical populations is reviewed by Page, Weiss, and Lietaer (chapter 11); the chapter provides sound evidence for the utilization of groups to treat a wide variety of clients. Bratton and Ray (chapter 12) review the child therapy research and remind us that children do indeed benefit from relationally based therapies. Accordino and Guerney (chapter 13) review their relationship enhancement therapy for couples and families; their psychoeducational model has become quite sophisticated since its inception in the 1960s and is one of the most highly researched members of the humanistic family.

Part 5: Therapeutic Issues and Applications begins with Watson's (chapter 14) assessment of the research on therapist empathy, which has, in recent years, been revisited by scholars and practitioners. With the emphasis on therapist technology in recent decades, Watson reminds us that there are few responses that are as fundamentally sound or useful than sensitive and accurate therapist empathy. Humanistic psychologists and therapists have been at the forefront in emphasizing the importance of the self-concept in influencing behavior. The literature on the self is reviewed by Purkey and Stanley (chapter 15). Breakthrough discoveries in the field of emotion and their applicability to psychotherapy are revolutionizing therapeutic practice. Greenberg and his colleagues have led the way in developing creative approaches to work with client emotion. In chapter 16, these exciting developments are reported by Greenberg, Korman, and Paivio. Asay and Lambert (chapter 17) review the literature on therapist relational variables, demonstrating clearly how important the qualities and attitudes of the therapist and the therapeutic alliance are in effecting client progress. Following is Gonzalez's review of the client's contribution to change (chapter 18) and the importance of tapping client resources. In the past decade, an increasing amount of evidence has demonstrated how substantially the client affects the process and outcome of therapy. In chapter 19, Prouty, who is a pioneer in psychotherapy of people with schizophrenia, reviews research indicating that psychotherapy can indeed enable people with such severe disorders to progress in their development and functioning.

In Part 6: Analysis and Synthesis, Stiles (chapter 20) sheds his perceptive light on where we as humanistic psychotherapists have been in our research endeavors and proposes promising future explorations. Finally, Seeman (chapter 21) sets forth a brilliant theoretical model and synthesis of humanistic therapy that serves as a beacon for understanding the person and engaging in effective practice.

In sum, the purpose of this volume is to provide university professors and researchers, graduate students, and practitioners with the compelling evidence of the effectiveness of humanistic therapies. In doing so, we hope to encourage graduate programs in psychology, counseling, marriage and family therapy, social work, psychiatric nursing, and related fields to expose students to therapeutic approaches that have had a profound impact on the well-being of persons in distress. It is also our hope that this text will encourage researchers and therapists to collaborate in the advancement of our knowledge of how psychotherapy might be optimally practiced.

ACKNOWLEDGMENTS

I would like to acknowledge the many people who have inspired and encouraged me in my professional development. Carl Rogers's impact on my thinking and therapeutic practice has been profound. He is my constant reminder to listen and seek to understand while providing a safe, supportive, and caring relationship for my client. Art Combs instilled faith and optimism in me that clients are inclined to move toward healthy behavior. Clark Moustakas taught me to use creative methods to tap my clients' resources and to value my own emergence as a person and therapist. Tom Gordon, a close friend and long-time tennis partner, taught me the value of democratic principles in working with children and families.

Jules Seeman, whom I consider to be one of our "best and brightest," has served as role model of an exemplary psychologist, teacher, researcher, and therapist for many years. As associate editor, he has been of enormous help to me in reviewing manuscripts for the present volume and in dealing with myriad issues that arose in the complex endeavor to develop and refine this book. Readers and many authors have Jules to thank for enhancing the qualities of the chapters in this handbook.

Enormous appreciation is due the countless people who have contributed to the development of humanistic psychotherapies. This international family stretches from the 1940s to the present and includes many whose writings and other contributions may not be represented or adequately represented in the present volume. It also includes those who, in their own quiet way, contribute to the development and provision of humanistic therapies as teachers, trainers, supervisors, and therapists.

I wish to thank the American Psychological Association for publishing this book. Margaret Schlegel in particular was instrumental for her support for the creation of the book and saw it through its first draft. Anne

Woodworth and Emily Welsh deserve special mention for their assistance in revising and bringing the book to its potential.

I want to express my extraordinary good fortune in having the constant sunshine, optimism, love, and sweetness provided by my delightful wife and soulmate Bobbi. She makes everything about my life better and easier. She has been a wonderful source of encouragement and support throughout the 4 years of the development of the book. Special thanks are also due to my parents, Esther and Russell Cain, who taught me to do a good job at whatever I undertook.

Finally, special appreciation goes to all of the clients who have taught us all we know about what helps in therapy and what does not. Specific thanks go the clients whose case studies or transcripts have been presented in the chapters of this book. Their identities have been disguised to protect their confidentiality.

David J. Cain

I

HISTORICAL AND CONCEPTUAL FOUNDATIONS

1

DEFINING CHARACTERISTICS, HISTORY, AND EVOLUTION OF HUMANISTIC PSYCHOTHERAPIES

DAVID J. CAIN

The origin of humanistic psychotherapies might be dated to December 11, 1940. On that day Carl Rogers, then 38, gave a speech titled "Newer Concepts in Psychotherapy" to the Psi Chi chapter of the University of Minnesota. Rogers was especially critical of many of the psychotherapy methods used at the time: advice giving, suggestion, persuasion, exhortation, and interpretation. He identified the "newer" approach he advocated as follows:

> The aim of this newer therapy is not to solve one particular problem, but to assist the individual to grow, so he can cope with the present problem. . . . It relies much more heavily on the individual drive toward growth, health and adjustment. . . . This newer therapy places greater stress on the emotional elements . . . than upon the intellectual aspects. . . . [It] places greater stress upon the immediate situation than upon the individual's past. . . . Finally this approach lays stress upon the therapeutic relationship itself as a growth experience. (see Kirschenbaum, 1979, p. 113)

The speech created a furor of excitement, praise, criticism, and puzzlement. Rogers would later come to identify the date of the Minnesota speech as the birth of client-centered therapy. What first seemed to be a critique of the long-standing methods of the past, along with some proposed advances, would, in fact, form the basis of a new school of thought. It is, arguably, the first attempt to identify the rudiments of many of the common elements that would be shared by humanistic approaches developed in the 1940s and beyond.

This chapter presents a brief history of the major schools of humanistic psychotherapy and identifies the primary concepts and characteristics shared

3

by humanistic approaches. It does not attempt to present a history of humanistic psychology in general, although mention is made of the major concepts that have affected the development of the family of humanistic psychotherapies. Although there are some important differences in the "humanistic family" of psychotherapies, this chapter emphasizes the most common shared characteristics while noting substantive variations.

Decisions about whose contributions should be emphasized were difficult. Every attempt was made to provide a balanced and representative presentation of all major humanistic therapeutic approaches. In general, three criteria were used in determining whose contributions would be emphasized: (a) the originality of the person's contribution, (b) the magnitude and pervasiveness of impact on the field of humanistic psychotherapies, and (c) the span of the leader's contribution. Because of Carl Rogers's profound and pervasive influence on the major schools of humanistic psychotherapy and on the field of psychotherapy in general, a significant portion of this chapter addresses the influence of his seminal ideas. First, I attempt to identify the shared characteristics of the humanistic family that most distinguish it from other approaches to psychotherapy.

DEFINING CHARACTERISTICS OF HUMANISTIC PSYCHOTHERAPIES

View of the Person

Humanistic therapists view the person as *self-actualizing*, endowed with an inherent tendency to develop his or her potential. Similarly, people are seen as *resourceful*, as having the capacity or potential to tap their internal experiences and external resources in a manner that leads to productive learning, growth, and effective behavior. There is an implicit *optimism* in the humanistic therapist's view of the person's capacity for constructive change. Combs (1999), speaking of people's fundamental drive toward fulfillment or health, stated, "clients can, will and *must* move toward health, *if* the way seems open to them to do so" (p. 14). Although humanistic therapists, especially the existentialists, do not deny the extremes of psychopathology that exist in people or their dark and destructive aspects, they are inclined to maintain their belief that their clients can be enabled to identify and develop their resources. People, as well as all forms of life, are viewed as *resilient* and tenacious in manifesting their natural inclination to survive and grow, even under the most adverse circumstances.

Humanistic therapists view people as *self-aware* and *free to choose* how they will live and *responsible* for the choices they make. Although a variety of factors make people's choices difficult and sometimes risky, in most instances they experience choice and agency as within their capacity. One of the main endeavors of humanistic therapists is to strengthen clients' belief that they can be the authors of their lives. People are also viewed as limited, to some degree, by their genetic and physical constitution, culture and life circumstances, and catastrophic events.

The person is viewed *holistically*, as an indivisible, interrelated organism who cannot be reduced to the sum of his or her parts. All individuals are *embodied* beings and, consequently, cannot be understood apart from their physical and emotional selves. Similarly, people are *contextual beings* who are best understood in their relationship to others and their environment in their immediate life space.

Each person is viewed as a *unique* entity, unlike any other person who has existed or will exist. Consequently, each client is understood in the context of his or her unique experiences and characteristics and responded to in a personalized manner.

People have a need to make sense of their experiences and find *meaning* in their lives. This premise is the basis for humanistic therapists' focus on clarifying the personal meaning of their clients' experiences and their search for purpose. Similarly, people create or *construct their realities* from their immediate experiences, recollections of their past, culture, and values. Their *capacity for creativity* enables them to evolve throughout the life span and become more complex and differentiated beings who can conceive of themselves and their worlds in new ways.

Humanistic therapists also view people as *primarily social beings* who have a powerful need to belong, to have a place in their families and social groups and feel valued. As Harry Stack Sullivan (1892–1949) emphasized, all behaviors, including psychopathology, are essentially interpersonal in nature. One of the most fundamental aspects of humanistic psychotherapy is its view that the therapist–client relationship is the fundamental source of constructive change in the client. People promote growth in others by the manner of their relating.

Values

A fundamental value of humanistic therapists is their belief that people have the right, desire, and ability to determine what is best for them and how they will achieve it. Embedded in humanistic therapies is a commitment to democratic principles in negotiating differences and solving problems when people are in conflict. Humanistic therapists are, therefore, strongly inclined to engage in behaviors that are collaborative and provide optimal freedom for their clients. Conversely, they are disinclined to use methods that are directive, persuasive, or covert.

Another primary value of humanistic therapists is their appreciation for a diversity of perspectives on "reality." There is no assumption of an ultimate or consensual reality but rather a belief that the same experiences can be interpreted in multiple ways. Reality is not a given; it is constructed from the raw data of experiences, tempered by one's collective experiences in interaction with a specific context at a particular moment by a person in a specific mental state. Similarly, humanistic therapists believe that there are many viable world views, belief systems, and lifestyles that people may embrace that enable them to live satisfying, functional, and useful lives. Consequently, psychotherapy must be individualized to fit with the personal goals, preferences, and values of an evolving client. Conversely, manualized or highly specific treatments for abstract psychological disorders as defined by the fourth edition of the *Diagnostic and Statistical Manual of Mental Disorders* (American Psychiatric Association, 1994) or other diagnostic systems are eschewed.

Actualizing Tendency

The foundational premise on which humanistic therapies are built is that people have an inherent actualizing tendency, a powerful impulse to maintain the self and develop its potential. Rogers's related concept of a formative tendency suggests that there is an inevitable directional course in people and all forms of life toward increased complexity, differentiation, evolution, completion, and wholeness. Maslow (1970) challenged psychology to reconsider its view of the person and to consider the magnificence of what people can be. By studying and describing self-actualizing people, Maslow showed us that it is indeed possible for people to reach extraordinary levels of development and evolution. He took the position that, given free choice, children will tend to choose what is good for their growth and experience satisfaction, pleasure, or delight in doing so. In other words, a growth tendency is self-maintaining and self-propelling because it is naturally satisfying to the person and enhances a sense of well-being. This belief in the actualizing tendency is fundamental to humanistic therapists because their efforts are focused on developing a relational climate that enables their clients to tap into and develop this enormous life source for survival and growth. Their faith in the client's potential results in humanistic therapists' disinclination to be directive but rather to act in ways that free clients to find their own directions, solve their own problems, and evolve in ways that are congruent to them.

Relational Emphasis

Every culture emphasizes that the way people treat each other has a critical relevance to their well-being and ability to function in life. Sixty years of practice and research in humanistic therapies have established the validity of the powerful growth-inducing power of a therapeutic relationship. The primary goal of humanistic therapists, therefore, is the creation of optimal therapeutic conditions for their clients. As Rogers (1980) eloquently stated, "Individuals have within themselves vast resources for self-understanding, and for altering their self concepts, basic attitudes, and self-directed behavior; these resources can be tapped if a definable climate of facilitative psychological attitudes can be provided" (p. 115). The "definable climate" includes the therapist's genuineness, authenticity, transparency, or congruence and appropriate self-disclosure; acceptance, nonjudgmental caring, liking, prizing, affirmation, respect, unconditional positive regard, or nonpossessive warmth; a genuine desire to understand the client's experience and accurate empathic communication of that experience. Other relational qualities and attitudes embraced by humanistic therapists include a collaborative relationship characterized by trust, safety, and support; receptivity to the client's and one's own experience and adaptivity; contact and engagement, I–thou encounter; therapist presence and immersion or indwelling in the client's experience; a therapeutic alliance, bond, authentic dialogue, and meeting; and optimism regarding the client's capacity for constructive change. With an ongoing relationship as its base, humanistic therapists strive to create optimal interpersonal and intrapersonal learning environments, believing that clients will identify what they need to learn and "learn how to learn."

Phenomenology

The field of phenomenology has had a profound influence on humanistic psychotherapy. Spiegelberg (1970) elegantly and succinctly defined *phenomenology* as "the direct investigation of and description of phenomena as consciously experienced, without theories about their causal explanation and as free as possible from unexamined preconceptions and presuppositions" (p. 810). Humanistic psychotherapists, especially the existentialists, have their phenomenological roots in the philosophical concepts and methods of German philosophers Edmund Husserl (1859–1938) and Martin Heidegger (1889–1976). Husserl, considered to be the founder of phenomenology, set out to develop a philosophical method that laid aside presuppositions in an endeavor to describe phenomena (the structures of consciousness) by focusing on "the things themselves" without concern about their causes. He developed the phenomenological method in an attempt to clarify the role of conscious experiencing in the creation of meaning and to develop a more adequate knowledge of reality. Husserl believed the task of phenomenology was to study essences or the qualities that define something.

Heidegger's primary concern was ontology, or the study of being or existence. He used the phenomenological method to discover what he believed to be fundamental categories of human existence (e.g., anxiety, guilt) and to address essential questions about the experience of being human (e.g., authenticity, meaning). Heidegger focused on interpreting the meaning of phenomena "in themselves" and in finding their hidden truths.

The phenomenological method, as described by Spinelli (1989) has three basic steps that might be applied to the therapeutic endeavor. I discuss these steps below.

Step 1: Epoche

In epoche, the therapist makes a conscious effort to suspend all beliefs and preconceptions, theoretical leanings, personal biases, hypotheses, previous knowledge or information, judgments, expectations, and assumptions in a spirit of minimizing interpretation of the client's experience. Toward this end, therapists *bracket*, or set aside, anything that may interfere with their ability to attend to clients' immediate experience. The therapist receives the client with curiosity, openness, and disciplined naivete as he or she endeavors to grasp the client's lived world.

Step 2: Description of Experience

The therapist's next goal is to *describe*, but not explain, the client's experience. Here, the therapist endeavors to describe in an atheoretical manner the subjective world of the client. Such description is likely to be concrete as opposed to abstract and as faithful as possible to the client's description of events, experiences, recollections, beliefs, feelings, and views. This requires considerable discipline and restraint on the part of the therapist because the therapist, like the client, is naturally inclined to make sense of or attribute meaning to the client's experience.

Step 3: Equalization

In this endeavor, the therapist refrains from assuming that any experience disclosed by the client is more primary or important than any other. Thus the therapist refrains from assuming or acting as if some of the client's experiences are central while others are peripheral. Instead each aspect of the client's experience is viewed as if it is potentially as significant as other aspects.

It is clear that the goal of the phenomenological method in the therapeutic enterprise is to illuminate the client's lived world, to grasp what it is like to be the client. The therapist's desire to understand the client accurately is crucial. Furthermore, therapists' capacity to respond to the client with sensitive and accurate empathy enables clients to reflect further on their experience and refine their understanding of it. The therapist appreciates that there are always multiple perspectives on reality and that the client is the expert on his or her life and the final source for determining the accuracy of the therapist's understanding.

As is probably clear, humanistic psychologists and psychotherapists tend to prefer ideographic, phenomenological, human science methods to comprehending the person, although they do not reject the contributions of positivistic, nomothetic, hypothesis-testing, statistically based, cause–effect, natural science approaches. Rather they embrace multiple ways of knowing and recognize the strengths and limitations of natural and human science approaches to further their understanding of the therapeutic process and outcome. As stated in the American Psychological Association (APA) Division 32 Task Force for the Development of Guidelines for the Provision of Humanistic Psychosocial Services (1997),

> We endorse the *human science* model of science . . . because it is more comprehensive, capable of embracing various forms of research and knowledge in a manner that allows complementarity in an integrated overall framework. The human science approach requires not less but more rigor, and is more scientific than the natural science model, because it is more inclusive and capable of apprehending a greater complexity. (p. 85)

Empathy

Therapist empathy is a critical factor in accurately illuminating, deepening, and enriching the client's experience. Empathy may be conceived as the therapist's desire and endeavor to understand what it is like to be the client and to communicate accurately that experience to the client. In light of the phenomenological orientation of humanistic therapists, empathy is a vital tool in grasping the nature and meaning of client experience. Therapist empathy is a response that has a multidimensional impact on the client. Accurate empathy enables therapist and client to grasp the cognitive aspect of the experience, particularly the client's views, core beliefs, and personal meanings. Empathy enables clients to focus on and decipher the unclear aspects of their feeling states. Because emotions can be understood as impulses to act, illuminating emotional experience helps clients get clear about their motivations, desires, and needs. Socially, the act of carefully attending to others in a nonjudgmental manner with a desire to understand is a powerful experience that typically results in their feeling valued and supported (see also Watson, this volume, chapter 14).

The Self

A fundamental concept and focus of humanistic theory and therapy is the *self*—the "I" or "me" of one's existence. As early as the 1940s, the self-concept was recognized as a pervasive and influential aspect of the client's experience. As Mahoney (1991) suggested, "All psychotherapies are psychotherapies of the self" (p. 235). Self-exploration, self-definition, reconstrual of the self, and the development of self-knowledge are the primary concerns of the humanistic therapist. The belief that behavior changes as the self-concept is altered has enormous influence in the therapeutic endeavor because it alerts therapists and focuses their attention on clients' immediate and ongoing sense of self and the role it plays in mediating their perceptions and behavior. As humans, we all strive and struggle to discover who we are and to form an identity that provides direction, stability, and worth.

There is probably nothing that occupies our mind more than our "self" and the imagined or actual view others have of us. Consequently, one's self plays a critical role in one's view of and manner of relating to others. Threat to the self often results in our tendency to preserve and defend it. One's relationship to oneself, to others, and to one's physical world constitutes the essence of our daily lives. As many humanistic therapists have observed, it takes courage to be oneself, to discover and live from one's core. The concept of congruence is closely related to the self of humanistic theories because it implies a correspondence between the self-concept and experience and between self and ideal self. When there is discrepancy between these experiences, discord and dysfunction are likely. Conversely, when people are integrated or whole in all aspects of their experiences, behavior, and view of self, a state of optimal functioning is likely. Humanistic therapists, therefore, strive to help their clients become aware of their incongruencies and to assist them to find ways to move toward integration and wholeness (see also Purkey & Stanley, this volume, chapter 15).

Emotion

One of the most distinguishing features of humanistic therapies is their emphasis on the importance of emotion. Humanistic therapists and researchers have been at the forefront in expanding our understanding of the critical role played by emotion in human behavior. Rather than view emotion primarily as something that interferes with functioning, humanistic therapists have embraced the importance of the adaptive nature of emotion in effective decision making and effective functioning. Antonio Damasio, a neurologist and author of *Descartes' Error*, provides evidence that "certain aspects of the process of emotion and feeling are indispensable for rationality [and] . . . take us to the appropriate place in a decision-making space, where we may put the instruments of logic to good use" (Damasio, 1994, p. xiii). Consequently, humanistic therapists "focus on the emotional and experiential dimensions of human functioning when it facilitates dialogue which takes clients to deeper levels of feeling and thinking" (Bohart et al., 1997, p. 95; see also Greenberg, Korman, & Paivio, this volume, chapter 16).

Meaning

Meaning is not a given but is constructed from the raw data of experience, including one's culture, values, perspectives, and personal history. Making sense of experience seems to be a fundamental need of all individuals. People are troubled by that which seems to elude their comprehension and search for a form of understanding that enables them to comprehend their behaviors and lives. Often the course and purposes of clients' lives is implicit but not clear. Humanistic therapists strive to enable their clients to grasp the larger meanings and patterns of their lives. Discovering that there are comprehensible threads of meaning to their lives enables clients to gain a sense of clarity, direction, and groundedness. As meanings and purposes become clear, clients develop a more centered self and a system of beliefs and values from which to operate.

The process of creating meaning in the client has been informed by constructivist theorists and therapists whose approach is fundamentally humanistic. "Humanistic" constructivists (e.g., Epting & Leitner, 1992) have grounded their ideas in George Kelly's (1905–1967) personal construct theory, which emphasizes that people create their own personal universes. On the basis of this premise, the goal of therapy is the restructuring of meaning in the client. Kelly's (1955) concept of *constructive alternativism* takes the view that "the events we face today are subject to as great a variety of constructions as our wits will enable us to contrive" (p. 1). There is an implicit optimism in constructivism because the therapist takes the position that clients have the capacity to create new meanings and new possibilities for living.

Holism

As mentioned earlier, the human organism is conceived as a constantly interconnected, indivisible whole. The person is viewed as a gestalt, a dynamic whole. Mind and body are inseparable. Views of the person as "part functions," such as cognition versus affect or mind versus body, are concepts used by psychologists for descriptive and analytical purposes rather than descriptions of real components of the person. A holistic view of a person eschews the simplifying and distorting tendencies associated with categorization and reductionism. When functioning optimally, clients have the experience of feeling "whole," "all-of-a-piece," and integrated. "The living organism . . . will always do the best it can to actualize its potentials . . . and it will do so as a *unit* along all dimensions of its functioning"

(Tageson, 1982, p. 35). As Seeman has articulated (see this volume, chapter 21), the human organism can be viewed most accurately as composed of interrelated systems.

Anxiety

Anxiety is an inevitable part of living and therefore must be a concern for humanistic therapists. Each of us must constantly deal with the uncertainties of living and the reality that we have limited control over some aspects of our lives. We must all grapple with the dread that our lives are finite and that we cannot predict when or how they will end. This realization heightens our concern about how we are living. If we can create our life in its current form, then we can also create it in another form. There is an inherent optimism in this realization (i.e., I could alter my life) but also the possibility for the existential guilt of missed opportunities and the existential anxiety of uncertainty. Humanistic therapists view existential anxiety as a potential source of growth in that it may heighten self-reflection and motivation. Although anxiety is often experienced as threatening and unpleasant, it may also be viewed as a warning system that alerts us to real or feared dangers to the self. Therefore, attending to the various manifestations of client anxiety as well as assessing its meanings is a critical endeavor of humanistic therapies. Rather than viewing anxiety as simply something that is distressing and dysfunctional, humanistic therapists accept its presence and strive to enable their clients to make constructive use of it for learning or to manage it more effectively when it interferes with functioning. Probably one of the most frequent acknowledgments humanistic therapists make about their clients' experiences is simply, "You're afraid." As Rollo May (1981) pointed out, freedom and anxiety are two sides of the same coin.

Freedom–Choice–Responsibility

Humanistic therapists view people as essentially free to choose the manner and course of their living and their attitude toward events. At the same time that people are free to choose, they are also responsible for their choices. As French writer and philosopher Jean-Paul Sartre (1905–1980) has commented, we are our choices. Therefore, freedom, choice, and the resulting responsibility for our choices are intertwined. Each choice we make inevitably means that another choice could not be made. Whatever one's choices, the choosing and the consequences cannot be avoided. As clients are enabled to realize that they are constantly choosing, as opposed to simply being carried along by or reacting to their experiences, they become empowered. They recognize that other paths are available to them. Thus, the existential questions of "How are you living?" and "Are you becoming the person you wish to be?" are often integral aspects of humanistic psychotherapy.

PRECURSORS OF HUMANISTIC THERAPIES

Humanistic psychotherapies have their roots in therapeutic systems dating to the early 1900s, especially those of Otto Rank, Alfred Adler, and the existential analysts. In the following sections, I address the impact of these precursors on the development of contemporary humanistic psychotherapies.

Otto Rank's Influence

Otto Rank (1884–1939) was Freud's closest disciple and served as secretary of the Vienna Psychoanalytic Society, but he broke away from Freud and psychoanalysis in 1926. Rank's *will therapy*, with its relational and existential emphasis, influenced many of the people who would become founders and leaders in the field of humanistic psychotherapies, including Carl Rogers, Rollo May, Paul Goodman, Frederick Allen, Carl Whitaker, and Irvin Yalom. Many of his ideas anticipated future developments in psychotherapy, including (a) an emphasis on conscious experience and emotion, especially fear and guilt; (b) the here-and-now; (c) awareness, choice, responsibility, and self-direction; (d) creativity and will in development of the self; (e) the "real" relationship as the core of therapy as opposed to the transferential relationship; and (f) fear of living (life fear) and fear of losing one's individuality and becoming helpless (death fear). Rank viewed the basic goal for the client as "the acceptance of the self with its individual ego and its volitional and emotional autonomy" (see Ford & Urban, 1963, p. 380).

Carl Rogers readily acknowledged that Otto Rank and his followers, Jessie Taft and Frederick Allen, had an influence on his thinking. In fact, Rogers invited Rank to make a presentation at the Child Study Department in Rochester in 1936. Rogers was most influenced by Rank's student, Jessie Taft, who identified her approach as *relationship therapy*. Taft's book, *The Dynamics of Therapy in a Controlled Relationship* (1933), was identified by Rogers as "a small masterpiece of writing and thinking" (see Kirschenbaum, 1979, p. 92). In 1937, Rogers commented about Taft's approach: "Its major value may be . . . the fresh viewpoint of non-interference and reliance upon the individual's own tendency toward growth which it has emphasized" (see Kirschenbaum, 1979, pp. 92–93). Rogers was also drawn to Rank's emphasis on the therapist's supportive and acceptant stance toward the client and the value placed on client self-insight. Many years later, Rogers reflected on the influence of Rank and his students as follows:

> I became infected with Rankian ideas and began to realize the possibilities of the individual being self-directing. This certainly fit in with the earlier ideas I had absorbed from Kilpatrick and John Dewey. . . . I came to believe in the individual's capacity. I value the dignity and rights of the individual sufficiently that I do not want to impose my way upon him. Those two aspects of the core idea haven't changed since that time. (see Kirschenbaum, 1979, p. 95)

Rollo May was impressed with Rank's emphasis on the importance of freedom and responsibility, and what Rank termed *creative will* in psychotherapy. May (1939) commented, "Rank holds that . . . the individual creates his own personality by creative willing, and that neurosis is due precisely to the fact that the patient cannot will constructively" and that "the neurotic type . . . suffers from the fact that he cannot accept himself, cannot endure himself" (pp. 52–53). May was also impressed with Rank's belief that the aim of psychotherapy is self-development.

Erving and Miriam Polster acknowledged the influence of Rank on Gestalt therapy. They commented, "Two of Rank's directions have special importance for the evolution of Gestalt therapy. . . . He asserted that the primary struggle in life is for personal individuation. . . . This struggle is waged in the individual's efforts to integrate his polar fears of separation and union"(E. Polster & Polster, 1973, p. 314). They also stated,

> Rank's interest in the developing sense of individual identity led to a change of focus in the interaction between patient and therapist. Acknowledgement of the human aspects of this interaction make him one of the major influences toward a humanistic orientation in psychotherapy—an important inheritance for Gestalt therapy. (E. Polster & Polster, 1973, p. 314)

Yalom (1980) quoted Rank on the importance of will as follows: "The task of the therapist is to function in such a way that the will of the patient shall not be broken but strengthened" (p. 297).

Moustakas (1995) viewed the denial of one's individuality as a cause of maladjustment and cited Rank as follows: "Psychologically, the problem of individuality is a will problem and a consciousness problem. The neurotic character represents not an illness but a developmental phase of the individuality problem, a personality denying its own will, not accepting itself as an individual" (p. 14).

Lieberman (1985), author of Rank's biography, *Acts of Will: The Life and Works of Otto Rank*, considered Rank to be an existentialist and noted that his therapy "envisioned a mutual relationship" whose aim was to "unify and free the crippled will ... and to develop a self, a distinct personality capable of making life a creative enterprise" (pp. 404–405).

Alfred Adler's Indirect Influence

Alfred Adler's (1870–1937) ideas made an impact on several of the founding fathers of humanistic psychology: Rollo May, Carl Rogers, and Abraham Maslow, as well as Viktor Frankl, Meddard Boss, and others. Rollo May, who studied with Adler in Vienna in the summers of 1932 and 1933, frequently cited Adler's ideas in *The Art of Counseling* (May, 1939). In a chapter titled "Empathy—Key to the Counseling Process," May credited Adler for his strong emphasis on empathy as the means by which the counselor comes to know and identify with the other, to "act and feel as if we were someone else" (May, 1939, p. 79). He later quoted Adler on the issue of judging others as follows: "Let us never allow ourselves to make any *moral* judgments ... concerning the worth of a human being" (May, 1939, p. 176). These two therapeutic endeavors—the desire to understand and nonjudgmental acceptance—constitute two key building blocks on which all humanistic therapies are built.

It is surprising that Adler has not had more direct influence on the development of humanistic therapies because he anticipated many of the ideas, attitudes, and therapeutic response that would later be embraced by them. These common characteristics include the following:

1. *Subjectivity:* As Ansbacher and Ansbacher (1956) noted, Adler's psychology was personalistic, ideographic, and subjective. For Adler, perception was largely determined by subjective values and interests. Adler viewed experience as the immediate subject matter of psychology.
2. *Holism:* Adler's psychology viewed living beings as connected wholes—biologically, philosophically, and psychologically. His view of the person was that of an indivisible unity. He rejected polarities such as mind–body and conscious–unconscious, believing that all functions or subsystems of the person are in the service of the whole person.
3. *Freedom:* Adler viewed people as free, choosing, and largely self-determining. He saw people as free to choose their life goals and free to determine whether or not they choose to contribute to the well-being of others.
4. *Meaning emphasis*: Adler believed that meaning was given to life by the individual and that the meanings the individual chooses will strongly influence the course of life. For Adler,

one's style of life largely reflected the purposes and meanings attributed to it.

5. *Phenomenology and empathy*: Psychopathology is viewed as a product of distorted perceptions and failure to learn. Although Adler did not use the term phenomenology, he attempted to grasp the client's world through empathy and stated, "We must be able to see with his eyes and listen with his ears" (see Ansbacher & Ansbacher, 1956, p. 14).

6. *Existentialism*: Adler believed that people strive to overcome or transcend themselves and life's limitations. In his view, people strive to overcome their inferiorities to achieve perfection and superiority. Development of the self was not seen as sufficient for actualization of one's potential but required social interest, a genuine concern for one's fellow human beings.

7. *Emphasis on therapeutic relationship*: Adler was an excellent role model of compassion toward humankind and his clients. He was nonjudgmental, patient, and kind, and he emphasized subjective understanding, a nonjudgmental attitude, empathy, and encouragement.

MAJOR APPROACHES TO HUMANISTIC PSYCHOTHERAPIES

Client-Centered Psychotherapy

The roots of client-centered therapy reach back to the late 1920s when Carl Rogers spent his formative years as a clinical psychologist in Rochester, New York. During the Rochester period from 1928 to 1939, Rogers worked at the Child Study Department of the Society for the Prevention of Cruelty to Children, becoming its director in 1929 at the age of 27.

Rogers was a pragmatist. As he found himself faced with large numbers of troubled children and parents, his guiding question was, "Does it work?" Rogers's approach to his clinical work was based on careful systematic observation as opposed to trial and error. Not content to rely on his subjective impressions, he carefully evaluated the effect of his work.

A number of clinical experiences influenced Rogers's thinking. One was environmental therapy, which might include the modification of the child's school or living environment. It might mean changing parental attitudes and behaviors, or even the removal of the child from his or her home if this was thought to be therapeutic. Rogers commented, "Most children, if given a reasonably normal environment which meets their own emotional, intellectual and social needs, have within themselves sufficient drive toward health to respond and make a comfortable adjustment to life" (see Kirschenbaum, 1979, p. 75). It appears that an important belief emerging in Rogers was the notion that individual growth was more likely to occur in a certain kind of environment. What Rogers called the "drive toward health" certainly has the sound of the actualizing tendency, perhaps the most important assumption on which client-centered therapy is built.

Toward the end of his Rochester years, Rogers identified in his first book, *The Clinical Treatment of the Problem Child* (1939), some of the basic elements that would form the foundation for what would be later known as client-centered therapy. As Kirschenbaum (1979) noted, these elements would form the basis for what Rogers would later identify as the therapist's qualities of empathic understanding, unconditional positive regard, and congruence. Rogers's experiences with children and parents led him to begin to realize that

> It is the client who knows what hurts, what directions to go, what problems are crucial. . . . It began to occur to me that unless I had a need to demonstrate my own cleverness and learning, I would do better to rely upon the client for the direction of movement in the process. (see Kirschenbaum, 1979, p. 89)

Rogers left Rochester and went to Ohio State University in 1939 as a full professor in the psychology department. Rogers established a practicum in counseling and psychotherapy in 1940 for graduate trainees, which was apparently the first such supervised training offered in a university setting.

While at Ohio State, Rogers wrote *Counseling and Psychotherapy: Newer Concepts in Practice* (1942), a classic textbook on basic therapeutic issues, methods, the therapy relationship, and the process of change. At the end of the first chapter, Rogers (1942) stated the basic hypothesis of his developing approach as follows: "*Effective counseling consists of a definitely structured, permissive relationship which allows the client to gain an understanding of himself to a degree which enables him to take positive steps in the light of his new orientation*" (p. 18). The descriptive terms *nondirective* and *client* were introduced to underscore the therapist's belief that the direction and locus of control in therapy were clearly centered in the person seeking help. This was a radical shift away from the interpretive and directive methods that were commonly used at the time. As Seeman (1965) stated, "The enduring process which Rogers set in motion in 1942 was a reexamination of the nature of therapy . . . which continues to this day" (p. 1215).

Rogers and his students were innovators in the early 1940s, experimenting with and refining the concepts and methods that would emerge as one of the most influential and controversial of therapeutic approaches. In his early stages of developing a "new" approach, a number of his proposals seemed to focus on what Rogers thought the therapist should *not* do or be. He was adamant in his belief that the therapist should not advise the client, interpret behavior, or attempt to direct or persuade the client to pursue a particular course of action. Rogers (1942) objected to these approaches because "they assume that the counselor is the one most competent to decide what are to be the goals of the individual, and what are the values by which the situation is to be judged" (p. 27). Rogers believed that *counselor-centered therapy* "may serve only to make the counselee more dependent, less able to solve new problems of adjustment" (see Kirschenbaum, 1979, p. 116) and more resistant to the counselor.

The therapeutic approach developed by Rogers in the early 1940s had many distinctive characteristics, a number of which continue to be basic to the practice of client-centered therapy and other humanistic approaches. Rogers made a major shift in emphasis in therapy by focusing on the *person* of the client rather than on the problem expressed. Another shift was toward the *feelings* expressed by the client as opposed to the client's thoughts. The therapist's *attitudes* of respect for and belief in the client's capacity for self-directed growth resulted in the therapist developing a dramatically different kind of relationship with the client. It was a relationship characterized by disciplined restraint and nonintrusiveness. The therapist as an individual stayed out of the relationship. Instead the therapist attempted to be a careful and *understanding listener*. To a large extent, the therapist's task was technical in emphasis. Although the therapist's *acceptance* of the client was viewed as critical, the accuracy and effectiveness of the therapist's *reflection and clarification of feelings* were clearly the primary focus during this phase of development.

Rogers and his students were the first to study the counseling process in depth. In 1940, with the assistance of Bernie Covner, the first audio readings of a therapy session were made on 78-rpm discs. These "live" and transcribed recordings provided case studies for training purposes as well as research studies. The case of Herbert Bryan, which constitutes the last 176 pages of *Counseling and Psychotherapy* (Rogers, 1942), was the first phonographically recorded verbatim transcript of an entire course of psychotherapy ever published. Although today we take for granted the usefulness of reviewing audio- and videotapes for training purposes, Rogers was the first to demystify psychotherapy by bringing it out into the open for study.

Finally, Rogers was a pioneer in carrying out and publishing research studies in counseling. It is probably fair to say that Rogers was primarily responsible for initiating research in the field of psychotherapy. Early in *Counseling and Psychotherapy*, Rogers (1942) stated that the book "endeavors to formulate a definite and understandable series of hypotheses . . . which may be tested and explored" (pp. 16–17). The research tradition established by Rogers and his students during this period has carried forward to the present to ensure the continued development and efficacy of client-centered therapy.

In 1945, Carl Rogers left Ohio State to create and direct the Counseling Center at the University of Chicago. There he continued to develop client-centered theory and practice while conducting research on its effectiveness. In *Twelve Therapists* (Burton, 1972), Rogers commented about his Chicago years:

> I believe I learned more and contributed more during the twelve years at the Center (1945–1957) than in any other period. . . . It was a period in which our basic views about the helping relationship came to fruition. . . . It was a germinal period for research hypotheses and theoretical formulations. . . . There was enormous freedom for creativity. I think it safe to say that anyone who worked for as much as a year in that climate regards his time there as one of the most significant experiences in his life. (p. 54)

In 1951, Rogers's third major book, *Client-Centered Psychotherapy*, was published. Applications of the client-centered approach to play therapy, group therapy, leadership and administration, teaching, and counselor training were advanced. In this period, Rogers further emphasized the attitudes of the therapist as primary, as opposed to technique, as well as the capacity of the client for constructive change. Rogers and client-centered therapists focused on creating a relationship that would release the client's natural tendency for self-actualization and growth. Increasing emphasis was placed on understanding the client's phenomenal world and its meaning.

Between 1943 and 1957, approximately 200 studies were conducted on client-centered therapy and its applications to children, groups, education, industry, and leadership. In 1954, the results of a group of studies were published in *Psychotherapy and Personality Change,* which was coedited by Rogers and Rosalind Dymond (see Rogers & Dymond, 1954). The studies that Rogers referred to as a "pioneering venture" were moderately supportive of client-centered hypotheses.

Rogers received considerable credit and praise for the research efforts he stimulated at the Counseling Center. Joseph Matarrazzo placed Rogers's research efforts in perspective in 1965 when he wrote: "His approach to the interview stimulated research more than the works of any single writer on the interview before or since" and that *Psychotherapy and Personality Change* was "probably the single most important research publication on interviewing (as found in psychotherapy) of the decade" (see Kirschenbaum, 1979, p. 219). Based primarily on his research contributions in psychotherapy, Rogers, along with Kenneth W. Spence and Wolfgang Kohler, was awarded the first Distinguished Scientific Contribution Award, presented by the American Psychological Association in 1956.

In 1956, Rogers added congruence to empathic understanding and unconditional positive regard as an important condition for therapeutic change. Also in 1956, Rogers developed his formulation of what he would call "The Necessary and Sufficient Conditions of Therapeutic Personality Change." This formulation, first published in 1957, represented the culmination of many years of development in Rogers's thinking and remains virtually unchanged to this day. It stated the following:

1. Two persons are in psychological contact.
2. The first, whom we shall term the client, is in a state of incongruence, being vulnerable or anxious.
3. The second person, whom we term the therapist, is congruent or integrated in the relationship.
4. The therapist experiences unconditional positive regard for the client.
5. The therapist experiences an empathic understanding of the client's internal frame of reference and endeavors to communicate this experience to the client.
6. The communication to the client of the therapist's empathic understanding and unconditional positive regard is to a minimal degree achieved.

Rogers's (1957) formulation stimulated an enormous amount of research and debate in the field of psychotherapy and quite possibly more than any other hypothesis advanced by any school of psychotherapy.

In the spring of 1957, Rogers accepted a position at the University of Wisconsin. Rogers and many of his colleagues were curious to see if his hypothesis about the necessary and sufficient conditions of personality change applied to people with serious mental illnesses. In 1957, he began to develop an ambitious research project on the treatment of individuals with schizophrenia. The results of the study showed no significant differences between the therapy group and the control group, although there was a correlation between high levels of the therapist conditions of congruence and empathy and successful outcome. Although much was learned about psychotherapy with people with schizophrenia, the research evidence for client-centered therapy was modest.

In 1959, Rogers published "A Theory of Therapy, Personality and Interpersonal Relationships" in Sigmund Koch's *Psychology: A Study of a Science*. This 72-page formal statement of his theory continues to stand as the most complete statement of Rogers's position. Rogers's fifth and most influential book, *On Becoming a Person*, was published in 1961. It contains many of Rogers's best-known and most influential papers. Some of his more provocative and incisive ideas on psychotherapy, education research, philosophy of science, interpersonal relations, family life, creativity, the process of growth, and the fully functioning person are contained in this book. Soon after its publication, there was an enormous outpouring of touching and appreciative responses from professionals and laypersons from every walk of life.

In the summer of 1963, Rogers resigned from the University of Wisconsin and moved to California. For several years, starting in 1964, Rogers involved himself in the encounter group movement and became a national leader in the field. The magazine *Psychology Today* identified him as a "grand master," and *Look* magazine referred to him as "an elder statesman of encounter groups." In 1970, *Carl Rogers on Encounter Groups* was published and clearly associated Rogers with encounter groups with both professionals and the general public. In 1972, Rogers received the first Distinguished Professional Contribution Award from the American Psychological Association. By receiving this reward, he became the first psychologist in history to receive both APA's Scientific Contribution Award and Distinguished Professional Contribution Award.

In the last 15 or so years of his life, Rogers became increasingly interested in broader social issues, especially peace. Beginning in 1974, Carl Rogers and his wife Natalie Rogers, along with several of their colleagues, initiated a series of large-group workshops, sometimes 2–3 weeks in length, to explore the implications of the person-centered approach for building communities in groups ranging from 75 to 800 people. For the first time, Rogers would use the phrase *person-centered* to describe these workshops, which would be offered all over the world for the next several years. As those workshops evolved, Rogers and the staff of facilitators provided less and less structure, instead leaving most, if not all, of the decision making to the entire community.

A Way of Being was published in 1980. It is a diverse collection of papers representing the evolution of Rogers's thought in the 1970s. Many of the papers were very personal statements of Rogers's growth and changing views. In a survey of clinical and counseling psychologists published in 1982 in the *American Psychologist* (Smith, 1982), Carl Rogers was identified as the most influential psychotherapist.

In 1986, the *Person-Centered Review*, an academic journal, was first published under my editorship. Up to this point Rogers had discouraged the creation of client-centered training programs, organizations, or journals, fearing that his approach would become formalized and dogmatic. By 1986, however, Rogers supported and welcomed the journal, even writing a brief commentary in the first issue (Rogers, 1986); he viewed the journal as a means to present new ideas and innovative methods, research, and critiques and to communicate with other person-centered scholars and practitioners worldwide.

Unfortunately, Carl Rogers was not able to pursue further the strongest commitments of his last years: to contribute whatever he could to the prevention of nuclear war and the accomplishment of world peace. On

January 20, 1987, the day of his fall and hospitalization (he broke his hip), Carl Rogers, at 85, was nominated by Congressman Jim Bates for the 1987 Nobel Peace Prize. A few weeks later, on February 4, 1987, Carl Rogers would die as he had hoped to—with his boots on, and, as always, looking forward. He had been relatively healthy and active until his death.

A number of other people have made substantial contributions to the development of client-centered therapy. Some of the most prominent contributors include Barrett-Lennard (1998), Bozarth (1998), Combs (1989), Gendlin (1996), Gordon (1955), Hart and Tomlinson (1970), Levant and Shlien (1984), Lietaer, Rombauts, and Van Balen (1990), Patterson (2000), Rice and Greenberg (1984), Seeman (1983), Tausch (1990), Wexler and Rice (1974), and Zimring and Raskin (1992).

Existential Psychotherapies

The Early Existential Influence: The Forefathers

One of the most prominent forefathers of the existential thrust in psychology and psychotherapy was Karl Jaspers (1883–1969), who was a leading exponent of German existentialism. Jaspers, a psychiatrist and philosopher, was greatly influenced by the works of Nietzsche and Kierkegaard. He was a strong subjectivist who asserted that personal experience is the only source of information about reality. He developed and advocated a descriptive phenomenology and stressed the importance of an "inward understanding" and a "living into the patients' experiences." Furthermore, Jaspers believed that one can discover one's authentic self only through encounter and reflection with another's authentic self. He distinguished between two states of being: Dasein and Existenz. *Dasein* referred to ordinary, everyday life, whereas *Existenz* referred to the richness of authentic being, including the experiences of freedom, infinite possibility, and loneliness. He emphasized the importance of transcending life's struggles by "being oneself," which implies a self-awareness in which one asserts oneself through choice, self-assertion, and decision. Like other European existential philosophers, Jaspers saw that people are continually confronted with the realities of suffering, death, guilt, and struggle, and he believed that one must find ways to transcend these dilemmas.

The Swiss psychiatrist, Ludwig Binswanger (1881–1966) is considered by Havens (1973) to be the foremost spokesman for existential psychiatry and by many as the founder of existential analysis. He was influenced by Heidegger's concept of "being-in-the-world" and by Buber's concepts of the "I–thou" relationship and the dialogical nature of human existence. Binswanger developed a form of psychotherapy called *Daseinanalyse* (analysis of being or existence), which had as its purpose the analysis of a person's ability to give meaning to his or her existence. For Binswanger (1975), being-in-the-world signified that people are not isolated entities but beings who are always in relation to others and the physical world around them.

With a focus on his clients' views of their world and immediate experience, Binswanger strove to enable them to grasp the meaning of their behavior, find direction, and discover a manner of living authentically in relationship to the world, others, and themselves. As a therapist, Binswanger advocated for equality in the relationship and for authentic encounter: "a being-together with one another" (see Ehrenwald, 1991, p. 377). He believed that a loving I–thou relationship characterized by mutuality, openness, and immediacy, as opposed to therapist technique, promoted expanded awareness and growth in the client. Conversely, Binswanger saw the loss of relatedness and isolation as factors that made a person vulnerable to psychopathology (Frie, 2000).

Binswanger identified the three dimensions of a person's world view: (a) *Umwelt*, the natural world, including the physical world we inhabit and our bodily states; (b) *Mitwelt*, the interpersonal worlds we inhabit in our daily contacts with others; and (c) *Eigenwelt*, one's own world, including one's relationship with oneself and one's personal perspective regarding the meaning of things in relation to self.

Meddard Boss (1903–1990), a Swiss psychiatrist who was analyzed by Freud, integrated existentialism with psychoanalysis in his book *Psychoanalysis and Daseinanalysis* (1963). Strongly influenced by Heidigger, Boss identified universal themes that people inevitably face in their lives. He stressed that people must coexist in and share the world with others and that they do so with varying degrees of openness and clarity. Boss believed that a person's basic mood state influenced his or her view of the world in that it affected the focus and content of awareness. He articulated the relationship between choice and guilt, pointing out that choosing one course inevitably requires the rejection of other possibilities and may result in guilt over the lost opportunities. Another basic theme he voiced was the finiteness of life and the consequent responsibility individuals have to make the most of their lives.

Modern Existential Contributions and Views

Contemporary views of existential psychotherapy share considerable common ground with their forefathers. Many contemporary existential therapists describe themselves as *existential–humanistic*, indicating that although their strongest roots are in existentialism, they have incorporated many aspects of North American humanistic psychotherapies. Some existential–humanistic therapists also retain some connection with psychoanalysis, mostly to the existential–analytic forerunners described above. Other practitioners (e.g., Irvin Yalom and Ernesto Spinelli) simply refer to themselves as existential therapists.

Existential psychotherapy focuses on important life themes and issues. It places a high premium on the quality of the therapeutic relationship as a healing agent, with an emphasis on the I–thou encounter and therapeutic dialogue. Like other humanistic therapies, it is discovery oriented, but existential therapists are more likely to engage in interpretation and challenge their clients to examine their lives. Existential therapists strive to enable clients to assess how their freedom is impaired, remove the obstacles to their freedom, increase their sense of choice, and engage their will. Existential therapy embraces an attitude toward living, one that faces the reality of death, advocates the search for meaning and purpose, and recognizes the freedom to choose and the ensuing responsibility for one's choices. Thus, conflict is a primary issue in existential therapy in that there is an inevitable conflict between the person and the givens of existence. Clients are challenged to wrestle with the basic question of how they are living, face the givens of their existence, confront the associated anxiety, and learn to live more fully, authentically, and responsibly.

Rollo May (1909–1994) is considered the founder of existential psychology and psychotherapy in the United States. In 1958, Rollo May, along with Ernest Angel and Henri Ellenberger, introduced existential psychotherapy to the United States in the book *Existence: A New Dimension in Psychology and Psychiatry*. As noted earlier, existential psychotherapy had its roots in Europe in the works of a number of psychiatrists and psychoanalysts who were dissatisfied with the impersonal, objective, and reductionistic elements of psychoanalysis practiced in the early 1900s. In the first chapter of *Existence*, May (1958) issued the following challenge: "Can we be sure . . . that we are seeing the patient as he really is, knowing him in his own reality; or are we seeing merely a projection of our own theories *about* him?" (p. 3). He stressed that the existential movement in psychiatry and psychology "arose precisely out of a passion to be . . . more empirical" and that "traditional scientific methods not only did not do justice to the data but actually tended to hide rather than reveal what was going on in the patient" (May, 1958, p. 8).

May (1958) offered an early definition of existentialism as "the endeavor to understand man by cutting below the cleavage between subject and object" (p. 11) and "an endeavor to grasp reality" (p. 19). For him, existentialism addressed the big questions and issues of life. May embraced the complexities and paradoxes that inevitably arise when one grapples with the human condition, often challenging limited and limiting views of the person. He said of his teacher and friend, Paul Tillich, that he "brought doubt to the faithful and faith to the doubters" (May, 1987, p. 114). This was May's endeavor: to raise doubt where there was certainty and to restore hope and faith where there was cynicism. A central theme of May's thinking is that people are both free and limited.

Schneider (1999) noted that as a therapist May's approach was characterized by the following:

> (1) A focus on freeing the client within the natural and self-imposed limits of living; (2) an emphasis on freedom and limitation . . . versus behavioral or childhood conflicts as the fundamental context to be addressed; (3) a stress on techniques that fit the person rather than the practitioner . . . ; (4) a stress on experiential contact (including that facilitated by the therapeutic relationship) to promote optimal healing; and (5) a stress on experiential awareness (or one's whole bodily understanding) prior to insight, decision and commitment. (p. 352)

Viktor Frankl (1905–1997), a psychiatrist who was born in Vienna, was profoundly influenced by his experiences in German concentration camps during World War II. He emphasized a person's freedom to choose and to find meaning in even the most restrictive and inhumane circumstances. In *Man's Search for Meaning*, originally published in 1946 as *From Concentration Camp to Existentialism*, he described the essence of logotherapy, which is based on the belief that a person's most fundamental goal is to understand the meaning of his or her existence. In this book, which has sold over 9 million copies in 23 languages, Frankl (1963) commented that logotherapy "focuses on the future . . . on the meanings to be fulfilled by the patient in his future" (pp. 152–153). He wrote, "in logotherapy the patient is actually confronted with and reoriented toward the meaning of his life," and he added, "the striving to find a meaning in one's life is the primarily motivational force in man" (p. 153). Regarding one's freedom, Frankl (1967) noted: "Man is not free of conditions. . . . But, he is, and always remains, free to take a stand toward these conditions; he always retains the freedom to choose his attitudes towards them" (p. 3).

Frankl stressed the importance of our values and that these values "pull" us and represent that which we strive for as personal commitments. Addressing the spiritual dimensions of human existence, especially the desire for a meaningful existence, Frankl (1963) stated, "A man's concern, even his despair, over the worthwhileness of life is a *spiritual distress* but by no means a *mental disease*" (p. 163).

Frankl developed the technique of *paradoxical intention*, the purpose of which is to enable clients to detach from their fears, engage their sense of humor, and deflate their anticipatory anxiety. It is a technique widely used in various forms of brief therapy and challenged the notions that lasting change can only come about through lengthy treatment and that the therapist must know and address the etiology of a symptom to relieve it.

R. D. Laing (1928–1989), a British psychiatrist, is probably best known for establishing a therapeutic community for individuals with severe mental illnesses and for *The Divided Self: An Existential Study in Sanity and Madness* (1969). Laing was one of the pioneers in exploring the meaning of the psychotic experience and probably the most radical and unorthodox of the existential therapists as he constantly pushed the envelope of therapeutic treatment. Laing had an extraordinary ability to be present with and make contact with even the most disturbed and recalcitrant of persons. He especially made strong contact with his client's face as a means of attuning himself to ("at-onement" as he called it) the "feel" or "tone" of the person before him and their interrelationship. He was receptive to and encouraging of clients' expression of immediate, lived experience. Laing was creative in searching for ways to reach clients where they were "stuck." His capacity for what he referred to as *therapeutic suspension*, a suspending of both belief and disbelief along with a disciplined naivete, enabled him to discover fresh and unanticipated meanings and resources in his clients.

James F. T. Bugental is viewed by many as one of existential–humanistic psychology's most prominent spokespersons. Bugental has long been a practitioner and advocate of long-term intensive psychotherapy. Central to his therapy is a powerful faith in a "life force" a tenaciousness in all of life that enables it to survive in extremely adverse conditions and manifest its potential. The therapist's job is to assist clients in clearing the way for their life force to open possibilities for authentic being. Bugental advocates against making the client an object of study or for the therapist to try to provide life for the client. Instead he emphasizes the importance of enlisting the client in mobilizing the life force. Consequently, he engages his clients in identifying and exploring important life *concerns*. Bugental (1999) defined *concern* as what matters in one's life and as the "process that arouses, energizes and guides searching" (p. 73).

In his most recent thoughts about psychotherapy, Bugental (1999) stated his fundamental conviction, "What is alive is what is now" (p. xi), and advocates that therapists focus their attention on the immediate subjective experiencing of the client instead of information about the client. Bugental (1999) contended that experiencing-centered therapy "is not about *what* you think; it is about *how* you live with yourself right now" (p. 1). Bugental's goal is to "intensify and expand" the client's subjectivity and consequent awareness. What *was* or *may be*—thoughts and feelings about the past and future—are occurring in the present moment. Rejecting historical determinism, Bugental believes that attention to clients' historical past tends to make them objects of study rather than consciously experiencing beings whose lives are continually flowing, unfolding, and evolving. Bugental's (1999) rationale for this present focus is that "Increased awareness of ourselves in the living moment means increased effectiveness of self-direction and increased satisfaction in living" (p. 24).

The moving force of therapeutic change, for Bugental, is the opening of perceptual boundaries, seeing vital aspects of one's life in fresh ways. Bugental views the client's symptoms or complaints as *constraints*. Clients experience distress because they feel limited in critical aspects of their lives. It follows, then, that a major goal of the therapist is to assist the client in identifying and removing constraints in their self and world constructs. In his view, "Psychotherapy . . . seeks to . . . disclose the underlying constraints and then . . . open out those constraints. In this way, the client finds possibilities where none seemed to exist before" (Bugental, 1999, p. 54). Bugental believes that a primary task of existential therapy is *searching*, an endeavor that requires clients to be fully present to themselves. For him, "this cycling of exploration-discovery-exploration is the *search* process" and is the driving force toward positive life transformation (Bugental, 1999, p. 54). Clients' concerns are likely to be resolved when new choices in views and behavior become evident.

Bugental (1999) summarized his position as follows:

> Human beings are most truly subjective presences and processes, rather than objective things solely manipulated by forces beyond their conscious knowing. . . . This recognition demands some shift in our image of the human, with a consequent change in our understanding of psychotherapy. That, in turn, calls for a move from emphasis on the objective, explicit and causative to a focus on the subjective, implicit and intentional. (p. 60)

Irvin Yalom is the author of *Existential Psychotherapy* (1980), a text that is considered by many to be the most comprehensive, in-depth explication of the existential approach to psychotherapy. Yalom (1980) defined existential psychotherapy as a "dynamic approach to therapy which focuses on concerns that are rooted in the individual's existence" (p. 5). For Yalom (1980), existential therapy emphasizes "conflict that flows from the individual's confrontation with the givens of existence" (p. 8). He identified these "givens" or ultimate concerns with which we must all grapple as (a) death, (b) freedom, (c) isolation, and (d) meaninglessness. Each of these ultimate concerns plays a critical role in client's pathology and in the therapeutic process.

Death represents one of life's inescapable truths that life fades and that we all fear the fading and ultimately the loss of life. As we embrace this truth, we open the possibility to reprioritize our lives and live more fully, authentically, and meaningfully. Vulnerability to and fear of death sometimes lead clients to create myths that they are special and, therefore, not subject to death; or clients create and maintain a belief in an ultimate rescuer who will save them from life's hardships, including death. *Freedom* to choose the course of one's life also implies responsibility for one's choices. A vital endeavor of existential therapy is for clients to recognize and accept responsibility for their lives and engage their wills in turning choice into action and commitment. *Isolation* or separateness refers to the experience of separation and aloneness that are sources of anxiety, dread, and powerlessness. Existential therapy addresses what the client can and cannot get from others and that the ultimate source of healing is in relationship. *Meaninglessness* is viewed by Yalom, Frankl, Maddi, and others as a significant substrate of many forms of psychopathology. A universal dilemma faced by all people is that while meaning and purpose seem essential to living, there is no inherent meaning in life. Therefore, each person must struggle to find personal meaning in his or her goals and manner of living. A primary task of existential therapists is to enable their clients to engage fully in their own lives while also looking for purposes beyond themselves.

Yalom (1980) presented a useful contrast between humanistic psychology, with its North American roots, and existential psychology, with its European roots, and articulated the differences in emphases:

> The existential tradition in Europe has always emphasized human limitations and the tragic dimensions of existence. . . . The United States (and the humanistic psychology it spawned) bathed in a Zeitgeist of expansiveness, optimism, limitless horizons and pragmatism. . . . The European focus is on limits, on facing and taking into oneself the anxiety of uncertainty and nonbeing. The humanistic psychologists, on the other hand, speak less of limits and contingency than of development of potential, less of acceptance than of awareness, less of anxiety than of peak experiences and oceanic oneness, less of meaning than self-realization, less of apartness and basic isolation than of I–Thou and encounter. (p. 19)

Yalom is best known for his unparalleled contribution to the field of group psychotherapy. His four editions of *The Theory and Practice of Group Therapy* are considered by many to be the standard in the field (e.g., Yalom, 1995). His interpersonal approach to group therapy integrates many aspects of existential therapy. His book, *Love's Executioner* (1989), a compilation of existential psychotherapy cases, was a national bestseller for several months.

Clark Moustakas is best known for his contributions to the development of child therapy. He, along with Frederick Allen (1942) and Virginia Axline (1947), were pioneers in what would later be known as humanistic approaches to child psychotherapy. Moustakas demonstrated the importance of the child therapist's creative use of self as a healing component of therapy with children. A vital aspect of his therapeutic attitude is captured in his poignant statement, "I have chosen to risk my own self in the hopes of knowing the glory of a voice that speaks for the first time" (Moustakas, 1975, p. i). In recent years, Moustakas has articulated an existential phenomenological model of psychotherapy composed of the following processes: (a) *initial engagement*, the development of a supportive, safe, and relaxed environment that encourages freedom of expression in the client; (b) *epoche*, a process in which the therapist intentionally puts aside preconceptions and attempts to take in the client and his or her experience as freshly as possible; (c) *phenomenological reduction*, a process of discovering the client's central issue or problem, the core theme that troubles the person; (d) *imaginative variation*, a process of entertaining possibilities, perspectives, and directions that might provide fresh frames of reference and meanings that enhance the self and carry forward the client's manner of living; (e) *synthesis*, an integrative process of bringing together experience and meanings; and (f) *plan of action*, transforming personal discovery into effective action. Moustakas and other existential therapists view therapy as a form of being-with the client in which a present therapist strives to engage in an authentic encounter (see also Walsh & McElwain, this volume, chapter 8).

Other significant contributors to existential psychotherapy include Binswanger (1975), Boss (1963), Deurzen-Smith (1988), May (1969), Schneider and May (1995), Spinelli (1997), and Strasser and Strasser (1997).

Gestalt Therapy

Frederick and Laura Perls

Frederick Perls (1893–1970) worked as an assistant to Kurt Goldstein, whose Gestalt psychology perspective, holistic approach, and concept of self-actualization affected his thinking. Lewin's field theory, phenomenology, and existentialism would all influence Perls's development of Gestalt therapy. Perls trained as a psychoanalyst at the Vienna and Berlin Institutes of Psychoanalysis. His training analyst in the early 1930s was Wilhelm Reich, who influenced Perls to focus on his clients' bodily experiencing as it related to their immediate living and problems. Other influential analysts under which he trained include Helene Deutsch, Karen Horney, and Otto Fenichel. After moving to South Africa in 1934 with his wife Laura because of the rise of Nazism, he established the South African Institute for Psychoanalysis in 1935. During his 12 years in South Africa, Perls met Jan Smuts, whose book *Holism and Evolution* influenced his creation of Gestalt therapy. The philosopher Sigmund Friedlander affected Perls's thinking with his writings on polarities and the importance of balance between them in personal functioning.

In 1946, Perls moved to New York City. In *Ego, Hunger and Aggression* (Perls, 1947), which blended holistic concepts with psychoanalysis, Perls articulated the goal of psychotherapy as "waking the organism to a fuller life." A few years later, *Gestalt Therapy* (1951) was published. It was written by Perls, Hefferline, and Goodman who, along with Laura Perls, established the New York Institute for Gestalt Therapy in 1952. *Gestalt Therapy* laid the foundation for the basic theory and practice of Gestalt therapy and remains a basic reference for its students. Perls would later establish several Gestalt training institutes of Gestalt therapy in the United States and Canada.

Laura Posner Perls (1905–1990), who was trained in psychology, was a cofounder of Gestalt therapy and wrote several chapters of *Ego, Hunger and Aggression* (Perls, 1947). Significant influences on her thinking included existential theologians Martin Buber and Paul Tillich. Although she wrote relatively little, much of the influence on Gestalt psychology of existentialism and phenomenology should be credited to her. In contrast to her husband, who placed a high premium on client awareness, Laura Perls emphasized contact and support in the therapeutic relationship.

Like many of the founders of humanistic therapies, Frederick Perls reacted adversely to the dogmatism and constraint of classical psychoanalysis. Perls drew from Gestalt psychology the notion that people naturally tend to perceive whole patterns as opposed to bits and pieces and that the whole is not equivalent to the sum of its parts. Furthermore, perception was viewed as an active and creative process. Consequently, to understand an individual's behavior, one must understand the person's subjective perceptions of reality. The Gestalt therapist's emphasis on enhancing the client's awareness was then a critical step in understanding the client's immediate experience. Another concept adopted from Gestalt psychology was that of *figure* (that which stands out) and *ground* (that which constitutes the background). Gestalt therapists engage their clients to focus their awareness on what emerges from the background as figure for them, the assumption being that what emerges often represents a need or something that is troubling the person. Yontef (1993) assessed the early phase of the development of Gestalt therapy as follows: In contrast to psychoanalysis, the early form of Gestalt therapy practiced in the late 1940s and 1950s emphasized "reality contact over transference, active presence over blank screen, dialogue and phenomenological focusing over free association and interpretation, field theory over mechanistic theory, and process theory over Newtonian and Aristotelian dichotomies" (Yontef, 1993, pp. 9–10).

During the 1960s, a different model of Gestalt therapy emerged, chiefly influenced by Perls. In the "anything goes" era of the 1960s, there was an anti-intellectual tone to the human growth movement. Perls was a gifted therapist who often had a powerful and constructive impact on those with whom he worked. He often elicited feelings of admiration and awe for his brilliance, charisma, and creativity, but he also elicited feelings of distaste.

Corey (1996) commented that Perls "was viewed variously as insightful, witty, bright, provocative, manipulative, hostile, demanding and inspirational" (p. 223). The flamboyant style of "Fritz" Perls became the model of Gestalt therapy—for better or for worse. His therapeutic style tended to be confrontational, dramatic, gimmicky, therapist orchestrated, abrasive, intense, and insensitive. Slogans such as "lose your mind, come to your senses" characterized the mentality of many Gestalt therapists during this period. As Yontef (1993) recalled,

> Gestalt therapy developed this theatrical and highly catharsis oriented approach. It was arrogant, dramatic, simplistic, promising quick change. . . . This turn-on, quick-change orientation was in marked contrast with the long term therapy of the early Gestalt therapists and . . . with the actual practice of skillful Gestalt therapists during the 1960s. (p. 11)

Toward the end of his life, Perls (1969) apparently recognized the damage that had been done to Gestalt therapy by its flamboyant practitioners and wrote: "A gimmick should be used only in the extreme case. . . . In Gestalt therapy, we are working to promote the growth process . . . and develop human potential. We do not talk of instant joy . . . [or] instant cure. The growth process . . . takes time" (p. 2). Since Perls's death in 1970, the practice of Gestalt therapy has softened and shifted its emphases toward the quality of the therapist–client relationship, dialogue, empathic attunement, tapping the client's wisdom and resources, an expansion of therapeutic styles, and development of theory, especially field theory and phenomenology. Another change in the 1970s and beyond was a deemphasis in technique (e.g., empty chair) that had been overidentified with what Gestalt therapy was.

Distinctive Characteristics and Contributions of Gestalt Therapy

Gestalt therapists have made substantial contributions to the theory and practice of humanistic psychotherapies. Some of the most prominent contributions include the following:

1. *The critical importance of contact with oneself, with others, and with one's environment:* In Gestalt therapy, *contact* refers to what the client is in touch with, the focal point of the client's awareness. The experience of contact involves a feeling of connection with others, oneself, or the external world while maintaining a sense of separation. Contact boundaries distinguish between one person and another, between people and objects, and between aspects of one's self. Authentic encounter between client and therapist is at the heart of the therapeutic process. The therapist relates with presence and immediacy,

sometimes sharing with the client his or her experience of the client. As E. Polster and Polster (1973) noted, "Contact is the lifeblood of growth, means for changing oneself and one's experience of the world" (p. 101). Healing is conceived as taking place in the meeting.

Contact boundary disturbances occur when the boundary between self and others or between self and objects becomes blurred or disturbed, resulting in the individual being out of balance and frustrated that his or her needs are not being met. Contact disturbances may take the form of accepting views or values uncritically (introjection), attributing parts of the self to others (projection), doing something to oneself that one wants to do to someone else or doing something for oneself that one wants the other to do for oneself (retroflection), avoidance of contact (deflection), and blurring or minimizing the differences between oneself and others (confluence). Helping clients repair disturbances in the contact process is a basic goal of Gestalt therapy.

2. *The importance of authentic relationship and dialogue*: Contemporary Gestalt therapists place a high value on the quality of the dialogical engagement. Gestalt therapy has been greatly affected by Martin Buber and his student Maurice Friedman. Buber's premise that healing occurs through meeting is at the heart of Gestalt therapy. In dialogic Gestalt therapy, the primary goal is to "meet" the client where he or she is in the moment and to make empathic contact with the client. The therapist's goal is not to "fix" the client but to engage in authentic dialogue. Yontef (1998) commented,

Dialogue is a special form of contact in which people are in touch with each other and share what they experience *without aiming for an outcome*, each appreciating the other as a separate source of experience and worthiness, both saying what they mean and meaning what they say. In dialogic contact the meeting is not an instrumental action done in order to reach some other goal, but rather contact with the other person is an end in and of itself. (p. 87)

It should be noted that, in Gestalt therapy, the client's sense of *self* is relational. There is no "I' or "me" or a "self" isolated from contact with others. Rather the self emerges from the field of which it is a part when it interacts with another or the physical environment.

Dialogical Gestalt therapy involves confirmation, inclusion, and presence. *Confirmation* refers to the therapist's imagining what it is like to be the client while affirming the client as a separate, independent, and distinctive person. *Inclusion* implies developing a "feeling for" the client's viewpoint and grasping his or her experience, without evaluation or judgment, while maintaining a separate sense of self. Therapist *presence* is manifested as the therapist expresses observations, preferences, feelings, personal experiences, and thoughts with the client as they seem relevant and with appropriate discrimination. Therapist confirmation, inclusion, and presence are firmly grounded in the therapist's respect, caring, and warmth for the client.

3. *Field theory, phenomenology, and awareness*: In field theory, events are understood by looking at the whole field of which the event is a part. The focus is on the description of the relationship of the parts to each other and to the whole. Because all parts of the field affect all other parts, one cannot understand behavior without understanding the field in which the behaving person exists at the moment. Consequently, a phenomenological approach is essential in field theory because the client's behavior can be understood only by understanding the client's subjective perceptions of reality in the given field. A goal of Gestalt therapy is to enhance the client's awareness of "what is" to achieve insight. By insight, Gestalt therapists mean a patterning of the perceptual field that clarifies significant realities for the client as they come into the foreground. It means seeing in fresh ways so new Gestalts are formed that open up alternative possibilities for behaving.

The client's awareness of immediate experience is central in Gestalt therapy. Yontef and Simkin (1989) contended that "*the only goal is awareness* . . . [which] includes knowing the environment, responsibility for choices, self-knowledge and self acceptance and the ability to contact" (1989, p. 327). Gestalt therapists focus on the client's awareness of sensations, the style of verbal expression, nonverbal behavior and body language, affective experiencing, and awareness of the client's wants and values. They emphasize experiencing and processing emotion as opposed to talking *about* emotion. The therapeutic process often involves the intensification of experience, a heightening of awareness that enables the clear emergence of emotion and personal needs. The heightening of emotion provides energy and helps orient clients toward action that will satisfy their needs.

4. *Therapeutic focus on the present, "here-and-now" experiencing of the client*: Past and future events are viewed through the lens

of the present. Thus, Gestalt therapy aims at enabling clients to explore their immediate awareness and to learn how they construct reality in the moment. Emphasis is on the what and how (as opposed to the why) of experiencing. The goal is to enable clients to attend to their immediate behavior and its impact, understand their manner of avoidance, and interact more authentically and effectively in the moment. Although Gestalt therapists are present centered with their clients, they also view clients in larger contexts, including personality patterns existing over time and in terms of the client's ongoing life story. An important concept in Gestalt therapy is the client's "unfinished business," which refers to feelings about prior experiences that have not been expressed or resolved. Working through such unfinished business means bringing the past into the present in such a way as to complete a gestalt and bring closure to the preoccupation with the prior experience. In this process, split off or disowned parts of the self and conflicted relations with significant others are processed with a goal of reconstructing and integrating these experiences.

5. *The creative and spontaneous use of active experiments and exercises to facilitate experiential therapeutic learning*: Gestalt therapists use a number of methods to help clients illuminate their experiences and its personal meaning. They have been enormously creative in developing a wide range of exercises and experiments. An *exercise* is a ready-made technique whose purpose is to evoke specific emotions, make something happen, or achieve a goal (e.g., exaggerating a gesture). An *experiment* is a procedure proposed for experiential exploration and discovery that grows naturally from the therapist–client interaction. The experiment is proposed with a spirit of "Let's try this out and see what might be learned." Experiments have the form of guided journeys in which what might be discovered is unknown and may be a surprise to the therapist and client. Gestalt therapy has been called "permission to be creative" by Zinker (1977, p. 3 ff.), suggesting that therapists rely on their spontaneity and inventiveness to develop exercises and experiments in the moment that have promise for facilitating phenomenological exploration.

The two best-known Gestalt experiments are the *empty-chair technique*, which is used to resolve unfinished conflicts with others, and the *two-chair technique*, which is used to resolve conflicts between different aspects of the self. Gestalt therapists place a high premium on the client's attending to that which is in their immediate awareness. Toward this end, clients are often asked "What are you aware of?" and then encouraged to "stay with it," followed by "Where are you now?" (or similar questions) to assist them in processing their immediate experience. Although Gestalt therapists use a great variety of experiments and techniques to facilitate experiential learning in the client, it would be incorrect to associate Gestalt therapy primarily with technique.

Contemporary Gestalt therapists value most highly the quality of the dialogic relationship and the focused processing of subjective experience.

Erving and Miriam Polster have played an enormous role in advancing the theory and practice of Gestalt therapy. They were instrumental in expanding the Gestalt approach to therapy and in "softening" the therapist's style. Their book *Gestalt Therapy Integrated* (1973) is considered to be seminal reading for serious practitioners of Gestalt therapy. Erving Polster assigns a prominent role for the client's self in therapy. He describes the "self" as a system of continuing contact that is fluid while still retaining a sense of constancy. The individual's complex of life experiences is formed into a Gestalt of the self that evolves over time. Polster identifies two forms of the self: (a) *essential selves*, which are conceived as the essences of one's existence and represent fundamental aspects of the person (e.g., thoughtful) that are affected relatively little by experience, and (b) *member selves*, or aspects of the self that are more responsive to environmental contingencies. Member selves are more fluid but could transform into an essential self.

In *Every Person's Life Is Worth a Novel* (1987), Erving Polster contends that people are story-telling beings and emphasizes the importance of clients telling their life stories. Noting that clients often tend to tell their stories in lifeless ways, Polster believed that the therapist's task is to help clients flesh out their stories and experience the richness of the dramas that are their lives unfolding. With the support of the therapist's fascination with their stories, clients are enabled to become more interesting and engaged with the therapist (and others). He (1987) commented,

> Sooner or later, when I have alertly hung around, the faded person will usually come out of hiding. For moments . . . he reveals something so arresting as to merit . . . even more widespread attention. In giving up the dulled image, such persons offer remarkably individualistic, suspenseful, and colorful memories, attitudes, expectations and insights. (p. 4)

With engaged immersion in his clients' story, Polster helps clients transform the ordinary storytelling into extraordinary living in the moment, thus providing the client with a glimpse of how they might live.

Miriam Polster has developed a model of client growth as a three-stage integrative process as follows:

1. *Discovery stage*: Clients reach new realizations about themselves or view old problems or situations in new ways. The therapist provides a high level of support in this stage.
2. *Accommodation stage*: Clients recognize that they have choices and begin experimenting with new ways of behaving. Clients shift their focus from themselves to interpersonal relations.
3. *Assimilation stage*: Clients progress from choosing and trying out new behaviors to learning how to influence their environment and become more active, assertive, and effective at getting what they need and want. Clients' awareness is more astute as they feel freer to act and move toward integration. Less therapist support is required at this stage as the client becomes more competent.

In *Eve's Daughters* (1992), Miriam Polster addressed the societal limitations that exist for women because of the lack of female heroes. She pointed out that most heroes are men, with women usually in supporting roles to men. Polster suggested a new view of heroism which she terms *neoheroism*. In this view, women's heroic accomplishments are on a par with those of men and are attained primarily by providing support, knowledge, and power that enables other women to achieve.

A number of other people who have made substantial contributions to Gestalt therapy include Fagan and Shepherd (1970), Kempler (1981), Simkin (1976), Yontef (1993), and Zinker (1977).

EVOLUTION OF HUMANISTIC PSYCHOTHERAPIES: ADVANCES IN THEORY AND THERAPEUTIC PRACTICE

All major schools of humanistic psychotherapies were well established by the mid-1960s. Since then, there have been substantial developments in theory and practice. In the next section, I review the most prominent advances in theory and practice, including the emergence of experiential therapies.

Art Combs's Contributions

Arthur W. Combs (1912–1999), a former student of Rogers, made an enormous contribution to the fields of humanistic psychology, education, and psychotherapy with the publication of 23 books and monographs in a career spanning over 60 years. He is best known for his *perceptual field approach*, which can be briefly stated as follows: "All behavior, without exception, is completely determined by and pertinent to the perceptual field of the behaving organism" (Combs, 1999, p. 21). Or as Combs (1997) preferred to say, "people behave according to how things seem to them, especially how they perceive themselves, the situations they are in and the purposes they are trying to achieve" (p. 240). He described the perceptual field as synonymous with the phenomenal field, the field of meaning, experiential field, private world, or the person's life space. Combs maintained that people are continuously engaged in a process of being and becoming and that their self or identity constantly strives for continuance and enhancement.

Combs articulated a comprehensive system of psychotherapy whose essence I attempt to describe here. Therapeutic change, in Combs's view, is dependent on constructive changes in the client's self-concept. Combs (1989) believed that people "can, will, must move toward health IF the way seems open for them to do so" (p. 22). The therapist's primary role is to create conditions for the client to draw from his or her natural motivation toward personal fulfillment. The provision of therapeutic conditions sets clients free to explore themselves and their worlds. The therapist's understanding and acceptance of the uniqueness of each client enable the therapist to appreciate differences and the need to create, with the client, an individualized course of therapy. Given Combs's belief that client behavior is a consequence of perception or personal meaning, then a primary task of the therapist is to enable clients to become aware of and clarify their personal meanings. Therapist empathy is the means by which the therapist makes inferences about the experiential world of the client. By attending to the clients' behavior, which is a consequence of their perceptions of themselves and their worlds, Combs (1989) maintained that "it should be possible to become aware of what people are thinking and feeling by *reading behavior backwards*" (p. 38). Thus, Combs asked himself, "How might a person think, feel or believe in order to behave as they are?"

As clients' meanings become clear, Combs encourages further exploration to provide an opportunity to develop more congruent and functional ways for them to view themselves and their worlds and achieve their goals. Regarding the fundamental importance of helping clients alter their perceptions, Combs (1989) stated, "Change in behavior without fundamental changes in the perceptual field provides only an illusion of progress [and] . . . clients quickly revert to behaviors more in line with their unchanged perceptual organization" (p. 44). Because Combs believes that the self-concept determines behavior, the fundamental change in the perceptual field that leads to constructive change is change in the client's self-perceptions. Combs (1989) made the point that the self-concept "lies at the very center of a person's existence [and is] one's most precious possession" (p. 49). Consequently, threat to the self is disruptive to the person's well-being and functioning. Combs maintains that therapy must challenge clients to confront themselves, their lives, and what is possible while minimizing threat. Thus, change in the self-concept "requires opening up experience, not narrowing it. It requires movement from what is to what may be" (Combs, 1989, p. 59).

Combs views the level of feeling expressed by clients as an indicator of the personal relevance and meaning of their experience. Accordingly, he stresses the importance of the therapist's attention to and processing of client emotion. Viewing psychotherapy as a learning experience, Combs believes that clients are most likely to engage in the therapeutic process when they have a "need to know." Thus, it becomes the therapist's job to facilitate clients' learning by following their lead regarding what is most relevant for them to know. Combs believes that the self of the therapist is the most critical factor in assisting clients to learn from their experience. He describes effective helpers as (a) people oriented, (b) holding positive views of people's capacity, (c) having positive self-concepts, and (d) having broader and larger purposes and priorities than less-effective helpers. Finally, Combs takes the position that effective therapists have a clear, comprehensive, and integrated system of belief guiding their work. Stating that "there are no universal right ways to counsel" (Combs, 1989, p. 156), he urged therapists to find their own voice as therapists and creatively fit their methods and responses to the needs and goals of their clients.

Focus on Emotion and Bodily Experience

Humanistic therapists focus intently on the emotional experiencing of their clients, on the assumption that emotions are their body's way of interpreting experience. Emotions, viewed as "impulses to act," provide essential information about clients' motives and desires while providing clues as to what might be needed for constructive change. Understanding emotion also provides clients insight into basic meaning structures that cannot be assessed accurately through purely cognitive analysis. Because the effective processing of emotional experiences are so essential to clients' therapeutic learning and well-being, humanistic therapists take the view that feelings are vital sources of information.

Conversely, most humanistic therapists place relatively less emphasis on cognitive analyses, believing that intellectual insight is usually not sufficient to effect constructive change. Clinical experience and research (e.g., Wallerstein, 1969) suggest that intellectual insight is of limited value or is insufficient for change. It is probably fair to say that most humanistic therapists believe that although cognitive insight may illuminate experience and its meaning, it is not likely to have much effect on the change process unless the emotional aspects of problematic experiences are felt, explored, and integrated.

Although humanistic therapists recognize the importance of processing client emotion, they vary considerably regarding how they respond to emotion. The main areas of difference are along the continuum of therapist directivity and technique used. A number of humanistic therapists, including Gendlin (1996), Rice (1974), Greenberg & Van Balen (1998), Prouty (1998), and Mahrer (1996), have developed increasingly refined methods for enabling clients to process their experiences. Next I review the experiential psychotherapies, those that place the highest emphasis on client processing of emotion and bodily states.

Experiential Therapies

Focusing-Oriented Experiential Psychotherapy

Eugene Gendlin made a major contribution to humanistic therapies by developing the process of experiential focusing (see Gendlin, 1996). He observed that successful clients focused on and processed their affective experience. On the basis of this learning, Gendlin gently encouraged his clients to attend to their bodily sense of their problem, believing that the body carries the problem in a physically felt form. By attending to the "felt sense" of the problem in a supportive relationship, along with some guidance from the therapist, the client's experience and its personal meaning would often unfold and become clear. When this sense of clarity was reached, the client's bodily response of relief or release confirmed the "rightness" of the understanding. The experience is one of cognitive and affective knowing coming together in a holistic and integrated manner. The use of experiential focusing was seen by many as a major innovation and advancement in client-centered and other humanistic therapies. Some, especially more traditional client-centered therapists, saw it as incompatible because it directed the client's process.

Laura N. Rice extended the client-centered response style by developing the method of evocative reflection, which she viewed as a more active, vivid, and powerful form of client-centered reflection. According to Rice (1974), the aim of evocative reflection is to "open up the experience and provide the client with a process whereby he can form successively more accurate constructions of his own experience" (p. 290). Believing that clients have had problematic experiences that have never been adequately processed, Rice (1974) identified the targets of therapy as "the set of schemes that are relevant to the recurrent situations in which the client reacts in unsatisfactory ways" (p. 293). The goal is to enable the client to reprocess experience in an undistorted manner that results in the reorganization of old and dysfunctional schemes. Rice (1974) believed that "if the client can fully explore his reactions to one such situation, and become aware of the elements in a more accurate and balanced form . . . the effect will be to force reorganization of all of the relevant schemes" (p. 294; see also Hendricks, this volume, chapter 7).

Process–Experiential Therapy

Leslie Greenberg, Robert Elliott, and their colleagues have blended the essence of client-centered therapy with elements of Gestalt therapy, existentialism, and Rice's and Gendlin's experiential methods into a therapy they have called *process–experiential therapy*. Greenberg describes process–experiential therapy as both relationally and task oriented. Therapist empathic attunement, bond, and collaboration on client goals and treatment tasks are seen as essential. The approach involves the client's working on therapeutic tasks with a process-directive therapist. Greenberg is clear in emphasizing that the client and the quality of the relationship always take precedence over the therapeutic tasks proposed, methods, or goals. The emphasis in process–experiential therapy is on processing emotion and the reconstruction of emotion schemes. "The primary objective in process–experiential therapy is to help clients integrate information from their emotional and cognitive systems to facilitate a more satisfactory adjustment. . . . Process–experiential therapists emphasize the role of emotion in personal development and functioning" (Watson, Greenberg, & Lietaer, 1998, p. 6; see also Elliott and Greenberg, this volume, chapter 9).

Mahrer's Experiential Approach

Alvin Mahrer has developed an experiential system that ventures to the borders of what is traditionally viewed as humanistic psychotherapy. With extensive roots in existential philosophy, his conceptualization offers a relatively simple model of personality consisting mainly of what is described as *potentials for experiencing*. Some of these "potentials" are close to the surface whereas others are deeper, with each relating to the others with varying degrees of compatibility and integration.

In Mahrer's (1996) experiential psychotherapy, the client locates a scene of powerful feeling. Then the client and the experiential therapist both enter into and live in the scene to discover the precise instant of peak powerful feeling to discover the underlying deeper potential for experiencing. After the client has entered the powerful scene, he or she is encouraged to be receptive and to welcome the experience. Mahrer contends that a critical, radical, qualitative, and quantum change occurs when the client wholly enters into his or her deeper potential for experiencing and when the client experiences, in the moment, what it is like to live and be a qualitatively whole new person in a qualitatively whole new personal world. Throughout the session, both the client and the therapist are living and experiencing scenes of powerful feeling, with virtually all of their attention on and in the scenes, as opposed to one another. The therapist is almost fully aligned or joined with the client and goes through the in-session changes right along with the client (A. R. Mahrer, personal communication, August, 2000).

One of Mahrer's notable contributions to humanistic therapy is his discovery-oriented approach to research on psychotherapy. The goal of this research is to discover the secrets of what psychotherapy can be. The key to this discovery-oriented research strategy is to answer four questions: (a) What are the excitingly new, highly impressive, magnificent changes that occur in psychotherapy sessions? (b) What are the steps or sequences in which these poignant in-session changes occur? (c) What are the exciting new ways in which these extraordinary in-session changes can be brought about? (d) In what new ways might these in-session changes be used?

Other important contributions to experiential psychotherapies include N. Friedman (1982), Gendlin (1962), Greenberg and Paivio (1997), Greenberg, Rice, and Elliott (1993), Greenberg, Watson, and Lietaer (1998), Hutterer, Pawlowsky, Schmid, and Stipsits (1996), Johnson (1996), Johnson and Greenberg (1994), Lietaer et al. (1990), Prouty (1994), Rennie (1998), Whitaker and Malone (1953), and Wright, Everett, and Roisman (1986).

Contributions to Children and the Family

Humanistic psychotherapists have made unique contributions to the remediation of family problems and the enhancement of family life. Two of the most prominent contributions, those of Virginia Satir and Tom Gordon, are presented in this section.

Virginia Satir (1916–1988) was a pioneer and founder of the development of family therapy. As a young child, she viewed herself as a parent "detective" and exhibited a curiosity about families that she retained throughout her accomplished professional career. As a young social worker, she railed against the pathology-oriented views of the person she was taught in her psychoanalytically oriented training. Satir (1982) recalled, "I felt I was doing some kind of 'name-calling' when I diagnosed. . . . The things . . . I was trained to look at were all negative. My sense told me somewhere there had to be something positive" (p. 16). By the early 1950s, Satir would eschew her "clinical professional self" to return to her "detective work," which meant being a careful listener and an observer who now looked for health in others and their families. She developed a communication theory based on her observation that there were significant discrepancies between what people said and their body language or nonverbal communication. These observations were instrumental in her development of family sculpting techniques.

The *primary survival triad* (composed of father, mother, and a child) was the conceptual cornerstone of Satir's approach. The triad was the source of the destructive or constructive messages children received from their parents. To survive in their families, children would do things that "worked against them." The goal of family therapy was to help families develop "nourishing" triads. Satir's task as a therapist was to observe the patterns of interactions between family members to understand the meaning and cause of the symptom.

In 1959, Satir joined Don Jackson, Gregory Bateson, John Weakland, Jay Haley, Jules Riskin, and others at the Mental Research Institute in Palo Alto, California. Later that year, Satir would develop the first formal training program in family therapy. In her training approach, Satir focused on the growth process—how it takes place, how it becomes distorted, and how it can be restored. She conceptualized growth as an ongoing process of *transformation and atrophy* in which people added on what they needed and let go of that which no longer fit. Satir (1982) commented, "I pay attention to the damage, but with the emphasis on what will develop health, instead if trying to get rid of what is wrong" (p. 22).

Satir's process model of family therapy rests on four basic assumptions: (a) People are geared toward growth, and symptoms represent blockages in freedom to grow within a family that is attempting to maintain its survival and balance; (b) people have all of the resources they need to thrive; (c) everyone and everything affects and is affected by everyone and everything in the system; and (d) therapy is a process that takes place between people and has positive change as its goal. Satir's initial endeavor is to make authentic contact with and to demonstrate her valuing of each family member. She envisions the therapist and family as joining forces to promote wellness. Although Satir views the therapist as the leader of the healing process, the therapist does not take charge of the family members. Rather, Satir strives to enable family members to disclose and study themselves, understand their communication and interactive patterns, reduce blaming, and recreate themselves in ways that enable all family members to develop and maintain a sense of wholeness and self-esteem.

Thomas Gordon was one of Carl Rogers's first students at Ohio State University, a colleague at the University of Chicago, and a long-time friend. Gordon was a pioneer in group-centered leadership, first publishing a chapter on the topic in 1951 in Rogers' *Client-Centered Therapy*. In 1955, Gordon published *Group-Centered Leadership: A Way of Releasing the Creative Potential of Groups*, an approach to leadership firmly grounded in democratic principles. Gordon (1995) expressed his conviction about the importance of democracy in relationships as follows: "Democracy *is* therapy. . . . The experience of living or working in a democratic relationship with others makes people healthy, while autocratic environments make people unhealthy" (p. 320).

In 1962, Gordon, a strong advocate for prevention in psychology, developed a training program for parents called Parent Effectiveness Training (PET). It is recognized as the first skills-based training program for parents. This program has four primary emphases: (a) Empathic listening and responding (active listening) to children when they are experiencing problems; (b) the expression of "I-messages" to encourage children to modify behavior that interferes with their parents' needs and that is unacceptable to them. The essence of an I-message is a nonblameful description of the child's behavior, an expression of the parent's feelings elicited by the behavior, and the tangible effect of the behavior on the parent; (c) a "no-lose" (democratic) problem-solving or conflict-resolution method to find mutually acceptable solutions to parent–child conflicts; and (d) a values consultation (expression of values the parent believes are in the child's best interests) from parent to child that is used at times when parents are concerned about behaviors of their children (e.g., poor grooming) that does not tangibly affect the parents' needs.

The effect of PET has been astounding in its pervasive and constructive impact on families (see also Bratton & Ray, this volume, chapter 12). As of 2000, the PET book has sold 4 million copies worldwide, and approximately 1.5 million people have taken the PET course or other effectiveness courses. Since 1962, Gordon, along with his wife Linda Adams and other colleagues, has developed additional courses for leaders, teachers, teenagers, women, couples, and families. Approximately 35,000 instructors have taught Gordon's approach in 43 countries and in 30 languages. In 1997, Gordon was nominated for the Nobel Peace Prize, and in 1999 he received the American Psychological Foundation's Gold Medal Award for Enduring Contribution to Psychology in the Public Interest.

Other humanistic therapists who have made important contributions to the treatment of children, couples, and families include Allen (1942), Axline (1947), Gaylin (1989), Johnson (1996), Johnson and Greenberg (1994), Kempler (1981), Moustakas (1997), O'Leary (1999), and Satir (1983; see also Johnson & Boisvert, this volume, chapter 10).

In the next section, I focus on one of the most characteristic values of humanistic therapists, the individualization of psychotherapy.

Individualizing Psychotherapy

Humanistic therapists tend to either reject or place relatively little value on diagnostic classification as a means of developing a course of therapy. They prefer "holistic, experiential diagnoses that attempt to understand persons as whole beings-in-context as opposed to preemptive labels that are concerned with inadequacies and illnesses . . . and believe that diagnostic labels are constructions placed upon the client and are not, in any way, reality itself" (Bohart et al., 1997, p. 83). Also, formal diagnostic labels are reductionistic and tend to simplify and obscure rather than illuminate clients' problems. The self-discovery that occurs in the client during the course of therapy is viewed as a more useful form of self-diagnosis in that it reflects the client's generation of personal knowledge. Because of the ideographic emphasis of humanistic therapies, strong emphasis is placed on individualizing therapy to the specific needs of the client.

Humanistic therapists do not, however, disregard the scientific evidence for sound practices in psychotherapy. They believe that "scientific knowledge may and should *inform* practice but it should never dictate it as an authority in a one way manner" (Bohart et al., 1997, p. 90). Consequently, primary importance is placed on the evidence generated in therapeutic dialogue to guide therapists' responses and the course of therapy.

One of the primary ways in which humanistic therapies have evolved is in their diversity, innovation, and individualization in practice. Ideally, therapists constantly monitor whether what they are doing "fits," especially whether their approach is compatible with their clients' manner of framing their problems and their belief about how constructive change will occur. Although the focus of humanistic therapists is primarily on the relationship and processing of experience, they may use a variety of responses and methods to assist the client as long as they fit with the client's needs and personal preferences.

Hubble, Duncan, and Miller (1999) and Duncan and Miller (2000) make a compelling case for the individualization of psychotherapy. Using an approach they describe as *client directed*, they maintain that therapy is most likely to be effective when therapists (a) develop a positive expectation for change; (b) embrace the view that all change is self-change; (c) enlist their clients as collaborative partners; (d) adopt their clients' view of their problems and their causes; (e) adopt their clients' goals for change, theory of change, and potential solutions and tailor the therapy accordingly; (f) identify and engage the client's competencies; (g) observe constructive change in the client, validate it when it is evident, and credit the client for his or her effort in effecting change; (h) encourage clients to incorporate resources outside of therapy; and (i) ask clients to be constructive critics of the therapist's performance. The comments of a 10-year-old client beautifully capture the essence of these authors' sentiments: "We have the answers, we just need someone to help us bring them to the front of our head. . . . It's a lot better to ask a person what they want to do and what they think will help" (Duncan & Miller, 2000, p. 63).

This way of being client centered has been supported in recent years by empirical research demonstrating that approximately 40% of the outcome of psychotherapy can be attributed to client factors or extratherapeutic factors (Asay & Lambert, 1999). Bohart and Tallman (1999) made a strong case for the client as an *active agent* of change, suggesting that the client's capacity for self-healing is the most potent factor in therapeutic change. As Bohart and Tallman (1999) stated, "the client's capacity for self-healing is the most potent factor in psychotherapy. It is the 'engine' that makes therapy work" (p. 91). In contrast, the therapist's contribution to the change process is estimated to account for 30% of the variance, and therapist technique was estimated to contribute only 15% of improvement (Asay & Lambert, 1999). As Bergin and Garfield (1994) observed, "it is the client more than the therapist who implements the change process. . . . As therapists have depended more on the client's resources, more change seems to occur" (pp. 825–826). A shift toward individualizing the manner of the therapist's response to the unique characteristics, needs, and strengths of the client would appear to be a significant advancement from Rogers's original "If . . . then" formulation, which focused primarily on therapist attitudinal conditions felt to be sufficient for all clients.

There have been a number of creative developments in humanistic concepts and theory in recent years. Some of the more notable advancements are addressed in the next section.

Creative Developments

Carl Rogers's theory of therapy, personality, and interpersonal relationships, published in 1959, remains as perhaps the most fundamental and comprehensive statement of humanistic therapy. Since Rogers's 1959 theory statement, a number of substantive modifications in client-centered and other humanistic theories of psychotherapy have been offered that build on or advance previous theory. Prouty (this volume, chapter 19) has placed greater importance on therapist contact with the client than Rogers's initial formulation. In a related vein, Watson (this volume, chapter 14) provides an expanded theory of how therapist empathy facilitates client change and differentiates various types of empathic responses. In line with Duncan and Miller (2000) and Hubble et al. (1999), I have suggested that therapists' adaptation to clients' learning and personal style are factors that enhance their ability to use therapy effectively (Cain, 1989).

Perhaps the most fundamental change in humanistic therapy has to do with the issue of therapist directiveness. The fundamental premise of therapist nondirectiveness has been challenged as being too confining for both therapists and clients and not fully in keeping with the more fundamental goal of enabling clients to experience freedom, choice, and control in their therapy and lives (Cain, 1990). Although traditional client-centered therapists maintain that a nondirective attitude is essential to practice, other humanistic theorists and practitioners have made a strong case for *process directiveness*. Based in part on research that shows that clients, on their own, often do not attend to and process critical aspects of their experiences without "process" guidance and assistance, many humanistic therapists, in collaboration with their clients, now propose a wide range of methods of processing experience for their clients' consideration. However, humanistic therapists never insist that clients follow their proposals and refrain from directing clients' content. Nor do they vary from their core belief and value that optimal therapist relational attitudes and qualities are essential to the promotion of client learning and growth.

The bedrock of most humanistic therapies is a basic premise that individuals have a natural tendency toward self-actualization. However, Greenberg (1998) and others have challenged the soundness of the concept of self-actualization and offered an alternative. Greenberg & Van Balen (1998) suggested that it is the "biologically adaptive emotion system that provides the scientific basis for the actualizing tendency and the associated organismic valuing process" (p. 46). Self-actualization is viewed by some humanistic therapists (e.g., M. Friedman, 1985) as having a strong interpersonal component and as a byproduct of confirming dialogue with another person. Seeman (1988) criticized the concept as being too general and abstract to be tested. In its stead, he proposed a human-system model composed of interrelated subsystems that are self-regulating. He contended that differences in the organism's efficacy in self-regulation affect the person's level of functioning. Seeman's (1988) working definition of self-actualization suggested that "*Persons are maximally actualizing when as total human systems they are functioning at peak efficacy*" (p. 309).

New syntheses of humanistic psychotherapy theory have been offered by a few authors. Seeman (see this volume, chapter 21) articulates a human-system model that has the power to "organize complex structures and also to account for their underlying unity" (p. 623). He identifies several subsystems that are "so intimately linked and mutually embedded that their function and their very definitions are interwoven with each other."(p. 623). Connection and communication within and between the subsystems provide for the possibility of optimal functioning. Human dysfunction is viewed as a result of impaired communication between the subsystems.

Greenberg and Van Balen (1998) offered a synthesis of client-centered, Gestalt, existential, and experiential theories of therapy. In their view, the person is a "symbolizing, meaning-creating being who acts as a dynamic system constantly synthesizing information from many levels of processing and from both internal and external sources into a conscious experience" (Greenberg

& Van Balen, 1998, p. 42). The person is also seen as an active agent who organizes his or her experiences into emotion-based schemes. Therapeutic change occurs as the result of therapist and client co-constructing new meaning through dialogue. In this view, integration of client emotion schemes and levels of processing enables the creation of new meanings. The self is viewed as a dynamic system that organizes "the elements of experience into a coherent whole [in] . . . a process of dynamic/dialectical synthesis" (Greenberg & Van Balen, 1998, p. 44). The notion of the self-concept is replaced by one's narrative constructions of one's identity. That is, the concept of self is the "ongoing process by which a person *makes sense of experience* and explains his or her actions" (Greenberg & Van Balen, 1998, p. 45). Dysfunction is viewed as resulting from three sources: (a) an inability to integrate aspects of experience and functioning in a coherent manner, (b) inability to symbolize adequately aspects of bodily experience, and (c) the activation of core maladaptive emotion schemes. Therapy is aimed at evoking maladaptive emotion schemes so they might be reprocessed and reconstrued, thereby enabling clients to resolve various difficulties in processing their experience.

CONCLUDING THOUGHTS

Starting with Carl Rogers's "Newer Concepts in Psychotherapy" presentation in 1940, the roots of what would become the first approach to humanistic psychotherapy were planted. In the past 60 years, a number of major humanistic therapies have been developed whose contribution to the field of psychotherapy has been pervasive and profound. Rogers taught us to listen and demonstrated the constructive impact on the client's well-being and growth of an optimal therapeutic relationship. For several decades, almost all graduate training programs in clinical and counseling psychology have emphasized the importance of developing empathic and relational skills in their students. The existential–phenomenological school has taught us, as psychotherapists and as human beings, that we create our realities from our subjective experiences and that we must all grapple with basic life issues such as our fundamental separateness and isolation, freedom–choice–responsibility, meaning, and the ultimate challenge of coming to terms with our inevitable death. Consequently, therapists of many persuasions have challenged their clients to live more authentic, meaningful, and richer lives. The Gestalt therapists have impressed on us the powerful impact of I–thou encounter and dialogue; the enlivening effect of heightened awareness of self, others, and environment; and the richness of living in the immediate and flowing present. Experiential therapists, with their focus on bodily and emotional states, have enabled us to understand that the "body knows" and that the processing of emotion is essential in clarifying our experiences, finding meaning, becoming grounded, and trusting our perceptions, judgment, and decision making. Relatedly, humanistic therapists have enabled us to understand the centrality of the self in mediating experience and behavior.

Humanistic psychologists fundamentally altered our view of the person. In contrast to a basically pathological and mechanistic view, Maslow and other humanistic scholars and practitioners enabled us to recognize that people can reach extraordinary levels of their potential and that they have enormous capacity for love, clarity of perception, acceptance of others, spontaneity, creativity, connection with others and all life forms, humor, freshness of experiencing, strong values and ethics, and capacity for transcendence. The current "positive psychology" movement surely owes a great debt to the optimistic view of people and their resourcefulness that has been advanced by humanistic psychologists. Humanistic therapists have always embraced a dual endeavor of enabling clients to resolve their problems *and* to become more optimally functioning beings.

Over approximately the past 25 years, humanistic therapies have evolved extraordinarily conceptually and in the sophistication of their therapeutic response styles and methods. A primary reason for this is the cross-fertilization within the humanistic family. Each humanistic therapy has benefited by incorporating and integrating some of the fundamental characteristics and strengths of other approaches while still retaining its own identity. Julius Seeman (this volume, chapter 21) perceptively describes humanistic therapies as process centered as opposed to content centered. Some of the most striking advances in our knowledge about effective therapeutic response have come from "microprocess" research addressing the immediate interactions between client and therapist. Similarly, human science research has provided a window to the inner experiences of the client and therapist that have refined and expanded our understanding of "what really happens." This more sophisticated understanding of therapy has enabled humanistic therapists to individualize therapy to fit the unique characteristics and needs of each client. Although humanistic therapists continue to view the quality of their relationship as the essential agent of change, they have become increasingly creative, adaptive, and discerning in the manner in which they respond to their clients. Therapist empathy, for example, has moved far beyond "reflection," as therapists have become more differentiated in their use of a variety of empathic response modes (Bohart & Greenberg, 1997).

Finally, there is cause for optimism in humanistic therapists. The large body of research evidence clearly shows that humanistic therapies are as effective or more effective than other major therapeutic approaches in treating a wide range of client problems. Both quantitative and qualitative forms of research have contributed to our ongoing understanding of what works and how it works. Most important, as our knowledge and skill advance, our clients have been the beneficiaries. As Carl Rogers might say about the evidence, "The facts are friendly."

REFERENCES

Allen, F. H. (1942). *Psychotherapy with children*. New York: Norton.

American Psychiatric Association. (1994). *Diagnostic and statistical manual of mental disorders* (4th ed.). Washington, DC: Author.

Ansbacher, H. L., & Ansbacher, R. R. (1956). *The individual psychology of Alfred Adler*. New York: Harper.

Asay, T. P., & Lambert, M. J., (1999). The empirical case for the common factors in therapy. In M. A. Hubble, B. L. Duncan, & S. D. Miller (Eds.), *The heart and soul of change* (pp. 23–55). Washington, DC: American Psychological Association.

Axline, V. M. (1947). *Play therapy*. New York: Houghton-Mifflin.

Barrett-Lennard, G. T. (1998). *Carl Rogers' helping system*. London: Sage.

Bergin, A. E., & Garfield, S. L. (Eds.). (1994). *Handbook of psychotherapy and behavior change* (4th ed.). New York: Wiley.

Binswanger, L. (1975). *Being in the world: Selected papers of Lugwig Binswanger*. New York: Basic Books.

Bohart, A. C., & Greenberg, L. S. (1997). *Empathy reconsidered: New directions in psychotherapy*. Washington, DC: American Psychological Association.

Bohart, A. C., O'Hara, M. M., Leitner, L. M., Wertz, F., Stern, E. M., Schneider, K., Serlin, I., & Greening, T. (1997). Guidelines for the provision of humanistic psychological services. *The Humanistic Psychologist, 25*, 64–107.

Bohart, A., & Tallman, K. (1999). *How clients make therapy work: The process of active self-healing*. Washington, DC: American Psychological Association.

Boss, M. (1963). *Psychoanalysis and daseinanalysis*. New York: Basic Books.

Bozarth, J. D. (1998). *Person-centered therapy: A revolutionary paradigm*. Ross-on-Wye, England: PCCS Books.

Bugental, J. F. T. (1999). *Psychotherapy isn't what you think*. Phoenix, AZ: Zeig, Tucker.

Burton, A. (1972). *Twelve therapists*. San Francisco: Jossey-Bass.

Cain, D. J. (1989). The paradox of nondirectiveness in the person-centered approach. *Person-Centered Review, 4*, 123–131.

Cain, D. J. (1990). Further thoughts about nondirectiveness and client-centered therapy. *Person-Centered Review, 5*, 89–99.

Combs, A. W. (1989). *A theory of therapy*. Newbury Park, CA: Sage.

Combs, A. W. (1997). Being and becoming: A field approach to psychology. *The Humanistic Psychologist, 25*, 233–243.

Combs, A. W. (1999). *Being and becoming*. New York: Springer.

Corey, G. (1996). *Theory and practice of counseling and psychotherapy*. Pacific Grove, CA: Brooks/Cole.

Damasio, A. R. (1994). *Descartes' error*. New York: Grossset/Putnam.

Deurzen-Smith, E. van. (1988). *Existential counselling in practice*. London: Sage.

Duncan, B. L., & Miller, S. D. (2000). *The heroic client: Doing client-directed, outcome-informed therapy*. San Francisco: Jossey-Bass.

Ehrenwald, J. (1991). *The history of psychotherapy*. Northvale, NJ: Jason Aronson.

Epting, F. R., & Leitner, L. M. (1992). Humanistic psychology and personal construct theory. *The Humanistic Psychologist, 20*, 243–259.

Fagan, J., & Shepherd, I. L. (1970). *Gestalt therapy now*. Palo Alto, CA: Science and Behavior Books.

Ford, D. H., & Urban, H. B. (1963). *Systems of psychotherapy*. New York: Wiley.

Frankl, V. E. (1963). *Man's search for meaning*. New York: Washington Square Press.

Frankl, V. E. (1967). *Psychotherapy and existentialism*. New York: Clarion.

Frie, R. (2000). The existential and the interpersonal: Ludwig Binswanger and Harry Stack Sullivan. *Journal of Humanistic Psychology, 40*, 108–129.

Friedman, M. (1985). *The healing dialogue in psychotherapy*. New York: Jason Aronson.

Friedman, N. (1982). *Experiential therapy and focusing*. New York: Half Court Press.

Gaylin, N. L. (1989). The necessary and sufficient conditions for change: Individual versus family therapy. *Person-Centered Review, 4*, 263–279.

Gendlin, E. T. (1962). *Experiencing and the creation of meaning*. New York: Free Press.

Gendlin, E. T. (1996). *Focusing-oriented psychotherapy*. New York: Guilford Press.

Gordon, T. (1955). *Group-centered leadership: A way of releasing the creative potential of groups*. Boston: Houghton-Mifflin.

Gordon, T. (1995). Teaching people to create therapeutic environments. In M. M. Sudh (Ed.), *Positive regard: Carl Rogers and other notables he influenced* (pp. 301–336). Palo Alto, CA: Science and Behavior Books.

Greenberg, L. S., & Paivio, S. C. (1997). *Working with emotions in psychotherapy*. New York: Guilford Press.

Greenberg, L. S., Rice, L. N., & Elliott, R. (1993). *Facilitating emotional change*. New York: Guilford Press.

Greenberg, L. S., & Van Balen, R. (1998). The theory of experience-centered therapies. In L. S Greenberg, J. C. Watson, & G. Lietaer (Eds.), *Handbook of experiential psychotherapy* (pp. 28–57). New York: Guilford Press.

Greenberg, L. S., Watson, J. C., & Lietaer, G. (1998). *Handbook of experiential psychotherapy*. New York: Guilford Press.

Hart, J. T., & Tomlinson, T. M. (1970). *New directions in client-centered therapy*. Boston: Houghton-Mifflin.

Havens, L. L. (1973). *Approaches to the mind*. Boston: Little, Brown.

Hubble, M. A., Duncan, B. L., & Miller, S. D. (1999). Directing attention to what works. In M. A. Hubble, B. L. Duncan, & S. D. Miller (Eds.), *The heart and soul of change* (pp. 407–447). Washington, DC: American Psychological Association.

Hutterer, R., Pawlowsky, G., Schmid, P. F., & Stipsits, R. (1996). *Client-centered and experiential psychotherapy*. Frankfurt: Peter Lang.

Johnson, S. M. (1996). *The practice of emotionally focused marital therapy*. New York: Brunner/Mazel.

Johnson, S. M., & Greenberg, L. S. (1994). *The heart of the matter: Perspectives on emotion in marital therapy*. New York: Brunner/Mazel.

Kelly, G. A. (1955). *The psychology of personal constructs*. New York: Norton.

Kempler, W. (1981). *Experiential psychotherapy within families*. New York: Brunner/Mazel.

Koch, S. (Ed.). (1959). *Psychology: A study of a science*. New York: McGraw-Hill.

Kirschenbaum, H. (1979). *On becoming Carl Rogers*. New York: Delacorte.

Laing, R. D. (1969). *The divided self*. Middlesex, England: Penguin.

Levant, R. F., & Shlien, J. M. (1984). *Client-centered therapy and the person-centered approach: New directions in theory, research and practice*. New York: Praeger.

Lieberman, E. J. (1985). *Acts of will: The life and work of Otto Rank*. New York: Free Press.

Lietaer, G., Rombauts, J., & Van Balen, R. (1990). *Client-centered and experiential psychotherapy in the nineties*. Leuven, Belgium: Leuven University Press.

Mahoney, M. J. (1991). *Human change processes*. New York: Basic Books.

Mahrer, A. R. (1996). *A complete guide to experiential psychotherapy*. New York: Wiley.

Maslow, A. H. (1970). *Motivation and personality*. New York: Harper & Row.

May, R. (1939). *The art of counseling*. New York: Abingdon-Cokesbury.

May, R. (1958). *Existence: A new dimension in psychiatry and psychology*. New York: Simon & Schuster.

May, R. (1969). *Love and will*. New York: Norton.

May, R. (1981). *Freedom and destiny*. New York: Norton.

May, R. (1987). *Paulus*. Dallas, TX: Saybrook Press.

Moustakas, C. E. (1975). *Who will listen?* New York: Ballantine Books.

Moustakas, C. E. (1995). *Being-in, being-for, being-with*. Northvale, NJ: Jason Aronson.

Moustakas, C. E. (1997). *Relationship play therapy*. Northvale, NJ: Jason Aronson.

O'Leary, C. J. (1999). *Counseling couples and families: A person-centered approach*. London: Sage.

Patterson, C. H. (2000). *Understanding psychotherapy: Fifty years of client-centered theory and practice*. Ross-on Wye, England: PCCS Books.

Perls, F. S. (1947). *Ego, hunger and aggression.* London: Allen & Unwin.

Perls, F. S. (1969). *Gestalt therapy verbatim.* Lafayette, CA: Real People Press.

Perls, F. S., Hefferline, R. F., & Goodman, P. (1951). *Gestalt therapy.* New York: Delta.

Polster, E. (1987). *Every person's life is worth a novel.* New York: Norton.

Polster, E., & Polster, M. (1973). *Gestalt therapy integrated.* New York: Bruner/Mazel.

Polster, M. (1992). *Eve's daughters: The forbidden heroism of women.* San Francisco: Jossey-Bass.

Prouty, G. (1994). *Theoretical evolutions in person-centered/experiential psychotherapy.* Westport, CT: Praeger.

Prouty, G. (1998). Pre-therapy and pre-symbolic experiencing: Evolutions in person-centered/experiential approaches. In L. S. Greenberg, J. C. Watson, & G. Lietaer (Eds.), *Handbook of experiential psychotherapy* (pp. 388–409). New York: Guilford Press.

Rennie, D. L. (1998). *Person-centered counselling: An experiential approach.* London: Sage.

Rice, L. N. (1974). The evocative function of the therapist. In D. A. Wexler & L. N. Rice (Eds.), *Innovations in client-centered therapy* (pp. 289–311). New York: Wiley.

Rice, L. N., & Greenberg, L. (1984). *Patterns of change.* New York: Guilford Press.

Rogers, C. R. (1939). *The clinincal treatment of the problem child.* Boston: Houghton-Mifflin.

Rogers, C. R. (1942). *Counseling and psychotherapy: Newer concepts in practice.* Boston: Houghton-Mifflin.

Rogers, C. R. (1951). *Client-centered psychotherapy.* Boston: Houghton-Mifflin.

Rogers, C. R. (1957). The necessary and sufficient conditions of therapeutic personality change. *Journal of Consulting Psychology, 21,* 95–103.

Rogers, C. R. (1959). A theory of therapy, personality and interpersonal relationships. In S. Koch (Ed.), *Psychology: A study of a science* (pp. 184–256). New York: McGraw Hill.

Rogers, C. R. (1961). *On becoming a person.* Boston: Houghton-Mifflin.

Rogers, C. R. (1970). *Carl Rogers on encounter groups.* New York: Harper & Row.

Rogers, C. R. (1972). My personal growth. In A. Burton (Ed.), *Twelve therapists* (pp. 28–77). San Francisco: Jossey-Bass.

Rogers, C. R. (1980). *A way of being.* Boston: Houghton-Mifflin.

Rogers, C. R. (1986). A comment from Carl Rogers. *Person-Centered Review, 1,* 3–5.

Rogers, C., & Dymond, R. F. (1954). *Psychotherapy and personality change.* Chicago: University of Chicago Press.

Satir, V. M. (1982). The therapist and family therapy: Process model. In A. M. Horne & M. M. Ohlsen (Eds.), *Family counseling and therapy* (pp. 12–42). Itasca, IL: Peacock.

Satir, V. (1983). *Conjoint family therapy* (3rd ed.). Palo Alto, CA: Science and Behavior Books.

Schneider, K. J. (1999). Rollo May: Liberator and realist. In D. Moss (Ed.), *Humanistic and transpersonal psychology* (347–354). Westport, CT: Greenwood Press.

Schneider, K. J., & May, R. (1995). *The psychology of existence*. New York: McGraw-Hill.

Seeman, J. (1965). Perspectives in client-centered therapy. In B. B. Wolman (Ed.), *Handbook of clinical psychology* (pp. 1215–1229). New York: McGraw-Hill.

Seeman, J. (1983). *Personality integration*. New York: Human Sciences Press.

Seeman, J. (1988). Self-actualization: A reformulation. *Person-Centered Review, 3*, 304–315.

Simkin, J. (1976). *Gestalt therapy mini-lectures*. Millbrae, CA: Celestial Arts.

Smith, D. (1982). Trends in counseling and psychotherapy. *American Psychologist, 37*, 802–809.

Spiegelberg, H. (1970). Phenomenology. In *Encyclopedia Britannica* (14th ed., pp. 810–812). Chicago: Encyclopedia Britannica.

Spinelli, E. (1989). *The interpreted world*. London: Sage.

Spinelli, E. (1997). *Tales of un-knowing*. New York: New York University Press.

Strasser, F., & Strasser, A. (1997). *Existential time-limited therapy*. Chichester, England: Wiley.

Taft, J. (1933). *The dynamics of therapy in a controlled relationship*. New York: Macmillan.

Tageson, C. W. (1982). *Humanistic psychology: A synthesis*. Homewood, IL: Dorsey Press.

Task Force for the Development of Guidelines for the Provision of Humanistic Psychological Services. (1997). Guidelines for the provision of humanistic psychosocial services. *The Humanistic Psychologist, 25*, 64–107.

Tausch, R. (1990). The supplementation of client-centered communication therapy with other valid therapeutic methods. In G. Lietaer & R. Van Balen (Eds.), *Client-centered and experiential therapies in the nineties* (pp. 65–85). Leuven, Belgium: Katholieke Universiteit te Leuven.

Wallerstein, R. S. (1969). *Forty-two lives in treatment*. New York: Guilford Press.

Watson, J. C., Greenberg, L. S., & Lietaer, G. (1998). The experiential paradigm unfolding. In L. S. Greenberg, J. C. Watson, & G. Lietaer (Eds.), *Handbook of experiential psychotherapy* (pp. 1–27). New York: Guilford Press.

Wexler, D. A., & Rice, L. N. (1974). *Innovations in client-centered therapy*. New York: Wiley.

Whitaker, C. A., & Malone, T. P. (1953). *The roots of psychotherapy*. New York: Brunner/Brunner.

Wright, L., Everett, F., & Roisman, L. (1986). *Experiential psychotherapy with children*. Baltimore: Johns Hopkins University Press.

Yalom, I. (1995). *The theory and practice of group therapy* (4th ed.). New York: Basic Books.

Yalom, I. (1980). *Existential psychotherapy*. New York: Basic Books.

Yalom, I. (1989). *Love's executioner*. New York: Basic Books.

Yontef, G. M. (1993). *Awareness dialogue and process*. Highland, NY: Gestalt Journal Press.

Yontef, G. M. (1998). Dialogic Gestalt therapy. In L. S. Greenberg, J. C. Watson, & G. Lietaer (Eds.), *Handbook of experiential psychotherapy* (pp. 82–102). New York: Guilford Press.

Yontef, G. M., & Simkin, J. S. (1989). Gestalt Therapy. In R. J. Corsini & Danny Wedding (Eds.), *Current psychotherapies* (4th Ed). Itasca, IL: Peacock.

Zimring, F. M., & Raskin, N. J. (1992). Carl Rogers and client/person-centered therapy. In D. K Freedhelm (Ed.), *History of psychotherapy* (pp. 629–656). Washington, DC: American Psychological Association.

Zinker, J. (1977). *Creative processes in Gestalt therapy*. New York: Vintage.

II
OVERVIEWS OF RESEARCH

2

THE EFFECTIVENESS OF HUMANISTIC THERAPIES: A META-ANALYSIS

ROBERT ELLIOTT

Humanistic therapies emphasize the values of self-determination, growth, pluralism, person-to-person relationship, wholeness, and experiencing as the basis of action and change. Although such values have sometimes been perceived as antithetical to quantitative investigation, Carl Rogers was in fact one of the pioneers in the investigation of the process and outcome of psychotherapy. Beginning in the late 1940s and early 1950s, he and his colleagues published some of the earliest controlled studies of therapy outcome (C. R. Rogers & Dymond, 1954). Unfortunately, client-centered therapists in North America largely lost interest in outcome research in the early 1960s. Furthermore, the other two major strands of humanistic therapy, Gestalt therapy and existential therapy, never developed research traditions of their own. As a result, from the late 1970s on, it became increasingly easy for mainstream psychologists and advocates of cognitive and behavioral therapies to dismiss humanistic therapies as irrelevant and lacking in empirical support. Today, there is a widely shared assumption in the field that humanistic therapies are ineffective, a "fact" that is put forward in most psychology textbooks and even reflected in psychology licensing exams (K. Davis, personal communication, October 11, 1996).

To make matters worse, in both North America and Europe, economic pressure on mental health services and scientific–political trends toward treatment standardization have led to calls for certain therapies to be officially recognized as effective, reimbursed by insurance, and actively promoted in training programs, at the expense of other therapies. The first wave of such attempts consisted of the Task Force on Promotion and Dissemination

I am grateful to the many researchers who sent me copies of published or unpublished outcome studies. Readers are urged to send me further information about humanistic therapy outcome research, new or old.

of Psychological Procedures (1995) in the United States and the so-called expert statement of Meyer, Richter, Grawe, von Schulenburg, and Schulte (1991) in Germany. These reports, however, were not kind to humanistic therapies and attempted to enshrine the supposed ineffectiveness of humanistic therapies as both scientific fact and health care policy.

Understandably, humanistic therapists (e.g., Bohart, O'Hara, & Leitner, 1998; Schneider, 1998) have responded to these challenges with some alarm. With good reason, they have challenged the assumptions and methods of the current research literature and current attempts to institute criteria for designating certain therapies as effective. However, the sometimes defensive and strident tone of these critiques can easily be read as implicit agreement with the judgment that humanistic therapies have no empirical support: After all, advocates of evidence-based psychotherapy must surely wonder, why would humanistic therapists confine themselves to general arguments, if they actually had data to prove their effectiveness?

Strangely, the argument from research evidence has been relatively neglected in the new "therapy wars." In spite of this, it is my contention that the widely held view of humanistic therapy as ineffective is incorrect. There is, in fact, a substantial body of research data that supports the effectiveness of humanistic therapies. Furthermore, this body of research is continuing to grow rapidly, with almost half of the available studies having appeared since 1990.

There are several explanations for the invisibility of humanistic therapy research: Some of the studies date from the 1950s and are unknown today. Some of the research uses new labels (e.g., process–experiential or emotionally focused). Many studies are buried in obscure corners of the literature or have been overlooked because they use single-group designs, generally ignored in meta-analyses. And much of this literature has only been published in German, making it inaccessible to monolingual North American psychologists.

This chapter is another in a series of meta-analytic reviews of research on the effectiveness of humanistic therapies, substantially updating earlier meta-analyses by Greenberg, Elliott, and Lietaer (1994) and Elliott (1996). Special features of this review that set it apart from previous meta-analyses of therapy outcome research include the following: (a) use of "change" or pre–post effect sizes, which allows the inclusion of single-group studies; (b) inclusion of a substantial number of previously unreviewed German-language studies; (c) use of statistical equivalence analysis ("proving the null hypothesis"; J. L. Rogers, Howard, & Vessey, 1993), which is particularly relevant to the question of comparative treatment effectiveness; and (d) application of statistical controls for the effects of researcher allegiance on research results.

The present analysis more than doubles the size of the sample of studies analyzed in Greenberg et al.'s (1994) original review, from 37 to 86. The additional studies include 24 not covered (or covered incompletely based on preliminary information) in the most recent review (Elliott, 1996), which was published in Germany. In attempting to be as complete as possible, I have now added a substantial number of German studies and investigations of process–experiential (PE) and emotionally focused therapy (EFT) for couples, as well as a smattering of older and recent studies.

This review addresses five sets of key questions regarding the effectiveness of humanistic therapies:

1. How much do clients in humanistic therapies change over the course of treatment? In which ways do clients change? Are the changes stable over time?
2. Do clients in humanistic therapies show more change than untreated control clients?
3. Do clients in humanistic therapies show amounts of change equivalent to that seen in nonhumanistic (and particularly cognitive–behavioral; CBT) therapies?
4. What study, client, and treatment characteristics affect amount of client change in humanistic therapies? These include research method (type of measure or control group, researcher location, and theoretical allegiance), client problem, and treatment characteristics (modality, setting, length, and therapist experience).
5. Do the major approaches to humanistic therapy ("pure" client-centered, nondirective–supportive treatments, PE, Gestalt, encounter, and other therapies) differ in their effectiveness?

METHOD

Studies Sampled

At this point, the analysis includes change effect size data from 99 therapy conditions in 86 studies, including 31 controlled studies with wait-list or no-treatment conditions, and 41 comparative treatment studies (including 51 comparisons with nonhumanistic treatments). Change effect size data were available on 357 measures, involving 5,030 clients.

Of the studies reviewed, 44 investigated client-centered therapy (CCT) in a relatively pure form, whereas 9 studied "nondirective" therapy with minor directive (e.g., relaxation training or education) elements. Fourteen studies examined task-focused PE therapies, 10 studies evaluated the closely related EFT for couples, 7 dealt with Gestalt therapy, 8 examined encounter/sensitivity groups, and another 7 looked at the outcome of various other experiential/humanistic therapies (e.g., focusing-oriented or cathartic). Nine of the studies reviewed were published prior to 1970; 19 were published in the 1970s and 26 in the 1980s; however, 45 (almost half) appeared in the 1990s, offering evidence for a revival of outcome research on humanistic and experiential therapies.

The average treatment length was 21.9 sessions (SD = 21.7, range = 2–100); the average number of clients studied was 50.8 (SD = 155.3; range = 6–1,426). Across the whole sample, researcher theoretical allegiances were most commonly prohumanistic (72%), although this breakdown varies across analyses.

Procedure

Measurement of Study Characteristics

For each study, characteristics of the treatments, clients, therapists, or the studies were rated to estimate the contribution of these features to effect size. I devised a set of rating scales using the categories listed in Exhibit 2.1.

Meta-Analysis of Change

Effect sizes were calculated for each measure or subscale by finding d, the difference between pretreatment and posttreatment/follow-up mean scores and dividing by the standard deviation. (For studies reported previously, the pretreatment standard deviation was used, but for the studies new to this report, pooled standard deviations are used, because these are more reliable.) Analyzing pre–post change effect sizes allows use of the largest number of studies, although the effects cannot be assumed to be equivalent to the between-groups post-only controlled effect sizes used in most meta-analyses (Lipsey & Wilson, 1993). Where means or standard deviations were not given, standard estimation procedures described by Smith, Glass, and Miller (1980) were used. After the original Greenberg et al. (1994) analysis, the D/STAT meta-analysis computer program was used for this purpose (B. T. Johnson, 1989). Effect sizes were calculated for each subscale of each outcome measure used, as long as the evaluative direction of the subscale could be determined (i.e., purely descriptive measures were not used).

After initial calculation, effect sizes were summarized as follows: First, pre–post effect sizes were averaged across subscales within measures for each of three assessment periods: posttherapy, early follow-up (less than a year), and late follow-up (a year or longer). These summary data were used for analyses of *measure effects*, to obtain estimates of the ways in which clients changed.

EXHIBIT 2.1
Rated Features of Studies

Measure type: 1 = individualized; 2 = clinician-rated symptoms/distress; 3 = client-rated symptoms/distress; 4 = social adjustment/interpersonal functioning; 5 = experiential functioning (e.g., self-awareness); 6 = self-image, self-esteem; 7 = personality, coping, health status; 8 = effect calculated from improvement ratings; and 9 = specific relationship quality.

Type of therapy: 1 = "pure" client-centered therapy; 2 = nondirective–supportive (client-centered with minor directive interventions, information); 3 = process–experiential therapy (e.g., task-focused process-directive treatments); 4 = Gestalt therapy; 5 = emotionally focused therapy for couples; 6 = encounter/sensitivity groups; and 7 = other experiential treatments (i.e., focusing-based, cathartic, or unspecified).

Comparison condition: This consists of the following two conditions.

Control condition: 1 = no treatment; 2 = wait-list control.

Nonexperiential treatments: 1 = cognitive–behavioral; 2 = psychodynamic; 3 = educational; and 4 = other or "usual" treatments.

Disorder or problem: 1 = mixed neurotic, psychosomatic, or interpersonal problems; 2 = depression; 3 = anxiety; 4 = normal populations with no or only minor problems; 5 = chronic or severe problems (schizophrenia, personality disorder); 6 = physical-based problems (e.g., weight, psychosocial adjustment to cancer); and 7 = relationship problems.

Treatment modality: 1 = individual; 2 = group; 3 = marital; 4 = program (i.e., inpatient multifaceted program with primarily experiential focus); and 5 = weekend marathon.

Setting: 1 = outpatient; 2 = inpatient.

Length of treatment: number of treatment sessions (weekend marathon = 10; inpatient = number of hospitalization days).

Therapist experience: 1 = para- or nonprofessional or bachelor-level; 2 = beginning graduate student or medical student; 3 = master's-level, intern, medical intern, or resident or advanced graduate student; 4 = new/recent PhD or psychiatrist; 1 to 9 years' postgraduate experience; 5 = experienced therapist with 10 or more years postgraduate experience.

Researcher allegiance (rated from author reputation or introduction): 1 = prohumanistic; 2 = neutral allegiance or can't tell; and 3 = against experiential.

Regional origin: 1 = North America; 2 = Germany/German-speaking country; 3 = U.K./British Commonwealth; 4 = other Europe; and 5 = other (e.g., Israel).

Assessment period: 1 = immediate posttherapy; 2 = early follow-up (1 to 11 months); and 3 = late follow-up (12 or more months).

Second, for analyses of *change (pre–post) effect size,* measures were averaged for each humanistic treatment condition for each of three assessment periods. Then, effect sizes were averaged across the three assessment periods to yield an overall change effect size value for each treatment in each study. In addition, standard correction and weighting formulas (Hunter & Schmidt, 1990) were applied to these effect sizes to obtain more precise estimates of overall effect.

Third, analyses of *controlled and comparative effect sizes* compared mean overall change effect sizes. Change effect sizes were also calculated for each control or comparative treatment condition, using the same procedures as above. Then, the overall change effect size for the control or comparative condition was subtracted from the overall change effect size for the humanistic treatment. Positive effect size values were assigned when the humanistic treatment showed a larger amount of change, whereas negative values were used to indicate less change than the control/comparative treatment condition.

Fourth, *equivalence analyses* were carried out for the key comparisons (e.g., between humanistic and nonhumanistic treatments). Equivalence analysis derives from biomedical research (especially pharmaceutical research) and has been adapted for psychosocial treatment research by J. L. Rogers et al. (1993). Elliott (1995), following Elliott, Stiles, and Shapiro (1993), proposed further adaptations, for meta-analysis of comparative treatment studies:

1. Set minimum clinically relevant difference: ES = ±0.4 *SD* (~4% of variance; 73% overlap of distributions; Cohen, 1988). This difference represents a point between a medium effect size of 0.5 (considered to be clinically meaningful) and a small effect size of 0.2 (considered to be too small to be clinically important).
2. Find mean (M_D) and standard deviation (SD_D) for the differences between pairs of change effect size values in the sample of comparative treatment studies being evaluated.
3. Calculate *t* for this difference (as one-group *t* test of the absolute value of the mean difference against a test value of 0.4), using the following formula:

$$t(.4) = \frac{(|M_D| - 0.4)}{SD_D/\sqrt{(n-1)}}.$$

4. If $p < .05$ (by two-tailed test), conclude treatments are clinically *equivalent.* If the difference is also significantly different from 0, conclude difference is statistically different but clinically *trivial.* If neither test is significant, conclude that the comparison is *equivocal* (neither different nor equivalent; Rogers et al., 1993).

RESULTS

How Much Do Clients in Humanistic Therapies Change During Treatment?

Overall change effect sizes are given in Table 2.1. The average change effect size obtained, across the 99 treatment groups and assessment periods, was 1.06 standard deviation, which means that the average treated client moved from the 50th to the 85th percentile in relation to the pretreatment population. Therefore, receiving treatment accounted for slightly more than 20% of the variance in client scores. This exceeds the 0.8 standard-deviation criterion cited by Cohen (1988) as a large effect size.

Next, standard correction and weighting formulas (Hunter & Schmidt, 1990) were applied to the overall effect size value to obtain more precise estimates (see Table 2.1). These analyses indicate little in the way of small sample bias (corrected ES = 1.01); weighting effect size by sample size,

TABLE 2.1
Summary of Overall Pre–Post Change, Controlled,
and Comparative Effect Sizes

Effect size (ES)	n	M	SD
Pre–post change ES			
By assessment point			
Post	89	1.03	0.59
Early follow-up (1–11 mos)	43	1.26	0.71
Late follow-up (≥ 12 mos)	25	1.15	0.55
Overall (mean ES)			
Uncorrected (M_g)	99	1.06	0.58
Corrected (M_d)	99	1.01	0.55
Weighted (M_{gw})	5,030[a]	0.85	0.43
Weighted/corrected (M_{dw})	5,030	0.80	0.45
Controlled ES (vs. untreated clients)[b]			
Uncorrected	36	0.99	0.72
Corrected	36	0.94	0.68
Weighted (M_{gw})	1,096	0.81	0.58
Weighted/corrected (M_{dw})	1,096	0.72	0.53
Comparative ES (vs. other treatments)[b]			
Uncorrected	48	0.00	0.62
Corrected	48	0.00	0.58
Weighted (M_{gw})	993	−0.01	0.58
Weighted/corrected (M_{dw})	993	0.00	0.44

[a]Number of clients in humanistic treatment conditions (used as weighting variable).
[b]Mean difference in change ESs for conditions compared; positive values indicate prohumanistic therapy results.

however, produced a somewhat smaller effect size of 0.85 standard deviation. This smaller weighted effect primarily reflects the contribution of large German studies with relatively small effect sizes, in particular two reported by Tscheulin (1995, 1996), with samples of 1,426 and 632, respectively.

The data also clearly demonstrate that during the posttherapy period clients maintained or perhaps even increased their posttreatment gains. As Table 2.1 indicates, change effect size was slightly larger at early follow-up (1–11 months posttreatment) than immediately after treatment ($n = 37$, $d = 0.16$, paired $t = 1.98$, $p < .06$). Similarly, effect sizes were larger at late follow-up (12+ months) compared with immediately posttreatment ($n = 19$, $d = 0.22$, paired $t = 3.52$, $p < .01$). However, equivalence analyses show that these further improvements can be considered to be trivial because they are significantly smaller (ts varied from 2.88 to 3.37, $p < .01$) than the 0.4 standard-deviation minimum clinically significant difference proposed by Elliott et al. (1993). Thus, the overall picture is one of large pre–post change that is maintained from posttest through later follow-ups.

Measure analyses provide useful information regarding the ways in which clients change in humanistic therapies and suggest large differences in amount of change, depending on what was measured and how it was measured. As Table 2.2 indicates, clients show the most change on measures of individualized problems (e.g., target complaints; $M = 2.54$). Clinicians' ratings of client symptoms and measures of the quality of specific relationship also showed large amounts of change and were significantly larger than at least one other type of measure. However, measures of personality or internal functioning produced the smallest average effect sizes (0.59 and 0.64, respectively). Further analyses revealed that different humanistic therapies differ significantly in their use of types of measure, suggesting a method confound between change measure and type of therapy.

TABLE 2.2
Pre–Post Effect Sizes Associated With Type of Change Measure

Type of measure	n	M	SD
Individualized	22	2.54	1.17
Improvement ratings	14	1.83	0.95
Symptoms, clinician	35	1.52	0.75
Specific relationship quality	31	1.31	0.95
Symptoms, client rated	101	0.93	0.59
Social adjustment/interpersonal	37	0.88	0.76
Self-esteem/beliefs	45	0.83	0.62
Experiential functioning	22	0.64	0.44
Personality/coping/health	50	0.59	0.45
Overall	357	1.07	0.71

Note. $F(8, 348) = 27.53$, $p < .01$; $eta^2 = .49$.

Do Clients in Humanistic Therapies Show More Change Than Untreated Control Clients?

General Comparisons

Pre–post or change effect size values do not tell us, of course, whether clients in humanistic therapies fared better than untreated clients, and thus make it more difficult to infer that therapy was responsible for changes made by clients. Therefore, I examined control-referenced effect sizes (differences between pre–post change effect sizes) in the 36 treated groups (from 31 studies) in which humanistic treatments were compared with wait-list or no-treatment controls (see Table 2.1). The mean controlled effect size for these studies was also large, 0.99, a value essentially the same as the mean change effect size value of 1.06. In fact, the average change effect in the 36 untreated conditions was 0.10, indicating that there was little or no improvement in the untreated clients in these studies; and in fact clients in 5 of the 36 untreated groups showed clinically significant deterioration (negative effect sizes of −0.40 or larger). The fact that controlled effect size results corroborated change effect size findings also supports the validity of using pre–post change effect size values, making it possible to draw on a much larger sample of studies. Finally, as with change effect size, corrections for sample size and bias produced comparable, though slightly smaller results.

Do Clients in Humanistic Therapies Show Change Equivalent to That Seen in Nonhumanistic Therapies?

Although impressive, the change and controlled effect size analyses reported so far do not address the issue of comparative treatment effectiveness, which is central to the current controversy about the effectiveness of humanistic therapies. For this, I analyzed 48 comparisons between humanistic and nonhumanistic therapies. (Three studies compared different humanistic therapies, e.g., Greenberg & Watson, 1998, and were therefore not included in these analyses.) The average difference in pre–post change between humanistic and nonhumanistic therapies was zero, indicating no overall difference. Once again, corrections for sample size and bias produced comparable results (see Table 2.1). In a majority of comparisons ($n = 28$), clients in humanistic and nonhumanistic therapies were within ±0.4 standard deviation of each other. However, there is significant heterogeneity in comparative effect sizes, as evidenced by 13 comparisons in which clients in the nonhumanistic treatments did substantially better (by at least 0.4 standard deviation) than clients in a humanistic therapy, whereas humanistically treated clients did substantially (≥ 0.4 standard deviation) better in the remaining 10 comparisons.

Applying equivalence analysis to this and other treatment comparisons makes it possible to "prove the null hypothesis" of equivalence between humanistic and nonhumanistic therapies. These analyses are summarized in Table 2.3 and include equivalence testing, indicated in the $t(0)$, $t(0.4)$, and Result columns. In the case of the overall comparison between humanistic and nonhumanistic therapies, the obtained zero difference is significantly less than ±0.4 standard deviation, the predetermined minimum substantive difference criterion, $t(0.4) = 4.40$, $n = 48$, $p < .001$. In other words, on the basis of this sample, it can therefore be concluded that humanistic and nonhumanistic treatments are, in general, *equivalent* in their effectiveness.

Cognitive–Behavioral (CB) vs. Humanistic Therapies

A significant center of controversy involves assumptions shared by many academic or CBT-oriented psychologists that humanistic therapies are inferior to CBTs. The comparative studies analyzed here did not exclu-

TABLE 2.3
Comparisons Between Treatments

Treatment comparison	n	M_D	SD_D	$t(0)$	$t(0.4)$	Result
Humanistic vs. nonhumanistic	48	0.003	0.62	0.04	−4.40**	Equivalent
Humanistic vs. non-CB	15	0.36	0.60	2.34*	−0.26	Better
Humanistic vs. CB	33	−0.16	0.58	−1.59	2.41*	Equivalent
CCT/nondirective– supportive vs. CB	23	−0.33	0.50	−3.12**	0.69	Worse
Pure CCT vs. CB	13	−0.28	0.51	−1.98†	0.84	Equivocal
Process-directive vs. CB	9	0.29	0.56	1.58	−0.58	Equivocal
Allegiance-controlled comparisons						
Humanistic vs. CB	33	−0.06	0.46	−0.70	4.26**	Equivalent
CCT/nondirective– supportive vs. CB	23	−0.05	0.48	−0.51	3.48**	Equivalent
CCT (pure) vs. CB	13	−0.09	0.49	−0.67	2.27*	Equivalent
Process-directive vs. CB	9	−0.04	0.46	−0.23	2.38*	Equivalent

Note. M_D = mean comparative effect size (difference between therapies); SD_D = standard deviation for the comparative effect sizes; $t(0)$ = usual one-group t value against a zero-difference null hypothesis; $t(0.4)$ = equivalence t value against a 0.4 standard-deviation difference null hypothesis. "Result" refers to the interpretation of the results of the equivalence testing: Equivalent = significantly less than 0.4 standard-deviation criterion but not significantly greater than zero; Equivocal = neither significantly different nor equivalent; Better or Worse = humanistic shows poorer or better outcome (significantly different from zero, but not significantly different from 0.4 standard-deviation criterion). CB = cognitive–behavioral therapy; CCT = client-centered therapy.
†$p < .10$. *$p < .05$. **$p < .01$.

sively use CBTs (only 33 out of 48 comparisons). Therefore, it can be argued that the effects of the CBTs were watered down by the inclusion of comparisons involving other types of therapy (i.e., psychodynamic, psycho-educational, and "treatment as usual"). This possibility is supported by the finding that humanistically treated clients do more poorly when pitted against CBTs than when they are compared with clients seen in non-CBTs (comparative $ES = -0.16$ vs. 0.36; $t = 2.87$, $p < .01$).

To clarify these issues, I undertook a series of subsidiary equivalence analyses (see Table 2.3). These analyses indicated that for the sample of 15 studies analyzed here humanistic therapies show pre–post effects statistically *superior* to non-CBTs. However, the 33 studies comparing humanistic to CBTs reveal a pattern of significant *equivalence* (i.e., significantly less than the ±0.4 minimum difference but not significantly greater than zero). Thus, these data support the claim that humanistic therapies in general are clinically equivalent to CBTs.

Nevertheless, in light of recent controversies in Germany over government recognition of *Gesprächtspsychotherapie* (the German version of CCT) as a valid treatment, more precise analyses were required. Specifically, it is important to address claims by Grawe, Donati, and Bernauer (1994) that CCT is less effective than CBT, based on their meta-analysis of 10 comparative treatment studies. In fact, when the focus is further narrowed to the 23 studies comparing CCT or nondirective–supportive therapies with CBT, a modest statistical superiority for CBT appears (comparative $ES = -0.33$); and the same result would probably appear for pure CCT if the sample were larger (-0.28; see Table 2.3). Thus, the present analysis (in contrast to that reported by Elliott, 1996) offers some apparent, modest support for Grawe et al.'s (1994) conclusions.

However, when "process directive" humanistic therapies (i.e., PE, EFT for couples, Gestalt, and focusing) are lumped together, these do significantly better against CBTs ($ES = 0.29$) than CCT and nondirective–supportive therapies do ($ES = -0.33$, $t = -3.05$, $p < .01$). (It should be noted that the direct comparison of process-directive humanistic to CBTs is itself equivocal, i.e., neither significantly different nor equivalent.) However, none of the mean effect size differences in Table 2.3 are in the medium range (~.5 standard deviation).

Despite the apparent modest superiority of CBTs to the less process-directive humanistic therapies, it appears likely that the significant differences found may reflect method factors, in particular, researcher allegiance effects. Therefore, I ran additional analyses statistically controlling for researcher allegiance, by removing variance in comparative effect sizes due to researcher allegiance. When this was done (see Table 2.3, bottom), the relatively small but significant treatment differences previously noted disappeared entirely. The result is again a set of "equivalence" findings: The allegiance-corrected mean comparative effect sizes are significantly less than the 0.4 criterion and not significantly greater than zero.

What Method, Client, and Treatment Characteristics Affect Client Change in Research on Humanistic Therapies?

Outcome effect sizes can potentially be affected by a variety of factors, including research method (type of measure, size of sample, regional origin of the research, year of study, and researcher theoretical allegiance), client problem, and treatment characteristics (modality, setting, length, and therapist experience). These factors are also likely to be confounded with differences between various forms of humanistic therapy.

Research Method

As noted earlier and in Table 2.2, there are large differences among types of *measure* used. Similarly, no treatment and wait-list *control group conditions* differ in controlled effect sizes, with humanistic therapies showing larger effect sizes against wait-list controls (controlled $ES = 1.21$, $n = 22$) than against no-treatment controls (controlled $ES = 0.64$, $n = 14$; $t = 2.82$, $p < .01$), probably because of differences in type of humanistic therapy and other study variables.

In addition, Table 2.4 offers results of correlations between effect sizes and various research method features. *Year of publication, regional origin of*

TABLE 2.4
Predictor Analyses: Correlations

Variable	Change ES	Controlled ES	Comparative ES
Year of publication	−0.06	0.29	−0.08
Regional origin (North America = 1; German-speaking = 2)	−0.13	−0.20	−0.04
Sample size (*n* of clients)	−0.12	−0.22	−0.03
Researcher allegiance (prohumanistic = 1; neutral = 2; against = 3)	0.01	−0.25	−0.61**
Setting (outpatient = 1; inpatient = 2)	−0.19	−0.20	−0.12
Therapist experience level	−0.12	0.06	−0.04
Therapy length (*n* of sessions)	−0.03	−0.33*	−0.03

Note. ES = effect size.
*$p < .05$. **$p < .01$.

the research, and *number of clients* in the sample showed no relation to pre–post change, controlled, or comparative effect size values. Interestingly, there was no support for Tscheulin's (1995) speculation that differences in typical change effect size may exist between German-language and North American research, stemming from differences in measures used (personality vs. symptom measures). Finally, *researcher theoretical allegiance* showed no association with change or controlled effect size but turned out to be a very strong predictor of comparative effect size ($r = .62, p < .01$). Proponents of humanistic treatments typically produced substantial, positive comparative effect sizes (mean $ES = 0.51, n = 15$), whereas advocates of nonhumanistic approaches typically found humanistic treatments to be less effective than other approaches (mean $ES = -0.43, n = 19$), and researchers whose allegiance was neutral, mixed, or indeterminate obtained "no difference" results (mean $ES = -0.03, n = 17$). As noted earlier, when researcher allegiance was controlled for, differences between humanistic and CBTs disappeared. (These allegiance effects are likely to include differential effort by trainers, supervisors, and therapists.)

Client Problems

Regarding the possible differential effectiveness of humanistic therapies with different client problems or disorders, the studies analyzed provided no overall significant differences (see Table 2.5).

Treatment Characteristics

Regarding treatment *modality*, change effect size and controlled effect size were significantly related to treatment modality (see Table 2.6), reflecting large effects found for the 10 studies of EFT for couples (change $ES =$

TABLE 2.5
Effect Size (ES) by Client Problem or Disorder

Problem/disorder	Change ES			Controlled ES			Comparative ES		
	n	M	SD	n	M	SD	n	M	SD
Mixed neurotic psychomatic/interpersonal	33	0.93	0.49	10	0.96	0.60	8	0.21	0.58
Depression	13	1.36	0.63	2	0.40	0.21	8	−0.01	0.92
Anxiety	7	1.14	0.23	0			7	−0.46	0.47
Normal/minor	17	0.97	0.62	13	0.80	0.42	9	0.02	0.48
Chronic/severe	12	0.88	0.51	1	0.33		7	−0.21	0.30
Physical/health	5	0.84	0.42	3	0.77	0.70	1	0.14	
Relationship	12	1.42	0.75	7	1.72	1.02	8	0.36	0.67
F(df)		2.17 (6,59)			1.91 (6,29)			1.44 (6,41)	
Eta²		.12			.25			.17	

Note. All *F* tests were nonsignificant.

TABLE 2.6
Effect Size (ES) by Treatment Modality

Modality	Change ES			Controlled ES			Comparative ES		
	n	M	SD	n	M	SD	n	M	SD
Individual	48	1.15	0.56	11	1.05	0.57	24	0.04	0.58
Group	20	0.81	0.58	11	0.55	0.39	17	−0.26	0.52
Couples	10	1.59	0.65	7	1.91	0.80	4	0.91	0.72
Program	11	0.93	0.33	1	0.33		2	−0.10	0.38
Weekend Marathon	9	0.69	0.34	6	0.70	0.31	1	0.06	
F(df)		5.11** (4,93)			7.60** (4,31)			3.50* (4,43)	
Eta²		.18			.50			.25	

*$p < .05$. **$p < .01$.

1.59; controlled *ES* = 1.91; comparative *ES* = 0.91). In addition, treatment length (number of sessions), setting, and therapist experience level were correlated with effect size to identify treatment characteristics that predict treatment effects (see Table 2.4). Contrary to expectations, *setting* and *therapist experience level* were unrelated to change, controlled, or comparative effect size. *Treatment length* did not correlate with change or comparative effect size but correlated negatively with controlled effect size, perhaps a function of more severely distressed clients being offered more sessions than those who were less distressed.

Do the Major Approaches to Humanistic Therapy Differ in Their Effectiveness?

Finally, the larger sample in this analysis yielded enough power to detect differences between types of humanistic treatment (see Table 2.7). Overall statistically significant differences (by *F* tests) were obtained, indicating the presence of meaningful differences among types of humanistic therapy. To identify particularly effective forms of treatment, I compared the mean of each type of therapy with the mean for all the remaining types. As Table 2.7 indicates, EFT for couples had significantly larger effects for change, controlled, and comparative effect sizes. PE therapy also had a significantly larger comparative effect size (0.61), although this was based on only four studies.

Finally, a process-directive dichotomy was created by grouping PE, EFT, Gestalt, and "other" (focusing and emotive) therapies together and contrasting them with a grouping of CCT and nondirective–supportive therapies (encounter groups were excluded from this analysis). This process-directiveness variable predicted change effect size ($r = .26$, $p < .05$), controlled effect size ($r = .47$, $p < .05$), and comparative effect size ($r = .44$,

TABLE 2.7
Effect Size (ES) by Humanistic Therapy Type

Therapy type	Change ES			Controlled ES			Comparative ES		
	n	M	SD	n	M	SD	n	M	SD
Client-centered	44	0.97	0.55	13	0.80	0.59	16	−0.22	0.48
Supportive/ nondirective	9	0.94	0.41	3	0.41	0.17	11	−0.31	0.55
Process– experiential	14	1.25	0.58	3	0.86	0.49	4	0.61[a]	0.46
Emotionally focused/ couples	10	1.59[a]	0.65	7	1.91[a]	0.80	4	0.91[a]	0.72
Gestalt	7	1.12	0.78	1	1.05		8	−0.11	0.33
Encounter	8	0.70	0.34	7	0.73	0.37			
Other	7	0.97	0.41	2	0.92	0.92	5	0.38	0.60
F(df)		2.75* (6,92)			3.72** (6,29)			5.79** (6,41)	
Eta²		.15			.43			.41	

[a]Significantly larger ES when compared with all other treatments combined ($p < .05$).
*$p < .05$. **$p < .01$.

$p < .01$), all in the medium-to-large effect size range. However, when researcher allegiance was controlled for, only change effect size ($r = .27$, $p < .05$) and controlled effect size ($r = .40$, $p < .05$) were significant (the effect for comparative effect size was reduced to essentially zero; $r = .04$).

DISCUSSION

In this, the largest meta-analysis of humanistic therapy outcome research to date, nearly 100 treatment groups were analyzed. The larger sample of studies reinforces the major conclusion of the two previous, smaller analyses (Elliott, 1995; Greenberg et al., 1994) that humanistic therapies are effective. This conclusion draws support from a variety of indicators:

1. Clients who participate in humanistic therapies show, on average, large amounts of change over time.
2. Posttherapy gains in humanistic therapies are stable; they are maintained over early (<12 months) and late (12 months) follow-ups.
3. In randomized clinical trials with untreated control clients, clients who participate in humanistic therapies generally show substantially more change than comparable untreated clients.
4. In randomized clinical trials with comparative treatment control clients, clients in humanistic therapies generally show

amounts of change equivalent to clients in nonhumanistic therapies, including CBT.

More specifically, on the contentious issue of the comparative effectiveness of humanistic versus CBT, the data analyzed here are consistent with the following tentative conclusions: (a) If researcher allegiance is ignored, CBTs show a modest superiority to CCT and nondirective–supportive treatments in the studies reviewed; (b) more process-directive therapies (PE, EFT for couples, and Gestalt) show a modest superiority over less process-directive therapies (CCT and nondirective–supportive, although this superiority is reduced when researcher allegiance is controlled for; and (c) process-directive therapies are at least equivalent in effectiveness to CBTs and may eventually turn out to be slightly superior. These modest differences, however, may all be due to researcher allegiance, because they largely disappear when researcher allegiance is statistically controlled. Thus, although more research is clearly needed, the present results clearly run against the claims of critics of client-centered and other humanistic approaches to therapy (e.g., Giles, 1993; Grawe et al., 1994).

This meta-analysis took a very different approach from that used by the APA Division 12 Task Force on Promotion and Dissemination of Psychological Procedures (1995; now known as the APA Division 12 Science and Practice Committee) and others (e.g., Nathan, 1996). Thus, if they wished, supporters of the empirically supported treatments movement could challenge this meta-analysis on several methodological issues. In the following discussion, I address many of these potential criticisms.

Criticism 1: This analysis relied heavily on uncontrolled studies. It could be argued that the uncontrolled studies are irrelevant because the specific causal influence of psychotherapy cannot be inferred from them.

Response: My position is that it is more scientific, as Smith et al. (1980) argued, to make use of as much data as possible. Allowing single-group studies made it possible to include large-scale naturalistic clinical effectiveness studies such as that of Tscheulin (1995), as well as pilot research on new treatments (e.g., W. R. Johnson & Smith, 1997). The absence of such naturalistic research is a key limitation of the APA Division 12 Science and Practice Committee criteria for designating treatments as empirically supported.

Furthermore, the present strategy made it possible to corroborate the main findings using three different types of meta-analysis, each with its complementary strengths and weaknesses. As noted, including pre–post change analysis of single-treatment groups allows a wider range of naturalistic treatment effectiveness samples but fails to control for differences in measures used in different studies or for other causes of the observed client change. Randomized clinical trials comparing different treatments make it easier to infer causal influence but are difficult to carry out in naturalistic clinical settings, often suffer from randomization failures, usually lack adequate statistical power, and are highly vulnerable to researcher allegiance effects (Luborsky et al., 1999). Controlled studies using untreated or wait-listed clients allow causal inference about the effects of therapy, appear to be much less influenced by researcher allegiance effects, and are easier to carry out than comparative treatment studies; however, they raise ethical problems with highly distressed clients and are often unacceptable in naturalistic clinical setting. The meta-analysis strategy used here was thus not weakened by using all three types of data; instead, the complementary methods allowed stronger conclusions to be made, because their results were highly consistent.

Criticism 2: Relatively few of the studies analyzed used treatment manuals. Therefore, it can be argued that it is not clear whether therapists actually performed the treatments they were claimed to have carried out in many of the studies included.

Response: Using treatment manuals does not ensure that therapists actually follow the manuals and does not ensure that therapists have been trained to perform a therapy competently. However, many of the studies included here (e.g., Greenberg & Watson, 1998) not only used treatment manuals but also carried out adherence or competence checks on therapist performance, which is more rigorous than simply using a treatment manual. In fact, because most humanistic therapies are process oriented, the main intervention strategies of CCT, PE, EFT, and Gestalt therapy have all been carefully described in the literature. Such careful process descriptions serve the same function as treatment manuals but are often more specific than descriptions of cognitive or behavioral therapy interventions.

Criticism 3: Many of the studies used clients with unspecified diagnoses or did not use standard DSM–IV (Diagnostic and Statistical Manual of Mental Disorders, 4th ed.; American Psychiatric Association, 1994) or the ICD-10 (International Classification of Diseases; World Health Organization, 1992) diagnostic categories. Consequently, it can be argued that few if any conclusions can be made about the treatment of specific disorders.

Response: The APA Division 12 Science and Practice Committee criteria for designating treatments as empirically supported are unscientific in their dismissal of all research prior to *DSM–III* (3rd ed.; American Psychiatric Association, 1983) and in their stipulation that specific diagnoses or problems be the focus of investigation (see Bohart et al., 1998). Mixed diagnostic groups are the rule in clinical practice, and substantial overlap exists between anxiety and depressive diagnoses as well as with Axis II diagnoses. Furthermore, diagnostic categories themselves hide substantial, important differences among clients. The ideal of single-diagnosis client groups is an illusion, which calls into question the entire 30-year scientific project of identifying specific treatments for specific disorders or problems. Given these considerations, older diagnostic categories, such as "neurotic," while imprecise, can be easily understood as roughly equivalent to today's garden-variety, moderate-level clinical presenting problems. These common problems include major depressive disorder, generalized anxiety disorder, and milder Axis II personality difficulties, all of which frequently overlap with one another. Furthermore, the present analysis found little if any differences between categories of clients, even when applied to studies using current diagnostic categories.

The most serious problem with the present results, however, is the problem of researcher allegiance effects. The present analyses support contentions by Luborsky et al. (1999) and others that researcher allegiance exerts a powerful effect in the current research literature and needs to be controlled for to ensure valid results. Although some (e.g., Gaffan, Tsaousis, & Kemp-Wheeler, 1995) have recently tried to downplay such effects, the evidence for researcher allegiance was strong in regard to the comparative outcome studies analyzed here. Furthermore, method differences (especially in type of measure selected) appear to be confounded with treatment type, making it impossible to determine whether treatment effects are artifacts of researcher allegiance or actually exist but are obscured by statistical control procedures.

PRACTICAL IMPLICATIONS

Some implications for the clinical practice of humanistic therapies emerge from these analyses.

1. Humanistic therapies as a group appear to be effective for helping distressed clients to change and need to be added to lists of "probably efficacious" treatments (Task Force on Promotion and Dissemination of Psychological Procedures, 1995) for a wide range of problems, including depression, anxiety, "mixed neurotic" problems, minor adjustment difficulties, and relationship difficulties (more research is needed on chronic/severe and health problems; see Table 2.5).
2. Humanistic therapies appear to be most strongly established as treatments of clinical depression and specific relational difficulties.
3. Process-directive humanistic therapies (i.e., PE, EFT, Gestalt, and focusing-oriented) appear to be particularly promising and should be more widely researched and used.

These results demonstrate that humanistic therapies have nothing to fear from research. The studies reviewed highlight the feasibility and desirability of carrying out research on humanistic therapies. It is clear that humanistic therapists can involve their clients in research without dehumanizing them. It is time for humanistic therapists to reclaim the tradition of therapy research that Carl Rogers helped start. Here are some practical suggestions for doing so.

1. The field needs more systematic outcome studies using randomized designs, carried out by CCT/experiential therapists or teams of researchers representing both humanistic and nonhumanistic theoretical orientations, to overcome researcher allegiance effects. Clearly, an impressive amount of work has been carried out, but more is needed to continue to support the case for the effectiveness of humanistic therapies.

2. A particularly promising approach to studying change in humanistic therapies is to use an individualized measure, such as the Personal Questionnaire (Elliott, 1995). Such measures allow clients to select their own problems, thus respecting their uniqueness and individuality. The results presented here indicate that such measures are quite sensitive to change. In addition, humanistic therapists should develop more measures of positive functioning and theory-relevant strengths and resources.

3. Finally, humanistic therapists can and should carry out research with their own clients, compiling series of single cases into naturalistic single-group pre–post studies, to assess the effects of new forms of therapy, to document the effects of applying an existing therapy to a new client population, to predict treatment responders, and to identify effective ingredients. Such research designs are an important route to developing further understanding of the applications and effects of humanistic therapies, adding to the overall store of "friendly facts" about these therapies. Humanistic therapists would be well served to build on recent trends toward renewed research on the "human science" of psychotherapy, research which serves clients and therapists alike by continuing a decades-long tradition of self-reflective investigation.

REFERENCES

References marked with an asterisk indicate studies included in this meta-analysis which were not included in Greenberg et al., 1994.

American Psychiatric Association. (1983). *Diagnostic and statistical manual of mental disorders* (3rd ed.). Washington, DC: Author.

American Psychiatric Association. (1994). *Diagnostic and statistical manual of mental disorders* (4th ed.). Washington, DC: Author.

*Baehr, G. O. (1954). The comparative effectiveness of individual psychotherapy, group psychotherapy, and a combination of these methods. *Journal of Consulting Psychology, 18,* 179–183.

*Barrett-Lennard, G. T. (1962). Dimensions of therapist response as causal factors in therapeutic change. *Psychological Monographs, 76*(43), 1–36.

*Beck, A. T., Sokol, L., Clark, D. A., Berchick, R., & Wright, F. (1992). A crossover study of focused cognitive therapy for panic disorder. *American Journal of Psychiatry, 149,* 778–783.

*Boeck-Singelmann, C., Schwab, R., & Tönnies, S. (1992). Klientenzentrierte Psychotherapie in form von Teamtherapie [Client-Centered Psychotherapy with co-therapist teams]. In M. Behr, U. Esser, F. Petermann, W. M. Pfeiffer, & R. Tausch (Eds.), *Personzentrierte Psychologie und Psychotherapie* [Person-Centered Psychology and Psychotherapy] (pp. 9–23). Köln, Germany: GwG-Verlag.

Bohart, A. C., O'Hara, M., & Leitner, L. M. (1998). Empirically violated treatments: Disenfranchisement of humanistic and other psychotherapies. *Psychotherapy Research, 8,* 141–157.

*Borkovec, R., & Costello, E. (1993). Efficacy of applied relaxation and cognitive–behavioral therapy in the treatment of generalized anxiety disorder. *Journal of Consulting and Clinical Psychology, 61,* 611–619.

*Bruhn, M. (1978). *Kurz- and läungerfristige Auswirkungen personenzentrierter Gesprächsgruppen (Encounter) bei Klienten einer psychotherapeutischen Beratungsstelle* [Short- and long-term outcomes of person-centered encounter group therapy with clients in a psychotherapy clinic]. Unpublished doctoral dissertation, Universität Hamburg, Hamburg, Germany.

Cohen, J. (1988). *Statistical power analysis for the behavioral sciences* (2nd ed.). Hillsdale, NJ: Erlbaum.

*Dessaulles, A. (1991). *The treatment of clinical depression in the context of marital distress.* Unpublished doctoral dissertation, University of Ottawa, Ottawa, Ontario, Canada.

*DiLoreto, A. (1971). *Comparative psychotherapy: An experimental analysis.* Chicago: Aldine-Atherton.

*Eckert, J., & Wuchner, M. (1996). Long-term development of borderline personality disorder. In R. Hutterer, G. Pawlowsky, P. F. Schmid, & R. Stipsits (Eds.), *Client-centered and experiential psychotherapy* (pp. 213–233). Frankfurt, Germany: Peter Lang.

Elliott, R. (1995). Therapy process research and clinical practice: Practical strategies. In M. Aveline & D. A. Shapiro (Eds.), *Research foundations for psychotherapy practice* (pp. 49–72). Chichester, England: Wiley.

Elliott, R. (1996). Are client-centered/experiential therapies effective? A meta-analysis of outcome research. In U. Esser, H. Pabst, & G. -W. Speierer (Eds.),

The power of the person-centered approach: New challenges, perspectives, answers (pp. 125–138). Köln, Germany: GwG Verlag.

*Elliott, R., Davis, K., & Slatick, E. (1998). Process–experiential therapy for post-traumatic stress difficulties. In L. Greenberg, G. Lietaer, & J. Watson (Eds.), *Experiential therapy: Processes and problem-focused interventions* (pp. 249–271). New York: Guilford Press.

Elliott, R., Stiles, W. B., & Shapiro, D. A. (1993). Are some psychotherapies more equivalent than others? In T. R. Giles (Ed.), *Handbook of effective psychotherapy* (pp. 455–479). New York: Plenum Press.

*Elliott, R., Wagner, J., Nathan-Montano, E., Urman, M., Slatick, E., Jersak, H., & Gutiérrez, C. (1999, April). *Outcome of process experiential therapy in a naturalistic treatment protocol.* Poster presented at the Medical College of Ohio Annual Symposium on Research in Psychiatry, Toledo, OH.

*Fife, B. L. (1978). Reducing parental overprotection of the leukemic child. *Social Science and Medicine, 12,* 117–122.

*Fleming, B. M., & Thornton, F. (1980). Coping skills training as a component in the short-term treatment of depression. *Journal of Consulting and Clinical Psychology, 48,* 652–654.

*Foulds, M. L. (1970). Effects of a personal growth group on a measure of self-actualization. *Journal of Humanistic Psychology, 10,* 33–38.

*Foulds, M. L. (1971a). Changes in locus of internal–external control: A growth group experience. *Comparative Group Studies, 1,* 293–300.

*Foulds, M. L. (1971b). Measured changes in self-actualization as a result of a growth group experience. *Psychotherapy: Theory, Research and Practice, 8,* 338–341.

*Foulds, M. L., Girona, R., & Guinan, J. F. (1970). Changes of ratings of self and others as a result of a marathon group. *Comparative Group Studies, 1,* 349–355.

*Foulds, M. L., & Guinan, J. F. (1973). Marathon group: Changes in ratings of self and others. *Psychotherapy: Theory, Research and Practice, 10,* 30–32.

*Foulds, M. L., Guinan, J. F., & Hannigan, P. (1974). Marathon group: Changes in scores on the California Psychological Inventory. *Journal of College Student Personnel, 14,* 474–479.

*Foulds, M. L., Guinan, J. F., & Warehime, R. G. (1974). Marathon group: Changes in perceived locus of control. *Journal of College Student Personnel, 14,* 8–11.

Gaffan, E. A., Tsaousis, I., & Kemp-Wheeler, S. M. (1995). Researcher allegiance and meta-analyses: The case of cognitive therapy for depression. *Journal of Consulting and Clinical Psychology, 63,* 966–980.

*Gallagher, J. J. (1953). MMPI changes concomitant with client-centered therapy. *Journal of Consulting Psychology, 17,* 334–338.

*Gibson, C. (1998). *Women-centered therapy for depression.* Unpublished doctoral dissertation, University of Toledo, Department of Psychology.

Giles, T. R. (Ed.). (1993). *Handbook of effective psychotherapy.* New York: Plenum Press.

Grawe, K., Donati, R., & Bernauer, F. (1994). *Psychotherapie im Wandel: Von der Konfession zur Profession* [Psychotherapy in transition: From confession to profession]. Göttingen, Germany: Hogrefe.

Greenberg, L. S., Elliott, R., & Lietaer, G. (1994). Research on humanistic and experiential psychotherapies. In A. E. Bergin & S. L. Garfield (Eds.), *Handbook of psychotherapy and behavior change* (4th ed., pp. 509–539). New York: Wiley.

*Greenberg, H., Seeman, J., & Cassius, J. (1978). Changes in marathon therapy. *Psychotherapy: Theory, Research and Practice, 15,* 61–67.

Greenberg, L. S., & Watson, J. (1998). Experiential therapy of depression: Differential effects of client-centered relationship conditions and process experiential interventions. *Psychotherapy Research, 8,* 210–224.

*Gruen, W. (1975). Effects of brief psychotherapy during the hospitalization period on the recovery process in heart attacks. *Journal of Consulting and Clinical Psychology, 43,* 223–232.

*Haimovitz, N. R., & Haimowitz, M. L. (1952). Personality changes in client-centered therapy. In W. Wolff & J. A. Precher (Eds.), *Success in psychotherapy* (pp. 63–93). New York: Grune & Stratton.

*Holden, J. M., Sagovsky, R., & Cox, J. L. (1989). Counselling in a general practice setting: Controlled study of health visitor intervention in treatment of postnatal depression. *British Medical Journal, 298,* 223–226.

Hunter, J. E., & Schmidt, F. L. (1990). *Methods of meta-analysis.* Newbury Park, CA: Sage.

*James, P. S. (1991). Effects of a communication training component added to an emotionally focused couples therapy. *Journal of Marital and Family Therapy, 17,* 263–275.

Johnson, B. T. (1989). *D/STAT: Software for the meta-analytic review of research literatures.* Hillsdale, NJ: Erlbaum.

*Johnson, S. M., & Talitman, E. (1997). Predictors of outcome in emotionally focused marital therapy. *Journal of Marital and Family Therapy, 23,* 135–152.

*Johnson, W. R. (1977). The use of a snake phobia paradigm and nonverbal behavior change in assessing treatment outcome: "The empty chair" versus systematic desensitization (Doctoral dissertation, Georgia State University, 1976). *Dissertation Abstracts International, 37,* 4146B. (University Microfilms No. 77-2933)

*Johnson, W. R., & Smith, E. W. L. (1997). Gestalt empty-chair dialogue versus systematic desensitization in the treatment of a phobia. *Gestalt Review, 1,* 150–162.

Lipsey, M. W., & Wilson, D. B. (1993). The efficacy of psychological, educational, and behavioral treatment: Confirmation from meta-analysis. *American Psychologist, 48,* 1181–1209.

Luborsky, L., Diguer, L., Seligman, D. A., Rosenthal, R., Krause, E. D., Johnson, S., Halperin, G., Bishop, M., Berman, J. S., & Schweizer, E. (1999). The researcher's own therapy allegiances: A "wild card" in comparisons of treatment efficacy. *Clinical Psychology: Science and Practice, 6*, 95–106.

*MacPhee, D. C., Johnson, S. M., & Van der Veer, M. C. (1995). Low sexual desire in women: The effects of marital therapy. *Journal of Sex and Marital Therapy, 21*, 159–182.

Meyer, A. E., Richter, R., Grawe, K., von Schulenburg, J. -M., & Schulte, B. (1991). *Forschungsgutachten zu Fragen eines Psychotherapeutengesetzes* [Research appraisal of questions of a psychotherapy law]. Hamburg, Germany: Universitaetskrankenhaus Eppendorf.

*Monti, P. M., Curran, J. P., Corriveau, D. P., DeLancey, A. L., & Hagerman, S. M. (1980). Effects of social skills training groups and sensitivity training groups with psychiatric patients. *Journal of Consulting and Clinical Psychology, 48*, 241–248.

*Munch, G. A. (1947). *An evaluation of non-directive psychotherapy: By means of the Rorschach and other indices.* Stanford, CA: Stanford University Press.

Nathan, P. E. (1996). Validated forms of psychotherapy may lead to better-validated psychotherapy. *Clinical Psychology: Science and Practice, 3*, 251–255.

*Paivio, S. C. (1997, December). *The outcome of emotionally-focused therapy with adult abuse survivors.* Paper presented at meeting of North American Society for Psychotherapy Research, Tucson, AZ.

*Paivio, S. C., & Greenberg, L. S. (1995). Resolving "unfinished business": Efficacy of experiential therapy using empty chair dialogue. *Journal of Consulting and Clinical Psychology, 63*, 419–425.

*Raskin, N. J. (1952). An objective study of the locus-of-evaluation factor in psychotherapy. In W. Wolff & J. A. Precher (Eds.), *Success in psychotherapy* (pp. 143–162). New York: Grune & Stratton.

Rogers, C. R., & Dymond, R. F. (Eds.). (1954). *Psychotherapy and personality change.* Chicago: University of Chicago Press.

Rogers, J. L., Howard, K. I., & Vessey, J. T. (1993). Using significance tests to evaluate equivalence between two experimental groups. *Psychological Bulletin, 113*, 553–565.

*Sachse, R. (1995). Zielorientierte Gesprächspsychotherapie: Effektive psychotherapeutische Strategien bei Klienten und Klientinnen mit psychosomatischen Magen-Darm-Erkrankungen [Goal-oriented client-centered psychotherapy: Effective psychotherapeutic strategies with male and female clients with psychosomatic stomach and intestinal diseases]. In J. Eckert (Ed.), *Forschung zur Klientenzentrierten Psychotherapie* [Investigation of client-centered psychotherapy] (pp. 27–49). Köln, Germany: GwG-Verlag.

*Salts, C. J., & Zonker, C. E. (1983). Effects of divorce counseling groups on adjustment and self concept. *Journal of Divorce, 6*, 55–67.

*Schefft, B. K., & Kanfer, F. H. (1987). The utility of a process model in therapy: A comparative study of treatment effects. *Behavior Therapy, 18*, 113–134.

Schneider, K. J. (1998). Toward a science of the heart: Romanticism and the revival of psychology. *American Psychologist, 53,* 277–289.

*Serok, S., & Zemet, R. M. (1983). An experiment of Gestalt group therapy with hospitalized schizophrenics. *Psychotherapy: Theory, Research and Practice, 20,* 417–424.

*Schwab, R. (1995). Zur Prozessforschung in der gesprächspsychotherapeutisicen Gruppentherapie: Überlegungen im Anschluss an empirische Ergebnisse aus Gruppen mis Einsamen [Process investigation in client-centered group therapy: Considerations in linking to empirical outcome from groups with the lonely]. In J. Eckert (Ed.), *Forschung zur Klientenzentrierten Psychotherapie* [Investigation of client-centered psychotherapy] (pp. 151–165). Köln, Germany: GwG-Verlag.

*Shaw, B. F. (1977). Comparison of cognitive therapy and behavior therapy in the treatment of depression. *Journal of Consulting and Clinical Psychology, 45,* 543–551.

*Shear, K. M., Pilkonis, P. A., Cloitre, M., & Leon, A. C. (1994). Cognitive behavioral treatment compared with nonprescriptive treatment of panic disorder. *Archives of General Psychiatry, 51,* 395–401.

*Sherman, E. (1987). Reminiscence groups for community elderly. *The Gerontologist, 27,* 569–572.

*Shlien, J. M., Mosak, H. H., & Dreikurs, R. (1962). Effect of time limits: A comparison of two psychotherapies. *Journal of Counseling Psychology, 9,* 31–34.

Smith, M. L., Glass, G. V., & Miller, T. I. (1980). *The benefits of psychotherapy.* Baltimore: Johns Hopkins University Press.

*Souliere, M. (1995). The differential effects of the empty chair dialogue and cognitive restructuring on the resolution of lingering angry feelings (Doctoral dissertation, University of Ottawa, 1994). *Dissertation Abstracts International, 56,* 2342B. (University Microfilms No. AAT NN95979)

*Speierer, G. -W. (1979). Ergebnisse der ambulanten Gesprächspsychotherapie [Outcome of outpatient client-centered psychotherapy]. *Fortschritte der Medizin, 97,* 1527–1533.

Task Force on Promotion and Dissemination of Psychological Procedures. (1995). Training in and dissemination of empirically-validated psychological treatments: Report and recommendations. *Clinical Psychologist, 48,* 3–23.

*Teusch, L. (1995). *Gesprächspsychotherapie in Kombination mit verhaltenstherapeutischer Reizkonfrontation bei Panikstörung mit Agoraphobie: Grundlagen und klinisch-experimentelle Überprüfung* [Client-centered psychotherapy in combination with behavioral exposure in panic disorder with agoraphobia: Theoretical basis and clinical-experimental demonstration]. Unpublished habilitation thesis, Medizinische Fakultät der Universität-GHS-Essen, Germany.

*Teusch, L., Böhme, H., & Gastpar, M. (1997). The benefit of an insight-oriented and experiential approach on panic and agoraphobia symptoms. *Psychotherapy and Psychosomatics, 66,* 293–301.

*Tscheulin, D. (Ed.). (1995). *Qualitätssicherung an der Hochgrat-Klinik Wolfsried* [Quality assurance at the Hochgrat Clinic, Wolfsried]. Wurzberg, Germany: Hochgrat-Klinik Wolfsried-Reisach GmbH.

*Tscheulin, D. (Ed.). (1996). *Zwischenbericht zur Effektqualitätssicherung an der Hochgrat-Klinik Wolfsried* [Interim report on effectiveness quality assurance at the Hochgrat Clinic, Wolfsried]. Wurzberg, Germany: Hochgrat-Klinik Wolfsried-Reisach GmbH.

*Walker, J. G., Johnson, S., Manion, I., & Cloutier, P. (1996). An emotionally focused marital intervention for couples with chronically ill children. *Journal of Consulting and Clinical Psychology, 64*, 1029–1036.

*Wolfus, B., & Bierman, R. (1996). An evaluation of a group treatment program for incarcerated male batterers. *International Journal of Offender Therapy and Comparative Criminology, 40*, 318–333.

World Health Organization. (1992). *The ICD-10 classification of mental and behavioural disorders: Clinical descriptions and diagnostic guidelines*. Geneva, Switzerland: Author.

*Yalom, I. D., Bond, G., Bloch, S., Zimmerman, E., & Friedman, L. (1977). The impact of a weekend group experience on individual therapy. *Archives of General Psychiatry, 34*, 399–415.

3

PROCESS–OUTCOME RESEARCH ON HUMANISTIC THERAPY VARIABLES

RAINER SACHSE AND ROBERT ELLIOTT

Process–outcome research on humanistic therapies, particularly client-centered and experiential therapies (CC/ET), has a long tradition. Initiated by Rogers (1957) and continued by Barrett-Lennard (1962) and Truax (1963), research aimed at evaluating the relevance of therapist characteristics and client processes to outcome has been widely pursued ever since. An important function of process–outcome research involves the empirical testing of therapy theory in relation to the following central research questions:

1. Is there a significant relationship between the use of humanistic *therapeutic strategies* and the outcome of the therapy? Do these therapeutic strategies lead to success?
2. A similar question may be asked with respect to the postulated within-therapy *client processes*: Do client processes thought to be relevant really have an impact on outcome?
3. Do the therapeutic interventions that the therapy theory claims to be relevant really influence relevant within-session client processes in the assumed way?

The first and second questions touch on classical, macrolevel process–outcome research work in client-centered psychotherapy, in which certain process variables of therapists or clients are used to predict overall outcome (see Orlinsky, Grawe, & Parks, 1994; Orlinsky & Howard, 1986). The third question concerns the immediate, in-session effects of interventions. In CC/ET, this corresponds almost entirely to Rice and Greenberg's (1984) task-analytic and Sachse's (1992b) microprocess analysis research programs.

In this chapter, we have two goals: First, we summarize the results of macrolevel process–outcome research, drawing on the CC/ET literature whenever possible (there is almost no process–outcome research on other humanistic therapies, e.g., existential). In our summary, we sometimes refer to research or reviews that include other therapies, when these involve key humanistic therapy variables such as therapist empathy. This is consistent with Rogers's (1957) assumption that change processes are generally consistent across treatments. We indicate when we are making use of research on other therapies (by stating this explicitly or prefacing citations with "cf."). Second, we summarize the main findings of Sachse's (1992b) microprocess research on therapist facilitation of client self-exploration, the key client microprocess, and CC/ET and related humanistic therapies. (Task analysis research is reviewed in this volume by Elliott & Greenberg, chapter 9).

MACRO LEVEL: SUMMARY OF HUMANISTIC PROCESS–OUTCOME RESEARCH

Studies examining the relationship between humanistic therapy processes and outcome include investigations into both therapist and client variables. To this end, global process measures outlining actions and attitudes of therapists or clients are typically correlated with therapeutic changes in clients. In reviewing this literature, four fields of research can be distinguished:

1. Research investigating the core therapist process variables (i.e., empathic understanding, acceptance, and congruence).
2. Research directed toward supplementary therapist processes (i.e., directiveness and therapist self-disclosure).
3. Research on key client process variables (i.e., intrapersonal exploration and experiencing).
4. Research on supplementary client processes (e.g., positive affective reactions to therapy, role involvement, defensiveness).

Research on the core therapist variables attempts to determine whether the "therapeutic conditions" of empathy, unconditional positive regard, and congruence as postulated by Rogers really produce constructive therapy results (for an overview, cf. Truax & Mitchell, 1971; see also Bozarth, Zimring, & Tausch, this volume, chapter 5). Similarly, research on core client variables tests theoretical postulates regarding the role of client self-exploration and level of experiencing in the process of constructive client change.

Aside from distinguishing client versus therapist variables and core versus supplementary variables, another significant factor in process–

outcome research is the question of perspective, that is, who assesses processes: therapist, client, or independent raters. In fact, rating perspective typically influences results (Orlinsky et al., 1994). Furthermore, as Orlinsky et al. noted, an external perspective is more convincing than evaluating one's own behavior and often provides stronger predictors of outcome. Thus, it follows that clients and raters are more capable of making valid assessments of therapist core variables than therapists themselves, while, analogously, the assessment of client self-exploration by therapists and raters is usually more credible than that of clients.

Central Therapeutic Variables: Empathy, Unconditional Positive Regard, and Genuineness

Empathic Understanding

Empathic understanding is a complex construct (Bohart & Greenberg, 1997). For example, there are at least five different forms of therapist empathic response: empathic understanding, empathic evocation, empathic exploration, empathic conjecture, and empathy-based interpretation (Greenberg & Elliott, 1997; see also Becker & Sachse, 1998). Empirical investigations have typically emphasized the first of these, empathic understanding (i.e., reflection). Examples of different approaches include Truax's (1961a) Accurate Empathy Scale, which uses independent raters to assess selected tape extracts (rater perspective), and the Barrett-Lennard Relationship Inventory (1962), which asks clients (and therapists) to judge whether they feel understood by the therapist (client perspective).

If empathic understanding is viewed as the ability of the therapist to understand the client, empirical results support the significance of this therapist attribute as a predictor of outcome (Barrett-Lennard, 1962; Halkides, 1958; Kiesler, Mathieu, & Klein, 1967; Mitchell, Bozarth, Truax, & Krauft, 1973; Tausch, Sander, Bastine, Freise, & Nagel, 1970; Truax, 1961a, 1963, 1966b; Truax, Carkhuff, & Kodman, 1965; Truax, Wittmer, & Wargo, 1971; van der Veen, 1967; see also Watson, this volume, chapter 14; cf. studies of nonhumanistic therapies by Cooley & Lajoy, 1980; Feitel, 1968; Gross & De Ridder, 1966; Kalfas, 1974; McClanahan, 1974; McNally, 1973; Melnick & Pierce, 1971; Peak, 1979; Schauble & Pierce, 1974; Stoffer, 1968).

This relationship becomes particularly clear if the therapist's understanding is assessed from the client's point of view, to determine whether the client thinks he or she has been understood. Two aspects, that the therapist is able to express understanding to the client and that the client feels understood by the therapist, thus appear to be fundamentally important. However, the possibility that these conditions may not always be mandatory is indicated by investigations that failed to find significant correlations between empathy and outcome (e.g., Bergin & Jasper, 1969; cf. Beutler, Johnson, Neville, Elkins, & Jobe, 1975; Mendola, 1982). Thus, it may be that therapist-expressed or client-perceived empathy does not facilitate solving certain problems or achieving certain goals, or with certain types of clients. However, such null findings may also stem from measurement problems (e.g., restricted range) or the fact that, beyond a "good-enough" level of empathy, more empathy does not necessarily mean better outcome.

Furthermore, the results vary greatly. For example, Tausch et al. (1970) found a large, highly significant correlation (.62), whereas Truax, Wargo, Frank, et al. (1966a) reported small correlations. However, the therapist variable *reflection of feelings* has not typically predicted therapy outcome (Rogers, 1975; cf. Elliott, Barker, Caskey, & Pistrang, 1982; Rounsaville, Weissman, & Prusoff, 1981). For example, in comparison with the Gestalt two-chair technique, reflection of feelings proved considerably less effective (Greenberg & Dompierre, 1981; Greenberg & Rice, 1981). Finally, other studies have found that a purely reflective, nondirective approach was less effective than one in which more directive therapist interventions occurred (Ashby, Ford, Guerney, & Guerney, 1957). Thus, Orlinsky and Howard (1986) concluded that reflection is "neither helpful nor harmful in itself" (p. 330). Clearly, reflection is not the same as empathy.

Finally, Orlinsky et al. (1994) discussed more recent studies of the relation between empathic understanding and outcome in various therapies. They found that 10 out of 11 studies showed significant correlations between the process characteristic *empathic understanding* and the outcome of the therapy (Bommert, Minsel, Fittgau, Langer, & Tausch, 1972, Horvath & Greenberg, 1989; Minsel, Bommert, Bastine, Nickel, & Tausch, 1972; Westermann, Schwab, & Tausch, 1983; cf. Buckley, Karasu, & Charles, 1981; Bugge, Hendel, & Moen, 1985; Burns & Nolen-Hoeksema, 1991; Dormaar, Dijkman, & de Vries, 1989; Gabbard, Howard, & Dunfee, 1986; Lafferty, Beutler, & Crago, 1989; Rabavilas, Boulougouris, & Perissaki, 1979). Correlations ranged between .14 and .60.

On the whole, then, this body of research indicates that understanding the client empathically is generally associated with positive outcome; it is sometimes highly effective but is never harmful. *For these reasons, empathic understanding can be considered to be a relevant basic condition in humanistic and other therapies.*

The pronounced variability of results, however, indicates that the effectiveness of empathic understanding is probably dependent on other factors: Apparently, this therapist variable does not yield identical results with all clients and problems (see Sachse, 1992b). For some clients, empathic understanding seems to initiate constructive processes, whereas other clients do not appear to benefit from it. It is therefore of great importance that researchers learn more about the conditions under which this strategy proves useful. However, it must also be noted that Rogers's (1957, 1959) theory requires that importance be attached to the simultaneous communication of *all* conditions: A nonsignificant correlation between empathy and success may also be due to the therapist not having adequately communicated the other conditions (cf. Watson, 1984).

Acceptance/Affirmation

The basic variable *acceptance* (also known as unconditional positive regard) actually consists of several aspects (Lietaer, 1984). For one thing, acceptance means to be interested in, to be on friendly terms with, and to refrain from rejecting the client regardless of what he or she says or does. However, acceptance also means accepting the contents expressed by the client and refraining from judging it negatively or positively. Similarly, acceptance does not involve agreement or endorsement but simply a non-judgmental attitude (Rogers, 1959; Tausch, 1973). These varying conceptualizations indicate that the therapist actions associated with acceptance are as a rule complex and implicit.

A number of studies of diverse treatments have found significant correlations between unconditional positive regard and outcome (Barrett-Lennard, 1962; Gomes-Schwartz, 1978; Mitchell et al., 1973; Truax, 1963; Truax, Wargo, Frank, et al., 1966b; Truax, Wargo, & Silber, 1966; van der Veen & Stoler, 1965; cf. Alexander, Barton, Schiavo, & Parsons, 1976; Board, 1959; Bottari & Rappaport, 1983; Brown, 1970; Cooley & Lajoy, 1980; Halkides, 1958; Rudy, 1983; Schauble & Pierce, 1974; Stoffer, 1968). However, this variable is not always associated with success (e.g., DiLoreto, 1971; Truax, Wargo, Frank, et al., 1966a; cf. Abramowitz & Abramowitz, 1974; Garfield & Bergin, 1971; Lerner, 1972; Mendola, 1982; Sloane, Staples, Cristol, Yorkson, & Whipple, 1975). Finally, Orlinsky et al. (1994) reported that 20 out of 24 mostly recent studies showed a significant positive relationship between therapist affirmation of the client (a slightly different variable) and outcome; one study reported a small negative correlation. The extent of the correlations varied greatly (between −.17 and .50).

Conclusions that can be drawn from these results are similar to those outlined for empathic understanding: The therapist's acceptance of the client constitutes a generally constructive therapeutic response. However, there is great variance in the results, indicating the operation of various other conditions and the need for more specific research.

Genuineness/Congruence

Genuineness or congruence on the part of the therapist means that the therapist has access to his or her own feelings and thoughts regarding the client and the therapeutic situation. The therapist does not avoid or deny these relevant experiences but is able to perceive and use them therapeutically (Truax & Mitchell, 1971).

Some studies do indicate a significant positive correlation between therapist genuineness and outcome (Barrett-Lennard, 1962; Mitchell et al., 1973; Truax et al., 1965; Truax, Wargo, Frank, et al., 1966a; cf. Gross & DeRidder, 1966; Halkides, 1958; McClanahan, 1974; McNally, 1973; Melnick & Pierce, 1971; Rucker, 1983). Typical of findings associated with positive results is the study by Tausch et al. (1970) in which genuineness (assessed by client report) strongly predicted outcome ($r = .51$). There are also studies showing the positive influence of the therapist characteristic of genuineness on client self-exploration (e.g., Truax & Carkhuff, 1965). Other studies, however, have found no connection between genuineness and therapy outcome (e.g., DiLoreto, 1971; cf. Garfield & Bergin 1971; E. E. Jones & Zoppel, 1982; Mendola, 1982; Sloane et al., 1975). Truax et al. (1965) even reported negative correlations. In their review, Orlinsky et al. (1994) found that three of five recent studies obtained significant relationships between genuineness and therapy outcome (Bommert et al., 1972; Westermann et al., 1983; cf. Ascher & Turner, 1979; Buckley et al., 1981; Lafferty et al., 1989). The reported correlations, however, were low (.30 maximum). Only 38% of the 60 available findings were in the positive direction.

Thus, therapist genuineness is a potentially effective therapist condition; however, much more than with empathy and acceptance, effects depend on unknown conditions that need to be investigated more closely, including conditions under which genuineness may even interfere with positive change. Beyond this, these variable results are consistent with Stiles and Shapiro's (1989) observation that greater "doses" of an effective therapeutic "ingredient" may not necessarily lead to better outcomes. For example, it may well be that certain clients are unable to put up with excessive genuineness on the part of the therapist. The overall pattern is that the core therapist variables cannot be regarded as universally necessary and adequate.

Other Therapist Process Variables

Therapeutic Alliance

Both therapist and client processes make up the therapeutic alliance. Here we review evidence regarding the therapist's contributions, including providing support, understanding, and affirmation. In various studies (Adler, 1988; Eckert & Biermann-Ratjen, 1990; Grawe, Bernauer, & Donati, 1990), correlations were found ranging between .35 and .50 between the client's appraisal of a constructive, trustful alliance and the outcome of the therapy. Orlinsky et al. (1994) found that 53% of the study findings reviewed showed a positive association between therapist contributions to alliance and outcome (67% of findings were significantly positive when viewed from the client perspective).

Beyond the core facilitative conditions reviewed earlier, the therapist's contribution to the therapeutic alliance comprises various individual concepts, which have also been found to predict outcome. These fall under the humanistic principle of presence or contact (Rogers, 1957) and include the following: (a) Therapist engagement (efforts to promote the process, active interventions, and showing interest) correlates positively with outcome; 57% of study results reviewed by Orlinsky et al. (1994) were positive. (b) Therapist collaboration (taking a mutual, invitational, negotiating stance) was positively associated with outcome in 43% of study results reviewed by Orlinsky et al.

Directiveness

Directiveness on the part of the therapist indicates the extent to which he or she influences the therapy process and content, by raising issues, asking questions, and suggesting content as opposed to encouraging the client to chose his or her own topics and modes of processing. Empirical results relating to directiveness vary: In the nonhumanistic therapy literature, some studies show a positive correlation between directiveness and outcome (e.g., Rabavilas et al., 1979), whereas other studies report negative correlations (e.g., Lafferty et al., 1989). For that reason, the specific form of directiveness has to be spelled out more precisely, as well as the conditions under which the directiveness is applied. If a distinction is made (cf. Greenberg, Rice, & Elliott, 1993) between process directiveness (the therapist directs processing work) and content directiveness (the therapist prescribes client content), a high degree of process directiveness on the part of the therapist has been found to be constructive (see section on Microprocess Research Methods; see also outcome research reviewed by Elliott, this volume, chapter 2).

Therapist self-disclosure refers to the extent to which a therapist communicates to the client his or her relevant experiences and reactions (cf. Jourard, 1971). Surprisingly, there has been little process–outcome research on therapist self-disclosure within the humanistic tradition, at least using actual therapy samples. C. E. Hill et al. (1988) found that therapist self-disclosure predicted immediate outcome, but this relation turned out to be confounded with client experiencing level. Orlinsky et al.'s (1994) review suggests that self-disclosure does not generally predict outcome and may even predict negatively. Therefore, therapist self-disclosure cannot be regarded as a generally effective therapeutic strategy; however, certain kinds of self-disclosure may be effective under certain circumstances (e.g., reassuring self-disclosures; C. E. Hill, Mahalik, & Thompson, 1989).

Special Methods for Enhancing Client Experiencing

Therapists may apply special techniques, such as two-chair dialogue, to activate the client's problems, emotions, and affective processing efforts. These therapeutic approaches have been found to be effective, correlating significantly with positive outcome (Clarke & Greenberg, 1986; C. E. Hill et al., 1988; Meyer, 1981, 1990; Tscheulin, 1983; cf. Buckley et al., 1981; G. E. Jones, Collins, Dabkowski, & Jones, 1988). Therapeutic interventions of this nature may thus complement the core therapist facilitative processes discussed earlier.

Central Client Processes

In humanistic therapies, especially CC/ET, the assessment of client processes and how they are linked to successful outcome of the therapy is of particular interest because it is theoretically assumed that the core therapeutic conditions initiate constructive processes in the client that, in turn, produce constructive outcomes. Theoretically, strong, positive correlations should thus link client process variables to the outcome of the therapy. Research into CC/ET has thoroughly investigated two core client process variables: self-exploration and experiencing.

Self-Exploration

The concept of intrapersonal or self-exploration primarily denotes that clients turn their attention to their internal experiences, clarify those experiences, discover new meanings, and develop intentions and plans for getting their needs met. In humanistic (and psychodynamic) therapies, self-exploration is considered an important part of the change process, leading to successful outcome. Rating scales of client self-exploration were originally developed or revised by Truax (1961b), Tausch et al. (1970), and Carkhuff (1969). These scales, however, have been criticized as too multidimensional (Bommert, 1987), and an investigation conducted by Tausch et al. (1972) showed a higher correlation between self-exploration and constructive changes if self-exploration was measured by means of the Carkhuff scale instead of the Truax scale.

Significant positive correlations between self-exploration and outcome have been found in the work of Bommert et al. (1972), Minsel et al. (1972), Sander et al. (1973), Schwartz (1975), Truax (1966a), and Truax and Carkhuff (1965, 1967). For example, Bommert et al. (1972) found a .33 correlation between self-exploration and increase in extraversion. Correlations between self-exploration and the increase of extraversion (.26) and the decrease of the values of the Psychasthenia scale of the Minnesota Multiphasic Personality Inventory (.30) were also detected by Sander et al. (1973). Self-exploration has been found to predict outcome in other studies as well (Doll et al., 1974; Feindt, 1978; Gomes-Schwartz, 1978; Kirtner & Cartwright, 1958a, 1958b; O'Malley, Suh, & Strupp, 1983; Schön, 1980; Schwartz, Eckert, Babel, & Langer 1978; cf. Schauble & Pierce, 1974). In studies using related constructs, Brinkerhoff (1991) found a correlation of .35 between explication of interpersonal conflicts and outcome, whereas Sachse (1991b, 1991c) reported a correlation of .49 between the greatest depth of processing achieved by clients and therapy outcome.

There are also empirical indications that client self-exploration can be learned in the course of the therapy (Bommert, Mann, & Strauss, 1975; Bruhn, 1975). Truax (1966a) reported that constructive outcome was associated with increase in self-exploration during therapy. Truax and Carkhuff (1965) also found that the level of self-exploration in the second session was a good predictor of the therapy success.

In reviewing research from a variety of humanistic and psychodynamic therapies, Orlinsky et al. (1994) found that 8 out of 14 studies obtained significant positive correlations between extent of client self-exploration and outcome (Bommert et al., 1972; Bruhn, Schwab, & Tausch, 1980; D. Hill, Beutler, & Daldrup, 1989; Minsel et al., 1972; Sachse, 1992b; Sander et al., 1973; Westermann et al., 1983; cf. Gaston, Marmar, Gallagher, & Thompson, 1991; Horowitz, Marmar, Weiss, Dewitt, & Rosenbaum, 1984; Marmar, Weiss, & Gaston, 1989; Rounsaville et al., 1987; Safran & Wallner, 1991; Torhorst & Stitz, 1988; Windholz & Silberschatz, 1988); correlations ranged between .30 and .57. It thus follows that self-exploration may have an influence on therapy success and as such is to be viewed as a relevant client process. However, it has become clear that self-exploration does not always and necessarily entail positive changes and that other processes play a major role as well.

Experiencing

Gendlin (1970, 1978) described personality change as a process developed by dealing intensively with one's own experiencing. The experiencing concept has been advanced by Gendlin (1970) and Klein, Mathieu, Gendlin, and Kiesler (1969) as a principal ingredient of a successful therapy (Sachse, Atrops, Wilke, & Maus, 1992). For example, Klein, Mathieu-Coughlan, and Kiesler (1986) found a .46 correlation between the *depth of experiencing* on the experiencing scale and the therapy outcome. Because a separate chapter in this book (see Hendricks, this volume, chapter 7) deals with experiencing/focusing, these processes are not discussed further here.

Other Client Process Variables: Contributions to Therapeutic Alliance

Several other client process variables have also been researched as predictors of outcome. All fall under the general rubric of client contributions to the therapeutic alliance.

Role Involvement

Role involvement on the part of the client is counted among the client characteristics of the therapeutic alliance and denotes the extent to which a client actively fulfills the client role, engages cooperatively, and shows commitment to the therapy process. Highly active participation by the client correlates positively with outcome (Gomes-Schwartz, 1978; O'Malley et al., 1983; cf. Bennum, Hahlweg, Schindler, & Langlotz, 1986; Kolb, Beutler, Davis, Crago, & Shanfield, 1985). Orlinsky et al. (1994) reported that 65% of 54 findings indicated that client role engagement predicted positive outcome.

Negativity/Passivity

It has been found, however, that a negative client attitude toward therapy or a high degree of client passivity in the therapy process correlates negatively with outcome (Sachse, 1982). A passive or negative attitude in clients with respect to therapy thus appears to prevent constructive changes in clients.

Openness Versus Defensiveness

The quality of concrete therapeutic work, and thus the success of the therapy, appears to be strongly influenced by the extent of a client's openness: whether he or she is willing to talk about problems, disclose, communicate, or process unpleasant aspects of self. Conversely, the therapy process is likely to be impaired by the client's tendency to avoid disagreeable aspects of self. It can be seen from empirical studies that openness on the part of client correlates positively and that client defensiveness correlates negatively with the outcome of the therapy (e.g., Bruhn, Schwab, & Tausch, 1980; Grawe et al., 1990; Westermann et al., 1983; cf. Henry, Schacht, & Strupp, 1986), with the respective correlations being very high and consistent. Orlinsky et al. (1994) reported 80% positive findings.

Positive Versus Negative Affective Reactions to Therapy

Studies also report that the client's emotional response to therapy is important for outcome. On the one hand, positive client reactions to sessions predict good outcome (cf. Andrews, 1990; Bennum et al., 1986). On the other hand, occasional negative reactions to a therapy session do not always have harmful consequences for the therapy (cf. Soldz, Budman, & Demby, 1992) and sometimes predict positive outcome (cf. G. E. Jones et al., 1988). Thus, minor annoyances do not appear to have impairing effects; only gravely negative emotional responses seem to have a destructive effect on outcome (cf. Nergaard & Silberschatz, 1989).

Other Client Processes

In addition, Orlinsky et al. (1994) noted that both *client affirmation* or liking of the therapist and *client expressiveness* predicted positive outcome in roughly two thirds of the available findings (69% and 63%, respectively). Although these processes were not part of Rogers's original formulation, they are consistent with later humanistic formulations emphasizing evocative (Rice & Saperia, 1984) and mutual processes (Jourard, 1971).

Relational Processes

The concept of therapeutic alliance is actually an interactional or relational one that draws heavily on humanistic principles of mutuality and psychological contact, as well as the specific relational components just reviewed. Numerous studies with a variety of nonhumanistic therapies show that the overall quality of the therapeutic alliance correlates well with outcome (e.g., Bachelor, 1991; Collins et al., 1985; Lansford, 1986; Safran & Wallner, 1991). Therefore, therapeutic alliance must be regarded as a significant, general component of a constructive and effective psychotherapy, as indicated by Orlinsky et al.'s (1994) report that 66% of findings were significantly positive. This is consistent with Horvath and Symonds' (1991) meta-analysis of 24 studies, which obtained an overall mean effect size of $r = .26$. One important relational "channel" of therapeutic alliance, communicative attunement (mutual understanding), has been found to predict positive outcome in a majority of studies (Orlinsky et al., 1994).

SUMMARY OF MICROPROCESS RESEARCH FINDINGS

Microprocess Research Methods

Microprocess studies examine the direct, immediate influence of therapeutic interventions on within-session client processes and also the effect that client actions have on the processing and planning activities of the therapist. The issues in microanalysis research involve questions such as "What client processes are triggered by what therapeutic interventions and under what conditions?" Thus, microlevel process research primarily involves establishing relations among process variables themselves, for example, between interventions the therapist makes and processes initiated within the client.

This research approach deviates, to a certain extent, from the nondirectiveness of early client-centered theory. That is, it is based on the belief in the therapeutic value of *process directiveness*. It assumes that therapists can constructively influence clients by attending to particular client markers and responding in ways that help the client to work productively on particular therapeutic tasks (Greenberg et al., 1993; Rice & Saperia, 1984; Sachse, 1992b). However, to verify this assumption, a global process–outcome strategy is not appropriate. Instead, processes on the microlevel must be analyzed and examined in relation to each other.

Research strategies and results from microanalysis studies performed in goal-oriented client-centered therapy (Sachse, 1992b; see also Toukmanian, 1986) are summarized here. These studies provide a broad range of process results illustrating the importance of therapeutic actions aimed at promoting client processes in problem-processing tasks involving self-explication (i.e., self-exploration). In this research, so-called "triples" are examined. A triple is a sequence of client–therapist–client (C-T-C) speaking turns. Client statements are rated on an 8-point Processing Mode scale and therapist statements on an 8-point Processing Proposal (PP) scale, each of which contains the following levels:

1. No processing of relevant contents discernible
2. Intellectualizing
3. Report
4. Assessment/evaluation
5. Personal assessment
6. Personal meaning
7. Explication of relevant structures of meaning
8. Integration.

Using these ratings, we can determined whether a therapist offers to the client (within a triple) a *deepening* PP (e.g., client Level 3; therapist Level 5), a *level-maintaining* PP (e.g., client Level 3; therapist Level 3), or a *flattening* PP (e.g., client Level 3; therapist Level 2). For example, a client (C) might say,

> C: Only yesterday I noticed again how terribly worried I get when I realize I'm telling somebody a story and he is not listening to me at all. (processing mode scale Level 5: personal assessment)

In responding, the therapist (T) may offer a PP on the *same level*:

> T1: You really feel that it bothers you?

On the other hand, the therapist may encourage the client to set in motion a more sophisticated, *deeper* clarification of his or her emotional processing performance, by saying:

> T2: What exactly do you feel then? (PP scale Level 6: personal meaning)
> or
> T3: What does it mean to you, to get terribly worried? (PP scale Level 7: explication of relevant structures of meaning)

As a consequence, the client is encouraged to assume an inwardly directed perspective, maintain the relevant focus, activate relevant emotion schemes, and eventually understand these processes. Finally, the therapist may also *distract* the client by asking mundane informational questions, corresponding to Level 3 (report of events). For example,

> T: How often did you notice it?
> T: Who was with you at that time?

The analysis thus determines whether the client's processing mode (from the first to the second client statement in a triple) *deepens* (e.g., client response 1: Level 3; client response 2: Level 5), whether the level is *maintained* (e.g., client response 1: Level 3; client response 2: Level 3), or *flattens* (e.g., client response 1: Level 3; client response 2: Level 2). The relation between the therapist's relative PPs and the client's response defines the process directive effect a therapist has on the quality of the client's explicating work, based in part on the context and the specific qualities of the therapeutic proposals (see Sachse, 1990a, 1990b, 1990c, 1992b; Sachse & Maus, 1991).

Results of Microanalysis Studies

The results of a large number of samples using microanalytic research strategies can be summarized as follows:

1. *Therapist responses influence client processing strongly and consistently.* In their clarification and problem-processing activities, clients make use of the therapists' proposals quite often (Sachse, 1988, 1990a, 1990b, 1990c, 1990d, 1991a, 1991b, 1991c, 1992a, 1992b, 1992c; Sachse & Maus, 1987, 1991). On average, 50%–60% of clients react to therapist deepening PPs by intensifying their processing efforts. With respect to level-maintaining PPs, 50%–70% of clients stayed at the same level of processing, whereas 60%–80% responded to therapists' flattening PPs by allowing their processing work to become less thorough, resulting in a relative impairment of their explication processes. Clients' frequent acceptance of their

therapists' proposals indicates that they *need* help in problem-processing tasks. One possibility is that clients are predominantly absorbed in dealing with their relevant *content*, so that little attention is left to simultaneously monitor, plan, and promote problem processing. Therefore, a "division of labor" between therapist and client appears to be expedient, with the client being the "content expert" and the therapist expertly guiding the process (see also Greenberg et al., 1993).

2. *The influence of the therapist may have positive or negative consequences.* Therapists influence clients both with respect to deepening the explication process (i.e., toward a more constructive problem processing) and with respect to flattening the process (i.e., toward a less constructive problem processing). This means that the therapist has a great deal of responsibility and must carry out interventions that are well aimed and positive in manner (Sachse, 1991b, 1991c, 1992b, 1992c). It is, therefore, of decisive importance what therapists actually do. As a consequence, it is not enough to judge the quality of a therapist response globally (in terms of core conditions). Rather, it is essential to examine whether the therapist's specific response enhances, maintains, or impairs the client's immediate processing. Both global manner of responding and attunement to the client's current level of processing are important.

3. *Clients do relatively little constructive explicating work on their own.* Without purposeful assistance by the therapist, clients rarely deepen their clarification process. If therapists make level-maintaining PPs, clients deepen the explication process in only 6%–10% of all cases. This is in line with the assumption that, for clients, the clarification process is difficult and generates ambivalence. It appears that clients generally do not seem to know how to deal with their own problems in a constructive way and seem often to lack sufficient capacity to concentrate simultaneously on both content *and* process. Moreover, they become aware that deepening the process means "facing up" to unpleasant or painful experiences. It is thus not very surprising that little progress seems to occur without deepening therapist interventions (Sachse, 1991b, 1991c, 1992b, 1992c; Sachse & Maus, 1991).

4. *Clients accept flattening PPs from therapists to a much higher degree than deepening ones.* Clients follow therapeutic PPs to a particularly high degree if these are *flattening* (at a lower level of processing) in nature. This emphasizes the importance

of the therapist acting as a responsible and competent process expert. But it also indicates that clarification processes are *ambivalent* experiences for clients. That is, when therapists allow or even encourage clients to dodge an issue, clients usually move away from reflecting on or processing important aspects of experience. Thus, it is essential that therapists effectively assist clients' inclinations to explore conflicting or difficult experiences (Sachse, 1991b, 1991c, 1992b, 1992c; Sachse & Maus, 1991).

5. *Quality and centrality of therapist understanding facilitates the effect of therapist PPs.* Clients are better able to profit from deepening PPs if the therapist has understood the client and anchored his or her intervention to the client's issues. If one analyzes the influence therapists exert on the client process, it is clear that empathic understanding is essential for any productive intervention. If the therapist does not understand what a client means in a particular context, or understands poorly, the client only occasionally accepts a deepening proposal (10%–20%). That is, clients can only be constructively guided if they feel themselves understood by the therapist. Conversely, flattening PPs are generally accepted, even if there is a lack of empathic understanding on the part of the therapist. This leads to the interesting conclusion that therapists can only promote clients' clarification process constructively if they understand their clients well, but they will usually disturb their clients' process with a flattening proposal, regardless of whether they understand their clients. Thus, it is much more difficult to promote than to disturb explicating client processes. Similarly, if a therapist responds sensitively to personally significant content, the client will more likely feel induced to process this content than if the therapist addresses peripheral content (Frohburg & Sachse, 1992; Sachse, 1991c, 1992b, 1992c).

6. *Understanding alone is not enough for good processing.* If a therapist communicates understanding of the client's central meaning, yet offers this in the form of a flattening PP, the client's processing effort is very likely to deteriorate. A good therapeutic understanding is therefore typically necessary but not sufficient for appropriate client processing (Sachse, 1992b; Sachse & Maus, 1991).

7. *Formal characteristics of the therapist's PPs also influence the client's explication process.* In addition, the following formal features of therapist PPs also affect client deepening, maintaining, or flattening:

- short instead of long interventions
- interventions that are unambiguous, well understandable, and not too complex
- *single* "instructions" given to the client one at a time, instead of multiple PPs.

In other words, even good PPs will be ineffective if the therapist's statements are long, complex, ambiguous, and difficult to follow (Sachse, 1993). It thus follows that an effective therapist should not only understand empathically but also speak empathically, that is, in a way that takes into consideration the client's ability to make use of the therapist's PP. Clients explicate their experiences more effectively when therapists make statements their clients can understand and use quickly and effortlessly without being distracted from relevant contents. If the therapist statements are too complex for the client, he or she will be forced to focus more on the therapist, which will interfere with client processing.

8. *The quality of the clients' explication process depends on the phase of therapy.* From the beginning to the middle of therapy, client's average depth of explication and acceptance of deepening PPs generally improves (Frohburg & Sachse, 1992).

9. *The quality of the explication process depends on the quality of the therapist–client relationship.* On average, the more trusting the therapist–client relationship, the better the client's performance in the explication process (Sachse et al., 1992; Sachse & Neumann, 1986, 1987). Clients who have not yet established a good therapeutic alliance with the therapist are significantly less likely to accept deepening PPs than those who have developed a good working relationship with the therapist.

10. *The client's processing performance depends on the nature of the disorder.* In comparison with clients with "mixed neuroses" (i.e., clients with varying anxiety or depressive disorders or interpersonal difficulties), clients suffering from psychosomatic disorders are less influenced by therapist interventions, use deepening PPs less effectively, and operate, on average, at a lower explication level. Psychosomatic clients may react less efficiently to interventions aimed at improving the explication process; however, in the absence of therapist prompting, they exhibit an explication level that is comparable with that of "neurotic" clients in the same situation. For these clients, a different therapeutic task is most effective, in particular, "metaprocessing work" (processing their processing).

Thus, therapists can help these clients focus on their processing difficulties and encourage them to work on their problems in a different manner (Sachse, 1994, 1995, 1997a, 1997b; Sachse & Atrops, 1989, 1991; Sachse & Rudolph, 1992).

11. *Difficulties in the explication process associated with psychosomatic disorders can be offset by specific therapeutic strategies.* If, in the initial phase (1st to 15th session) of the therapy, therapists concentrate strongly on promoting processing efforts when working with clients suffering from psychosomatic disturbances, these clients *no longer* show difficulties with the explication process in the middle of the therapy. That is, they no longer differ from the neurotic clients as far as acceptance of deepening PPs is concerned, but they do differ significantly from clients with psychosomatic disorders whose therapists refrained from improving the processing work (Sachse, 1998).

IMPLICATIONS FOR PRACTICE

The empirical results reviewed here entail a number of practical implications, particularly as they suggest types of therapeutic responses, actions, and strategies that appear to lead to good outcome or process characteristics within the therapy. Therefore, the results are not purely descriptive in nature but rather form the basis for recommendations to therapists regarding what they should actually do to promote constructive client self-exploration. In addition, they also hint at what a therapist should avoid doing in order not to interfere with constructive client processes.

To begin with, in regards to the basic conditions of CC/ET, it can be said that *empathic understanding* is an essential humanistic therapy response. Empathic understanding on the part of the therapist is important (a) to understand the client's "inner frame of reference," including what he or she is saying as well as his or her central concerns, problems, and understandings of self and world; and (2) to develop a working understanding of the client that enables the therapist to adjust himself or herself to the client.

As far as the client is concerned, empathic understanding helps the client to understand and reconstruct his or her own problems, constructions, and motives and facilitates changing his or her views, convictions, and objectives. In fact, it seems clear that *self-exploration* and *experiencing* are significant client processes that influence a constructive outcome. A constructive therapy outcome will also be fostered by the client's commitment to the therapeutic work (as opposed to a passive receiving attitude) and openness toward both self and therapist.

In view of the important role of these client processes, therapists must learn how to influence these aspects positively. A positive client attitude toward the therapy can be improved by (a) realizing the basic conditions of empathy, prizing, and genuine presence and (b) helping the client to process his or her difficulties productively.

When a client has realized that the therapeutic work yields new awareness, new understandings, and new possibilities for action, this will positively influence his or her attitude toward the therapy, as well as his or her cooperation in the therapy. It can thus be assumed that the more effective the therapy from the client's viewpoint, the better the client's work in the therapy. All these aspects speak for active, process–directive actions by the therapist, aimed at meeting the client where his or her content focus is, but also trying to promote the client's problem processing in a precise manner that focuses attention exactly where the client needs active assistance.

Thus, the research reviewed indicates that empathic understanding continues to be an indispensable approach in humanistic therapy that should not be abandoned. However, the data likewise show that empathic understanding is not equally important to all clients. Expressed differently, there seem, on the one hand, to be clients or client tasks in which something more than traditional client-centered empathic understanding would be more effective. It may be important for a given client (e.g., someone with borderline processes) to be "empathically accompanied" by the therapist and to experience that the therapist understands him or her. On the other hand, there may be other clients (e.g., with psychosomatic problems or decisional conflicts) who may not be optimally helped by this approach. For such clients, it may be important for the therapist to direct the clarification process more actively, for instance, through empathic formulations, experiential teaching, metaprocessing, or two-chair work.

Furthermore, *acceptance* of the client by the therapist is also an essential prerequisite for constructive work in psychotherapy. Acceptance creates a basis for constructive therapeutic work by both therapist and client. Something similar applies to *genuineness*. This characteristic is also an important factor for many clients, helping to establish a trusting, secure therapeutic alliance.

Although the research reviewed points to the importance of empathy, acceptance, and genuineness, additional therapeutic strategies appear to be needed to influence outcome favorably. This is also consistent with the results of microanalysis studies indicating that clients without specifically targeted help from therapists usually do not process their problems effectively. Accordingly, it seems clear to us that humanistic therapists should manifest more than empathy, acceptance, and genuineness in their therapeutic work. Only if a therapist carries out precise process–directive interventions that deepen the client's self-exploration will the client's work become optimal for dealing with relevant problems. This implies

1. an active endeavor on the part of the therapist to promote the client and the therapy process, in which
2. the therapist acts in a competent and trustworthy way and directs the client's explication process through carefully targeted interventions, in order to
3. actively influence the client's clarification process while honoring client content as much as possible.

By adopting this approach, the therapist abandons a nondirective attitude but actually acts in a much more client-centered manner in that he or she facilitates client work on issues in which the client actually wants help and encourages the client to improve his or her self-regulation capabilities.

The results of microanalytic studies show that therapists can and should exert a significant influence on client self-exploration processes. Because clients typically find it quite difficult to clarify, check, and modify their own motives, goals, and convictions, therapists should offer active assistance to support clients' processing efforts.

As an example of the process–directive influence of the therapist on the client's level of self-exploration, we present below an excerpt from the beginning of Session 12 in a successful process–experiential treatment of a 19-year-old woman with severe posttraumatic stress difficulties (Elliott, Davis, & Slatick, 1998). The level of client processing mode and therapist PPs (Sachse & Maus, 1987) are given in brackets after each speaking turn, using the 8-point scale described earlier:

> T1: OK, so where are you today? [Level 5 PP: personal assessment]
> C1: Um (laughs). Nothing's really happened this week. (long pause) Um. But, like on my way in here, you know, I thought that nothing had happened this week and that made me realize that nothing big *ever* happens, *any* week. You know, that that's not my problem, I don't get hysterical once a week you know. [Level 4: general assessment; flattening in relation to T1]
> T2: So that's not what it's about, all right. [Level 4, maintaining C1 level]
> C2: Right, my problem is that, it's always there. It's mild, but it's always there, you know. I mean it's not drastic, you know. [Level 4, maintaining C1 level]
> T3: Right, it's not some raw trauma or something. [Level 4, maintaining C2 level]
> C3: Right, it's just a constant. [Level 4, maintaining C2 level]
> T4: And that's the *fear* you're talking about. (long pause) So that's what we talked about working on today, (C: Uh-huh.) for the next

three sessions. (long pause) So where would you like to start with that? [Level 5: personal assessment; deepening proposal; moves from simple empathy to explicit process direction]

C4: Um (laughs) (pause), I don't know. I kept thinking, like on the way in here today that (pause) nothing is going to change, you know. [Level 5; follows deepening proposal; displays openness]

T5: You had a sense, "Well, what's the point in this?" Right? "What am I doing?" And that's painful. I can see that's painful for you. Yeah, yeah. (pause) The sense of being stuck with things how they are. Can you talk from the sadness, from the hurt about that? [Level 6: Personal meaning or feeling; deepening proposal; with acceptance affirmation]

C5: (long pause) I just, think of my life and I just, (pause) I don't want to spend it living in fear. [Level 6; follows deepening proposal]

T6: (Gently:) Uh-huh, you don't want it to be like it is now, do you? And when you think about that, you feel, what?, a great sense of loss, a real hurt about that? (pause) Yeah. Can you stay with that hurt and sadness for a minute, and just feel what that's about and what that's like? [Level 7: Explication of relevant structures of meaning; deepening proposal]

C7: (pause) I mean, the simplest way to put it is, I'm afraid of living, I mean of everything, I mean to the point where I get terrified by the thought of dying, you know . . . [Level 7; follows deepening proposal]

This excerpt poignantly illustrates the process–directive influence of the therapist in facilitating client entry into painful, trauma-related experiencing. The therapist's PPs illustrated the therapist variables discussed earlier, including empathic attunement and acceptance; therapist reference to central client contents (trauma-related fear and emotional pain); and therapist use of explicit process directives ("Can you stay with that hurt . . . and feel what that's about?"). For her part, the client displayed the key client process variables reviewed here: self-exploration, openness, and an active involvement in the process of therapy, all contributing to the therapeutic alliance.

CONCLUSION

As our review indicates, humanistic therapy variables have figured prominently in research relating therapeutic processes to outcomes, and these variables have been extensively investigated. This is true for process–outcome relationships and for the influence of therapeutic interventions on the processing work of clients. All told, empirical research has confirmed most of the relevant theoretical assumptions of client-centered psychotherapy. It also has launched a self-correction process in CC/ET: Empirical results have stimulated the development of new theoretical models, which in turn have led to new research paradigms and further results. It can be concluded, therefore, that process research in CC/ET has not only been comprehensive but also very successful, as it has augmented the basic approach.

Furthermore, the research reviewed here supports the proposition that a competent implementation of the therapeutic principles of humanistic therapy will give rise to positive therapy outcomes for clients in humanistic and other therapies. Moreover, it can reasonably be expected that the effectiveness of humanistic therapies can be further enhanced by pursuing the directions indicated by the findings reviewed here, to the benefit of both clients and their therapists.

REFERENCES

Abramowitz, S. I., & Abramowitz, C. V. (1974). Psychological mindedness and benefit from insight-oriented group therapy. *Archives of General Psychiatry, 30*, 610–615.

Adler, J. (1988). *The client's perception of the working alliance.* Unpublished doctoral dissertation, University of British Columbia, Vancouver, Canada.

Alexander, J. F., Barton, C., Schiavo, R. S., & Parsons, B. V. (1976). Systems-behavioral interventions with families of delinquents: Therapists characteristics, family behavior, and outcome. *Journal of Consulting and Clinical Psychology, 44*, 656–664.

Andrews, J. D. (1990). Interpersonal self-confirmation and challenge in psychotherapy. *Psychotherapy, 27*, 485–504.

Ascher, L. M., & Turner, R. M. (1979). Paradoxical intention and insomnia: An experimental investigation. *Behavioral Research and Therapy, 17*, 408–411.

Ashby, J. D., Ford, D. H., Guerney, B. G., & Guerney, L. F. (1957). Effects on clients of a reflective and a leading type of psychotherapy. *Psychological Monographs, 71*(24) (Whole No. 453).

Bachelor, A. (1991). Comparison and relationship to outcome of diverse dimensions of the helping alliance as seen by client and therapist. *Psychotherapy, 28*, 534–549.

Barrett-Lennard, G. T. (1962). Dimensions of therapist response as causal factors in therapeutic change. *Psychological Monographs, 76*, 562 (Whole No. 562).

Becker, K., & Sachse, R. (1998). *Therapeutisches Verstehen: Effektive Strategien therapeutischer Informationsverarbeitung* [Therapeutic understanding: Effective strategies for therapeutic information processing]. Göttingen, Germany: Hogrefe.

Bennum, I., Hahlweg, K., Schindler, L., & Langlotz, M. (1986). Therapists' and clients' perceptions in behavior therapy: The development and cross-cultural analysis of an assessment instrument. *British Journal of Clinical Psychology, 25,* 275–283.

Bergin, A. E., & Jasper, L. G. (1969). Correlates of empathy in psychotherapy: A replication. *Journal of Abnormal Psychology, 74,* 477–481.

Beutler, L. E., Johnson, D. T., Neville, C. W., Jr., Elkins, D., & Jobe, A. M. (1975). Attitude similarity and therapist credibility as predictors of attitude change and improvement in psychotherapy. *Journal of Consulting and Clinical Psychology, 43,* 90–91.

Board, F. A. (1959). Patients' and physicians' judgement of outcome of psychotherapy in an outpatient clinic. *Archives of General Psychology, 1,* 185–196.

Bohart, A. C., & Greenberg, L. S. (1997). Empathy and psychotherapy: An introductory overview. In A. C. Bohart & L. S. Greenberg (Eds.), *Empathy reconsidered: New directions in psychotherapy* (pp. 3–31). Washington, DC: American Psychological Association.

Bommert, H. (1987). *Grundlagen der Gesprächspsychotherapie* [Foundations of client-centered therapy] (4th ed.). Stuttgart, Germany: Kohlhammer.

Bommert, H., Mann, F., & Strauss, H. (1975). Zusammenhänge zwischen Erwartungshaltungen und psychischen Veränderungen [Relation between expectancy behavior and psychological change]. *Zeitschrift für Klinische Psychologie, 4,* 239–249.

Bommert, H., Minsel, W. R., Fittgau, B., Langer, I., & Tausch, R. (1972). Empirische Kontrolle der Effekte und Prozesse der Klientenzentrierten Gesprächspsychotherapie bei psychoneurotischen Klienten [Empirical control of the effects and processes of client-centered therapy with neurotic clients]. *Zeitschrift für Klinische Psychologie, 1,* 48–63.

Bottari, M. A., & Rappaport, H. (1983). The relationship of patient and therapist-reported experiences of the initial session to outcome: An initial investigation. *Psychotherapy: Theory, Research and Practice, 20,* 355–358.

Brinkerhoff, L. J. (1991). *Application of the core conflictual relationship method to an analysis of significant events in an experiential therapy of depression.* Unpublished doctoral dissertation, University of Toledo, OH.

Brown, R. D. (1970). Experienced and inexperienced counselors' first impression of clients and case outcome: Are first impressions lasting? *Journal of Counseling Psychology, 17,* 550–558.

Bruhn, M. (1975). *Die Veränderung der intrapersonellen Kommunikation bei Klienten der Gesprächspsychotherapie* [Change in interpersonal communication in clients in client-centered therapy] Unpublished thesis. Unveröffentlichte Diplomarbeit, Universität Hamburg.

Bruhn, M., Schwab, R., & Tausch, R. (1980). Die Auswirkung intensiver personenzen-trierter Gesprächsgruppen bei Klienten mit seelischen Beeinträchtigungen [Effects of intensive person-centered therapy in clients with self-derogation]. *Zeitschrift für Klinische Psychologie, Forschung und Praxis, 9,* 266–280.

Buckley, P., Karasu, T. B., & Charles, E. (1981). Psychotherapists view their personal therapy. *Psychotherapy, Research, and Practice, 18*, 299–305.

Bugge, I., Hendel, D. D., & Moen, R. (1985). Client evaluation of therapeutic processes and outcome in a university mental health center. *Journal of American College Health, 33*, 141–146.

Burns, D. D., & Nolen-Hoeksema, S. (1991). Coping styles, homework compliance, and the effectiveness of cognitive–behavioral therapy. *Journal of Consulting and Clinical Psychology, 59*, 305–311.

Carkhuff, R. R. (1969). *Helping and human relations* (Vol. 12). New York: Holt, Rinehart & Winston.

Clarke, K. M., & Greenberg, L. S. (1986). Differential effects of the gestalt two-chair intervention and problem solving in resolving decisional conflict. *Journal of Counseling Psychology, 33*, 11–15.

Collins, J. F., Ellsworth, R. B., Casey, N. A., Hyer, L., Hickey, R. H., Schoonover, R. A., Twemlow, S. M., & Nesselroade, J. R. (1985). Treatment characteristics of psychiatry programs that correlate with patient community adjustment. *Journal of Clinical Psychology, 412*, 299–308.

Cooley, E. J., & Lajoy, R. (1980). Therapeutic relationship and improvement as perceived by clients and therapists. *Journal of Clinical Psychology, 36*, 562–570.

DiLoreto, A. O. (1971). *Comparative psychotherapy: An experimental analysis.* Chicago: Aldine-Atherton.

Doll, G., Feindt, K., Kühne, A., Langer, I., Sternberg, W. -D., & Tausch, A. -M. (1974). Klientenzentrierte Gespräche mit Insassen eines Gefängnisses über Telefon [Client-centered dialogue with prison inmates by telephone]. *Zeitschrift für Klinische Psychologie, 3*(1), 39–56.

Dormaar, J. M., Dijkman, C. I., & de Vries, M. W. (1989). Consensus in patient–therapist interaction: A measure of the therapeutic relationship related to outcome. *Psychotherapy and Psychosomatics, 51*, 69–76.

Eckert, J., & Biermann-Ratjen, E. -M. (1990). Client-centered therapy versus psychoanalytic psychotherapy: Reflections following a comparative study. In G. Lietaer, J. Rombauts, & R. van Balen (Eds.), *Client-centered and experiential psychotherapy in the nineties* (pp. 457–468). Leuven, Belgium: Leuven University Press.

Elliott, R., Barker, C. B., Caskey, N., & Pistrang, N. (1982). Differential helpfulness of counselor verbal response modes. *Journal of Counseling Psychology, 29*, 354–361.

Elliott, R., Davis, K., & Slatick, E. (1998). Process–experiential therapy for post-traumatic stress difficulties. In L. Greenberg, G. Lietaer, & J. Watson (Eds.), *Handbook of experiential psychotherapy* (pp. 249–271). New York: Guilford Press.

Feindt, K. (1978). *Überprüfung des Therapieerfolges und Untersuchung der Prozesse von Gesprächspsychotherapien mit Klienten geringer Schulbildung* [An examination of therapeutic success and the process of client-centered therapy with clients in primary school]. Unpublished doctoral dissertation, University of Hamburg, Hamburg, Germany.

Feitel, B. (1968). *Feeling understood as a function of a variety of therapist activities.* Unpublished doctoral dissertation, Teachers College, Columbia University.

Frohburg, I., & Sachse, R. (1992). Steuerungseffekte im Verlauf der Psychotherapie oder: Wann arbeiten Klienten am intensivsten an der Klärung eigener Motive? [Control effects in the process of therapy, Or: When do clients work intensively on the clarification of their motives?] In R. Sachse, G. Lietaer, & W. B. Stiles (Eds.), *Neue Handlungskonzepte der Klientenzentrierten Psychotherapie* [New action-concepts in client-centered psychotherapy] (pp. 95–108). Heidelberg, Germany: Asanger.

Gabbard, C. E., Howard, G. S., & Dunfee, E. J. (1986). Reliability, sensitivity to measuring change, and construct validity of a measure of counselor adaptability. *Journal of Counseling Psychology, 33,* 377–386.

Garfield, S. L., & Bergin, A. E. (1971). Therapeutic conditions and outcome. *Journal of Abnormal Psychology, 77,* 108–114.

Gaston, L., Marmar, C. R., Gallagher, D., & Thompson, L. W. (1991). Alliance prediction of outcome beyond in-treatment symptomatic change as psychotherapy processes. *Psychotherapy Research, 1,* 104–113.

Gendlin, E. T. (1970). A theory of personality change. In Y. T. Hart & T. M. Tomlinson (Eds.), *New directions in client-centered psychotherapy* (pp. 129–173). Boston: Houghton-Mifflin.

Gendlin, E. T. (1978). *Focusing.* New York: Everest House.

Gomes-Schwarz, B. (1978). Effective ingredients in psychotherapy: Prediction of outcome from process variables. *Journal of Consulting and Clinical Psychology, 46,* 1023–1035.

Grawe, K., Bernauer, F., & Donati, R. (1990). Psychotherapien im Vergleich. Haben wirklich alle einen Preis verdient? [Psychotherapy in comparison: Have all really earned prizes?] *Zeitschrift für Psychologie, Psychosomatik und medizinische Psychologie, 40,* 102–114.

Greenberg, L. S., & Dompierre, L. M. (1981). Specific effects of Gestalt two chair dialogue on intrapsychic conflict in counseling. *Journal of Counseling Psychology, 28,* 288–294.

Greenberg, L. S., & Elliott, R. (1997). Varieties of empathic responding. In A. C. Bohart & L. S. Greenberg (Eds.), *Empathy reconsidered: New directions in psychotherapy* (pp. 167–186). Washington, DC: American Psychological Association.

Greenberg, L. S., & Rice, L. N. (1981). The specific effects of a gestalt intervention. *Psychotherapy: Theory, Research and Practice, 18,* 31–37.

Greenberg, L. S., Rice, L. N., & Elliott, R. (1993). *Facilitating emotional change: The moment-by-moment process.* New York: Guilford Press.

Gross, W. F., & DeRidder, L. M. (1966). Significant movement in comparatively short-term counseling. *Journal of Counseling Psychology, 13,* 98–99.

Halkides, G. (1958). *An experimental study of four conditions necessary for therapeutic change.* Unpublished doctoral dissertation, University of Chicago.

Henry, W. P., Schacht, T. E., & Strupp, H. H. (1986). Structural analysis of social behavior: Application to a study of interpersonal process in differential psychotherapeutic outcome. *Journal of Consulting and Clinical Psychology, 54,* 27–31.

Hill, C. E., Helms, J. E., Tichenor, V., Spiegel, S. B., O'Grady, K. E., & Perry, E. S. (1988). Effects of therapist response modes in brief psychotherapy. *Journal of Counseling Psychology, 35,* 222–233.

Hill, C. E., Mahalik, J. R., & Thompson, B. J. (1989). Therapist self-disclosure. *Psychotherapy, 26,* 290–295.

Hill, D., Beutler, L. E., & Daldrup, R. (1989). The relationship of process to outcome in brief experiential psychotherapy for chronic pain. *Journal of Clinical Psychology, 45,* 951–957.

Horowitz, M. J., Marmar, C., Weiss, D., Dewitt, D., & Rosenbaum, R. (1984). Brief psychotherapy of bereavement reactions: The relationship of process to outcome. *Archives of General Psychiatry, 41,* 438–448.

Horvath, A. O., & Greenberg, L. S. (1989). Development and validation of the working alliance inventory. *Journal of Counseling Psychology, 36,* 223–233.

Horvath, A. O., & Symonds, B. D. (1991). Relation between working alliance and outcome in psychotherapy: A meta-analysis. *Journal of Counseling Psychology, 38,* 139–149.

Jones, E. E., & Zoppel, C. L. (1982). Impact of client and therapist gender on psychotherapy process and outcome. *Journal of Counseling and Clinical Psychology, 50,* 259–272.

Jones, G. E., Collins, S. W., Dabkowski, E. A., & Jones, K. E. (1988). The discriminability of temporal patterns used in the Whitehead Discrimination Procedure. *Psychophysiology, 25,* 547–553.

Jourard, S. M. (1971). *Self-disclosure: An experimental analysis of the transparent self.* New York: Wiley.

Kalfas, N. S. (1974). Client-perceived therapist empathy as a correlate of outcome. *Dissertation Abstracts International, 34,* 5633A.

Kiesler, D. J., Mathieu, P. L., & Klein, M. H. (1967). Patient experiencing level and interaction chronograph variables in therapy interview segments. *Journal of Consulting Psychology, 31,* 224.

Kirtner, W. L., & Cartwright, D. S. (1958a). Success and failure in client-centered therapy as a function of client personality variables. *Journal of Consulting Psychology, 22,* 259–264.

Kirtner, W. L., & Cartwright, D. S. (1958b). Success and failure in client-centered therapy as a function of initial in-therapy behavior. *Journal of Consulting Psychology, 22,* 329–333.

Klein, M. H., Mathieu, P. L., Gendlin, E. T., & Kiesler, D. L. (1969). *The experiencing scale: A research and training manual* (Vols. I and II). Madison: University of Wisconsin Press.

Klein, M. H., Mathieu-Coughlan, P., & Kiesler, D. J. (1986). The experiencing scales. In L. S. Greenberg & W. M. Pinsof (Eds.), *The psychotherapeutic process: A research handbook* (pp. 21–72). New York: Guilford Press.

Kolb, D. L., Beutler, L. E., Davis, C. S., Crago, M., & Shanfield, S. B. (1985). Patient and therapy process variables relating to dropout and change in psychotherapy. *Psychotherapy, 22*, 702–710.

Lafferty, P., Beutler, L. E., & Crago, M. (1989). Differences between more and less effective psychotherapists: A study of selected therapist variables. *Journal of Consulting and Clinical Psychology, 57*, 76–80.

Lansford, E. (1986). Weakenings and repairs of the working alliance in short-term psychotherapy. *Professional Psychology: Research and Practice, 17*, 364–366.

Lerner, B. (1972). *Therapy in a ghetto*. Baltimore: Johns Hopkins University Press.

Lietaer, G. (1984). Unconditional positive regard: A controversial basic attitude in client-centered therapy. In R. F. Levant & J. M. Shlien (Eds.), *Client-centered therapy and the person-centered approach: New directions in theory, research and practice* (pp. 5–41). New York: Praeger.

Marmar, C. R., Weiss, D. S., & Gaston, L. (1989). Toward the validation of the California therapeutic Alliance Rating System. *Psychological Assessment, 1*, 46–52.

McClanahan, L. D. (1974). Comparison of counseling techniques and attitudes with client evaluation of the counseling relationship. *Dissertation Abstracts International, 34*, 5637A.

McNally, H. A. (1973). An investigation of selected counselor and client characteristics as possible predictors of counseling effectiveness. *Dissertation Abstracts International, 34*, 6672A–6673A.

Melnick, B., & Pierce, R. M. (1971). Client evaluation of therapist strength and positive–negative evaluation as related to client dynamics, objective ratings of competence and outcome. *Journal of Clinical Psychology, 27*, 408–410.

Mendola, J. J. (1982). Therapist interpersonal skills: A model for professional development and therapeutic effectiveness. *Dissertation Abstracts International, 42*, 4201B.

Meyer, A. -E. (1981). The Hamburg short psychotherapy comparison experiment. *Psychotherapie, Psychosomatik, Medizinische Psychologie, 35*, 77–270.

Meyer, A. -E. (1990, June). *Nonspecific and common factors in treatment outcome: Another myth?* Paper presented at the 21st Annual Meeting of the Society for Psychotherapy Research, Wintergreen, VA.

Minsel, W. -R., Bommert, H., Bastine, R., Nickel, H., & Tausch, R. (1972). Weitere Untersuchung der Auswirkung und Prozesse klienten-zentrierter Gesprächspsychotherapie [Further investigation of the effects and processes of client-centered psychotherapy]. *Zeitschrift für Klinische Psychologie, 1*, 232–250.

Mitchell, K. M., Bozarth, J., Truax, C. B., & Krauft, C. (1973). *Antecedents to psychotherapeutic outcome* (National Institute of Mental Health Final Report

No. MH 12306). Little Rock: University of Arkansas, Arkansas Rehabilitation Research and Training Center.

Nergaard, M. O., & Silberschatz, G. (1989). The effects of shame, guilt, and the negative reaction in brief dynamic psychotherapy. *Psychotherapy, 26*, 330–337.

O'Malley, S. S., Suh, C. S., & Strupp, H. H. (1983). The Vanderbilt psychotherapy process scale: A report of the scale development and a process–outcome study. *Journal of Consulting and Clinical Psychology, 51*, 581–586.

Orlinsky, D. E., Grawe, K., & Parks, B. K. (1994). Process and outcome in psychotherapy. In A. E. Bergin & S. L. Garfield (Eds.), *Handbook of psychotherapy and behaviour change* (4th ed., pp. 270–376). New York: Wiley.

Orlinsky, D. E., & Howard, K. I. (1986). Process and outcome in psychotherapy. In S. L. Garfield & A. E. Bergin (Eds.), *Handbook of psychotherapy and behavior change* (3rd ed., pp. 311–384). New York: Wiley.

Peak, T. H. (1979). Therapist–patient agreement and outcome in group therapy. *Journal of Clinical Psychology, 35*, 637–646.

Rabavilas, A. D., Boulougouris, J. C., & Perissaki, C. (1979). Therapist qualities related to outcome with exposure in vivo in neurotic patients. *Journal of Behaviour Therapy and Experimental Psychiatry, 410*, 293–294.

Rice, L. N., & Greenberg, L. (Eds.). (1984). *Patterns of change*. New York: Guilford Press.

Rice, L. N., & Saperia, E. P. (1984). Task analysis of the resolution of problematic reactions. In L. N. Rice & L. S. Greenberg (Eds.), *Patterns of change* (pp. 29–66). New York: Guilford Press.

Rogers, C. R. (1957). The necessary and sufficient conditions of therapeutic personality change. *Journal of Consultative Psychology, 21*, 95–103.

Rogers, C. R. (1959). A theory of therapy, personality and interpersonal relationships as developed in the client-centered framework. In S. Koch (Ed.), *Psychology: A study of science* (Vol. 3, pp. 184–256). New York: McGraw-Hill.

Rogers, C. R. (1975). Empathic: An unappreciated way of being. *Counseling Psychologist, 5*(2), 2–10.

Rounsaville, B. J., Chevron, E. S., Prusoff, B. A., Elkin, I., Imber, S., Sotsky, S., & Watkins, J. (1987). The relation between specific and general dimensions of the psychotherapy process in interpersonal psychotherapy of depression. *Journal of Consulting and Clinical Psychology, 55*, 379–384.

Rounsaville, B. J., Weissman, M. M., & Prusoff, B. A. (1981). Psychotherapy with depressed outpatients: Patient and process variables as predictors of outcome. *British Journal of Psychiatry, 138*, 67–74.

Rucker, I. E. V. (1983). Counseling outcomes and perceived social influence: Validity of the counselor rating form extended. *Dissertation Abstracts International, 43*, 2355–2356B.

Rudy, J. P. (1983). Predicting therapy outcome using Benjamins' structural analysis of social behavior. *Dissertation Abstracts International, 43*, 534B.

Sachse, R. (1982). Der Begriff des "Klientenzentrierten Handels" und seine thera-peutischen Konsequenzen: Vier Thesen für ein erweitertes Verständnis [The notion of "client-centered exchange" and its consequences: Four theses for extending understanding]. *GwG-Info, 49,* 44–50.

Sachse, R. (1988). Das Konzept des empathischen Verstehens: Versuch einer sprachpsychologischen Klärung und Konsequenzen für das therapeutische Han-deln [The concept of empathic understanding: An attempt at psycholinguistic clarification and its consequences for therapeutic exchange]. *Orientierung an der Person: Diesseits und Jenseits von Psychotherapie* (Vol. 2, pp. 162–174). Köln, Germany: GwG.

Sachse, R. (1990a). Acting purposefully in client-centered therapy. In P. J. D. Drenth, J. A. Sergeant, & R. -J. Takens (Eds.), *European perspectives in psychol-ogy* (Vol. 1, pp. 65–80). New York: Wiley.

Sachse, R. (1990b). Concrete interventions are crucial: The influence of therapist's processing-proposals on the client's intra-personal exploration. In G. Lietaer, J. Rombauts, & R. van Balen (Eds.), *Client-centered and experiential psychotherapy in the nineties* (pp. 295–308). Leuven, Belgium: Leuven University Press.

Sachse, R. (1990c). The influence of processing proposals on the explication process of the client. *Person-Centered Review, 5,* 321–344.

Sachse, R. (1990d). Schwierigkeiten im Explizierungsprozeß psychosomatischer Klienten: Zur Bedeutung von Verstehen und Prozeßdirektivität [Troubles in the explication process in psychosomatic clients: The implications from under-standing and process directiveness]. *Zeitschrift für Klinische Psychologie, Psycho-pathologie und Psychotherapie, 38,* 191–205.

Sachse, R. (1991a). Gesprächspsychotherapie als "affektive Psychotherapie": Be-richt über ein Forschungsprojekt [Client-centered psychotherapy as an "affect-ive psychotherapy": Report on a research project]. Part 1 in *GwG Zeitschrift 83,* 30–42. Parl 2 in *GwG Zeitschrift 84,* 32–40.

Sachse, R. (1991b). Spezifische Wirkfaktoren in der Klientenzentrierten Psychother-apie: Zur Bedeutung von Bearbeitungsangeboten und Inhaltsbezügen [Specific change processes in client-centered psychotherapy: The implications from processing proposal level and content]. *Verhaltenstherapie und psychosoziale Praxis, 23,* 157–171.

Sachse, R. (1991c). Zielorientiertes Handeln in der Gesprächspsychotherapie: Steuerung des Explizierungsprozesses von Klienten durch zentrale Bearbei-tungsangebote des Therapeuten [Goal-oriented treatment in client-centered therapy: Control of the explication process in clients by means of the central content of therapy]. In D. Schulte (Ed.), *Therapeutische Entscheidungen* [Thera-peutic decisions] (pp. 89–106). Göttingen, Germany: Hogrefe.

Sachse, R. (1992a). Differential effects of processing proposals and content refer-ences on the explication process of clients with different starting conditions. *Psychotherapy Research, 2,* 235–251.

Sachse, R. (1992b). *Zielorientierte Gesprächspsychotherapie: Eine grundlegende Neu-konzeption* [Goal-oriented client-centered psychotherapy: A new fundamental conceptualization]. Göttingen, Germany: Hogrefe.

Sachse, R. (1992c). Zielorientiertes Handeln in der Gesprächspsychotherapie: Zum tatsächlichen und notwendigen Einfluß von Therapeuten auf die Explizierungsprozesse bei Klienten [Goal-oriented treatment in client-centered psychotherapy: The actual and necessary influence of therapists on the explication process of clients]. *Zeitschrift für Klinische Psychologie, 21,* 286–301.

Sachse, R. (1993). The effects of intervention phrasing of therapist–client communication. *Psychotherapy Research, 3,* 260–277.

Sachse, R. (1994). Veränderungsprozesse im Verlauf Klientenzentrierter Behandlung psychosomatischer Patienten [Change processes in the process of client-centered treatment of psychosomatic patients]. In K. Pawlik (Ed.), *Kongreß der Deutschen Gesellschaft für Psychologie* [Congress of the German Psychological Association] (pp. 601–602). Hamburg, Germany: Psychologisches Institut der Universität Hamburg.

Sachse, R. (1995). *Der psychosomatische Patient in der Praxis: Grundlagen einer effektiven Therapie mit "schwierigen" Klienten* [The psychosomatic patient in practice: Principles of effective therapy with "difficult" clients]. Stuttgart, Germany: Kohlhammer.

Sachse, R. (1997a). Clientgerichte Psychotherapie bij psychosomatische stoornissen [Client-centered psychotherapy with psychosomatic disorders]. *Tijdschrift voor Clientgerichte Psychotherapie, 35,* 5–32.

Sachse, R. (1997b). Zielorientierte Gesprächspsychotherapie bei Klienten mit psychosomatischen Störungen. Therapiekonzepte und Ergebnisse [Goal-oriented client-centered psychotherapy for clients with psychosomatic disorders]. *Gesprächspsychotherapie und Personenzentrierte Beratung, 28,* 90–107.

Sachse, R. (1998). Treatment of psychosomatic problems. In L. Greenberg, G. Lietaer, & J. Watson (Eds.), *Experimental psychotherapy: Differential intervention* (pp. 295–327). New York: Guilford Press.

Sachse, R., & Atrops, A. (1989). Focusing: Beziehungs-oder Bearbeitungsangebot? [Focusing: Relationship or processing proposal?] In M. Behr, F. Petermann, W. M. Pfeiffer, & C. Seewald (Eds.), *Jahrbuch für Personenzentrierte Psychologie und Psychotherapie* [Yearbook for person-centered psychology and psychotherapy] (Vol. 1, pp. 107–119). Salzburg, Austria: Müller.

Sachse, R., & Atrops, A. (1991). Schwierigkeiten psychosomatischer Klienten bei der Klärung eigener Emotionen und Motive: Mögliche Konsequenzen für die therapeutische Arbeit [Difficulties of psychosomatic clients with the clarification of emotions and motives: Possible consequences for therapeutic work]. *Psychotherapie, Psychosomatik, Medizinische Psychologie, 41,* 155–198.

Sachse, R., Atrops, A., Wilke, F., & Maus, C. (1992). *Focusing: Ein emotionszentriertes Psychotherapieverfahren* [Focusing: An emotion-centered psychotherapy procedure]. Bern, Switzerland: Huber.

Sachse, R., & Maus, C. (1987). Einfluß differentieller Bearbeitungsangebote auf den Explizierungsprozeß von Klienten in der klientenzentrierten Psychotherapie [The influence of differential processing proposals on the explication process in clients in client-centered psychotherapy]. *Zeitschrift für Personenzentrierte Psychologie und Psychotherapie, 6,* 75–86.

Sachse, R., & Maus, C. (1991). *Zielorientiertes Handeln in der Gesprächspsychotherapie* [Goal-oriented treatment in client-centered psychotherapy]. Stuttgart, Germany: Kohlhammer.

Sachse, R., & Neumann, W. (1986). Prognostische Indikation zum Focusing aufgrund von Selbstexploration und Selbsterleben von Klienten in Klientenzentrierter Psychotherapie [Prognostic indication for focusing on the basis of self-exploration and self-experience by clients in client-centered psychotherapy]. *Zeitschrift für Personenzentrierte Psychologie und Psychotherapie, 5,* 79–85.

Sachse, R., & Neumann, W. (1987). Prognostische Indikation zum Focusing aufgrund von Klienten-Prozeßerfahrungen in Klientenzentrierter Psychotherapie [Prognostic indication for focusing on the basis of client process-skill in client-centered psychotherapy]. *Bochumer Berichte zur Klinischen Psychologie,* No. 2.

Sachse, R., & Rudolph, R. (1992). Gesprächspsychotherapie mit psychosomatischen Klienten? Eine empirische Untersuchung auf der Basis der Theorie der Objektiven Selbstaufmerksamkeit [Client-centered psychotherapy with psychosomatic clients? An empirical investigation based on the theory of objective self-perceptiveness]. *Jahrbuch für Personenzentrierte Psychologie und Psychotherapie, 3,* 66–84.

Safran, J. D., & Wallner, L. K. (1991). The relative predictive validity of two therapeutic alliance measures in cognitive therapy. *Psychological Assessment, 3,* 188–195.

Sander, K., Langer, L., Bastine, R., Tausch, A., Tausch, R., & Wieceskowski, W. (1973). Gesprächspsychotherapie bei 73 psychoneurotischen Klienten mit alternierenden Psychotherapeuten ohne Abwahlmöglichkeit [Client-centered psychotherapy with 73 psychoneurotic clients seen by alternative psychotherapists without the possibility of dropping out]. *Zeitschrift für Klinische Psychologie, 20,* 218–229.

Schauble, P. G., & Pierce, R. M. (1974). Client in-therapy behavior: A therapist guide to progress. *Psychotherapy: Theory, Research and Practice, 11,* 229–234.

Schön, H. (1980). *Ergebnisse und Prozesse der Gesprächspsychotherapie unter Berücksichtigung des nichtsprachlichen Psychotherapieverhaltens* [Outcomes and processes of client-centered therapy under considerations of inarticulate psychotherapy behavior]. Hamburg, Germany: Lüdke.

Schwartz, H. -J. (1975). *Prozeßforschung in klientenzentrierter Gesprächspsychotherapie: Bedingungen des Behandlungseffektes im Anfangsgespräch* [A process investigation into client-centered psychotherapy: Agreement on treatment effects in opening dialogue]. Unpublished doctoral dissertation, Universität Hamburg, Hamburg, Germany.

Schwartz, H. -J., Eckert, J., Babel, M., & Langer, L. (1978). Prozessmerkmale in psychotherapeutischen Anfangsgesprächen: Eine Analyse neuer Merkmalskonzepte in der Gesprächspsychotherapie [Process markers in psychotherapeutic opening dialogue: An analysis of a new marker concept in client-centered psychotherapy]. *Zeitschrift für Klinische Psychologie, 7,* 65–71.

Sloane, R. B., Staples, F. R., Cristol, A. H., Yorkson, N. J., & Whipple, K. (1975). *Psychotherapy versus behavior therapy.* Cambridge, MA: Harvard University Press.

Soldz, S., Budman, S., & Demby, A. (1992). The relationship between main actor behaviors and treatment outcome in group psychotherapy. *Psychotherapy Research, 2,* 52–62.

Stiles, W. B., & Shapiro, D. A. (1989). Abuse of the drug metaphor in psychotherapy process–outcome research. *Clinical Psychology Review, 9,* 521–543.

Stoffer, D. L. (1968). *An investigation of positive behavioral change as a function of genuineness, non-possessive warmth, and empathic understanding.* Unpublished doctoral dissertation, Ohio State University.

Tausch, R. (1973). *Gesprächspsychotherapie* [Client-centered psychotherapy]. Göttingen, Germany: Hogrefe.

Tausch, R., Kühne, A., Langer, I., Dolli, G., Feindt, K., & Sternberg, W. (1972). *Effekte psychologisch hilfreicher Gespräche mit sogenannten Strafgefangenen* [The effect of psychological helping dialogue with so-called convicts]. Unpublished manuscript.

Tausch, R., Sander, K., Bastine, R., Freise, H., & Nagel, K. (1970). Variablen und Ergebnisse bei client-centered Psychotherapie mit alternierenden Psychotherapeuten [The variables and results of client-centered psychotherapy with alternative therapists]. *Psychologische Rundschau, 21,* 29–38.

Toukmanian, S. G. (1986). A measure of client perceptual processing. In L. Greenberg & W. Pinsof (Eds.), *The psychotherapeutic process* (pp. 107–130). New York: Guilford Press.

Torhorst, A., & Stitz, S. (1988). Therapieverlaufsstudie bei Patienten nach Suizidversuch unter Berücksichtigung linguistischer Untersuchungsergebnisse [A therapy process study of patients after suicide attempts under the consideration of linguistic research results]. *Suizidprophylaxe, 15,* 211–220.

Truax, C. B. (1961a). *A scale for the measurement of accurate empathy* (Psychiatric Institute Bulletin, Vol. 1, No. 12). Madison: University of Wisconsin.

Truax, C. B. (1961b). *A tentative scale for the measurement of depth of intrapersonal exploration* [Discussion papers]. Madison: University of Wisconsin, University Psychiatric Institute.

Truax, C. B. (1963). Effective ingredients in psychotherapy: An approach to unrevealing the patient–therapist interaction. *Journal of Counseling Psychology, 10,* 256–263.

Truax, C. B. (1966a). *Depth of intrapersonal exploration in psychotherapy: Comparisons between schizophrenic cases and counseling cases and between relatively unsuccessful psychotherapeutic outcomes.* Unpublished manuscript.

Truax, C. B. (1966b). Therapist empathy, warmth and genuineness and patient personality change in group psychotherapy: A comparison between interaction unit measures, time sample measures, and patient perception measures. *Journal of Clinical Psychology, 22*, 225–229.

Truax, C. B., & Carkhuff, R. R. (1965). The experimental manipulation of therapeutic conditions. *Journal of Consulting Psychology, 29*, 119–124.

Truax, C. B., & Carkhuff, R. R. (1967). *Toward effective counseling and psychotherapy: Training and practice.* Chicago: Aldine.

Truax, C. B., Carkhuff, R. R., & Kodman, F. (1965). Relationship between therapist-offered conditions and patient change in group psychotherapy. *Journal of Clinical Psychology, 21*, 327–329.

Truax, C. B., & Mitchell, K. M. (1971). Research on certain therapist interpersonal skills in relation to process and outcome. In A. E. Bergin & S. L. Garfield (Eds.), *Psycho-therapy and behaviour change* (pp. 299–344). New York: Wiley.

Truax, C. B., Wargo, D. G., Frank, J. D., Imber, S. D., Battle, C. C., Hoehn-Saric, R., Nash, E. H., & Stone, A. R. (1966a). Therapist empathy, genuineness, and warmth and patient therapeutic outcome. *Journal of Consulting Psychology, 30*, 395–401.

Truax, C. B., Wargo, D. G., Frank, J. D., Imber, S. D., Battle, C. C., Hoehn-Saric, R., Nash, E. H., & Stone, A. R. (1966b). Therapists' contribution to accurate empathy, nonpossessive warmth and genuineness in psychotherapy. *Journal of Consulting Psychology, 30*, 331–334.

Truax, C. B., Wargo, D. G., & Silber, L. D. (1966). Effects of group psychotherapy with high accurate empathy and nonpossessive warmth upon female institutionalized delinquents. *Journal of Abnormal Psychology, 71*, 267–274.

Truax, C. B., Wittmer, J., & Wargo, D. G. (1971). Effects of the therapeutic conditions of accurate empathy and nonpossessive warmth on hospitalized mental patients during group therapy. *Journal of Clinical Psychology, 27*, 137–142.

Tscheulin, D. (1983). Psychotherapie mit verdeckter Strategie—Bemerkungen zu A. Auckenthalers "Psychotherapie ohne Strategien" [Psychotherapy with hidden strategy: Commentary on A. Auckenthaler's "Psychotherapy without strategies"]. In D. Tscheulin (Ed.), *Beziehung und Technik in der klientenzentrierten Therapie* [Relationship and technique in client-centered therapy] (pp. 45–49). Weinheim, Germany: Beltz.

van der Veen, F. (1967). Basic elements in the process of psychotherapy: A research study. *Journal of Consulting Psychology, 31*, 295–303.

van der Veen, F., & Stoler, N. (1965). Therapist judgment, interview behavior, and case outcome. *Psychotherapy: Theory, Research and Practices, 2*, 158–163.

Watson, N. (1984). The empirical status of Rogers's hypotheses of the necessary and sufficient conditions for effective psychotherapy. In R. F. Levant & J. M. Shlein (Eds.), *Client-centered therapy and the person-centered approach: New directions in theory, research and practice* (pp. 17-40). Westport, CT: Praeger.

Westermann, B., Schwab, R., & Tausch, R. (1983). Auswirkungen und Prozesse personenzentrierter Gruppenpsychotherapie bei 164 Klienten einer psychotherapeutischen Beratungsstelle [The consequences and processes of person-centered group therapy with 164 clients in various psychotherapy clinics]. *Zeitschrift für Klinische Psychologie, 12*, 273–292.

Windholz, M., & Silberschatz, G. (1988). Vanderbilt Psychotherapy Process Scale: A replication with adult outpatients. *Journal of Consulting and Clinical Psychology, 56*, 56–60.

4

EXPERIENCING PSYCHOTHERAPY: GROUNDED THEORY STUDIES

DAVID L. RENNIE

Inquiry in humanistic psychotherapy has involved the development of research approaches consistent with its values. A major value is the emphasis this type of inquiry places on the experience of therapy. Qualitative research methods are in harmony with this emphasis. This chapter describes how the application of the grounded theory approach to qualitative research has helped to elucidate what it is like to be in therapy.

The term *qualitative* research has to do with a human science approach to social science, in contrast to *quantitative* research, which is more in keeping with the natural science approach (Fischer, 1977; Giorgi, 1970; Rennie, 1995). Directed especially toward understanding the meaning of human experience and conduct, qualitative research typically uses as its "data" various verbal texts and expresses the understandings derived from study of these texts in verbal language as well. It is perhaps more responsive than is most quantitative research to the observation made by Giddens (1976) that the social sciences involve a double hermeneutic. This means that the social sciences involve the study of a preinterpreted world made up of the same condition that is brought to the study of it—human social conduct. Thus, the social sciences turn back on themselves, or are reflexive, in ways not seen in the natural sciences. Still, assumptions having to do with how knowledge is developed (i.e., epistemology) vary widely among qualitative researchers. Some take a more realist stance and express positivism when developing research procedures (e.g., Hill, Thompson, & Williams, 1997). Others subscribe to a relativist epistemology and see the approach as *quite* interpretive, or constructionistic (see Madill, Jordan, & Shirley,

Appreciation is extended to Kimberly Watson for her helpful comments.

117

2000; McLeod, 2001). Still others see it as a way of reconciling realism and relativism (e.g., Kvale, 1996; Rennie, 2000b). Qualitative research is time consuming and so, when it is directed toward the experience of aggregates of individuals, the number of people studied is usually small by quantitative research standards. Because of the unique features of qualitative research, much energy has been put into the development of methodological principles guiding the approach (e.g., Henwood & Pidgeon, 1992; Stiles, 1993). Recently such principles have been incorporated into a set of guidelines for the publication of qualitative research studies in psychology and related fields (Elliott, Fischer, & Rennie, 1999).

A prominent form of qualitative research, the *grounded theory* method, was developed by two sociologists, Barney Glaser and Anselm Strauss (1967), who were critical of the conventional method in sociology. They worked out a set of procedures designed to ground theory in facts as an antidote to what they saw as the usual practice of testing rationally developed theory with facts. In their initial methodology, Glaser and Strauss saw the method mainly as a form of induction and that the method has more to do with the context of discovery than the context of verification (see Reichenbach, 1949). More recently, Strauss and an associate, Juliette Corbin, modified the method to include an interplay between induction and deduction, much to the distress of Glaser (see Glaser, 1992; Rennie, 1998a, 2000b; Strauss & Corbin, 1990). In any case, even under this modification, the method retains many of the features of qualitative research given above. Meanwhile, the grounded theory method has been adapted to psychological inquiry (e.g., Rennie, Phillips, & Quartaro, 1988).

Most of the studies reviewed in this chapter entailed the basic procedures constituting the method as originally conceived by Glaser and Strauss (1967). In these procedures, texts of various sorts (such as transcripts of interviews) are broken into units of meaning, and commonalities of meaning among the units are conceptualized as categories in response to the *constant comparative analysis* of the units. That is, the units of meaning are compared systematically with each other, and the categories generated from these comparisons are compared as well. As such interpretation proceeds, the growing list of categories eventually is judged sufficient to account for the meaning apparent in additional texts. At this point, one can conclude that the categories are saturated and can bring the gathering of texts to a close. Meanwhile, the grounded theory analyst attempts to be aware of initial conceptions (i.e., biases) about the phenomenon under study. Initially, in particular, effort is made to put such conceptions aside as much as possible (i.e., to *bracket* them) during the study in an attempt to address the meaning of the text under analysis in an open-ended way. Similarly, new ideas, hypotheses, and hunches coming to the analyst are bracketed and recorded as *theoretical memos*. In the initial phase of the analysis, these memos are kept separate from the filing system used to record the categories and meanings attached to them. As the analysis continues, however, the memos are drawn on during constant comparative analysis of the categories as a way of conceptualizing higher order categories and the relations among them. Flowing out of this activity is the conceptualization of a *core category* that gathers together the meaning of all other categories and their relations. This core category is the main organizer of the theory of the social phenomenon being studied.

Although the grounded theory method has been applied to the study of couples counseling (Burr, 1994), family therapy (Tanji, 1996), and group therapy (Bolger, 1999), with the exception of the study by Bolger, the following review is restricted to its use in the study of the experience of individual psychotherapy. In this review, I arranged these studies into four sections: studies on the experience (a) of a course of therapy as whole, (b) of an hour of therapy, (c) of spontaneous events occurring within a session, and (d) of therapist-directed tasks in sessions. As will be seen, most of these studies have focused exclusively on the client's experience, although some have addressed the therapist's experience as well.

EXPERIENCE OF A WHOLE COURSE OF THERAPY

Three studies have called on clients to recall aspects of psychotherapy in the light of having completed a whole course of therapy. Phillips (1984) was interested in clients' impressions of the contributors to change over the course of therapy. Schneider (1985) inquired into clients' recollections of the positive and negative qualities of their therapists. More recently, Bolger (1999) studied the experience and resolution of emotional pain.

Sources of Change in Psychotherapy

Phillips (1984) examined the extent to which events occurring both inside and outside therapy were thought by former clients to have contributed to change. He selected, from a number of volunteers to the study, 3 clients who appeared similar in many ways and contrasted them with 4 other clients who were different in many respects. The 5 women and 2 men who were selected had been in therapy at a university counseling center, a behavior modification clinic, or in private practice. Two clients had been engaged in person-centered therapy, 2 were in cognitive therapy, 2 were in therapy with inexperienced therapists with little specifiable orientation, and 1 client who had undergone years of therapy had been engaged primarily with psychoanalytic and behavioral approaches. In his inquiry, Phillips (1984) was presented with reports such as the following:

And if you talk to somebody else, that forces you to go deeper. . . . If I'm not going to be honest there's no point in me going through with this. . . . I mean I wasn't doing it for fun. . . . I mean I took it very seriously. I was doing it for myself. It was a sort of present to myself . . . the excitement of becoming more aware of what's going on . . . the pleasure of discovering. (pp. 57–58)

Phillips (1984) found that, although he probed into extratherapy events and conditions that contributed to change during the course of therapy, the respondents had little to say in this regard. Instead, they talked mainly about what they were able to get from their therapists that they were not able to get from friends and acquaintances. The core category that he conceptualized to represent the overall meaning of the interviewees' reports was *self-focus*. The respondents indicated that they saw their therapy as a special occasion enabling them to pay attention to themselves. Phillips interpreted the reports to mean that this self-focus entailed a process of change involving (a) awareness of problems and issues, (b) motivation to change, (c) pursuit of change, (d) acquisition of new understandings, (e) acquisition of new behaviors, and (f) changes in the interpersonal environment. More concretely grounded in the reports and interpreted to support the process model were categories having to do with (a) the interviewees themselves (openness, hope, and respect for the therapist), (b) the therapist (attending, caring support, separateness, techniques, and consistency), and (c) the relationship with the therapist (humor and insight).

Thus, the interviewees mainly spoke more about in-therapy than out-side-therapy influences on them when they were in therapy. They also addressed their experience of themselves and of the relationship with the therapist more than the experience of encountering therapeutic technique.

Clients' Positive and Negative Appraisals of Therapists

Schneider (1985) conducted an investigation involving a combination of empirical phenomenological psychology (Giorgi, 1975) and the grounded theory method. He was interested in learning about clients' positive and negative appraisals of therapists in a way that was not constrained by the views of the researcher. He interviewed 9 women and 6 men, 13 of whom were counselors themselves, all of whom, on average, had completed a course of long-term humanistic therapy 3.7 years prior to the study. Eight of the interviewees evaluated their therapy as successful, 1 judged it as poor, and the rest rated it as fair.

Among the positive appraisals Schneider (1985) was given was the following comment: "One thing that I really felt positive about . . . was that she gave me feedback. . . . And as she gave me feedback, she also let me know that that's the way she's seeing it. . . . I didn't have to take it as ultimate truth" (p. 73). Alternatively, another interviewee who evaluated his therapist negatively remarked, "It would've been better if she hadn't disclosed the things she was unresolved with" (p. 119).

The analysis of such reports resulted in the conceptualization of four main themes regarding the therapist: (a) personal involvement, (b) technical restructuring, (c) authoritativeness, and (d) role modeling. Therapists who were appraised positively were high on these themes, whereas those who were judged negatively were low on them. Those who were *personally involved* conveyed genuineness, support, acceptance, and deep understanding. Their clients had felt less defensive, more genuine, responsible, and acceptant of their feelings. These clients had also understood themselves better and took themselves more seriously. Therapists who engaged in *technical restructuring* conveyed cognitive and experiential skills. This intervention helped interviewees to shift their perspectives on matters of concern, to feel clearer about precipitating events and more capable of perceiving options, and to become more aware of their responses and impact on others. Practitioners who displayed *authoritativeness* conveyed firmness and self-assurance. In response, the interviewees had felt secure, receptive to influence, and psychologically edified. Finally, by virtue of how they were as people and how they conducted themselves, positively appraised therapists were taken as *role models* personally, socially, and professionally.

Therapists who were appraised negatively were interpreted to be unsatisfactory in terms of the four themes. These counselors expressed either too much or too little personal or technical involvement. They did not know when to withdraw and when to intervene. They failed to bring personal and professional resources forward and burdened their clients with personalities that lacked integration, maturity, and responsibility.

Significantly, whether positive or negative, the former clients reported that the impact of their therapists on them was profound and lasted for a long time after the therapy ended. Overall, Schneider (1985) found that the interviewees evaluated their therapists mainly in terms of the relationship that they had with them. Within this relationship, it was important for the therapist to be a good listener, accepting, natural, and actively involved in the therapy. Interventions such as intuitively timed interpretations, exercises, and therapeutic games facilitated gains that may not have occurred in a more permissive relationship. Schneider interpreted these accounts to provide support for the claim made by existential–analytical and experiential therapists that the person-centered attitudes of empathy, unconditional positive regard, and genuineness are necessary but inefficient, and sometimes insufficient. At the same time, he acknowledged that this interpretation was contingent on his having spoken to sophisticated former clients and recommended that his study be followed by one directed toward the experience of people less familiar with counseling theory and practice.

Emotional Pain

The experience of emotional pain, and of its resolution, was examined by Bolger (1999). She recruited 7 White women between 32 and 42 years of age who were professionally employed and self-supporting. Most were adult children of alcoholics. They were in group therapy for the resolution of emotional pain, with Bolger sitting in as a participant observer. Participants were interviewed immediately following a group session and then 6 months later, as a follow-up. The participants' reports were interpreted to mean that they had developed a *covered self* that served to protect a *hidden self*, through the use of "covers" and "containers." The women used this defensive strategy as a way of dealing with a *broken self*. The covered self could be broken in any of a number of ways: retraumatization, remembering past traumatic events, talking about them, or hearing others talk about them. As Bolger (1999) described the experience,

> Pain was initially experienced at a visceral level, as being opened suddenly and unnaturally against one's will, like "being ripped apart". . . . There was also a feeling of "breaking apart", "having a nervous breakdown", or "losing myself" completely, as if one might disintegrate. (p. 352)

Some of the participants had undergone a resolution of broken self, into a *tranformed self*. The broken self was interpreted to be the core category gathering together the meaning of experienced pain, and the covered self and transformed self were conceptualized as higher order categories integrally related to the core category. These categories were interpreted to subsume 11 main categories, 13 submain categories, and 99 descriptive categories. From this hierarchy, Bolger (1999) developed a process model of working through emotional pain. In this model, initial pain leads to the covered self, which gets *ruptured*, resulting in *surfacing/exposing*, causing *brokenness*, leading to *loss of control*, and then *alarm*. At this point, the individual either (re)covers the pain or allows it, the latter then enabling expression of it, which may eventuate in transformed self. Bolger observed that the moves to transformed self were not taken by everyone in her sample. She remarked:

> The process of working through pain outlined in this study bears similarity to the model developed by Greenberg and Safran (1987). Allowing pain appeared to facilitate change, and participants expressed relief at surviving the experience. Both the identification of needs and a shift in belief about the self seemed to be important in the change process. However, although pain forced a positive change in some, for others it had been wholly destructive. I was surprised to learn how powerful and persisting the impact of previous painful experiences could be. Even the constructive effects of feeling pain were not enough to overcome

the negative impact of some former painful experience. . . . The results confirmed that both the fear of annihilation and the fear of seeing the self mediated the avoidance of pain. What was clarified for me was that the fear of annihilation functioned to disallow pain, while the fear of seeing the self interfered with staying with the pain, even when it was allowed. In addition, overcoming the fear of annihilation was not facilitative of change. Change happened when individuals were able to overcome the fear and shame evoked when seeing themselves. Facing Myself and Questioning emerged as critical processes that kept individuals focused on themselves, once the fear of not surviving was overcome. (Bolger, 1999, pp. 358–359)

Thus, Bolger's study illustrates how clients' reports on the experience of therapy add richness to understandings of what is involved in therapeutic change and resistance to it.

THE EXPERIENCE OF AN HOUR OF PSYCHOTHERAPY

I conducted a study on clients' moment-to-moment experiences of an hour of therapy. In a research interview, either a videotape or audiotape of a therapy session that the clients had just completed was played back to the client in the presence of a researcher–interviewer. The interviewees were asked to stop the tape at any point of recalled significance or interest and to report what they recollected. Thus, the inquiry procedure was an adaptation of Kagan's (1975) technique of Interpersonal Process Recall (IPR) and paralleled an adoption of the same technique for related purposes by Elliott (1986). Both the therapy session and the IPR interview were tape-recorded, and the latter was analyzed in terms of the grounded theory method, with the therapy transcript serving as context (Rennie, 1990, 1992, 1994a, 1994b, 1994d, 1998b, 2000a).

The interviewees were mostly university students going to the counseling center at each of two major Canadian universities, although some of the participants were with a private practitioner. The therapies were primarily person centered and experiential, although cognitive therapy and behavior therapy were represented as well. Fourteen people were interviewed in all, with 2 participants interviewed about two separate therapy sessions each, for a total of 16 interviews. Three of these interviews involved 2 of my clients. I interviewed all participants other than my own clients. The core category conceptualized in the grounded analysis was *client's reflexivity* (see below). It subsumed four main categories: (a) client's relationship with personal meaning, (b) client's perception of the relationship with the therapist, (c) client's experience of the therapist's operations, and (d) client's experience of outcomes. The relationship with personal meaning was further interpreted to involve both the pursuit and avoidance of meaning. The relationship with the therapist was interpreted to entail deference to the therapist and nonspecific relationship factors (see Frank, 1971). The relationship with the therapist's operations was understood to involve the experience of operations bearing on (a) the client's sense of identity, (b) the client's agency, and (c) the therapist's relationship with the client. Finally, the main category of the client's experience of outcomes involved the impact of the therapy and impact of the inquiry. These main categories and their properties in turn were interpreted to be supported by 51 fourth-level categories (for their specific nature, see Rennie, 1992).

The reflexivity attributed to clients has been defined as self-awareness and agency within that self-awareness (Rennie, 1992, 1998b, 2000a).[1] The interviewees' reports consistently indicated that the most salient, recalled aspect of their experience was their active self-reflection as they dealt with their own experience and with the presence and conduct of the therapist. Moreover, in this self-reflection they listened to their feelings when proceeding from moment to moment in the interaction with the therapist. Although often rapid and subtle, this feeling-of-one's-way was interpreted to amount to decision making. It is this decisional aspect of the client's experience that has led to the formulation that agency is integral to the client's reflexivity. Once embarking on a given line of thought (whether expressed to the therapist or followed covertly), related thoughts, memories, associations, and feelings emerged in line with the topic. Thus, they followed a path or track of thought and feeling (see also Gendlin, 1974, 1996; Pearson, 1974; Wexler, 1974). When on the path, this pursuit was often nonreflexive, which means that they were not aware that they were engaged in the pursuit as such. Rather, they were "just doing it" (see Searle, 1983). In this state, the presence and contributions of the therapist, if in line with the track, were hardly noticed but nevertheless had a prompting effect. Thus, the experience of therapy was characterized by an ongoing shifting back and forth between a reflexive sense of where to go next, on the one hand, and a nonreflexive pursuit of that line of meaning until it came to a close, on the other hand.

The ending of the nonreflexive pursuit of a line of meaning appeared to come about either because the intention originating the path of thought came to fulfillment or because the path was disturbed in some way. An

---

[1]*Reflexivity* has been defined as "a turning back on oneself, a form of self-awareness" (Lawson, 1985, p. 9). When the clients participating in the study revealed how active they had been internally in their interactions with their therapists, I initially conceptualized the core category representing the clients' experience as *clients' agency*. Later, I decided that this category did not represent adequately the self-referencing that was involved in the agency. It was for this reason that I opted for *clients' reflexivity*, with the amendment to the usual definition of reflexivity to the effect that agency is involved in it.

example of an intention in the process of fulfillment was a "point" that a client wished to make, such as the conclusion of a statement or the climax of a story.

Alternatively, *disturbances* were either internal or external. *Internal* disturbances were unexpected distressing thoughts and feelings arising during the tracking of experience. For example, the clients may have become upset while telling a story, causing a shift from being immersed in the story to being aware of being upset. In contrast, *external* upsets happened when the therapist's activity was not in line with the track. To illustrate, a client's smooth immersion in a story was interrupted when her therapist failed to support her sufficiently during a brief moment when she needed it (Rennie, 1994d). In either case, the clients "snapped out of" the nonreflexive pursuit to deal with the disturbance.

When the disturbance was internal, the clients had to decide on courses of action such as continuing the pursuit despite the upset, easing the upset by not disclosing the feeling or the memory/association that triggered the upset, or by changing the subject. When external, the disturbance usually placed clients in an awkward position. In general, they got out of it by either ignoring the therapist's response, giving token acknowledgment of it until they could safely get back on track, or dropping what they were thinking about and attending fully to the therapist. When the last response happened, it was with a sense of loss, and they experienced considerable relief if the therapist managed to return to the track. Thus, one client was derailed when the therapist asked a question that the client did not understand and was placed back on track when the therapist rephrased the question (see the illustrative dialogue toward the end of the chapter).

I also came to understand that disjunctions created by the therapist interacted powerfully with the client's relationship with the therapist. Clients who felt good about their therapist generally could take therapist-induced disjunctions in stride. These clients rested on the realization that, if things did not work out in this particular moment, they would come out all right in the end. Alternatively, clients who had troubled relationships with their therapists were prone to overreact to such a disjunction because they felt that it both arose from the negative aspects of the relationship and was evidence of it. Such an attribution was made by a client being seen by a therapist who strenuously urged her to be assertive in her interpersonal relationships. The client resisted this advocation to a certain extent. Meanwhile, the therapist answered the telephone a lot during their sessions, which irritated the client. Although she realized that the idea was "wild," as she put it, she suspected that the therapist engaged in this behavior to demonstrate how to be assertive when talking to someone over the telephone.

The reports revealed that the most significant experience often was not expressed to the therapist. One the one hand, some interviewees reported that they were thinking faster than they could talk. As one remarked, her engagement with herself was *her* process. She decided that her therapist did not need to know about it and that, besides, she could work more quickly when not conveying all of her thoughts to him. On the other hand, when uncomfortable with aspects of their experience, the clients communicated only what they felt they could express. This constraint was especially true of moments when the clients had negative reactions to the therapist's manner or approach. It was evident that the clients had a strong tendency to defer to the therapist (Rennie, 1990, 1994a, 1994c, 1998b; see also the studies by Rhodes, Hill, Thompson, & Elliott, 1994; Watson & Rennie, 1994, addressed below). This deference was expressed in a number of ways. They respected the therapist's judgment even when not agreeing with it. They made allowances. They followed the therapist's lead. They attempted to understand the therapist's frame of reference to make the therapist's work easier. They resisted criticizing or challenging the therapist; and so on. Interestingly, some clients revealed that, although what the therapist did was unpleasant, it was not appraised as negative. They realized that what a therapist did was good for them even though they did not like it, as when a Gestalt therapist encouraged them to participate in exercises to facilitate contact with painful emotions. In this circumstance, the relationship with the therapist was crucial. In the presence of a relationship, the interviewees willingly complied, albeit usually with initial resistance, whereas in an unsettling relationship, they complied with an inwardly grudging diffidence.

The study is thus a reminder that clients are self-aware agents in interaction with their therapists. Moreover, in this vein it illustrates that (a) clients often do not disclose to the therapist all that they are experiencing, and (b) some of what they do not disclose has to do with their sense of the therapist. Accordingly, it points to the importance of nonverbal cues indicating covert experience. The study also calls for therapists to discuss openly with their clients the nature of the communication between them and their clients. As addressed elsewhere (Rennie, 1998b), communication may be thought to involve purposes and impacts (see Elliott, James, Reimschuessel, Cislo, & Sack, 1985). Accordingly, therapists may either inquire into the purpose behind the client's communication or reveal the purpose of their own communication. Alternatively, they may either ask about the impact of their communication or reveal the impact of the client's communication. Such communication about communication has been termed *metacommunication* by Watzlawick, Beavin, and Jackson (1967; see also Kiesler, 1996). In turn, the study helps to elucidate how metacommunication may facilitate the establishment, maintenance, and repair of the working alliance (cf. Bordin, 1979; Rennie, 1998b; Rhodes et al., 1994; Safran, Muran, & Wallner Samstag, 1994; Watson & Greenberg, 1994).

THE EXPERIENCE OF SPONTANEOUS EVENTS WITHIN A THERAPY SESSION

Four studies have been conducted on the experience of particular kinds of events occurring spontaneously in therapy. The events in question have to do with misunderstanding, storytelling, metaphor, and therapists' imagery.

Misunderstanding

Rhodes et al. (1994) conducted a study of the experience of being misunderstood by the therapist. A total of 16 women and 3 men, who were all therapists or therapists-in-training, described in writing an event that had occurred in their therapy in which they felt that they had been misunderstood (3 of the study's authors included themselves among the 19 participants). The therapists involved in the study were psychodynamic ($n = 13$), psychodynamic/humanistic ($n = 3$), humanistic ($n = 2$), and eclectic ($n = 1$). In a research approach that drew in part on the grounded theory method, the written accounts were interpreted in terms of the pathway-to-change model borrowed from comprehensive process analysis (Elliott, 1989). This model characterizes change in therapy as occurring in significant therapeutic events. The components of an event involving change are its long-term background, immediate context, precipitant, experience of the event, client action, ensuing therapist action, resolution, and ensuing process. The investigators found that the accounts were quite different depending on whether the participants appeared to have resolved the misunderstanding event, which led to the conduct of separate analyses for the 11 resolvers and 8 nonresolvers.

The consensual understanding arrived at by Rhodes et al. (1994) was as follows: The misunderstanding occurred when the therapist either gave what the client had not wanted in that moment or did not give what the client had wanted. Whether the misunderstanding was resolved depended to a great extent on the client's relationship with the therapist. On the whole, the resolvers reported having a good relationship. Thus, although some of the resolvers initially *went underground* (i.e., they quashed their inner negative reaction to the therapist), roughly half of the resolvers spoke up against the therapist immediately. Moreover, most of those who went underground eventually expressed their negativity. In response, the therapists of the resolvers accommodated the criticism by apologizing and negotiating where to go from there. The result was that most of the resolvers continued to work with the therapist after the immediate resolution and to profit from it. In contrast, half of the nonresolvers specifically mentioned a poor relationship, and only one indicated a good relationship. Most of these clients went underground and stayed there. Indeed, a majority of them ended the therapy. Although the termination was not attributed entirely to the event, it seemed clear that it had contributed to it. This account supports the understanding given to Schneider (see page 121, this chapter) on the profundity of the impact of therapy on sophisticated clients.

Storytelling

As an extension of my main study, I focused on the experience of telling a story to the therapist (Rennie, 1994d). I came to understand that storytelling was a way of dealing with inner disturbance. For clients who intended to get into their disturbance, telling a story was a way of preparing to address it directly. The structure of the story "housed," as it were, a number of internal experiences related to the disturbance (such as memories, associations, ideas, and appraisals). In this way, storytellers could engage the experiences without necessarily having to express them. Through this avenue, then, they could touch on and, to a certain extent, come to terms with the disturbance privately. This preliminary work made it easier for them to address the disturbance openly. Thus, it was as if they used the story to "get their feet in the water." In the bargain, they also found that the act of telling the story was therapeutic in its own right. Not only did they achieve emotional relief, they also managed to gain some insight in the course of their private work with their inner disturbance.

Alternatively, there were some clients who could not avoid an inner disturbance arising from a life event but who were disinclined to enter into their disturbance. These clients *altered* the actual story of the life event that had given rise to the disturbance. Thus, this strategy was a kind of "belief management." There was enough ambiguity about the painful event to enable them to construe it in a way that made it less painful. Interestingly, the intensity with which they told their stories seemed to indicate that they were enveloped in creative tension until the story was complete. This tension was reflected in a low tolerance for interference by the therapist until it was completed. Ironically, these participants disclosed that, as much as they wished to create more acceptable stories, they were aware of what they were doing and of the alternative story (the "true" story), even though they did not give *that* story to the therapist. Thus, the alteration of the true story carried them to insight despite their intention to the contrary.

Metaphor

A study of both the client's and the therapist's experience of metaphor in therapy was conducted by Angus (1992; Angus & Rennie, 1988, 1989). Lakoff and Johnson's (1980) definition of metaphor guided the selection of metaphor in therapy discourse. Accordingly, metaphor was considered to be a figure of speech that invokes a transaction between differing contexts of meaning and construct systems. Thus, one may remark, "He's a lion," where the lion as the dominant species on the African plains is related to a man who is considered more powerful than those around him. From each of the single sessions of the four therapy dyads, Angus chose 5 client-produced and 6 therapist-produced metaphors, or roughly three metaphors per dyad. An IPR inquiry was made into the client's and the therapist's experience of the particular metaphors they produced. Examples of the 11 metaphors chosen for study were "giving a litany," "on a broomstick," "having a tantrum," "a witch," and "an ogre." The therapists participating in the study entailed 1 psychoanalyst, 1 Gestalt therapist, and 2 eclectics working within a person-centered and psychodynamic framework. All 4 therapists were men. The 4 clients were 3 women studying at a university and 1 salesman. With a combination of grounded theory analysis (Glaser & Strauss, 1967) and empirical phenomenological psychology (Fessler, 1978), the coordination of clients' and the therapists' perspectives led to the conceptualization of two global themes: *metaphoric communicative interaction* and *associated meaning contexts.*

The first global theme came from the realization that, for half of the dyads, there was conjunction in the meaning of a metaphor as experienced by both the client and the therapist, whereas for the other half, there was disjunction in the meaning. Whether meaning conjunction or disjunction occurred was contingent on the style of communication between the therapist and the client. Meaning conjunction arose from a collaborative style of communication, in which the therapist actively worked with both the client's and his own experience in trying to make sense of the metaphor and in developing it further. In this case, the therapist shared his personally held meanings in a tentative way, which stimulated similar exploratory work by the client. During this give-and-take, the client and therapist collaboratively teased out the ways in which the metaphor seemed to catch the nuances of the client's experience. Alternatively, in noncollaborative communicative interaction, the therapist conducted a kind of Socratic inquiry evidently designed to stimulate the client to come to an understanding of the meaning of the metaphor that the therapist had already decided was "true" of a particular set of issues. Thus, the ultimate purpose of these interactions boiled down to the therapist's attempt to persuade the client to come to the former's point of view.

The second global theme, associated meaning context, referred to the embeddedness of metaphors in a network of associated memories, incidents, feelings, and images. The elements of this network were articulated either in the therapy session itself or in the inquiry session about it. The participants' reports were interpreted to indicate that metaphor symbolized inner experience in three ways: (a) It was an associative link in that it led to the elaboration of specific memories or images related to an inner experience; (b) it symbolized and made apparent a unique set of values and characteristics on which clients implicitly drew when addressing themselves, thus providing a framework for the client's self-identity; and, last, (c), it figuratively characterized the client's role-relationship patterns. These patterns were represented as inner dialogues between particular speaker–listener pairs making up the experiential social world of the client. As an example, the client producing the ogre metaphor internally engaged in a dialogue between his fantasized billy-goat self and his ogre or troll mother. Overall, as associated meaning context, the use of metaphor provided the client and therapist with a succinct way of referring to the complex fabric making up the meaning of the client's experience.

Therapist's Imagery

Shaul (1994) conducted a study of the impact of therapists' imagery on the psychotherapeutic process. Four therapists were involved in the study. Two were process–experiential, 1 was person-centered, and 1 was psychodynamic in orientation; all had between 3 and 15 years of experience. The clients were 2 men and 2 women, between the early 20s and early 30s in age. Shaul audio-recorded a single session for each dyad. He arranged for the therapists to indicate when they experienced an image by giving an auditory sign of some sort, such as a clearing of the throat. Within no more than a few hours after the session, the investigator conducted an IPR interview with the therapist, focusing on two such images that were judged by the therapist to be especially significant in some way. In this IPR interview, once the moment when a given image had been experienced was located on the tape, the tape was rolled back to approximately 4 minutes prior to that moment. The therapist was asked to recall what he or she had experienced during this period prior to the visual image. As the tape rolled forward, the replay entered the moment of the visual image, and the therapist was asked to recall what had been experienced at that moment. The inquiry about the given image ended with the therapist being asked to recall what he or she had experienced during the 4 minutes after the moment of imagery. To illustrate, one of the therapists reported that, when listening to his client talk about her desire to satisfy both herself and her parents over a matter that was concern to the client, he had experienced an image of her walking on a fence:

> As I envision her walking on the fence, I sense that she wants me to help her somehow balance on this fence instead of choosing a side. She also appears quite scared in the image. I can see her face and she looks quite scared, you know, like something terrible, really awful, will happen

if she ends up on either side. It really struck me, I mean, I felt a strong sense that the client in the image wanted to stay on that fence and would rather balance precariously than try to get down, kind of like a scared cat up a tree. (Shaul, 1994, pp. 60–61)

As it turned out, of the eight imagery events, only three were directly shared with the clients. In the other incidents, the therapists had decided to work with and to share their sense of the *meaning* of the image, without actually imparting the image.

On completion of the IPR interview with the therapist, Shaul replayed the same tape footage to the therapist's client. Parallel to what had been done with the therapist, the client was asked to recall what had been experienced from moment to moment during that section of the therapy session. This procedure was repeated for the four dyads. In addition, Shaul administered the Working Alliance Inventory (Horvath & Greenberg, 1986) to both the clients and the therapists. He also had raters use the Client Experiencing Scale (Klein, Mathieu, Gendlin, & Kiesler, 1969) to appraise the client's processing of experience during the period of the therapy session under study. Having in hand both the therapists' and the clients' reports of their experience, Shaul proceeded to do separate grounded theory analyses of the therapists' and clients' experiences. He also integrated the two analyses in a way that was informed by the returns from the Working Alliance Inventory and the Experiencing Scale.

Shaul (1994) conceptualized *Working With the Image* as the core category subsuming the many categories representing the therapist's experience. The main properties of this category were understood to be: (a) imagery generation, (b) construction of meaning, (c) decision regarding intervention, (d) intervention, and (e) evaluation of intervention. It is noteworthy that although the therapist's reports were cast in such a way as to make a linear process model appropriate the same was not true of the clients' reports. A "holographic" model, as Shaul put it, seemed more fitting for the latter in the sense that what was true of the whole of the client's experience was true of each part of it as well. The core category of the clients' experiences was conceptualized as *Client's Processing: Responding to the Therapist's Challenge*. This category gathered together as its main properties (a) the client's analysis of therapist's activity, (b) the internal check, (c) the client's evaluation of the therapeutic alliance, and (d) the client's evaluation of the therapeutic process.

The overall analysis led to the understanding that, whether the therapist disclosed the actual image or made an intervention derived from his or her interpreted meaning of the image, the clients experienced a positive shift in their understanding of their experience. This pattern, derived from the participants' accounts, was corroborated by the pattern of Experiencing Scale scores, judged by raters who were "blind" to the grounded theory analyses. Moreover, as would be expected, the clients who benefited the most from the therapist's imagery-based intervention were those who reported the most satisfactory relationships with their therapist. This impression was corroborated by the Working Alliance Scale scores. Shaul concluded that therapist's imagery appears to serve as an *empathic lens*, or exquisite articulation of the client's experience.

THE EXPERIENCE OF THERAPIST-DIRECTED TASKS

A task prescribed by the process–experiential approach to therapy (Greenberg, Rice, & Elliott, 1993) is the analysis of *problematic reactions* (Rice & Saperia, 1984). The concept of problematic reaction refers to the client's overreaction to an interpersonal event that occurred outside therapy. Thus, a client might remark, "It was such a small thing, but I was completely devastated." The task is to delve into the reaction to determine its meaning and resolve it, under the therapist's direction. Specifically, once a problematic reaction is identified, the therapist uses the technique of systematic evocative unfolding (Rice, 1974)—a form of empathic responding entailing the use of imagery and vivid language—as a way of helping the client to reexperience the problematic event and to understand its meaning.

A study was conducted on the client's subjective experience of undergoing the task of attempting to resolve a problematic reaction (Watson & Greenberg, 1994; Watson & Rennie, 1994). Watson recruited 8 clients from both a university counseling center and undergraduate psychology classes of a major Canadian university to undergo a 12- to 16-week course of process–experiential therapy, offered by her and two colleagues. At the end of the second and seventh session, the clients were asked to bring to the next session a problematic reaction that they had experienced in the previous week. Thus, the third and eighth sessions were devoted to the task of resolving the problematic reaction in response to the therapeutic technique of systematic unfolding. After each of these two therapy sessions, the clients were asked to review the audiotape of their session and to locate and rank three significant moments when something had shifted for them. Within no more than 2 days following the session, an IPR interview was used to inquire into the experience of these moments (if the moments were not moments of addressing the problematic reaction, then the IPR interviewer took the liberty of directing the client's attention to such moments). Watson was the IPR interviewer of the clients of the other two therapists, whereas I interviewed her two clients.

The grounded theory analysis of the clients' reports led to the conceptualization of a core category titled *Inquiry Into Self*. This category was understood to have two main properties: *client operations* and *session momentum*.

Client operations was understood to subsume: (a) symbolic representation of experience, (b) reflexive self-examination, (c) making new realizations, and (d) revisioning self. Session momentum was interpreted to have two properties, positive and negative (Watson & Rennie, 1994).

In terms of their operations when in the role of clients, the interviewees reported that, once they began to comply with the therapist's directive to recall as vividly as possible the details of the problematic event, they found themselves faced with the need to articulate adequately their experience. It was important to use the right words. They attempted to match the words they were using against the visual images and felt-senses they were experiencing while recollecting the event. While trying to make sense of their experience, they came to new realizations about themselves. Furthermore, when the exploratory process went well, they came to see themselves and their relationship with others in a new light. This was an achievement that connected in complex ways with the resolution of the problematic reaction.

Regarding the second main category, session momentum, it was evident from the interviewees' reports that complying with the task was not always easy. Compliance meant that they had to deal with their experience in the therapist's way, not their way, and it was necessary to get involved in the task before it began to work for them. Watson and Greenberg (1994) interpreted this aspect in terms of the concept of the working alliance as advanced by Bordin (1979). Within this interpretation, they generalized the experience of being confronted with the task of resolving problematic reactions to the several tasks developed in process–experiential therapy (e.g., two-chair work as a way of resolving conflicts involved in unfinished business; see Greenberg et al., 1993). Watson found that most of the clients deferred to the therapist's judgment. In their deference, some experienced an initial period of adjustment but found themselves, with growing excitement and momentum, engaged in a path to clarification and resolution of their disturbance. Alternatively, others had difficulty with the task, complaining that the therapist's pressing for the details of the problematic event got in the way of their preferred way of dealing with it. Watson and Greenberg (1994) pointed out that in work of this sort it is important to distinguish between the task and the bond components of the working alliance and to give priority to the latter. Thus, it is best to make metacommunicative probes into the state of the bond to ascertain willingness to engage in the task, as a way of ascertaining when the client is ready to begin in the task work. In this way, the working alliance is maintained.

On the whole, Watson's study (Watson & Greenberg, 1994; Watson & Rennie, 1994) led to the understanding that clients' participation in the activity of dealing with their problematic reactions is more complex than has been outlined by the performance model advanced by Rice and Saperia

(1984), based on analysis of the discourse between the client and the therapist. As discussed by Watson and her colleagues, this finding is not surprising in the sense that much of what clients experience in therapy is covert. Thus, it is not to be expected that such activities are revealed through the discourse with the therapist. Instead, to access them, one must obtain clients' reports on their inner experience.

IMPLICATIONS OF THE RESEARCH FOR THE PRACTICE OF PSYCHOTHERAPY

As seen throughout, the above studies accessed the experience of psychotherapy—usually the client's experience but at times the therapist's as well. The studies were thus close to the actual practice of therapy and, accordingly, shed new light on practice. Although what follows is not in any way meant to be completely representative of the implications that may be drawn from these studies, seven main points are presented:

1. Although the characterization is not total by any means, clients in therapy are self-aware agents. Their agency is engaged when they match their experience against their sense of the therapist's understanding of it and act in terms of their sense of their best interests in the light of this complex evaluation. This understanding of the active role clients play in the conduct of therapy reinforces and elucidates Carl Rogers's and the existential–humanistic therapists' prizing of clients' self-determination. It also imposes a constraint on the tenability of attempts to develop "causal" therapist-driven performance models of change. Clients will always respond in their own ways to the tasks assigned by the therapist, and it is difficult if not impossible for any model of change to take into account the myriad options available to clients by virtue of their agency. Thus, the most that could be expected from a model of change is a gross estimation of change. Looking at this matter another way, a plausible explanation for the well-known finding that there are surprisingly few differences among the outcomes of various approaches to therapy is that clients creatively use whatever approach is applied to them (see Bohart & Tallman, 1996).

2. On the other side of the coin, the reports given by the clients and former clients in these studies have indicated consistently that they felt they benefited from their therapist's agency

so long as it was compatible with their own. Indeed, some participants indicated that the therapist's agency was in keeping with their ideal agency and that they consequently forced themselves to comply with the therapist's agency. This understanding thus supports the existential–humanistic and feminist emphases on real encounter. It also supports the process-directiveness of the experiential therapies, provided this directiveness is consistently and sensitively negotiated. By the same token, experiential therapists are especially called on to be alert to the nuances of the working alliance; the same point reasonably seems generalizable to any structuring/interventive/interpretive approach to therapy.

3. The client's relationship with the therapist is crucial. Clients evidently pay much more attention to the relationship with the therapist than to the therapist's techniques. Indeed, it is evident from these studies that technique is often inseparable from the relationship with the therapist. This point is almost a hallmark of Schneider's (1985) study, but it is borne out in a variety of ways in the other studies as well. This revelation by clients supports the emphasis given by humanistic therapists to the therapeutic relationship and, within it, the importance of congruence and transparency. It also suggests, however, that humanistic therapists need not be concerned that technique gets in the way of contact with the client: The results from these studies suggest that technique is taken in stride by clients so long as it is in keeping with their experience and is used in a good working relationship. Accordingly, it seems appropriate for the therapist to probe metacommunicatively into the status of the alliance from time to time.

4. Clients' experience is often covert. Although it is often the case that the client's thoughts are at one with his or her discourse, it is also true that the client has thoughts that are not expressed. Moreover, this privacy may occur in the best of working alliances. Even these alliances do not require the client to be completely transparent. The right to privacy is taken for granted by partners in other kinds of relationships, and a psychotherapy relationship is no exception. The exercise of this right to privacy has obvious implications for psychotherapy research involving the study of discourse in psychotherapy. It also underscores the importance of signs of covert experience, such as the paralinguistic aspects of the discourse and body language, as every skillful practitioner knows so well.

These studies thus give compelling evidence of the potential gains to be made from sensitive initiatives that probe beneath the unspoken.

5. Clients have a strong tendency to defer to the therapist's authority. Clients may rail inwardly against *any* approach, depending on their preferences, without letting the therapist know about their discontent because of the power dynamics entailed in the relationship with the therapist. Again, this understanding underscores the importance of not taking for granted that the therapy is going well and of checking on how the client experiences the relationship, from time to time, in a way designed to defuse the power differential between the client and therapist.

6. Clients appear to experience storytelling as beneficial. Moreover, the benefits are in many ways experienced privately. This understanding sheds a new light on the role of storytelling in therapy. The activity can easily be viewed by therapists as superficial, leading them to want to shift clients into a more "direct" way of dealing with their experience. Instead, it appears that therapists might do better to be patient with storytelling: In the best of circumstances, a story may be used rather deliberately by the client as a way of entering into a more direct focus on disturbing experience. Alternatively, at worst, even if a story is used defensively, productive returns may flow from the activity, despite the client's intention to the contrary. As seen, this may be the case because clients may "see through" their own defensiveness while they are engaged in it, thereby achieving insight despite their desire to avoid it.

7. Overall, then, clients' reflexivity, covert experience, sensitivity to the therapeutic relationship, and deference to the therapist all point to the importance of accessing the client's reactions to the therapist's manner and approach. As was concluded by the authors of many of the above studies, the best way to achieve this compatibility is by metacommunicating with the client about the joint experience of the therapy. It needs to be pointed out in this regard that metacommunication always takes the client away from the direct experience of therapy and so should be used sparingly. Still, as a way of getting on track therapy that is off the rails, it seems indispensable once it is realized that the derailing may be experienced only covertly. This line of thinking is rather new for both person-centered and process–experiential therapists. Carl Rogers

checked on whether or not he understood the client but generally did not let the client in on what he, Rogers, was up to, apart from conveying his general values and beliefs. Alternatively, although the work of Watson and Greenberg (1994) may mark a shift in direction, because of process–experiential therapists' interest in getting at unreflected experience, they have tended to be skeptical of reflexivity in any form, including metacommunication.

Some of these principles are exemplified by the following exchange between one of my clients and myself. In reviewing the exchange after it occurred, I judged that my responses involved four modes: (a) commentary on the process in which the client seemed to be engaged in the moment (process identification), (b) suggestions on how the client might proceed in his inquiry into his experience (process direction), (c) metacommunication, and (d) empathic support. (For elaboration on these modes, see Rennie, 1998b.) The client was a male undergraduate, and the episode to follow had to do with his concern about feeling tense in social situations (C represents the client; T represents me, the therapist.)

T: I heard you say that you went to the group because of just one person. (Empathy)
C: Just because I was friends.
T: I see. (Empathy)
C: I knew one person pretty casually.
T: Mm hm, I see. So then, it's when you're with people with whom you're not familiar that the pressure gets really intense. (Empathy)
C: Right.
T: Mm hm. (Empathy)
C: Where I feel real threatened.
T: Can you identify what it is about that, that's so threatening? (Process direction)
C: I want to look good in their eyes. I want me to look good.
T: Even though you don't mean anything to them. (Empathy)
C: Yeah. I, uh, yeah.
T: You're smiling at that. (Process identification)
C: Well, they do mean something to me. Not as a friend but (pause). Huh! I don't even know what they do. Maybe it's just my own self-esteem.
T: Would you like to examine that for a moment? (Process direction)
C: Uh. (pause)
T: Did the way I phrased that stop you? (Metacommunication)
C: Yeah.
T: Yeah. All right. Can I try again? (Metacommunication)

C: Sure.

T: How does self-esteem enter into it? (Empathy and tacit process direction)

C: OK. That's better (chuckles). Uh, well, there's no reason why I should want to look good in their eyes . . .

T: Mm hm. (Empathy)

C: . . . for any reason other than I should want them to see me as being good. And the only reason why I should want them to see me as good and intelligent, or whatever, is so I can feel better. Because if I really felt I was good, then the threat wouldn't be there. They wouldn't see it. If they wouldn't see it, then that would be their mistake.

T: Mmmmf! (Empathy)

C: So (unclear) reassurance.

T: Yeah. So we're back again to, uh, defining yourself in terms of other people's expectations of you. (Process identification)

C: Yeah. In this situation—it's a threatening situation, and I think all people would feel threatened. But I'm definitely kind of accentuating it. (Pause)

T: So, does all consideration of that stop there, or does it lead to anything? (Empathy and tacit process direction)

C: It leads to, again, the fact that I can recognize why I feel that way, and what situations make me feel that way. If I could take the time to think why I feel that way, it would again give me the choice of acting in a role of acting as myself. In a situation where I feel threatened, the important thing would be to think it through. That would give me the choice. (Pause)

T: So (pause) I don't know how to phrase this. What would be required of you to be able to do that? Or how would you do that? (Metacommunication and process direction)

C: The first step would be to recognize when I feel that way.

T: When you feel threatened? (Empathy)

C: Right.

T: Yes. (Empathy)

C: And identify why.

T: Yes. Now let's just stop there. (Process direction)

C: OK.

T: Could you go about identifying how you feel threatened? (Process direction)

C: I know when I, uh—it's a feeling in my stomach, I get a (pause)

T: Can you describe that feeling? (Process direction)

C: It's like really intense butterflies. Really, uh (Pause).

T: Intense butterflies. Do you mean almost nauseous?

C: Mmm. Yeah (chuckles, then pauses) A little.

T: Not to the point where you want to throw up? (Empathy)

C: No. But (therapist interrupts)

T: It's a churning. (Empathy)
C: Yeah, it's a churning. It churns. I don't feel nauseous but I do feel sick to my stomach.
T: Mmm. It's that strong. (Empathy)
C: Oh, yeah. Yeah. At times. Definitely.
T: That's a pretty strong cue. (Empathy) (Rennie, 1998b)[a]

In an IPR interview of the client, conducted by a colleague, the client positively appraised this exchange, remarking "It was really important and it allowed me to focus and to be able to identify when I feel threatened and how to deal with it" (Rennie, 1998b, p. 87). If one takes this remark at face value, it would seem that the client had found the exchange useful.

CONCLUSION

The grounded theory studies reviewed in this chapter reveal that the experience of therapy is rich and complex. On the one hand, clients appreciate the guidance offered by their therapists so long as it is congruent with expectations and aspirations. On the other hand, clients very actively use the therapy interview as an occasion for their own work on themselves, often carried out covertly. The studies also reveal that clients are finely tuned to the nuances of the relationship with the therapist and often make concessions to the therapist to keep the relationship intact.

These understandings have been derived from interpretations of reported recollections of the conscious experience of therapy. Thus, the studies are limited to what the participants were aware of and were willing to disclose. For students of therapy who believe that the most important sources of distress are beyond the reach of the client's awareness, clients' accounts of their experiences would hold little interest. On this score, perhaps the greatest significance of these grounded theory studies is that they serve as a reminder that, apart from any unconscious mechanisms and processes that may influence experience and conduct, the client's consciousness is also important.

Finally, the grounded theory method draws on intensive study of the experience of individual participants in its attempt to derive an understanding of what is common among them. It has been observed that this approach to inquiry is similar to the one used by clinicians (Kvale, 1999; Maione & Chenail, 1999; Rennie, 1994c) in that they, too, gather a general understanding from a series of cases. It has also been observed that practitioners

---

[a] From *Person-Centred Counselling: An Existential Approach* (pp. 84–86), by D. L. Rennie, 1998, London: Sage. Copyright 1998 by Sage. Reprinted with permission.

tend to disregard conventional research reports in favor of case studies and theoretical works (see, e.g., Morrow-Bradley & Elliott, 1986). Reports of grounded theory studies anchor general formulations in specific instances of lived experience given in participants' own words. Moreover, the results of a grounded theory are conveyed in ordinary language rather than through numerics, which makes the meaning of grounded theories studies more immediate. Thus, clinicians may find that when compared with conventional research reports grounded theory reports have more direct applicability, and thus greater appeal. In this event, studies such as those reviewed in this chapter may help to close the gap between research and practice—humanistic or otherwise.

REFERENCES

Angus, L. E. (1992). Metaphor and communicative interaction in psychotherapy: A multimethodological approach. In S. G. Toukmanian & D. L. Rennie (Eds.), *Psychotherapy process research: Paradigmatic and narrative approaches* (pp. 187–210). Newbury Park, CA: Sage.

Angus, L. E., & Rennie, D. L. (1988). Therapist participation in metaphor generation: Collaborative and non-collaborative styles. *Psychotherapy, 25,* 552–560.

Angus, L. E., & Rennie, D. L. (1989). Envisioning the representational world: The client's experience of metaphoric expressiveness in psychotherapy. *Psychotherapy, 26,* 373–379.

Bohart, A., & Tallman, K. (1996). The active client: Therapy as self-help. *Journal of Humanistic Psychology, 36,* 7–30.

Bolger, E. A. (1999). Grounded theory analysis of emotional pain. *Psychotherapy Research, 9,* 342–362.

Bordin, E. (1979). The generalizability of the psychoanalytic concept of the working alliance. *Psychotherapy: Theory, Research and Practice, 16,* 252–260.

Burr, R. G. (1994). Emotional processes of marital attachment: A grounded theory. *Dissertation Abstracts International, 55*(04), 1662B. (University Microfilms International No. 9424354)

Elliott, R. (1986). Interpersonal Process Recall (IPR) as a process research method. In L. S. Greenberg & W. M. Pinsof (Eds.), *The psychotherapeutic process: A research handbook* (pp. 503–527). New York: Guilford Press.

Elliott, R. (1989). Comprehensive process analysis: Understanding the change process in significant therapy events. In M. Packer & R. B. Addison (Eds.), *Entering the circle: Hermeneutic investigation in psychology* (pp. 165–184). Albany, NY: SUNY Press.

Elliott, R., Fischer, C. T., & Rennie, D. L. (1999). Evolving guidelines for the publication of qualitative research in psychology and related fields. *British Journal of Clinical Psychology, 38,* 215–229.

Elliott, R., James, E., Reimschuessel, C., Cislo, D., & Sack, N. (1985). Significant events and the analysis of immediate impacts. *Psychotherapy, 22,* 620–630.

Fessler, R. (1978). A phenomenological investigation of psychotherapeutic interpretation. *Dissertation Abstracts International, 39*(06), 2981–2982B. (University Microfilms International No. 7823870)

Fischer, C. T. (1977). Historical relations of psychology as an object-science and as a subject-science: Toward psychology as a human science. *Journal of the History of the Behavioral Sciences, 13,* 369–378.

Frank, J. D. (1971). Therapeutic factors in psychotherapy. *American Journal of Psychotherapy, 25,* 350–361.

Gendlin, E. T. (1974). Client-centered and experiential therapy. In D. A. Wexler & L. N. Rice (Eds.), *Innovations in client-centered therapy* (pp. 211–246). New York: Wiley.

Gendlin, E. T. (1996). *Focusing-oriented psychotherapy: A manual of the experiential method.* New York: Guilford Press.

Giddens, A. (1976). *New rules for sociological method.* New York: Basic Books.

Giorgi, A. (1970). *Psychology as a human science: A phenomenologically based approach.* New York: Harper Row.

Giorgi, A. (1975). Application of phenomenological method in psychology. In A. Giorgi, C. Fischer, & E. Murray (Eds.), *Duquesne studies in phenomenological psychology* (Vol. 2, pp. 82–103). Pittsburgh: Duquesne University Press.

Glaser, B. G. (1992). *Emergence vs. forcing: Basics of the grounded theory analysis.* Mill Valley, CA: Sociology Press.

Glaser, B. G., & Strauss, A. (1967). *The discovery of grounded theory: Strategies for qualitative research.* Chicago: Aldine.

Greenberg, L. S., Rice, L. N., & Elliott, R. (1993). *Facilitating emotional change: A moment-by-moment process.* New York: Guilford Press.

Greenberg, L. S., & Safran, J. (1987). *Emotion in psychotherapy.* New York: Guilford Press.

Henwood, K. L., & Pidgeon, N. F. (1992). Qualitative research and psychological theorizing. *British Journal of Psychology, 83,* 97–111.

Hill, C. E., Thompson, B. J., & Williams, E. N. (1997). A guide to conducting consensual qualitative research. *The Counseling Psychologist, 25,* 517–572.

Horvath, A. O., & Greenberg, L. S. (1986). The development of the Working Alliance Inventory. In L. S. Greenberg & W. M. Pinsof (Eds.), *The psychotherapeutic process: A research handbook* (pp. 529–556). New York: Guilford Press.

Kagan, N. (1975). *Interpersonal Process Recall: A method for influencing human interaction.* (Available from N. Kagan, Educational Psychology Department, University Park, Houston, TX, 77004)

Kiesler, D. J. (1996). *Contemporary interpersonal theory and research: Personality, psychopathology and psychotherapy.* New York: Wiley.

Klein, M. H., Mathieu, P., Gendlin, E. T., & Kiesler, D. J. (1969). *The Experiencing Scale: A research and training manual* (Vol. 1). Madison: University of Wisconsin, Extension Bureau of Audiovisual Instruction.

Kvale, S. (1996). *InterViews: An introduction to qualitative research interviewing.* Thousand Oaks, CA: Sage.

Kvale, S. (1999). The psychoanalytic interview as qualitative research. *Qualitative Inquiry, 5,* 87–113.

Lakoff, G., & Johnson, M. (1980). *Metaphors we live by.* Chicago: University of Chicago Press.

Lawson, H. (1985). *Reflexivity: The post-modern predicament.* La Salle, IL: Open Court.

Madill, A., Jordan, A., & Shirley, C. (2000). Objectivity and reliability in qualitative analysis: Realist, contextualist, and radical constructionist epistemologies. *British Journal of Psychology, 91,* 1–20.

Maione, P. V., & Chenail, R. J. (1999). Qualitative inquiry in psychotherapy: Research on the common factors. In M. A. Hubble & S. D. Miller (Eds.), *The heart and soul of change: What works in therapy* (pp. 57–88). Washington, DC: American Psychological Association.

McLeod, J. (2001). *Qualitative research in counselling and psychotherapy.* London: Sage.

Morrow-Bradley, C., & Elliott, R. (1986). Utilization of psychotherapy research by practicing psychotherapists. *American Psychologist, 41,* 188–197.

Pearson, P. H. (1974). Conceptualizing and measuring openness to experience in the context of psychotherapy. In D. A. Wexler & L. N. Rice (Eds.), *Innovations in client-centered therapy* (pp. 139–170). New York: Wiley.

Phillips, J. R. (1984). Influences on personal growth as viewed by former psychotherapy patients. *Dissertation Abstracts International, 46,* 2820B.

Reichenbach, H. (1949). *Theory of probability* (E. H. Hutton & M. Reichenbach, Trans.). Berkeley: University of California Press.

Rennie, D. L. (1990). Toward a representation of the client's experience of the psychotherapy hour. In G. Lietaer, J. Rombauts, & R. Van Balen (Eds.), *Client-centered and experiential psychotherapy in the nineties* (pp. 155–172). Leuven, Belgium: Leuven University Press.

Rennie, D. L. (1992). Qualitative analysis of the client's experience of psychotherapy: The unfolding of reflexivity. In S. G. Toukmanian & D. L. Rennie (Eds.), *Psychotherapy process research: Paradigmatic and narrative approaches* (pp. 211–233). Newbury Park, CA: Sage.

Rennie, D. L. (1994a). Clients' accounts of resistance: A qualitative analysis. *Canadian Journal of Counselling, 28,* 43–57.

Rennie, D. L. (1994b). Clients' deference in psychotherapy. *Journal of Counseling Psychology, 41,* 427–437.

Rennie, D. L. (1994c). Human science and counselling psychology: Closing the gap between research and practice. *Counselling Psychology Quarterly, 7,* 235–250.

Rennie, D. L. (1994d). Storytelling in psychotherapy: The client's subjective experience. *Psychotherapy, 31,* 234–243.

Rennie, D. L. (1995). On the rhetorics of social science: Let's not conflate natural science and human science. *The Humanistic Psychologist, 23,* 322–332.

Rennie, D. L. (1998a). Grounded theory methodology: The pressing need for a coherent logic of justification. *Theory & Psychology, 8,* 101–119.

Rennie, D. L. (1998b). *Person-centred counselling: An experiential approach.* London: Sage.

Rennie, D. L. (2000a). Aspects of the client's conscious control of the psychotherapeutic process. *Journal of Psychotherapy Integration, 10,* 151–167.

Rennie, D. L. (2000b). Grounded theory methodology as methodical hermeneutics: Reconciling realism and relativism. *Theory & Psychology, 10,* 481–502.

Rennie, D. L., Phillips, J. R., & Quartaro, G. K. (1988). Grounded theory: A promising approach to conceptualization in psychology? *Canadian Psychology, 29,* 139–150.

Rhodes, R. H., Hill, C. E., Thompson, B. J., & Elliott, R. (1994). A retrospective study of the client perception of misunderstanding of events. *Journal of Counseling, 41,* 473–483.

Rice, L. N. (1974). The evocative function of the therapist. In D. A. Wexler & L. N. Rice (Eds.), *Innovations in client-centered therapy* (pp. 289–312). New York: Wiley.

Rice, L. N., & Saperia, E. (1984). Task analysis of the resolution of problematic reactions. In L. N. Rice & L. S. Greenberg (Eds.), *Patterns of change: Intensive analysis of psychotherapy process* (pp. 29–66). New York: Guilford Press.

Safran, J. D., Muran, J. C., & Wallner Samstag, L. (1994). Resolving therapeutic alliance ruptures: A task analytic investigation. In A. O. Horvath & L. S. Greenberg (Eds.), *The working alliance: Theory, research, and practice* (pp. 225–255). New York: Wiley.

Schneider, K. J. (1985). Clients' perceptions of the positive and negative characteristics of their counselors. *Dissertation Abstracts International, 45*(10), 3345B. (University Microfilms International No. NN84217).

Searle, J. (1983). *Intentionality: An essay in the philosophy of mind.* Cambridge, England: Cambridge University Press.

Shaul, A. N. (1994). Therapists' symbolic visual imagery: A key to empathic understanding. *Dissertation Abstracts International, 54,* 5953B. (University Microfilms International No. NN84217)

Stiles, W. B. (1993). Quality control in qualitative research. *Clinical Psychology Review, 13,* 593–618.

Strauss, A., & Corbin, J. (1990). *Basics of qualitative research: Grounded theory procedures and techniques.* Thousand Oaks, CA: Sage.

Tanji, J. M. (1996). The application of Milan systemic family therapy in a training context: A grounded theory study. *Dissertation Abstracts International, 56*(09), 3460A. (University Microfilms International No. 9600758)

Watson, J. C., & Greenberg, L. S. (1994). The alliance in experiential therapy: Enacting the relationship conditions. In A. O. Horvath & L. S. Greenberg (Eds.), *The working alliance: Theory, research, and practice* (pp. 153–172). New York: Wiley.

Watson, J. C., & Rennie, D. L. (1994). A qualitative analysis of clients' subjective experience of significant moments in therapy during the exploration of problematic reactions. *Journal of Counseling Psychology, 41,* 500–509.

Watzlawick, P., Beavin, J. H., & Jackson, D. D. (1967). *Pragmatics of human communication.* New York: Norton.

Wexler, D. A. (1974). A cognitive theory of experiencing self-actualization, and therapeutic process. In D. A. Wexler & L. N. Rice (Eds.), *Innovations in client-centered therapy* (pp. 49–116). New York: Wiley.

III

MAJOR THERAPEUTIC
APPROACHES

5

CLIENT-CENTERED THERAPY: THE EVOLUTION OF A REVOLUTION

JEROLD D. BOZARTH, FRED M. ZIMRING, AND REINHARD TAUSCH

The purpose of this chapter is to review research in client-centered therapy (CCT). Our review reveals that research in CCT has played a seminal role in the investigations of psychotherapy and is integrally intertwined with outcome research in psychotherapy. Research of psychotherapy outcome suggests that the most viable treatment is emergent, determined, and acted on by the client and facilitated by the centrality of the client–therapist relationship and client's resources. This is the primary intention and focus of CCT. Four distinct periods characterize the research associated with CCT: (a) nondirective therapy (1940–1951), (b) the client-centered relationship (1951–1957), (c) conditions of therapy (1957–1987), and (d) common factors revisited (1987–1999).

Carl R. Rogers revolutionized the field of psychotherapy and counseling. He did this by proposing a theory that focused on the client as the agent for self-change. Rogers's (1951, 1959) theory of humans in the process of actualization was embraced by humanistic psychology. Rogers's stance, however, was more radical than most other humanistic schools of psychotherapy. Rogers emphasized the client and client resources as the focus of the theory and the client–therapist relationship as the healing catalyst. Rogers's radical view that the clients are always their own best experts about their lives differed from most other schools of psychotherapy, including other humanistic schools.

Rogers also altered the face of psychotherapy by initiating scientific research of psychotherapy process and outcome. He and his colleagues were

We are indebted to the editorial and conceptual contributions of Kathy Moon and Amy Shenkel.

147

the first to examine audio recordings of therapy sessions to determine what actually took place in therapy. They examined therapy outcome through the hard criteria of behavioral improvement and clinical assessment using quantitative research designs. As such, the demystification of psychotherapy began.

THE FIRST PERIOD: NONDIRECTIVE THERAPY (1940–1951)

This period was characterized by Rogers's belief that rapport with and acceptance by the therapist facilitated the client's own acceptance of self. Rogerian therapy underscored the idea that the client, rather than the therapist, was the director of the treatment. This approach was labeled *nondirective*. Research during this period was directed toward investigations of nondirective therapy.

This period included the first major efforts to explore psychotherapy through quantitative research designs. Previous qualitative studies, which provided detailed examination of therapy sessions by means of audio recordings, were now extended to include quantitative studies.

In *Counseling and Psychotherapy*, Rogers (1942) accentuated his intention of operating within the scientific paradigm. He made predictions about therapeutic change and used hypothesis tests. His initial hypothesis was that if therapists accept, recognize, and clarify the feelings expressed by the clients, then there will be movement from negative to positive feelings, followed by insight and positive actions initiated by the clients. In describing his hypothesis, Rogers emphasized three aspects of the therapist's role: (a) the importance of responding to expressed feelings rather than to content, (b) the acceptance of the client's feelings by the therapist, and (c) the clarification of the client's expressed feelings. These hypotheses could be examined with detailed scrutiny through the newly discovered media of audio recordings. The first step of quantitative research on psychotherapy sessions was set through analysis of the verbal interchange between clients and therapists.

Directive and Nondirective

One area of investigation was to describe therapist and client discourse and their interactions. Initial interest was in the therapist and whether nondirective therapists were different from other therapists. Porter (1943) found that judges were able to reliably differentiate verbal classifications between counselors on a directive–nondirective continuum. The same method was applied a year later by Gump (1944) to client-centered and psychoanalytic recordings with similar results.

Snyder (1945) studied both client and therapist verbal behaviors in 48 interviews from six different cases, five of which were considered successful. He found nondirective therapists to be consistently nondirective. Analysis showed movement in the client from early to late interviews in such areas as emergence of understanding or insight, increased planning activity, and positive feelings. These findings supported Rogers's predictions and served as a springboard for further research.

Interaction of Client and Counselor

Bergman's (1950) study of the interaction of client and counselor responses is indicative of findings in this area. Using category systems, Bergman found that structuring or interpretive counselor statements were followed by clients' abandonment of self-exploration, whereas counselor responses that were classified as reflecting feeling were followed by clients' continual self-exploration or insight. Snyder (1945) found that nondirective responses by therapists were more likely to be followed by clearer statements of problems by clients.

The supplementation of findings of quantitative studies were also supported by qualitative studies. For example, qualitative observations by Snyder (1947) revealed that clarification of the client's feelings created experiences of self-acceptance.

Relationships of Attitudes Between Self and Others as Affected by Therapy

In a series of coordinated research identified as the Parallel Studies Project that occupied an entire issue of the *Journal of Consulting Psychology* (Raskin, 1949), several methods and questions were applied to 10 completely recorded cases. Quantitative and qualitative studies were included in this coordinated research project.

In a replication of Snyder's (1945) study with these 10 cases, Seeman (1949) discovered that 85% of the therapists' behaviors were nondirective, compared with 63% for the therapists in Snyder's cases. In the same project, Sheerer (1949) devised categories to record acceptance of self and others. Judges reliably recorded client statements and tested for an increase in the acceptance of self and subsequent acceptance of others. On the basis of her findings, Sheerer (1949) concluded that the individual's evaluation of others plus the degree of acceptance and respect are significantly related to attitudes toward self (p. 175). Stock (1949) found a correlation between the way that clients feel about themselves and others. Hoffman (1949) investigated the growth of maturity in clients as therapy progressed. Maturity was defined as whether the client was behaving with little or no control over himself or herself or the environment, and behaving with substantial self-direction and responsibility. Ten cases were divided into a successful group and an unsuccessful group. Successful clients significantly improved in maturity, whereas the 5 least successful clients did not improve.

Self-Reference and Client–Therapist Relationship

Raimy (1948) concluded that self-concept changed as a result of therapy. Cases judged successful showed positive change in self-concept. Unsuccessful cases did not show such change.

The research during this period therefore identified nondirective therapy as related to increased understanding, more positive feelings, greater self-exploration, improved self-concepts, and improved maturity of clients. Nondirective therapy was found to be as effective but not more effective than Adlerian therapies in one dissertation. Another dissertation (Heine, 1953) and a later journal article (Shlien, Mosak, & Dreikurs, 1962) buttressed this finding. These studies were forerunners to the pervasive conclusion of decades of therapy research that outcome is related to common factors rather than to particular therapies (Hubble, Duncan, & Miller, 1999; see also The Fourth Period, below). One key contribution of research during this period lay in the demonstration that the methods of science could be successfully brought to bear on the data of therapy.

THE SECOND PERIOD: THE CLIENT-CENTERED RELATIONSHIP (1951–1957)

For Rogers, in this period, the basic motivating force of the individual was freed when the therapist assumed the internal frame of reference of the client. Rogers shifted from emphasizing clarification of the client's feelings to emphasizing broader understanding of the way in which the client views the world. Research focused on the individual's frame of reference that ranged from self-concept studies to effectiveness studies. Coordinated research and more rigorous and extensive research designs were also developed during this period.

This period began with publication of *Client-Centered Therapy* (Rogers, 1951). In this book, Rogers emphasized that the therapist's attitude, rather than any particular technique, was central to successful therapy. Rogers extended his belief that individuals possess an innate, fundamental motivating inner force for change toward increased self-actualization. The foundation of the theory was clarified with the postulate that the client knows best the problems and the direction to take. The investigation of this hypothesis was undertaken from the following perspectives.

Central Importance Given to the World of the Client

In this period, there was increased emphasis on the importance of the client's world as the client views it. CCT was not to be viewed as a problem-centered therapy. Rather, it was centered on personality change that then enabled clients to solve problems and to more successfully engage new problems. Research moved toward investigating hypotheses related to the centrality of the client as a person.

Using Q-Sort instrumentation, Heine (1953) asked clients of psychoanalytic, nondirective, and Adlerian therapists to describe changes they experienced and to identify their reasons for the changes. Regardless of therapy orientation, the clients reported similar changes. When clients of psychoanalytic therapists reported their reasons for change, they tended to focus on therapist technique, whereas clients of nondirective therapists tended to attribute change to qualities of the therapeutic atmosphere.

Several studies were reported in detail in *Psychotherapy and Personality Change* (Rogers & Dymond, 1954). The book reports one of the first coordinated series of controlled research projects designed to assess changes in psychotherapy. Clients were placed into a therapy group and a *wait-list* or *own control* group. The second group deferred the beginning of therapy for 60 days. In addition, two comparable groups were formed as *equivalent control* groups. Measures used included counselor ratings, projective tests (scored by independent diagnosticians), independent observer judgments, and self-reports. The self-report instruments were primarily based on the methods of Stephenson (1953), which were further developed by Butler and Haigh (1954). Multiple outcome measures were administered, and the interrelationship of outcomes was assessed. The first group of studies was concerned with client changes in self-perception. Does therapy result in a change in self-perceptions so clients may view themselves as being more like their ideal? With Q-Sort measurement methodology, the results indicated that the relationship of the client group before therapy was low and increased significantly in relation to the control group after therapy. To investigate the change in the self and ideal self, Rogers and Dymond (1954) selected a subpopulation as improved on the combined basis of the Thematic Apperception Test diagnostic rating and counselor judgments. The clients who were more improved on both measures were less discrepant between self and ideal self.

Although this was a bold venture in research design during this period, there was one scathing critique of the coordinated studies project (Meltzoff & Kornreich, 1970). Meltzoff and Kornreich suggested that the studies provided little tangible evidence about the efficacy of psychotherapy because of the lack of a randomly assigned control group, reliance of self-report data, and the presence of biased samples. They cited the most crucial flaw in the design as the lack of a randomly assigned control group. Although technically a viable argument, the valence of the argument has become a moot point. The fact is that there have been few studies in the 45 years of psychotherapy outcome research following this series of studies that meet this criteria. Their critique of self-report data reflects their own bias. Viable data and self-report data have become increasingly accepted even by advocates of true design research.

Transitions to Common Conditions Research

One of the first studies to look for common conditions related to successful therapy was conducted at Johns Hopkins Hospital in Baltimore, Maryland. Whitehorn and Betz (1954) conducted a retrospective study that compared the interpersonal manner of 7 successful psychiatrists with 7 similarly trained, unsuccessful psychiatrists in their work with patients with schizophrenia. The successful psychiatrists had an improvement rate of 75%, whereas the unsuccessful psychiatrists had an improvement rate of only 27%. The evidence indicated that the successful therapists were warm and attempted to understand the subjective, phenomenological experiences of their patients. In contrast, less-successful therapists related to their patients in a more impersonal manner, focusing on matters other than patients' experiences, such as symptoms of pathology. This was one of the first studies that did not involve therapists who were identified as client centered.

In summary, most of the therapists in the studies were client-centered therapists. Most of the studies examined some aspect of client-centered theory, and most of the designs were among the first attempts for sophisticated scientific method research. Although the designs could be critiqued on the criterion of the true design research model, this critique can be made of most designs since that time. As Rogers (Rogers & Dymond, 1954) indicated, the research in the coordinated study was not good research. Rather, it was the best there was at the time. Ironically, it turns out that the research of this period was just as rigorous as most of the psychotherapy outcome research over the next 4 decades.

Successful CCT was found to increase self-acceptance and personal worth of clients. Comparisons with other therapies, particularly Adlerian therapy, found comparable outcome results. The research started to expand to examination of common therapist factors regardless of theoretical orientation.

THIRD PERIOD: CONDITIONS OF THERAPY (1957–1987)

This period was characterized by a shift of research emphasis from examining CCT to examining attitudinal conditions of therapists of all persuasions. In an article titled "The Necessary and Sufficient Conditions of Therapeutic Personality Change," Rogers (1957) set forth a hypothesis that evoked more than 3 decades of research. This was a landmark proposal for CCT, for psychotherapy, and for helping relationships in general. The core of the article was two-pronged. First, the conditions postulated by Rogers became the central intention for client-centered therapists (Rogers, 1959). Second, these conditions are postulated to be essential for all theories of therapy and for all helping relationships that involve therapeutic personality change as a goal. This is postulated even when other theories focus on other central issues. Rogers's (1957) article has been dubbed the "integration statement" (Bozarth, 1998; Stubbs & Bozarth, 1996) and the "conditions of therapy theory" (Barrett-Lennard, 1998). The conditions described by Rogers (1957) are the following:

1. Two persons are in psychological contact.
2. The first, whom we shall term the client, is in a state of incongruence, being vulnerable or anxious.
3. The second person, which we shall term the therapist, is congruent or integrated in the relationship.
4. The therapist experiences unconditional positive regard for the client.
5. The therapist experiences an empathic understanding of the client's internal frame of reference and endeavors to communicate this experience to the client.
6. The communication to the client of the therapist's empathic understanding and unconditional positive regard is to a minimal degree achieved. (p. 96)

Rogers's (1957) definitions of the three therapist attitudes are the following:

Congruency (or genuineness) is the state of the therapist during the therapy session where "within the relationship (the therapist) is freely and deeply himself, with his actual experience accurately represented by his awareness of himself . . . [and] . . . the therapist is what he actually is, in this moment of time."
Unconditional Positive Regard is "the extent that the therapist finds himself experiencing a warm acceptance of each aspect of the client's experience as being a part of that client."
Empathic Understanding is "To sense the client's private world as if it were your own, but without ever losing the "as if" quality."(pp. 97–99)

Rogers hypothesized that these conditions were both necessary and sufficient for the initiation of a process of constructive personality change. By "necessary," he meant that constructive personality change would not take place if any of these conditions were not present. By "sufficient," he meant that these conditions were adequate for constructive change to occur.

Much of the outcome research involving CCT shifted from inquiry regarding the differences among therapies toward examination of therapist attitudes. Samples of therapists in most published studies after Rogers's (1957) integrative statement are not client-centered therapists (Bozarth, 1983). Most of the research that was considered to be client centered actually focused on attitudinal conditions regardless of therapists' theoretical persuasions.

A Core of Studies

Contributions by Halkides (1958) and Barrett-Lennard (1962) led the way for additional measurement developments (Rogers, Gendlin, Kiesler, & Truax, 1967; Truax & Carkhuff, 1967). Halkides devised scales for ratings by judges on audiotapes of the conditions. She also found that the three conditions were related to successful cases. Barrett-Lennard (1962) developed the Relationship Inventory, which assessed clients' perceptions of the conditions. Barrett-Lennard found that clients improved to the extent that they perceived their therapists as understanding, congruent, positive, and having unconditional regard for them. The Relationship Inventory, which was developed to measure the client's perception of the relationship, has been validated and improved over the years (Barrett-Lennard, 1998). It has also been used in research all over the world and translated into more than 15 languages (Barrett-Lennard, 1999).

Other studies were reported in areas outside of psychotherapy outcome research. For example, one study (Gaylin, 1966) demonstrated change in creativity variables after 20 sessions of CCT.

From 1957 to 1963, Rogers and his colleagues at the University of Wisconsin undertook the daunting task of studying the client-centered approach in psychoses. Although the overall results revealed few significant differences as reported elsewhere (see Prouty, this volume, chapter 19), several studies (Barrett-Lennard, 1999; Truax & Mitchell, 1971; van der veen, 1965, 1967, 1970), using the original Wisconsin data, found various outcome measures positively associated with the core attitudes. The direction of client-centered research was influenced in several ways. First, the Wisconsin project was Rogers's last major quantitative research project. Second, coordinated efforts to research CCT virtually disappeared in the United States after this project. Third, the "therapist-offered conditions" were perpetuated as a viable research endeavor for psychotherapy outcome. Fourth, scales used became the mainstay for later development of interpersonal skills training programs and for continued research (Bozarth, 1998). Fifth, the data revealed that "successful" clients perceived higher conditions of congruence and empathy in their therapists, whereas clients who deteriorated perceived lower conditions (Rogers et al., 1967). The Wisconsin project, identified by some as a failure because of the overall lack of significant findings (see Prouty, this volume, chapter 19), added substance and direction to research of the necessary and sufficient conditions in psychotherapy outcome.

Lietaer (1988, 1990) and Bozarth (1983) concluded that CCT research in the United States during the 1970s and 1980s was limited in volume and shrinking with the passing years. Bozarth concluded that this was, in part, due to the fact that most sampled therapists were not client-centered therapists (a fact that continues throughout research in the United States). Bergin (1971) identified eight selected studies on client-centered psychotherapy from 1957 to 1967, including the Wisconsin study (Rogers et al., 1967), and another four studies with control groups from 1954 to 1965, including Rogers and Dymond's (1954) study. By the time of the second edition of the *Handbook of Psychotherapy and Behavior Change* (Garfield & Bergin, 1978), the chapters on evaluation of therapeutic outcomes (Bergin & Lambert, 1978) and on therapist variables related to process and outcome (Parloff, Waskow, & Wolfe, 1978) had little discussion about CCT. Likewise, later reviews (Bergin & Garfield, 1994; Garfield & Bergin, 1986) revealed few studies on CCT. Outcome studies on CCT were reported in some theses and dissertations at this time, but most were not published in the professional literature. Lietaer noted the increasing diversity and divergence from Rogers's theory. Specifically, he identified the thrust of the works of Wexler and Rice (1974), Gendlin (1973), Carkhuff (1972), and Gordon (1970) as examples of such diversity and divergence. Two of these directional thrusts are considered elsewhere (see this volume, Hendricks, chapter 7; Greenberg, Korman, & Paivio, chapter 16). Studies of training models identified as human relations and interpersonal skills models are not included in this review. Most of these models were developed from Rogers's (1957) hypothesis of the necessary and sufficient conditions and were perpetuated by the training proposals of Truax and Carkhuff (1967). Their review of research supported the notion that the conditions cited by Rogers resulted in constructive personality change in a wide variety of clients, "including college underachievers, juvenile delinquents, hospitalized schizophrenics, college counselees, mild to severe neurotics, and the mixed variety of hospitalized patients" (p. 100). Many of their references are reported in a later review of psychotherapy outcome research (Truax & Mitchell, 1971). Some of their major references are cited throughout the present chapter. Truax and Carkhuff proposed training methods that might promote these core conditions of therapists. Other publications then deviated from Rogers's

TABLE 5.1
Research on Client-Centered Therapy in Germany

Author	Population/Focus	Design	Results
I-1. Rudolph, Langer, and Tausch (1980)	Clients of psychotherapeutic ambulance Psychological Institute III, University of Hamburg; higher scores in neuroticism and introversion, psychasthenia, and anxiety (MMPI), 37% with psychosomatic complaints, 36% sexual difficulties, 45% work difficulties.	149 clients (37 first waiting 17 weeks + control group); 80 client-centered therapists, with 50% little experience. Average of 11 sessions during 17 weeks. Every client had 2 therapists. After 4 sessions, the client could choose only one therapist; 75% chose the more experienced therapist.	Significant positive changes in test scores and problem lists. This was related to high end of at least 2 of Rogers's 3 dimensions of therapists (rated by tapes and by clients). Changes were not dependent on kind and degree of disturbances or test characteristics; 44% variance of changes predictable by client ratings of therapists after 4 sessions.
I-2. Bommert, Minsel, Fittkau, Langer, and Tausch (1972)	Clients of psychotherapeutic ambulance Psychological Institute III, University of Hamburg; higher scores in subtests of EPI and MMPI.	44 clients (22 first waiting 9 weeks + control group); 13 psychotherapists (psychologists). Average 6 psychotherapeutic sessions during 8–9 weeks.	Significant positive changes on MMPI and scales of EPI. Empathy of therapists (related by clients) correlated .44 with positive changes in neuroticism and introversion, regard of therapist with self-rated changes of clients, self-exploration of clients correlated with positive changes in anxiety (MMPI).
I-3. Minsel et al. (1972)	Clients (mostly students) asking for psychotherapeutic help.	55 clients (20 first waiting 9 weeks + control group); 19 psychotherapists (psychologists). Average 6 psychotherapeutic sessions during 8–9 weeks.	Significant positive changes on MMPI and on Eysenck Personality Inventory (EPI). Self-exploration of clients (rated by tapes) correlated significantly with positive changes in neuroticism and extroversion and with empathy of therapists (tape rated).
I-4. Doll et al. (1974)	Male prisoners with striking disturbances on Eysenck Personality Inventory and Personal Orientation Inventory.	25 prisoners received 6 therapeutic sessions by telephone (30 min); 6 client-centered therapists (control group, 36 prisoners).	Increase in self-acceptance and decrease in tendency to lie. Those who had all sessions compared with less than 6 sessions showed decrease in psychoneuroticism and decrease in aggressiveness.

Study	Sample	Results
I-5. Ronnecke et al. (1976)	Elderly, mean age 74 years, living alone, low income, with help from state administration. Offered 8 psychotherapeutic telephone sessions (30 min during 8 weeks).	24 elderly women in therapy group, compared with 29 in waiting group, 17 client-centered psychologists.	Life satisfaction of those talking with psychologists was significantly increased. After 8 telephone sessions and 8 weeks later, 65% elderly women reported positive changes in many important areas of their daily lives.
I-6. A. M. Tausch, Kettner, Steinbach, and Tönnies (1973)	Therapy group = 29 disadvantaged kindergarten children and 30 disadvantaged pupils (mean age = 8.3 years). Control group = 28 disadvantaged children and 19 pupils.	7 weeks individual client-centered therapy (10 min weekly) and group therapy (2–5 children; 30 min weekly) by 5 client-centered therapists. Before and after therapy various tests, interviews with 1–2 adults and ratings from teachers.	Compared with control groups, counseled children/pupils showed significant positive changes in emotional stability, social cooperation, verbal spontaneity, and perceptual accuracy in intelligence tests. Self-exploration of pupils correlated with accurate emphatic understanding and positive regard by psychologists.
II-1. Boeck-Singelman, Schwab, and Tönnies (1992)	Clients of psychotherapeutic Psychological Institute III, University of Hamburg. Mean age 30 years, unfavorable test scores in depression, nervousness (EPI), and in Tennessee Self-Concept Scale. 65% clients had body complaints, 46% took medicine regularly, 13% high alcohol consumption.	53 clients (19 first waiting 4 months + control group); 55 client-centered therapists. Every client had 2 therapists in every session (a woman and a man), always 1 experienced and 1 student therapist.	Therapy clients had significant, positive changes in self-concept and in psychosomatic complaints. No significant changes in waiting group. In global self-rating of clients (Strupp), 67% of clients were satisfied with therapy, and 90% saw the therapy as important and helpful. 17 clients could be reached by mail 1 year. The improvement was stable: 85% held the presence of the 2 therapists in the sessions as favorable. Arguments: Men and women, more independence from only one therapist, supplementation of therapists. The majority of the therapists perceived team therapy as good possibility for learning. The groups of more improved clients perceived the experienced therapist as significantly more empathic and contruent than the group with small or no improvement.

continued

TABLE 5.1
Continued

Author	Population/Focus	Design	Results
II-2. Schaefer (1992)	Clients of psychotherapeutic Psychological Institute III, University of Hamburg. Mean age 35 years, no students. Unfavorable test scores: 71% complaints in partnership, 51% in work, 39% family. Focus: Can the outcome of therapy be made better through organizational conditions?	86 clients in therapy group and 27 in waiting control group; 17 experienced and 86 learning therapists. I. Every client had after 5 and 10 sessions an interview for clarification with an outside psychologist. Half of therapy group had 2 therapists (team therapy). Other half of therapy group could choose between 2 therapists teams.	I. The clarification speeches with a psychologist had very good effects, especially by clients with slow progress and little satisfaction with the therapy. II. The possibility to choose between 2 therapist's teams had good effects regarding dropout (7% vs. 32% without the possibility) and also on the outcome: 64% who could choose were markedly improved vs. 36% of those who could not choose.
II-3. Tausch (1988)	Transcripts of psychotherapeutic sessions of Carl Rogers, David Burns, and Wilhelm Gerl, a focusing therapist. To what extent do these therapists focus on cognitions and emotions?	Therapists and their clients' utterances were separately rated for the amount of cognitions and emotions on 5-point scales.	Carl Rogers: mean in every utterance, 3.3 for cognitions, 2.3 emotions. David Burns: 4.3 for cognitions, 1.5 emotions. Wilhelm Gerl: 1.7 for cognitions, 2.8 emotions (focusing therapist). In 67% of his responses, Rogers attended more to the clients' cognitions than emotions; in 25%, this was equal, and in 19%, more emotions than cognitions. In 65% of the following utterances, his clients expressed more cognitions than emotions; in 25%, equal; and in 19%, more emotions than cognitions. A high level of empathy for the clients' cognitions and emotions was present in 23% of Rogers's responses, 8% of Burn's responses, and 5% of Gerl's responses. These facts can correct misunderstanding of the term *feelings* in client-centered therapy.

| II-4. Eckert, Schwartz, and Tausch (1977) | Clients of psychotherapeutic Psychological Institute III, University of Hamburg. Purpose of research: What are the experiences and emotions of clients during the psychotherapeutic session? Are they predicting the outcome of the therapy? | 25 clients with clear positive changes after therapy and 25 clients with only few changes, elected from a total of 97 clients with 80 client-centered therapists (Rudolph et al., 1980). Both extreme groups did not differ in test scores by the beginning of the therapy. Clients marked their experiences on 14 items after each session. The behavior of clients and therapists was rated by tapes. | The experiences of positive and negative extreme groups of clients differed drastically. (Also in the first session, the positive group had clearly more favorable experiences.) Clients with positive changes saw their problems in a new light, felt themselves in the session more relaxed, and were more optimistic. The cognitions changed more in the beginning sessions, later the emotional experiences. Self-exploration of the clients (rated by tapes) had a correlation of .53 with changing perceptions and cognitions. Deep emotional engagement of the clients (rated by tapes) correlated with satisfying experiences. Empathy, activity, and concreteness of therapists (rated by tapes) correlated (.49–.56) with clients' satisfaction with the session. |
| II-5. Sander, Tausch, Bastine, and Nagel (1969) | Clients of psychotherapeutic Psychological Institute III, University of Hamburg, asking for therapeutic help. Focus: Is empathy of therapist a main condition for self-exploration of client? | 12 clients; 4 client-centered therapists. The therapists diminished their empathy for 10 min. Rating of tapes in empathy and self-exploration before, during, and after the diminished empathy. | The significantly diminished empathy of therapists was connected with significantly diminished self-exploration. The normal high empathy of therapists was connected with the amount of self-exploration as before the experimental phase. High empathy (measured by tapes with the Truax scale) can be seen as a main condition for high self-exploration and therefore for chances of favorable outcome. |

continued

TABLE 5.1
Continued

Author	Population/Focus	Design	Results
II-6. Fox and Tausch (1983)	120 adults, ages 18–50 years, 53% married, 45% workers and employees, without asking for help. Focus: Proof of Rogers's hypothesis that the 3 core conditions of therapy are also core conditions of helpful relationship in other areas (here in partnerships).	The adults filled out questionnaires on how they perceived their partners and about their satisfaction in various areas of partnership/ marriage.	With the partnership, satisfied persons ($n = 60$, median) vs. unsatisfied persons ($n = 60$, median) perceived their partner favorable in empathy 90% (vs. unsatisfied perssion, 27%); in regard-caring, 98% vs. 68%; in nondirectivity, 97% vs. 67%; and in helpful activities, 100% vs. 58%. More striking were the differences between satisfied and unsatisfied persons in percentage of very favorable perception: empathy, 28% vs. 2%; regard-caring, 75% vs. 10%; and helpful activities, 45% vs. 7%.
II-7. Caspari and Tausch (1979)	416 adults not seeking therapeutic help. Focus: Is there a connection between facade–genuineness in daily behavior and psychic discomfort.	416 adults filled out a scale with items for facade–genuineness in daily behavior and other psychological tests.	Facade (vs. genuineness) in daily behavior correlated significantly with depression (.56), neuroticism (.49), and nervousness (.44). There was also a correlation between amount of facade and perceptions of the behavior of parents as cold, incongruent, and authoritarian (.22).

Note. I = outcome research; II = process-outcome research and related questions; EPI = Eysenck Personality Inventory; MMPI = Minnesota Multiphasic Personality Inventory.

primary assumptions of client authority and client direction (Carkhuff, 1967, 1969; Egan, 1975; Gordon, 1970, 1976; Gordon & Burch, 1974; Guerney, 1977).

Representative Research Outside of the United States

Lietaer (1990) suggested that contributions to the psychological literature on CCT were increasing in Germany (e.g., Helm, 1980; R. Tausch & Tausch, 1981), the Netherlands, and Belgium (Lietaer, van Praag, & Swildens, 1984; Van Balen, Leijssen, & Lietaer, 1986) in contrast to the lesser increase in the United States. Literature included clinical reports and research studies in group therapy with clinical populations as well as individual therapy.

Studies of person-centered group therapy with clinical populations are reported in the chapter on humanistic group research (see Page, Weiss, & Lietaer, this volume, chapter 11). Page et al. present nine European reports and another 12 studies as well as the results of two reviews of additional studies on person-centered clinical groups. Barrett-Lennard (1998) reported in detail research on client-centered group therapy, as did R. Tausch and Tausch (1990, 1998). Nearly all of these studies reveal positive results favoring the effectiveness of CCT and *conditions therapy theory* related to group psychotherapy.

Individual therapy fared as well in a cluster of studies supervised by Reinhard Tausch (see Table 5.1). The studies are well designed and, for the most part, incorporate large numbers of clients of diverse diagnoses, control groups, and a large number of client-centered therapists.

A study with 149 clients and 80 client-centered therapists and wait-list control clients (Rudolph, Langer, & Tausch, 1980) found that the person-centered psychotherapists who exhibited high levels of two of the three conditions of empathy, warmth, and genuineness had clients with positive changes. The presence of high levels of only one condition was associated with no or unfavorable change. This point reflects Rogers's (1957, 1959) hypothesis that more than one condition is necessary for client change. Additional findings in this particular study are of interest. They include the following: (a) Client changes were not dependent on the kind of disturbances or extent of test characteristics, (b) clients who quit therapy did so largely because of the unfavorable conditions of their therapists, and (3) client change could be predicted after the fourth contact by perceptions of the therapist and of client feelings about sessions.

Eckert, Schwartz, and Tausch (1977) recorded the self-reported experiences of clients after each of nine sessions with client-centered therapists. The favorable experiences of clients who were considered "more changed" differed considerably from those who "hardly changed."

The former clients revealed greater depth of self-exploration and perceived more empathic understanding from their psychotherapists.

Ronnecke et al. (1976) conducted a study of client-centered psychologists involved in telephone sessions with older people and found positive psychological change. Life satisfaction and attitudes of elderly people toward death and dying were examined. Findings included significant increases in life satisfaction after speaking with psychologists and improved psychological change after receiving counseling. The most helpful talking conditions were from helpers who had average levels of empathy and were involved in their own self-exploration. Likewise, Doll et al.'s (1974) study of prison inmates who received telephone counseling revealed that striking psychological disturbances could be helped by client-centered counseling. Different telephone research (Parikh, Steinbach, Tausch, & Teegen, 1973) involved the assessment of counselor helpers who commented on standardized counseling problems. Voice and speech samples were evaluated by 50 evaluators and by clients in a day clinic. Results revealed that assessment of speech quality by both groups showed a preference for voice quality that encouraged acceptance and that presented clear statements.

Other studies of individual therapy found the following: (a) Psychoneurotic clients in the experimental group showed significant reduction on psychoneuroses and introversion tests over the wait-list control group (N = 81; Minsel et al., 1972). (b) Psychoneurotic clients in the experimental group who received an average of six contacts with 1 of 13 client-centered therapists showed significant positive change over the no-treatment control group (N = 42; Bommert, Minsel, Fittkau, Langer, & Tausch, 1972). (c) Psychoneurotic clients (N = 12) exposed to a 10-minute reduction in accurate empathy showed significantly reduced self-exploration and an increase in cursory talk. Resumption of empathy was accompanied by a return of client's self-exploration (Sander, Tausch, Bastine, & Nagel, 1969).

Throughout this period, the studies by Tausch and his colleagues as well as others in Europe are quite positive. Positive findings are consistent in the areas of individual psychotherapy (see Table 5.1); group psychotherapy; and groups with cancer patients, prisoners, judges, teachers, and geriatric individuals. The findings extend to encounter groups, education, and daily life activities (Bergeest, Steinbach, & Tausch, 1977; Boeck-Singelman, Shwab, & Tönnies, 1992; Caspari & Tausch, 1979; Fox & Tausch, 1983; A. M. Tausch, Kettner, Steinbach, & Tönnies, 1973; R. Tausch, 1978). The studies include large samples of person-centered therapists, a rarity in the majority of later research in the United States.

An Analysis of the Research

An analysis of the research in psychotherapy outcome was undertaken to search for pronounced patterns of research during separate units of time. Using symbolic interactionism (Blumer, 1969) and constant comparative analysis (Glaser & Strauss, 1967), Stubbs and Bozarth (1994) discovered five categories of research focus from 1950 to 1993. These categories reveal the permeating influence of the Rogerian hypothesis on research in psychotherapy effectiveness. They also reveal a discordant connection between research results and the direction of outcome research over the years. This discordant connection resulted in the suppression of the research results supporting Rogers's hypothesis of the necessary and sufficient conditions. We discuss the categorical analysis below.

1. *Psychotherapy is no more effective than no psychotherapy* (1950s and 1960s; Eysenck, 1952, 1966). Eysenck's hypothesis that psychotherapy is no more effective than no psychotherapy stimulated considerable reaction and criticism (Bergin, 1971; Fay & Lazarus, 1992; Rosenweig, 1954). The general conclusions of research in this category suggested that psychotherapy is more effective than no psychotherapy. Somewhat unheralded and unrealized, the research on Rogers's hypothesis of the necessary and sufficient conditions became an important part of the responses to Eysenck. This is elaborated in Category 3.

2. *The core conditions (empathic understanding, unconditional positive regard, and congruence) are necessary and sufficient for therapeutic personality change* (1960s and 1970s). The research on this hypothesis was consistently supported (Lambert, DeJulio, & Stein, 1978; Truax & Mitchell, 1971) and continued to be supported through the late 1970s and the 1980s (e.g., Orlinsky & Howard, 1986; Patterson, 1984) in the face of more equivocal reviews to be noted later. Studies and reviews continued to support Rogers's hypothesis during this time. Truax and Mitchell (1971) presented 14 studies (8 of which were individual therapy) consisting of 992 participants. They identified 125 specific outcome measures favoring the hypothesis (66 of 158 were statistically significant). They report an analysis of the long-term effects of higher and lower levels of empathy, warmth, and genuineness experienced by the clients of the Wisconsin project (Truax & Mitchell, 1971, p. 329). Their data over 9 years indicate that hospital patients seen

by therapists low on the conditions tended not to get out of the hospital and that clients of these same therapists who did get out tended to return.

Lambert, Shapiro, and Bergin (1986) concluded that the attitudinal qualities "seem to make up a significant portion of the effective ingredients of psychotherapy" (p. 202). Orlinsky and Howard (1986) concluded their review of the research on the attitudinal conditions by stating that "generally, 50 to 80 per cent of the substantial number of studies in this area were significantly positive, indicating that these dimensions were very consistently related to patient outcome" (p. 365).

The series of studies in Germany by Tausch and colleagues (R. Tausch, 1990) as well as other studies in Europe provide additional strong support for Rogers's hypothesis of conditions therapy theory. (See Table 5.1 and previous narrative review.)

Miller, Taylor, and West (1980) studied the effects of focused versus broad-spectrum behavioral therapy with problem drinkers in an effort to control their alcohol consumption. They collected data on therapist empathy as a secondary inquiry and found that the level of therapist empathy was highly correlated (.82) with outcome. Another example of the importance of relationship variables was the more recent study by the National Institute of Mental Health, which was conducted to compare various treatments for depression (Blatt, Zuroff, Quinlan, & Pilkonis, 1996). Blatt et al. compared the effects of the administration of a drug (imipramine), cognitive–behavioral therapy (CBT), interpersonal therapy, and "ward management," which served as a placebo. The placebo effect involved a therapist who spent time talking to patients about ward management. There were no significant differences between the effects of the three active treatments. The best prediction of success at the end of any of the active treatments was whether the patient perceived the therapist as empathic at the end of the second interview. Drug treatment was significantly more successful if the patient viewed the therapist as empathic after the second interview.

Research supported Rogers's postulates on the necessary and sufficient conditions with a wealth of studies. Such overwhelming evidence would suggest that further investigation be continued. This was not, however, the case.

3. *Psychotherapy is for better or for worse* (early 1960s). Somewhat unheralded and unrealized, the research on Rogers's hypothesis of the necessary and sufficient conditions became an important

part of the responses to Eysenck (1952, 1966). Several reviewers pointed to the adverse effects of some therapists. Truax and Carkhuff (1967) concluded that psychotherapy was "for better or for worse" (p. 143). The review by Truax and Mitchell (1971) included a call for attrition in the ranks of "psychonoxious practitioners" while increasing the number of helpful counselors (p. 301). On the basis of a separate research review, Bergin (1971) concluded that the previous four decades of the practice of psychotherapy has had an effect that is modestly positive. However, Bergin (1971) pointed out that "the average group data on which this conclusion is based obscure the multiplicity of processes occurring in therapy, some of which are now known to be either unproductive or actually harmful" (p. 263). Lambert et al. (1986) also found evidence to support the position that psychotherapy is for better or for worse and that some therapists are detrimental enough to clients to affect outcome data. These findings were consistent with those in Period 1 identifying certain therapist behaviors as thwarting therapeutic outcome. It is interesting that research on this rather dire finding, which suggests that therapists low on the conditions postulated by Rogers were detrimental to their clients, virtually disappeared with the advent of the thrust for "specificity" studies in the 1980s and 1990s.

4. *The core conditions are necessary but not sufficient for therapeutic personality change* (late 1970s and early 1980s). Reviews during the middle 1970s through the 1980s included some that offered equivocal conclusions for Rogers's hypothesis of the necessary and sufficient conditions. Change in the direction of research began in the middle 1970s paralleling these equivocal reviews. The conclusions of the equivocal reviews that were supported with some data were that (a) "more complex relationships exist among therapists, patients, and techniques" (Parloff et al., 1978, p. 273) and that (b) the conditions need to undergo more thorough investigation (Bozarth, 1983; Mitchell, Bozarth, & Krauft, 1977; Watson, 1984). Opinions predicated on other theoretical formulations rather than on data included the view that the core conditions were nonspecific and similar to placebo effect (Luborsky, Singer, & Luborsky, 1975; Shapiro, 1971) and that "the conditions are neither necessary nor sufficient although it seems clear that such conditions are facilitative" (Gelso & Carter, 1985, p. 220). Issues that need resolution were cited by Beutler, Crago, and Arismendi (1986) as the need to find "an acceptance of an optimal level of

therapeutic skill, common methods of measurement, and the creation and control of levels of the facilitative skills" (p. 276). For the most part, the equivocal reviews founded on examination of the research data pointed to the need for more extensive examination of the complex phenomena. They called for more rigorous methodological designs to confirm the quasi-designs of most of the studies. Among the critical observations, Mitchell et al. (1977) discovered that many of the studies reporting the levels of the conditions were comparisons between therapists "who are non-facilitative and those who are barely facilitative" (p. 498) as operationally defined by the scales. This phenomenon was previously observed in two national studies sponsored by the National Institute of Mental Health and Rehabilitation Services Administration: The Arkansas Psychotherapy Study (Mitchell et al., 1977, pp. 484–488) and a comparably designed study of rehabilitation counselors (Bozarth & Rubin, 1975). One interpretation of this finding is that the attitudinal conditions are quite robust; that is, that in most instances the levels of the conditions can be minimally facilitative and still make a difference in client outcome. Patterson (1984) analyzed the reviews of therapist variables in relation to outcome. He pointed to the specific bias of the reviews and concluded that the effects of the necessary and sufficient conditions are grossly underestimated.

Stubbs and Bozarth (1994) did not find one direct study that supported the assertion that the conditions are not sufficient. Nevertheless, this presumption seemed to affect (or perhaps served as a rationalization for) the direction of research. The research shifted from examining the attitudinal conditions and common variable factors to investigating specificity. This shift was clearly not predicated on previous research results.

5. *There are specific techniques that are uniquely effective in treating particular disorders* (late 1989s and 1990s). The search for the effectiveness of techniques and for specificity virtually paralleled a decrease in published studies on the Rogerian hypothesis of the necessary and sufficient conditions. On the face of it, studies in CCT and the conditions therapy theory were no longer viable inquiries in the United States.

After the middle 1980s, the Rogerian hypothesis was investigated by only a dozen outcome studies that emphasized therapists' empathy (Sexton & Whiston, 1994). These studies were all positive. They included a study of therapist variables that found that emotional adjustment, relationship attitudes, and empathy were most predictive of effective therapists (Lafferty, Beutler, & Crago, 1989). Positive therapy outcome in several studies was linked to such constructs as understanding and involvement (Gaston & Marmar, 1994), warmth and friendliness (Gomes-Schwartz, 1978), and similar constructs (Bachelor, 1991; Gaston 1991; Windholtz & Silbershatz, 1988). Empathy was strongly related to improvement for clients with depression who were being treated by CBT (Burns & Nolen-Hoeksema, 1992). Despite the many positive findings, the equivocal reviews of the conditions therapy research influenced rationale for research toward specificity of treatment. The focus on specificity research replaced inquiry on the common factors.

In summary, this period can be characterized as a major shift of the research from CCT to research on Rogers's (1957) integration or conditions therapy hypothesis. The studies examined the attitudinal conditions experienced by the therapists toward their clients regardless of the therapists' theoretical orientations. The studies reflect the pervasive effect of Rogers's hypothesis of the necessary and sufficient conditions for therapeutic personality change on psychotherapy outcome research. In addition, the studies overwhelmingly support the relationship of these conditions to successful psychotherapy outcome. This holds true even though many of the studies involve therapists who are minimally high on the conditions.

This period is also characterized by an extreme shift in the direction of research. The shift from examination of common factors to examination of specific treatment for particular dysfunction is unfounded by the research evidence.

THE FOURTH PERIOD: COMMON FACTORS REVISITED
(1987–1999)

The investigations of specificity research have ironically returned full cycle to Rogers's basic premises. Research on specific variables include numerous studies in the 1990s that cite person-centered therapies as effective with a range of client problems. The studies include therapies that hold the conditions as central in the treatment process and are derivatives of the client-centered tradition (e.g., experiential therapy and process–experiential therapy). The studies include investigations of alcoholism, anxiety disorders, and personality disorders (see Bohart, 1994; Swildens, 1990). The effectiveness of person-centered psychotherapy has been reported in studies that include treatments of anxiety, psychosomatic problems, agoraphobia, interpersonal difficulties, depression, cancer, and schizophrenia (Borkovek et al., 1987; Elliott, 1997; Grawe, Caspar, & Ambuhl, 1990; Meyer, 1981; Prouty, 1990; Teusch, & Boehme, 1991). In studies of person-centered therapy with specific problems or particular groups, person-centered therapies proved to be as viable as the more goal-oriented therapies. Furthermore, CCT compared favorably over the years in time-limited treatment (Lambert & Anderson, 1996; Shlien et al., 1962).

Stubbs and Bozarth (1994) concluded: "Over four decades, the major thread in psychotherapy efficacy research is the presence of the therapist attitudes hypothesized by Rogers" (p. 120). Duncan and Moynihan (1994) independently buttressed this assessment of Rogers's (1957) hypothesis in a report titled, "Applying Outcome Research: Intentional Utilization of the Client's Frame of Reference." Using outcome research to develop a treatment model, they concluded that the major operational variable is the utility of intentionally using the client's frame of reference. Their model parallels CCT in method and intention (Bozarth, 1998, pp. 168–169). Duncan and Moynihan's article parallels an explosion of psychological literature that identifies the common factors of client–therapist relationship and client resources as the basis for most psychological improvement (Asay & Lambert, 1999; Duncan, Hubble, & Miller, 1997; Hubble et al., 1999; Lambert, 1992; Miller, Duncan, & Hubble, 1997).

The clear message of five decades of research identifies the relationship of the client and therapist in combination with the resources of the client (extratherapeutic variables) that respectively account for 30% and 40% of the variance in successful psychotherapy. Techniques account for 15% of the success variance, comparable with a 15% success rate related to placebo effect.

In summary, the reviews of outcome research of this period reveal that (a) effective psychotherapy is predicated on the relationship of the therapist and client in combination with the inner and external resources of the client (common factors; Hubble et al., 1999); (b) type of therapy and technique add little to the effect of the relationship and client resources if not accompanied by common factors (Hubble et al., 1999); and (c) relationship variables that are most often related to effectiveness are the conditions of empathy, genuineness, and unconditional positive regard (Bozarth, 1998; Patterson, 1984; Stubbs & Bozarth, 1994).

IMPLICATIONS OF RESEARCH FOR PRACTICE

The variables of the client–therapist relationship and the resources of the client identified by research in psychotherapy outcome have been and are the express focus of CCT. The foundation block of the person-centered approach is the self-authority and self-determination of the client. It is the client who directs and orchestrates the process and progress. The "instructions" of CCT theory are that the therapist must be genuine and experience empathic understanding of the client's frame of reference and experience unconditional positive regard toward the client. If the client is in relationship with the therapist, is incongruent at the time, and perceives these experiences in a congruent therapist, then the client will discover his or her inner and outer resources. The dedication of the therapist to empathically experience the client's frame of reference creates an absolute loyalty to the client's direction, pace, and manner. There are many examples of Rogers's response patterns representing his communication of empathy and regard to his clients (Bozarth, 1984, 1990, 1997; Brodley, 1977, 1991, 1994, 1996, 1999; Brodley & Brody, 1990; Brody, 1991; Farber, Brink, & Raskin, 1996; Merry, 1996; Rogers, 1951, 1975; Teich, 1992). However, it is the therapists' attitudes rather than any particular response system that creates the therapeutic climate for growth (Bozarth, 1998; Bozarth & Brodley, 1986; Rogers, 1957, 1975). Limited space prohibits discussion concerning response systems in this chapter. The reader is referred to Brodley's writings for in-depth reference to this topic. The following examples offer two different types of interactions in which the therapists' intentions are to experience the client's frame of reference and to experience unconditional positive regard toward the client.

The Case of Sylvia

The following is an example of a client–therapist relationship and the development of the client's utilization of her own resources. Carl Rogers demonstrates accepting and empathic attitudes in the therapeutic relationship as well as using the more predominant empathic understanding response pattern of many client-centered therapists. This example is offered to demonstrate typical empathic understanding responses and also as an example of some struggle by Rogers to maintain his empathic stance. He deviates slightly from empathic understanding responses that are often characteristic of responses by classical client-centered therapists.

This transcript is presented from a full text that is presented in another publication (Farber et al., 1996, pp. 261–274) that is followed by two commentaries.[1] Although the demonstration is with an individual dealing

---

[1]From *The Psychotherapy of Carl Rogers: Cases and Commentary*, by B. A. Farber, D. C. Brink, and P. M. Raskin, 1996, pp. 261–274. Copyright 1996 by Guilford Press. Reprinted with permission.

with moderate problems, Rogers's responses and relationship with the individual is similar to his work with "more difficult" clients (see Mr. Brown in the Farber et al. casebook). From their unique perspectives, both commentaries in the casebook (by Maureen O'Hara and David Cain) of Sylvia's session view some of Rogers's responses as insertions of his own bias and as having missed the mark on occasion. Such speculations, whether accurate or not, are well taken in that we are reminded of the true healing source, the client. When the therapist trusts the client for direction and trusts in the client's individual process, the client is able to correct or ignore the therapist's imperfections.

This is the fifth interview of Carl Rogers (C.R.) with Sylvia, which was recorded in 1976 (Farber et al., 1996, pp. 261–274). The fourth interview was held on the previous day. There were three interviews a year earlier. Part of the session is shown as it was recorded, with comments offered by Sylvia and Rogers after reviewing the transcript. Comments are in brackets.

C.R.: Well, where would you like to start this morning?

Sylvia: Well, uh, I want to tell you about something that I've been thinking about and that it's a, a sharing more than telling you a problem.

C.R.: M-hm, m-hm.

[C.R.: So often clients and counselors get the feeling that the relationship is one which must be filled only with problems. Sylvia gives a little indication of that, this is just a sharing, it's not a problem.]

Sylvia: And that is, I just recently noticed in myself that I've been learning. (C.R.: M-hm.) And that's a big deal. Uh, I hear people say that all the time, "Oh, I've learned so much, I learned this, and I learned that, and that was such a learning experience." And I, all these years that I've been growing up, I haven't felt any learning, and I feel, "Well, what did you learn and how did you know that you learned it?" And it was a mystery to me. (C.R.: Uh-huh.) And just the last few weeks, or, actually I've been realizing the last year, mainly, is that I learned some things and I know I've learned them, and I know that, OK, that I'm at this point and with a certain situation or idea, and that 6 months ago or 3 months ago it was different. (C.R.: Uh-huh.) And so I'm feeling my learning, and that's really exciting.

C.R.: It's the awareness of it that's new. (Sylvia: Uh-huh.) That you're beginning to realize, "Hey, I am different in this respect, I've learned something."

[C.R.: A relationship should be one in which good feelings have just as much place as bad feelings, and here she is bringing out some very positive feelings about herself, which is a healthy and valid part of a counseling relationship. It's always exciting to me to hear a client telling of positive steps which he or she has been taking, and here Sylvia sounds confident because she is doing something that she has decided to do in her own way, not necessarily following all the books, but doing what she feels and experiences is right.]

Sylvia: I've changed. (C.R.: Uh-huh.) And I can see the difference and feel the difference. (C.R.: Uh-huh.) Yeah.

C.R.: What are some of those differences?

Sylvia: Well (small laugh), um, I, I've made a decision to be more strict with my children and to, uh, to listen to them but decide that I'm their mother and I know many things they don't, and that I will make many more decisions than I've made in the past. And uh—

C.R.: M-hm, m-hm. Sounds as though you feel a bit stronger that way.

Sylvia: Yes. And, and I've been trying it. (C.R.: Uh, m-hm.) Trying being the more strict person and it's working beautifully. (C.R.: Uh-huh.) Uh, they at first they, you know have their little resistance or whatever it is, but then we go on with the program, which is my program more, and I feel a lot better about that as being, uh, uh, helping children to adjust to the world.

C.R.: Sounds, sounds as though you feel more like a grown-up mother.

Sylvia: M-hm. Capable. (C.R.: M-hm.) Of making appropriate decisions. (C.R.: M-hm.) For them. And another area is sex. And, uh, and I, I've done a lot of things in the past year, in the past mainly year that I haven't done before. That is, I've had intercourse with a few different men and put myself in situations where before I was absolutely unwilling to do because of my fears and, and I've learned some things about myself, like I know a lot more right now today about what kind of sexual relationship, what kind of intimate relationships that I want to have with men and that feels good. (C.R.: M-hm.) Beca—, and, um, and it only came through, uh, risking. I mean there was no, it only came through trying things out, there was no amount—(C.R.: Uh-huh, Uh-huh.) There was no amount of therapy or reading or thinking or talking that helped me to learn those things, but it was feeling strong enough within myself that I could take chances.

C.R.: So risking has been the road to learning in the sexual area.

Sylvia: Yes. Uh-huh. (C.R.: M-hm.) And it is with my children, and it is with relating to people in many ways, not just sexually. (C.R.: M-hm.) Other ways too.

C.R.: M-hm.

[C.R.: Sylvia is showing a lot of risking behavior. She is risking a good deal to talk about things like this on film. But what's more important is that she has come to the point in her own life where she realizes that her own experience is the best guide for her. Not books, not therapy, not anything outside of herself. It is her own experience from which she can learn, and here she is learning in a very sensitive and personal area and is willing to share that with us.]

Sylvia: Reaching out to people and approaching strangers and uh—

C.R.: Taking all kinds of risks that you hadn't before.

Sylvia: Some. More, which, I mean I, I don't know about all kinds.

C.R.: Yeah.

Sylvia: Quite a few, and it's been exciting and hard.

C.R.: And I guess that leads to a, um, a deeper kind of learning, at any rate a learning that you feel more sure of. I get, I get a sense of assurance in what you're talking about. Assurance in you.

[C.R.: One thing that has been true with Sylvia is in every interview we have had is that she thinks carefully about what she says, she thinks carefully about what I say, and when what I say is not correct, doesn't match her experience, she's quite willing to correct me. She is very precise in both describing her own feelings and also in making sure that my response to them is accurate.]

Sylvia: Well, yes. Yes and no. And I, I feel more im—, like I was saying before, I feel more mature and more, and I'm more aware of my immaturity. (C.R.: M-hm.) They're both, uh, a part of each other. (C.R.: M-hm.) And uh, does that make—does that, I guess I'm thinking that it just sounds crazy.

C.R.: No, I don't—

Sylvia: To say that I feel more mature because I know I'm how, I know more about how immature I am.

C.R.: Uh-huh. No, that makes a lot of sense to me.

[Sylvia: I was surprised that what I said made sense to him. I think that I thought that it made sense to me, but that doesn't necessarily mean it would make sense to other people. I mean, it made sense in my own system. It felt good that he could understand me, and he knew I valued that it made sense to him too.]

[C.R.: It's important to Sylvia to make sure she is accurately understood. Can anyone understand how she can be more mature by being aware of her immaturity? Well, to me, that is quite understandable, but it's clear that she wants to make certain that my understanding extends to that degree.]

Sylvia: It does.

C.R.: Uh-huh. Because you're, you're, uh, more aware of all aspects of yourself, and it sounds more acceptant of them too. "Yes, I'm mature in certain ways and here are some ways I know I'm immature."

Sylvia: M-hm. And I didn't know that before, or I, I knew I felt uncomfortable that I didn't understand it. (C.R.: M-hm.) But that is related to something I've been thinking about, I think, about being here with you and, uh, and telling myself two things. One is, "Oh, you're just a," I'm just a dependent personality, you know, Carl Rogers or blah-blah-blah-blah, don't I don't run my own life. I go for help a lot. And then I tell myself I'm always being so strong and so together and having everything so worked out in my head that I don't allow myself to be, to be helpless in a situation where it might be good for me. Like right here now, with you, I would like to be more helpless, which to me means open, I think. (C.R.: M-hm, m-hm.) To what to us, and, uh, and I see myself being, uh, together and not being helpless. [Sylvia: I think at that point I was feeling concern that I was just gonna go to another session of being, oh, in control of things and rattling on and on. I probably made a conscious decision that I have to do something to, to break that and, uh, which was talk about it, talk about my fear. My fear was a concern that I wouldn't learn anything.]

C.R.: M-hm. Sounds as though you, you voice that as a conflict, but it sounds as though really you're more on the, on the side of the second aspect that, uh, uh, to be open and, and in that sense helpless and vulnerable, I guess might be a possible term too, uh, is something you, you really believe that is what you are, rather than that you're a totally dependent person and really helpless and have to, have to run for help. I sort of get the feeling you like this aspect of you that is able to be with me in a way that is, uh, more open, more vulnerable perhaps.

Sylvia: Well, I like it, and I also scold myself for being dependent, so there is—

C.R.: There are two sides, uh-huh.

Sylvia: There is something missing in the middle to connect, and I, it seems like you might have been talking about that and I still didn't hear it.

C.R.: M-hm. So really to get it more accurately, you scold yourself for, for being dependent, for, for wanting to be here, for example, with me, and yet at the same time you, you feel, uh, well, that's good, I, I really like that, but where's the, where's the integration of those two, uh, points of view.

Sylvia: M-hm.

[Sylvia: That seemed to me like a very excellent, uh, not paraphrase, but when he, you know, tells me back what he thinks I meant. It, um, solidified what I expressed in the previous comment about that there was something missing. It made more sense to me.] That's right. (Small laugh) May I hold your hands again?

C.R.: Sure. M-hm.

Sylvia: We feel an old feeling.

C.R.: OK.

[Sylvia: When we did the filming in A ——————, we held each other's hands the whole time, and I imagine it occurred to me that it might be good to do that again. I feel good. At that time, I, I wanted to get away from being in my head so completely the whole time, experiencing.]

[C.R.: I felt very comfortable during this holding of hands. Uh, I'm reminded of a friend of mine who said that he did eye therapy and, uh, in a sense that is what this was. Our eyes were very much in contact, and, uh, I think as much was going on at a nonverbal way as in a verbal way. It was a close relationship, and we both experienced it that way.]

Sylvia: (Clears throat) I would like to be less, uh, less strong right now. I would like to give myself the gift of not having to be sensible and reasonable and—(C.R.: M-hm, m-hm.) Also the protection, protect, protect myself.

C.R.: M-hm, m-hm, m-hm. Really would be giving yourself a gift if you could just kind of let go and not, uh, not be so competent and able—

[C.R. It seems clear that the reason she wants to hold my hands is that she wants to experience something that is very frightening to her, namely to drop her competent, reasonable, strong self and let herself be some of the weakness and vulnerability that she is.]

Sylvia: M-hm, m-hm. And I think that it helps to touch you, to, to, to let go of the should, of my shoulds. (Small laugh)

C.R.: M-hm, m-hm. And you feel some contact and maybe you can say, "Well, maybe I don't have to be so strong, so—" (Sylvia: M-hm.) "Maybe I can just let go more."

Sylvia: Yes. (Small laugh) (20-second pause) I want to get away from all, um, my rationalizing right now this minute, and I don't know how to do that except to shut up. (C.R.: M-hm, m-hm.) And, so it is not like I have so much a desire to sit and not talk and look in your eyes as I have a desire to not be the way I am all the time. (C.R.: M-hm.) And I don't know yet what else to do.

C.R.: You have to be kind of silent, to let go of that rational and rationalizing part of you.

[C.R. In the interviews that we held a year ago, the silences were very long and Sylvia found a great deal of security and, uh, seemed to profit a great deal from holding my hands during the interview, and here she returns to the pattern of a year ago. It's another indication of the fact that these interviews with her perhaps rest more solidly on just the fact of the relationship than they do even on the content of what she's saying and talking about.]

Sylvia: M-hm. (20-second pause) It feels easier to focus on, uh, in this position that I'm in now with you, I feel more focused, yeah.

C.R.: M-hm. Are there any things that sort of come bubbling up?

Sylvia: Yeah, I know it is something I want to talk about.

C.R.: OK. M-hm. (10-second pause) but it's not easy, huh.

Sylvia: No, it's not easy, and I'm enjoying the richness of feeling— (C.R.: M-hm.) Your hands this way and letting go of some more of, of the camera business and the—(C.R.: M-hm, m-hm.) And, uh, and the fear about bringing up something that (laughs) (clears throat) and knowing that in about 15 minutes, it'll all seem, um, I don't know, not quite as serious.

[Sylvia: It just had to take its own time for me to get where I could feel like I could say the words that I needed to say. It was almost like waiting and just like, uh, you know, what else is new while I'm waiting? For something that took a natural process that it had to take.]

C.R.: M-hm.

[C.R.: If anyone has a doubt about the value of silences, it should be removed by this interchange. Sylvia is saying, "I'm doing more work when I'm silent than I am when I'm talking."]

[Sylvia: His specific comments or the content of his comments is not necessarily helpful as opposed to not helpful. But what it does do that is valuable is that it gives me something to bounce against. It's a stimulation to better focus myself.]

Sylvia: There's something I've been wanting to talk over with you.

C.R.: OK.

Sylvia continues with discussion of her attraction to Black men and to the Black culture and the implications that she perceives this to create for her. Rogers's interaction and response repertoire changes little from that depicted above even though this appeared to be a more difficult area for her to discuss.

This session is an illustration of the way in which CCT as a therapy (if not *the* therapy) emphasizes the client–therapist relationship and dedication to the client's resources. In addition, the session emphasizes therapy as more than a focus on problems; it can call on the therapist's willingness (in this case, Rogers), on the client's request, to share himself, and on the therapist's willingness to correct his understandings. Most importantly, the therapist's responses and acceptance facilitate the client's internal and external resources. It is the client who orchestrates her own direction and process.

The Case of Gerald

The next example is that of CCT with a client who was in a state mental hospital (Bozarth, 1999) in the late 1950s. The vignette demonstrates the therapist's commitment to the client's frame of reference in a way that did not necessarily involve the usual empathic understanding response repertoire. The sessions involved long silences, brief discussions about a job search, and the therapist's periodic fear of the client. Gerald was a 21-year-old who was diagnosed with schizophrenia when admitted to the hospital 2 years before his contact with the therapist. The therapist was a psychiatric rehabilitation counselor who conducted therapy and had access to resources to assist clients with vocational training and job placement. Gerald (G) was referred by his doctor and by his work supervisor. Gerald worked as a garbage collector in the hospital but was periodically transferred to a locked ward because of violent behavior toward staff and other patients. The following is part of the therapist's (T) report:

We sat mostly in silence over a half dozen or so sessions. We then continued one to three times a week for over a year. Silence continued to be a large part of the sessions. The sessions ranged from twenty minutes to an hour. Although an hour was scheduled for him, he usually left before thirty minutes. I would say things to him or ask questions every once in awhile. He would briefly respond. I could often "feel" anger exuding from him. I would tell him occasionally that I was sometimes afraid of him. He kept returning. Here is an example of one of our interchanges that is reconstructed from written notes:

The therapist talked with Gerald's doctor. Surprisingly, the doctor said Gerald could have an off grounds pass if the therapist agreed and monitored Gerald during that time. The following week, Gerald was interviewed at the employment office. I waited for him in the car. He felt that the interview went well. During the next session the following week, Gerald had an announcement:

G: Well, I think I'll get out of here pretty soon.

T: Out of the hospital?

G: Yeah, doctor said when I get a job, I can get out.

(Pause of five or so minutes)

T: So I guess it is up to me to get you out of here?

[After a few minutes pause, both of us laughed with a mutual understanding. It was this experience of laughter with Gerald that both of us acknowledged his need to depend upon me at certain times and my willingness to accommodate him. (Here, the relationship was enhanced with a nonverbal experience between them.)]

G: I think I'll work a little while yet here; they will pay me a little now to work on the truck. They like my work.

The sessions carried on for awhile this way. During the last session, Gerald talked about his family and that he might go back with them. Shortly after that, he was suddenly discharged. He had a job and was going to live with his family. He stopped by to see me but I was not there.

Three years later, the therapist received a letter from Gerald that thanked the therapist for his help and for "believing in me." He did not give details but reported doing well. This was not the end of information about him though. More than 15 years later, the therapist was chairing a university graduate program in another state. He was cleaning up old student files that had gathered years before his arrival and came across Gerald's name. It had to be Gerald because of his previous residence and other factors as well as his last name. He had been in military service, honorably discharged, and received his graduate degree in a helping profession. It is still difficult to believe that this coincidence occurred 15 years after therapy.

There were no great empathic understanding responses in the dialogue, no noticeable "moments of movement," but Gerald had a relationship with someone who supported him and went with Gerald's feelings, expressions, and internal frame of reference on a moment-to-moment basis, sometimes when logic might dictate otherwise. Gerald's resources, both internal and external, were predominant factors. His motivation to get out of the hospital and his eventual perception of his family as supportive of him were variables that supported his own theory of change. Many potent factors must have come into his life over the years. Nevertheless, Gerald viewed the relationship as helpful to him over 3 years later. His motivation to get out of the hospital and his desire to work, along with a new type of family support that was not available to him earlier in his hospital stay, were later variables that supported his own "theory of change" (Hubble et al., 1999).

CONCLUSION: EVOLUTION OF A REVOLUTION

This chapter reviewed research in CCT. Our focus was on quantitative research with few references to the wealth of qualitative studies that first defined the examination of psychotherapy sessions. Our discoveries went beyond our focus on the results of quantitative studies. These discoveries were the following:

1. Rogers and his colleagues revolutionized the field of psychotherapy with their seminal studies of the verbal interchange in psychotherapy sessions and with their use of qualitative and quantitative research methods.
2. Rogers and his colleagues introduced scientific hypothesis testing research to the field of psychotherapy.
3. Several periods of client-centered research are identified: (a) nondirective therapy (1940–1951), (b) the client-centered relationship (1951–1957), (c) conditions of therapy (1957–1987), and (d) common factors revisited (1987–1999). The first period, nondirective therapy, was characterized by the idea that rapport and acceptance facilitated the client's own acceptance of self. The client rather than the therapist was the person to be in charge. The research identified nondirective therapy as being related to increased understanding, more positive feelings, greater self-exploration, improved self-concepts, and improved maturity of clients. Nondirective therapy was found to be as effective as other therapies.

   The second period, the client-centered relationship, was characterized by a shift from clarification of feelings to focus on the client's frame of reference. Research ranging from self-concept studies to effectiveness variables confirmed many of Rogers's hypotheses.

   The third period, conditions of therapy, revealed a radical shift of research from client-centered therapy to conditions therapy. Conditions therapy referred to the necessary and sufficient condition and was hypothesized to be the foundation of all successful therapy. The results overwhelmingly support the relationship of the attitudinal conditions to successful psychotherapy outcome.

The fourth period, common conditions revisited, offered strong evidence that the factors most associated with successful psychotherapy are the relationship of the client and therapist and the resources of the client.

4. There was little research on CCT after Rogers's (1957) hypothesis of the necessary and sufficient conditions of therapeutic personality change (the attitudinal conditions), and after the Wisconsin investigation of psychotherapy with patients hospitalized with psychoses (Rogers et al., 1967). The research shifted to studies of the attitudinal conditions of therapists regardless of theoretical orientations.

5. The research on the attitudinal conditions started shortly before the third period, and research on these attitudes dominated psychotherapy outcome studies during 1950 through 1970.

6. There is substantial research supporting Rogers's attitudinal conditions. This is particularly true from the middle 1950s through the 1970s.

7. Rigorously designed studies in Germany (see R. Tausch & Tausch, 1990) confirm the effectiveness of the attitudinal conditions and of CCT.

8. The confirmation of the attitudinal conditions over two decades was dismissed with the rationale that the conditions had been found to be "necessary but not sufficient." This assumption was predicated on less than a half dozen reviews that primarily called for increased rigor of research designs. There was, in fact, no research evidence to support the contention of the conditions being necessary but not sufficient.

9. Psychotherapy outcome was dominated with specificity research during the 1990s. This research effort ignored the findings of the previous 3 decades of research.

10. Specificity studies that included secondary common factors (e.g., empathy) identified common factors as being related most often to positive outcome. This fact, and the results of the research in the previous period, lay a strong foundation for support of the basic foundation of CCT, namely, the attitudinal conditions.

11. Research reviews of psychotherapy outcome in the late 1990s (see Hubble et al., 1999) found that successful outcome was predominantly related to the variables of the client–therapist relationship and to the extratherapeutic variables of the cli-

ent. The extratherapeutic variables include client resources and client happenstance.

In short, psychotherapy outcome research supports the major tenets of CCT. The therapeutic relationship and the client's resources are the crux of successful therapy and the foundation of CCT. It is clear that Rogers's specific hypothesis of the necessary and sufficient conditions and his conditions therapy theory have received much more empirical support than some of the equivocal reviews of the middle 1970s imply. Research has supported the theory that a congruent therapist's experience of empathic understanding of the client's frame of reference and experience of unconditional positive regard are related to positive outcome. The potency of these conditions becomes even more apparent with realization that most studies compare therapists who are rated as minimally high with therapists who are rated low on the conditions. Few studies in the United States since the early 1960s have included client-centered therapists who focus on Rogers's postulates of the necessary and sufficient conditions as central to therapeutic change. Some studies in Europe, especially Germany, have included client-centered therapists.

It is our contention that the empathic stance of the therapist fosters the relationship. In addition, empathy helps clarify, identify, and promote extratherapeutic variables. Empathy also promotes the relationship in a way that is more apt to keep the attention on the "client's theory of change" (Hubble et al., 1999) rather than on the therapist's objectives. This point is accentuated with the model of the intentional utilization of the client's frame of reference proposed by Duncan and Moynihan (1994), a model based on psychotherapy outcome research. Their model is essentially a reiteration of Rogers's theory. We believe that Rogerian empathy, which is inseparable from unconditional positive regard (Bozarth, 1997), is the most viable "utilization" of the client's frame of reference.

What are the implications of the research for the training of psychotherapists? The most important aspect of training is to develop the attitudes of the therapist as a dedicated servant to the client's perception of the world. First and foremost, the research supports the therapist who attends to the therapeutic relationship and to the client's own resources. It is the client who discovers personal power from relationship with the therapist and from his or her own inner resources. The most viable training goal in CCT is that of enabling therapists to develop their own unconditional positive self-regard to experience unconditional positive regard and emphatic understanding toward their clients. A most powerful learning about the therapeutic relationship can come from the opportunity for the therapist to experience the remarkable potency of going with the client's internal frame of reference without interruption, intervention, supplementation, and expertise.

Decades of research on CCT and, especially, on the necessary and sufficient conditions of therapeutic personality change suggest that the real potency of successful therapy is the client, and the therapist's attention to the individual client's frame of reference fosters the client's utilization of inner and outer resources. CCT offers a viable model for this endeavor.

REFERENCES

Asay, T. P., & Lambert, M. J. (1999). The empirical case for the common factors in therapy: Qualitative findings. In M. A. Hubble, B. L. Duncan, & S. D. Miller (Eds.), *The heart and soul of change: What works in therapy* (pp. 23–55). Washington, DC: American Psychological Association.

Bachelor, A. (1991). Comparison and relationship to outcome of diverse dimensions of the helping alliance as seen by client and therapist. *Psychotherapy: Theory, Research and Practice, 28,* 534–549.

Barrett-Lennard, G. T. (1962). Dimensions of therapist response as casual factors in therapeutic change. *Psychological Monographs, 76*(43, Whole No. 562).

Barrett-Lennard, G. T. (1998). *Carl Rogers' helping system: Journey and substance.* London: Sage.

Barrett-Lennard, G. T. (1999). *Relationship inventory resource bibliography.* Unpublished manuscript.

Bergeest, H. G., Steinbach, I., & Tausch, A. M. (1977). Psychic help for aged people of day-care centers by attending person-centered encounter groups. *Acta Gerontology, 7,* 305–313.

Bergin, A. E. (1971). The evaluation of therapeutic outcomes. In A. E. Bergin & S. L. Garfield (Eds.), *Handbook of psychotherapy and behavior change* (pp. 217–270). New York: Wiley.

Bergin, A. E., & Garfield, S. L. (1994). Overview, trends and future issues. In A. E. Bergin & S. L. Garfield (Eds.), *Handbook of psychotherapy and behavior change* (4th ed. pp. 821–821). New York: Wiley.

Bergin, A. E., & Lambert, M. J. (1978). The evaluation of therapeutic outcomes. In S. L. Garfield & A. E. Bergin (Eds.), *Handbook of psychotherapy and behavioral change: An empirical analysis* (2nd ed., pp. 139–189). New York: Wiley.

Bergman, D. V. (1950). *The relationship between counseling method and client self-exploration.* Unpublished master's thesis, University of Chicago.

Beutler, L. E., Crago, M., & Arizmendi, T. G. (1986). Research on therapist variables in psychotherapy. In S. L. Garfield & A. E. Bergin (Eds.), *Handbook of psychotherapy and behavior change* (3rd ed., pp. 257–310). New York: Wiley.

Blatt, S. J., Zuroff, D. C., Quinlan, D. M., & Pilkonis, P. A. (1996). Interpersonal factors in brief treatment of depression: Further analyses of the National Institute of Mental Health treatment of depression collaborative research program. *Journal of Consulting and Clinical Psychology, 64,* 162–171.

Blumer, H. (1969). *Symbolic interactionsim: Perspective and method*. Englewood Cliffs, NJ: Prentice Hall.

Boeck-Singelman, C., Schwab, R., & Tönnies, S. (1992). Klientzentrierte Psychotherapie in Form von Team-therapie [Client-centered psychotherapy in the form of team therapy]. *Jahrbuch fur personzentriente Psychologie und Psychotherapie, 3*(9), 9–23.

Bohart, A. (1994). The person-centered therapies. In A. S. Gurman & S. B. Messer (Eds.), *Modern psychotherapies* (pp. 59–75). New York: Guilford Press.

Bommert, H., Minsel, W., Fittkau, B., Langer, I., & Tausch, R. (1972). Empirische controlle der effekte und prozesse klientzentrierter gesprachspsychotherapie bei psychoneurotischen klienten [Empirical control for effect and process of client-centered psychotherapy with neurotic clients]. *Zeitschrift fur Klinische Psychologie, 1*, 48–63.

Borkovek, T. D., Matthews, A. M., Chambers, A., Ebrahimi, S., Lytle, R., & Nelson, R. (1987). The effects of relaxation training with cognitive or non-directive therapy and the role of relaxation-induction anxiety in the treatment of generalized anxiety. *Journal of Consulting and Clinical Psychology, 55*, 883–888.

Bozarth, J. D. (1983). Current research on client-centered therapy in the USA. In M. Wolf-Rudiger & H. Wolfgang (Eds.), *Research on psychotherapeutic approaches: Proceedings of the First European Conference on Psychotherapy Research* (pp. 105–115). Frankfurt: Peter Lang.

Bozarth, J. D. (1984). Beyond reflection: Emergent modes of empathy. In R. Levant & J. M. Shlien (Eds.), *Client-centered therapy and the person-centered approach: New directions in theory, research, and practice* (pp. 59–75). New York: Praeger.

Bozarth, J. D. (1990). The evolution of Carl Rogers as a therapist. *Person-Centered Review, 2*, 11–13.

Bozarth, J. D. (1997). Empathy from the framework of client-centered theory and the Rogerian hypothesis. In A. C. Bohart & L. S. Greenburg (Eds.), *Empathy reconsidered: New directions in psychotherapy* (pp. 81–102). Washington, DC: American Psychological Association.

Bozarth, J. D. (1998). *Person-centered therapy: A revolutionary paradigm*. Ross-on-Wye, England: PCCS Books.

Bozarth, J. D. (1999, July). *Forty years of dialogue with the Rogerian hypothesis of the necessary and sufficient conditions*. Paper presented at the annual meeting of the Association for the Development of the Person-Centered Approach, Ruston, LA.

Bozarth, J. D., & Brodley, B. T. (1986). Client-centered psychotherapy: A statement. *Person-Centered Review, 1*, 262–271.

Bozarth, J. D., & Rubin, S. E. (1975). Empirical observations of rehabilitation counselor performance and outcome: Some implications. *Rehabilitation Counseling Bulletin, 19*, 294–298.

Brodley, B. T. (1977). *The empathic understanding response process*. Unpublished manuscript, University of Chicago.

Brodley, B. T. (1991, July). *Some observations of Carl Rogers' verbal behavior in therapy interviews*. Paper presented at the annual meeting of the Second International Conference on Client-Centered and Experiential Therapy, Stirling, Scotland.

Brodley, B. T. (1994). Some observations of Carl Rogers' behavior in therapy interviews. *Person-Centered Journal, 1*, 37–47.

Brodley, B. T. (1996). Empathic understanding and feelings in client-centered therapy. *Person-Centered Journal, 3*, 22–30.

Brodley, B. T. (1999). Reasons for responses expressing the therapist's frame of reference in client-centered therapy. *Person-Centered Journal, 6*, 4–27.

Brodley, B. T., & Brody, A. F. (1990, August). *Understanding client-centered therapy through interviews conducted by Carl Rogers*. Paper presented at the 98th Annual Convention of the American Psychological Association, Boston.

Brody, A. F. (1991). *Understanding client-centered therapy through interviews conducted by Carl Rogers*. Unpublished equivalency thesis, Illinois School of Professional Psychology.

Burns, D. D., & Nolen-Hoeksema, S. (1992). Therapy empathy and recovery from depression in cognitive behavioral therapy: A structural equation model. *Journal of Consulting and Clinical Psychology, 60*, 441–449.

Butler, J. M., & Haigh, G. V. (1954). Changes in the relation between self-concepts and ideal concepts consequent upon client-centered counseling. In C. R. Rogers & R. F. Dymond (Eds.), *Psychotherapy and personality change* (pp. 55–75). Chicago: University of Chicago Press.

Carkhuff, R. R. (1967). *Beyond counseling and therapy*. New York: Holt, Rinehart & Winston.

Carkhuff, R. R. (1969). *Helping and human relations: A primer for lay and professional helpers: Vol. 1. Selection and training*. New York: Holt, Rinehart & Winston.

Carkhuff, R. R. (1972). The development of systematic human resource development models. *The Counseling Psychologist, 3*, 4–11.

Caspari, G., & Tausch, R. (1979). Der Zusammenhang seelischer Beeintrachtigungen mit unechtem-fassadenhaftem Verhalten [The relationship of mental impairments with defensive behavior]. *Zeitschrift fur Klinische Psychologie, 8*, 245–255.

Doll, G., Feindt, K., Kruhne, A., Langer, I., Sternberg, W., & Tausch, A. (1974). Klientenzentrierte Gesprache mit Insassen eins Gefangnisseş uber telefon [Client-centered counseling with inmates in prison by telephone]. *Zeitschrift fur Klinesche Psychologie, 3*(1), 39–56.

Duncan, B. L., Hubble, M. A., & Miller, S. D. (1997). *Psychotherapy with "impossible" cases: The efficient treatment of therapy veterans*. New York: Norton.

Duncan, B. L., & Moynihan, D. (1994). Applying outcome research: Intentional utilization of the client's frame of reference. *Psychotherapy, 31*, 294–301.

Eckert, J., Schwartz, H. J., & Tausch, R. (1977). Client experiences and the correlation these have with psychic changes in person-centered psychotherapy. *Zeitschrift fur Klinische Psychologie, 6*, 177–184.

Egan, G. (1975). *The skilled helper: A model for systematic helping and interpersonal relating.* Belmont, CA: Wadsworth.

Elliott, R. (1997). Are client-centered/experiential therapies effective? A meta-analysis of outcome research. In U. Esser, H. Pabst, & G. W. Speierer (Eds.), *The power of the person centered approach* (pp. 125–138). Koln, Germany: GwG Verlag.

Eysenck, H. J. (1952). The effects of psychotherapy: An evaluation. *Journal of Consulting Psychology, 16,* 319–324.

Eysenck, H. J. (1966). *The effects of psychotherapy.* New York: International Science Press.

Farber, B. A., Brink, D. C., & Raskin, P. M. (1996). *The psychotherapy of Carl Rogers: Cases and commentary.* New York: Guilford Press.

Fay, A., & Lazarus, A. A. (1992, August). *On necessity and sufficiency in psychotherapy.* Paper presented at the 100th Annual Convention of the American Psychological Association, Washington, DC.

Fox, R., & Tausch, R. (1983). Important psychological qualities in partnerships: An empirical examination of the theory of interpersonal relations by Carl Rogers. *Zeitschrift fur Personzentrierte Psychologie und Psychotherapie, 2,* 499–508.

Garfield, S. L., & Bergin, A. E. (Eds.). (1978). *Handbook of psychotherapy and behavior change* (2nd ed.). New York: Wiley.

Garfield, S. L., & Bergin, A. E. (Eds.). (1986). *Handbook of psychotherapy and behavior change* (4th ed.). New York: Wiley.

Gaston, L. (1991). The reliability and criterion-related validity of the patient version of the California Psychotherapy Alliance Scale. *Journal of Consulting and Clinical Psychology, 3,* 68–74.

Gaston, L., & Marmar, C. (1994). The California Psychotherapy Alliance Scales. In A. O. Horvath & L. S. Greenberg (Eds.), *The working alliance: Theory, research and practice* (pp. 85–108). New York: Wiley.

Gaylin, N. L. (1966). Psychotherapy and psychological health: A Rorschach function and structure analysis. *Journal of Consulting Psychology, 30,* 494–500.

Gelso, C. J., & Carter, J. A. (1985). The relationship in counseling and psychotherapy: Components, consequences, and theoretical antecedents. *The Counseling Psychologist, 13,* 155–433.

Gendlin, E. T. (1973). Experiential psychotherapy. In R. J. Corsini (Ed.), *Current psychotherapies* (pp. 317–352). Itasca, NY: Peacock.

Glaser, B., & Strauss, A. (1967). *The discovery of grounded theory: Strategies for qualitative research.* Chicago: Aldine.

Gomes-Schwartz, B. (1978). Effective ingredients in psychotherapy: Prediction of outcome from process variables. *Journal of Consulting and Clinical Psychology, 46,* 196–197.

Gordon, T. (1970). *P.E.T.: Parent effectiveness training.* New York: Wyden.

Gordon, T. (1976). *T.E.T. in action.* New York: Wyden.

Gordon, T., & Burch, N. (1974). *T.E.T.: Teacher effectiveness training.* New York: Wyden.

Grawe, K., Caspar, F., & Ambuhl, H. (1990). The Bernese comparative psychotherapy study. *Zeitschrift fur Klinische Psychologie, 19,* 287–376.

Guerney, B. G. (1977). *Relationship enhancement: Skill training programs for therapy, problem, prevention, and enrichment.* San Francisco: Jossey-Bass.

Gump, P. V. (1944). *A statistical investigation of one psychoanalytic approach and a comparison of it with non-directive therapy.* Unpublished master's thesis, Ohio State University, Columbus, OH.

Halkides, G. (1958). *An experimental study of four conditions necessary for therapeutic change.* Unpublished doctoral dissertation, University of Chicago.

Heine, R. W. (1953). A comparison of patients' reports on psychotherapeutic experience with psychoanalytic, non-directive and Adlerian therapists. *Psychotherapy, 7,* 16–23.

Helm, J. (1980). *Gesprachpsychotherapie* [Counseling Psychotherapy]. Darmstadt, Germany: Stierhaupt.

Hoffman, A. E. (1949). A study of reported behavioral changes in counseling. *Journal of Consulting Psychology, 13,* 190–195.

Hubble, M. A., Duncan, B. L., & Miller, S. D. (1999). *The heart and soul of change: What works in therapy.* Washington, DC: American Psychological Association.

Lafferty, P., Beutler, L. E., & Crago, M. (1989). Differences between more and less effective psychotherapists: A study of select therapist variables. *Journal of Consulting and Clinical Psychology, 57,* 76–80.

Lambert, M. J. (1992). Psychotherapy outcome research. In J. C. Norcross & M. R. Goldfried (Eds.), *Handbook of psychotherapy integration* (pp. 94–129). New York: Basic Books.

Lambert, M. J., & Anderson, E. M. (1996). Assessment for the time-limited psychotherapies. *Annual Review of Psychiatry, 15,* 23–47.

Lambert, M. J., DeJulio, S. J., & Stein, D. M. (1978). Therapist interpersonal skills: Process, outcome, methodological considerations, and recommendations for future research. *Psychological Bulletin, 85,* 467–489.

Lambert, M. J., Shapiro, D. A., & Bergin, A. E. (1986). The effectiveness of psychotherapy. In S. L. Garfield & A. E. Bergin (Eds.), *Handbook of psychotherapy and behavior change* (3rd ed., pp. 157–212). New York: Wiley.

Lietaer, G. (1988). *Centrum voor client-centered psychotherapie en counseling* [The client-centered/experiential/person-centered approach 1950–1987: Bibliographical survey]. (Available from G. Lietaur, Blijde Inkonstsraat 13, 3000 Leuven, Belgium)

Lietaer, G. (1990). The client-centered approach after the Wisconsin project: A personal view on its evolution. In G. Lietaer, J. Rombauts, & R. Van Balen (Eds.), *Client-centered and experiential psychotherapy in the nineties* (pp. 19–45). Leuven, Belgium: Leuven University Press.

Lietaer, G., van Praag, P. P., & Swildens, J. C. A. G. (1984). *Client-centered psychotherapie in beweging* [Client-centered psychotherapy in action]. Leuven, Belgium: Acco.

Luborsky, L., Singer, B., & Luborsky, L. (1975). Comparative studies of psychotherapies: Is it true that "everyone has won and all must have prizes"? *Archives of General Psychiatry, 32*, 995–1008.

Meltzoff, J., & Kornreich, M. (1970). *Research in psychotherapy*. New York: Atherton Press.

Merry, T. (1996). An analysis of ten demonstration interviews by Carl Rogers: Implications for the training of client-centered counselors. In R. Hutterer, G. Pawlowsky, P. F. Schmid, & R. Stipsits (Eds.), *Client-centered and experiential psychotherapy: A paradigm in motion* (pp. 273–283). Frankfurt: Peter Lang.

Meyer, A. E. (1981). The Hamburg short psychotherapy comparison experiment. *Psychotherapy and Psychosomatics, 35*, 81–207.

Miller, S. D., Duncan, B. L., & Hubble, M. A. (1997). *Escape from Babel: Toward a unifying language for psychotherapy practice*. New York: Norton.

Miller, S. D., Taylor, C. A., & West, J. C. (1980). Focused versus broad-spectrum behavior therapy for problem drinkers. *Journal of Consulting and Clinical Psychology, 48*, 590–601.

Minsel, W., Bommert, H., Bastine, R., Langer, I., Nickel, H., & Tausch, R. (1972). Weitere Untersuchung der Auswirkungen und Prozesse klientzentrierter Gesprachspsychotherapie [Further investigations into the outcomes and process of client-centered psychotherapy]. *Zeitshrift fur Klinische Psychologie, 1*, 232–250.

Mitchell, K. M., Bozarth, J. D., & Krauft, C. C. (1977). A reappraisal of the therapeutic effectiveness of accurate empathy, non-possessive warmth, and genuineness. In A. S. Gurman & A. M. Razin (Eds.), *Effective psychotherapy: A handbook of research* (pp. 482–502). New York: Pergamon.

Orlinsky, D. E., & Howard, K. I. (1986). Process and outcome in psychotherapy. In S. L. Garfield & A. E. Bergin (Eds.), *Handbook of psychotherapy and behavior change* (3rd ed., pp. 311–381). New York: Wiley.

Parikh, B., Steinbach, I., Tausch, A. M., & Teegen, F. (1973). Dimensionen der Stimm-und Sprechweise von Beratern-helfern am telefon, Zusammenhang mit personlichkeitsvariablen sowie bevorzugung durch Rat-u. Hilfesuchende [Dimensions of manner of voice and speaking of advisors on the telephone in correlation with personality variables as well as preference for advice and help seeking]. *Zeitscrift fur Klinische Psychologie, 2*, 145–150.

Parloff, M. B., Waskow, I. E., & Wolfe, B. E. (1978). Research on therapist variables in relation to process and outcome. In S. L. Garfield & A. E. Bergin (Eds.), *Handbook of psychotherapy and behavior change: An empirical analysis* (2nd ed., pp. 233–282). New York: Wiley.

Patterson, C. H. (1984). Empathy, warmth, and genuineness in psychotherapy: A review of reviews. *Psychotherapy, 21*, 431–438.

Porter, E. H., Jr. (1943). The development and evaluation of a measure of counseling interview procedures. *Educational and Psychological Measurement, 111*, 105–126.

Prouty, G. F. (1990). Pre-therapy: A theoretical evolution in the person-centered/ experiential psychotherapy of schizophrenia and retardation. In G. Lietaer, J. Rombauts, & R. Van Balen (Eds.), *Client-centered and experiential psychotherapy in the nineties* (pp. 645–658). Leuven, Belgium: Leuven University Press.

Raimy, V. C. (1948). Self-reference in counseling interviews. *Journal of Consulting Psychology, 12*, 153–163.

Raskin, N. J. (1949). An analysis of six parallel studies of the therapeutic process. *Journal of Consulting Psychology, 13*, 206–219.

Rogers, C. R. (1942). *Counseling and psychotherapy*. Boston: Houghton-Mifflin.

Rogers, C. R. (1951). *Client-centered therapy: Its current practice, implications, and theory*. Boston: Houghton-Mifflin.

Rogers, C. R. (1957). The necessary and sufficient conditions of therapeutic personality change. *Journal of Consulting Psychology, 21*, 95–103.

Rogers, C. R. (1959). A theory of therapy, personality, and interpersonal relationships as developed in the client-centered framework. In S. Koch (Ed.), *Psychology: A study of science: Vol. 3. Formulation of the person and the social context* (pp. 184–256). New York: McGraw Hill.

Rogers, C. R. (1975). Empathic: An unappreciated way of being. *The Counseling Psychologist, 5*(2), 2–10.

Rogers, C. R., & Dymond, R. F. (1954). *Psychotherapy and personality change*. Chicago: University of Chicago Press.

Rogers, C. R., Gendlin, G. T., Kiesler, D. V., & Truax, C. B. (1967). *The therapeutic relationship and its impact: A study of psychotherapy with schizophrenics*. Madison: University of Wisconsin Press.

Ronnecke, B., Becker, M., Bergeest, H. G., Freytag, C., Jurgens, G., Steinbach, I., & Tausch, A. M. (1976). Counseling by telephone with old people, conducted by person-centered psychologists and lay-helpers. *Zeitschrift fur Gerontologie, 9*, 455–462.

Rosenzweig, S. A. (1954). A transvaluation of psychotherapy: A reply to Hans Eysenck. *Journal of Abnormal Social Psychology, 49*, 298–304.

Rudolph, J., Langer, I., & Tausch, R. (1980). Empirical investigation of psychic effects and conditions of person-centered therapy with individual clients. *Zeitschrift fur Klinische Psychologie, 9*, 23–33.

Sander, K., Tausch, R., Bastine, R., & Nagel, K. (1969). Auswirkung experimenteller Anderung des psychotherapeutenverhaltens auf Klienten [Results of experimental changing of psychotherapeutic conditioning of clients]. *Zeitschrift fur Experimentelle und Angewandte Psychologie, 16*, 334–344.

Schäefer, H. (1992). Klarende zwischen gesprache und alternative Therapeutenwahl durch die Klienten [Clarifying between counseling and alternative therapeutic choices for the client]. *Jahbuch Personzentrierte Psychologie und Psychotherapie, 3*, 24–37.

Seeman, J. A. (1949). Study of the process of non-directive therapy. *Journal of Consulting Psychology, 13*, 157–168.

Sexton, T. L., & Whiston, S. C. (1994). The status of the counseling relationship: An empirical review: Theoretical implications and research directions. *The Counseling Psychologist, 22*(1), 6–78.

Shapiro, A. K. (1971). Placebo effects in medicine, psychotherapy and psychoanalysis. In A. E. Bergin & S. C. Garfield (Eds.), *Handbook of psychotherapy and behavior change: Empirical analysis* (pp. 437–473). New York: Wiley.

Sheerer, E. T. (1949). An analysis of the relationship between acceptance of and respect for self and acceptance of and respect for others in ten counseling cases. *Journal of Consulting Psychology, 13,* 169–175.

Shlien, J. M., Mosak, H. H., & Dreikurs, R. (1962). Effect of time limits: A comparison of two psychotherapies. *Journal of Counseling Psychology, 9,* 31–34.

Snyder, W. U. (1945). An investigation of the nature of non-directive psychotherapy. *Journal of General Psychology, 33,* 192–223.

Snyder, W. U. (1947). *Casebook of non-directive counseling.* Boston: Houghton Mifflin.

Stephenson, W. (1953). *The study of behavior.* Chicago: University of Chicago Press.

Stock, D. (1949). An investigation into the relationships between the self-concept and feelings directed toward other persons and groups. *Journal of Consulting Psychology, 13,* 176–180.

Stubbs, J. P., & Bozarth, J. D. (1994). The dodo bird revisited: A qualitative study of psychotherapy efficacy research. *Journal of Applied and Preventive Psychology, 3,* 109–120.

Stubbs, J. P., & Bozarth, J. D. (1996). The integrative statement of Carl Rogers. In R. Hutterer, G. Pawlowsky, P. Schmid, & R. Stipsits (Eds.), *Client-centered and experiential psychotherapy: A paradigm in motion* (pp. 25–33). New York: Peter Lang.

Swildens, J. C. A. G. (1990). Client-centered psychotherapy for patients with borderline symptoms. In G. Lietaer, J. Rombauts, & R. Van Balen (Eds.), *Client-centered and experiential psychotherapy in the nineties* (pp. 623–636). Leuven, Belgium: Leuven University Press.

Tausch, A. M., Kettner, V., Steinbach, I., & Tönnies, S. (1973). Effects of client-centered and group talks with underprivileged kindergarten and elementary school children. *Psychologie in Erziehung und Unterricht, 20,* 77–88.

Tausch, R. (1978). Facilitative dimensions in interpersonal relations: Verifying the theoretical assumptions of Carl Rogers in school, family, education, client-centered therapy, and encounter groups. *College Student Journal, 12,* 2–11.

Tausch, R. (1988). The relationship between emotions and cognitions: Implications for therapist empathy. *Person-Centered Review, 3,* 277–291.

Tausch, R. (1990). The supplementation of client-centered communication therapy with other valid therapeutic methods. In G. Lietaer & R. Van Balen (Eds.), *Client-centered and experiential therapies in the nineties* (pp. 65–85). Leuven, Belgium: Katholieke Universiteit te Leuven.

Tausch, R., & Tausch, A. M. (1981). *Erziehungspsychologie. Begegnung von Person zu person* [Educational psychology]. Gottingen, Germany: Hogrefe.

Tausch, R., & Tausch, A. M. (1990). *Gespraechspsychotherapy* [Counseling psychology] (9th ed.). Gottingen, Germany: Hogrefe.

Tausch, R., & Tausch, A. M. (1998). Erzehunpsychologie [Educational psychology] (11th ed.). Gottingen, Germany: Hogrefe.

Teich, N. (1992). *Rogerian perspectives: Collaborative rhetoric for oral and written communication.* Norwood, NJ: Ablex.

Teusch, P., & Boehme, L. (1991). Results of a one-year follow up of patients with agoraphobia and/or panic disorder treated with an inpatient therapy program with client-centered basis. *Psychotherapie-Psychosomatic Medizinische Psychologie, 41,* 68–76.

Truax, C. B., & Carkhuff, R. R. (1967). *Toward effective counseling and psychotherapy: Training and practice.* Chicago: Aldine.

Truax, C. B., & Mitchell, K. M. (1971). Research on certain therapist interpersonal skills in relation to process and outcome. In A. E. Bergin & S. L. Garfield (Eds.), *Handbook of psychotherapy and behavior change* (pp. 299–344). New York: Wiley.

Van Balen, R., Leijssen, M., & Lietaer, G. (1986). Droom enwerkelijkheid in client-centered psychotherapie [Dream analysis in client-centered psychotherapy]. Leuven, Belgium: Acco.

van der veen, F. (1965, September). *Dimensions of client and therapist behavior in relation to outcome.* Paper presented at the 73rd Annual Convention of the American Psychological Association, Chicago.

van der veen, F. (1967). Basic elements in the process of psychotherapy: A research study. *Journal of Consulting and Clinical Psychology, 31,* 295–303.

van der veen, F. (1970). Client perception of therapist conditions as a factor in psychotherapy. In J. T. Hart & T. M. Tomlinson (Eds.), *New directions in client-centered therapy* (pp. 214–222). Boston: Houghton Mifflin.

Watson, N. (1984). The empirical status of Rogers' hypothesis of the necessary and sufficient conditions for effective psychotherapy. In R. F. Levant & J. M. Shlien (Eds.), *Client-centered therapy and the person-centered approach: New directions in theory, research, and practice* (pp. 17–40). New York: Praeger.

Wexler, D. A., & Rice, L. N. (Eds.). (1974). *Innovations in client-centered therapy.* New York: Wiley.

Whitehorn, J. C., & Betz, B. J. (1954). A study of psychotherapeutic relations between physicians and schizophrenic patients. *American Journal of Psychiatry, 111,* 321–331.

Windholtz, J. J., & Silbershatz, G. (1988). Vanderbilt Psychotherapy Process Scale: A replication with adult outpatients. *Journal of Consulting and Clinical Psychology, 37,* 369–376.

6

CONTACTING GESTALT THERAPY

UWE STRÜMPFEL AND RHONDA GOLDMAN

From both a theoretical and practical perspective, Gestalt therapy focuses on the process of human contact. Awareness of one's own experience in the therapeutic dialogue directly affects both the client's own inner dialogue and his or her personal interactions in the world and in the process of healing. Gestalt therapy developed within the humanistic tradition and is phenomenological and process oriented in its approach. This tradition emphasizes growth and the self, although its concept of self is distinct from other humanistic psychotherapies (see also Purkey & Stanley, this volume, chapter 15). Gestalt therapy has traditionally seen the processing of emotion as basic to change. Process–experiential therapy (see Elliott & Greenberg, this volume, chapter 9) adapted fundamental Gestalt concepts and methods into its approach and has continued to emphasize and develop work with emotion in psychotherapy (L. S. Greenberg & Paivio, 1997; L. S. Greenberg, Rice, & Elliott, 1993; see also L. S. Greenberg, Korman, & Paivio, this volume, chapter 16). Research on Gestalt therapy over the past 25 years has focused on both efficacy research and investigations into emotional processes in therapeutic dialogue and their relationship to outcome in therapy. Major questions of concern to researchers have focused on how intense moments of contact, particularly in the context of emotional expression of inner conflict, lead to conflict resolution and a reduction in clients' suffering.

SELF AND CONTACT IN GESTALT THERAPY

Gestalt therapy is based on phenomenology, field theory, and dialogue. Although Friedrich Perls (1893–1970), the main founder of Gestalt therapy, practiced as a psychoanalyst at the beginning of his career, he and his wife Laura (1905–1990) and the American philosopher and writer Paul Goodman (1911–1972) developed a completely new approach to psychotherapy. Working within a phenomenological framework, they placed inter- and intrapersonal contact, and its disturbances, at the center of their psychotherapeutic practice. From their perspective, the therapist enters the therapeutic relationship in a personal manner. Feelings are an intrinsic part of contact, and lively awareness of impulses, feelings, and needs facilitate the client's attaining satisfaction. In dialogue, the therapist and client practice awareness of present feelings and needs and explore alternative means for achieving gratification. In this vein, different forms of dialogue are explored in an imaginative and sometimes playful manner. The therapist may invite clients to enter an internal dialogue with themselves or to contact memories of significant others when past relationships have remained unresolved (L. S. Greenberg et al., 1993; Hycner & Jacobs, 1995; Yontef, 1998; Zeigarnik, 1927). The Gestalt concept of self reflects this central preoccupation with the contact process and its interruptions. In the theoretical writings of Perls, Hefferline, and Goodman (1951), the self only comes into existence in the course of the contact process.

One of the fundamental tenets of Gestalt therapy is its concept of the self as drawn from Lewin's (1917) field theory. Field theory posits an interdependence of phenomena and a constant shifting of boundaries; the field is always in motion, as people continually construct their worlds in a subjective manner. According to field theory, the subject, referred to as the *organism*, recognizes itself as part of the field, contacting the environment at its boundaries. Emerging wishes and needs are as much a part of the field as actual options for attaining satisfaction.

The Gestalt psychologists' work with perceptual phenomena gave rise to other concepts, namely *figure* and *background*. Both figure and background continually reconfigure themselves in the field; new figures are always emerging while old ones recede into the background. For example, a person's body boundaries return to the background when he or she is absorbed in an exciting film and disappear completely when the person falls asleep. Within the field, the boundaries between figure and background shift in a continual process of change. Emerging excitations and impulses form and become figural until the internal and external possibilities for satisfaction of needs are realized. Gestalt therapy, integrating Lewin's principle of interdependency and the Gestalt psychologist's concept of figure and background, views human activity as being constantly affected by the whole field. The contact boundary and its movement are influenced by the total field of impulses, emotions, wishes, and perceived options for achieving satisfaction. This holistic notion informs the definition of self as "the contact boundary at work; its activity is forming figures and grounds" (Perls et al., 1951,

p. 235). In the following two sections, we introduce a process diagnosis that is integral to Gestalt therapy. This process diagnosis entails the analyses of four stages of the contact process and various disturbances of the self.

Stages of the Self in Contact

The entire process of contacting, beginning from the first emergence of impulses to final actions toward gratification, is referred to as the *contact* or the *need* cycle. It can be described in four stages: (a) *Fore contact* is the emergence of initial impulses and their transformation into emotions— impulses gain intention and guide further action; (b) *contacting* refers to the selection, decision making, and transformation of motoric energy into movement; (c) *final contact* is the consummation of contact and ensuing gratification; and (d) *postcontact* is the assimilation by the personality of all experiences that have entered awareness. The self is in a continuing dynamic process of unfolding at the contact boundary and is a result of all these activities.

This description of the need cycle illustrates how Friedrich Perls originally understood the process by which people make healthy intra- and interpersonal contact. It is experienced at the boundary between the organism and its environment. More recent interpretations of contact include Yontef's (1998) concept of *dialogue*—a special form of contact in which people get in touch with each other and share what they experience as an end in itself. This dialogical engagement is considered to be the basis of effective therapy (Hycner & Jacobs, 1995). Yontef's concept of dialogue reflects the influence of Buber's (1984) philosophy on Gestalt therapy. In other conceptualizations, dialogue occurs between two aspects of the self, and contact refers to the liveliness of the interaction between these parts and the extent to which feelings are currently felt (L. S. Greenberg et al., 1993).

Disturbances in the Contact Cycle

Disturbances to the healthy contact cycle are seen as the basis of pathology and thus become the focus of therapy. Perls and others have identified different forms of interruption, including introjection, projection, and retroflection, that occur at different points in the contact cycle. *Introjection* refers to the uncritical acceptance of principles, dogmas, or taboos (such as "you must not be angry") that result in the inhibition of experience. *Projection* refers to the process by which people find aspects of the self to be unacceptable and disown them by attributing them to people in the environment, experiencing their feelings as those of another. A person's aggressive feeling toward another, for example, may not be identified as his or her own but experienced as aggression from another. In a different manner, people may interrupt contact through *retroflection*, which means turning emotions intended for someone in the environment back against oneself. It may be more acceptable to hurt oneself than express anger or dissatisfaction to another.

Within the therapy session, therapists stay in contact with clients as they make contact with themselves, supporting them to explore their impulses, wishes, and needs in the background that are pressing to become figural. Awareness of impulses and emotions is fundamental to the therapeutic endeavor and is seen as providing a window to all aspects of the functioning of the self. In the therapeutic process, the client becomes more fully conscious through both awareness work and experiments that therapists construct and propose in the session. Experiments aim to bring awareness to contact interruptions through different exercises, such as chair dialogues designed to increase awareness and better integrate different aspects of the personality, and through dream work that is designed to increase awareness of the encoded messages of dreams and bodily expression.

Developments Since Perls

Originally, Gestalt therapy was mainly practiced in groups. Considered an innovative setting central to Gestalt therapy's identity and character, the group setting was assigned a decisive role in the healing process. Early groups paid little attention to group dynamics, however, because they were not seen as essential to the process of change. Early group work is best described as individual therapy within the group (see Lieberman, Yalom, & Miles, 1973, for an early survey). According to a survey carried out by Frew (1988), almost all Gestalt therapists participated in groups in their own training. Modern training institutes continue to offer the group format or use a combination of individual or group therapy for learning purposes. The first training institute for Gestalt therapists was founded in 1952, in New York, followed by institutes in Cleveland, Ohio, and in Esalen, California, on the West Coast of the United States. Each of these institutes became associated with different styles within Gestalt therapy. Two major trends have emerged over the last 40 years. First, individual therapy has been taken out of the group and is now the most widely practiced form of Gestalt therapy. Second, partly due to the influence of Kurt Lewin (1890–1947), who first observed and described group dynamics, both interpersonal and systemic dynamics have become increasingly important in group work.

Sreckovic (1999) identified three streams in Gestalt therapy: (a) the growth-oriented tradition, (b) the social therapeutic tradition, and (c) the clinical tradition. Each tradition still exists today. The growth-oriented tradition is the most leader-driven form of therapy (the "Guru model") and is practiced in a series of sporadic workshops whose format and techniques are partially structured in advance. This original style of group work was long associated with the West Coast of the United States. The social therapeutic tradition focuses more on self-exploration in the group. The clinical tradition signifies an increased emphasis on professionalism, more formal diagnosis of client problems, and long-term treatment with a focus on client process. This tradition originated in New York, and current or recent practitioners include Jim Simkin, Gary Yontef, and Erving Polster. Erving and Miriam Polster have made a number of theoretical and practical contributions to Gestalt therapy (Polster & Polster, 1973). Their theoretical ideas regarding the concept of self and contact disturbances were hotly discussed but not generally accepted. Their practical contributions that have been highly influential include a more accepting and less confrontational style. Yontef (1998), in a discussion of the development of the new model of Gestalt therapy, describes it as softer, more dialogic, and relationship oriented. Since the 1970s, the mainstream practice of Gestalt therapy has been influenced primarily by North American therapists. Gestalt therapy's emphasis on immediate emotional experiences and group work has proved attractive to many European therapists. For this reason, Gestalt therapy, second to client-centered therapy (CCT), has become the most widely practiced humanistic psychotherapy in Europe.

RESEARCH ON GESTALT THERAPY

This review section begins with research illuminating moment-by-moment processes, or *microprocesses*, followed by a section summarizing studies relating microprocesses to long-term *macroprocesses*, or outcome data. Finally, in a third section, outcome studies on specific clinical subgroups are summarized, including comparative studies with other psychotherapeutic treatments and long-term follow-up studies. The criterion used for a study's inclusion in this review is that the description of the investigated treatment or intervention contain the term *Gestalt therapy*.

Microprocesses

Research on microprocesses in therapy have focused on the expressive and emotional dimensions in the moment-by-moment process of Gestalt therapeutic dialogue. This kind of research primarily explores therapeutic processes occurring immediately before and after therapists' single statements (microinterventions). Both Mahrer (Mahrer, Nifakis, Abhukara, & Sterner, 1984; Mahrer, Sterner, Lawson, & Dessaulles, 1986; Mahrer, White, Howard, Gagnon, & MacPhee, 1992; Mahrer, White, Howard, & Lee, 1991) and

Boulet (Boulet, Souliere, & Sterner, 1993; Boulet, Souliere, Sterner, & Nadler, 1992), and to some extent other authors (Brunink & Schroeder, 1979; Kemmler, Schelp, & Mecheril, 1991; Lesonsky, Kaplan, & Kaplan, 1986; Mecheril & Kemmler, 1992; Viney, 1994), have described "important moments" of therapeutic dialogue. Using a method of categorizing and clustering therapeutic statements, these researchers identified moments of intense emotional expression. Mahrer et al. (1991) demonstrated that as the tension in therapeutic dialogue intensifies, it leads to important moments when therapists actively focus on (a) heightened emotional expression and (b) the use of challenging and confrontational interpretations of the way clients interact with therapists. Building on this methodology, Teschke (1996) undertook a phenomenological analysis of video recordings of long-term therapies to further understand important turning points in the therapeutic process that lead to a strengthening of the therapeutic alliance. He used separate groups of raters (therapists, clients, and independent observers) to identify these moments through consensus. A content analysis of these moments placed them in an overall sequential context showing how they trigger a qualitative change in the relation between therapist and client in terms of greater trust. Teschke (1996) concluded that existential moments occur when mutual spontaneity and authenticity are relied on to guide therapy. Angus and Rennie (1989) studied the impact of therapists' use of metaphor on therapy sessions. In the course of interviews, researchers played recordings of selected passages containing metaphors to therapists and clients separately to trigger their recall of in-session feelings, experiences, and insights. Findings suggested that metaphors increased clients' awareness of their implicit feelings and convictions and helped them to access childhood memories, fantasies, and emotions. This in turn led to a stronger alliance between client and therapist.

From Microprocesses to Macroprocesses

Leslie S. Greenberg and colleagues have provided a substantial contribution to the field of research on Gestalt therapy. Much of this research has involved the development of models of Gestalt therapeutic interventions (Clarke & Greenberg, 1986; Goldman & Greenberg, 1991; L. S. Greenberg, 1980; L. S. Greenberg et al., 1993), whereas later studies linked these models with therapeutic outcome (L. S. Greenberg & Foerster, 1996; L. S. Greenberg & Watson, 1998a, 1998b). To explicate typical models that illustrate how these dialogues progress in the therapy session, researchers have adopted a process research strategy called *task analysis* (L. S. Greenberg, 1984). The method involves a cyclic procedure of constant comparison between theoretical categories and the empirical data of therapy sessions (L. S. Greenberg & Foerster, 1996; Singh & L. S. Greenberg, 1992). Research has led to the development of two main models over the years. One is the *two-chair* method for dialogue between conflicting aspects of the personality or "splits" (L. S. Greenberg et al., 1993). The other is the *empty-chair* method for unfinished business with a significant other from the past (L. S. Greenberg et al., 1993; Paivio & Greenberg, 1995). Research has been conducted that investigates whether resolution of dialogues as described by the models relates to changes at the end of therapy.

The Two-Chair Method for a Conflict Split

Within a session, a split is identified through the client's verbal responses indicating that two parts of the self are in conflict, one that is evaluating or interrupting and another that is referred to as the experiencing self. There is also indication of tension and struggle, which is often manifested in negative or bad feelings (L. S. Greenberg, 1984). The model for the two-chair dialogue (L. S. Greenberg, 1992; L. S. Greenberg et al., 1993) is derived from the Gestalt therapy concepts of "topdog" and "underdog." L. S. Greenberg et al. (1993) adopted the terms *critic and self* or *experiencing chair* to refer to the two aspects of the self. The critic refers to introjections of others' views, external standards, and injunctions. This part is characterized as strict, critical, and harsh. The experiencing aspect of self is expressed as compliant on the surface and usually obscures more primary underlying feelings and needs. In the first stage of the dialogue, harsh criticism is expressed. There is often a defensive response from the experiencing aspect of self that belies more vulnerable feelings. Advancement of the dialogue from this point involves the therapist directing the critic to be more specific and an encouragement of the experiencing part to express feelings of sadness or outrage. Work with these more basic emotion processes can often lead to recollections in which memories typically emerge from past misunderstandings. It is sometimes the case that the critic becomes inflexible, adhering to its principles and maintaining a recalcitrant and harsh position. Gestalt therapists refer to this as being "stuck" or the impasse. It is usually accompanied by expressions of hopelessness in the client. This must be worked through gently and precisely by using awareness and active expression exercises. Ultimately, it is the full expression of basic emotions and accompanying needs that moves the critic to become more tolerant. This is referred to as a softening of the critic and paves the way for subsequent resolution.

The chair dialogue is often initiated within the context of real-life situational conflicts, such as "I want to get closer to you but I cannot." In working through the dialogue, a deeper, more fundamental conflict emerges, such as "Be careful, you will get hurt." As the dialogue progresses to resolution, the two aspects of self are both expanded and reconfigured, thereby allowing for a fuller, more integrated functioning of the self to be negotiated, such as "You may get hurt but it is worth being close and I will support you."

In a range of studies, Greenberg and colleagues have compared the two-chair dialogue method with focusing, empathic mirroring, and cognitive problem solving. Comparisons with empathic mirroring have indicated that the two-chair method leads to greater depth of experiencing, greater change in awareness (L. S. Greenberg, 1975; L. S. Greenberg & Rice, 1981), and improved conflict resolution (L. S. Greenberg & Clarke, 1979; L. S. Greenberg & Dompierre, 1981). Comparisons with experiential focusing showed that two-chair work produced significantly greater depth of experiencing but that both treatments produced significant shifts in awareness (L. S. Greenberg & Higgins, 1980). Comparisons with behavioral problem solving indicated that the two-chair method was more effective in reducing indecision. Both treatments were superior to a wait-list control for facilitating movement through the stages of decision making (Clarke & Greenberg, 1986).

In a number of studies comparing successful and unsuccessful conflict resolution episodes, L. S. Greenberg (1980, 1983, 1984) found higher levels of experiencing and more focused and emotional patterns of vocal quality (Rice, Koke, Greenberg, & Wagstaff, 1979) in the successful episodes. To further understand the relationship between resolution processes and outcome, L. S. Greenberg and Webster (1982) studied 31 clients who completed a 6-week program working on intrapsychic conflicts related to a decision. Clients were classified as resolved or nonresolved on the basis of the presence or absence of three crucial components of resolution from the model: (a) criticism in the other chair, (b) expression of felt wants by the self, and (c) softening of the previously harsh critic in the other chair. Resolvers were found to be significantly less undecided and less anxious after treatment than were nonresolvers. After the session in which the critic softened, resolvers reported greater conflict resolution, less discomfort, greater mood changes, and greater goal attainment than nonresolvers.

The Empty-Chair Method for Unfinished Business

The model for the unfinished business dialogue is based on the Gestalt principles that there is a dynamic relation between figure and ground and that significant unmet needs represent "unclosed gestalts" that have not fully receded from awareness (Perls et al., 1951; Polster & Polster, 1973; Zeigarnik, 1927). According to Greenberg et al. (1993), when schematic emotion memories of significant others are triggered, the person reexperiences unresolved emotional reactions. The empty-chair dialogue is a therapeutic means of encountering the unfinished situation in imagination, especially if the other is unavailable (Perls et al., 1951). The marker of unfinished business is the current experiencing of lingering bad feeling that is related to a significant other but not directly expressed. Its unfinished quality is often evidenced by statements of giving up or nonverbal signs of restricting emotion (L. S. Greenberg & Safran, 1987). Facing an empty chair, the person contacts the imaginary other to express previously inhibited painful emotion. This often involves overcoming an interruptive process wherein affect is stimulated until it is difficult to ignore while accompanying unmet needs are legitimized and expressed. Resolution involves a restructuring of relevant self–other schemas leading to a new understanding of the other and self-affirmation.

An analogue study (King, 1988) comparing the effects of empty-chair dialogue and empathic reflection for unfinished business showed that, 1 week after the session, the empty-chair work resulted in a greater increase in tolerance for the significant other and self-confidence in relation to the significant other. L. S. Greenberg and Foerster (1996) showed that successful conflict resolution involves an intense expression of feelings and needs and a shift in perception of "the other." In an initial study relating process to outcome, Paivio and Greenberg (1995) demonstrated that in a 12-session treatment for clients with unfinished business with a significant other, those who engaged in the empty-chair dialogue with an imagined other had better psychotherapeutic outcomes than those assigned to a psychoeducational treatment. Three further process–outcome studies investigating the empty-chair treatment demonstrated that those clients who had resolution sessions had better sessions following the resolution sessions and better overall treatment outcome than those whose dialogues did not resolve (L. S. Greenberg & Foerster, 1996; Malcolm & Greenberg, 1998; Pedersen & Greenberg, 1996).

The Gestalt empty-chair and two-chair dialogues have been integrated into a new experiential therapy called *process–experiential* (PE) therapy (L. S. Greenberg et al., 1993; see Elliott & Greenberg, this volume, chapter 9). In two successive clinical trials, PE therapy has been compared with CCT and shown to be effective in alleviating depression (see Macroprocesses: Outcome Research section below for further detail). A study investigating the effects of Gestalt two-chair and empty-chair interventions on the therapeutic process (Watson & Greenberg, 1996) showed that PE therapy sessions in which chair dialogues occurred showed significantly greater depth of experiencing, emotional intensity, and a greater degree of problem resolution when compared with CCT sessions.

Macroprocesses: Outcome Research

The following summary of outcome research data documents findings from more than 2,000 clients, half of whom participated in Gestalt therapy and half of whom underwent other kinds of therapy or were untreated controls. Research findings are presented here according to the following clinical subgroups: (a) affective disturbances, (b) psychiatric disturbances and personality disorders, (c) psychosomatic disturbances, (d) substance abuse, and (e) other populations. Both group and individual therapy studies are reviewed in each of these subsections. Finally, the results of long-term follow-up studies are summarized. The comparative studies reviewed compare Gestalt therapy with either CCT or cognitive–behavioral therapy (CBT). A comprehensive overview including meta-analytic data can be found in Strümpfel (in press).

Affective Disturbances

A number of studies have investigated the effects of Gestalt therapy on affective disturbances. Beutler and colleagues (Beutler, Engle, et al., 1991; Beutler, Machado, Engle, & Mohr, 1993; Beutler, Mohr, Grawe, Engle, & MacDonald, 1991) conducted a study on group therapy for depression. Beutler's study involved a three-way comparison of CBT, focused experiential therapy (FEP; a manualized form of Gestalt group therapy), and supportive, self-directed therapy (S/SD). S/SD is an instructed self-help program that was designed to support clients' individual initiatives directed toward healthier functioning with a minimum of therapist's authority and control. With this goal, clients received weekly phone calls from nonprofessionals (graduates) and completed homework in the form of a self-paced reading program in popular psychological literature. Beutler and colleagues (Beutler, Engle, et al., 1991; Beutler, Mohr, et al., 1991) also categorized coping strategies as either internalizing (self-punishment, worry, and compartmentalization) or externalizing (acting out, projecting, and direct avoidance). A variable called *resistance potential*, defined as the extent of opposition behavior to directives from an authority, was also investigated. Findings showed that clients with depression who externalize benefited more from S/SD than from CBT, whereas clients who internalize benefited more from CBT. FEP (manualized Gestalt treatment) produced middle-range results with both externalizers and internalizers, suggesting its flexibility as a form of treatment with both coping strategies. Low-resistance clients benefit more from FEP than from CBT. FEP and CBT showed no difference in the reduction of symptomatology (Beutler, Engle, et al., 1991; Beutler et al., 1993; Beutler, Mohr, et al., 1991; Rosner, Frick, Beutler, & Daldrup, 1999). Results were stable at 3 and 12 months after therapy.

Mulder et al. (1994) compared cognitive and Gestalt group treatment for outpatients with HIV/AIDS who are experiencing depressive symptoms and anxiety. Investigators looked at changes in affective conditions, symptom variables, emotional expression, psychiatric symptoms, coping strategies, and social support sought by the patients. No differences were discernible between the two therapies in immediate treatment effects or at follow-up except in the patient's subjective evaluations. Mulder et al. (1994), who used Gestalt therapy as a control for CBT, concluded that for their sample Gestalt therapy was a good alternative option.

As mentioned earlier, two studies have been conducted comparing CCT and PE therapy for depression (L. S. Greenberg & Watson, 1998a, 1998b). PE treatment uses a client-centered relational base but integrates specific Gestalt interventions at client markers indicating affective–cognitive problems. In both studies, outcome was measured by changes in depressive symptoms, overall symptoms, self-esteem, and interpersonal problems. In Greenberg and Watson's (1998a) study, PE therapy produced quicker changes within clients by the middle of the treatment than CCT on all outcome indices. At the end of therapy, both groups showed significant improvements, and there was no difference between them in the reduction of depressive symptoms. However, clients in the PE group showed greater improvement in self-esteem, interpersonal functioning, and overall levels of symptom distress. At the 6-month follow-up, the groups were indistinguishable on all outcome indices.

Goldman, Greenberg, and Angus (2000) replicated L. S. Greenberg and Watson's (1998a) study and similarly found that both treatments were successful in alleviating depression. In this study, however, PE therapy showed greater improvement in the reduction of depressive symptoms, but there was no difference between the groups in the reduction of overall symptom distress or improvement in self-esteem or interpersonal functioning. Further analysis was conducted that combined the investigators from the two studies. This allowed for a more powerful analysis that compared 36 clients in each treatment group. Results indicated that PE therapy showed greater improvement on all outcome indices: greater reduction of depressive symptoms and overall symptomatology, as well as improvement in interpersonal functioning and self-esteem (Goldman et al., 2000).

Studies of Gestalt treatment for the treatment of simple phobia have also met with success. Johnson and Smith (1997) selected 23 first-year students from a state university on the basis of their responses on subjective and objective measures of simple phobia. The participants were randomly assigned to one of three treatment groups: Gestalt empty-chair dialogues, systematic desensitization, and a no-treatment control. Following treatment, measures were taken of participants' avoidance behavior and their subjective experience. Participants in both treatment groups showed significant reductions in phobic symptoms, as compared with the no-treatment control group. Johnson and Smith concluded that Gestalt empty-chair dialogue is an effective treatment for simple phobia. Ongoing research by Butollo, Krusmann, Maragkos, and Wentzel (1997) that is testing the effects of a combination of behavioral and Gestalt therapy for anxiety and phobias shows promising interim findings. Furthermore, Pauls and Reicherts's (1999) study indicates positive effects for Gestalt treatment for a range of disturbances such as compulsiveness, depression, and anxiety disorders.

The above studies demonstrate that Gestalt therapy in private practice, manualized Gestalt therapy, and PE therapy (a treatment that integrates Gestalt interventions) are effective for a range of affective disorders. To date, the effects of Gestalt treatment on depressive disorders have been investigated most extensively; however, more recent studies have demonstrated similar success in the treatment of anxiety disorders.

Psychiatric Disturbances and Personality Disorders

Gestalt therapy has also been shown to be effective in work with more seriously disturbed psychiatric inpatients. Three studies with small groups of mixed psychiatric patients (Hartmann-Kottek, 1979) and individuals with schizophrenia (Serok, Rabin, & Spitz, 1984; Serok & Zemet, 1983) demonstrate the effectiveness of Gestalt group therapy for severely disturbed inpatients. Serok and Zemet (1983) documented a moderate improvement in the reality perception of individuals with schizophrenia after a 10-week Gestalt treatment in comparison with an untreated group who showed no improvement. In a second study (Serok et al., 1984), in which a Gestalt treatment group was again compared with an untreated control group, individuals with schizophrenia showed a reduction in disturbances in 17 out of 18 measured dimensions. Improvement was demonstrated in the following problem areas: (a) perception of self and others, (b) self and personality functions, (c) nursing staff's evaluation of the prevalence of verbal and physical attacks, and (d) positive contact and communication. Hartmann-Kottek (1979) conducted a study on personality changes with patients experiencing severe personality disturbances such as schizophrenia, severe depression, and compulsiveness. After a 2-month inpatient Gestalt treatment, scores on all but one scale of the personality questionnaires showed a return to the average range. Positive gains were maintained 12 months after discharge, with the exception of one patient.

Group therapy has also been shown to be effective in treating psychiatric outpatients with serious personality disturbances (H. Greenberg, Seeman, & Cassius, 1978). Clients were assigned to either a Gestalt or a control group. Clients in the Gestalt groups showed significant improvement in personality dysfunction, self-image, and interpersonal relationships and assessed the therapy as very helpful. Results are supported by those of Yalom, Bond, Bloch, Zimmerman, and Friedman (1977), who investigated the impact of weekend therapy groups, including a Gestalt group, on individual therapy with moderately disturbed clients. They found a positive effect of weekend Gestalt group therapy on individual therapies as rated by patients and their individual therapists.

Esser, Bellendorf, Groß, Neudenberger, and Bommert (1984) conducted an investigation into the effects of two therapy treatments on 30 clients whose profiles were described as psychoneurotic but similar to those of a psychiatric sample. One treatment combined CCT with selected evocative Gestalt interventions, whereas the other was a CCT treatment alone. Twenty therapists acted as their own controls, seeing clients in both groups for ten 45-minute sessions. Researchers were especially interested in the effect of *evocative Gestalt interventions* on client depth of experiencing. Results showed a significantly higher level of experiencing in clients treated by the combination of CCT and Gestalt evocative interventions, although a significant correlation between depth of experiencing and client success was not demonstrated. Researchers were in fact surprised by this lack of relationship as the study was an attempt to replicate an earlier study that had in fact shown a significant correlation between experiencing and outcome.

The process–outcome study of Cross and colleagues (Cross, Sheehan, & Khan, 1980, 1982; Sheehan & Cross, 1981) is a well-known example of individual therapy with psychiatric outpatients. Patients were assigned to either a combination of Gestalt therapy and transaction analysis (TA) or CBT for a 3-month period. Focusing on macroprocesses in therapy, Cross and colleagues examined the extent to which clients sought support outside therapy sessions from other professional and nonprofessionals, such as friends or priests. Clients in the TA/Gestalt therapy group tended to seek less additional help initially than the clients who received CBT. Findings showed, however, that in the course of 3 months, the CBT clients lost contact with more people to whom they had turned for help than did those in the TA/Gestalt group. Clients in the latter group were able to maintain more contacts in their existing support network. Posttherapy results revealed no significant difference between groups in changes in target symptoms, social and personality functions, and psychiatric estimates of change. It is interesting to note that the TA/Gestalt therapy, while not particularly symptom oriented, did show slightly stronger symptom reduction at the end of the study and greater improvement based on global estimates of therapists. Follow-up data taken 4 and 12 months after treatment revealed no statistical differences between the two groups (Cross et al., 1982). These results are promising in light of the fact that behavioral therapy is traditionally regarded as the treatment of choice for strongly disturbed patients.

Psychosomatic Disturbances

A number of studies carried out in psychosomatic clinics have investigated the effects of Gestalt treatment for both psychosomatic disturbances and chronic pain. A study by Heinl (1998) included 123 patients who were experiencing chronic back pain. Sixty of the patients were divided into three treatment groups. Another 30 patients were divided into two wait-list control groups, whereas the remaining 33 patients were further divided into two control groups. Treatment groups received approximately 40 hours of Gestalt therapy over 5 days. Measures of orthopedic complaints, body sensations, social and other behavior, personality, and pain experience were given. Assessments were conducted at pre- and posttreatment, as well as 10 weeks and 12 months after therapy had been completed. Two statistical analyses of the data were undertaken: The first concerns change on the different variables of the measures named above (Müller & Czogalik, 1995); the second analysis concerns the effects of different treatment factors (Czogalik, Landerer, & Bechtinger-Czogalik, 1995). Improvements were shown in all areas of treatment and were stable at follow-up 1 year after treatment. The greatest changes were found in (a) affective disturbances, (b) distress in experience and behavior, and (c) physical well-being. Changes in clients' reported experience of pain were not as great as change in other psychosocial symptoms. Factor analysis conducted on the 1-year and 2-year follow-up revealed an increase in patients' feelings of acceptance, security, and protection within the group. Similar results were found in analysis of research conducted by Sandweg and Riedel (1998) over a 5-year period in a orthopedic and psychosomatic clinic. During this period, 220 patients were treated with Gestalt therapy. The study included follow-up questionnaires returned 1 and 3 years after therapy had been completed. Patients answered questions about complaints that had originally brought them into the clinic. As with Heinl's (1998) study, greater reductions were found in psychosocial symptoms than in pain itself. However, this result may have been a statistical artifact, because neither study used standardized measures of pain experience. In both studies however, 55% of patients did report a reduction in pain after receiving Gestalt therapy. Another investigation of Gestalt treatment in the context of medical treatment for functional intestinal pain showed that Gestalt therapy led to a reduction in the amount of medication needed to treat the pain (Teegen, Johannsen, & Voght, 1986).

Substance Abuse

Research studies have indicated that Gestalt therapy is effective in the treatment of substance-dependent populations, although results of such studies should be interpreted with care, because much of the therapy has been conducted within the milieu of hospital treatment programs. It is thus not clear whether positive results are the effect of the Gestalt treatment or other social, work, and medical therapies. Nevertheless, Moran, Watson, Brown, White, and Jacobs (1978) studied the psychological and physiological effects of 10 hours of Gestalt and body group therapy for individuals with alcoholism within the context of hospital treatment programs. Positive outcome of this short treatment was evidenced in improvement in blood pressure, anxiety, hysterical symptoms, disturbed feelings, and self-image. Röhrle, Schmölder, and Schmölder (1989) studied the effects of a group therapy that included Gestalt elements integrated in other approaches on depressive symptoms and personality dysfunction in a chemically dependent population. Results revealed a reduction in depressive symptoms and improved personality development at the end of treatment. Treatment gains were maintained at the 4-year follow-up assessment. Another study (Ludwig & Vormann, 1981) on Gestalt and social therapy for chemical dependents showed a long-term abstinence rate of 70% up to 9 years after discharge. The positive effects of Gestalt therapy are further substantiated by findings from an individual Gestalt postcare project with opiate and other substance dependents (Broemer, Rosenbrock, & Szabo, in press). Results have thus far indicated a high patient compliance rate for the program along with an abstinence rate of over 80%.

Other Populations

Gestalt therapy has also been demonstrated to be effective with a range of other populations. Felton and Davidson (1973) gave 61 high school low achievers a 5-month Gestalt treatment. Compared with a control of 18 untreated but similarly disturbed sophomores, therapy led to the adolescents adopting a significantly increased sense of responsibility for their own feelings, actions, and the consequences of their actions, which was in turn directly related to improved academic achievement. Literature has demonstrated that children's learning disabilities and personal maladjustments are often related to relationship difficulties between parents, child-rearing practices, and parents' perceptions of their children. In a study with 23 parents who regarded their children as "problematic," Little (1986) showed that this labeling was often linked with parenting styles based on overly harsh and restrictive attitudes. She reported an improvement in parental styles, including intrinsic valuing of the children, after 5 months of Gestalt treatment, compared with an untreated control group.

Other studies testing Gestalt therapy as a means of preventive psychosocial health care have yielded promising results. For example, in an investigation on relationship treatments for married couples, Jessee and Guerney (1981) compared a Gestalt treatment with a relationship enhancement treatment that taught married couples specific communication and problem-solving skills. Although some changes were difficult to interpret because of sampling errors, both treatments proved highly effective on all variables, such as quality of communication and problem resolution. In a comprehensive study with 250 women, Lobb (1992) showed that women given Gestalt group therapy as part of preparation for childbirth were in labor for much shorter periods of time and, as a result, experienced less pain and had a more positive image of themselves and their relationships than women who received no Gestalt therapy. In his work with senior citizens, Petzold (1979) demonstrated the positive effects of Gestalt therapy with a group of 40 clients, age between 68 and 82, who demonstrated an increased ability to rebuild lost social contacts and achieve more socially integrated lives.

Follow-Up Studies

Two major follow-up studies of Gestalt therapy have been recently completed. One was conducted in Austria with 431 outpatients (Schigl, 1998, 2000), and a second was conducted in Germany where 800 inpatients were treated with experiential therapy that integrated Gestalt interventions (Mestel & Votsmeier-Röhr, 2000). Schigl took the *Consumer Reports* study (Seligman, 1995) as a model for her survey of clients who had completed Gestalt therapy. She supplemented Seligman's questionnaire with two standardized scales. The advantages of a study of this kind are size and the natural quality of therapy. However, the heterogeneity of the sample makes drawing specific conclusions more difficult. For example, the length of therapies varied between 10 and 190 weeks, with an average of 70 weeks. Approximately two thirds of the patients suffered from depression or depression-related states or grief. Almost half of the patients listed conflict with their partners and sexual issues as most problematic, whereas the second most frequent complaint was anxiety and, in some cases, panic. Factor analysis demonstrated that improvements achieved after Gestalt therapy were equal across symptom groups. Of the clients, 73% showed a strong to mid-range improvement in the symptoms and problems that led them to seek therapy; only 5% suffered a worsening in their symptoms. In the areas of social behavior and professional performance, 80% of clients reported substantial increases in feeling pleased with their lives, as well as increased self-esteem and self-respect; they also felt that had more insight into their problems. Another important finding was that half of those clients who had taken psychotropic medication had stopped it at the time of follow-up. The number of clients taking tranquilizers fell by as much as 76%. Ninety percent of all clients reported that they had learned strategies in Gestalt therapy with which to successfully combat any reappearing symptoms.

Mestel and Votsmeier-Röhr (2000) conduced a follow-up study in which 800 patients with depression were questioned between 1 and 3 years after the completion of inpatient psychotherapy. The difficulty in assessing the meaning of the outcome here is similar to the two inpatient studies reported above (Moran et al., 1978; Röhrle et al., 1989). Although Mestel and Votsmeier-Röhr (2000) named Gestalt therapy as their primary experiential modality, one does not know which therapy elements were used when. Outcome instruments used were the Beck Depression Inventory, Symptom

Checklist 90–Revised, Inventory of Interpersonal Problems, and the Structural Analysis of Social Behavior (SASB). As in Schigl's (1998, 2000) study, findings revealed strong to mid-range improvement on the depressive and general symptom index and the self-acceptance scales of the SASB but less improvement on interpersonal problems. These major studies by Schigl (1998, 2000) and Mestel and Votsmeier-Röhr (2000), with their proximity to therapeutic and clinical reality, both support each other and the long-term effects of Gestalt therapy and experiential therapy with Gestalt interventions.

Of 12 studies reported in this Outcome Research section that were carried out under controlled conditions and assessed follow-up data, only 1 study showed evidence of relapse. This was a short treatment that lasted for 10 hours (Moran et al., 1978). Of the remaining, 11 studies, the majority of which conducted follow-up interviews between 4 and 12 months posttherapy, demonstrated stable effects or continued improvement.

FROM RESEARCH TO PRACTICE

Concentration on present experiences is the basic endeavor of Gestalt therapy. In a present moment a client's whole world may unfold; everything she or he has become may be reflected in it. As emotions emerge, surprising and immediate insights may occur. Experiencing is far more important than the therapist's interpretations. For this reason, Gestalt therapists often invite their clients to engage in experiments that will lead to new and valuable emotional experiences.

Emotional Expression

In psychotherapy in general, the importance of emotions has become widely recognized. Within their experimental gestalt framework, L. S. Greenberg and Paivio (1997) provided a theory of emotions based on the role of what they call *emotion schemes* together with a classification of emotions (see also Greenberg, Korman, & Paivio, this volume, chapter 16). In harmony with the concepts of the contact cycle, *emotion schemes* are defined as complex configurations of emotions that govern and guide how one processes one's world. Research has demonstrated the importance of emotions both in the resolution of conflicts and in the success of the therapy process as a whole (Watson & Greenberg, 1996). One of the most important processes in Gestalt therapy is the client's acceptance of his or her own emotions as opposed to the denial, suppression, or projection of them. Perls (1947) first highlighted the importance of emotion in his discussion of aggression turned against the self as an indicator of pathological process.

Most Gestalt therapists today evaluate expressions of pure aggression as cathartic but less curative than originally believed (Beutler, Frank, Schieber, Calvert, & Gaines, 1984). Anger expression, however, that is accompanied by the expression of other previously entangled emotions such as grief and sadness is seen as highly therapeutic, particularly in working through trauma. In Gestalt terms, one says that "emotions must achieve their own separate Gestalt," suggesting that both anger and sadness must each have distinct and full expression to facilitate healing. L. S. Greenberg and his colleagues (Goldman & Greenberg, 1997; L. S. Greenberg & Paivio, 1997; Malcolm & Greenberg, 1998) have articulated and demonstrated how the expression of such primary emotions is associated with the acknowledgment and expression of unmet needs that facilitates either forgiveness or holding the other accountable in trauma work. Similarly, Mulder et al. (1994) demonstrated that the expression of emotions is decisive for coping with traumatization in work with clients suffering from terminal illnesses such as HIV/AIDS. Viola and McCarthy (1994) integrated the Gestalt therapeutic method of dramatization with other interventions in their work with survivors of both the Vietnam and Gulf wars.

Methods and Techniques

Isadore From (1984) warned decisively against reductionist methods wherein Gestalt therapy is represented as the sum of its various techniques. However, although this is a holistic approach, distinct methods and interventions can be identified (From, 1984). The therapist discourages the client from making on-the-spot interpretations, as well as thinking and rationalizing that prevent awareness of emotions and sensory experience. An emphasis away from plans for the future, talking about the past, or thinking in abstractions is encouraged. Awareness can also be achieved by experimenting with the expression of impulses and feelings (Naranjo, 1993). As Gestalt therapy evolved, a number of micro- and macrotechniques have been developed. Microtechniques describe what the therapist does on a moment-to-moment basis, whereas macrotechniques are experiments such as two-chair and empty-chair interventions. We describe some of the most salient types of microtechniques below.

In *repetition* responses, the therapist suggests that the client repeat a gesture, verbal expression, or particular aspect of body language. For example, a client with depression who has no access to his or her feelings might shrug his or her shoulders often. The therapist may ask the client to repeat this gesture several times, while at the same time asking the client about his or her feelings. This may help the client to share with the therapist his or her feelings of profound resignation.

Exaggeration and *elaboration* techniques are based on the same principles of awareness. Clients are asked to repeat and intensify a particular behavior to bring unconscious emotional processes into awareness. Automated aspects of functioning that are not processed in awareness can be brought to the client's attention in this way. If a client tends to grin, the therapist may ask the client to concentrate on his or her facial expression and exaggerate it.

Identification involves the client concentrating on a sensory experience, such as a headache, a feeling of tension, sickness in the stomach, or an element within a dream. This is one of the earliest techniques of Gestalt therapy and can be introduced by the therapist in a number of ways, such as "What do your tears say?" or "Can you give your loneliness a voice?" Identification may be regarded as a projective technique in which primary emotions or reactions like disgust and contempt are discovered and symbolized.

Representing or *dramatizing* is a technique in which clients are asked, for example, to assume the roles of influential people in their lives in staging a family scene. This is often practiced in groups in which different roles may be adopted by different people, but this technique is also effective in individual therapy. This technique is partially informed by psychodrama practices and the possibilities for dramatization are limitless. The enactment of inner conflict helps activate emotional processes and provides a tangible, living stage for the client. Habitual patterns of conflict that have been rigidly repeated over a lifetime become conscious, enabling the client to break the chain of repeated dysfunctional behavior. Dramatizations are also practiced within the context of both the empty-chair and two-chair method. For a more full description of Gestalt therapy techniques, see L. S. Greenberg et al. (1993).

The following case example illustrates the macrointervention of the empty-chair and two-chair dialogues; the microinterventions are embedded within the dialogues. The following dialogues are excerpts from a case with a 27-year-old woman with depression. She has two young children, and her husband is a compulsive gambler. She initially feels both responsible and abandoned when he goes out to gamble, leaving her alone with the children and draining the family of financial assets. Her father was also a compulsive gambler, and her mother had always "put up with it," silently suffering with her pain. On two occasions prior to therapy, the client had left her husband, and her family had basically responded with the message that a good wife "stands by her man." The following dialogue illustrates a sample of an empty-chair dialogue used by the therapist (T) in which the client (C) is working with unfinished business with her mother and in which she eventually forgives her mother (microinterventions are identified throughout in brackets).

C: (toward mother) You expected so much from me; you made me believe that you knew what was right for me, that I should always take care of the children, my younger brothers.

T: Tell her what you missed out on. [identification]

C: (crying) I wanted to be myself. I wanted you to accept me as an individual.

T: Tell your mom what you wanted to hear. [expression of need]

C: (crying) I wanted to hear you say you loved me.

T: Tell her what it was like for you.

C: (crying) It was lonely and confusing, knowing that I did as you said, and I always tried to please you but you never expressed your love. [identification]

T: You feel a lot of sadness with her love not coming to you.

C: I also believe that at the time, it was hard for her. I know what she was going through with my father 'cause of what I went through, um . . . just being stuck in her own confusion because of his gambling.

T: Okay, come over here, and be your mom and tell her how it was for you that you were not able to love her. [dramatization]

C: I was uh very occupied by your father's gambling.

(Later in dialogue—as her mother again:)

C: (crying) I was wanting something I wasn't getting from your father. I wanted to make him see that his family was important. I just felt despair.

T: You felt desperate to try to turn things around.

C: (crying) and um . . . I'm sorry that I didn't allow you to do other things, to have other relationships with your friends or anyone, I needed your help at home . . . as much as you needed your own time with your friends.

In this dialogue, the therapist is encouraging the client to fully express her sadness and acknowledge her unmet need for approval and love from her mother. This allows her to achieve a new understanding of her mother's struggles and how those may have contributed to her inability to be more giving with her daughter. The therapist is encouraging the client's construction of new meaning particularly in relationship to her mother.

What follows is a two-chair work dialogue in which the same client is working with a self-evaluative split. In this excerpt, a shift (softening of the critic or harsh topdog) begins to take shape. (Microinterventions are identified throughout in brackets.)

C: I feel I don't count, that I don't know anything, that I am stupid.

T: OK, come back over here (to critic chair). Make her feel stupid. [dramatizing]

C: You don't count, you're stupid, you are worthless.

T: Again, make her not count. [exaggeration]

C: You're stupid. It doesn't matter what you say, there's no meaning to what you say; you just don't know anything.

> T: OK, come back to this chair. How do you feel when she puts you down and ridicules you? [encouraging emotional expression]
>
> C: Oh (sigh), I just feel like she is right and that is just the way it is.
>
> T: Do you notice when you say this that your shoulders kind of hunch and you slump in your chair. Hunch over like that some more. What is it like to feel so hopeless? [repetition]
>
> C: I just feel so alone (client begins to cry).
>
> T: Yeah, it hurts, give the loneliness a voice. What do you want to say to her? [identification and encouraging emotional expression]
>
> C: It hurts when you talk to me like this (sobbing).
>
> T: Yeah, it hurts when she talks to you like this. What do you want from her? [encouraging emotional expression]
>
> C: I want you to accept me unconditionally. I want you to listen to me.

Later in the dialogue,

> T: Now change back over here (to critic chair). She says she wants to feel she counts and she wants to be heard, accepted. What do you say?
>
> C: Okay, um, yes that is fair [beginning of softening of critic]
>
> T: So, what are you saying, that you understand her need?
>
> C: (crying) Um, yeah, I'm sorry. You don't deserve to be treated like that. [elaboration of softening]

In this dialogue, the therapist helps the client move beyond her feelings of hopelessness to access her primary feelings of sadness and loneliness and accompanying need for approval. Identification and validation of these emotions help to strengthen the self, which allows her to stand up to her critical self. Later in the dialogue, when the client moves into the other chair, her critical self softens and becomes more accepting. As the dialogue ends, the client is beginning to access underlying needs for nurturance.

By the end of a 16-week therapy, the client was no longer depressed and did not feel guilty or responsible when her husband gambled. She showed significant improvement in her self-esteem and interpersonal relationships.

Dreamwork

A survey conducted in Florida on the use of dreamwork by psychotherapists (Keller et al., 1995) showed that the Gestalt method is used more often than the Freudian approach. Prominent Gestalt therapists, such as Polster and Polster (1973), give work with dreams a central place in Gestalt therapy. A number of techniques are used to give dreamwork immediacy. The client is asked to start by telling the dream as if it is occurring in the present, which helps the dreamer relate more directly to the dream's content. The client may also be asked to act out the dream, to identify with a figure or a mood, and to narrate his or her dream experiences from a subjective perspective.

The following dialogue excerpt, extracted from a dream seminar by Fritz Perls (P), exemplifies this type of dreamwork. The participant, Nora (N), is a member of the seminar and is familiar with Gestalt interventions such as identification and dramatization.

> N: In my dream I was in an incomplete house and the stairs have no rails. I climb up the stairs and get very high, but they go nowhere. I know that in reality it would be awful to climb that high on these stairs. In the dream it's bad enough, but it's not that awful, and I always wonder how I could endure it.
> P: Okay. Be this incomplete house, and repeat the dream again.
> (Although familiar with Gestalt methods, Nora shows difficulty getting into the method of identification.)

Later in the dialogue,

> N: I am the house and I'm incomplete. And I have only the skeleton, the parts and hardly the floors. But the stairs are there. And I don't have the rails to protect me. And yet I do climb and—
> P: No, no. You're the house. You don't climb.
> N: Yet I'm climbed on. And I end somewhere on the top, and it—and it leads nowhere and—
> P: Say this to Nora. You're the house, and talk to Nora.
> N: You're climbing on me and you're getting nowhere. And you might fall. Usually you fall.
> P: . . . Now say the same thing to some people here, as the house. "If you try to climb on me . . ."
> N: If you try to climb on me, you'll fall.
> P: Can you tell me more what you're doing to them if they're trying to live in you and so on . . . (Nora sighs) Are you a comfortable house to live in?
> N: No, I am open and unprotected and there are winds blowing inside. (voice sinks to whisper) And if you climb on me you'll fall. And if you'll judge me . . . I'll fall.
> P: You begin to experience something? What do you feel?
> N: I want to fight.
> P: Say this to the house.
> N: I want to fight you. I don't care about you. I do. I don't want to. (crying) . . . I don't want to cry and I don't want you—I don't even want you to see me cry. (cries) . . . I'm afraid of you . . . I don't want you to pity me.
> P: Say this again.
> N: I don't want you to pity me. I'm strong enough without you, too. I don't need you and—I, I wish I don't need you.

Emotions that arise in the course of the telling of the dream are an important source of information that provide insight for the dreamer. Dreams are understood as clients' projections, representing the functioning of the self and the dreamer's existential situation in life. In this example, the client describes an incomplete house and becomes sad and later angry while she identifies with this element. The reworking of dreams offers an opportunity for the client to reintegrate neglected aspects of the self. Perls (1969) commented on Nora's dream:

> Nora's projection is the incomplete house. She does not experience herself at the beginning as an incomplete house. It's projected as if she is living in this house. But she herself is the incomplete house. . . . If you're capable of projecting yourself totally into every little bit of the dream—and really become that thing—then you begin to reassimilate, to re-own what you have disowned, given away. The more you disown the more impoverished you get. Here is an opportunity to take back. The projection often appears as something unpleasant. . . . But if you realize, "This is my dream. I'm responsible for the dream. I painted this picture. Every part is me," then things begin to function and to come together, instead of being incomplete and fragmented. (p. 98)

Later in the session, Perls helps the client contact her self-support functions. Through the method of identification, Nora starts to realize that she, as the house, has the potential for solid foundations and surroundings.

> P: Can you tell this to the group. That you have solid foundations?
> N: You can walk and it's safe, and you could live with it if you don't mind being a little bit uncomfortable. I'm dependable.
> P: So what do you need to be complete?
> N: I don't know. I . . . I don't think I need, I . . . I just feel I . . . I want more.
> P: Aha. How can we make the house a bit warmer?
> N: Well, cover it, close—put windows in it; put walls, curtains, nice colors—nice warm colors.

Working with the client's experience is characteristic of Gestalt therapy. Experiencing is indivisible from emotional processes. On both a micro and macro level, Gestalt therapy has a range of interventions aimed at confronting spontaneously arising emotions in the contact process, and thereby supporting clients in deepening their experience.

CONCLUSION

From the beginning, Gestalt therapy has undergone different developments; however, the basic elements of active dialogical work can be historically traced to the theoretical and practical work of the founding practitioners. Gestalt theory and practice have directly informed research and have been influential in the development of new experiential therapies within the humanistic approach. Gestalt psychotherapeutic techniques have entered a new field of operations with further specifications and delineations. We see this in the moment-by-moment work with emotional processes and the specific use of Gestalt interventions in PE therapy. This development also leads to a renewed awareness of common roots within the humanistic tradition (see Cain, this volume, chapter 1). A good example of this is the use of process diagnosis within PE therapy, a practice that may be used in both Gestalt therapy and CCT (see Elliott & Greenberg, this volume, chapter 9). There seem to be interesting benefits to be gained from the integration of different humanistic approaches under one roof.

The review of empirical research on Gestalt therapy included 60 studies. Both process and outcome studies have advanced the theory and practice of Gestalt therapy. Process research is well suited to the process orientation of Gestalt therapy and has produced models that describe Gestalt techniques, such as in vivo dialogues that exaggerate oppositional tensions and encourage subsequent emotional expression and meaning creation. Important research strategies have been developed to investigate how complex therapeutic processes enable change in therapy by mapping the resolution processes in chair dialogues.

Great advances have also been made in outcome research. Outcome studies have shown the effects of Gestalt therapy for a range of clinical subgroups. Of the studies reviewed, 75% used pure Gestalt therapy as the treatment condition. The remaining 25% reflected the modern psychotherapeutic practice of combining Gestalt therapeutic interventions with other approaches as in PE therapy. Outcome studies have shown the effects of Gestalt therapy to be equal to or greater than other therapies for a variety of disorders. Whereas the methodological weaknesses of earlier studies sometimes obscured the strength of effects, newer studies have shown Gestalt therapy to be most promising, especially with affective and personality disturbances, and most recently, with psychosomatic disturbances and chemical addictions. Furthermore, the effects of therapy are stable in the follow-up studies 1 to 3 years after the cessation of treatment. Gestalt therapy has proved itself to be a viable and effective method for working with emotional disturbances as they arise in different psychological disorders, ranging from mild to moderate problems to severe psychiatric disturbances.

Different aspects of Gestalt therapeutic theory and therapy would benefit from future empirical investigation and exploration. Gestalt therapy works through the medium of present dialogue and experimental tools that are called on in response to emerging impulses and emotional difficulties. Just as process research has given useful insights into emotional change processes, it may also be effective in producing models of the contact process and its interruptions. In addition, further research into the nature of the emotional change processes associated with outcome is recommended. Within the field of humanistic psychotherapy, research and development in Gestalt therapy have shown how powerful and effective therapy can be in helping people lead healthier and more fulfilling lives.

REFERENCES

Angus, L. E., & Rennie, D. L. (1989). Envisioning the representational world: The client's experience of metaphoric expression in psychotherapy. *Psychotherapy, 26,* 372–379.

Beutler, L. E., Engle, D., Mohr, D., Daldrup, R. J., Bergan, J., Meredith, K., & Merry, W. (1991). Predictors of differential response to cognitive, experiential, and self-directed psychotherapeutic procedures. *Journal of Consulting and Clinical Psychology, 59,* 333–340.

Beutler, L. E., Frank, M., Schieber, S. C., Calvert, S., & Gaines, J. (1984). Comparative effects of group psychotherapies in a short-term inpatient setting: An experience with deterioration effects. *Psychiatry, 47,* 66–76.

Beutler, L. E., Machado, P. P. P., Engle, D., & Mohr, D. (1993). Differential Patient × Treatment maintenance among cognitive, experiential, and self-directed psychotherapies. *Journal of Psychotherapy Integration, 3,* 15–30.

Beutler, L. E., Mohr, D. C., Grawe, K., Engle, D., & MacDonald, R. (1991). Looking for differential treatment effects: Cross-cultural predictors of differential psychotherapy efficacy. *Journal of Psychotherapy Integration, 1,* 121–142.

Boulet, D., Souliere, M., & Sterner, I. (1993). Good moments in Gestalt therapy: A descriptive analysis of two Perls sessions. *Canadian Journal of Counselling, 27,* 191–202.

Boulet, D. B., Souliere, M. D., Sterner, I., & Nadler, W. P. (1992). Development of a category system of good moments in Gestalt therapy. *Psychotherapy, 29,* 554–563.

Broemer, H., Rosenbrock, H., & Szabo, K. (in press). ATHERNA—*Erfahrungen und Ergebnisse der ambulanten Therapie mit Drogenabhängigen* [ATHERNA–Experiences and results of outpatient therapy for chemical dependents]. Berlin, Germany: Drogenhilfe Tannenhof Berlin.

Brunink, S. A., & Schroeder, H. E. (1979). Verbal therapeutic behavior of expert, psychoanalytically oriented, Gestalt, and behavior therapist. *Journal of Counseling and Clinical Psychology, 47,* 567–574.

Buber, M. (1984). *Das dialogische Prinzip* [The dialogical principle]. Heidelberg, Germany: Verlag Lambert Schneider.

Butollo, W., Krusmann, M., Maragkos, M., & Wentzel, A. (1997). Integration verschiedener therapeutischer Ansatze bei Angststörungen: Verhaltens und Gestalttherapie [Integrating different therapeutic approaches for anxiety disorders: Behavior therapy and Gestalt therapy]. In P. Hoffmann, M. Lux, C. Probst, M. Steinbauer, J. Taucher, & H. -G. Zapotoczky (Eds.), *Klinische Psychotherapie* [Clinical psychotherapy] (pp. 274–283). Vienna, Austria: Springer.

Clarke, K. M., & Greenberg, L. S. (1986). Differential effects of the Gestalt two-chair intervention and problem solving in resolving decisional conflict. *Journal of Counseling Psychology, 33*, 11–15.

Cross, D. G., Sheehan, P. W., & Khan, J. A. (1980). Alternative advice and counsel in psychotherapy. *Journal of Consulting and Clinical Psychology, 48*, 615–625.

Cross, D. G., Sheehan, P. W., & Khan, J. A. (1982). Short- and long-term follow-up of clients receiving insight-oriented therapy and behavior therapy. *Journal of Consulting and Clinical Psychology, 50*, 103–112.

Czogalik, D., Landerer, W., & Bechtinger-Czogalik, S. (1995). *Wirkfaktoren eines gestalttherapeutisch orientierten Kurzzeitgruppentherapieseminars für Patienten mit chronischen Rückenschmerzen (nach H. Heinl) aus der Sicht der teilnehmenden Patienten* [Factors contributing to treatment in H. Heinl's Gestalt oriented short term group therapy for chronic back pain, from the patients' point of view]. Heidelberg, Germany: Forschungsbericht [Research report].

Esser, P., Bellendorf, E., Groß, A., Neudenberger, W., & Bommert, H. (1984). Auswirkungen einer erlebnisorientierten Psychotherapie auf Prozeß- und Erfolgsmerkmale unter besonderer Berücksichtigung der Klientenvariable "Experiencing" [Consequences of an experience oriented psychotherapy according to process and success factors with special consideration for the client variable "experiencing"]. *Zeitschrift für Personenzentrierte Psychologie und Psychotherapie, 3*, 221–231.

Felton, G. S., & Davidson, H. R. (1973). Group counseling can work in the classroom. *Academic Therapy, 8*, 461–468.

Frew, J. (1988). The practice of Gestalt therapy in groups. *Gestalt Journal, 11*, 77–96.

From, I. (1984). Reflections on Gestalt therapy after thirty-two years of practice: A requiem for Gestalt. *Gestalt Journal, 7*, 4–12.

Goldman, R., & Greenberg, L. S. (1991). *The validation of the experiential therapy adherence measure*. Unpublished master's thesis, York University, Toronto, Ontario, Canada.

Goldman, R., & Greenberg, L. S. (1997). Case formulation in experiential therapy. In T. Eells (Ed.), *Handbook of psychotherapy case formulation* (pp. 402–429). New York: Guilford Press.

Goldman, R., Greenberg, L. S., & Angus, L. E. (2000, June). *Results of the York II comparative study testing the effects of process–experiential and client-centered therapy for depression*. Paper presented at the 31st Annual Meeting of the Society for Psychotherapy Research, Chicago.

Greenberg, H., Seeman, J., & Cassius, J. (1978). Personality changes in marathon therapy. *Psychotherapy: Theory, Research and Practice, 15*, 61–67.

Greenberg, L. S. (1975). A task analytic approach to the study of psychotherapeutic events (Doctoral dissertation, York University). *Dissertation Abstracts International, 27*, 4647B.

Greenberg, L. S. (1980). The intensive analysis of recurring events from the practice of Gestalt therapy. *Psychotherapy: Theory, Research and Practice, 17*, 143–152.

Greenberg, L. S. (1983). Toward a task analysis of conflict resolution in Gestalt therapy. *Psychotherapy: Theory, Research and Practice, 20,* 190–201.

Greenberg, L. S. (1984). A task analysis of intrapersonal conflict resolution. In L. Rice & L. Greenberg (Eds.), *Patterns of change* (pp. 67–123). New York: Guilford Press.

Greenberg, L. S. (1992). Task analysis: Identifying components of intrapersonal conflict resolution. In S. G. Toukmanian & D. L. Rennie (Eds.), *Psychotherapy process tesearch: Paradigmatic and narrative approaches* (Vol. 143, pp. 22–50). Newbury Park, CA: Sage.

Greenberg, L. S., & Clarke, K. M. (1979). Differential effects of the two-chair experiment and empathic reflections at a conflict marker. *Journal of Counseling Psychology, 26,* 1–8.

Greenberg, L. S., & Dompierre, L. M. (1981). Specific effects of Gestalt two-chair dialogue on intrapsychic conflict in counseling. *Journal of Counseling Psychology, 28,* 288–294.

Greenberg, L. S., & Foerster, F. S. (1996). Task analysis exemplified: The process of resolving unfinished business. *Journal of Counseling and Clinical Psychology, 64,* 439–446.

Greenberg, L. S., & Higgins, H. M. (1980). Effects of two-chair dialogue and focusing on conflict resolution. *Journal of Counseling Psychology, 27,* 221–224.

Greenberg, L. S., & Paivio, S. C. (1997). *Working with emotions in psychotherapy,* New York: Guilford Press.

Greenberg, L. S., & Rice, L. N. (1981). The specific effects of a Gestalt intervention. *Psychotherapy: Theory, Research and Practice, 18,* 31–37.

Greenberg, L. S., Rice, L. N., & Elliott, R. (1993). *Facilitating emotional change.* New York: Guilford Press.

Greenberg, L. S., & Safran, J. D. (1987). *Emotion in psychotherapy: Affect, cognition, and the process of change.* New York: Guilford Press.

Greenberg, L. S., & Watson, J. (1998a). Experiential therapy of depression: Differential effects of client-centered relationship conditions and process experiential interventions. *Psychotherapy Research, 8*(2), 210–224.

Greenberg, L. S., & Watson, J. C. (1998b). Forschung zur gestalttherapeutischen Behandlung von Depressionen [Research on a Gestalt therapeutic treatment of depression]. In R. Fuhr, M. Sreckovic, & M. Gremmler-Fuhr (Eds.), *Das Handbuch der Gestalttherapie* (pp. 1121–1135) [Handbook for Gestalt therapy]. Cologne, Germany: Edition Humanstische Psychologie.

Greenberg, L. S., & Webster, M. C. (1982). Resolving decisional conflict by Gestalt two-chair dialogue: Relating process to outcome. *Journal of Counseling Psychology, 29,* 468–477.

Hartmann-Kottek, L. (1979). Schwerpunkt Gestalttherapie im Grenzgebiet der Psychiatrie [Gestalt therapy in the area of psychiatry]. *Psychiatrie und Medizinische Psychologie, 29,* 1–13.

Heinl, H. (1998). Behandlungsergebnisse bei Integrativer Therapie [The results of treatment with integrative therapy]. In H. Riedel & P. Henningsen (Eds.), *Die Behandlung chronischer Rückenschmerzen. Kongreßband zur 6. Fachtagung der Stiftung "Psychosomatik der Wirbelsäule" in Heidelberg* (pp. 103–169) [The treatment of chronic back pain. 6th congress of the foundation "Psychosomatik der Wirbelsaule" in Heidelberg]. Blieskastel, Germany: Stiftung Psychosomatik der Wirbelsäule.

Hycner, R., & Jacobs, L. M. (1995). *The healing relationship in Gestalt therapy: A dialogic/self psychology approach.* Highland, NY: Gestalt Journal Press.

Jessee, R. E., & Guerney, B. G. (1981). A comparison of Gestalt and relationship enhancement treatments with married couples. *American Journal of Family Therapy, 9,* 31–41.

Johnson, W. R., & Smith, E. W. L. (1997). Gestalt empty-chair dialogue versus systematic desensitization in the treatment of phobia. *Gestalt Review, 1,* 150–162.

Keller, J. W., Brown, G., Maier, K., Steinfurth, K., Hall, S., & Piotrowski, C. (1995). Use of dreams in therapy: A survey of clinicians in private practice. *Psychological Report, 76,* 1288–1290.

Kemmler, L., Schelp, T., & Mecheril, P. (1991). *Sprachgebrauch in der Psychotherapie* [Use of language in psychotherapy]. Bern, Switzerland: Huber.

King, S. (1988). *The differential effects of empty-chair dialogue and empathic reflection for unfinished business.* Unpublished master's thesis, University of British Columbia, Vancouver, Canada.

Lesonsky, E. M., Kaplan, N. R., & Kaplan, M. L. (1986). Operationalizing Gestalt therapy's processes of experiential organization. *Psychotherapy, 23,* 41–49.

Lewin, K. (1917). Kriegslandschaft [Warlandscape]. *Zeitschrift für angewandte Psychologie, 7,* 440–447.

Lieberman, M. A., Yalom, I. D., & Miles, M. B. (1973). *Encounter groups: First facts.* New York: Basic Books.

Little, L. F. (1986). Gestalt therapy with parents when a child is presented as the problem. *Family Relations: Journal of Applied Family and Child Studies, 35,* 489–496.

Lobb, M. S. (1992). Childbirth as rebirth of the mother. *Gestalt Journal, 15,* 7–38.

Ludwig, G., & Vormann, G. (1981). Katamnestische Untersuchung für die Therapeutischen Gemeinschaften der STEP-Gem. Gesellschaft für Sozialtherapie und Pädagogik für den Zeitraum, 1973–1980 [Follow-up investigation for the therapeutic communities of the STEP community. Society of social thearpy and pedagogy, 1973–1980]. *Informationen aus der Therapiekette Niedersachsen, 1,* 29–39.

Mahrer, A. R., Nifakis, D. J., Abhukara, L., & Sterner, I. (1984). Microstrategies in psychotherapy: The patterning of sequential therapist statements. *Psychotherapy, 21,* 465–472.

Mahrer, A. R., Sterner, I., Lawson, K. C., & Dessaulles, A. (1986). Microstrategies: Distinctively patterned sequences of therapist statements. *Psychotherapy, 23,* 50–56.

Mahrer, A. R., White, M. V., Howard, M. T., Gagnon, R., & MacPhee, D. C. (1992). How to bring about some very good moments in psychotherapy sessions. *Psychotherapy Research, 2,* 252–265.

Mahrer, A. R., White, M. V., Howard, M. T., & Lee, A. C. (1991). Practitioner methods for heightening feeling expression and confrontational strength. *Psychotherapy in Private Practice, 9,* 11–25.

Malcolm, W., & Greenberg, L. S. (1998). *Relating process to outcome in the resolution of unfinished business in process–experiential therapy.* Unpublished doctoral dissertation, York University, Toronto, Ontario, Canada.

Mecheril, P., & Kemmler, L. (1992). Vergleich des sprachlichen Umgangs mit Emotionen in Gestalttherapie und Psychoanalyse. Ergebnisse einer empirischen Untersuchung [Comparison of the use of language about emotions in Gestalt therapy and psychoanalysis. Results of an empirical investigation]. *Integrative Therapie, 4,* 346–362.

Mestel, R., & Votsmeier-Röhr, A. (2000). *Long-term follow-up study of depressive patients receiving experiential psychotherapy in an inpatient setting.* Paper presented at the 31st Annual Meeting of the Society for Psychotherapy Research, Chicago.

Moran, M., Watson, C. G., Brown, J., White, C., & Jacobs, L. (1978). Systems releasing action therapy with alcoholics: An experimental evaluation. *Journal of Clinical Psychology, 34,* 769–774.

Mulder, C. L., Emmelkamp, P. M. G., Antoni, M. H., Mulder, J. W., Sandfort, T. G. M., & de Vries, M. J. (1994). Cognitive–behavioral and experiential group psychotherapy for asymptomatic HIV-infected homosexual men: A comparative study. *Psychosomatic Medicine, 3,* 271–288.

Müller, I., & Czogalik, D. (1995). *Veränderungen nach einer Integrativen Therapie bei Patienten mit chronischen Rückenschmerzen. Eine Evaluationsstudie* [Changes occurring after an integrative therapy for patients with chronic back pain. An evaluative study]. Düsseldorf, Germany: Abschlußbericht für das Fritz Perls Institut.

Naranjo, C. (1993). *Gestalt therapy: The attitude and practice of an atheoretical experimentalism.* Nevada City, CA: Gateways/IDHHB.

Paivio, S. C., & Greenberg, L. S. (1995). Resolving unfinished business: Efficacy of experiential therapy using empty-chair dialogue. *Journal of Consulting and Clinical Psychology, 63,* 419–425.

Pauls, H., & Reicherts, M. (1999). Empirische Forschung in der Gestalttherapie am Beispiel eines praxisorientierten Forschungsprojektes [Example of empirical research on Gestalt therapy in a practice oriented project]. In R. Fuhr, M. Sreckovic, & M. Gremmler-Fuhr (Eds.), *Das Handbuch der Gestalttherapie* [Handbook of Gestalt Therapy] (pp. 1137–1160). Cologne, Germany: Edition Humanistische Psychologie.

Pedersen, R., & Greenberg, L. S. (1996). *Verification of a model of the resolution of unfinished business.* Unpublished master's thesis, York University, Toronto, Ontario, Canada.

Perls, F. S. (1947). *Ego, hunger, and aggression.* London: Allen & Unwin.

Perls, F. S. (1969). Gestalt therapy verbatim. Moab, UT: Real People Press.

Perls, F. S., Hefferline, R. F., & Goodman, P. (1951). *Gestalt therapy: Excitement and growth in the human personality.* New York: Julian Press.

Petzold, H. (1979). Zur Veränderung der sozialen Mikrostruktur im Alter-eine Untersuchung von 40 "sozialen Atomen" alter Menschen. [Towards change in the micro structure of social life in old age–a study of 40 "social atoms" with old people]. *Integrative Therapie, 1–2,* 51–78.

Polster, E., & Polster, M. (1973). *Gestalt therapy integrated.* New York: Brunner/ Mazel.

Rice, L., Koke, C. J., Greenberg, L. S., & Wagstaff, A. K. (1979). *Manual for client vocal quality* (Vols. 1, 2). Toronto, Ontario, Canada: York University, Toronto Counseling Development Centre.

Röhrle, B., Schmölder, H., & Schmölder, H. (1989). Merkmale sozialer Netzwerke als Kriterien zur Nachuntersuchung von Patienten einer therapeutischen Gemeinschaft [Characteristics of social networks in a follow-up study of patients in a therapeutic community]. *Zeitschrift für Klinische Psychologie, Psychopathologie und Psychotherapie, 37,* 3, 291–302.

Rosner, R., Frick, U., Beutler, L. E., & Daldrup, R. (1999). Depressionsverläufe in unterschiedlichen Psychotherapieformen—Modellierung durch Hierarchische Lineare Modelle (HLM) [Courses taken by depression in different forms of psychotherapy–model construction with hierarchical line models]. *Zeitschrift für Klinische Psychologie, 28,* 112–120.

Sandweg, R., & Riedel, H. (1998). Gibt es Prädiktoren für den Erfolg bei der Behandlung chronischer Schmerzen? [Are there predictors for the success of treatments for chronic pain?] In H. Riedel & P. Henningsen (Eds.), *Die Behandlung chronischer Rückenschmerzen: Grundlagen, Therapiekonzepte, offene Fragen* [The treatment of chronic back pain: Basic principles, therapeutic concepts, open questions] (pp. 171–197). Blieskastel, Germany: Psychosomatik der Wirbelsäule.

Schigl, B. (1998). *Evaluationsstudie zur Integrativen Gestalttherapie: Wirkungen und Wirkfaktoren—aus katamnestischer Sicht ehemaliger KlientInnen* [Evaluative study on integrative Gestalt psychotherapy]. Vienna, Austria: Endbericht zum Forschungsprojekt der Fachsektion für Integrative Gestalttherapie im ÖAGG.

Schigl, B. (2000). Wirkungen und Wirkfaktoren von Gestalttherapie aus katamnestischer Sicht der KlientInnen [Effects and treatment factors of Gestalt therapy from the follow-up point of view of former clients]. *Psychotherapie Forum, 8,* 79–87.

Seligman, M. E. P. (1995). The effectiveness of psychotherapy: The *Consumer Reports* study. *American Psychologist, 50,* 965–974.

Serok, S., Rabin, C., & Spitz, Y. (1984). Intensive Gestalt group therapy with schizophrenics. *International Journal of Group Psychotherapy, 34*, 431–450.

Serok, S., & Zemet, R. M. (1983). An experiment of Gestalt group therapy with hospitalized schizophrenics. *Psychotherapy: Theory, Research and Practice, 20*, 417–424.

Sheehan, P. W., & Cross, D. G. (1981). Alternative advice and support provided during and following short-term insight-oriented therapy and behavior therapy. *Academic Psychological Bulletin, 3*, 371–385.

Singh, M., & Greenberg, L. S. (1992, June). *Development and validation of a measure of the resolution of unfinished business: Relating session change to outcome.* Paper presented at the annual meeting of the Society for Psychotherapy Research, Berkeley, CA.

Sreckovic, M. (1999). Geschichte und Entwicklung der Gestalttherapie [History and development of Gestalt theapry]. In R. Fuhr, M. Sreckovic, & M. Gremmler-Fuhr (Eds.), *Das Handbuch der Gestalttherapie* [Handbook for Gestalt Therapy] (pp. 15–178). Cologne, Germany: Edition Humanistische Psycholgie.

Strümpfel, U. (in press). *Forschungsergebnisse zur Gestalttherapie* [Research findings on Gestalt therapy]. Cologne, Germany: Edition Humanistische Psychologie.

Teegen, F., Johannsen, A., & Voght, K. -H. (1986). Modifikation von Beschwerdehäufigkeit, -intensität und Medikamentenverbrauch bei Klienten mit funktionellen Bauchbeschwerden [Changes in the frequency and intensity of complaints and the use of medicines in the case of clients with functional stomach complaints]. *Integrative Therapie, 1–2*, 39–48.

Teschke, D. (1996). Existentielle Momente in der Psychotherapie [Existential moments in psychotherapy]. In *Fortschritte in der Psychologie: Vol. 18.* Münster, Germany: LIT Verlag.

Viney, L. L. (1994). Sequences of emotional distress expressed by clients and acknowledged by therapist: Are they associated more with some therapists than others. *British Journal of Clinical Psychology, 33*, 469–481.

Viola, J. M., & McCarthy, D. A. (1994). An eclectic inpatient treatment model for Vietnam and Desert Storm veterans suffering from posttraumatic stress disorder. *Military Medicine, 159*, 217–220.

Watson, J. C., & Greenberg, L. S. (1996). Pathways to change in the psychotherapy of depression: Relating process to session change and outcome. *Psychotherapy, 33*, 262–274.

Yalom, I. D., Bond, G., Bloch, S., Zimmerman, E., & Friedman, L. (1977). The impact of a weekend group experience on individual therapy. *Archives of General Psychiatry, 34*, 399–415.

Yontef, G. (1998). Dialogic Gestalt therapy. In L. S. Greenberg, J. Watson, & G. Lietaer (Eds.), *Handbook of experiential psychotherapy* (pp. 82–102). New York: Guilford Press.

Zeigarnik, B. (1927). Das Behalten erledigter und unerledigter Handlungen [Remembering completed and uncompleted actions]. *Psychologische Forschung, 9*, 1–85.

7

FOCUSING-ORIENTED/EXPERIENTIAL PSYCHOTHERAPY

MARION N. HENDRICKS

C: But why in the hell do I get so scared? I mean, I'm just sick to think I have to meet him. I get this feeling like some pressure's gonna come on me. Like . . . like when I was talking to him on the phone today, he goes, "I've really missed you." Wouldn't you think that would make me feel good?

T: It feels like pressure, you say. Can you sense what is the quality of that pressure?

C: I don't know. I mean . . . I . . . I just feel like . . . like he could make me do something that I didn't want to. Or something. Now what could he make me do that I don't wanta do? I don't know.

T: Why don't we just slow down and see if you can sense that. It feels like pressure, like you could do something you don't wanta do. What is your sense of all that?

C: Gee, I'm not sure . . . (deep breath) . . . (long pause) . . . this is kinda dumb; you know, I'm thinking that . . . (tears) . . . I mean, what if I even liked him *more* or something? Or something. I don't know what it is (tears).

T: That you might like him more . . .

C: Uhum . . .

When clients do well in humanistic psychotherapy, this is how they usually sound, regardless of the orientation of their therapist. They pause and grope for words or images. They pay attention to an unclear, but bodily sensed aspect of how they are in a situation. They do not just think about the situation and they do not drown in emotions. They attend to what is called a *bodily felt sense* of a situation or problem. Words or images arise directly from that sense. What comes is often a surprise. A new aspect of experience emerges, a small step of change that brings a body response, like a slight physical easing of tension, or tears, or a deeper breath. This a called *felt shift*. This kind of process is one "motor of change" in psychotherapy. Focusing-oriented/experiential psychotherapy is an interaction in which clients can contact their direct experience in this manner. The emphasis on client experiencing marks the beginning and continuing development of humanistic psychology. This major root of humanistic psychotherapy grew out of a collaboration in the 1950s at the University of Chicago between Carl Rogers, the founder of client-centered psychotherapy, and philosopher Eugene Gendlin. Coming from the philosophical tradition of Wilhelm Dilthey (1833–1911), John Dewey (1859–1952), Maurice Merleau-Ponty (1908–1961), and Richard McKeon (1900–1985), Gendlin developed a Philosophy of the *Implicit* (Gendlin, 1997) and applied it to the work Rogers was doing. He asked what is actually going on when empathic conditions are present. Out of this interaction came a further theory of personality change (Gendlin, 1964) and psychotherapy (Gendlin, 1996), which involved a fundamental shift from looking at content—*what* the client discusses—to the manner of process—*how* the client is relating to experience. From examining hundreds of transcripts and hours of taped psychotherapy interviews, Gendlin and Zimring (1994) formulated the *experiencing level* variable. A Process Scale and eventually the Experiencing Scale (Klein, Mathieu, Gendlin, & Kiesler, 1969; Klein, Mathieu-Coughlan, & Kiesler, 1986) were developed to measure this variable. The hypothesis was that clients who are more successful in therapy would show an increasing ability to refer directly to bodily felt experience, as illustrated in the example above. To the surprise and dismay of Gendlin and colleagues, some findings indicated that experiencing level early in therapy predicted outcome. Clients who began therapy already able to speak from their inner experience did well, and those who started unable to do this did not necessarily learn and had a poorer outcome. In response to the problem that failure could be predicted from the outset, therapists developed specific instructions to teach people how to do this important process, which was termed *focusing* (Gendlin, 1981).

The importance of emotion and the relationship with the therapist have been acknowledged as central to psychotherapy, beginning with Freud's initial emphasis on abreaction and transference. These lines were further developed through the work of Otto Rank and Carl Rogers. Rogers (1959) saw therapy as involving personality change along "a continuum which reaches from rigidity and fixity of psychological functioning . . . to psychological flow and changingness" (p. 96). Going even further in the direction of a process definition of therapy, Gendlin (1996) wrote,

Therapy does not consist mainly of familiar, already defined kinds of experience, whether dreams or emotion, actions or images. Therapy is rather a process that centrally involves experience *before* it becomes one of these defined "packages" and again *afterward* when it dips back into the zone at the edge of consciousness. (p. 4)

Gendlin's contribution was the articulation of the *felt sense*, as distinct from emotions, and his specification of exactly how the therapeutic interaction supports this focusing process. Over the past 40 years, focusing has been applied and researched in other areas, from medicine, business, schools, creative writing, and churches to experiential thinking.

EXPERIENCING: A NEW UNDERSTANDING OF BODY AND ENVIRONMENT

Experiencing refers to what you can sense in your body right now as you read this. Human beings have bodies that live in situations, not just in physical space. A little bit of good news in the mail about a situation you are worried about changes your body. You have been living in that interaction, even though the other person, the letter writer, is in another part of the world. This also happens when someone suddenly understands something you have been trying to say to them. You feel the relief in your body when they get it. Experiencing is neither just "inside" you or just "out there." Human activities are both bodily and environmental. Breathing *is* the air and *is* your lungs. If there is no air, breathing stops and eventually the body structure disintegrates. Living organisms cannot continue to exist apart from activity. It is a powerful philosophical move to put activity or interaction as the basic, first term. It gives us concepts modeled on humans, rather than on mathematical units (Gendlin, 1997). The unit model of our atomistic science has great power in relation to machines, but it is inadequate to understand people. Experiencing is an ongoing process.

Felt Sense: How the Body Is Wise

When we pay attention to our bodily experiencing, we find that it has in it the complexity of how we are living with others. At first this is an unclear, whole sense in your body that does not yet have words or parts but is felt quite distinctly. Stop now for a minute and pay attention to your whole sense of a friendship with someone with whom you love to spend time. It has a distinct feel, before you have yet thought any words. Now sense your relationship with someone who is difficult for you. Again, you have a distinct felt sense, but different from the first one. This fuzzy sense is an intricate mesh of past history, current meanings, the other person, the physical setting, the relationship, and much more. All this is implicitly present. This body sense is not like a cramped muscle, but the body as it lives in a situation. This is called a *felt sense*. It is neither just thinking nor just emotion. It refers to meanings felt in the body.

Carrying Forward: Implied Next Steps of Living

Living implies its own next steps in a highly ordered sequence. In digestion, eating implies saliva in the mouth, which implies juices in the stomach, which implies absorption of nutrients by the blood, which implies elimination of toxins and wastes. If the events that are implied do not occur, there is a disruption of this very fine order. There is trouble. Our felt experiencing has this same implying of next steps in our interactions. Our bodies can also imply brand new action steps. Carl Rogers observed that when therapists expressed empathy, unconditional regard, and congruence, some clients seemed to naturally grow into fuller living, without any content directives by the therapist. He called this the *self-actualizing tendency*. Now we can understand this more exactly when we see that living organisms imply exact next steps.

Reconstituting Blocked Process in Psychotherapy

When a needed interaction is lacking and the implied sequence cannot occur, the body continues to imply its forward living. Sometimes, we can respond to ourselves to change the situation. If we cannot, we may need a new interaction in which our living can be carried forward. Our concern in psychotherapy is to participate in such an interaction. Because a person's experiencing involves language, culture, other human beings, symbols, dreams, actions, or interpersonal behavior, any of these avenues may carry blocked experiencing forward. This is why many different kinds of therapy modalities can be helpful. The interaction with the therapist may provide the opportunity for stopped aspects of the client's living to flow into further process.

Felt Shift: When the Body Eases

When process is blocked, a person goes on in whatever way is still possible, but often with a sense of constriction and pain. When what is implied can eventually occur, this is felt as relief in the body. The attention both therapist and client pay to the client's felt sense allows exact words, images, gestures, or new action steps to arise from the felt sense to carry the body forward into fuller living. This brings an easing in the body that is called a *felt shift*. With many such small shifts, life changes.

Focusing and Experiencing: Defining and Measuring a Process Variable

Research in the client-centered/experiential tradition goes back 40 years. Initially, it consisted of content analyses. The shift to process variables (Gendlin & Zimring, 1994), about *how* the client related to experience, led Rogers to redefine the self in process terms. Clients who self-actualize in successful therapy should become "able to live more fully and acceptantly in the process of experiencing, and to symbolize the meanings which are implicitly in the immediate moment" (Rogers, 1959, p. 102).

Reliability and validity were developed for the Experiencing Scale. Judges were trained separately through standardized materials. The scale measures a continuum, from externalized narrative to inwardly elaborated feeling statements, but this may not be a single variable measure. Middle stages measure the presence of emotions, but focusing on a felt sense is distinctly different from emotions. This begins at Stage 4. The following are excerpts from Klein et al.'s (1969) training manual:

> *Stage 1:* The content is not about the speaker. The speaker tells a story, describes other people or events in which he or she is not involved or presents a generalized or detached account of ideas.
>
> *Stage 2:* Either the speaker is the central character in the narrative or his or her interest is clear. Comments and reactions serve to get the story across but do not refer to the speaker's feelings.
>
> *Stage 3:* The content is a narrative about the speaker in external or behavioral terms with added comments on feelings or private experiences. These remarks are limited to the situations described, giving the narrative a personal touch without describing the speaker more generally.
>
> *Stage 4:* Feelings or the experience of events, rather than the events themselves, are the subject of the discourse. The client tries to attend to and hold onto the direct inner reference of experiencing and make it the basic datum of communications.
>
> *Stage 5:* The content is a purposeful exploration of the speaker's feelings and experiencing. The speaker must pose or define a problem or proposition about self explicitly in terms of feelings. And must explore or work with the problem in a personal way. The client now can focus on the vague, implicitly meaningful aspects of experiencing and struggle to elaborate it.
>
> *Stage 6:* The subject matter concerns the speaker's present, emergent experience. A sense of active, immediate involvement in an experientially anchored issue is conveyed with evidence of its resolution or acceptance. The feelings themselves change or shift.

Stage 7: Experiencing at stage seven is expansive, unfolding. The speaker readily uses a fresh way of knowing the self to expand experiencing further. The experiential perspective is now a trusted and reliable source of self-awareness and is steadily carried forward and employed as the primary referent for thought and action. (pp. 6, 56–63)

Sachse and Neumann (1983) developed a Focusing Rating Scale (FRS), which was validated indirectly against the Experiencing Scale with a correlation of .90. Clients who are able to focus immediately in response to standard instructions were also found to be high on the Experiencing Scale. Focusing distinguishes high and low experiencing. Sachse and Neumann also designed three paper-and-pencil measures that correlate highly with each other and with the FRS. A Post-Focusing Questionnaire and a Post-Focusing Checklist (Wolf & VandenBos, 1971) are two more paper-and-pencil measures. Lambert and Hill (1994) stated, "Perhaps the most widely used and best-researched observer-rated measure(s) of client involvement in the therapy process [is] the Experiencing Scale" (p. 94).

RESEARCH STUDIES

Ninety-one studies are reviewed in this chapter in relation to three research questions: (a) Does experiencing level correlate with psychotherapy outcome? (b) Does focusing correlate with outcome? and (c) Can we teach low-experiencing clients to focus?

Experiencing Level and Session and Therapy Outcomes

Twenty-seven studies have shown that higher experiencing correlates with more successful outcome in therapy. Higher experiencing from averaged, early, middle, and late sessions of therapy and increases in experiencing level over the course of therapy all show this correlation. However, many studies found the correlation only in one of these phases of therapy and not in the others. Outcome has been measured by therapist and client reports, independent evaluations, and objective measures. The positive relation between experiencing level and success has been found with clients in a variety of therapeutic orientations and diagnostic categories. One study (Richert, 1976) showed a negative correlation between experiencing and client satisfaction measured by self-statements at the end of therapy. Leijssen (1996) found no correlation between peak experiencing level measured at the start, middle, or end of therapy and successful therapy outcome, measured by therapist and client ratings on a five-stage improvement scale. The experiencing level and outcome studies are summarized in Table 7.1, listed chronologically by date.

TABLE 7.1
Experiencing Level and Outcome

Study	Experiencing Ratings	Orientation Population	Outcome Measures and Findings
Kirtner and Cartwright (1958)	Manner of process rated for first therapy hour	42 university counseling center clients: CC	Higher process manner in first session differentiated success and failure cases, measured by therapist rating on a 9-point scale.
Tomlinson (1959)	Process scale early sessions, $r = .47-.63$	20 cases: CC	High process early in therapy correlates with better outcome on multiple criteria.
Gendlin, Jenney, and Shlein (1960)	Counselor ratings on "content" vs. "process" scale, 7th and last sessions	39 university counseling center clients, 16 therapists: CC	Counselors rated successful clients higher on 3 process items: express feelings rather than talk about them; uses the therapy relationship as a source of new experience; and uses the relationship as an instance of difficulties the client has in living. Finding is for the last session ratings, not found for 7th-session ratings.
Walker, Rablen, and Rogers (1960)	Process scale change, $r = .83$	6 cases: 3 high success and 3 low success	Successful group, judged by counselor ratings and objective measures, shows more change to higher levels of process.
Tomlinson and Hart (1962)	Process scale early and late sessions, $r = .65$	5 more success, 5 less success; replicated Walker study	High process in early and late sessions discriminates the more- and less-successful cases on multicriteria outcome measures. Therapist and client outcome ratings and Q sort: 4 of 5 in more successful group at Stage 4 and above; in less successful group, none reach Stage 4.
Truax and Carkhuff (1965)	Depth of intrapersonal exploration scale ratings of every 5th session	14 schizophrenic patients	The greater the patient's intrapersonal exploration, the greater degree of constructive personality change, measured by change of pre- and posttests and time spent hospitalized.

continued

TABLE 7.1 Continued

Study	Experiencing Ratings	Orientation Population	Outcome Measures and Findings
Ryan (1966)	Experiencing change, $r = 77$	Diverse 32 university counseling center clients	Higher experiencing in clients relates to better outcome, measured by Hunt Kogan Movement Scale and Terminal Counselor Ratings of Client Self-Perception.
Rogers, Gendlin, Kiesler, and Truax (1967)	Experiencing average for treatment course, $r = .76$; .79	14 schizophrenics; control group	Higher experiencing correlated with therapist and client ratings of success, scores on the MMPI Schizophrenic scale, and time out of hospital.
Tomlinson and Stoler (1967)	Change	Schizophrenics and neurotics	Success correlates with increased experiencing for whole group. Neurotics higher than schizophrenics.
Van der Veen (1967)	Process scale: case means over 5 sessions spread across the therapy	15 schizophrenics; also analyzed subgroups of most and least successful	Higher average process level related to better combined outcome score and MMPI change score and clinicians rating score. Slope scores not significant. Most successful subgroup showed more patients reaching high stages of the process scales.
Gendlin, Beebe, Cassens, Klein, and Oberlander (1968)	Experiencing scale early sessions and change	Reanalysis of 8 neurotics and 12 schizophrenics	Higher experiencing in early sessions and more increase in success. Schizophrenic group starts lower on experiencing than neurotic group.
Fishman (1971)	Experiencing late, $r = .92$; early ns	Dynamic	Therapist, client, and independent measures of success correlate with high experiencing in late sessions.
Kiesler (1971)	Sessions 1–30 rated on experiencing (included reanalysis of Rogers's data for psychotic clients), $r = .79$	38 clients (12 psychotic, 26 neurotic): CC, Adlerian, Freudian, and electic	More successful clients have higher experiencing in both groups: Successful neurotics have highest experiencing, followed by less successful neurotics; more successful schizophrenics are next, and less successful schizophrenics last. Neurotics higher on experiencing than schizophrenics at all points. No overlap. However, the mean scores of all clients were in the low stages of the scale (1.77–2.44).

Study	Experiencing measure	Sample	Results
Custers (1973); cited in Klein et al., 1969	Experiencing change, early ns	Neurotic	More change to higher experiencing over the course of therapy relates to better outcome, measured by MMPI and Q-sort scores.
Richert (1976)	Experiencing samples from latter half of therapy	26 clients, 13 therapists	Higher experiencing level relates to less satisfaction at end of therapy, measured by pre–post change in clients' satisfaction with self-descriptions that included positive and negative self-statements.
Bommert and Dahlhoff (1978)	Experiencing at mid-early sessions	Neurotic	Successful group had a mean of 4.18. Less successful 3.51 for mid-therapy sessions. Early session no relation between experiencing and success.
Jennen (1978)	Late $r = .80$ change	13 patients	Higher experiencing relates to better outcome on Inner Support scale of Personal Orientation Inventory.
Greenberg and Rice (1981)	Experiencing during two-chair work	Gestalt	In split resolution, both chairs start out at low experiencing and reach high experiencing as resolution occurs.
Luborsky (1982; cited in Klein et al., 1986)	Early peak composite residual gain	Dynamic	Whole sample no relation of experiencing to success. In a subsample of male outpatients, more successful had higher peak experiencing.
Nixon (1982)	Pretherapy	Primal	Client ratings of success correlate with higher experiencing in a pretherapy consultation session.
Elliott et al. (1982, 1983)	Average over therapy, 10 sessions	Eclectic-psychodynamic, single case	Higher experiencing ratings highly correlated with client overall session effectiveness ratings.
Greenberg (1983)	Experiencing during two-chair work	Gestalt 14 resolution, 14 nonresolution	Higher experiencing in 14 instances of two-chair resolution compared with 14 instances of nonresolution.
Ikemi, Kira, Murayama, Tamura, and Yuba (1986)	Experiencing on least and most successful sessions	5 dyads, 5 focusing sessions	Focusers selected most and least successful sessions. Experiencing higher in successful sessions.

continued

TABLE 7.1 Continued

Study	Experiencing Ratings	Orientation Population	Outcome Measures and Findings
Johnson and Greenberg (1988)	Experiencing scale	Emotionally focused marital	Good outcome associated with higher experiencing in "blaming spouse."
Kubota and Ikemi (1991)	Experiencing rating of video segments	18 physicians, 14 students	Sessions rated as successful by the clients had higher client experiencing peak levels.
Leijssen (1996)	Experiencing ratings from start, middle, and end of therapy	40 clients: CC	No correlation between peak experience and therapist or client ratings on 5-stage improvement scale.
Warwar (1996)	One low- and one high-experiencing session for each client	16 depressed, 16–20 sessions divided into CC or process–experiential	High experiencing sessions correlated with better session outcomes. Therapeutic modality not related to success of sessions.
Goldman (1997)	2nd-session experiencing, theme-related experiencing ratings for second half of therapy, $r = .78$	35 depressed, 17 CC, 18 process–experiential	Higher experiencing in 2nd session predicts outcome. Second half of therapy theme-related experiencing at Stage 4 and even more at Stage 6 correlates with success on residual gain scores on Beck Depression Inventory, Symptom Checklist 90–Revised, and at Stage 6 with Rosenberg Self-Esteem Scale.
Adams (1999)	Therapist Experiencing Scale	34 depressed, CC, or process–experiential	Therapist higher-experiencing level correlates with successful client outcome measured on Self-Esteem Scale, Beck Depression Inventory, and Symptom Checklist 90–Revised.

Note. All studies are significant at $p = .05$ or better unless noted. r = interjudge reliability obtained on experiencing ratings; CC = client-centered therapy; MMPI = Minnesota Multiphasic Personality Inventory; *ns* = nonsignificant.

Klein et al. (1969) said of the early studies, "experiencing . . . ratings of brief therapy segments are consistently and highly reliable, and yield a meaningful differentiation between more and less successful cases and between neurotics and schizophrenics" (p. 11). Seeman (1996) reviewed and summarized the results of seven of the early studies. He concluded that "initial high levels of experiencing are likely at a better than chance level to facilitate a fruitful therapy outcome and that increase in level of [experiencing] during therapy is associated with positive therapy outcome" (p. 15).

In an elegantly designed recent study using residual gain scores on outcome measures and hierarchical regression analyses, Goldman (1997) found that higher experiencing in Stage 2 correlated with greater reduction in depression symptoms. However, theme-related experiencing levels, at Stage 4 and even more so at Stage 6 in the last half of therapy, are even stronger predictors for reduction in depressive symptoms, and Stage 6 predicts an increase in self-esteem. This study advances the research method by the use of theme-related experiencing. Rather than the usual procedure of random sampling from sessions, segments are identified in which the client is speaking about important themes. These segments are then rated for experiencing level. As in some of the early studies, higher experiencing in initial sessions predicts success, but further increases in experiencing during therapy strengthen successful outcome. Another recent study (Warwar, 1996) took one high-experiencing and one low-experiencing session from each of 14 clients with depression and found that higher experiencing sessions correlated with better session outcomes. Similarly, Kubota and Ikemi (1991) found that sessions rated as successful by clients had higher client experiencing levels. Comparing instances of two-chair conflict resolution with nonresolution in Gestalt therapy, Greenberg (1983) found that experiencing was higher for the resolution group during the "merging" phase. Adams (1999) found that higher *therapist* experiencing level during sessions correlated with increased self-esteem and decreased symptoms in clients at termination of therapy.

Focusing and Psychotherapy Outcome

Twenty-three studies found that focusing, measured by instruments other than the Experiencing Scale, correlated with successful outcome. One study (Loynes, 1984) found that focusing did not correlate with outcome measures of client hostility or depression.

In a Belgian study, Leijssen (1996) audiotaped 810 sessions from 26 clients over 6 years and conducted a series of analyses. In an initial study, she examined sessions with explicitly positive and negative evaluations by client and therapist. To be included as positive, the client had to say something spontaneously about the helpfulness of the session, without the therapist asking. Transcripts of the complete sessions were read, and focusing was judged as present when the therapist gave a focusing instruction and the client accepted the invitation, or when the client spontaneously did one of the six steps of focusing. Seventy-five percent of positive sessions contained focusing, and only 33% of negative sessions contained focusing.

In a second analysis, all of the clients who successfully terminated therapy in less than 20 sessions were studied. Leijssen (2000) noted,

> Remarkable was the prominent use of focusing in all eight cases. Almost every session acquired an intense experience-oriented character and the client discovered aspects of the problem which had remained hitherto out of reach. All these clients achieved contact with their bodily felt experience without being flooded by it. Four of these clients seemed to find a personal form of self-transcendency during focusing. (p. 10)

Sachse's (Sachse, Atrops, Wilke, & Maus, 1992) research over many years has not been reviewed in depth in the United States. He found that clients who received focusing instructions as part of client-centered therapy (CCT) had significantly better outcomes on Therapist Success Ratings, Client Ratings of Success, and the Client Change in Behavior and Experience Questionnaire than clients who received only CCT. In a second phase, Sachse's FRS was applied to tape-recorded *first* sessions for each client in the focusing group. Clients were rated on how far they were able to progress in the steps of focusing, and then were divided into high (Stage 4 and above) and low groups. The clients in the high-focusing subgroup scored better on the Therapist Success Rating and the Client Change in Behavior and Experience Questionnaire. Focusing ability in the first session predicted outcome. It was concluded that just the introduction of focusing instructions into CCT has a significant, positive effect on successful therapy outcome. The study also supports the finding that focusing predicts success from the beginning of therapy.

Sachse (1990) found that "depth" of client experiencing in the middle phase of therapy is related to success, measured by objective personality tests, and even more so with therapist estimates of success. In further studies, the therapists of successful clients made significantly more "deepening processing proposals" than the therapists of less successful clients, and a higher percentage of the successful clients responded to them. Iberg (1998) also found that client-rated focusing events were related to improvement in therapy, measured on the Symptom Checklist Outcome Questionnaire. Lietaer and Neirinck (1986) asked clients in postsession questionnaires what they felt had happened in sessions that were "really helpful." A content analysis was done using a category system derived from the data. A cluster of focusing-related factors (deep exploration of experience, experiencing fully, and fruitful self-exploration) were most often identified as helpful and best discriminated the most from least successful sessions.

Focusing-oriented therapy has been found to correlate with successful outcome for prison inmates (Goldman, Bierman, & Wolfus, 1996; Wolfus & Bierman, 1996), patients with psychoses (Egendorf & Jacobson, 1982; Gray, 1976; Hinterkopf & Brunswick, 1975, 1979, 1981), the elderly (Sherman, 1990), and patients with health-related issues (Grindler & Flaxman, 1999; Holstein & Flaxman, 1997; Shiraiwa, 1999). Focusing achieved desensitization as effectively as the use of behavior therapy in a single case study design (Weitzman, 1967), and focusing was equivalent to rational–emotive therapy in successful stress management (Weld, 1993). Focusing and Gestalt therapy were both found to be effective in resolving a specific therapy task and on outcome measures, compared with a control group, but Gestalt therapy was more effective than focusing alone (Greenberg & Higgins, 1980). Focusing was included as part of the process–experiential therapy treatment condition in several studies (Elliot et al., 1990; Greenberg & Watson, 1998) that showed change effects comparable with behavioral studies of patients with depression.

Can Clients Be Taught to Focus and to Increase Experiencing Level?

This question is important, given the replicated finding that focusing or higher experiencing in first or early sessions predicts successful outcome and that short-term successful clients focus during every session. Thirty-nine studies found that focusing or experiencing level can be increased by training or specific therapist interventions.

Durak, Bernstein, and Gendlin (1997) measured client experiencing in two therapy sessions before and two after focusing training. The whole group was higher on experiencing after training. Of the 10 clients who started at an experiencing level below 3, 6 clients were rated as effectively trained. Of these 6 clients, 4 were then successful in therapy. Of the 4 clients who started low and were not successfully trained, 1 succeeded. Of the 7 clients who were high on experiencing in pretraining sessions, 6 were successful in outcome. This study indicates that people who come into therapy without the ability to focus can be trained to do so and are then able to succeed in therapy.

Eleven more studies (Bierman et al., 1976; Clark, 1980; Gibbs, 1978; Hinterkopf & Brunswick, 1975, 1979, 1981; Leijssen, 1996; McMullin, 1972; Olsen, 1975; Schoeninger, 1965; VandenBos, 1973) found that experiencing level or focusing ability can be increased by training, although the increase is not always maintained after training is completed. Clients identified a number of factors that helped them focus: having a listener who refers to the focuser's experiencing and who helps the focuser find a right distance from the problem, creating a safe space (Tamura, 1987, 1990) and trusting one's experiencing, and "clearing a space" (Morikawa, 1997).

Therapists Can Help Clients Focus During Sessions or Can Hinder Them

In a series of studies, Sachse (1990) conducted fine-grained analyses and found that therapist *processing proposals* can deepen or flatten subsequent client responses. He developed a Client Processing Scale and a Therapist Processing Scale, based on Gendlin's experiencing theory. The higher stages represent focusing. The Therapist Processing Scale rates the level that the therapist intended to facilitate in the client. Sachse established reliabilities between .79 and .94. An initial study analyzing 1,520 triplets (client–therapist–client statement units) from 152 clients at mid-therapy found that clients deepened their process 70% of the time when the therapist made a deepening proposal and flattened their process 73% of the time when the therapist made a flattening proposal. As mentioned earlier, therapists of more successful clients made more deepening proposals than did those of less successful clients, and the more successful clients accepted the deepening proposals their therapists made more often than did less successful clients. These findings are corroborated by three studies (Adams, 1999; Hitz, 1994; Yakin, 1970) that used the Experiencing Scale to analyze triplets. Elliott and colleagues (Elliott, Cline, & Shulman, 1982; Elliott, Klein, & Mathieu-Coughlan, 1983) found greater residual gain in experiencing following therapist interventions rated as high in helpful experiencing, depth, and empathy.

Two studies (Gibbs, 1978; Jennen, 1978) found that therapist qualities of empathy, depth, or high therapist experiencing level correlated with higher client experiencing level. One study (McMullin, 1972) showed that even when therapists were instructed to deliberately not express empathy or positive regard, client experiencing level still increased when focusing instructions were given. Most researchers have looked at the effect of therapist interventions or conditions on client experiencing. Several studies looked at the impact of higher client experiencing on the client's perception of the therapist. Van der Veen (1967) found that higher experiencing clients perceived their therapists as more congruent and that client experiencing level predicted the perception of the therapist's congruence and empathy 3 months later. Elliott et al. (1982, 1983) found that higher client experiencing segments correlated with the following therapist statement being rated as more helpful by both therapist and client. It appears that experiencing level of clients may affect a therapist's own capacity to be helpful.

Other studies found focusing training or higher experiencing level in trainee therapists, compared with controls, correlated with more empathy

(Corcoran, 1981), better ability to sustain facilitative communication during action-oriented skills training (Rennie, Brewster, & Toukmanian, 1985), and scoring higher on spontaneity, feeling reactivity, regard, and facilitativeness, rated by volunteer clients (Swaine, 1986; p = .06–.09).

Therapist interventions in other orientations increased experiencing level or focusing ability from pre- to postmeasures or compared with controls. This included good psychoanalytic interpretations (Fretter, 1985; Silberschatz, 1977), Gestalt (Greenberg, 1980; Greenberg & Rice, 1981), guided daydream (Smith, 1980), encounter group training (Tetran, 1981; cited in Klein et al., 1986), and reevaluation co-counseling (Riemer, 1975). Meditation (King, 1979) plus focusing, as well as galvanic skin response biofeedback training plus focusing (Henderson, 1982), increased experiencing more in comparison with focusing instructions alone. Gestalt two-chair work increased experiencing more than focusing instructions with empathic responses did. Not only did the Gestalt work increase experiencing level, but it moved it into the higher range, which is focusing (Greenberg & Higgins, 1980). Except for this study, it is not clear whether any of these other interventions increased focusing ability or just emotional involvement, because stage data for the increase are not reported.

Training Therapists to Focus Helps Their Clients Focus

Sachse (personal communication, June 29, 1998) developed a training model for therapists. He hypothesized that therapists who focus and also understand it theoretically will be better able to help clients focus. Standardized focusing instructions are not as helpful as when the therapist adjusts the focusing intervention to "fit" a particular client. Forty therapists received focusing training for 6 months and were rated for focusing ability on the FRS. The therapists then did focusing sessions with their clients. These sessions were judged for "realized fit"—the therapist's capacity to give client-specific focusing invitations. The intent was to help the client arrive at a felt shift by working with intervening process steps. The therapist must respond to both the content and process, in what Sachse called *process empathy*. Therapist focusing ability and technical knowledge score predicted ability to fit instructions to the client at a highly significant correlation of .75 (p = .001). Two further studies (R. Sachse, personal communication, 1999) found a high correlation between the therapist fit ability and the client's ability to focus. Focusing or high experiencing has physiological, cognitive, attentional, and personality correlates that are beyond the scope of this chapter.

Some of the early outcome studies can be faulted methodologically because reliability is low, sample sizes are small, and control groups are lacking, or there is a small spread of experiencing level, with few clients reaching the higher ranges (Brodley, 1988). Higher experiencing can improve therapy outcome without reaching the focusing stage, but if clients at Stage 4 and above are looked at separately, as in Goldman's (1997) study, the correlations with successful outcome are even stronger.

For clients who can focus immediately, usually the therapy process is quickly and successfully established. Helping the client trust this already-developed capacity leads to steps of change. For clients who lack this ability, learning it becomes a crucial issue.

FROM RESEARCH TO PRACTICE

The Interaction Is First

The basic criterion of focusing-oriented psychotherapy is whether the client's experience is being carried forward in the moment in the particular interaction with the therapist. As therapists, we want to interact with our client in such a way that the client can contact a bodily felt sense of life situations. To do this requires that we respond to that which is vague and unclear, at the edge of the client's attention. If we predefine or rely on a technique or model to form our responses, we will not be able to hear what is sensed by the client but not yet articulated. Many clients have only a fragile connection to their felt sense. If we do not respond to it, then they cannot enter into it further.

Listening Is the Baseline

As therapists, we listen to the person's experience, rather than to our ideas about the person. We say back what the client *intends* to convey. This allows the client to resonate the words or images against the felt sense and correct them or see what emerges next. We listen to the texture and intricacy in experience and respond to the unclear edge from which steps of change come. What will carry forward the client's experience is very exact. Just this word, action, or image touches or moves something, while many others do not. We try to protect the emergent process, knowing it is more likely than anything we might come up with to carry experience forward. Therefore, the therapist's baseline behavior is an empathic listening attitude. This attitude includes the basic Rogerian concept of empathy but adds a sensitivity to the not-yet-articulated but directly sensed edge of the client's experience.

When the Client and Therapist Both Respond to the Felt Sense

In the session below, we see what focusing looks like when it is working. Sometimes we think of focusing in steps. Although not formally named in this example, the client forms a *felt sense*, *asks* (inner questions are directed into the felt sense), *symbolizes* (lets words or images emerge from it), *resonates* (checks to see if there is a response in the body to the words), and *receives* (makes welcoming, nonjudgmental room inside for what has come). There are a series of small felt shifts and beginning small steps of change. This client (C) is in her early 30s and has related a dream. The therapist (T) invites the client to get a felt sense of the whole thing.

T1: Can you sense where in all that you want to pay attention? [Focusing question]

C1: (Silence as she checks inside.) The only place I can really *connect to feeling-wise* is if I say to myself . . . "maybe my infinite energy doesn't have to come through being sexual, maybe I can let it . . . maybe it just wants to come now . . ."

[The client has found the issue that has a bodily felt dimension, rather than just words.]

T2: I want to say that back to you . . . [Saying back welcomes the person, and exactly whatever content came and lets the client resonate the words with her felt sense.] You get a real feeling response when you say, "maybe now the spiritual can come in its own form, it doesn't have to come only through being sexual."

C2: Yes. And that's very hard for me but that *feels like the right place.* [What she means by "place" is a felt sense in her body. What she means by "right" is a quality of resonance. Her body says, "yes, that is right," and she also senses that there is more that wants to open right at that point.]

T3: Oh, *there's something that's hard about that.*

[The therapist is acknowledging the client's felt sense. Notice that he says "something." He and the client are both comfortable with the edge being unclear. The therapist has no need for the content to be clear before it arises.]

C3: (Silence as she asks herself what is in this sense of "hard") . . . There's *some way that I don't want to let go* of it only coming through the sexual space . . . [Beginning symbolization from felt sense. She doesn't yet know in what way this is true, but can sense there is "some" way. It is sensed but not yet in words.] . . . like . . . that's the only place I've known it coming through, so to let loose at all . . . maybe then I won't have it at all . . . *That's where it is* [Felt shift] . . . (begins to cry— a whole body response) . . . It's like . . . it's so important to have a channel. [Creates a metaphor] So if they came along and said, "well move over here and you can have an even wider channel. . . ." It's so scary (sobs) cause (sobs) what if you lose the only channel you have . . .

T4: I see.

C4: *There's more there* [Felt sense]. . . . *What is that?* [She is asking into her felt sense. This is not a cognitive or deductive question.] . . . *Why is that so scary?* [Again she is asking right into her felt sense, which then starts to open.] . . . It's also *something in it like.* . . . (sobs) Keeping the channel only sexual also narrowed how much energy could come through or something . . . some part of it is really scary. . . . *Maybe I could really live in relation to that energy all the time* if I didn't restrict it to that channel [Symbolization]. [Felt shift]

T5: Scary to live in relation to it all the time?

[The therapist is confused by the fact that this content is the *opposite* of the previous statements. There is an exact experiential order in this kind of process but it is different than the order of logic.]

C5: Uh hum . . . I've always been hidden. It's saying, "don't do that anymore. . . . Look! . . . *Let your energy be visible, use it, live in it, that would be such a change in who I am!* . . . Be in it in the daylight. [Change step] [She is being more visible right now.]

T6: Uhmm . . . let it manifest, perceive it, see it . . . [Welcoming, reflecting]

C6: Right . . . (big sigh) . . . (crying) . . . take it seriously . . . (big sigh, breath, quieter . . . laughs) . . . that old energy still wants to pull me down and back into that dark hole . . . but, it's a little more free, it's moved a little, it's like, "oh, maybe there is a road."

When people focus they use language in a new way. Notice the frequent use of open pronouns such as *something, it,* and *some.* Words are being used to point toward the felt sense that is not in words but is tangibly present. There is no way to use content words yet, without closing the felt sense.

When the Therapist Fails to Respond to the Client's Felt Sense

Unfortunately, it can happen that the client is close to focusing and the therapist does not recognize the client's felt sense. Because the therapist is the expert, the client may become confused, feel inadequate, defer to the therapist's authority, and disconnect from his or her direct experience. We saw in Sachse's study that a "flattening" response by the therapist leads to a flattening of experiential depth in 73% of subsequent client responses. There is an unhappy stalemate, which the therapist may interpret as resistance on the client's part, when it really is an undeveloped capacity in the therapist that is the problem.

C1: And yet I feel . . . *there's something underneath it all but I don't know what* . . . [Felt sense] and if I kind of knew what it was . . . I might feel differently, I don't know. But it's *vague right now.*

T1: Okay. If things could be a little more *definite.* If you were really able to *identify the cause* . . . you really think that you'd be able to *cope* with it then. But right now you can't seem to put your finger on what the *real problem* is.

C2: Yuh . . . and . . . that . . . like when you say that . . . that makes me mad because I feel . . . you know like I'm . . . intelligent. I can figure things out. And yet . . . right now I don't know what the hell's going on with me.

The therapist is unable to respond to the client's felt sense, which is the rich, intricate, not-yet-known place from which movement would come. The client has given a clear prescription of what needs to happen next. She literally tells the therapist that if she could just sense more into this unclear place underneath it all, she has a sense that something would move from there. Because the therapist does not know about this level of process, he uses his words in a cognitive, closed, defined way that cannot point to or invite the client's felt sense to open. The client is left self-critical and, probably, rightfully, angry at the therapist. This kind of interaction under-scores the need for therapists to develop this sensitivity as part of their training. The therapist could have pointed to the felt sense, "You can sense something right there underneath . . ." which would have helped the client stay next to her felt sense so that it might open.

When Clients Do Not Focus

There has been a great elaboration over the years of how to help clients learn to focus when it is not spontaneously present (Hendricks, 1986; Leijssen, 1990, 1998; Weiser Cornell, 1996; Wiltschko, 1996). Because a felt sense is initially a vague body sense of a whole situation, it can be elusive, especially compared with intense, obvious emotions or to interpretations that let people feel they understand themselves. The following excerpts illustrate some typical difficulties faced by clients and how we as therapists can respond to help a felt sense form.

Getting a Felt Sense Instead of Just Thinking or Reporting

When clients do not know how to focus, there are several typical problems. Clients can be stuck in ideas about themselves instead of seeing what is actually in their felt experience. The client below felt fearful in his legal work and offered ideas about why he might be afraid. The therapist invites the client to sense directly into that whole thing he calls "fear." The client is unable to do so and continues to get involved in ideas about it. The therapist again invites him to form a felt sense. He is able to briefly do so, but then jumps back up to the level of ideas and analyzing. But this has been a beginning.

> T1: So *wait for a minute* and let's see if we *can sense what the fear is.* Can you do that? Is that a right question? *Where in all this would you like to sense into it more?*
> C: (Client does not stop and form a felt sense. He continues on with his ideas and analysis.) Yeah. I think that's right. I know in the last

sessions there's been a tremendous duality in the images we found. Freedom and resistance. Adult and baby. An assertive pushing out into the world and a pushing away. Which would also be freedom and separateness.

T2: So there are all kinds of ideas about it, but let's *just stay with sensing the fear. Can you feel it right now? Can you sense that whole thing about work that feels fearful in your body right now?*

C3: (Silence) *Part of the scary feeling is a vague sense* [Felt sense] of being adrift and groping.

T3: Adrift and groping . . .

C4: *Like I'm in outer space and I can't grab onto anything* . . . [Words coming from felt sense and creating a metaphor.]

T4: Can you just check that image of you groping and can't grab anything in your body. Does that feel right?

C5: Very much. [Resonating] . . . And now that I have it I remember having similar kinds of images in different sessions in different ways.

A client like this will often say things like, "Well, I probably feel this way because of the way my parents treated me when I was little" or "My therapist says I must have been very angry as a child to have withdrawn so much." Such clients do not have their own direct sense. Connections do not emerge from their own process but are imposed on their experience either by themselves or by the therapist. This kind of client is also likely to narrate many reports of events during the week with no reference to personal felt meaning of the events.

Getting Distance Instead of Drowning in Emotions

The other dead-end in therapy comes when clients drown in emotions. They just reexperience painful events or feelings. Focusing distinguishes between emotions and a felt sense. An emotion is narrower and tends to be the "universal" response to given situations; for example, if someone dies, one is sad. To get a felt sense, one must step back and form one's own complex, unclear sense of some "whole thing." This will be particular to the individual. The elderly client below has suffered from a very severe depression all of his life and has been completely identified with intensely painful emotions.

C1: I feel very upset. I cannot take action. I didn't call him and follow through. I never follow through. I've been this way my whole life. I think this is related to my mother always saying to me, "Dan, remember, you are very sick." I feel terrible. Now I will be depressed all week. I don't want to leave feeling like this! (The client is angry, agitated, and depressed.)

This is familiar. Any approach to his relationship with his mother sends him down a chute of extreme bad feeling. He may not sleep well and his agitation and depression interfere with his life for several days. He is unable to process this experience. He is simply retraumatized each time.

> T1: Well, this is an old place, where you just slide into that bad feeling. That's an old familiar place. We don't need it. Let's see. *Why don't you put that outside of you. That was her, not you. Let's put that whole thing about her out there* on the other side of the room.
>
> C2: (Looking slightly startled and puzzled.) I didn't know I could do that!
>
> T3: Well you can just take that *whole thing about her and put it all as far away as you need to get it out of your body. How about across the river in New Jersey?*
>
> C3: (*Client begins to laugh!*) *Yeah! I think that would be good!* (*Gestures with his hands as he pushes that whole thing about her out from his stomach area* toward the river.) [Clearing a space and getting distance.]
>
> T4: You have a right to have some space for you.
>
> C4: I do? (Slightly tearful) That's the first time in my life I ever had the feeling that I didn't have to accept that. [Small felt shift with body easing.]

This client gradually became able to discern when he was not at the right distance from emotions. Falling into emotions is not focusing, nor are abreaction or catharsis.

Friendly Focusing Attitude Instead of the Inner Critic

Getting a felt sense and letting it unfold requires an inner attitude of friendliness, waiting, listening, and tolerating not yet knowing what will come. Many people have trouble maintaining this attitude. They attack or disrupt themselves. Often, just at the point when clients come to the edge of what they know, they back away with a comment like, "Oh, I don't know" or "This is too stupid" or "It's too vague" or "It's not clear." It is just at this edge, when they are finished with what they have already thought, that a felt sense can form. A self-attacking attitude is one of the major blocks to focusing. Therapists have many ways to help clients move past these disruptions. Below is a simple example in which the client begins the session attacking herself and the therapist ignores the self-attack and the content details of her story. Instead, the client is invited to step back and form her felt sense of the whole situation. She is able to do so. What unfolds from her felt sense surprises her and is a small felt shift. Notice how differently the client feels and how much better connected to herself she is after this simple exchange.

> C1: I feel like no one wants to relate to me. Like *something is wrong with me* and I don't know what. Like *I am a monster.* [Self-attack] I know what set off the feeling. Maybe I should tell you that. I feel like I'm never going to have just regular relationships. Last night at church

. . . (She tells of a brief conversation with a friend about babysitters in which she ended up feeling criticized by her friend.)

T1: So, can you just step back a little and get a sense for that whole situation, that whole thing with her. What is your sense of the situation?

C2: (She is quiet, getting a felt sense, and then begins to cry.) *Oh! I know what it is. I was so excited!* [Symbolization from felt sense.] My daughter wants to babysit so much and I thought it was going to happen. And I feel like I spoiled it . . . I felt so excited I think I didn't pay attention to what was coming back to me from her. I just kept talking because I was so excited and I wanted it to happen. . . . *Actually now that I think of it, I did feel sort of like I didn't really agree with some of the way she was thinking* about child care. I remember feeling like *she seemed sort of overly protective or rigid in her approach.*

T2: So, in your excitement you really didn't pay attention to some of your own signals. You actually didn't like what she was saying, but you didn't stop and pay attention to your own feeling.

C3: Yeah . . . that's right . . . I feel better now that I have a sense of what happened for me.

The emergence of the words, "Oh! I know what it is. I was so excited!" is a small felt shift. The words are new and surprising to the client. The content "excitement" is quite different from "I am a monster." And the movement of the felt sense into words that carry her forward in her body is felt as relief and tears, a whole body response. Change is directly felt in the body in this kind of therapy. The client does not need to speculate about whether she is changing. It is an immediate experience.

Implied Forward Direction and the Emergence of Steps

Sometimes the felt sense does not respond to waiting and sensing into it with the question, "What is in this whole sense?" Then we can ask a different kind of question. We ask, "What is needed here?" or "What would be right to happen next?" These are not abstract, intellectual questions, but rather focusing questions that ask directly into the felt sense of what would carry life forward now in this situation. The organism implies next steps. Then we wait and see if something forms. The example below marks a turning point in therapy for a client with a severe posttraumatic stress disorder when her body responds to the question, "What does it need now?" The client has been unable to find a proper distance from her abuse experience and so cannot focus on it. She has flashbacks, partially dissociated states, is chronically hypervigilant, and feels terror most of the time. She feels deep grief that, even though she functions at a high-level job, normal life is passing her by and she will never be able to have children because she cannot tolerate sexual contact with her husband. When she focuses, what always comes is her longing to have a child. She is 38 years old.

C: The tension level has been even more than usual and it's unbearable even the way it usually is. There's a racing in my chest. Nothing we are doing is touching this. Nothing touches it. I'm taking something like twenty pills a day right now and nothing is any different than it's ever been. I don't know what to do.

Therapist and client spend about 40 minutes trying to find some way to work with this tension, to no avail. The client is unable to get a felt sense of it and nothing else helps either. She remains locked in this awful tension state that has no psychological content. The therapist then asks the client this other kind of focusing question, trying to engage her body's own knowledge or implying of what is needed now.

T1: So, why don't you gently bring your attention in the front part of your body. Keeping your attention there, let's see if we can *get a sense, maybe an image of what would help. Let's ask inside, "What does it need now for all this whole thing to gently ease, so you can feel OK in your body?"*
C1: (Long silence) *I get two things* [Words emerging from the felt sense.] . . . . One is if I didn't have to leave until I wasn't worried anymore about leaving. If I didn't have to be aware of the clock ticking. . . . And I got another thing. A dog—a Collie. (She begins to cry.) [Felt shift with body response.] I don't know if I've told you but when I was a kid and so scared all the time, so terrified, I used to ask my parents for a dog, a Collie, like Lassie. Lassie sat on Timmie's bed and would have protected him from anyone coming in the window, so no one could hurt him. And Lassie was his friend and kept him company too. I used to feel a Collie could make me less scared and be my friend. Every single Christmas, every birthday, anytime I would ever get anything, I would ask them for just that one thing, a dog. They always said if I did something a certain way or for long enough or whatever, they would give me one. But they never did. They always said I didn't do whatever it was good enough or some other excuse. (She is still crying.)
T2: So you knew even then, as that little person, something that would help, but they wouldn't do it.
C2: Dan (her husband) says they were really mean not to give it to me.
T3: Yeah, I was just feeling the same thing. I feel mad at them. But, *that whole thing is what comes now. A feeling that if you had your own Lassie that would help, would let the tension ease inside.* [Therapist is returning to the felt sense. By saying it back the client can reconnect to it.]
C3: I asked Dan could we get a Collie. He said yes. But I'm the one who always nixes it. (She gives many practical reasons why it would be difficult.)
T4: But, maybe it would be right, now. *You have a feeling sense that getting a dog would make you feel more safe in the inside place and like there was company.* [Again the therapist is returning to the point at which there was an opening, a felt sense of what would help.]

C4: Yeah. Last week Dan and I were in the bookstore. He found me reading a book on training Collies. He said, "I'll buy it for you." I said, "Naw. That's OK."

T5: So, maybe you could start with getting the book? [Therapist is suggesting a small step of change.]

C5: Yeah, maybe. Dan said he was scared if I got a dog I would stop trying to get pregnant.

T6: No, it isn't like that. Having a warm living creature to love and take care of would help your body relax into getting pregnant. . . . *Maybe it would be right to let yourself have* that now. . . . You could get a dog for yourself now. [Therapist is still trying to protect and make room for the step that came, so it isn't overwhelmed by all these objections.]

C6: Maybe I could get that small kind of Collie that only grows to two feet.

T7: Well, how about not compromising, but really doing what that place needs?

C7: (She is quiet for awhile. A laugh wells up in her body.) Hey! For Christmas! I could get my Lassie for Christmas.

T8: Oh yes! That's just right.

Notice that the client feels better in her body. She has cried and laughed. Her body is no longer locked in contentless agitation. The client's felt sense has responded to our focusing question of what is needed to ease this whole awful tenseness. The therapist tries hard to get the client to receive, protect, and make room for this step that her body has formed. Getting a dog is certainly not the therapist's idea or a traditional formula for treating this kind of problem. It emerged from the intricate complexity of this person, now.

Four months later, the client commented,

C: The other day I was looking at Tucker [her Collie], how big she is and I was thinking about how we roll around on the grass and wrestle and squeal and chase each other. I thought, "Gee, I'm glad you're not some little fluff dog. You're my real Lassie." . . . I thought of you saying to me . . . remember how I said, "Well maybe I could get a toy Collie," and you said, "How about not compromising. How about getting your real Lassie." I think that's a metaphor for a lot of things.

Twenty months later in a note to her therapist, the client wrote,

You've probably looked at the picture I sent. . . . Leah (her baby daughter) is getting big. . . . She is such a joy to me. I can't even put it into words in any kind of right way. I just hold her and cuddle her and thank God every day for her. I wish we had about four!

Focusing touches a level in us that has its own direction and momentum. When we as therapists can get out of the way, the organism creates and implies precise next interactions. We are too often trained to relate to our client's experiencing through concepts or techniques. We are supposed to be "experts." In our anxiety to perform well, we can impose our concepts, missing the experiential intricacy and the unfolding inherent in the client's own process. The small needed steps of change that emerge directly from the client's felt sense of the problem are more creative and exact than we can generate.

CONCLUSION

Clients from different cultures, in a variety of therapy orientations, with a variety of diagnoses, do better if they focus. The therapeutic relationship can allow this capacity to develop and be sustained, until it becomes available to clients in their everyday living. Focusing-oriented/experiential therapy works with a level of human process that is still not well known. It is not emotion, not thoughts, not literal body sensations. It is rather a felt sense of our situations. This process can probably be found by every human being. Having learned focusing, one spends time with a bodily sense of a situation, problem, difficulty, or puzzle, without yet having words or symbols. At such an unclear edge, new and creative steps of living emerge. This could be a dancer waiting for next steps in her choreography, or a poet sensing for the right word, or a physicist pursuing an implicit sense of the answer to a puzzle. As therapists, we can sometimes point to this felt sense level by asking the client the simple question, "How does that whole situation feel in your body?" This may immediately deepen the process. More often, small responses over a period of time enable a client to focus.

The research developed in a historical sequence: from the early studies relating experiencing to outcome, to the formulation of focusing, and then to the many studies on teaching focusing to clients, therapists, and others. Recent clusters of sequential studies in Canada, Belgium, and Germany have produced studies with good reliabilities and more sophisticated designs that build on and replicate the findings of the early studies. Successful therapy outcome and session outcome, measured by therapist, client, and objective ratings correlate with experiencing or focusing. Focusing also relates to health, physiological, and personality measures. This accumulation of theory, research, and practice anchored in experiencing has influenced many subsequent developments in the humanistic psychotherapies. The kind of experiencing going on in the client and the therapist's capacity to respond to the client's bodily felt sense and implicit meanings appear to be factors across orientations. A wider implication of the new kind of concepts is the development of a first-person science that will move beyond orientations and identify central processes. There may be social implications in the capacity to discern one's own sense of a situation and allow steps to emerge rather than to be imposed. This capacity frees people from predefined forms, whether they be those of the internal critic or the external oppression of societal roles or ideologies.

REFERENCES

Adams, K. (1999). The effects of therapist's experiential focus (Doctoral dissertation, York University, Toronto, Ontario). *Dissertation Abstracts International.*

Bierman, R., Davidson, B., Finkleman, L., Leonidas, J., Lumly, C., & Simister, S. (1976). *Toward meeting fundamental human needs: Preventive effects of the human service community.* Unpublished report, Guelph, Ontario, Canada.

Bommert, R., & Dahlhoff, H. D. (1978). *Das Selbsterleben (Experiencing) in der Psychotherapie* [Experiencing in Psychotherapy]. Munich: Urban & Schwarzenber.

Brodley, B. (1988, May). *Does early-in-therapy level predict outcome?* Paper presented at the Second Annual Meeting of the Association for the Development of the Person-Centered Approach, New York City.

Clark, D. B. (1980). Effects of experiential focusing with psychotherapy patients. *Dissertation Abstracts International, 41*(2-B), 684. (University Microfilms No. 8017688).

Corcoran, K. (1981, July). Experiential focusing and human resource development: A comparative study of pre-conceptual and conceptual approaches to the training of empathy. *Dissertation Abstracts International A, 42/01,* 384. (University Microfilms No. AAC 8112725).

Durak, G., Bernstein, R., & Gendlin, E. T. (1997, Fall/Winter). Effects of focusing training on therapy process and outcome. *The Folio: A Journal for Focusing and Experiential Therapy, 15,* 7–14.

Egendorf, A., & Jacobson, L. (1982). Teaching the very confused how to make sense: An experiential approach to modular training with psychotics. *Psychiatry, 45,* 336–350.

Elliot, R., Clark, C., Wexler, M., Kemeny, M., Brinkerhoff, V., & Mack, C. (1990). The impact of experiential therapy of depression: Initial results. In G. Lietaer, J. Rombauts, & R. Van Balen (Eds.), *Client-centered and experiential psychotherapy in the nineties* (pp. 549–577). Leuven, Belgium: Leuven Uniersity Press.

Elliott, R., Cline, J., & Shulman, R. (1982). *Effective processes in psychotherapy: A single case study using four evaluative paradigms.* Unpublished manuscript, University of Toledo.

Elliott, R., Klein, M. H., & Mathieu-Coughlan, P. L. (1983, July). *A sequential analysis of empathy and experiencing: A case study.* Paper presented at the meeting of the Society for Psychotherapy Research, Sheffield, England.

Fishman, D. (1971, September). *Empirical correlates of the Experiencing Scale.* Paper presented at the 79th Annual Convention of the American Psychological Association, Washington, DC.

Fretter, P. B. (1985). The immediate effects of transference interpretations on patients' progress in brief, psychodynamic psychotherapy (Doctoral dissertation, University of San Francisco). *Dissertation Abstracts International, 46* (6-A), 1519.

Gendlin, E. T. (1964). Personality change. In P. Worchel & D. Byrne (Eds.), *A theory of personality change* (pp. 102–148). New York: Wiley.

Gendlin, E. T. (1996). *Focusing-oriented psychotherapy.* New York: Guilford Press.

Gendlin, E. T. (1997). *A process model.* New York: Focusing Institute.

Gendlin, E. T. (1981). *Focusing.* New York: Bantam.

Gendlin, E. T., Beebe, J., III, Cassens, J., Klein, M., & Oberlander, M. (1968). Focusing ability in psychotherapy, personality, and creativity. In M. M. Shlien (Ed.), *Research in psychotherapy* (Vol. III, pp. 217–241). Washington, DC: American Psychological Association.

Gendlin, E. T., Jenney, R., & Shlien, J. M. (1960). Counselor ratings of process and outcome in client-centered therapy. *Journal of Clinical Psychology, 17,* 73–77.

Gendlin, E. T., & Zimring, F. (1994). The qualities or dimensions of experiencing and their change. *Person-Centered Journal, 1*(2), 55–67.

Gibbs, B. (1978). Effects of therapist and subject experiencing levels on the therapeutic process (Doctoral dissertation, California School of Professional Psychology). *Dissertation Abstracts International, 40*(8-B), 3927.

Goldman, R. (1997). Change in thematic depth of experiencing and outcome in experiential psychotherapy (Doctoral dissertation, York University, Ontario, Canada). *Dissertations Abstracts International, 58*(10-B), 5643.

Goldman, R., Bierman, R., & Wolfus, B. (1996, June). *Relating without violence (RWV): A treatment program for incarcerated male batterers.* Poster session presented at the meeting of the Society for Psychotherapy Research, Amelia Island, FL.

Gray, J. P. (1976). *The influence of experiential focusing on state anxiety and problem-solving ability.* Unpublished doctoral dissertation, California School of Professional Psychology, Los Angeles.

Greenberg, L. S. (1980). An intensive analysis of recurring events from the practice of Gestalt therapy. *Psychotherapy: Theory, Research and Practice, 17,* 143–152.

Greenberg, L. (1983). Toward a task analysis of conflict resolution in Gestalt intervention. *Psychotherapy: Theory, Research and Practice, 20,* 190–201.

Greenberg, L. S., & Higgins, H. M. (1980). The differential effects of two-chair dialogue and focusing on conflict resolution. *Journal of Counseling Psychology, 27,* 221–225.

Greenberg, L., & Rice, L. (1981). The specific effects of a Gestalt intervention. *Psychotherapy: Theory, Research and Practice, 18,* 31–37.

Greenberg, L., & Watson, J. C. (1998). Experiential therapy of depression: Differential effects of client-centered relationship conditions and process experiential interventions. *Psychotherapy Research, 8,* 210–224.

Grindler-Katonah, D., & Flaxman, J. (1999). *Focusing: An adjunct treatment for adaptive recovery from cancer*. Unpublished manuscript, Illinois School of Professional Psychology.

Henderson, J. (1982). The effect of training with biofeedback and experiential focusing on increasing experiencing ability (Doctoral dissertation, University of Southern California). *Dissertation Abstracts International, 43*(6-A), 1836.

Hendricks, M. N. (1986, May). Experiencing level as a therapeutic variable. *Person-Centered Review, 1*, 141–161.

Hinterkopf, E., & Brunswick, L. K. (1975, Spring). Teaching therapeutic skills to mental patients. *Psychotherapy: Theory, Research and Practice, 12*, 8–12.

Hinterkopf, E., & Brunswick, L. (1979, Winter). Promoting interpersonal interaction among mental patients by teaching them therapeutic skills. *Psychosocial Rehabilitation Journal, 3*(1), 20–26.

Hinterkopf, E., & Brunswick, L. K. (1981, Fall). Teaching mental patients to use client-centered and experiential therapeutic skills with each other. *Psychotherapy: Theory, Research and Practice, 18*, 394–402.

Hitz, L. C. (1995). *Effects of changes in experiencing level of therapist responses on client experiencing*. Dissertation Abstracts International: Section B: The Sciences & Engineering, 55, 8–B.

Holstein, B., & Flaxman, J. (1997, Fall/Spring). The effect of focusing on weight loss. *The Folio: A Journal for Focusing and Experiential Therapy, 15*(2), 29–46.

Iberg, J. R. (1998). *Exploring the relationships between focusing-oriented therapy and the OQ 45.2*. Unpublished manuscript.

Ikemi, A., Kira, Y., Murayama, S., Tamura, R., & Yuba, N. (1986). Rating the process of experiencing: The development of a Japanese version of the Experiencing Scale. *Japanese Journal of Humanistic Psychology, 4*, 50–64.

Jennen, M. G. (1978). *Relationship and interaction between therapist conditions, client depth of experiencing during therapy and constructive personality change in individual psychotherapy*. Unpublished manuscript.

Johnson, M. E., & Greenberg, L. S. (1988). Relating process to outcome in marital therapy. *Journal of Marital and Family Therapy, 14*, 175–183.

Kiesler, D. J. (1971). Patient experiencing level and successful outcome in individual psychotherapy of schizophrenics and psychoneurotics. *Journal of Consulting and Clinical Psychology, 37*, 370–385.

King, J. W. (1979). *Meditation and the enhancement of focusing ability*. Unpublished doctoral dissertation, Northwestern University, Evanston, IL.

Kirtner, W. L., & Cartwright, D. S. (1958). Success and failure in client-centered therapy as a function of initial in-therapy behavior. *Journal of Consulting Psychology, 22*, 329–333.

Klein, M. H., Mathieu, P. L., Gendlin, E. T., & Kiesler, D. J. (1969). *The Experiencing Scale: A research and training manual*. Madison: Wisconsin Psychiatric Institute.

Klein, M. H., Mathieu-Coughlan, P., & Kiesler, D. J. (1986). The Experiencing Scales. In L. Greenberg & W. Pinsof (Eds.), *The psychotherapeutic process: A research handbook* (pp. 21–71). New York: Guilford Press.

Kubota, S., & Ikemi, A. (1991). The manner of experiencing and the perceived relationship: A study of one-shot interviews. *Japanese Journal of Humanistic Psychology, 9,* 53–66.

Lambert, M. J., & Hill, C. E. (1994). Assessing psychotherapy outcomes and processes. In A. E. Bergin & S. L. Garfield (Eds.), *Handbook of psychotherapy and behavior change* (p. 94). New York: Wiley.

Leijssen, M. (1990). On focusing and the necessary conditions of therapeutic personality change. In G. Lietaer, J. Rombauts, & R. Van Balen (Eds.), *Client-centered and experiential psychotherapy in the nineties* (pp. 225–250). Leuven, Belgium: Leuven University Press.

Leijssen, M. (1996). *Focusingprocessen in clientgericht-experientiele psychotherapie* [Focusing processes in client-centered-experiential psychotherapy]. Unpublished doctoral dissertation, Katholieke Universiteit Leuven, Leuven, Belgium.

Leijssen, M. (1998). Focusing microprocesses. In L. S. Greenberg, J. C. Watson, & G. Lietaer (Eds.), *Handbook of experiential psychotherapy* (pp. 121–154). New York: Guilford Press.

Leijssen, M. (2000). Die Staerken und Grenzen von Focusing: Einige Forschungsergebnisse [The power and limitations of focusing]. In H. J. Feuerstein, D. Mueller, & A. Weiser Cornell (Eds.), *Focusing im Prozess* [Focusing in process] (pp. 217–236). Cologne, Germany: GwG Verlag und FZK Verlag. (An English version, *The Power and Limitations of Focusing: A Few Research Findings,* is available from The Focusing Institute, 34 East Lane, Spring Valley, NY 10977)

Lietaer, G., & Neirinck, M. (1986, November). Client and therapist perceptions of helping processes in client-centered/experiential psychotherapy. *Person-Centered Review, 1,* 436–455.

Loynes, J. L. (1984). *Effects of experiential focusing on anger experiences of separated or divorced men.* Unpublished doctoral dissertation, Michigan State University.

McMullin, R. E. (1972). Effects of counselor focusing on client self-experiencing under low attitudinal conditions. *Journal of Counseling Psychology, 19,* 282–285.

Morikawa, Y. (1997). Making practical the focusing manner of experiencing in everyday life: A consideration of factor analysis. *Journal of Japanese Clinical Psychology, 15*(1), 58–65.

Nixon, D. (1982). *The relationships of primal therapy outcome with experiencing, voice quality and transference.* Unpublished doctoral dissertation, York University, Toronto, Ontario, Canada.

Olsen, L. E. (1975). *The therapeutic use of visual imagery and experiential focusing in psychotherapy.* Unpublished doctoral dissertation, University of Chicago.

Rennie, D. L., Brewster, L. J., & Toukmanian, S. G. (1985, January). The counsellor trainee as client: Client process as a predictor of counselling skill acquisition. *Canadian Journal of Behavioural Science, 17,* 16–28.

Richert, A. (1976, April). Expectations, experiencing and change in psychotherapy. *Journal of Clinical Psychology, 32,* 438.

Riemer, R. (1975). *Effects of brief reevaluation counseling on experiential focusing.* Unpublished doctoral dissertation, California School of Professional Psychology.

Rogers, C. (1959). A tentative scale for the measurement of process in psychotherapy. In E. A. Rubinstein & M. B. Parloff (Eds.), *Research in psychotherapy* (pp. 96–107). Washington, DC: American Psychological Association.

Rogers, C. R., Gendlin, E. T., Kiesler, D., & Truax, C. B. (1967). *The therapeutic relationship and its impact: A study of psychotherapy with schizophrenics.* Madison: University of Wisconsin Press.

Ryan, R. (1966). *The role of the experiencing variable in the psychotherapeutic process.* Unpublished doctoral dissertation, University of Illinois.

Sachse, R. (1990). The influence of therapist processing proposals on the explication process of the client. *Person-Centered Review, 5,* 321–347.

Sachse, R., Atrops, A., Wilke, F., & Maus, C. (1992). *Focusing: Ein emotionszentriertes Psychotherapie-Verfahren* [Focusing: An emotion-centered psychotherapeutic technique]. Bern, Switzerland: Verlag Hans Huber.

Sachse, R., & Neumann, W. (1983, December). ProzeBmodell zum focusing unter berucksichtigung spezifischer probleme [Process model for focusing under consideration of specific problems]. *GwG-info: Informationsblatter der Gesselschaft fur wissenschaftliche Gesprachspsychotherapie, 53,* 51–73.

Schoeninger, D. W. (1965). *Client experiencing as a function of therapist self-disclosure and pre-therapy training in experiencing.* Unpublished doctoral dissertation, University of Wisconsin, Madison.

Seeman, J. (Fall 1996/Winter 1997). Level of experiencing and psychotherapy outcome. *The Folio: A Journal for Focusing and Experiential Therapy, 15,* 15–18.

Sherman, E. (1990). Experiential reminiscence and life-review therapy with the elderly. In G. Lietaer, J. Rombauts, & R. Van Balen (Eds.), *Client-centered and experiential psychotherapy in the nineties* (pp. 709–732). Leuven, Belgium: Leuven University Press.

Shiraiwa, K. (1999). Focusing and support group activities for those who live with cancer. *The Folio: A Journal for Focusing and Experiential Psychotherapy, 18,* 47–50.

Silberschatz, G. (1977). *The effects of the analysts neutrality on the patient feelings and behavior in the psychoanalytic situation.* Unpublished doctoral dissertation, New York University.

Smith, D. (1980). The effect of guided daydreams on the experiencing and imagery of patients in psychotherapy (Doctoral dissertation, Fuller Theological Seminary, School of Psychology). *Dissertation Abstracts International, 41*(4-B), 1528.

Swaine, W. T. (1986). Counselor training in experiential focusing: Effects on empathy, perceived facilitativeness and self-actualization. *Dissertation Abstracts International, 47*(4-A), 1197.

Tamura, R. (1987). Floatability: A focuser variable related to success in focusing. *Japanese Journal of Humanistic Psychology, 5*, 83–87.

Tamura, R. (1990). The interrelation between the focuser–listener relationship and the focuser's floatability during focusing. *Journal of Japanese Clinical Psychology, 8*, 16–25.

Tomlinson, T. M. (1959). *A validation study of a scale for the measurement of the process of personality change in psychotherapy.* Unpublished master's thesis, University of Wisconsin.

Tomlinson, T. M., & Hart, J. T., Jr. (1962). A validation study of the process scale. *Journal of Consulting Psychology, 26*(1), 74–78.

Tomlinson, T. M., & Stoler, N. (1967). The relationship between affective evaluation and ratings of outcome and therapy process with schizophrenics. *Psychotherapy, 4*, 14–18.

Truax, C. B., & Carkhuff, R. R. (1965). Client and therapist transparency in the psychotherapeutic encounter. *Journal of Counseling Psychology, 12*(1), 3–9.

VandenBos, G. R. (1973). *An investigation of several methods of teaching "experiential focusing."* Unpublished doctoral dissertation, University of Detroit.

Van der Veen, F. (1967). Basic elements in the process of psychotherapy: A research study. *Journal of Consulting and Clinical Psychology, 31*, 395–403.

Walker, A., Rablen, R., & Rogers, C. (1960). Development of a scale to measure process change in psychotherapy. *Journal of Clinical Psychology, 16*, 79–85.

Warwar, N. (1996). The relationship between level of experiencing and session outcome in client-centered and process-experiential therapies (Depression). *Dissertation Abstracts International.* (University Microfilms No. MAI Vol 34–06).

Weiser Cornell, A. (1996). *The power of focusing.* Oakland, CA: New Harbinger.

Weitzman, B. (1967). Behavior therapy and psychotherapy. *Psychological Review, 74*, 300–317.

Weld, S. E. (1993). Stress management outcome: Prediction of differential outcome by personality characteristics. *Dissertation Abstracts International, 54*(1-B), 513.

Wiltschko, J. (1996). Focusing therapy: Part 1. Some basic statements. *The Folio: A Journal for Focusing and Experiential Therapy, 14*, 55–77.

Wolf, L., & vandenBos, G. (1971). *Experiential focusing: New research tools.* Unpublished paper. (Available from The Focusing Institute, 34 East Lane, Spring Valley, NY 10977)

Wolfus, B., & Bierman, R. (1996). An evaluation of a group treatment program for incarcerated male batterers. *International Journal of Offender Therapy and Comparative Criminology, 40*, 318–333.

Yakin, P. (1970). *A test of Gendlin's theory of personality change.* Unpublished doctoral dissertation, University of Chicago.

8

EXISTENTIAL PSYCHOTHERAPIES

RUSSELL A. WALSH AND BRIAN McELWAIN

What is existential psychotherapy, and in what sense is it one of the humanistic psychotherapies? Although there is no simple answer to either query, this chapter highlights issues that can assist one in answering such questions. By deferring to the reader, we have adopted a decidedly existential stance, acknowledging important questions without presuming universal answers. Indeed, the posing of, and reflecting on, questions of meaning makes a course of psychotherapy existential. Faith in clients' abilities to discern their own answers makes existential therapy a humanistic endeavor.

And so, with our faith in the reader's ability to tolerate the ambiguity of foundational questions without definitive answers, we explore issues of importance to existentialists. To begin this process, we must address the ambiguity inherent in defining the "essence" of existential psychotherapy.

DEFINING THE "ESSENCE" OF EXISTENTIAL THERAPY

Existential psychotherapists share a basic concern with the philosophical foundations of their work with people. Answers to fundamental philosophical questions shape the theory and practice of all clinicians (Boss, 1979; Cannon, 1991; Cohn, 1984). For existential psychotherapists, such questions are informed by the writings of philosophical scholars such as Søren Kierkegaard, Friedrich Wilhelm Nietzsche, Edmund Husserl, Martin Heidegger, Martin Buber, Jean-Paul Sartre, Maurice Merleau-Ponty, Paul Johannes Tillich, and Emmanuel Levinas. Each of these authors grappled with questions about the essential nature and meanings of human existence. However, among these philosophers, as well as their clinical counterparts, there is considerable variability in the answers to those questions (Cohn, 1984; Misiak & Sexton, 1973; Norcross, 1987; Willis, 1994). It is thus appropriate to speak of existential psychotherapies rather than of a single existential psychotherapy.

A core theme within existentialism and the related field of phenomenology is concern for the uniqueness and irreducibility of human experience. Accordingly, existential phenomenologists are critical of the application of natural scientific methods to the study of human beings. Existentialists argue that natural scientific methods are inadequate to the task of understanding the meaningful complexities of human experience (Boss, 1979; May & Yalom, 1995; Norcross, 1987). For example, many such methods presuppose that all people operate in the same mechanistic way, that their behaviors are wholly determined by past and present, and that a person's subjective experience is of secondary importance. Existentialists and phenomenologists consider such accounts of individuals to be violently objectifying and reductive. Thus, they argue that if science is to be pursued with human beings as subjects, then their *subjectivity* must be respected. These psychotherapists and scholars have advocated the development of a suitably *human science* that respects the uniqueness of individuals and the distinctions between human beings and other objects of scientific investigations (Cannon, 1991).

Given the existential assumption that each human experience is unique, there is little interest in generalizing across individuals for "universally valid" laws of behavior. Thus, it can be said that existential thought is radically antisystematic (Hoeller, 1990). In fact, many of those who are identified as existential therapists do not consider existential psychotherapy to be an independent school of therapy. Indeed, existential therapists may incorporate techniques from psychoanalysis (e.g., Boss, 1963) to client-centered therapy (e.g., Willis, 1994) to more directive-strategic approaches (e.g., Frankl, 1967). Such techniques, however, are practiced in light of an existential attitude (van Kaam, 1966), a stance toward human beings that can be organized according to some common themes. These themes include assumptions about *human freedom and its attenuation, intersubjectivity, temporality*, and *being as becoming*, as well as the concepts of *existential anxiety, existential guilt*, and *authenticity*. In the following pages, we outline these assumptions and concepts and discuss their relevance in terms of the *therapeutic relationship, understanding, liberation*, and therapist *flexibility*. We then review research supporting these ideas and discuss the practical implications of existential psychotherapies.

Human Freedom and Its Attenuation

The most common and fundamental assumption that existentialists make about human beings is that all individuals are, in significant respects, free. However, the freedom about which existentialists speak is not the absolute autonomy portrayed so optimistically by some humanistic psychotherapists (Lowenstein, 1993). Existentialists also emphasize limitations, frailty, and the tragic dimensions of human experience to a much greater degree than their humanistic colleagues (Yalom, 1980). Indeed, the moniker *existential–humanistic* is often used to denote a therapeutic approach that tempers the humanistic notion of individual freedom with an existential focus on context and responsibility.

For existentialists, being human is "factical"—embodied, limited, and situated in a sociohistorical context. Thus, freedom is understood as the choices one makes within one's particular situation, which then shape the situations one encounters in the future (Cannon, 1991; du Plock, 1997; van Deurzen-Smith, 1988). Indeed, people are unable to avoid the continual process of making choices that determine who they are and who they will be (Frankl, 1967; Lowenstein, 1993; Yalom, 1989). However, it is important to remember that people are always thrown into situations that they have not independently brought on themselves (Keen, 1970). An inescapable paradox of human existence is that it can be described in both object and subject terms; that is, there are always both given and chosen aspects of any particular moment.

Intersubjectivity

The dual, subject–object nature of human existence has, in contemporary Western societies, been obscured by the natural scientific approach that views people as merely objects for study. Thus, many existential psychotherapists focus on human subjectivity as a kind of corrective to an exclusively objectifying view of people. Objects in the world are not free, but subjects in the world are. So existential psychotherapists tend to take people's private, inner experience of themselves more seriously than many other therapists (Keen, 1970; Washington, 1972). From such an internal frame of reference, a person's experience, perceptions, thoughts, feelings, and values are imbued with determinative significance that overshadows the objective facts as seen by external observers (Bugental, 1987). Existential psychotherapists tend not to view people in terms of mechanisms that cause them to act in particular ways. Rather, they prefer to think of people in terms of their own uniquely meaningful "lived worlds" (C. T. Fischer, 1991).

Despite the foregoing emphasis on the subject side of the subject–object dialectic, it must be remembered that the notions of "subjects" and "objects" are abstractions. Existentialists seek an understanding of human existence that precedes the splitting apart of subject and object (C. T. Fischer, 1991; May, 1958; Prochaska, 1979). Minds, psyches, and subjectivities are inseparable from the worlds (i.e., meaningful contexts) in which they exist (Boss,

1979). Human beings always find themselves in relationship with others, and their experiences in relationships provide all of the raw materials from which their own subjective experiences are constructed. Thus, it makes little sense to attempt to understand people apart from the fundamentally intersubjective contexts into which they are thrown and the histories that they carry with them into the consulting room (Cohn, 1984; du Plock, 1997).

Temporality

Existentialists have articulated an understanding of *lived time* that goes beyond the commonsense notion that time passes as a continuous sequence of moments in which the future becomes present and is left behind as past (Boss, 1979). Instead, it is more "experience-near" to say that the past and future always exist in a person's present experience (Cohn, 1984; du Plock, 1997). Boss (1979) articulated the human experience of temporality as simultaneously being expectant of one's future, being aware of the present moment, and holding on to what has passed. This is not to say that all three temporal dimensions will always be equally open to a person at any given time, as often one dimension becomes figural while the others are unattended as ground. Additionally, existentialists have tended to reevaluate the relative significance of past, present, and future. In the light of deterministic science, the past is seen as causally determinative of the present and the future. In contrast, existential thought suggests that the immediate future is the crucially important temporal dimension of human existence. Human beings are always aiming toward certain ends. Indeed, the capacity of individuals to transcend their past and present situations and to imagine possible futures forms the very basis of human freedom (May, 1958). However, this should not be taken as a denial of the significance of the past or present. Cannon (1991) articulated the following understanding of human temporality: The future (as meaning) and the past (as ground) are equally significant in contributing to a person's choices in the present. Instead, it is more experience-near to say that the past and future always exist in the present experience of a person (Cohn, 1984; du Plock, 1997).

Becoming

Given the assumption of human freedom, it follows that existentialists conceptualize people as dynamic rather than as determined, predictable mechanisms. Indeed, for psychotherapy to be meaningfully practiced, therapists of all theoretical orientations must at least implicitly assume that people are capable of change (Cohn, 1984). The uniqueness of the existential position is its assumption that radical change is possible at any point because the essence of being human is not to have an essence. One's self is always, in principle, fluid—despite one's security-motivated efforts to be stable and "true to one's self" (Strasser & Strasser, 1997). Thus, although some therapeutic approaches seek to repair damaged "self-structures," existential psychotherapies may help clients let go of a confining sense of who one "really" is (Cannon, 1991). Such letting go accepts the continuous unfolding, or becoming, of oneself, as well as the human potential to explore and incorporate new possibilities.

Existential Anxiety and Existential Guilt

In further contrast to more conventional clinicians, existential psychotherapists view anxiety and guilt as potentially instructive signals that can be used toward the end of living more authentically (Handley, 1996) rather than as symptoms to be managed or eliminated. More specifically, *existential anxiety* is seen as the normal and unavoidable product of being confronted with the "givens of existence"—death, freedom and responsibility, existential isolation, and meaninglessness (Yalom, 1980). The concerns that people take to psychotherapy can often be understood as resulting from rigid patterns of defense against the anxiety-producing awareness of the givens of existence. These defensive patterns may result in severely restrictive stances in relation to the world (Boss, 1963; Bugental, 1965; Colm, 1966). People may be motivated to impose limitations on their own freedom of thought, feeling, and action to avoid direct experiences of existential anxiety. Existential guilt arises from one's failure to face existential givens and one's responsibility with respect to those givens (May, 1958; van Kaam, 1966).

Existential anxiety and existential guilt are invaluable insofar as they serve to mobilize what Bugental (1987, 1999) referred to as a person's *concern*, that is, the pain, hope, commitment, and inwardness that provide both the impetus and the intuitive guidance for pursuing significant life change. Deeply experienced concern demands action.

Authenticity

A basic goal of an existential psychotherapy is the reduction of duplicity (Bergantino, 1981) or bad faith (Sartre, 1953). *Bad faith* involves self-deception by recognizing either one's freedom or one's limitations to the exclusion of the other, that is, imagining one's self to be either purely an object at the whim of external forces or as a purely transcendent and autonomous subject (Cannon, 1991; Sartre, 1953). Authenticity involves a radical openness to the world, to others, and to one's own experience; it involves honest and direct confrontation with the givens of existence toward the end of living in conscious harmony with them (Bugental, 1965; Norcross, 1987; Prochaska, 1979). The resolution of pathological symptoms occurs when one moves from a self-deceptive posture to one that involves the empowering experience of one's sense of personal agency (Keen, 1970). Thus, authenticity involves not being true to some limiting notion of one's "real self" but rather being open and true to one's experience of the world (Cohn, 1995). In this sense, authenticity is analogous to the humanistic notion of genuineness. However, some degree of inauthenticity is accepted as an inescapable aspect of human experience, and an appreciation of the universality of such existential dilemmas enables therapists to engage their clients as equals.

The Therapeutic Relationship

In light of the inescapably relational character of human existence, it should come as no surprise that many existential psychotherapists regard the quality of the therapeutic relationship as of paramount importance. Thus, several have emphasized the process of interaction between client and therapist over the content of what is said in the consulting room (e.g., Bugental, 1978; Yalom, 1989). The therapeutic relationship is itself the force that fosters a kind of corrective emotional experience (Moss, 1989; Yalom, 1989). It is assumed that all substantial human relationships are based on emotional contact (Willis, 1994) and that transformation in psychotherapy requires having a new experience in relation to the therapist, not intellectual explorations or explanations (Boss, 1963). In this view, then, much is made of the therapist's *presence* and its role in facilitating a genuine *encounter* between the people who are present in the consulting room. On the part of the therapist, Spinelli (1994) emphasized being there, being with, and being for a client in an exceptionally respectful manner over efforts to do anything to or for a client. Bugental (1987) hoped that both client and therapist will be optimally present, that is, both open to being deeply and personally affected by the other and willing to disclose their own experience as it pertains to the therapeutic encounter. Without dismissing the relational distortions to which the terms transference and countertransference refer, an existential approach emphasizes the "real relationship," which involves mutual investment and risk on the part of both client and therapist (Bugental, 1978; May, 1983).

Understanding

Another major theme regarding the practice of existential psychotherapy is the emphasis on understanding in two different senses. First, several writers have stressed that all technical concerns in the practice of psychotherapy must be subordinated to the development of an empathic grasp of the client's experience (e.g., Corey, 1985; May, 1958; Misiak & Sexton, 1973;

Washington, 1972). In the broadest terms, the existential psychotherapist seeks to engage, understand, and illuminate a client's self-and-world construct system, that is, a client's implicit visions of himself or herself and of the character of the world in which he or she lives (Bugental, 1999). These are the operating assumptions that lend form and stability to one's experiences across time in the face of the innumerable possibilities that confront a person at any given moment. However, existential psychotherapists must not presume that they ever understand their clients in any certain or final sense given the dynamic character of human existence (Spinelli, 1997). They must continually be willing to call into question anything that they presume to understand and, thus, take for granted about their clients as they assist their clients in doing likewise toward their own liberation. The existential psychotherapists' emphasis on understanding involves attempting to "make the unconscious conscious" toward the end of helping people to more intentionally direct the course of their lives (May, 1983). It should be noted that existential psychotherapists assume that because people are generally caught up in the acts of conducting their daily lives, they are quite imperfectly aware of the ways in which they engage with the world (van Deurzen-Smith, 1997). Typically, people do not reflect on (or even recognize) their engagement with the world as such, but by attending to what is happening within and around oneself, one can discover much that usually remains hidden within one's experience. In the radical terms of Sartre (1953), the existential psychotherapist illuminates the ways in which clients have already chosen to become exactly who they find themselves to be. In this light, it would be a mistake to say that the existential therapist helps clients become more responsible for themselves. Rather, we would say that the therapist helps clients recognize the ways in which they are always already responsible and, thus, invites them to pursue more intentionally their continual process of self-construction (van Deurzen-Smith, 1988).

Psychotherapeutic Liberation

Increasing the compass of conscious choice is held by existentialists to be liberating (May, 1983). The therapist's task is to clarify the choices being made by the clients and to avoid colluding with clients' beliefs that they are inadequate to the task of directing their own lives (Prochaska, 1979). The existential psychotherapist's hope is that increased awareness of one's choices will contribute to a growing sense of potency in which one previously felt compelled to react to external forces (Bugental, 1987). Thus, Bugental (1999) used a focus on the present, momentary experience of the client in the consulting room to illuminate the unrecognized choices that the client is continually making. Bugental's intense focus on the *living moment* aims to foster greater awareness of the choices being made and to help the client to overcome repetitive patterns by developing awareness of them in the very moment of their activation.

Van Kaam (1966) pointed out that personal freedom involves not only being able to change one's behaviors but also intentionally doing things that one had previously done mechanically or unconsciously. The existential psychotherapist illuminates clients' experience of themselves as passive victims and works to foster a sense of active agency (May & Yalom, 1995). As a result, clients can move from relatively constricted to much more flexible approaches to the dynamic contingencies of living. However, such experiential transformation depends on the therapist's own liberation, both personally and with respect to therapeutic technique (Bergantino, 1981).

Therapeutic Flexibility

In light of each person's uniqueness and the dynamic character of human life, the practice of an existential psychotherapist will necessarily be characterized by its flexibility across clients, situations, and time (May, 1958; Washington, 1972). Because no two "cases," moments, or therapeutic relationships will be the same, a therapist must not mechanically use interventions (du Plock, 1997; Willis, 1994). C. T. Fischer (1991) described the practice of existential psychotherapy as involving a disciplined openness, methodological eclecticism, and theoretical pluralism This fits with depictions of psychotherapy as having much more in common with the work of an artist than that of a scientist or technician (Bergantino, 1981; Bugental, 1987). An existential psychotherapist may use a wide variety of interventions so long as they are used in light of an "existential attitude" and in the context of an authentic relationship with the client (May & Yalom, 1995; Moss, 1989). Thus, there are substantial variations in practice across existential psychotherapists as each develops a flexible style given his or her own unique set of experiences, values, and aptitudes (Bergantino, 1981). In all cases, however, the existential psychotherapist's practice will be sensitively responsive to the uniqueness of the given client and moment.

RESEARCH REVIEW

For the most part, existential psychotherapies have not been researched by means of quantitative, nomothetic, "empirical"[1] methods (Yalom, 1980).

---

[1]"Empirical" is set in quotes because its literal meaning, "based on experience," contrasts with its present use in reference to quantitative procedures. Indeed, qualitative and discovery-oriented methods are arguably more empirical in that they describe experience without resorting to abstract, quantitative transformations.

Instead, the theoretical and philosophical scholarship cited earlier, as well as qualitative research (e.g., Fessler, 1983; Hanna, Giordano, Dupuy, & Puhakka, 1995; Rahilly, 1993) and case study reports (Bugental, 1976; du Plock, 1997; Schneider & May 1995; Spinelli, 1997; Yalom, 1989), provide existential psychotherapists with compelling evidence in support of their clinical practices. However, within natural science research literature, there are also findings consonant with the common themes of existential psychotherapy. We therefore summarize both mainstream and alternative research results that support existential psychotherapy.

Existential Assumptions: Human Freedom, Intersubjectivity, Temporality, and Becoming

Freedom and responsibility are implicitly assumed in all approaches to psychotherapy. Despite the deterministic rhetoric of much discourse about psychotherapy, the possibility of change through conversation, rather than solely through manipulation of environmental determinants, would make little sense without the assumption of client freedom and responsibility. Indeed, even radically behavioral therapies involve the client as an agent of change; in most cases, clients are instructed to reflect on and revise the contingencies of their own behavior. Such "psychoeducation" is comprehensible only in light of a client who is reflexively aware and adaptable, one who is willing to apply the therapist's teachings.

Research explicitly relevant to the notions of client freedom and responsibility in psychotherapy can be found in qualitative studies by Rennie (1990, 1992, 1994) and Watson and Rennie (1994), as well as in Bohart and Tallman's (1996) research. These authors demonstrated that successful psychotherapy as understood by clients involves a process of self-reflection, considering alternative courses of action, and making choices. Other research concerning client variables has demonstrated the significant role played by clients in determining the success or failure of psychotherapy (Garfield, 1994; Lambert, 1992). This finding is far from surprising if one acknowledges client freedom and responsibility. Indeed, it is only from the stance of an "objective" expert imbued with the power to change "helpless" clients that this evidence could be startling. Unfortunately, such a stance, at odds with an understanding of human beings as active agents, remains evident in much of the discourse about psychotherapy and in psychotherapy research. As procedures for documenting and evaluating psychotherapy become increasingly objectivistic and intervention focused, the importance of clients' freedom and responsibility may be further obscured.

The implications of intersubjectivity for understanding human beings have been largely ignored by traditional research methods in psychology. The distinction drawn between the "naive" perspective of participants and the "objective" standpoint of researchers has led to a privileging of the latter (Morawski, 1988). With respect to psychotherapy research, this means that clients' perspectives have been dismissed as biased, whereas researchers' observations have been assumed to be objective and reliable (e.g., Jacobson & Christensen, 1996). To remedy this problem, some researchers have explored clients' accounts of the psychotherapy process (Rennie, 1990, 1992, 1994; Watson & Rennie, 1994; see also Rennie, this volume, chapter 4). Others have sought to incorporate multiple perspectives of the same psychotherapy (Caskey, Barker, & Elliott, 1984; Fessler, 1983; Walsh, 1994). These studies have shown that clients' perspectives often differ from those of therapists and "objective" observers. This divergence of viewpoints, a problem for logical positivists, suggests the importance of recognizing the intersubjective foundations of psychotherapy and psychotherapy research (Elliott & Shapiro, 1992; Omer & Strenger, 1992; Strupp, 1996; Walsh, Perucci, & Severns, 1999). Thus, recent evidence suggests that the subjectivity of clients is an important but often neglected component of the psychotherapy process.

The past 2 decades have seen a broadening of research approaches to accommodate a view of humans as reflexive, relational, embodied beings. These human science research approaches (e.g., Giorgi, Barton, & Maes, 1983; Giorgi, Fischer, & Murray, 1975; Giorgi, Fischer, & von Eckartsberg, 1971; Giorgi, Knowles, & Smith, 1979; Messer, Sass, & Woolfolk, 1988; Packer & Addison, 1989) attempt to explore the inescapable relationship between person and world that defines human existence. Concurrent with these developments in research methods, accounts of psychotherapy across various theoretical approaches have emphasized the intersubjective character of relationships both within and outside of therapy (Friedman, 1992; Goncalves, 1994; Griffith & Griffith, 1994; Mahoney, 1991; Stolorow, Atwood, & Brandchaft, 1995). This awareness is in many ways far from new, as the person-in-relation was acknowledged by such psychotherapists as Harry Stack Sullivan (1953) and R. D. Laing (1965). Nevertheless, the explosion of interest in interpersonal or relational approaches to psychotherapy suggests a new appreciation for this existential theme.

Research regarding temporality in the context of psychotherapy has been constrained by positivistic understandings of time as an objective variable (e.g., Howard, Kopta, Krause, & Orlinsky, 1986; Seligman, 1995). However, the human experience of time has been shown clearly to be variable across individuals and situations. Flaherty (1991), for example, explored the experience of *protracted time* and showed that individuals' engagement with their circumstances shaped their experience of the passage of time. Similarly, Allison and Duncan (1988) found that the passage of time at work was experienced differently by people engaged in tasks at hand and those disinterested and bored with their jobs. These findings compare with research by Maslow (1968) and Csikszentmihalyi (1990), who showed that lived time changes during peak or flow experiences.

Research on the relativity of lived time is complemented by research concerning narrative and its role in human experience (e.g., Polkinghorne, 1994). This literature has shown that people achieve a sense of meaning and purpose through storytelling and that stories reflect the experience of temporality (Gergen, 1994; McLeod, 1997). Gergen (1994), for example, showed that memories are structured according to the narrative forms through which recollection occurs. Such storied memories are not veridical representations of past events but organizing structures for individuals' experiences (Spence, 1982). Narratives entail a *historical dimension* and an *anticipatory thrust* that give meaning to the present through constructing a past that projects a particular future (Neimeyer, 1994). This temporal dimension of narrative allows for revisions of both historical events and the significance of those events during the course of psychotherapy (Spence, 1982). It is, in other words, human temporality and its embeddedness in narrative forms that allow for change and the reconstruction of meaning through therapeutic discourse.

Evidence supporting the notion of becoming can be found implicitly in all psychotherapy research and, more directly, in studies of personality. All psychotherapies are intended to produce some sort of change. Although existential psychotherapies may be criticized for their lack of behavioral change criteria, the change of interest to existentialists is far more broad and transformative. This change is an expanding of the person's world such that the dynamic nature of experience can be embraced rather than endured. Such change is seen as constant and continuous, rather than once and for all.

Psychotherapy research concerning significant change events over the course of psychotherapy (Rice & Greenberg, 1984) is compatible with existential understandings of change. This research has shown that psychotherapy comprises many small and significant changes—a reality that is missed when researchers focus exclusively on the final outcome. To complicate matters, research has suggested that such change events are relative to the "eye of the beholder" (Walsh, Perucci, & Severns, 1999). Thus, it appears that the process of becoming can be discerned no more objectively than any other aspect of human experience.

The notion of becoming stands in contrast to that of a static and enduring personality or self. A shift toward a sense of human beings as dynamic, rather than fixed, is evident in the areas of personality and developmental psychology. C. T. Fischer (1994), for example, advocated an approach to psychological assessment that acknowledges and documents the mutable character of personality. Moreover, theory and research regarding the role of narrative in the construction of a meaningful sense of self (Hermans, 1993; McAdams, 1996; Van den Broek & Thurlow, 1991) support the understanding of human beings as continually engaged in a process of becoming. This process has been shown to be inherently indeterminate and dynamic (Thorne & Latzke, 1996). As a result, lives are always subject to revision, redirection, and transformation.

Existential Concepts: Existential Anxiety, Guilt, and Authenticity

Research supporting the concepts of existential anxiety, guilt, and authenticity can be found in both qualitative and quantitative research literatures. The experience of anxiety and its potential for transformation have been documented in a series of studies by W. F. Fischer (1989). Fischer used empirical–phenomenological methods to analyze participants' accounts of situations wherein they experienced anxiety. His results showed that anxiety arose when participants' self-understandings were challenged by circumstances. Subsequently, they experienced a sense of being blocked concurrent with bodily symptoms. Typically, these individuals tried to ignore their physical symptoms by engaging in a flurry of activity. Fischer identified two distinct styles of living out this anxiety: In the first, fear of "being overwhelmed by the unthinkable" leads one to "turn away from the possibility of reflecting upon it," whereas in the second, which "typically occurs in the presence of some empathic friend or other . . . one explores and appropriates the ambiguity that has been revealed" (W. F. Fischer, 1989, p. 135). This leads to change in "one's understanding of who one is [and] of what one's relations with the world are all about" (p. 135).

W. F. Fischer's (1989) research fits readily with the existential understanding of the transformative potential of anxiety when it is tolerated, explored, and shared. It also supports the notion of existential guilt as a sign—which an individual can either heed or ignore—that the problem is a challenge inviting change. Other relevant research along these lines includes studies of Gendlin's (1981) focusing technique whereby clients attend to problematic bodily experiences, as well as research by Clarke (1989) regarding the process of meaning creation in therapy. Studies pertaining to Gendlin's focusing technique (Greenberg, Elliott, & Lietaer, 1994; see also Hendricks, this volume, chapter 7) have shown the therapeutic power of "dwelling" with distressing experience and incorporating that experience through understanding. In their review of research by Oishi and Murayama (1989), Greenberg et al. (1994) summarized three conditions identified as important to focusing: "concentrating while being relaxed, dwelling in the body sense and putting this into words, and experiencing a comfortable psychological climate with the therapist" (p. 525). In a related vein, Clarke's (1989) research delineated three indicators for meaning-making events in psychotherapy: emotional arousal; a challenged cherished belief; and confusion, surprise, or lack of understanding (Greenberg et al., 1994). Taken together, these findings complement W. F. Fischer's (1989) conclusion that anxiety and its shadow, existential guilt, when explored in the presence of an empathic listener, can lead to transformation through the reconstruction of meaning.

The concept of authenticity has support in reviews of research literature as well as in studies involving client and therapist recollections of psychotherapy. Goldfried and Padawer (1982), for example, identified client self-awareness as one of three basic change principles common across the psychotherapy literature (with the other two principles being a warm, supportive therapeutic relationship and renewal of the client's sense of hope). Similarly, Rennie (1992) analyzed the experiences of clients and identified the pursuit of personal meaning to be a predominant theme, with clients' scrutiny of their own processes and experiences of heightened awareness as some of the most common elements. Likewise, Lietaer's (1992) study of helping and hindering processes in therapy (according to clients and therapists) led to the following characterization of successful psychotherapy:

> Through exploring their own inner world with the empathic facilitation of their therapists, clients come to face, accept, and integrate hitherto denied aspects of their experience. This process of self-exploration . . . opens new possibilities and encourages them to behave in new ways. (p. 147)

These and other studies (Jones, Parke, & Pulos, 1992; McCullough et al., 1991; Taurke et al., 1990) support the notion that openness to one's experience of the world and the empowering experience of oneself as an agent—aspects of authenticity—are important components of the process of change in effective psychotherapy.

Therapeutic Implications: Relationship, Understanding, Liberation, and Flexibility

The importance of the therapeutic relationship has been demonstrated repeatedly in psychotherapy research. The client–therapist relationship has been evaluated under the term *therapeutic alliance*, which includes the therapeutic bond between client and therapist as well as shared understandings of goals and tasks (Bordin, 1976). The therapeutic alliance has been shown to be a major contributor to clinical outcome regardless of therapists' theoretical orientations (Beutler, Machado, & Neufeld, 1994; Horvath & Greenberg, 1994; Orlinsky, Grawe, & Parks, 1994). As Orlinsky et al. (1994) pointed out in their extensive review of psychotherapy process research, evidence supporting the power of the therapeutic bond comes from more than 1,000 process–outcome findings. Among these studies, the strongest relationships are evident in studies that took the client's perspective into account.

Understanding as a component of effective psychotherapy is supported by research exploring empathy. In studies of client–therapist interactions defined by participants as helpful, both clients' feeling understood by their therapists and their coming to understand themselves were identified as crucial (Greenberg et al., 1994). In a study of significant events in psychotherapy, Elliott, Clark, and Kemeny (1991; cited in Greenberg et al., 1994) found that clients and therapists rated feeling understood as the most important therapeutic component. The therapeutic power of understanding was similarly demonstrated in research by Dormaar, Dijkman, and DeVries (1989) and Lafferty, Beutler, and Crago (1989). In fact, a recent review of psychotherapy research regarding therapist variables led Beutler et al. (1994) to reaffirm Patterson's (1983) conclusion that "there are few things in the field of psychology for which the evidence is so strong as that supporting the necessity if not sufficiency, of the therapist conditions of accurate empathy, respect, or warmth, and therapeutic genuineness" (p. 243).

Liberation, though couched in various terms, has also been shown to be a crucial aspect of effective psychotherapy. Whether characterized as making the unconscious conscious, altering maladaptive cognitions, or even changing behavioral contingencies, all therapists help clients let go of harmful or self-limiting patterns in favor of alternative possibilities. In a qualitative study of people who experienced significant change both in and out of therapy, Hanna et al. (1995) identified *transcendence*, or moving beyond limitations, as the essential structure of each change. Moreover, this transcendence consisted of insight (defined as " penetrating, pervasive, global and enduringly stable understanding which included a new perspective on the self, world, or problem") and "psychological or metacognitive acts such as intending, deciding, willing, detaching, and confronting" (Hanna et al., 1995, p. 148). In a related research (Goldfried, 1980; cited by Drozd & Goldfried, 1996), a group of prominent psychotherapists of various theoretical orientations identified *corrective experiences* as key to therapeutic change. These corrective experiences were seen as opportunities for clients to "experience themselves in a new way, to discover that they can survive what is dreaded or feared, that they can once again experience themselves as agents of their experience, rather than victims" (Greenberg & Rhodes, 1991, cited in Drozd & Goldfried, 1996, p. 177). These findings highlight the importance of liberation as an outcome of effective psychotherapy.

It is difficult to find evidence supporting the value of flexibility in the efficacy studies of the mainstream psychotherapy literature. As Seligman (1995) pointed out, well-controlled efficacy studies ignore the flexibility that is inherently part of the psychotherapy process. Instead, consistency across therapists and clients is sought through the use of treatment manuals (e.g., Chambless, 1996; Moras, 1993). The irrelevance of such manuals to the actual practices of psychotherapists has been highlighted by a number of psychologists (Bohart, O'Hara, & Leitner, 1998; Fensterheim & Raw, 1996; Havik & VandenBos, 1996). As an alternative, they have advocated research addressing the effectiveness of psychotherapy as actually practiced by psychotherapists.

In adapting their methods to the needs of their clients, practicing psychotherapists are likely to adopt an eclectic, pluralistic, or integrative approach. Surveys have shown that a large number of psychotherapists describe their approach with one of these terms (Jensen, Bergin, & Greaves, 1990). Thus, most psychotherapists turn away from rigid schools of therapy and comparative outcome studies (which continue in the face of consistent findings of equivalence across therapies). Instead, they turn toward their clients and seek to understand their experience. This turn is decidedly existential.

FROM RESEARCH TO PRACTICE

From an existential perspective, every course of psychotherapy is unique. The notion of manualized psychotherapy is therefore an oxymoron. Arguably more important than *what* existential psychotherapists do is the manner in which they do it. This *how* of the existential psychotherapies—the existential attitude—is one that "calls for continual attention to the patient's inner experience, and it recognizes that the prime instrument needed for that attention is the therapist's own subjectivity" (Bugental, 1987, p. 3). From this standpoint, "the therapist's primary function is not that of provoking attitudinal or behavioral change in the client, but of clarifying the client's lived experience of being-in-the-world" (Spinelli, 1997, p. 88). Thus, the therapist maintains an attitude of curiosity and respect for the client's experience and invites the client to explore and reflect on his or her existence. This attitude is *not* a technique. It is an openness that emerges through the co-constitution of an empathic, empowering therapeutic relationship.

Existential psychotherapies tend to be insight- rather than symptom-oriented, although exploring symptoms as attempts to ward off existential anxieties may be useful (Cohn, 1995; Handley, 1996; May & Yalom, 1995). An existential psychotherapist would be much less concerned with curing symptoms than with explicating their latent meanings as illuminating the structure of a client's life (Sipiora, 1988–1989). Some have gone so far as to suggest that existential psychotherapists should not even be concerned with facilitating change because such considerations will create pressures that interfere with the real purpose of existential psychotherapy: clarification of a person's attitude toward the givens of existence (Strasser, 1996; van Deurzen-Smith, 1988). The existential therapist helps illuminate ways in which clients avoid full openness to the world and to their experience of it (including their relationship with the therapist), that is, how and why they constrict their lives without recognizing that they have done so (Bugental, 1965; May, 1958; Prochaska, 1979). Thus, existential therapists help their clients explore and set aside their surface anxieties and guilt-motivated defenses so that they may recognize and accept their existential anxiety and guilt (Colm, 1966; Willis, 1994).

To clarify what existential psychotherapists do, we consider examples from two published case studies. However, we want to emphasize the uniqueness of these (and any) particular cases. Maurice Friedman has recounted (in Schneider & May, 1995) his work with Dawn, a 40-year-old graduate student and married mother who came to therapy with marital difficulties, symptoms of depression, and a history of physical and psychological abuse by her parents. Over a period of 4 years, Friedman's psychotherapy included individual therapy, couples therapy, and family therapy. In their long-term work together, Friedman and Dawn explored her troubled family relationships (past and present); facilitated Dawn's emotional expression, particularly with respect to feelings of anger; explored the significance of Dawn's decision to separate from her husband; and discussed Dawn's plans for and struggles with graduate school. In addition, Friedman brought in a divorce mediator, referred Dawn to a psychiatrist for antidepressant medication, and encouraged Dawn to write down and reflect on her dreams. In describing his multifaceted work with Dawn, Friedman emphasized that

> The goal of Dawn's therapy was neither to preserve her (marital) relationship . . . nor to establish her in a new long-term relationship. . . . Nor was it any specific matter, such as overcoming her anxiety and depression. . . . What was essential, rather was the relationship of trust that developed between us. (see Schneider & May, 1995, p. 312)

Thus, for Friedman, as for most existential therapists, therapeutic techniques and behavioral goals are secondary to the therapist–client relationship. This difference from other therapies is one of emphasis. Where other therapists might seek to foster a collaborative relationship to implement particular interventions, existential therapists view *the relationship as the therapy*, and only secondarily consider using various techniques. Friedman characterizes his technical eclecticism as follows:

> My approach to Dawn's therapy was at times insight-oriented, at times process-oriented, and at times support-oriented. But it always evolved from the relationship and returned back to my relationship with her. . . . I did not simply impose these actions on Dawn but explored with her when it was helpful. . . . Thus choosing therapeutic goals and objectives became a responsibility that Dawn and I shared. (see Schneider & May, 1995, p. 312)

Dawn evaluated her own psychotherapy and concluded,

> When I think about our therapeutic relationship, it is the process that stands out in my memory, not the content. . . . He always responded to me as simply "me" and did not classify me or categorize me or try to fix me because there was something wrong. (see Schneider & May, 1995, p. 313)

In characterizing her experience of the therapeutic process, Dawn remarked, "If the therapist can be human and fallible, that gives me permission to be human and fallible, too" (see Schneider & May, 1995, p. 313). For Dawn, this humanness meant that "because he doesn't need to be my teacher, I am now able to be my own teacher" (p. 314).

As this example demonstrates, existential psychotherapy is truly collaborative, flexible, and integrative. Rather than feigning a collaborative relationship so that the therapist can strategically pursue an agenda, the existential therapist avoids the role of "expert" and tolerates with the client the uncertainty of unknowing (Spinelli, 1997). However, this unknowing stance does not imply passivity on the part of the therapist. Indeed, some existential psychotherapists apply didactic methods such as Socratic dialogue (Frankl, 1967) and characterize existential psychotherapy as a practical tutorial in the art of living (van Deurzen-Smith, 1988). The goal of these methods is to empower clients to reflect on their lived experience, to explore the meaning of the choices they have implicitly made, and to consider alternative courses of action.

A second practical example can be found in Irvin Yalom's (1989) bestselling book, *Love's Executioner*. In a chapter titled, "I Never Thought It Would Happen To Me," Yalom described his work with Elva, an elderly, embittered widow highly critical of everyone and everything, so much so that Yalom had difficulty in building a therapeutic alliance. It was not until Elva faced the "crisis" of a purse-snatching following her lunch with three friends that an opportunity for transformation—of Elva, Yalom, and their relationship—presented itself.

Elva's expression of grief following the robbery, "I never thought it would happen to me," was explored for its broader meaning within the context of her life. As a result of this exploration, Yalom came to understand Elva's struggles in new ways:

> "When you say you never thought it would happen to you, I know just what you mean," I said. "It's so hard for me, too, to accept that all these afflictions—aging, loss, death—are going to happen to me, too."
>
> Elva nodded, her tightened brow showing that she was surprised at my saying anything personal about myself.
>
> "You must feel that if Albert were alive, this never would have happened to you." I ignored her flip response that if Albert were alive

she wouldn't have been taking those three old hens to lunch. "So the robbery brings home the fact that he's really gone."

Her eyes filled with tears, but I had the right, the mandate, to continue. "You knew that before, I know. But part of you didn't. Now you really know that he's dead. He's not in the yard. He's not out back in the workshop. He's not anywhere. Except in your memories."

Elva was really crying now, and her stubby frame heaved with sobs for several minutes. She had never done that before with me. I sat there and wondered, "Now what do I do?" (Yalom, 1989, p. 150)

In response to this question, Yalom eyed Elva's purse and called into question its enormous size; reconsidering the robbery, he wondered aloud if she had not been asking for trouble by carrying that large bag. When Elva defiantly argued that she needed everything contained in her bag, Yalom challenged her to show him. Elva responded by emptying her purse onto Yalom's table. The two of them laughed as they inventoried the contents, including doggie bags, cologne bottles, a roll of dimes, knitting needles, several pairs of sunglasses, and a host of other "necessary" items. This process of sharing was, according to Yalom, nothing short of intimate:

> When the great bag had finally yielded all, Elva and I stared in wonderment at the contents set out in rows on my table. We were sorry the bag was empty and that the emptying was over. She turned and smiled, and we looked tenderly at each other. It was an extraordinarily intimate moment. In a way that no patient had ever done before, she showed me everything. And I had accepted everything and asked for even more. I followed her into every nook and crevice, awed that the old woman's purse could serve as a vehicle for both isolation and intimacy: the absolute isolation that is integral to existence and the intimacy that dispels the dread, if not the fact, of isolation.
>
> That was a transforming hour. Our time of intimacy—call it love, call it love making—was redemptive. In that one hour, Elva moved from a position of forsakenness to one of trust. She came alive and was persuaded, once more, of her capacity for intimacy. (Yalom, 1989, p. 151)

Yalom's example underscores the power of a collaborative and creative relationship that can develop between client and therapist. While acknowledging the difference in the relative power between therapist and client, many existential psychotherapists emphasize mutuality within a respectful therapeutic relationship (Willis, 1994). This involves an experientially egalitarian engagement of two (or more) people who are in many fundamental respects quite similar (Moss, 1989). Although clients may often think of themselves as far from equal with their therapists, an effective course of psychotherapy is presumed to facilitate a growing sense of equality on the part of the client (van den Berg, 1971). Therapist self-disclosure makes more sense from this perspective and, indeed, would seem to be inevitable; the crucial questions are when, why, what, and how a therapist should disclose (Willis, 1994). A most important aspect of any self-disclosure on the part of the therapist, however, is that it be genuine and, thus, that it contributes to a more authentic relationship. In light of this goal, it is important that the therapist not attempt to shield a client from all things negative in a misguided attempt to manifest unconditional positive regard. A truly authentic human encounter will necessarily involve tensions and perhaps outright conflict, and these should not be avoided or minimized; ultimately, the client and the therapist must be free to express both their positive and negative feelings in relation to one another (Colm, 1966). The aim of such an existential psychotherapy is to help clients recover their willingness to live more openly and freely through the experience of such an encounter with their psychotherapist.

Yalom's (1989) work with Elva also demonstrates the healing power of understanding the unique and implicit meanings of a client's experience. From an "objective" perspective, the act of emptying an overstuffed purse would seem mundane and of little relevance to the goals of psychotherapy. In this instance, however, for both Elva and Yalom, this shared act created an opportunity for liberation. Of course, as Yalom acknowledged, his decision to challenge Elva regarding her purse was a creative response that followed his reflection, "Now what do I do?" This clear recognition of unknowing allowed the flexibility and spontaneity necessary for a novel therapeutic encounter. And this improvised encounter emboldened Elva to explore fundamental issues concerning isolation, intimacy, and trust.

CONCLUSION

The existential approach to psychotherapy seeks to understand the unique meanings of clients' lived experiences. Such understanding does not depend on abstract theorizing or diagnostic conceptualization; instead, it involves exploration of clients' implicit understandings of their own experiences. This emphasis on understanding, combined with faith in its ability to facilitate transformation, makes existential therapy a humanistic approach.

Existential psychotherapists believe that people cannot be fully understood from an external or objective frame of reference (Corey, 1985); thus, they focus less on particular symptoms and more on the meanings of whatever concerns their clients bring to therapy (Bugental, 1978; Schneider & May, 1995). In doing so, existential psychotherapists agree with Strupp (1996, p. 1018) in his conclusion that "many patients turn to psychotherapy less for the cure of traditional disorders as described in the *Diagnostic and Statistical Manual of Mental Disorders* . . . but (at least ostensibly) more for the purpose of finding greater meaning in their lives, combating existential anxieties, or 'actualizing' themselves." As clients come to understand the implicit choices they have made and their stance with respect to others, they can collaborate with their therapists to explore alternative possibilities. The existential therapist may borrow many techniques from other therapeutic approaches. These techniques, however, remain secondary to the genuine relationship between client and therapist—a relationship based on the shared understanding that "we are, all of us, in this together" (Yalom, 1989, p. 14). This collaborative approach constitutes "a very different kind of psychotherapy" that is "no longer based on a repair model" (Bugental, 1976, p. 9). Instead, as described by Rollo May (cited in Bugental, 1976, p. 13), "The therapist's being able to help the patient recognize and experience his own existence [is] the central process of therapy."

REFERENCES

Allison, M. T., & Duncan, M. C. (1988). Women, work, and flow. In M. Csikszentmihalyi & I. S. Csikszentmihalyi (Eds.), *Optimal experiences: Psychological studies of flow in consciousness* (pp. 118–137). Cambridge, England: Cambridge University Press.

Bergantino, L. (1981). *Psychotherapy, insight, and style: The existential moment.* Boston: Allyn & Bacon.

Beutler, L. E., Machado, P. P., & Neufeldt, S. A. (1994). Therapist variables. In A. E. Bergin & S. L. Garfield (Eds.), *Handbook of psychotherapy and behavior change* (4th ed., pp. 229–269). New York: Wiley.

Bohart, A. C., O'Hara, M., & Leitner, L. M. (1998). Empirically violated treatments: Disenfranchisement of humanistic and other psychotherapies. *Psychotherapy Research, 8,* 141–157.

Bohart, A. C., & Tallman, K. (1996). The active client: Therapy as self-help. *Journal of Humanistic Psychology, 36,* 7–30.

Bordin, E. S. (1976). The generalizability of the psychoanalytic concept of the working alliance. *Psychotherapy: Theory, Research, and Practice, 16,* 252–260.

Boss, M. (1963). *Psychoanalysis and Daseinsanalysis* (L. Lefebre, Trans.). New York: Basic Books.

Boss, M. (1979). *Existential foundations of medicine and psychology* (S. Conway & A. Cleaves, Trans.). Northvale, NJ: Aronson.

Bugental, J. F. T. (1965). *The search for authenticity: An existential–analytic approach to psychotherapy.* New York: Holt, Rinehart & Winston.

Bugental, J. F. T. (1976). *The search for existential identity.* San Francisco: Jossey-Bass.

Bugental, J. F. T. (1978). *Psychotherapy and process: The fundamentals of an existential–humanistic approach.* New York: Random House.

Bugental, J. F. T. (1987). *The art of the psychotherapist.* New York: Norton.

Bugental, J. F. T. (1999). *Psychotherapy isn't what you think: Bringing the psychotherapeutic engagement into the living moment.* Phoenix, AZ: Zeig, Tucker.

Cannon, B. (1991). *Sartre and psychoanalysis: An existentialist challenge to clinical metatheory.* Lawrence: University of Kansas.

Caskey, N., Barker, C., & Elliott, R. (1984). Dual perspectives: Clients' and therapists' perceptions of therapist responses. *British Journal of Clinical Psychology, 23,* 281–290.

Chambless, D. L. (1996). In defense of empirically supported psychological interventions. *Clinical Psychology: Science and Practice, 3,* 230–235.

Clarke, K. M. (1989). Creation of meaning: An emotional processing task in psychotherapy. *Psychotherapy, 26,* 139–148.

Cohn, H. W. (1984). An existential approach to psychotherapy. *British Journal of Medical Psychology, 57,* 311–318.

Cohn, H. W. (1995). Misconceptions in existential psychotherapy. *Journal of the Society of Existential Analysis, 6,* 20–27.

Colm, H. (1966). *The existentialist approach to psychotherapy with adults and children.* New York: Grune & Stratton.

Corey, G. (1985). *Theory and practice of group counseling* (2nd ed.). Monterey, CA: Brooks/Cole.

Csikszentmihalyi, M. (1990). *Flow: The psychology of optimal experience.* New York: HarperPerennial.

Dormaar, J. M., Dijkman, C. I., & DeVries, M. W. (1989). Consensus in patient–therapist interactions: A measure of the therapeutic relationship related to outcome. *Psychotherapy and Psychosomatics, 51,* 69–76.

Drozd, J. F., & Goldfried, M. R. (1996). A critical evaluation of the state-of-the-art in psychotherapy outcome research. *Psychotherapy, 33,* 171–180.

du Plock, S. (1997). Introduction. In S. du Plock (Ed.), *Case studies in existential psychotherapy and counselling* (pp. 1–11). New York: Wiley.

Elliott, R., & Shapiro, D. A. (1992). Client and therapist as analysts of significant events. In S. G. Toukmanian & D. L. Rennie (Eds.), *Psychotherapy process research: Paradigmatic and narrative approaches* (pp. 163–186). Newbury Park, CA: Sage.

Fensterheim, H., & Raw, S. D. (1996). Psychotherapy research is not psychotherapy practice. *Clinical Psychology: Science and Practice, 3,* 168–171.

Fessler, R. (1983). Phenomenology and "the talking cure": Research on psychotherapy. In A. Giorgi, A. Barton, & C. Maes (Eds.), *Duquesne studies in phenomenological psychology* (Vol. IV, pp. 33–46). Pittsburgh: Duquesne University Press.

Fischer, C. T. (1991). Phenomenological–existential psychotherapy. In M. Hersen, A. E. Kazdin, & A. S. Bellack (Eds.), *The clinical psychology handbook* (2nd ed., pp. 534–550). New York: Pergamon.

Fischer, C. T. (1994). *Individualizing psychological assessment.* Hillsdale, NJ: Erlbaum.

Fischer, W. F. (1989). An empirical–phenomenological investigation of being anxious: An example of the phenomenological approach to emotion. In R. Valle & S. Halling (Eds.), *Existential–phenomenological perspectives in psychology* (pp. 127–136). New York: Plenum.

Flaherty, M. G. (1991). The perception of time and situated engrossment. *Social Psychology Quarterly, 54,* 76–85.

Frankl, V. E. (1967). *Psychotherapy and existentialism: Selected papers on logotherapy.* New York: Simon & Schuster.

Friedman, M. (1992). *Dialogue and the human image: Beyond humanistic psychology.* Newbury Park, CA: Sage.

Garfield, S. L. (1994). Research on client variables in psychotherapy. In A. E. Bergin & S. L. Garfield (Eds.), *Handbook of psychotherapy and behavior change* (4th ed., pp. 190–228). New York: Wiley.

Gendlin, E. T. (1981). *Focusing.* New York: Bantam Books.

Gergen, K. J. (1994). *Realities and relationships: Soundings in social construction.* Cambridge, MA: Harvard University Press.

Giorgi, A., Barton, A., & Maes, C. (1983). *Duquesne studies in phenomenological psychology* (Vol. IV). Pittsburgh: Duquesne University Press.

Giorgi, A., Fischer, C., & Murray, E. (1975). *Duquesne studies in phenomenological psychology* (Vol. II). Pittsburgh: Duquesne University Press.

Giorgi, A., Fischer, W. F., & Von Eckartsberg, R. (1971). *Duquesne studies in phenomenological psychology* (Vol. I). Pittsburgh: Duquesne University Press.

Giorgi, A., Knowles, R., & Smith, D. L. (1979). *Duquesne studies in phenomenological psychology* (Vol. III). Pittsburgh: Duquesne University Press.

Goldfried, M. R., & Padawer, W. (1982). Current status and future directions in psychotherapy. In M. R. Goldfried (Ed.), *Converging themes in psychotherapy* (pp. 3–49). New York: Springer.

Goncalves, O. F. (1994). From epistemological truth to existential meaning in cognitive narrative psychotherapy. *Journal of Constructivist Psychology, 7,* 107–118.

Greenberg, L., Elliott, R., & Lietaer, G. (1994). Research on experiential psychotherapies. In S. Garfield & A. Bergin (Eds.), *Handbook of psychotherapy and behavior change* (4th ed., pp. 509–539). New York: Wiley.

Griffith, J. L., & Griffith, M. E. (1994). *The body speaks: Therapeutic dialogues for mind–body problems.* New York: Basic Books.

Handley, N. K. (1996). Anxiety: An existential perspective. *Journal of the Society for Existential Analysis, 7*(2), 27–49.

Hanna, F. J., Giordano, F., Dupuy, P., & Puhakka, K. (1995). Agency and transcendence: The experience of therapeutic change. *The Humanistic Psychologist, 23,* 139–160.

Havik, O. E., & VandenBos, G. R. (1996). Limitations of manualized psychotherapy for everyday clinical practice. *Clinical Psychology: Science and Practice, 3,* 264–267.

Hermans, H. J. (1993). Telling and retelling one's self-narratives: A contextual approach to life-span development. *Human Development, 35,* 361–375.

Hoeller, K. (1990). An introduction to existential psychology and psychiatry. In K. Hoeller (Ed.), *Readings in existential psychology and psychiatry* (pp. 3–19). Seattle, WA: Review of Existential Psychology and Psychiatry.

Horvath, A. O., & Greenberg, L. S. (Eds.). (1994). *The working alliance: Theory, research, and practice.* New York: Wiley.

Howard, K. I., Kopta, S. M., Krause, M. S., & Orlinsky, D. E. (1986). The dose–effect relationship in psychotherapy. *American Psychologist, 41,* 159–164.

Jacobson, N. S., & Christensen, A. (1996). Studying the effectiveness of psychotherapy: How well can clinical trials do the job? *American Psychologist, 51,* 1031–1039.

Jensen, J. P., Bergin, A. E., & Greaves, D. W. (1990). The meaning of eclecticism: New survey and analysis of components. *Professional Psychology: Research and Practice, 21,* 124–130.

Jones, E. E., Parke, L. A., & Pulos, S. M. (1992). How therapy is conducted in the private consulting room: A multidimensional description of brief psychodynamic treatment. *Psychotherapy Research, 2,* 16–30.

Keen, E. (1970). *Three faces of being: Toward an existential clinical psychology.* New York: Appleton-Century-Crofts.

Lafferty, P., Beutler, L. E., & Crago, M. (1989). Differences between more and less effective psychotherapists: A study of selected therapist variables. *Journal of Consulting and Clinical Psychology, 57,* 76–80.

Laing, R. D. (1965). *The divided self.* Baltimore: Pelican.

Lambert, M. J. (1992). Psychotherapy outcome research. In J. C. Norcross & M. R. Goldfried (Eds.), *Handbook of psychotherapy integration* (pp. 94–129). New York: Basic.

Lietaer, G. (1992). Helping and hindering processes in client-centered/experiential psychotherapy. In S. G. Toukmanian & D. L. Rennie (Eds.), *Psychotherapy process research: Paradigmatic and narrative approaches* (pp. 134–162). Newbury Park, CA: Sage.

Lowenstein, L. F. (1993). Humanism–existentialism as a basis of psychotherapy. *International Journal of Mental Health, 22,* 93–102.

Mahoney, M. J. (1991). *Human change processes: The scientific foundations of psychotherapy.* New York: Basic Books.

Maslow, A. H. (1968). *Toward a psychology of being.* New York: Van Nostrand Reinhold.

May, R. (1958). Contributions of existential psychotherapy. In R. May, E. Angel, & H. F. Ellenberger (Eds.), *Existence: A new dimension in psychiatry and psychology* (pp. 37–91). New York: Basic Books.

May, R. (1983). *The discovery of being: Writings in existential psychology.* New York: Norton.

May, R., & Yalom, I. D. (1995). Existential psychotherapy. In R. J. Corsini & D. Wedding (Eds.), *Current psychotherapies* (5th ed., pp. 262–292). Itasca, IL: Peacock.

McAdams, D. P. (1996). Personality, modernity, and the storied self: A contemporary framework for studying persons. *Psychological Inquiry, 7,* 295–321.

McCullough, L., Winston, A., Farber, B. A., Porter, P., Pollack, J., Vingiano, W., & Trujillo, M. (1991). The relationship of patient–therapist interaction to outcome in brief psychotherapy. *Psychotherapy, 28,* 525–533.

McLeod, J. (1997). *Narrative and psychotherapy.* London: Sage.

Messer, S., Sass, L., & Woolfolk, R. (Eds.). (1988). *Hermeneutics and psychological theory: Interpersonal perspectives on personality, psychotherapy, and psychopathology.* New Brunswick, NJ: Rutgers University.

Misiak, H., & Sexton, V. S. (1973). *Phenomenological, existential, and humanistic psychologies: A historical survey.* New York: Grune & Stratton.

Moras, K. (1993). The use of treatment manuals to train psychotherapists: Observations and recommendations. *Psychotherapy, 30,* 581–586.

Morawski, J. G. (1988). Impossible experiments and practical constructions: The social bases of psychologists' work. In J. G. Morawski (Ed.), *The rise of experimentation in American psychology* (pp. 72–93). New Haven, CT: Yale University Press.

Moss, D. (1989). Psychotherapy and human experience. In R. S. Valle & S. Halling (Eds.), *Existential–phenomenological perspectives in psychology: Exploring the breadth of human experience* (pp. 193–213). New York: Plenum.

Neimeyer, R. A. (1994). The role of client-generated narratives in psychotherapy. *Journal of Constructivist Psychology, 7,* 229–242.

Norcross, J. C. (1987). A rational and empirical analysis of existential psychotherapy. *Journal of Humanistic Psychology, 27,* 41–68.

Oishi, E., & Murayama, S. (1989). A study on "experiential words" of the focuser: Discussions of what determines the meaning of focusing. *Research Bulletin of Educational Psychology, 34,* 181–188.

Omer, H., & Strenger, C. (1992). The pluralistic revolution: From one true meaning to an infinity of constructed ones. *Psychotherapy, 29,* 253–261.

Orlinsky, D. E., Grawe, K., & Parks, B. K. (1994). Process and outcome in psychotherapy—Noch einmal. In A. E. Bergin & S. L. Garfield (Eds.), *Handbook of psychotherapy and behavior change* (4th ed., pp. 270–376). New York: Wiley.

Packer, M., & Addison, R. (1989). *Entering the circle: Hermeneutic investigation in psychology.* Albany: State University of New York Press.

Patterson, M. L. (1983). *Nonverbal behavior: A functional perspective.* New York: Springer-Verlag.

Polkinghorne, D. E. (1994). Narrative and self-concept. *Journal of Narrative Life History, 1,* 135–153.

Prochaska, J. O. (1979). *Systems of psychotherapy: A transtheoretical analysis.* Homewood, IL: Dorsey.

Rahilly, D. A. (1993). A phenomenological analysis of authentic experience. *Journal of Humanistic Psychology, 33,* 49–71.

Rennie, D. L. (1990). Toward a representation of the client's experience of the psychotherapy hour. In G. Lietaer, J. Rombauts, & R. Van Balen (Eds.), *Client-centered and experiential therapy in the nineties* (pp. 155–172). Leuven, Belgium: Leuven University Press.

Rennie, D. L. (1992). Qualitative analysis of the client's experience of psychotherapy. In S. G. Toukmanian & D. L. Rennie (Eds.), *Psychotherapy process research: Paradigmatic and narrative approaches* (pp. 211–233). Newbury Park, CA: Sage.

Rennie, D. L. (1994). Storytelling in psychotherapy: The client's subjective experience. *Psychotherapy, 31,* 234–243.

Rice, L. N., & Greenberg, L. S. (Eds.). (1984). *Patterns of change: Intensive analysis of psychotherapy process.* New York: Guilford Press.

Sartre, J. -P. (1953). *Existential psychoanalysis.* New York: Philosophical Library.

Schneider, K. J., & May, R. (1995). *The psychology of existence: An integrative, clinical perspective.* New York: McGraw-Hill.

Seligman, M. E. P. (1995). The effectiveness of psychotherapy: The *Consumer Reports* study. *American Psychologist, 50,* 965–974.

Sipiora, M. P. (1988–1989). Solicitude, discourse, and the unconscious: Toward a Heideggerian theory of therapy. *Review of Existential Psychology and Psychiatry, 31*(1–3), 35–49.

Spence, D. P. (1982). *Narrative truth and historical truth: Meaning and interpretation in psychoanalysis.* New York: Norton.

Spinelli, E. (1994). *Demystifying therapy.* London: Constable.

Spinelli, E. (1997). *Tales of unknowing: Eight stories of existential therapy.* New York: New York University Press.

Stolorow, R. D., Atwood, G. E., & Brandchaft, B. (1995). *The intersubjective perspective.* Northvale, NJ: Jason Aronson.

Strasser, F. (1996). Time-limited existential therapy: A structural view. *Journal of the Society for Existential Analysis, 8*(1), 45–56.

Strasser, F., & Strasser, A. (1997). *Existential time-limited therapy: The wheel of existence.* New York: Wiley.

Strupp, H. H. (1996). The tripartite model and the *Consumer Reports* study. *American Psychologist, 51,* 1017–1024.

Sullivan, H. S. (1953). *The interpersonal theory of psychiatry.* New York: Norton.

Taurke, E. A., Flegenheimer, W., McCullough, L., Winston, A., Pollack, J., & Trujillo, M. (1990). Change in patient affect/defense ratio from early to late sessions in brief psychotherapy. *Journal of Clinical Psychology, 46,* 657–668.

Thorne, A., & Latzke, M. (1996). Contextualizing the storied self. *Psychological Inquiry, 7,* 372–376.

van den Berg, J. H. (1971). What is psychotherapy? *Humanitas, 7,* 321–370.

Van den Broek, P., & Thurlow, R. (1991). The role and structure of personal narratives. *Journal of Cognitive Psychotherapy, 5,* 257–274.

van Deurzen-Smith, E. (1988). *Existential counselling in practice.* Newbury Park, CA: Sage.

van Deurzen-Smith, E. (1997). *Everyday mysteries: Existential dimensions of psychotherapy.* New York: Routledge.

van Kaam, A. (1966). *The art of existential counseling.* Wilkes-Barre, PA: Dimension.

Walsh, R. (1994). The study of values in psychotherapy: A critique and call for an alternative method. *Psychotherapy Research, 5,* 313–326.

Walsh, R., Perucci, A., & Severns, J. (1999). What's in a good moment: A hermeneutic study of psychotherapy values across levels of psychotherapy training. *Psychotherapy Research, 9,* 304–326.

Washington, C. A. (1972). Existential theory and the psychiatric counselor. *The Psychiatric Forum, 3,* 35–40.

Watson, J. C., & Rennie, D. L. (1994). Qualitative analysis of clients' subjective experience of significant moments during the exploration of problematic experiences. *Journal of Counseling Psychology, 41,* 500–509.

Willis, R. J. (1994). *Transcendence in relationship: Existentialism and psychotherapy.* Norwood, NJ: Ablex.

Yalom, I. D. (1980). *Existential psychotherapy.* New York: Basic.

Yalom, I. D. (1989). *Love's executioner and other tales of psychotherapy.* New York: Basic Books.

9

PROCESS–EXPERIENTIAL PSYCHOTHERAPY

ROBERT ELLIOTT AND LESLIE S. GREENBERG

The process–experiential (PE) approach to psychotherapy (Greenberg, Rice, & Elliott, 1993) integrates client-centered therapy (CCT) and Gestalt therapy traditions, fostering a creative dialectic between the client-centered emphasis on creating a genuinely empathic and prizing therapeutic relationship (Rogers, 1961) and the active, task-focused, process-directive style of Gestalt therapy (Perls, 1969). Moreover, PE therapy updates these two process-oriented treatments by incorporating contemporary theoretical perspectives. In addition, PE therapy is a research-informed treatment (see Grawe, 1997), based on a 25-year-old program of research (Rice & Greenberg, 1984). In this chapter, we review the current status of the PE approach, briefly summarizing its theory, existing outcome and process research, and practice. Wherever possible in our presentation, we have tried to integrate theory, research, and practice, because these three activities are inextricably interwoven in PE therapy.

PROCESS–EXPERIENTIAL THEORY

Theoretical Foundations

PE therapy weds traditional humanistic assumptions with contemporary emotion theory, dialectical constructivism, and process orientation. The following are five key characteristics of PE therapy.

1. PE therapists endorse a set of key *humanistic values*, including self-determination, the primacy of experiencing, continuing psychological growth throughout the life-span, pluralism and egalitarianism, holism, and authentic person-to-person relationships (cf. Greenberg & Rice, 1997; Tageson, 1982).

2. The major contemporary foundation of PE therapy is *emotion theory* (Greenberg & Paivio, 1997; Greenberg & Safran, 1987, 1989), which holds that emotion is fundamentally adaptive in nature, thereby helping the organism to process complex situational information rapidly and automatically to produce action appropriate for meeting important organismic needs (e.g., self-protection, support). Thus, the PE approach is an emotionally focused treatment (and is sometimes referred to as *emotionally focused therapy*; Greenberg & Paivio, 1997).

Specifically, PE therapy makes use of two key emotion-theoretical concepts: emotion schemes and emotion reactions (these are described in greater detail later in the volume, chap. 16, by Greenberg, Korman, & Paivio). In brief, *emotion schemes* are implicit, idiosyncratic organizational structures that serve as the basis for human experience and self-organization (Greenberg & Paivio, 1997; Greenberg et al., 1993). In the PE approach, the therapist helps clients reflect on, understand, and reevaluate their emotion schemes, through careful empathic listening and evocative or expressive interventions.

However, not all emotional expression is the same, and so different kinds of *emotion reactions* require different therapist intervention (see Greenberg, Korman, & Paivio, this volume, chap. 16; see also Greenberg & Paivio, 1997; Greenberg & Safran, 1989). Assessing these different emotion processes requires close empathic attunement to the nuances of the client's expression and to the perceived situation in which the emotion emerged. Each type of emotion process must be worked with differently (Greenberg & Paivio, 1997). For example, primary adaptive anger needs to be accessed and more fully allowed, whereas secondary reactive anger requires empathic exploration of what other, more primary emotions (e.g., sadness or fear) may underlie the anger.

3. The PE approach is based on a *dialectical constructivist* theory of self and therapy. This form of constructivism is a pluralist, neo-Piagetian perspective, in which the person is viewed as a system in which various elements continuously interact to produce experience and action (Greenberg & Pascual-Leone, 1995, 1997). The clinical implication of this view of the change process is, first of all, that it is useful for the therapist to help the client develop clear separation between the client's different modules, self-organizations, or "voices." In particular, PE therapy encourages the emergence of underrecognized as-

pects of self, so that these aspects can be brought into contact with more dominant, often dysfunction-producing aspects. By accessing underrecognized internal resources and fostering these in interaction with maladaptive dominant aspects, an internal self-challenge is created. This generates new experiences, leading to a restructuring of emotion schemes. This dialectic process can be seen most clearly in PE therapy's use of the Gestalt two-chair dialogue for conflict splits. However, interaction between different aspects of the client runs through most PE tasks (Elliott & Greenberg, 1997).

4. PE therapy is an *empirically supported psychotherapy* (but in a broader sense than has been meant by Chambless & Hollon, 1998, and others): PE therapy is the product of extensive psychotherapy process–outcome research programs initiated by Rice, Greenberg, and Elliott, reviewed in Greenberg, Elliott, and Lietaer (1994) and Elliott (1999). Adapting the method of task analysis from research on cognitive problem solving, Rice and Greenberg (1984) carried out a series of studies in which they developed and tested microprocess models of the steps clients typically pass through in the process of successfully resolving internal conflicts (Greenberg, 1984) and puzzling or problematic reactions (Rice & Saperia, 1984). Similarly, Elliott's research on therapist response modes (Elliott et al., 1987) and client within-session experiences (e.g., Elliott, James, Reimschuessel, Cislo, & Sack, 1985) also provided the descriptive basis for those elements of the PE approach.

5. PE therapy is also characterized by (and takes its name from) its *process orientation*, that is, its emphasis on the unfolding of moment-to-moment process both within the client's and therapist's inner experiencing and in the interaction between them. Furthermore, PE therapy makes use of research-derived descriptive models of the steps clients pass through on their way to resolving particular therapeutic tasks. These models act as *roadmaps* for the way in which the therapist can facilitate client progress toward resolution of a particular therapeutic task.

Treatment Principles

Greenberg et al. (1993) proposed six treatment principles, listed below, which derive from the theoretical foundations just described and which guide the practice of PE therapy. These treatment principles provide the most condensed summary of the PE theory of practice. The first three principles involve facilitating a therapeutic relationship, whereas the last three involve helping the client to engage in work on specific therapeutic tasks. The relationship always takes precedence over the pursuit of a task. (See Greenberg et al., 1993, for more details.)

1. *Empathic attunement: Enter and track the client's immediate and evolving experiencing.* From the therapist's point of view, empathic attunement involves a series of internal actions by the therapist, including letting go of previously formed ideas about the client, actively entering the client's world, resonating with the client's experience, and grasping what is most crucial or poignant for the client at a particular moment. The therapist does not take the client's message as something to be evaluated for truth, appropriateness, or psychopathology, but rather tries to maintain a genuine understanding of the client's internal experience as it evolves from moment to moment.

2. *Therapeutic bond: Express empathy and genuine prizing.* Following Rogers (1957) and others, the therapeutic relationship is seen as a key element in a PE approach. For this reason, the therapist seeks to express his or her empathic attunement to the client, as well as to develop and to communicate acceptance or prizing of the client and genuine presence with the client.

3. *Task collaboration: Facilitate mutual involvement in goals and tasks of therapy.* An effective therapeutic relationship also entails involvement by both client and therapist in the overall treatment goals, immediate within-session tasks, and specific therapeutic activities carried out in therapy. In general, the therapist accepts the goals and tasks presented by the client, working actively with the client to describe the emotional processes involved in them (Greenberg & Paivio, 1997).

4. *Experiential processing: Facilitate optimal client experiential processing (modes of engagement).* A key insight of PE therapy is the understanding that optimal client in-session activities vary between and within therapeutic tasks. Therefore, the therapist helps the client to work in different ways at different times. We refer to these different ways of working as *modes of engagement* (Greenberg et al., 1993). Six main client modes of engagement can be distinguished:

- Attending: allowing and evoking awareness of experience.
- Experiential search: attending to and symbolizing emerging, unclear experiences.

- Active expression: expressing and owning emotional reactions in relation to their appropriate objects.
- Interpersonal contact: experiencing the helpful presence of the therapist.
- Self-reflection: developing a meaning perspective or coherent narrative about experience.
- Carrying forward into action: translating emerging awareness into daily life.

The PE therapist continually uses "micromarkers" to make momentary "microprocess diagnoses" of the mode of engagement most likely to be optimal at that particular moment in therapy.

5. *Task completion: Facilitate client completion of key therapeutic tasks.* In addition, the PE therapist helps the client to identify and resolve important therapeutic tasks, especially those related to key treatment foci. Research on PE therapy has consistently found that clients who resolve key therapist tasks have better outcomes (Greenberg et al., 1994; Watson & Greenberg, 1996). Thus, the therapist begins by helping the client to develop clear treatment foci, then tracks the client's current task within each session. Typically, the therapist gently persists in helping the client stay with key therapeutic tasks. It is important, however, to avoid rigid adherence to a particular current task.

6. *Growth/choice: Foster client growth and self-determination.* Finally, as a humanistic therapy with existential roots, the PE approach emphasizes the importance of clients' agency in choosing their actions and constructing their experiences (Greenberg & Paivio, 1997). Thus, the therapist supports the client's potential and motivation for self-determination, mature interdependence, mastery, and self-development by listening carefully for and helping the client to explore "growing edges" of new experience. Choice is commonly facilitated by encouraging the client to make in-session decisions about the goals, tasks, and activities of therapy.

THE EFFECTIVENESS OF PROCESS–EXPERIENTIAL THERAPY

Overview and Meta-Analysis of Process–Experiential Outcome Research

The outcome of individual PE therapy has been the subject of at least 11 separate studies with various clinical populations. To date, clients with major depression have been the most common subject (e.g., Gibson, 1998; Greenberg & Watson, 1998; Jackson & Elliott, 1990). In addition, the outcome of PE therapy with the following target problems has also been investigated:

- childhood abuse and other unresolved relationships with significant others (Clarke, 1993; Paivio, 1997; Paivio & Greenberg, 1995)
- crime-related posttraumatic stress disorder (PTSD; Elliott, Davis, & Slatick, 1998)
- decisional conflicts (Clarke & Greenberg, 1986; Greenberg & Webster, 1982)
- interpersonal difficulties (Lowenstein, 1985; Toukmanian & Grech, 1991).

These studies are summarized in Table 9.1, which updates previous reviews by Elliott (1996) and Greenberg et al. (1994). The studies involved a variety of different forms of PE therapy; some emphasized a particular therapeutic task (Clarke, 1993; Clarke & Greenberg, 1986; Greenberg & Webster, 1982; Lowenstein, 1985; Paivio & Greenberg, 1995; Toukmanian & Grech, 1991), whereas others used a wider range of tasks (Elliott, Davis, & Slatick, 1998; Gibson, 1998; Greenberg & Watson, 1998; Jackson & Elliott, 1990; Paivio, 1997).

In the present review, meta-analyses of three previously reviewed studies were updated in light of additional data (e.g., long-term follow-ups), and three new studies were added, and all studies were reanalyzed using more conservative meta-analytic methods. Our current review once again yielded very large pre-to-post effect sizes (ESs) for PE therapy (mean ES = 1.34 standard deviation), but somewhat lower than reported in previous reviews (Elliott, 1996: mean ES = 1.96; Greenberg et al., 1994: mean ES = 1.84).

The main reason for the smaller effect size is that we are now distinguishing between individual PE therapy and Greenberg and Johnson's (1988) closely related emotionally focused therapy (EFT) for couples. If comparison with other individual treatments of common adult outpatient problems (e.g., CCT or cognitive–behavioral therapy; CBT) is the primary concern, then it may be somewhat misleading to lump conjoint EFT with individual PE therapy. (Current data suggest that CCT, Gestalt therapy, and PE therapy have pre-to-post effect sizes of roughly the same size, in the range of 1.1 to 1.3 standard deviations; see this volume, Elliott, chapter 2.)

There are as yet relatively few controlled and comparative outcome studies, but the existing studies have yielded impressive and uniformly positive effect sizes. Two controlled studies exist, both showing a large advantage for clients in PE therapy versus in wait-list control groups. In a brief treatment of decisional conflicts, Clarke and Greenberg (1986) found a substantially

TABLE 9.1
Outcome Research on Process–Experiential Psychotherapy

Study	Treatment (length)	Population (n)	Type of[a] Measure	Mean Change[b] ES
Clarke (1993)	Meaning creation (8)	Childhood sexual abuse (9)	Exp; Slm	—[c]
Clarke and Greenberg (1986)	Experiential two-chair (2)	Decisional conflicts (16)	Adj	Post: 1.14
Jackson and Elliott (1990)	Process-experiential (16)	Depression (15)	Adj, CSy, Exp, Slm, SSy, TC	Mid (11): 0.64 Post (11): 1.36 FU 6 months (8): 2.05 FU 18 months (8): 1.80
Elliott, Davis, and Slatick (1998)	Process-experiential (16)	Crime-related PTSD (6)	SSy, Exp	Mid (5): 0.35 Post (5): 0.82 Post 6 months (5): 0.93
Gibson (1998)	Feminist process–experiential (12)	Depression (6)	SSy, CSy, Adj	Post (4): 0.50
Greenberg and Watson (1998)	Process-experiential (16)	Depression (17)	SSy, Slm, Adj, TC	Mid (4): 1.25 Post (5): 2.49 FU 6 months (5): 1.88
Greenberg and Webster (1982)	Experiential two-chair (6 max)	Decisional conflicts (31)	Adj, SSy	Post (3): 2.07 FU 1 month (3): 2.16
Lowenstein (1985)	Client-centered + evocative unfolding (5)	Interpersonal + anxiety (12)	Slm, SSy, TC	Post (4): 0.94
Paivio (1997)	Emotionally focused therapy (20)	Childhood sexual abuse (22)	SSy, Adj, Rel, TC, Slm	Post (7): 1.59
Paivio and Greenberg (1995)	Process-experiential chair work (12)	Unresolved relationship issues (17)	SSy, Adj, TC, Rel, Slm	Post: 1.65 FU 4 months: 1.57
Toukmanian and Grech (1991)	Perceptual processing experiential (10)	Interpersonal problems (18)	Slm, Exp	Post (3): 0.70

Note. Mean effect size (ES) = 1.33 standard deviation.

[a]Exp = measures of experiential functioning; Adj = social adjustment or interpersonal problems measures; CSy = clinician ratings of symptoms; SSY = self-ratings of symptoms; Slm = self image measures; Rel = measures of relationship quality (e.g., marital); TC = target complaint or individualized problem measures. [b]ESs for multiple outcome measures were first averaged within instruments, then across instruments for each treatment group and each assessment period. Number of instruments at different assessments is given in parentheses. Pooled standard deviations are used to calculate ESs. FU = follow-up (followed by time period in months). [c]Pre–post ES could not be calculated from data provided (comparative ES = 0.76).

larger effect for a two-chair-based early form of PE therapy (controlled ES = 1.14). Paivio (1997), working with a much more clinically distressed population of adult survivors of childhood sexual abuse, also found a very large controlled effect size favoring PE treatment (ES = 1.29).

PE therapy has been studied in five comparative outcome studies, four of them in contrast with nonexperiential interventions. Two studies found that PE therapy was superior to group psychoeducational treatments. Toukmanian and Grech (1991) found more improvement in clients with interpersonal difficulties treated with a perceptual-processing-based PE treatment (i.e., empathic exploration task, see below; ES = 0.55), whereas Paivio and Greenberg (1995) reported much greater positive change in empty-chair-based PE therapy for clients with unresolved issues with significant others (ES = 1.24). In another two studies of very brief treatments, PE therapies were significantly more effective than CBTs. Clarke and Greenberg (1986) found that a brief two-chair-based PE therapy was superior to behavioral problem solving (comparative ES = 0.57) for clients with decisional conflicts. Clarke (1993) also reported results from a small-sample study in which a brief PE therapy emphasizing a meaning-creation task produced a substantially larger effect size than a cognitive restructuring treatment (ES = 0.76). Finally, Greenberg and Watson (1998) found that clinically depressed clients treated with PE therapy improved somewhat more than clients who received CCT (i.e., without specific treatment tasks; ES = 0.33).

Thus, the existing literature, though still relatively sparse, suggests that PE therapy is superior to wait-list and some common alternative treatments. Overall, there now is strong support for PE therapy as a treatment of depression (see below), and some evidence also supports its use for unresolved issues related to abuse. Although relatively little research has been carried out with other clinical populations, based on the research to date, PE therapy appears to be a promising treatment.

Outcome Research on Process–Experiential Therapy With Depression

The results of Jackson and Elliott's (1990) initial study on the use of PE therapy to treat clinical depression yielded promising results. Researchers followed 15 clients over 12–20 sessions of PE treatment for depression. They found substantial and clinically significant change on the Beck Depression Inventory (BDI), the Hamilton Rating Scale for Depression, the Symptom Checklist 90–Revised, the Rosenberg Self-Esteem Scale, and the Social Adjustment Scale, among others.

Subsequently, the York 1 Depression Study compared the effectiveness of PE psychotherapy with one of its components, CCT, in the treatment of adults with major depression. The experiential treatment consisted of the client-centered conditions, plus the use of specific PE interventions.

Although there was no difference between treatments on the BDI and target complaints, the PE treatment was more effective on broader indices of change at termination. It resulted in greater improvement in clients' self-esteem, interpersonal functioning, and reduced symptom distress. It also produced quicker change, with clients showing greater change on all indices at mid-treatment. At 6-month follow-up, treatment gains were maintained, but there were no longer any significant differences between groups, because clients in CCT had improved to the point at which they resembled the PE clients.

The results show that both treatments demonstrated pre–post effect sizes equivalent to those found for other therapeutic approaches in the treatment of depression (see Table 9.1; Greenberg et al., 1994; Robinson, Berman, & Neimeyer, 1990). Furthermore, in light of the absence of change in untreated depressed clients, as indicated by the small effect sizes reported in depressed control groups (Nietzel, Russell, Hemmings, & Gretter, 1987), these results can be interpreted as providing preliminary evidence for the probable efficacy of experientially oriented treatments for depression.

Finally, preliminary results on two other PE studies of depression are available: Goldman, Greenberg, and Angus (1999) replicated the York 1 Study, again with large pre–post effects for PE therapy (ES = 1.69) and greater posttreatment improvement for PE versus CCT (ES = 0.74). In addition, Watson and Stermac (1999) reported generally equivalent results for PE versus CBT, with slightly greater improvement for clients in PE therapy.

THE RESEARCH-INFORMED PRACTICE OF PROCESS–EXPERIENTIAL THERAPY

Experiential Response Modes

The actual practice of PE therapy is best described at two complementary levels: (a) experiential response modes, which occur at the level of individual therapist responses, and (b) PE tasks, which encompass substantial portions of therapy sessions. We incorporate relevant research into our discussion of these two levels of practice.

In carrying out the treatment principles described earlier, therapists use a number of specific actions or response modes. Both Davis (1995) and Goldman (1991) have developed measures of therapist experiential response modes. Where possible, we illustrate the main types of therapist response used in PE therapy with examples from a key change session involving Beth, a 19-year-old client with crime-related PTSD (examples from Elliott, Urman, Jersak, & Gutiérrez, 1998).

1. *Empathic understanding*. Consistent with its client-centered heritage, an important form of therapist response in the PE approach is empathic reflection and following, enacted by therapist (T) responses that seek to communicate understanding of the client's (C) message, including simple reflections and related responses ("Uh-huh's"). For example, Beth said about her inability to do things on her own,

C: I mean that's the biggest grief, that's my biggest sadness.
In response, the therapist reflected with,
T: That's what you grieve for, is the loss of independence.

2. *Empathic exploration responses*. The most characteristic PE intervention is empathic exploration (Greenberg et al., 1993). These responses simultaneously communicate understanding and help clients move toward the unclear or emerging edges of their experience. Empathic exploration responses take a number of different forms, including evocative and open-edge reflections, exploratory questions, "fit" questions (to check understanding), and empathic conjectures. Here is a brief excerpt illustrating empathic exploration responses, taken from a two-chair exercise between Beth's strong previctimization self and her weak postvictimization self:

C: I just want enough of who I used to be, so that I could live like a human being.
T: "I don't feel like a human being right now. I feel like some kind of something else that's not human." [First-person *evocative reflection* spoken as the postvictimization self.]
C: (Jus') like a paranoid little, girl, ya know.
T: It's like what you want from that part is some of the courage. Is that right? [*Empathic conjecture*, intended to direct the client's attention back to her current, postvictimization self; followed by a *"fit" question* to determine the accuracy.]

A little later, the therapist offers two *exploratory questions*, addressed to the lost, previctimization self, to help the client to enact this part of herself:

T: What's that like? What do you feel in that part?
C: Happy. (laughs softly)

3. *Process directives*. The difference between CCT and PE therapy is most apparent in the use of a variety of process directives. Although PE therapists rarely suggest possible solutions to client life problems, they often suggest in a nonimposing way that the client try engaging in particular *in-session* activities. These responses include experiential teaching (giving orient-

ing information or treatment rationales), attention suggestions (directives to attend to immediate experience), action suggestions (directives to do or try something in the sessions), task structuring (used to set up therapeutic tasks), and task focusing (used to help the client "stay with" or "come back to" a therapeutic task after a sidetrack). Many of these are illustrated in this sample of process directives used to help the client Beth to grieve and reaccess her lost, previctimization "strong self":

T: [Early in session; *attention suggestion* about her discouragement at not overcoming her fears:] Can you stay with that hurt and sadness for a minute, and just feel what that's about and what that's like?

T: [Later in session; *experiential teaching* about a potentially useful therapeutic strategy:] One way to try to work with the grief is to put that part of you that you've lost in the chair and talk to her. There are other ways but that is one way that occurs to me.

T: [Introducing chairwork; *task structuring*; points to "other" chair:] So there's the "normal" Beth.

Later, a *task focus* response is used to redirect the client after a client sidetrack:

C: Whenever we needed to drive somewhere, I drove. When we needed to get something, I got it.

T: So this is the strong Beth, and somehow, you're gone, you went away.

Finally, near the end of the session, the therapist helps the client reintegrate her lost, previctimization self, using a series of *action suggestions*, in this exchange:

T: Can you go over and *be* in (the strong) part?
C: I would but I wouldn't know how.
T: Tell her "I'd like you to have that strength."
C: I'd like you to have my strength.
T: What's that feel like? [Exploratory question]
C: Like a, like a mom.

Experiential "homework" is a final kind of process directive, as in the following example from Susan, a client who has sudden inexplicable episodes of suicidal feelings:

T: During the next week, it might be useful for you to try to pay attention to what is going on when you have these "black funnel" experiences, and see if you can remember exactly what is going through your mind right before them.

In addition to chair work, process direction is also common in experiential focusing (Clark, 1990).

4. *Experiential presence.* Therapist empathic attunement, prizing, genuineness, and collaborativeness—attitudes involved in

fostering the therapeutic relationship—are primarily communicated through the therapist's genuine "presence" or manner of being with the client. The exact configuration of therapist paralinguistic and nonverbal behaviors, including silence, vocal quality, and appropriate posture and expression, is difficult to describe. There is, however, a distinctive, easily recognized PE style: For example, the therapist typically uses a gentle, prizing voice (and sometimes humor) to deliver process directives, whereas empathic exploration responses often have a tentative, pondering quality. Presence is also indicated by direct eye contact at moments of connection between client and therapist.

Therapist *process* and *personal disclosure* responses are really explicit forms of experiential presence response, in that they are commonly used to communicate relationship attitudes. For example, the therapist began the first session of Beth's therapy with a process disclosure of excitement:

T: . . . So I'm excited about giving it [the therapy] a try.

In the fifth session, the therapist used a personal disclosure to help the client explore her experience of her crime-related fear:

T: You know it reminds me of, you know, those creepy old science fiction horror movies about things that take possession of people.

Davis (1995) found that about 3% of therapist responses were disclosures.

In a study of client-designated significant events in the treatment of depression, Davis (1995) found that more than three quarters of PE therapists' responses were either empathic understanding (57%) or empathic exploration (19%), and that process-directing responses occurred about at a rate of about 8%; the other response types occurred less than 5% of the time. In contrast, Benjamin (1979), Goldman (1991), and Hirscheimer (1996) all found a much higher level of process directing in two-chair work tasks (around 40%). This discrepancy is probably due to differences in the samples (two-chair work vs. general PE practice).

5. *Nonexperiential responses.* Although therapist responses such as interpretation, extratherapy advisement, reassurance, or confrontation are important in various psychodynamic or cognitive therapies, these content directive responses are typically avoided or minimized. These responses compromise the treatment principles described earlier, particularly growth/choice and empathic attunement, and are generally irrelevant or interfere with client experiential work. Nevertheless, occasionally such nonexperiential responses may be needed, for exam-

ple, for clinical management of suicidality. In these cases, the therapist makes his or her nonexperiential response briefly and tentatively, as a disclosure of a personal perspective. Davis (1995) found about 5% of therapist responses to be nonexperiential.

Research on Process–Experiential Tasks

PE therapy integrates a variety of different experiential tasks, drawn from CCT, Gestalt therapy, and existential therapy traditions. These tasks all include three elements: (a) a *marker* of a problem state signaling the client's *wish* to work on a particular experiential task; (b) a *task intervention* sequence of actions carried out by client and therapist in working on the task; and (c) a desired *resolution* or end state. We find it useful to divide PE tasks into three groupings: basic exploratory tasks, active expression tasks, and interpersonal tasks (see Table 9.2; for more detail, see Elliott et al., 1998; Greenberg et al., 1993).

The study of particular task interventions within the task-analytic paradigm (Rice & Greenberg, 1984) is the strongest area of PE therapy research.

Evocative Unfolding of Problematic Reactions

The problematic reaction point (PRP) marker has been shown to be identifiable with high reliability (95% agreement between raters; Greenberg & Rice, 1991). Rice and colleagues demonstrated that when the incident is vividly reevoked and reprocessed more slowly and completely, clients recognize that their reactions were a direct response to their subjective construals of the eliciting stimulus (Rice & Saperia, 1984). This recognition leads to the further understanding of a broader style of functioning that is interfering with meeting needs and goals. An empirically derived model of the above components of resolution of problematic reactions has been established (Rice & Saperia, 1984) and is central to PE treatment.

Research on this task has provided evidence for its effectiveness. In an initial analog study, Rice and Saperia (1984), comparing the effects of purely empathic responding with evocative unfolding, found that clients' ratings for the evocative sessions were significantly higher. In a further study (Lowenstein, 1985), clients with anxiety and interpersonal problems were seen at a counseling center for brief, time-limited CCT. Therapists used evocative unfolding to respond to a PRP marker in either the third or fourth session. The evocative session was rated by the clients as significantly higher on depth than the other two middle sessions. Evocative unfolding sessions were also rated significantly higher on a scale assessing the degree of shift

TABLE 9.2
Process–Experiential Tasks: Markers, Interventions and End States

Task Marker	Intervention	End State
Basic exploratory tasks		
Problem-relevant experience (e.g., interesting, troubling, puzzling)	Empathic exploration	Clear marker, or new meaning explicated
Experiential–processing difficulty (e.g., overwhelmed, blank, stuck, unclear)	Experiential focusing (including clearing a space)	Productive experiencing (therapeutic focus; enhanced working distance; symbolization of felt sense)
Narrative marker (internal pressure to tell difficult life stories, e.g., trauma)	Facilitating retelling	Relief, restoration of narrative gaps
Problematic reaction point (puzzling overreaction to specific situation)	Systematic evocative unfolding	New view of self-in-the-world functioning
Meaning protest (life event violates cherished belief)	Meaning work	Revision of cherished belief
Active expression tasks		
Self-evaluative split (self-criticism, tornness)	Two-chair dialogue	Self-acceptance, integration
Self-interruption split (blocked feelings, resignation)	Two-chair enactment	Self-expression, empowerment
Unfinished business (lingering bad feeling regarding significant other)	Empty-chair work	Forgive other or hold other accountable, affirm self/separate
Interpersonal tasks		
Vulnerability (painful emotion related to self)	Empathic affirmation	Self-affirmation (feels understood, hopeful, stronger)
Therapy complaint (questioning goals or tasks; disrupted bond with therapist)	Alliance dialogue (each explores own role in difficulty)	Alliance repair (stronger therapeutic bond or investment in therapy; greater self-understanding)

in their own perspective (Lowenstein, 1985). On final outcome, the clients who had successfully resolved the PRP in the "task-focused" evocative session had significantly greater reduction in state anxiety.

In a sequential analysis study, Wiseman and Rice (1989) found that therapist interventions specific to the particular step of the PRP task had a highly significant effect on client-experiencing level, thus supporting the validity of the previously developed model of how PRP tasks are resolved.

In addition, evocative task-focused sessions were rated as deeper and more valuable than comparable nontask sessions. Clients also rated the evocative sessions as producing significantly greater shifts in self-understanding and sense of progress.

Two-Chair Dialogue for Conflict Splits

This task intervention addresses a class of client difficulties in which two emotion schemes or aspects of the self are in opposition. Conflict split markers have been shown to be identifiable with very high reliability (100% agreement between raters; Greenberg, 1984). To determine the effectiveness of the Gestalt two-chair dialogue in resolving splits, research has compared it with interventions drawn from other therapeutic orientations. In a number of controlled analogue and therapy studies, the two-chair method was found to be more effective than client-centered empathy (Greenberg & Clarke, 1979; Greenberg & Dompierre, 1981; Greenberg & Rice, 1981), cognitive–behavioral problem solving (Clarke & Greenberg, 1986), and experiential focusing (Greenberg & Higgins, 1980).

To identify how the change takes place, Greenberg (1980, 1983, 1984) conducted a series of intensive analyses of client performances in successful episodes of conflict resolution and compared these with unsuccessful episodes. In the first study, the two sides of the conflict were found to function as independent systems, proceeding at different levels of experiencing. One side, called the *other chair*, contained clients' criticisms and expectations and proceeded at lower levels of experiencing than did the second side, called the *experiencing chair*. When resolution occurred, the two sides converged, becoming indistinguishable in their experiencing level and moving to a higher level of experiencing. This pattern revealed itself consistently throughout nine events in the three clients studied.

Greenberg (1984) then used additional process ratings to evaluate and elaborate the model into one containing six components necessary for conflict resolution. In this refined model, the critic, through role playing, first identifies its harsh, critical evaluations of the experiencing part of the self. The experiencing part, in turn, expresses its affective reactions to the harsh criticism. The harsh critic then moves from general statements to more concrete and specific criticisms of the person or situation. Specific behaviors may be criticized and specific changes demanded. In response to these criticisms, the experiencing chair begins to react in a more differentiated fashion until a new aspect of its experience is expressed. A sense of direction then emerges for the experiencer, which is expressed to the critic as a want or a need. The critic next moves to a statement of standards and values. At this point in the dialogue, the critic softens. This is followed by a negotiation or an integration, or both, between the two parts.

To investigate the relationship between resolution processes and outcome, Greenberg and Webster (1982) selected three essential components of resolution from the model: criticism in the other chair, expression of felt wants in the experiencing chair, and softening in the other chair. These components were used to classify clients as having either resolved or failed to resolve one or more conflict splits during the course of therapy. Resolvers were found to be significantly less undecided and less anxious after treatment than were nonresolvers. Resolvers also showed greater improvement on target complaints and behavioral change. After the particular session in which the critic softened, resolvers reported greater conflict resolution, less discomfort, greater mood change, and greater goal attainment than nonresolvers.

Empty-Chair Dialogue for Unfinished Business

The marker of unfinished business has been shown to be identified with high reliability (90% agreement; Greenberg & Rice, 1991). The process of resolution has been modeled, and components that distinguish resolved from unresolved events have been established (Foerster, 1991). Critical components of the resolution of unfinished business appear from this preliminary study to be the arousal of intense emotion, the declaration of a need, and a shift in view of the significant other.

An analogue study (King, 1988) compared the effects of empty-chair dialogue and empathic responding to unfinished business. This study showed a delayed effect for empty-chair dialogue: One week after the session, the empty-chair work resulted in a greater increase in tolerance for the significant other and in self-confidence in relation to the significant other. Results from a study of the in-session process also revealed that empty-chair sessions were characterized by significantly greater depth of experiencing than empathic responding sessions (Maslove, 1989).

Following these preliminary studies, empirical task-analysis procedures were used to develop and successively refine a model of the successful resolution of unfinished business: First, there is a statement of chronic unresolved feeling; then a memory of a specific episode with the other is evoked. The emotional reactions associated with this episodic memory are then symbolized, differentiated, and expressed. The process completes itself with the construction of a new narrative of self as stronger, and other as more responsive.

Foerster (1991) carried out the original validation of this model, and Pedersen (1996) replicated and extended it with a separate group of participants. Foerster (1991) found that the discriminating components are the intense expression of primary emotion, expression of previously unmet interpersonal needs, a shift in view of the other, and resolution. The components of blame/complaint/hurt and enactment of negative frustrating other did not discriminate between the two groups, as these elements were usually present at the beginning of all empty-chair dialogues. It is only as clients engage more deeply in the process that evidence of change begins to be seen. In addition, it was confirmed that resolvers demonstrated greater depth of client experiencing. A shift in interpersonal process ratings was also found, in that clients who resolved their unfinished business became less hostile and more assertive and friendly toward the other while in the self chair. In the other chair, they became less hostile and controlling, and more affiliative. Together, the studies by Foerster (1991) and Pedersen (1996) validated the model as proposed, supporting the theory that the refined model does in fact describe the key components of client performance in the resolution of unfinished business.

The next step was Paivio and Greenberg's (1995) efficacy study comparing an empty-chair-based treatment with a psychoeducational intervention for resolving unfinished business. The empty-chair intervention was found to be significantly more effective in reducing target complaints, general symptoms, and interpersonal distress, as well as in achieving unfinished business resolution.

A series of more intensive analyses of the same data set were then carried out: First, Singh (1996) used Foerster's (1991) findings to develop a self-report measure specifically designed to assess the degree of resolution of unfinished business with a significant other. The findings from an item analysis, exploratory factor analysis, and tests of construct and concurrent validity provided support for the scale as a measure of degree of resolution of unfinished business. Singh also demonstrated that change reported from the three best sessions predicted overall treatment outcome.

Next, using the core conflictual relationship theme (Luborsky & Crits-Cristoph, 1990) and structural analysis of social behavior (Benjamin, 1982) methods to compare early versus late sessions of empty-chair dialogue, McMain (1995) found that changes in representation of self (increases in self-autonomy, self-affiliation, and positive responses to the significant other) were predictive of treatment outcome at posttherapy and 4-month follow-up.

Greenberg and Hirscheimer (1994) also used the Degree of Resolution Scale (DRS; Greenberg et al., 1993) to rate client process over the course of treatment. The DRS consists of seven increasing degrees of resolution through which clients proceed in empty-chair work. Hirscheimer (1996) demonstrated that high levels of resolution (as defined by raters' in-session ratings on the DRS) were significantly related to client self-report of positive treatment outcomes at posttherapy and 4-month follow-up. These results supported the reliability and predictive validity of the DRS as a measure of client degree of resolution in unfinished business tasks.

Hirscheimer (1996) also found that clients who demonstrated moderate or high emotional expression during empty-chair work were more than twice as likely to resolve compared with clients who demonstrated low emotional expression. Intense expression of emotion in itself, however, did not directly predict symptom change, increased self–other affiliation, or self-autonomy. This suggests that the effect of intense emotional expression is mediated through empty-chair task resolution rather than directly affecting outcome.

Finally, Malcolm (1999) used a set of process measures independent of the model to assess the resolution of unfinished business, including measures of vocal quality, level of experiencing, shifts in social interaction, and degree of emotional arousal. In this study, 13 clients whose empty-chair dialogues contained at least five of the six components of the model (including resolution) were defined as the resolved group and were compared with an equal number of clients randomly selected from the remaining pool of clients who had fewer than five components of the model in their empty-chair dialogue. Analyses of covariance demonstrated that resolvers showed statistically significant improvements at termination on a variety of outcome measures. In short, this series of studies on empty-chair work for unfinished business supports the validity and clinical utility of the model of resolution developed by Greenberg and colleagues (Greenberg et al., 1993; Greenberg & Foerster, 1996).

Creation of Meaning in Meaning Protests

Meaning-creation work occurs when a client protests an unexpected, often traumatic, life event (Clarke, 1989, 1991). Using task analysis to develop a performance model of therapeutic meaning-creation work, Clarke (1989) first defined the marker for this event as containing three indicators: the presence of strong emotional arousal (positive or negative emotion); an indication of a confronted or challenged cherished belief; and an indication of confusion, surprise, or lack of understanding. She then developed an empirical model consisting of three phases: specification, exploration, and revision.

An analogue study (Clarke, 1989) of this process contrasted the effects of the focused use of meaning-symbolization interventions with ordinary empathic reflection in meaning crisis. As hypothesized, meaning symbolization led to deeper levels of experiencing, more focused voice, greater reduction in discomfort, and more positive inner feeling and clarity than did empathic reflection.

Clarke (1996) subsequently evaluated some of the performance patterns in successful and unsuccessful meaning-creation events. Results confirmed that four specific component processes distinguish between successful and unsuccessful meaning-making events. These processes involve the exact symbolization of both the cherished belief and the client's emotional reaction, as well as the generation of a hypothesis about the origin of the belief and the evaluation of the present tenability of the cherished belief. These components were measured using client experiencing, client vocal quality, and verbal imagery. Verbal imagery ratings were significantly higher at the moment of meaning-making in successful events than in unsuccessful events, supporting the idea that therapists help by providing symbols that link visual imagery to verbal processing. Finally, as noted earlier, Clarke (1993) carried out a small comparative treatment outcome study in which a brief meaning-creation-focused treatment for incest survivors led to more change than a cognitive restructuring treatment.

Focusing for Unclear or Painful Felt Sense

Two studies on the use of experiential focusing (Gendlin, 1996) in PE therapy have been carried out: Horton and Elliott (1991), in research with clients with depression, found that focusing was the most common PE task, reported by therapists in 52% of sessions. Clark (1990) carried out an intensive qualitative study of significant events involving focusing. She found that the "handle" step of focusing (in which clients label their experience) was the most important in these events. The clients themselves tended to be unassertive, to be self-critical, and to have problems in interpersonal relationships, but they showed a general ability to contact their inner experiences spontaneously. In the course of these events, clients became clearer about the nature of their difficulties.

General Research on Frequency and Discriminability of Process–Experiential Tasks

Horton and Elliott (1991) reported that clients with depression in PE therapy presented at least one specific task marker in almost every session (96%); the most common were internal conflicts and unclear feelings. Horton and Elliott also provided data on the relative use of four different therapist task interventions: More than three quarters of all sessions contained at least one of the four techniques; after focusing, the most common tasks were empty-chair work (30%), two-chair work (29%), and unfolding (23%).

Research on the Effective Processes in Process–Experiential Therapy

Process–Outcome Research

Relatively little process–outcome research has so far been done on PE therapy. *Client engagement* in treatment has been studied most often. Brinkerhoff (1991) found more explication of interpersonal conflicts in successful cases in PE therapy. Greenberg and Adler (1989) found that client self-ratings on a measure of client involvement were a promising predictor of outcome. In addition, Watson and Greenberg (1996) reported that the emergence of a clear task focus by the fifth session predicted successful outcome.

Similarly, Goldman (1998) related pre–post changes in the *depth of experiencing* to outcome of clients with depression. Previous research has often failed to find clear increases in client experiencing over successful treatments (Klein, Mathieu-Coughlan, & Kiesler, 1986). Goldman and Greenberg (1997), however, argued that successful brief PE therapy works by addressing client core themes, rather than by means of gradual and cumulative change in overall personality functioning (e.g., enhanced experiencing), as argued by Rogers. They proposed that client experiencing should therefore be rated on core thematic episodes. To test this proposal, Goldman identified segments in which clients were addressing core themes and found that changes across therapy in theme-related experiencing predicted outcome. She also found that change in experiencing from early to late in therapy was superior to the working alliance in predicting outcome (Goldman, 1998).

Horton and Elliott (1991), in the only study to examine the relationship between PE *therapist interventions* and treatment outcome, reported disappointing results: Therapist ratings of specific tasks did not predict outcome, but self-ratings of basic facilitative interventions (e.g., empathic understanding, empathic exploration) did. Finally, Greenberg and Adler (1989), using a sample of broadly humanistic treatments, found that clients' perceptions of the *working alliance* correlated with outcome.

Helpful Factors Research

In addition to process–outcome research, another, more direct method for understanding what is effective or change-producing in experiential–humanistic therapies is to ask clients to identify aspects or incidents that were helpful or hindering. This approach typically uses postsession or posttreatment open-ended questions.

Using qualitative analyses of mid-treatment interview data of clients with depression, Mancinelli (1993) identified "a safe working environment" as the core helpful process in PE therapy of depression. This core category was made up of three subordinate factors: relational safety, engagement in exploratory therapeutic work, and a sense of resulting progress. If any one of these factors was missing, the client did not feel helped. Three other analyses of data from the same study examined postsession questionnaires administered to clients: (a) Elliott, Clark, and Kemeny (1991) carried out a content analysis of clients' postsession descriptions of most helpful events in PE therapy. They found that the most common types of helpful event involved self-awareness, client self-disclosure, and therapist basic experiential techniques. (b) In contrast, Elliott et al. (1990) also found that when clients and therapists were given quantitative rating scales to evaluate the effects of significant events, both awarded the highest ratings to the client feeling understood (followed by self-awareness and either closer to therapist or supported). (c) Finally, in a study of clients' postsession ratings of therapeutic impact, Elliott and Wexler (1994) found that, consistent with their ratings of significant events, relationship impacts (e.g., supported) received higher ratings than task impacts (e.g., awareness) and that the highest-rated relationship impact was feeling understood.

Practical Implementation of Process–Experiential Therapy

Appropriate Clients

On the basis of our clinical experience, as well as the research conducted to date, we believe that PE therapy is most appropriate for use in outpatient settings with clients experiencing mild-to-moderate levels of clinical distress and symptomatology. Some clients seem to enter therapy with processing styles that allow them to engage almost immediately in the attending, experiential search, and active expression modes of engagement so critical to this approach. Such clients may present a variety of diagnoses and problems, including depression, PTSD, anxiety, low self-esteem, internal conflicts, and lingering resentments and difficulties with others.

Treatment Length

As described here, the PE approach is appropriate as either a brief therapy or a longer term treatment, although relationship elements appear to play a relatively larger role in longer treatments with clients with long-standing personal or interpersonal difficulties (e.g., narcissistic or borderline processes).

CHALLENGES AND CONTINUING DEVELOPMENT

The development of PE therapy has been accompanied by challenges and controversy. The first challenge derives from the location of PE therapy midway between client-centered and Gestalt traditions and styles of relating to clients. On the one hand, traditional client-centered therapists see PE therapy as too directive and regard it as having sacrificed the core client-centered tenets of nondirectiveness and unconditionality. On the other hand, traditional Gestalt therapists have been inclined to regard PE therapy's emphasis on empathic attunement and prizing as fostering dependency in clients. It is our impression that both of these external perceptions are changing. Nevertheless, we and our colleagues and students continue to struggle with conflicts between our "client-centered" and "process–directive" selves, for example, in the current trend to provide a greater role for experiential teaching in PE therapy.

A second challenge comes with the ever-growing sophistication and complexity of PE theory and practice. As we noted earlier, PE therapy has developed increasing complexity, making it more difficult to master. It is important to keep in mind that a process-oriented, multitask approach such as PE therapy is complex and requires time to learn (Elliott & Davis, in press). At the same time, there is also a risk that some students will become too technically focused, at a cost to the relational contact or I–thou relationship between therapist and client. We continue to explore strategies for helping students and others learn the PE approach.

A third challenge comes from those who criticize PE therapy as "too pure" for today's integrative practice of therapy. We agree that it is sometimes necessary to make use of nonexperiential interventions, for example, to help clients cope with immediate life crises. We have also observed that students often adopt a too-rigid, negative understanding of PE therapy as a collection of "don'ts" ("don't give advice, interpret, reassure, disagree, and so on"). In our view, it is important to clarify when experiential work is appropriate and when and how to integrate strategies from other therapeutic traditions, for example, when to encourage clients with depression to seek medication or behavioral activation. At issue is how to incorporate other approaches while still retaining theoretical coherence and relational consistency.

In spite of these challenges, PE therapy seems to have appeal for therapists who are interested in the adaptive power of emotion or who share its humanistic values of focusing on people's internal resources and strengths. At the same time, its task-focused nature and empirical support appeal to cognitive–behavioral therapists who wish to broaden their approach, whereas its emphasis on implicit experience and the therapeutic relationship are compatible with psychodynamic psychotherapies. In an era of increasing demands for brief, effective treatments, the PE approach offers a viable development of the humanistic tradition in psychotherapy, while at the same time appealing to therapists from other traditions. The continuing efforts described in this chapter, in the areas of theory development, research, training, and extension to new clinical populations, are all part of a larger project to help establish humanistic–experiential treatments as empirically supported and generally respected psychotherapies for the 21st century.

REFERENCES

Benjamin, L. S. (1979). Use of structural analysis of social behavior (SASB) and Markov chains to study dyadic interactions. *Journal of Abnormal Psychology, 88,* 303–319.

Benjamin, L. S. (1982). Use of structural analysis of social behavior (SASB) to guide intervention in psychotherapy. In J. C. Anchin & D. J. Kiesler (Eds.), *Handbook of interpersonal psychotherapy* (pp. 190–212). New York: Pergamon Press.

Brinkerhoff, L. J. (1991). *Application of the core conflictual relationship method to an analysis of significant events in an experiential therapy of depression.* Unpublished doctoral dissertation, University of Toledo.

Chambless, D. L., & Hollon, S. D. (1998). Defining empirically supported therapies. *Journal of Consulting and Clinical Psychology, 66,* 7–18.

Clark, C. A. (1990). A comprehensive process analysis of focusing events in experiential therapy (Doctoral dissertation, University of Toledo, 1990). *Dissertation Abstracts International, 51,* 6098B.

Clarke, K. M. (1989). Creation of meaning: An emotional processing task in psychotherapy. *Psychotherapy, 26,* 139–148.

Clarke, K. M. (1991). A performance model of the creation of meaning event. *Psychotherapy, 28,* 395–401.

Clarke, K. M. (1993). Creation of meaning in incest survivors. *Journal of Cognitive Psychotherapy, 7,* 195–203.

Clarke, K. M. (1996). Change processes in a creation of meaning event. *Journal of Consulting and Clinical Psychology, 64,* 465–470.

Clarke, K. M., & Greenberg, L. S. (1986). Differential effects of the Gestalt two-chair intervention and problem solving in resolving decisional conflict. *Journal of Counseling Psychology, 33,* 11–15.

Davis, K. L. (1995). The role of therapist actions in process–experiential therapy. (Doctoral dissertation, University of Toledo, 1994). *Dissertation Abstracts International, 56,* 519B.

Elliott, R. (1996). Are client-centered/experiential therapies effective? A meta-analysis of outcome research. In U. Esser, H. Pabst, & G. W. Speierer (Eds.), *The power of the person-centered-approach: New challenges, perspectives, answers* (pp. 125–138). Köln, Germany: GwG Verlag.

Elliott, R. (1999). The origins of process–experiential therapy: A personal case study in practice-research integration. In S. Soldz & L. McCullough Vaillant (Eds.), *The sometime relationship of research to practice: Psychotherapy researchers' personal reflections* (pp. 33–49). Washington, DC: American Psychological Association.

Elliott, R., Clark, C., & Kemeny, V. (1991, July). *Analyzing clients' postsession accounts of significant therapy events.* Paper presented at the meeting of the Society for Psychotherapy Research, Lyon, France.

Elliott, R., Clark, C., Wexler, M., Kemeny, V., Brinkerhoff, J., & Mack, C. (1990). The impact of experiential therapy of depression: Initial results. In G. Lietaer, J. Rombauts, & R. Van Balen (Eds.), *Client-centered and experiential psychotherapy towards the nineties* (pp. 549–577). Leuven, Belgium: Leuven University Press.

Elliott, R., & Davis, K. (in press). Therapist experiential processing in process-experiential therapy. In F. Caspar (Ed.), *The inner processes of psychotherapists: Innovations in clinical training.* Stanford, CA: Oxford University Press.

Elliott, R., Davis, K., & Slatick, E. (1998). Process–experiential therapy for post-traumatic stress difficulties. In L. Greenberg, G. Lietaer, & J. Watson (Eds.), *Handbook of experiential psychotherapy* (pp. 249–271). New York: Guilford Press.

Elliott, R., & Greenberg, L. S. (1997). Multiple voices in process–experiential therapy: Dialogues between aspects of the self. *Journal of Psychotherapy Integration, 7,* 225–239.

Elliott, R., Hill, C. E., Stiles, W. B., Friedlander, M. L., Mahrer, A., & Margison, F. (1987). Primary therapist response modes: A comparison of six rating systems. *Journal of Consulting and Clinical Psychology, 55,* 218–223.

Elliott, R., James, E., Reimschuessel, C., Cislo, D., & Sack, N. (1985). Significant events and the analysis of immediate therapeutic impacts. *Psychotherapy, 22,* 620–630.

Elliott, R., Urman, M., Jersak, H., & Gutiérrez, C. (1998, June). *"I'd like you to have my strength": A conversational analysis of the process of re-owning the lost self in process–experiential traumawork.* Paper presented at meeting of the Society for Psychotherapy Research, Snowbird, UT.

Elliott, R., & Wexler, M. M. (1994). Measuring the impact of treatment sessions: The Session Impacts Scale. *Journal of Counseling Psychology, 41,* 166–174.

Foerster, F. S. (1991). *Refinement and verification of a model of the resolution of unfinished business.* Unpublished master's thesis, York University, Toronto, Ontario, Canada.

Gendlin, E. T. (1996). *Focusing-oriented psychotherapy: A manual of the experiential method.* New York: Guilford Press.

Gibson, C. (1998). *Feminist experiential therapy of depression: Outcome and helpful factors.* Unpublished dissertation, Department of Psychology, University of Toledo.

Goldman, R. (1991). *The validation of the experiential therapy adherence measure.* Unpublished master's thesis, York University, Toronto, Ontario, Canada.

Goldman, R. (1998). Change in thematic depth of experience and outcome in experimental psychotherapy. *Dissertation Abstracts International, 58*(10), 5643B. (Ann Arbor, MI: ProQuest Digital Dissertations No. AAT NQ22908)

Goldman, R., & Greenberg, L. S. (1997). Case formulation in process–experiential therapy. In T. D. Eells (Ed.), *Handbook of psychotherapy case formulation* (pp. 402–429). New York: Guilford Press.

Goldman, R., Greenberg, L. S., & Angus, L. (1999, June). *Initial results from the York II comparative study on experiential psychotherapy of depression.* Paper presented at meeting of the Society for Psychotherapy Research, Braga, Portugal.

Grawe, K. (1997). Research-informed psychotherapy. *Psychotherapy Research, 7,* 1–20.

Greenberg, L. S. (1980). An intensive analysis of recurring events from the practice of Gestalt therapy. *Psychotherapy: Theory, Research and Practice, 17,* 143–152.

Greenberg, L. S. (1983). Toward a task analysis of conflict resolution in Gestalt therapy. *Psychotherapy: Theory, Research and Practice, 20,* 190–201.

Greenberg, L. S. (1984). A task analysis of intrapersonal conflict resolution. In L. Rice & L. Greenberg (Eds.). *Patterns of change* (pp. 67–123). New York: Guilford Press.

Greenberg, L. S., & Adler, J. (1989, June). *Clients' perceptions of the working alliance.* Paper presented at the Society for Psychotherapy Research, Toronto, Ontario, Canada.

Greenberg, L. S., & Clarke, D. (1979). The differential effects of the two-chair experiment and empathic reflections at a conflict marker. *Journal of Counseling Psychology, 26,* 1–8.

Greenberg, L. S., & Dompierre, L. (1981). The specific effects of Gestalt two-chair dialogue on intrapsychic conflict in counseling. *Journal of Counseling Psychology, 28,* 288–296.

Greenberg, L. S., Elliott, R., & Lietaer, G. (1994). Research on humanistic and experiential psychotherapies. In A. E. Bergin & S. L. Garfield (Eds.), *Handbook of psychotherapy and behavior change* (4th ed., pp. 509–539). New York: Wiley.

Greenberg, L. S., & Foerster, F. (1996). Resolving unfinished business: The process of change. *Journal of Consulting and Clinical Psychology, 64,* 439–446.

Greenberg, L. S., & Higgins, H. M. (1980). The differential effects of two-chair dialogue and focusing on conflict resolution. *Journal of Counseling Psychology, 27,* 221–225.

Greenberg, L. S., & Hirscheimer, K. (1994, November). *Relating process to outcome in unfinished business.* Paper presented at the meeting of the North American Society for Psychotherapy Research, Santa Fe, NM.

Greenberg, L. S., & Johnson, S. M (1988). *Emotionally focused therapy for couples.* New York: Guilford Press.

Greenberg, L. S., & Paivio, S. (1997). *Working with emotions in psychotherapy.* New York: Guilford Press.

Greenberg, L. S., & Pascual-Leone, J. (1995). A dialectical constructivist approach to experiential change. In R. Neimeyer & M. Mahoney (Eds.), *Constructivism in psychotherapy* (pp. 169–191). Washington, DC: American Psychological Association.

Greenberg, L. S., & Pascual-Leone, J. (1997). Emotion in the creation of personal meaning. In M. Power & C. Brewin (Eds.), *The transformation of meaning in psychological therapies* (pp. 157–174). Chichester, England: Wiley.

Greenberg, L. S., & Rice, L. N. (1981). The specific effects of a Gestalt intervention. *Psychotherapy: Theory, Research and Practice, 18,* 31–37.

Greenberg, L. S., & Rice, L. N. (1991). *Change processes in experiential psychotherapy* (NIMH Grant No. 1RO1MH45040). Toronto, Ontario, Canada: York University.

Greenberg, L. S., & Rice, L. N. (1997). Humanistic approaches to psychotherapy. In P. Wachtel & S. Messer (Eds.), *Theories of psychotherapy: Origins and evolution* (pp. 97–129). Washington, DC: American Psychological Association.

Greenberg, L. S., Rice, L. N., & Elliott, R. (1993). *Facilitating emotional change: The moment-by-moment process.* New York: Guilford Press.

Greenberg, L. S., & Safran, J. D. (1987). *Emotion in psychotherapy.* New York: Guilford Press.

Greenberg, L. S., & Safran, J. D. (1989). Emotion in psychotherapy. *American Psychologist, 44,* 19–68.

Greenberg, L. S., & Watson, J. (1998). Experiential therapy of depression: Differential effects of client-centered relationship conditions and active experiential interventions. *Psychotherapy Research, 8,* 210–224.

Greenberg, L. S., & Webster, M. C. (1982). Resolving decisional conflict by means of two-chair dialogue: Relating process to outcome. *Journal of Counseling Psychology, 29,* 468–477.

Hirscheimer, K. (1996). *Development and verification of a measure of unfinished business.* Unpublished master's thesis, Department of Psychology, York University, Toronto, Ontario, Canada.

Horton, C., & Elliott, R. (1991, November). *The experiential session form: Initial data.* Paper presented at the meeting of the North American Society for Psychotherapy Research, Panama City, FL.

Jackson, L., & Elliott, R. (1990, June). *Is experiential therapy effective in treating depression?: Initial outcome data.* Paper presented at the meeting of the Society for Psychotherapy Research, Wintergreen, VA.

King, S. (1988). *The differential effects of empty-chair dialogue and empathic reflection for unfinished business.* Unpublished master's thesis, University of British Columbia, Vancouver, Canada.

Klein, M. H., Mathieu-Coughlan, P., & Kiesler, D. J. (1986). The Experiencing Scales. In L. Greenberg & W. Pinsof (Eds.), *The psychotherapeutic process* (pp. 21–71). New York: Guilford Press.

Lowenstein, J. (1985). *A test of a performance model of problematic reactions and an examination of differential client performances in therapy.* Unpublished master's thesis, Department of Psychology, York University, Toronto, Ontario, Canada.

Luborsky, L., & Crits-Christoph, P. (1990). *Understanding transference: The CCRT method.* New York: Basic Books.

Malcolm, W. (1999). *Relating process to outcome in the resolution of unfinished business in process experiential psychotherapy.* Unpublished doctoral dissertation, Department of Psychology, York University, Toronto, Ontario, Canada.

Mancinelli, B. (1993). *A grounded theory analysis of helpful factors in experiential therapy of depression*. Unpublished master's thesis, Department of Psychology, University of Toledo.

Maslove, V. J. (1989). *The differential effects of empathic reflection and the Gestalt empty-chair dialogue on depth of experiencing when used with an issue of unfinished business*. Unpublished master's thesis, University of British Columbia, Vancouver, Canada.

McMain, S. (1995). *Relating changes in self–other schemas to psychotherapy outcome*. Unpublished doctoral dissertation, York University, Toronto, Ontario, Canada.

Nietzel, M. T., Russell, R. L., Hemmings, K. A., & Gretter, M. L. (1987). Clinical significance of psychotherapy for unipolar depression: A meta-analytic approach to social comparison. *Journal of Consulting and Clinical Psychology, 55*, 156–160.

Paivio, S. (1997, December). *The outcome of emotionally-focused therapy with adult abuse survivors*. Paper presented at the meeting of the North American Society for Psychotherapy Research, Tucson, AZ.

Paivio, S. C., & Greenberg, L. S. (1995). Resolving "unfinished business": Efficacy of experiential therapy using empty chair dialogue. *Journal of Consulting and Clinical Psychology, 63*, 419–425.

Pedersen, R. A. (1996). Verification of a model of the resolution of unfinished business (Gestalt therapy). *Masters Abstracts International, 34*(06), 2480. (Ann Arbor, MI: ProQuest Digital Dissertations No. AAT MM10301)

Perls, F. S. (1969). *Gestalt therapy verbatim*. Moab, UT: Real People Press.

Rice, L. N., & Greenberg, L. (Eds.) (1984). *Patterns of change*. New York: Guilford Press.

Rice, L. N., & Saperia, E. P. (1984). Task analysis and the resolution of problematic reactions. In L. N. Rice & L. S. Greenberg (Eds.), *Patterns of change* (pp. 29–66). New York: Guilford Press.

Robinson, L. A., Berman, J. S., & Neimeyer, R. A. (1990). Psychotherapy for the treatment of depression: A comprehensive review of controlled outcome research. *Psychological Bulletin, 108*, 30–49.

Rogers, C. R. (1957). The necessary and sufficient conditions of therapeutic personality change. *Journal of Consulting Psychology, 21*, 95–103.

Rogers, C. R. (1961). *On becoming a person*. Boston: Houghton Mifflin.

Singh, M. (1996). Unfinished business resolution: Development, measurement and application. *Dissertation Abstracts International, 56*(07), 4057B. (Ann Arbor, MI: ProQuest Digital Dissertations No. AAT NN97418)

Tageson, C. W. (1982). *Humanistic psychology: A synthesis*. Homewood, IL: Dorsey Press.

Toukmanian, S. G., & Grech, T. (1991). *Changes in cognitive complexity in the context of perceptual-processing experiential therapy* (Report No. 194). Toronto, Ontario, Canada: York University, Department of Psychology.

Watson, J. C., & Greenberg, L. S. (1996). Pathways to change in the psychotherapy of depression: Relating process to session change and outcome. *Psychotherapy, 33,* 262–274.

Watson, J. C., & Stermac, L. (1999, June). *Comparing changes in clients' levels of depression, self-esteem, and interpersonal problems in cognitive–behavioural and process–experiential therapy.* Paper presented at the meeting of the Society for Psychotherapy Research, Braga, Portugal.

Wiseman, H., & Rice, L. N. (1989). Sequential analyses of therapist–client interaction during change events: A task-focused approach. *Journal of Consulting and Clinical Psychology, 57,* 281–286.

IV
THERAPEUTIC MODALITIES

10

TREATING COUPLES AND FAMILIES FROM THE HUMANISTIC PERSPECTIVE: MORE THAN THE SYMPTOM, MORE THAN SOLUTIONS

SUSAN JOHNSON AND CHRISTINE BOISVERT

A humanistic approach to therapeutic change naturally lends itself to working with couples and families. This approach has always emphasized the strengthening of relational bonds, the creation of empathy, and engagement with one's own emotional experience and with intimate others. Humanistic therapists have always focused on the fact that personal growth and empowerment occur in relationships with intimate others. They have always viewed those relationships as more than the sum of their parts, as having a life of their own. This perspective is consonant with the systemic viewpoint that has formed the basis of so much of couples and family therapy. Humanistic practices exemplify the notion that people are formed and transformed by their relationships with others.

This chapter includes client-centered and experiential approaches as well as approaches generally defined as humanistic, such as relationship enhancement (see Guerney, 1977). The most delineated and empirically tested interventions are emotionally focused couples therapy (EFT; Greenberg & Johnson, 1988; Johnson, 1996) and relationship enhancement therapy (RE; Guerney, 1977, 1994). These approaches are the focus of this chapter. Humanistic therapists have been defined in part by their antipositivist ideals and a rejection of manualized techniques and outcome analyses. Humanistic therapists reject invariant procedures uniformly applied and allow clients to teach them about their idiosyncratic experience. However, the position taken here is that it is still possible to stipulate interventions and empirically examine how these interventions affect clients' relationships. Indeed this is necessary, if humanistic approaches to couples and family therapy are not to be marginalized in the field as a whole.

The approaches discussed in this chapter follow the basic premises of humanistic thought, namely

1. *The therapeutic alliance is healing in and of itself and should be as egalitarian as possible.* The acceptance and validation of clients' experience is the key element in therapy. In couples and family modalities, this involves an active effort to validate each family member's experience in a way that allows that client's innate self-healing tendencies to flourish.

2. *The goal of therapy is to offer an opportunity for growth and an expanded sense of agency.* The therapist articulates the moments when choices are made in the relationship drama and encourages clients to consider new alternatives in their ways of viewing and responding to intimate others. The essence of humanism is a belief in the ability of human beings to make creative, healthy choices, if given the opportunity. This approach focuses on clients' strengths in being able to actively face their issues and make new choices. Therapy has to encompass more than the alleviation of symptoms and finding remedies for dysfunction. It involves a second level of change (Watzlawick, Weakland, & Fisch, 1974) in which the elements in a system are reorganized so that the whole system is transformed and oriented toward health and growth.

3. *The collaborative dialogue of therapy generates new meanings for clients that prime new responses to partners and family members.* New meanings are associated with compelling new emotional experiences. As the Task Force (1997) for the provision of humanistic social services suggested, apparent irrationality is most fully rational when joined with the body and with emotion (p. 73). The humanistic focus on whole individuals in context dictates that the integration of emotion, cognition, and body experience is an essential part of the goal of therapy. Clients are then encouraged to stay close to and learn from their emotional experience.

4. *The therapy process is essentially constructivist.* The therapy process explores the construction of experience in the here and now and how this experience then plays a part in creating interactions with others. Intense personal encounters in the here and now of the therapy session create new realities and foster the articulation of new elements of self. It is accepted

that there are multiple realities to be constructed and multiple aspects of self to be developed and owned.

RECENT DEVELOPMENTS IN HUMANISTIC COUPLES AND FAMILY THERAPIES

In couples and family therapy, there has been such a focus on what happens *between* family members that the private joys and pains of individuals are rarely mentioned (Nichols, 1987) and the person becomes lost in the system (Krause, 1993). As a result, systemic therapies have been accused of being impersonal and of relying on abstract formulas to address that most personal and emotionally salient territory: intimate relationships. In contrast, the humanistic interventions of EFT and RE address both the person and the system. These approaches aim to help couples and families create more engaged and empathic relationships that promote personal growth and a relational context characterized by safety and support.

Both RE and EFT are also consonant with recent developments in the study of the nature of relationship distress and the nature of adult intimacy. In the past decade, our understanding of relationship distress has grown exponentially. The empirical work of John Gottman (1994) and his colleagues (Gottman, Coan, Carrere, & Swanson, 1998) has stressed the power of negative emotional arousal during disagreements to predict long-term satisfaction in marriage. The facial expression of negative emotion and particular rigid interactional patterns, such as the expression of criticism and contempt, responded to by stonewalling and defensiveness, predict separation with impressive accuracy (90%) in this research. Like the humanistic perspective, this research particularly stresses the deleterious effects of avoidance and defensiveness and lack of empathic responsiveness between partners. Empirical researchers and humanistic theorists seem to agree that the core elements in relationship distress are conflicts characterized by blame rather than empathy, defensiveness that narrows emotional processing, and lack of emotional engagement that can soothe and nurture (Gottman et al., 1998).

A major development in the understanding of adult intimacy is the recent application of attachment theory to adult relationships (Bartholomew & Perlman, 1994; Bowlby, 1969; Hazan & Shaver, 1987). The research on attachment theory, which is outlined in detail and related to couples and family therapy elsewhere (Johnson, 1996; Johnson & Whiffen, 1999), supports the humanistic contention that relationships characterized by presence, accessibility, and emotional attunement create a secure base and a safe haven that optimizes individual growth and adaptation. For example, research on attachment suggests that a sense of security allows individuals to process information effectively, and thus construct coherent, consistent, and meaningful stories about past and present relationships. These stories then foster people's sense of efficacy and allow them to tolerate and process painful emotions (Main, 1991).

The essential tenets of attachment theory fit well with the humanistic perspective. This theory views partners or family members as becoming stuck in fight, flight, or freeze responses as a result of being unable to form a secure bond. Humanistic therapists would expect similar results to those found in the research on intimate attachments: For example, the more adolescents feel that they can count on their parents, the more they can meta-communicate and see things from the parents' perspective when conflict arises in the relationship (Kobak & Cole, 1991). Safety and a sense of being valued in close relationships build a positive sense of self and foster open, direct, and coherent communication (Kobak, Ruckdeschel, & Hazan, 1994). This theory, like the humanistic perspective, depathologizes people's need for each other and focuses on the negative effects of defended, avoidant, or highly anxious and coercive ways of engaging significant others (Bowlby, 1969, 1988).

CURRENT HUMANISTIC INTERVENTIONS

Relationship Enhancement

The RE approach can be used to address relationships between parents and children (filial family therapy) and relationships between partners. RE integrates humanistic principles with more behavioral skill-building approaches. This approach is based on the assumption that when, and only when, therapists can change the nature of a client's interpersonal interactions with significant others, then they can produce fundamental, enduring changes in personality (Guerney, 1994, p. 126). Both RE and EFT assume that the power of intimates to generate stronger emotions may give them more leverage to help each other. Such leverage may promote personal growth and new definitions of self.

Consistent with humanistic theory, the avoidance and disowning of emotional responses and needs are considered problematic in relationships in both RE and EFT approaches. Cavedo and Guerney (1998) noted that RE reflects the Rogerian view that defense mechanisms triggered by threats to the person's self-concept become problematic and begin to distort reality. However, acceptance and empathy, offered by the therapist and by one's partner, reduce such defenses and promote insight. An essential difference, however, between RE and EFT is that in RE the therapist not only provides empathic acceptance to foster open communication but also actively trains the couple in providing such acceptance. The therapist becomes not just a genuine affirming other but also a skills coach. The therapist teaches the couple skills such as how to listen with empathy, how to negotiate problems, and how to resolve conflicts. Even though such direct skill building is not usually associated with humanistic approaches, Guerney (1994) noted that these skills are taught in such a way as to pull clients toward deeper levels of experiential processing. He stressed that what is being fostered in RE is emotional attunement and empathic connection with a speaker rather than mechanical paraphrasing. The goal is to further the other's self-acceptance and self-understanding as well as to promote contact between partners.

The skills taught in RE are the following:

1. Expressive skills, for example, stating one's desires assertively.
2. Empathic skills that facilitate listening to others.
3. Discussion and negotiation skills.
4. Coaching skills to help others master RE skills and end the cycles of hostility and blame.
5. Conflict resolution skills to devise creative solutions.
6. Changing self-skills to reduce unwanted behaviors.
7. Helping others change skills to support others in implementing their agreements.
8. Generalization and maintenance skills.

As Guerney (1988) stated, these skills are demonstrated and then practiced by the couple or family with direct feedback and reinforcement from the therapist. The overall goal is to decrease interactions that create anxiety and emotional insecurity and increase participants' capacity to show love and win love (p. 104). The therapist focuses on the whole person's thoughts, feelings, and behavior and the interpersonal context. The therapist is more than a skills coach. His or her acceptance of clients' feelings fosters their own ability to accept and explore their emotions. RE can be implemented in a full 30-hour format or an abbreviated format (15 hours) in group and individual formats.

Emotionally Focused Couples Therapy

EFT is a brief systematic approach to modifying distressed couples' constricted interaction patterns and emotional responses and to fostering the development of a secure emotional bond (Greenberg & Johnson, 1988; Johnson, 1996). EFT integrates the intrapsychic perspective afforded by humanistic experiential approaches with a more interpersonal systemic perspective and melds these perspectives into change strategies that are formulated in a 9-step change process. In this process, newly formulated emotional responses are expressed in such a way as to create a shift in how partners engage with their spouse. Those who habitually withdraw are helped to reengage, and hostile partners are supported to become more open and vulnerable. Specific shifts in interaction are choreographed that prime an increased emotional responsiveness between partners. For example, a generally hostile wife is encouraged to "soften," that is, to express her fear and vulnerability in an open way that touches her spouse and elicits caring responsiveness from him. New constructive cycles of contact and caring can then begin.

EFT focuses on how the processing of emotional experience creates and reflects interaction patterns and influences the meaning ascribed to those patterns, particularly how the self and the other are defined in this context. New emotional experience, generated in the safe and accepting environment of the session, promotes new responses to the partner. The therapist is a process consultant who, by empathically attuning to and validating each partner, creates a safe place that allows each partner to become more engaged with his or her own experience and with the other. From the Rogerian perspective, for example, a male partner may be encouraged to move from an incongruent position of asking for closeness in an aggressive way (because he believes that showing vulnerability is weak and will result in rejection) to one in which he becomes aware of and accepting of his needs for caring and expresses these needs in a manner that pulls his partner closer to him. When he is able to do this, his partner's perception of him changes, his sense of self is modified, and his responses become more flexible and more conducive to relationship repair. Change in EFT is presumed to occur, not from insight, catharsis, or improved skills per se, but from the formulation and expression of new emotional experience that transforms the nature of the dialogue and thus the interactional drama.

EFT is a relatively brief intervention (10 to 12 sessions in empirical studies). The therapist focuses on three tasks: (a) the creation and maintenance of a collaborative alliance, (b) the accessing and reformulating of emotional responses, and (c) the shaping of new interactions based on these responses. In the first task, the therapist fosters the trust and confidence that allows clients to fully engage in therapy. He or she does this by taking a collaborative and respectful stance toward the client, by being genuine and transparent, and by nonjudgmental empathy. In the second task, the therapist focuses on the emotion that is most poignant and salient in the session. Most often this emotion is associated with attachment needs and fears and plays a central role in patterns of negative interaction. The therapist stays close to the leading edge of the client's experience and uses the experiential interventions (Perls, 1973; Rogers, 1951), reflection, evocative questions, validation, heightening, and empathic interpretation to expand that experience. Reactive responses such as anger then move into the background while more primary emotions such as a sense of grief or fear become the focus of attention. In the third task, the therapist tracks and reflects the patterns of interaction, identifying the negative cycles, such as criticize/attack followed by defend/distance, that constrain the responses of the partners to each other. The therapist then assigns expressive tasks in the session that restructures the dialogue between partners. These expressive tasks can be viewed from the Gestalt perspective as experiments in new kinds of interaction. They can also be viewed in more systemic terms (Minuchin & Fishman, 1981) as reframing and the direct choreographing of new relationship events. Problems are reframed in terms of cycles and patterns and in terms of attachment needs and fears. So the therapist will ask a partner to share specific fears with his or her partner, thus creating a new kind of dialogue that fosters empathic attunement and acceptance. These tasks and interventions are outlined in detail elsewhere, together with transcripts of therapy sessions (Johnson, 1998, 1999; Johnson & Greenberg, 1995).

The three stages of change in EFT are (a) negative cycle deescalation; (b) restructuring interactions, which involve both the reengagement of withdrawn partners and the softening of more blaming partners; and (c) consolidation and integration of change. Once the alliance is established in the first stage of therapy, the goal is to identify and deescalate negative cycles and to explore the underlying emotions that organize these cycles. At the end of this stage, the couple have gained a meta-perspective on their interactions and can clearly describe the negative cycles that maintain their distress. They begin to see their cycle, rather than each other, as the problem. The second stage, restructuring interactions, involves the shaping of new emotional experiences and new interactions. In this stage, more withdrawn partners reengage in the relationship and actively express their needs, and more blaming partners can ask for their attachment needs to be met in a way that primes the other's compassion and responsiveness. This latter event has been found to be associated with recovery from relationship distress in EFT (Johnson & Greenberg, 1988). At the end of this stage, bonding events occur in which each partner confides in and seeks comfort from the other, becoming mutually accessible and responsive. In this stage, the relationship is reorganized and redefined. The last stage of treatment involves the consolidation of new responses and cycles of interaction and supporting the couple to solve concrete problems that have been destructive to the relationship. These problems are more manageable because they are no longer infused with negative affect and issues of relationship definition.

Humanistic Family Therapy

The most powerful ingredient in earlier formulations of humanistic family therapy was considered to be the therapist's ability to remain genuine and congruent. Self-disclosure, openness, and spontaneity were seen as more important than theory and technique. The therapist attempted to choreograph genuine encounters between family members that might expand the rigid patterns of interaction in the family. The denial of impulses and the suppression of emotions were viewed as the root of family problems (Whitaker & Keith, 1991). A healthy family was one that could adapt to changing circumstances and could acknowledge differences between members. These interventions did not lend themselves to empirical research, and there are only anecdotal reports of outcomes in these forms of experiential family therapy (Duhl & Duhl, 1981; Napier & Whitaker, 1978).

There are RE studies that illustrate more manualized and empirically based humanistic interventions. There is also a study in progress to extend the findings of Diamond and Siqueland (1995), and there is a completed preliminary study of emotionally focused family therapy (EFFT) by Johnson, Maddeaux, and Blouin (1998). The latter two interventions are based on attachment theory. As stated previously, this theory is consonant with humanistic perspectives. Attachment theory is supported by empirical research on adolescent development and the evolution of problems such as anxiety and depression in adolescence (Atkinson & Zucker, 1997; Mikulincer, Florian, & Weller, 1993). Both of the interventions formulated by Diamond and Siqueland (1995) and Johnson et al. (1998) focus on safe attachment and reengagement rather than on issues such as individuation and the defusing of enmeshment. A brief description of EFFT, perhaps the best validated of these more recent interventions, follows.

The EFFT therapist helps clients explore and reprocess the emotional responses, particularly attachment insecurities, that underlie the interactions between the child identified with the problem and the parents. The goal is to create a secure base that fosters children's growth and development. The more secure the adolescent–parent relationship is, the more tolerance there is of differences and the more confident and autonomous the adolescent can be. The family is seen together at the beginning and end of therapy (10 to 12 sessions), but the rest of the therapy process involves triads, for example, the parents and the symptomatic adolescent, or involves dyads, for example, two siblings or a parent and a child. Key change events might involve, for example, a depressed adolescent first being able to confide her fears of failure and how her father's disapproval paralyses her and evokes the need to hide. She can then ask her father for his approval and respect. Her father might then be able to confide that he harangues his daughter as a response to his own fears that he has failed as a parent and does not belong in the family. In this encounter, new emotions are formulated and shared, and rigid interactions such as criticize/withdraw evolve into dialogues in which both participants feel more connected and reassured.

This work is consonant with the work of Virginia Satir. Satir used ropes and blindfolds to dramatize constricting family roles (Satir & Baldwin, 1983), whereas the EFFT therapist is more likely to use images and descriptions of the steps in a particular family's patterns of interaction. However, like Satir, the EFFT therapist choreographs new sequences of interaction and, like Satir, this therapist mainly views the rigid stances in distressed families in terms of fear. As Satir suggested, resistance is often the fear of going somewhere one has never been (quoted by Simon, 1989, pp. 38–39).

RESEARCH ON HUMANISTIC COUPLES AND FAMILY THERAPIES

The number of instances in which humanistic couples and family interventions have been specified and tested are relatively few. In a recent meta-analysis, Shadish and his colleagues (Shadish et al., 1993) noted that humanistic couples and family therapies failed to show positive treatment effects and that this finding gave serious cause for concern (p. 999). On inspection of the eight studies used in Shadish et al.'s meta-analysis, five were unpublished dissertation projects, one was behavioral (Alexander & Parsons, 1973), and one contained clients with personality disorders (Ford & West, 1979). The collection of studies used by Shadish et al. does not seem to give an adequate representation of the state of humanistic couples and family therapy in the 1990s. In fact, both RE and EFT interventions have demonstrated considerable effectiveness in empirical studies.

RESEARCH ON RE

Considering the results of research on RE (which are addressed in greater detail in chap. 13, this volume), it is interesting to note that Smith, Glass, and Miller (1980) reported the average effect size for psychotherapy studies as 0.85. A recent meta-analysis of general relationship enrichment outcomes, which would logically be smaller than those found for distressed couples and families, found an average effect size of 0.44 (Giblin, Sprenkle, & Sheehan, 1985). However, the average effect size for RE is reported in the above meta-analysis as 0.96, and Hahlweg and Markman (1988) noted an even higher effect size of 1.14 for RE in their meta-analysis. These effect sizes are then higher than other enhancement approaches and higher than many remedial psychotherapy approaches. Giblin et al. (1985) also noted that enhancement approaches such as RE seem to have significant impact. RE has also shown superior results with couples in a group format when compared with a reciprocal reinforcement approach (Wieman, 1973) and a Gestalt approach (Jessee & Guerney, 1981). Schlinder, Hahlweg, and Revenstorf (1983) also used the expressive and empathic skills elements of the RE program and found that both group and dyadic formats were effective when compared with no-treatment controls.

RE has been used in a variety of populations and across levels of problem severity. These include prevention programs, such as programs to help couples change negative parenting practices (Rose, Battjes, & Leukefeld, 1984) and programs to prevent relapse from psychotic breakdown and alcoholism (Matter, McAllister, & Guerney, 1984; Vogelsong, Guerney, & Guerney, 1983). In general, the quality of the research on RE has been high with random assignment, the use of control groups, and follow-up assessment. It would be fruitful to examine which ingredients of RE are particularly associated with change (Guerney & Maxson, 1990) and expand this intervention to new populations.

RESEARCH ON EFT OUTCOMES

At present, there are only two clearly delineated treatments for marital distress that have been empirically tested in a number of studies and generally accepted as efficacious (Baucom, Shoham, Mueser, Daiuto, & Stickle, 1998). These are behavioral marital therapy (BMT) and EFT. Of these two, EFT is the most recently formulated, having been first described in the literature in 1985 (Johnson & Greenberg, 1985a). To date, eight studies have examined the impact of EFT on distressed couples, as assessed by a wide range of measures, including indices of psychological and dyadic adjustment, intimacy, and target complaints about the relationship. The majority of these studies have been randomized clinical trials in which EFT was compared with other treatments or with wait-list controls (Denton, Burleson, Clarke, Rodriguez, & Hobbs, 2000; Dessaulles, 1991; Goldman & Greenberg, 1992; James, 1991; Johnson & Greenberg, 1985a; Walker, Johnson, Manion, & Cloutier, 1996); in two studies, treated couples served as their own controls (Johnson & Greenberg, 1985b; Johnson & Talitman, 1997).

Additionally, to examine the extent to which EFT may affect relationship issues other than marital distress, two randomized clinical trials have explored the ability of EFT to enhance intimacy in maritally adjusted couples (Dandeneau & Johnson, 1994) and to modify low sexual desire in female partners (MacPhee, Johnson, & Van der Veer, 1995). All EFT trials have included treatment integrity checks on tapes of therapy sessions to verify that therapist interventions followed treatment manuals. All studies have had very low attrition rates.

The main goal of EFT is to alleviate a couple's relationship distress. We therefore concentrate our presentation on treatment effects by focusing on distress as measured by the Dyadic Adjustment Scale (DAS; Spanier, 1976), the most commonly used measure of dyadic adjustment. In all studies in which the primary focus of treatment was marital distress (i.e., excluding the Dandeneau & Johnson, 1994, and the MacPhee et al., 1995, studies), EFT has significantly improved dyadic adjustment, compared both with wait-list controls and with a couple's pretreatment DAS scores. Using the criteria suggested by Jacobson and Truax (1991) for assessing clinically significant change, the overwhelming majority of EFT-treated couples reported clinical improvement on the DAS, and in most studies over half of the EFT-treated couples met criteria for recovery (i.e., no longer distressed). Additionally, there appears to be only rare instances in which EFT-treated couples experienced deterioration in their relationship over the course of treatment. The results discussed above are summarized in Johnson, Hunsley, Greenberg, and Schindler (1999). Overall these results clearly exceed the oft-reported finding that only approximately half of couples seen in marital therapy outcome research show clinical improvement (Hahlweg & Markman, 1988; Jacobson & Addis, 1993).

There have been a number of recent reviews of the marital therapy outcome literature, both traditional literature reviews (Lebow & Gurman, 1995; Piercy & Sprenkle, 1990) and meta-analytic reviews (Dunn & Schwebel, 1995; Shadish et al., 1993). However, because of the recency of publication for some of the articles describing the effects of EFT, these reviews do not provide an overview of the efficacy of EFT. A meta-analysis on the randomized clinical trials of EFT in which couples were seeking treatment for their relationship distress has been completed, using DAS scores, to obtain a general estimate of the size of EFT treatment effects (Johnson et al., 1999). Only randomized clinical trials of EFT were included in the analysis because there is evidence that effect sizes derived from other types of research designs may underestimate the true effects of treatment (Shadish & Ragsdale, 1996). The weighted mean effect size attained a statistically significant value of 1.3. This is a large effect size for psychotherapy research and exceeds published estimates of 0.95 (Shadish et al., 1993) for the effect size of BMT, the most frequently researched form of couples therapy. To ensure that these results are stable, although based on only four studies, a fail-safe sample size was calculated (Rosenthal, 1984). This calculation yields an estimate of the number of studies reporting nonsignificant findings that would be required to reduce the overall effect size estimate found in this analysis to a nonsignificant level. The fail-safe sample size for the EFT findings is 56; that is, 56 studies reporting nonsignificant results would be required to yield an overall effect size that was statistically nonsignificant.

Not only is EFT clearly effective in reducing marital distress, but there also seems to be a tendency for couples to continue to improve after the termination of treatment. For example, in the most recent study (Johnson & Talitman, 1997), 70% of couples were found to be recovered at 3-month follow-up, an improvement over the 50% who were recovered at the end of therapy. The same kind of increase occurred in the first EFT study (Johnson & Greenberg, 1985a; 46% at termination, 73% recovered at follow-up) and in Walker et al.'s (1996) study (38% recovered at termination, 70% at follow-up). A 2-year follow-up of the couples involved in Walker et al.'s (1996) study has also been completed, with very positive results (Clothier, Manion, Walker, & Johnson, in press). In contrast to such findings, Jacobson and his colleagues (Jacobson, Follette, & Ellwood, 1984) estimated that approximately one third of couples receiving BMT in four studies were recovered (i.e., nondistressed) after treatment. The results on EFT seem to exceed the results for BMT from the point of view of the proportion of couples who improve and recover from marital distress.

Although EFT is primarily designed to alter marital functioning, there are initial data indicating that EFT interventions also reduce depressive symptoms (Dessaulles, 1991; MacPhee et al., 1995; Walker, 1994). For example, in a study with distressed parents of chronically ill children, 44% of both treatment and control parents were in the clinical range for depression (as measured by the Beck Depression Inventory) at pretreatment. At 5-month follow-up, only 9% of the treated parents were scoring in the clinical range for depression compared with 54% of controls. However, 10 sessions of EFT failed to significantly increase the sexual adjustment of couples in which the female partner was experiencing low sexual desire (MacPhee et al., 1995).

Process Research: How Does EFT Work?

Turning from outcome research to the study of the process of change, in general, there has been little research addressing the process of change in couples therapy. However, four studies of the process of change in EFT have been reported in the literature. The first study (Johnson & Greenberg, 1988) examined the process of therapy in "best" sessions for three couples whose DAS scores increased by an average of 47 points (i.e., approximately 2.5 standard deviations) in the original EFT outcome study (Johnson & Greenberg, 1985a) and compared it with the three lowest-change couples who did not show significant improvement on the DAS. Videotapes of best sessions (chosen by the couples) were rated by independent raters for levels of experiencing (Klein, Mathieu, Gendlin, & Miesler, 1969) and for affiliative and autonomous responses in interactions using the Structural Analysis of Social Behavior (Benjamin, 1986). A particular change event, a softening, in which a previously critical partner expresses vulnerability and asks for comfort and connection from his or her partner, was also defined using these measures. The high-change couples showed significantly higher levels of experiencing in "best" sessions. A chi-square analysis also found that blaming partners in the high-change couples were more likely to demonstrate a more affiliative and less coercive position toward their spouse in the session. On average, five softening change events were found in the sessions of the successful couples, whereas none were found in the sessions of the low-change couples. These results confirmed the relevance of encouraging couples to explore their emotional responses and engage in tasks in which they disclose attachment needs in a manner that facilitates emotional engagement with their partner. Three additional small studies of EFT change processes demonstrated the same kinds of effects (Greenberg, Ford, Alden, & Johnson, 1993).

Differential Effectiveness in EFT in Different Kinds of Couples

There are certain couples for whom EFT is not recommended, for example, couples for whom abuse is an ongoing part of the relationship and for whom the expression of vulnerability may not be respected. The results of a recent study on predictors of success in EFT (Johnson & Talitman, 1997) also provide some initial evidence on who is likely to benefit most from EFT. Hierarchical multiple regression analyses were used in this study to assess the unique contribution of the predictor variables to improvement or recovery from marital distress, beyond that due to initial satisfaction level. In addition to posttreatment assessment, a 3-month follow-up was conducted. The main results were as follows:

1. The quality of the alliance with the therapist was a strong predictor of success in EFT. The task-relevance aspect of the alliance was more predictive of improvement than was a positive bond or a sense of shared goals.
2. The quality of the alliance was a more powerful predictor of treatment success than was initial distress level. Initial distress level accounted for only 4% of the outcome variance in couples' posttreatment satisfaction at follow-up, whereas alliance scores accounted for 29% of the variance at follow-up.
3. In contrast to these results, initial distress level seems to be the best predictor of long-term success in other couples therapies, accounting for as much as 46% of the variance in couple satisfaction (Whisman & Jacobson, 1990). Engagement in the

tasks of therapy seems more important in EFT than initial distress level.

4. Men who were over 35 years of age reported greater satisfaction at follow-up and made more gains in therapy, perhaps finding issues of intimacy and attachment more relevant than did younger male partners. In contrast, research on BMT found an inverse relationship between age and outcome (Jacobson & Addis, 1993).

5. A female partner's initial level of faith that her partner still cared for her predicted the couple's adjustment and intimacy levels at follow-up. This is consistent with evidence that emotional disengagement, rather than factors such as the inability to resolve disagreement, is predictive of couple distress and instability (Gottman, 1994) and lack of success in couples therapy (Jacobson & Addis, 1993). This may be particularly true for women given their role as caretakers of close relationships.

6. Lack of emotional expressiveness or awareness did not inhibit progress in EFT; in fact, EFT seemed to be particularly helpful for men who were described by their partners as inexpressive.

7. Traditionality in relationships (i.e., in which the male partner is oriented to independence and the female to affiliation) also did not inhibit progress in EFT.

Overall, then, these findings suggest that a female partner's level of faith in her spouse's caring and the couple's ability to engage in an alliance with the therapist and respond to the tasks of EFT are important prognostic indicators for the EFT therapist. These factors appear to be more important than initial distress level or factors such as emotional inexpressiveness. Future research is necessary to substantiate these findings.

The studies completed on EFT have several strengths. They have, in general, used random assignment to group, valid control groups, treatment implementation checks with very acceptable interrater reliability, reliable measures of process and outcome, follow-up analyses, and appropriate research methodology. One methodological limitation is that all but one study involved one or both of the developers of EFT as a research investigator. More research is needed in which EFT is evaluated by investigators less associated with its development, and such research is beginning to emerge (Denton et al., 2000). How EFT might be tailored to individual differences is also just beginning to be described in the literature (Johnson & Whiffen, 1999). Additional questions remain as to how successful EFT can be in affecting individual symptomatology that often accompanies relationship distress. From clinical data, it appears that EFT may be useful for couples struggling with posttraumatic stress disorder, such as incest survivors, or victims of violence (Johnson & Williams-Keeler, 1998).

Research on Humanistic Family Therapy

Research on humanistic family therapy, as stated previously, is almost nonexistent. Humanist family therapists have considered therapy an art rather than a science; however, art does have principles and procedures, and it is not necessarily true that humanistic therapies defy manualization (Task Force, 1997) This is particularly true now that there are clear empirical maps to inform us as to the pivotal factors in relationship distress and the nature of attachment ties.

A recent preliminary study on EFFT with bulimic adolescents (13 clients; mean age = 17 years) is perhaps the beginning of a new and more empirically validated set of humanistic family therapies. The clients for this study were recruited from the waiting list of young women seeking treatment in an outpatient eating disorder clinic of a large teaching hospital. The group therapy condition was used as an established reference treatment because it had already been tested on a larger sample (Blouin, Perez, & Blouin, 1988). Approximately 32% of those contacted refused to participate in the study because they had kept their eating disorder a secret from their family. Therapists were committed to the treatment they provided and were supervised by an expert in the group therapy treatment, or in the case of EFFT, by Susan Johnson, the first author of this chapter. This study found that EFT significantly reduced bulimic symptomatology (Johnson et al., 1998). Symptoms were measured using the Eating Disorders Inventory (EDI; Garner, Olmsted, & Polivy, 1983) and the Bulimic Symptom Checklist (BSC; Blouin, Perez, & Blouin, 1988), and associated mood disturbance as measured by the Symptom Checklist–90–Revised (Derogatis, 1992) and the Beck Depression Inventory (Beck, Steer, & Garbin, 1988). EFFT reduced bulimic symptoms as much as a control group that was given a cognitive–behavioral group treatment for bulimia. In particular, binge frequency was reduced by 52% with total remission in 44% of clients, and vomiting was reduced by 65% with complete remission in 67% of cases. The effect sizes for binge frequency on the BSC and the bulimia subscale on the EDI were 0.87 and 1.1, respectively. These are respectable effect sizes for psychotherapy outcome. These results, although preliminary, are superior to those reported in the literature for individual cognitive therapy (Garner et al., 1993). However, because this was a preliminary investigation, no follow-up was conducted so it is unclear how lasting the effects were.

RE has been implemented in a format in which parents are trained in relationship skills such as empathy. This intervention changed maternal responses and the behavior of emotionally disturbed children under 10 years old (Guerney & Stover, 1971). In a study by Sywulak (1977) in which similar clients were used as their own controls, significant gains were recorded and maintained at 3-year follow-up (Sensue, 1981). Group family therapy for adolescents has also been found to be effective. For example, mother–daughter pairs were assigned to three conditions: RE, a group discussion (both 13 sessions), and a no-treatment control. Clients were treated in groups of three mother–daughter pairs. The RE group showed significantly greater gains than the other groups in all areas and maintained these gains at 6-month follow-up (Guerney, Vogelsong, & Coufal, 1983). RE has also been used effectively with father–son pairs (Ginsberg, 1984).

FROM RESEARCH TO PRACTICE

In this section, the focus is on EFT, because the practice of RE is elaborated elsewhere (this volume, chap. 13) and EFFT is very similar to, if less articulated than EFT. In general, research suggests that if the couples therapist focuses on the three tasks of EFT—creating a collaborative, empathic alliance; helping partners to expand key emotional responses and shaping new interactions; and bonding experiences—therapy will be successful. The quality of the therapeutic alliance seems to be a powerful predictor of success in EFT (Johnson & Talitman, 1997). The couple's response to and engagement in the tasks set by the therapist was the most significant predictive element of this alliance. In process research, change events that involve deeper experiencing, emotional disclosure, and new interactions involving reaching out to the partner in an affiliative way were associated with the highest levels of change. It seems most useful then to briefly consider each of these therapeutic tasks and to outline how change occurs in the most researched change event in EFT, a softening.

Task 1: Creation of a Collaborative Alliance

The EFT therapist's first task is to find a way to empathically attune to and connect with both partners in a troubled relationship in a manner that builds safety and trust. Therapists immerse themselves in each client's experience, without making judgments, and encourage partners to follow their lead. The therapist attempts to be personally present and transparent and honor each person's struggle to deal with the distress in the relationship. A map of relationships taken from attachment theory helps the EFT therapist remain nonjudgmental. This theory assumes that specific attachment fears and defenses against these fears are narrowing clients' processing of their experience and the ways they engage their spouse. All through therapy, the therapist allows partners to teach him or her about how they construct their experience of self, other, and the relationship dance. The challenge, in couples and family therapy, is to validate each partner's experience of the relationship and the other without invalidating that other.

As a tense, angry husband, Dennis, turns to the therapist in the first session and says in an aggressive way, "I don't want a fat wife." His slim wife, Diane, weeps and whispers about being depressed. The therapist replies, "Could you help me understand, this worries you, that your wife might get fat." He nods. The therapist (T) continues,

> T: Could you tell me, how do you feel when you talk about this? Is it the same feeling as when you talk about how upset you get when she walks around in her comfy old nightie? (He nods.) You get agitated? Like right now you are drumming your hand against your leg?
> Husband: (He stares out the window.) She doesn't care, she doesn't care what she looks like with me.
> T: I'm not quite sure I understand. You get upset because the way it hits you is that she doesn't care if you find her attractive? (He nods emphatically.) It's like you don't matter? Your desiring her doesn't matter?
> Husband: It's like she's already left me. (He tears; his wife looks puzzled.)
> T: So, all these comments about weight and what your wife wears, they come up when you get upset and start to feel unsure of her feelings for you? And then you try to push her to do what you say, to show you that she wants to look pretty for you. (He puts his head down on his chest and mumbles agreement.) (The therapist turns to the wife:) This must be very difficult for you, Diane, you just see him being critical and giving you orders, I guess?
> Wife: I just feel suffocated. I like to wear my old nightie sometimes. He's so controlling. I just withdraw.
> T: Aha. You feel controlled and you have to shut him out to protect yourself. (She agrees.) You don't see his worry. Then I guess, when you withdraw, which you have to do to feel like you can breathe your own air, maybe, Doug feels even more because you seem distant, and this pattern starts all over again?

The focus on the husband as a person who is in the process of becoming (Rogers, 1961, p. 55) helps the therapist not to get caught in judging his behavior. The therapist's empathic stance allows the wife to piece together how each partner's responses create the dance that maintains their distress and frame the dance, not the partners, as the problem. Validating each partner's emotional experience and their need to protect themselves, and describing the negative cycle that has taken hold of their relationship, is a key part of the first stage of EFT, cycle deescalation. The safety and acceptance the therapist provides and the description of the cycle moves the relationship toward greater equilibrium and cements the alliance. The therapist has to continually monitor the alliance with both partners as they move through the change process.

Task 2: Accessing and Reprocessing of Emotional Experience

The EFT therapist helps partners to expand and deepen their experience of self and other in their relationship. The therapist focuses on and stays at the leading edge of emotional experience as it comes up in present encounters between the spouses and in stories of key incidents that become present and alive when discussed in the session (Johnson & Greenberg, 1994). By tracking clients' immediate experience and fitting that experience into a new meaning frame, perhaps the most core humanistic intervention, the therapist reorganizes how the clients experience the relationship and, eventually, how they engage with each other. Experience seems to be reorganized in several ways: (a) What was figure becomes ground (frustration may take a back seat to the expression of fear); (b) new elements reconfigure an experience (a recognition of hopelessness makes new sense of a withdrawal response) as empathy brings marginalized elements into focus; (c) a new context frames elements differently (the therapist's validation of fear makes it less shameful and more easily explored); and (d) undifferentiated experience, for example, experience implicit in a nonverbal gesture, may be explicated. An example of the last experience takes place when a therapist asks a distressed wife what happens for her when her partner starts to cry and she looks blank and then replies, "It's like, Ping!" She has no clear sense or symbol for her experience. The therapist supports this client to stay close to key cues: her partner's weeping, her bodily sense of recoil, and the voice in her head that says, "You hurt him; you are toxic; no wonder he withdraws from you." The therapist and the client then piece together the helplessness and self-blame that is, for this client, an inevitable part of being close. This new encounter with her own experience then leads into a new encounter with her partner, when she can tell him about her helplessness and ask for the reassurance she longs for. In EFT, the goal of therapy is for clients to be able to formulate their own attachment longings and needs and communicate them to their spouse.

Task 3: Restructuring Interactions

The EFT therapist tracks and reflects the process of interaction just as he or she reflects the process of inner experiencing. The therapist frames particular responses within the negative interaction cycle, such as withdrawal, in the light of attachment needs and fears. As partners enter the second stage of therapy, during which the goal is to shift interactional positions, the therapist choreographs new forms of engagement. These are based on the new formulations of key responses to the partner. So a withdrawn partner, having heard the therapist's focused, heightened synopsis of his emotional experience, is able to acknowledge, "Yes, I am afraid of my wife. So I run and hide. I stay invisible." Then, on the therapist's invitation, he is able to tell his wife, " I don't let you in. I won't risk your rejection." This spouse thus actively owns and asserts what has before been tacit and implicit. As he shares this, his stance evolves into, "And I don't want to spend all my life in hiding. I want you to put your guns away." The therapist supports him to encounter his wife in a new way, and the therapists supports her to hear and accept this new stance. The shifts in position in the second stage of therapy involve reengaging withdrawn partners and softening more critical partners. The latter shift is a turning point in therapy and usually results in bonding events that redefine the attachment dance between partners and lead into the final, consolidation stage of the therapy process. In such a change event, new bonding interactions are choreographed by the therapist and form an antidote to the original negative cycle.

A Change Event: Softening the More Blaming Spouse

In a change event, the previously withdrawing partner stays engaged as the other partner moves through owning his or her blaming responses, exploring the emotions that prime such responses, and formulating needs and fears that are usually not openly expressed. So a blaming partner may start with saying to her spouse, "You are so cold, how could anyone be married to you." She then moves into being able to acknowledge her rage and her hostility, as in "I'll show you, you can't shut me out." In a softening event, however, this partner is able to go further and get in touch with the desperation she feels when her spouse turns his back on her. She can then articulate the sense of loss and vulnerability that characterizes her core experience of the relationship. As she shares this with her spouse, key schemas about self and other also become accessible and can be modified, for example, "I have no right to ask for comfort: I am basically unlovable." As the blaming spouse brings new elements of herself into the interaction, stating, "I long for you to hold me," she evokes new responses in her partner. This partner no longer sees her as dangerous, but as needing his love and protection. When, with the therapist's support, he is able to offer this, powerful new cycles of caring, comfort, and connection are initiated. These events are a classic example of change in the humanistic mold. As a blaming partner engages more fully with her own experience and emotional needs, and as these needs are accepted, first by the therapist and then by the spouse, she is able to expand the way she constructs her experience, her sense of self, and her way of engaging with her spouse. A softening event might unfold as follows:

T: What happens to you, Claire, when Peter tells you he wants to come closer now, and he wants you to lean on him more? [Evocative question, attachment focus.]

Claire: (She folds her arms across her chest, looks down, and speaks very softly.) I don't know.

T: (Peter leans toward her.) As he says, "Lean on me, Claire, I'm here," what happens? You curl up, hum? [Heightening, reflection of body response, evocative question.]

Claire: I hear him. I feel confused. What did he say?

T: It's hard for you to hear what he is saying, to believe he is really here for you? [Reflection, maintain focus.]

Claire: (Looks at the therapist and straightens her body. Her voice is colder.) That's an illusion, a delusion. I should give up on that. I should take care of myself. (She tears.)

T: (In soft slow voice:) Some part of you says, don't even hope for that, that's too risky, to hope. Am I hearing it right? (She nods.) No one has ever been there to take care of you, hum? [Interpretation, expanding client's experience, heightening of client's fear.]

Claire: Right. It's not worth it.

T: It feels better just to give up on getting that caring, hum? Not to even let yourself hope, risk. Feels safer. (She agrees.) But then there is the tear, the tear on your cheek? Some part of you still longs, still feels the loss. (Claire weeps.) To hope is scary and not to hope is terrible and lonely, is that it? [Interpretation, heightening, reflection, and validation of conflict.]

Claire: I can't risk it. I don't believe in magic.

T: What do you think Peter, do you hear your wife's fear and hopelessness? (He nods.) Can you tell her please? [Choreograph interaction around wife's fear.]

Peter: I want you to let yourself hope for us. We were magic once, a long time ago. I think we were.

T: What is happening Claire, as you hear him say that? [Evocative question.]

Claire: It's like he's a long way off. I can hardly hear him.

T: Can you tell him, please? It's so hard to hear your voice, all the fear and despair gets in the way. [Interpretation, frame fear as the problem, set interactional task.]

Claire: (She raises her head and looks at Peter. Long pause.) If I let myself hope, . . . you'll be there for a day, maybe two and then . . . I can't be hurt again like that, I'll drown in it.

T: (Softly:) It's so hard to risk, to reach for the magic, it might disappear, like before? Feels like you'd die if that happened, hum? (She nods and weeps.) So can you tell him, it's so dangerous, like swimming in deep water to risk letting you in, to hope you'll come close, can you tell him? [Heightening, reflection, validation, set interactional task.]

Claire: (She sighs deeply.) Yes, it's so risky. I'm not sure I can do it.

T: How could he help, right now how could he help with that fear, Claire? [Frame him as helper.]

Claire: I need to know he understands, that he sees . . .

T: That he sees how scared you are? (Turns to Peter.) Peter, can you reassure your wife, can you help her with her fear? You look very sad right now, is that right? [Keep focus on fear, choreograph responsiveness from Peter, reflect his emotion.]

Peter: Yes, (leans toward his wife) I know I disappeared, just when you needed me, after the baby was born. I know I let you down. I want you to try to hope for us, to give me a chance? I want to hold you, to take away the fear. (She bursts into tears.) Can I hold you? (She nods.) He stands up and pulls her to her feet and holds her.

The session ends there, and in the next session Claire recounts and reprocesses a key incident during which she felt her hopes for a safe attachment with Peter were dashed. She also expresses her fear that others have been uncaring because she was defective in some way. Peter reassures her all through the session and all through the next week. When the couple come in again, they talk of new moments of trust and closeness and move on to discuss the future of the relationship. They have moved into Stage 3, the consolidation of change.

CONCLUSION

Recent forms of humanistic couples and family interventions, such as RE, EFT, and EFFT, suggest that it is possible to integrate a therapist stance of empathic responsiveness and genuineness with systematized sets of interventions and rigorous research into the effects of therapy. These approaches share certain characteristics. Both RE and EFT reverse the trend of including more and more people in the family therapy session and often focus on enhancing the quality of specific dyadic relationships. Both RE and EFT are also relatively directive compared with traditional humanistic therapies. Perhaps this reflects the nature of the modality. Rombauts and Devriendt (1990) noted that, in general, client-centered couples therapists tend to be more active and directive than might be the norm in individual therapy. Individual humanistic therapies have also become more directive as a result of research that supports the effectiveness of extensions of client-centered and Gestalt interventions, such as process–experiential approaches (Greenberg, Elliott, & Lietaer, 1998). However, it is striking that although proponents of less-directive humanistic masters such as Rogers have focused on less-directive interventions like reflection, excerpts of Rogers's work appear to be remarkably similar to the present-day practice of EFT. For example, the excerpt of Rogers's interventions included in Lietaer (1994) and in his own writings (Rogers, 1961) include techniques such as heightening and conjecture, which expand and add to clients' articulation of their experience. These techniques, combined with reflection, are the cornerstones of EFT practice. However, the setting of tasks in EFT, when the therapist asks one client to express certain emotions to another, and the practice of skills in RE, are more directive than usual Rogerian practices. The teaching of skills can be seen as an extension of Rogers's concept that the therapist serves as a model to the client. The practice of skills and engagement in the interactional tasks set by the EFT therapist can also be viewed in the context of traditional humanistic practice as experiments in new ways of being (Perls, 1973).

Both EFT and RE focus on the power of the therapist's empathy and acceptance to create a secure base for the couple or family as they grow toward a new relationship. Both of these approaches address emotion and evoke the power of emotional experience to rapidly reorganize specific behaviors. Both also use the expression of emotion to redefine the nature of bonds between intimates. Both approaches look beyond problems and symptoms and aim to foster personal growth through secure relationships. They focus on validating clients' strengths and see positive life tendencies behind clients' negative feelings and disturbing behavior (Leitaer, 1994, p. 41). The essence of humanistic therapies is a faith in people's ability to grow, develop new meanings, and enrich their sense of self. As Rogers (1975) suggested, identity requires the existence of another by whom one is known. Being seen and known then encourages growth and expands one's sense of self.

The field of couples and family therapy appears to be moving away from more mechanistic, impersonal ways of viewing relationships that arose as part of systems theory (Merkel & Searight, 1992) and toward postmodern views that echo the humanistic perspective (Anderson, 1997; Barton, 1994). Postmodern epistemology, with its emphasis on reality as constructed by the individual and in relationships with others, and the voice of feminism writers converge with humanistic theorists in advocating a return to collaborative alliances with couples and families. There has been a turning away from the image of the therapist as strategist and all-knowing expert. Social constructionism, feminism, and humanism all stress the healing power of genuineness, empathy, and positive regard. In general, the field of couples and family therapy seems to be returning to a more humanistic view of the therapy process. It is returning to an emphasis on the therapist's empathic responsiveness. There is an increasing awareness that this responsiveness offers clients a structure that more fully captures and better organizes the experiences and meanings with which they are struggling. This return to the wisdom offered by the humanistic perspective encourages therapists to learn with and from their clients about the mysteries and challenges of creating loving relationships with life partners and family members.

REFERENCES

Alexander, J. F., & Parsons, B. V. (1973). Short term behavioral interventions with delinquent families: Impact on family process and recidivism. *Journal of Abnormal Psychology, 81*, 219–225.

Anderson, H. (1997). *Conversation, language and possibilities.* New York: Basic Books.

Atkinson, L., & Zucker, K. (1997). *Attachment and psychopathology.* New York: Guilford Press.

Bartholomew, K., & Perlman, D. (Eds.). (1994). *Attachment processes in adulthood: Advances in personal relationships* (Vol. 5). London: Jessica Kingsley.

Barton, A. (1994). Humanistic contributions to the field of psychotherapy: Appreciating the human and liberating the artist. In F. Wertz (Ed.), *The humanistic movement: Recovering the person in psychology* (pp. 221–232). Washington, DC: American Psychological Association.

Baucom, D. H., Shoham, V., Mueser, K., Daiuto, A. D., & Stickle, T. R. (1998). Empirically supported couple and family interventions for marital distress and adult mental health problems. *Journal of Consulting and Clinical Psychology, 66*, 53–88.

Beck, A. T., Steer, A. R., & Garbin, M. G. (1988). Psychometric properties of the Beck Depression Inventory: Twenty-five years of evaluation. *Clinical Psychology Reviews, 8*, 77–100.

Benjamin, L. S. (1986). Adding social and intra-psychic descriptors to Axis I of *DSM–III*. In T. Millon & G. Klerman (Eds.), *Contemporary directions in psychopathology* (pp. 215–232). New York: Guilford Press.

Blouin, A. G., Perez, E. L., & Blouin, J. H. (1988). Computerized administration of the Diagnostic Interview Schedule. *Psychiatry Research, 23*, 335–344.

Bowlby, J. (1969). *Attachment and loss: Vol. I. Attachment.* New York: Basic Books.

Bowlby, J. (1988). *A secure base.* New York: Basic Books.

Cavedo, C., & Guerney, B. G., Jr. (1999) Relationship enhancement enrichment and problem-prevention programs: Therapy-derived, powerful, versatile. In R. Berger and M. T. Hannah (Eds.), *Preventive approaches in couples therapy* (pp. 73–105). Bristol, PA: Brunner/Mazel.

Clothier, P., Manion, I., Walker, J., & Johnson, S. (in press). Emotionally focused interventions for couples with chronically ill children: A two-year follow-up. *Journal of Marital & Family Therapy.*

Dandeneau, M., & Johnson, S. (1994). Facilitating intimacy: A comparative outcome study of emotionally focused and cognitive interventions. *Journal of Marital and Family Therapy, 20,* 17–33.

Denton, W. H., Burleson, B. R., Clarke, P. E., Rodriguez, C.P., & Hobbs, B. V. (2000). Outcomes of emotionally focused therapy for couples in a training clinic. *Journal of Marital and Family Therapy, 26,* 65–78.

Derogatis, L. R. (1992). *SCL-90-R: Administration, scoring and procedures manual.* Towson, MD: Clinical Psychometric Research.

Dessaulles, A. (1991). *The treatment of clinical depression in the context of marital distress.* Unpublished doctoral dissertation, University of Ottawa, Ottawa, Canada.

Diamond, G., & Siqueland, L. (1995). Family therapy for the treatment of depressed adolescents. *Psychotherapy: Theory, Research and Practice, 32,* 77–90.

Duhl, B. S., & Duhl, F. J. (1981). Integrative family therapy. In A. S. Gurman & D. P. Kniskern (Eds.), *Handbook of family therapy* (pp. 96–123). New York: Brunner/Mazel.

Dunn, R. L., & Schwebel, A. I. (1995). Meta-analytic review of marital therapy outcome research. *Journal of Family Psychology, 9,* 58–68.

Ford, B. G., & West, L. W. (1979). Human relations training for families: A comparative strategy. *Canadian Counsellor, 13,* 102–107.

Garner, D. M., Olmsted, M. P., & Polivy, J. (1983). Development and validation of Multidimensional Eating Disorder Inventory for anorexia nervosa and bulimia. *International Journal of Eating Disorders, 2,* 15–34.

Garner, D., Rockert, W., Davis, R., Garner, M., Olmsted, M., & Eagle, M. (1993). A comparison between cognitive–behavioral and supportive–expressive therapy for women with bulimia nervosa: Short-term outcome. *American Journal of Psychiatry, 150,* 37–46.

Giblin, P., Sprenkle, D., & Sheehan, R. (1985). Enrichment outcome research: A meta-analysis of premarital, marital and family interventions. *Journal of Marital and Family Therapy, 11,* 257–271.

Ginsberg, B. (1984). Filial therapy with retarded children and their families. *American Psychology Bulletin, 6,* 332–334.

Goldman, A., & Greenberg, L. (1992). Comparison of integrated systemic and emotionally focused approaches to couples therapy. *Journal of Consulting and Clinical Psychology, 60,* 962–969.

Gottman, J. (1994). An agenda for marital therapy. In S. M. Johnson & L. S. Greenberg (Eds.), *The heart of the matter: Perspectives on emotion in marital therapy* (pp. 256–295). New York: Brunner/Mazel.

Gottman, J., Coan, J., Carrere, S., & Swanson, C. (1998). Predicting marital happiness and stability from newlywed interactions. *Journal of Marriage and the Family, 60,* 5–22.

Greenberg, L. S., Elliott, R., & Lietaer, G. (1998). *Handbook of experiential psychotherapy.* New York: Guilford Press.

Greenberg, L. S., Ford, C., Alden, L., & Johnson, S. M. (1993). Change processes in emotionally focused therapy. *Journal of Consulting and Clinical Psychology, 61*, 78–84.

Greenberg, L. S., & Johnson, S. M. (1988). *Emotionally focused therapy for couples.* New York: Guilford Press.

Guerney, B. G., Jr. (1977). *Relationship enhancement: Skill training programs for therapy, problem prevention and enrichment.* San Francisco: Jossey-Bass.

Guerney, B. G., Jr. (1988). Family relationship enhancement: A skill training approach. In L. A. Bond & B. W. Wagner (Eds.), *Families in transition: Primary prevention programs that work* (pp. 99–134). Beverly Hills, CA: Sage.

Guerney, B. G., Jr. (1994). The role of emotion in relationship enhancement marital/family therapy. In S. Johnson & L. Greenberg (Eds.), *The heart of the matter: Perspectives on emotion in marital therapy* (pp. 124–150). New York: Brunner/Mazel.

Guerney, B. G., & Maxson, P. (1990). Marital and family enrichment research: A decade review and look ahead. *Journal of Marriage and the Family, 52*, 1127–1135.

Guerney, B. G., & Stover, L. (1971). *Filial therapy: Final report.* Silver Spring, MD: Ideals.

Guerney, B. G., Vogelsong, E., & Coufal, J. (1983). Relationship enhancement versus a traditional treatment: Follow-up and booster effects. In D. Olson & B. Miller (Eds.), *Family studies review yearbook* (Vol. 1, pp. 738–756). Beverly Hills, CA: Sage.

Hahlweg, K., & Markman, H. J. (1988). Effectiveness of behavioral marital therapy: Empirical status of behavioral techniques in preventing and alleviating marital distress. *Journal of Consulting and Clinical Psychology, 56*, 440–447.

Hazan, C., & Shaver, P. (1987). Conceptualizing romantic love as an attachment process. *Journal of Personality and Social Psychology, 52*, 511–524.

Jacobson, N. S., & Addis, M. E. (1993). Research on couples and couples therapy: What do we know? Where are we going? *Journal of Consulting and Clinical Psychology, 61*, 85–93.

Jacobson, N. S., Follette, W. C., & Elwood, R. W. (1984). Outcome research in behavioral marital therapy: A methodological and conceptual reappraisal. In K. Hahlweg & N. S. Jacobson (Eds.), *Marital interaction: Analysis and modification* (pp. 113–129). New York: Guilford Press.

Jacobson, N. S., & Truax, P. (1991). Clinical significance: A statistical approach to defining meaningful change in psychotherapy research. *Journal of Consulting and Clinical Psychology, 59*, 12–19.

James, P. (1991). Effects of a communication training component added to an emotionally focused couples therapy. *Journal of Marital and Family Therapy, 17*, 263–276.

Jessee, R., & Guerney, B. G. (1981). A comparison of Gestalt and relationship enhancement treatments with married couples. *American Journal of Family Therapy, 9*, 31–41.

Johnson, S. M. (1996). *The practice of emotionally focused couples therapy: Creating connection*. New York: Brunner/Mazel.

Johnson, S. (1998). Emotionally focused couple therapy. In F. Dattilio (Ed.), *Case studies in couple and family therapy: Systemic and cognitive perspectives* (pp. 450–472). New York: Guilford Press.

Johnson, S. M. (1999). Emotionally focused couples therapy: Straight to the heart. In J. Donovan (Ed.), *Short term couple therapy* (pp. 13–42). New York: Guilford Press.

Johnson, S., & Greenberg, L. (1985a). The differential effectiveness of experiential and problem solving interventions in resolving marital conflict. *Journal of Consulting and Clinical Psychology, 53*, 175–184.

Johnson, S., & Greenberg, L. (1985b). Emotionally focused couples therapy: An outcome study. *Journal of Marital and Family Therapy, 11*, 313–317.

Johnson, S. M., & Greenberg, L. S. (1988). Relating process to outcome in marital therapy. *Journal of Marital and Family Therapy, 14*, 175–183.

Johnson, S. M., & Greenberg, L. S. (1994). Emotion in intimate interactions: A synthesis. In S. M. Johnson & L. S. Greenberg (Eds.), *The heart of the matter: Perspectives on emotion in marital therapy* (pp. 297–234). New York: Brunner/Mazel.

Johnson, S. M., & Greenberg, L. S. (1995). The emotionally focused approach to problems in adult attachment. In N. S. Jacobson & A. S. Gurman (Eds.), *The clinical handbook of marital therapy* (2nd ed., pp. 121–141). New York: Guilford Press.

Johnson, S., Hunsley, J., Greenberg, L., & Schindler, D. (1999). Emotionally focused couples therapy: Status and challenges. *Clinical Psychology: Science and Practice, 6*, 67–79.

Johnson, S., Maddeaux, C., & Blouin, J. (1998). Emotionally focused family therapy for bulimia: Changing attachment patterns. *Psychotherapy: Theory, Research and Practice, 35*, 238–247.

Johnson, S., & Talitman, E. (1997). Predictors of outcome in emotionally focused marital therapy. *Journal of Marital and Family Therapy, 23*, 135–152.

Johnson, S. M., & Williams-Keeler, L. (1998). Creating healing relationships for couples dealing with trauma: The use of emotionally focused marital therapy. *Journal of Marital and Family Therapy, 24*, 25–40.

Johnson, S. M., & Whiffen, V. (1999). Made to measure: Adapting emotionally focused couples therapy to partner's attachment styles. *Clinical Psychology: Science and Practice, 6*, 366–381.

Klein, M. H., Mathieu, P. L., Gendlin, E. T., & Miesler, D. J. (1969). *The Experiencing Scale: A research and training manual* (Vol. I). Madison: University of Wisconsin, Bureau of Audio Visual Instruction.

Kobak, R., & Cole, H. (1991). Attachment and meta-monitoring. In D. Cicchetti & S. Toth (Eds.), *Disorders and dysfunctions of the self* (pp. 267–297). Rochester, NY: University of Rochester Press.

Kobak, R., Ruckdeschel, K., & Hazan, C. (1994). From symptom to signal: An attachment view of emotion in marital therapy. In S. Johnson & L. Greenberg (Eds.), *The heart of the matter: Perspectives on emotion in marital therapy* (pp. 46–71). New York: Brunner/Mazel.

Krause, I. B. (1993). Family therapy and anthropology: A case for emotions. *Journal of Family Therapy, 15,* 35–56.

Lebow, J. L., & Gurman, A. S. (1995). Research assessing couple and family therapy. *Annual Review of Psychology, 46,* 27–57.

Lietaer, G. (1994). Authenticity, congruence and transparency. In D. Brazier (Ed.), *Beyond Carl Rogers* (pp. 17–46). London: Constable.

MacPhee, D. C., Johnson, S. M., & Van der Veer, M. C. (1995). Low sexual desire in women: The effects of marital therapy. *Journal of Sex and Marital Therapy, 21,* 159–182.

Main, M. (1991). Meta-cognitive knowledge, meta-cognitive monitoring and singular (coherent) vs multiple (incoherent) models of attachment. In J. S. Stevenson-Hinde, C. M. Parkes, & P. Marris (Eds.), *Attachment across the life cycle* (pp. 127–159). London: Routledge.

Matter, M., McAllister, W., & Guerney, B. G. (1984). Relationship enhancement for the recovering couple: Working with the intangible. *Focus on Family and Chemical Dependency, 7,* 21–23.

Merkel, W. T., & Searight, H. R. (1992). Why families are not like swamps, solar systems or thermostats: Some limits of systems theory as applied to family therapy. *Contemporary Family Therapy, 14,* 33–51.

Mikulincer, M., Florian, V., & Weller, A. (1993). Attachment styles, coping strategies and post-traumatic psychological distress: The impact of the Gulf War in Israel. *Journal of Personality and Social Psychology, 64,* 817–826.

Minuchin, S., & Fishman, H. C. (1981). *Family therapy techniques.* Cambridge, MA: Harvard University Press.

Napier, G., & Whitaker, C. A. (1978). *The family crucible.* New York: Harper & Row.

Nichols, M. P. (1987). *The self in the system.* New York: Brunner/Mazel.

Perls, F. (1973). *The Gestalt approach and eyewitness to therapy.* Ben Lomond, CA: Science and Behavior Books.

Piercy, F. P., & Sprenkle, D. (1990). Marriage and family therapy: A decade review. *Journal of Marriage and the Family, 52,* 1116–1126.

Rogers, C. (1951). *Client-centered therapy.* Boston: Houghton-Mifflin.

Rogers, C. (1961). *On becoming a person: A therapist's view of psychotherapy.* Boston: Houghton-Mifflin.

Rogers, C. (1975). Empathy: An unappreciated way of being. *The Counselling Psychologist, 5,* 2–10.

Rombauts, J., & Devriendt, M. (1990). Conjoint couple therapy in client centered practice. In G. Lietaer, J. Rombauts, & R. Van Balen (Eds.), *Client centered and experiential psychotherapy in the nineties* (pp. 847–863). Leuven, Belgium: Leuven University Press.

Rose, M., Battjes, R., & Leukefeld, C. (1984). *Family skills* (Family Life Skills Training for Drug Abuse Prevention Booklet). Rockville, MD: National Institute on Drug Abuse.

Rosenthal, R. (1984). *Meta-analytic procedures for social research.* Beverly Hills, CA: Sage.

Satir, V. M., & Baldwin, M. (1983). *Satir step by step: A guide to creating change in families.* Palo Alto, CA: Science and Behavior Books.

Schindler, L., Hahlweg, K., & Revenstorf, D. (1983). Short and long term effectiveness of two communication training modalities with distressed couples. *American Journal of Family Therapy, 11,* 54–64.

Sensue, M. E. (1981). *Filial therapy follow-up study.* Unpublished doctoral dissertation, Pennsylvania State University.

Shadish, W. R., Montgomery, L. M., Wilson, P., Wilson, M. R., Bright, I., & Okwumabua, T. (1993). Effects of family and marital psychotherapies: A meta-analysis. *Journal of Consulting and Clinical Psychology, 61,* 992–1002.

Shadish, W. R., & Ragsdale, K. (1996). Random versus nonrandom assignment in controlled experiments: Do you get the same answer. *Journal of Consulting and Clinical Psychology, 64,* 1290–1305.

Simon, R. (1989). Reaching out to life: An interview with Virginia Satir. *Family Therapy Networker, 13,* 36–43.

Smith, M., Glass, G., & Miller, T. (1980). *Benefits of psychotherapy.* Baltimore: John Hopkins University Press.

Spanier, G. B. (1976). Measuring dyadic adjustment: New scales for assessing the quality of marriage and similar dyads. *Journal of Marriage and the Family, 38,* 15–28.

Sywulak, A. E. (1977). *The effect of filial therapy on parental acceptance and child adjustment.* Unpublished doctoral dissertation, Pennsylvania State University.

Task Force for the Development of Guidelines for the Provision of Humanistic Psychosocial Services. (1997). Guidelines for the provision of humanistic psychosocial services. *The Humanistic Psychologist, 24,* 64–107.

Vogelsong, E., Guerney, B. G., & Guerney, L. (1983). Relationship enhancement therapy with inpatients and their families. In R. Luber & C. Anderson (Eds.), *Family intervention with psychiatric patients* (pp. 48–68). New York: Human Sciences Press.

Walker, J. (1994). *A marital intervention program for couples with chronically ill children.* Unpublished doctoral dissertation, University of Ottawa, Ottawa, Canada.

Walker, J., Johnson, S., Manion, I., & Cloutier, P. (1996). An emotionally focused marital intervention for couples with chronically ill children. *Journal of Consulting and Clinical Psychology, 64,* 1029–1036.

Watzlawick, P., Weakland, J., & Fisch, R. (1974). *Change: Principles of problem formation and problem resolution.* New York: Norton.

Wieman, R. J. (1973). *Conjugal relationship modification and reciprocal reinforcement: A comparison of treatments for marital discord.* Unpublished doctoral dissertation, Pennsylvania State University.

Whisman, M. A., & Jacobson, N. S. (1990). Power, marital satisfaction, and response to marital therapy. *Journal of Family Psychology, 4,* 202–212.

Whitaker, C. A., & Keith, D. (1991). Symbolic–experiential family therapy. In A. S. Gurman & D. P. Kniskern (Eds.), *Handbook of family therapy* (pp. 187–224). New York: Brunner/Mazel.

11

HUMANISTIC GROUP PSYCHOTHERAPY

RICHARD C. PAGE, JAMES F. WEISS, AND GERMAIN LIETAER

There is a large amount of research in the professional literature that supports the effectiveness of humanistic group therapy. Unfortunately, the utility of humanistic group therapy with clinical populations is not widely recognized by the psychological community. This chapter describes what the research shows about the effectiveness of humanistic group therapy. We hope to demonstrate concretely the specific ways this research details how humanistic group therapy helps clients make positive behavioral and attitudinal changes.

BASIC CONCEPTS OF HUMANISTIC GROUP THERAPY

The primary therapy theories that are reviewed in this chapter as humanistic theories of group therapy include person-centered (or client-centered; CCT) group therapy, Gestalt group therapy, and existential group therapy. These theories are included under the humanistic rubric because they share common assumptions about human nature and the therapeutic processes that are central to effective psychotherapy. All of these theories emphasize that people have free will and the ability to make choices that are growth producing. These theories also stress the importance of self-awareness in therapy because it is assumed that people who are self-aware can make better choices. Person-centered, Gestalt, and existential therapies all emphasize the idea that people are capable of acting in responsible and caring ways in interpersonal relationships. All of these theories state that human beings have an innate drive toward growth that enables them to benefit from therapy. For a complete description of the individual approaches of these three types of humanistic therapies in this volume, refer to chapters 1 and 5 for person-centered therapy, chapter 6 for Gestalt therapy, and chapter 8 for existential therapy.

In the book *Creating Contact, Choosing Relationship: Dynamics of Unstructured Group Therapy* that examines the common assumptions of person-centered therapy, Gestalt therapy, existential therapy, and other theories, Page and Berkow (1994) stressed that self-actualization is an important theme in the group therapy literature and should be conceptualized in ways that account for the negative as well as the positive aspects of human direction. To operate effectively in a group, the therapist must trust the abilities of the group members to help one another grow in positive directions. Unless this is the case, the therapist may try to exert more control over the group process than is helpful. When this occurs, it works against the therapeutic potential of the group, which operates most effectively when the members are free to help one another and determine their own directions for growth. Existential, person-centered, and Gestalt group therapies attempt to capitalize on group members' potential to help themselves become more satisfied and fulfilled individuals. One of the advantages of group therapy compared with individual therapy is that the members have the opportunity to learn about interpersonal relationships by actually experiencing these relationships in a group with one another.

Humanistic group therapies provide an atmosphere in which people can discuss personal problems and engage in interpersonal learning. Gestalt, person-centered, and existential theories all stress the importance of the present moment in the group. The past can be brought up in therapy, but the present, here-and-now encounters that members have with one another and with the therapist allow them to engage in interpersonal learning that is powerful because it is immediate. Existential and person-centered group therapies generally emphasize that it is important for the therapist to allow the members to encounter one another in the group without having activities conducted by the leader. The members are encouraged to assume the primary responsibility for what is discussed in their group and for the overall direction of the group. This type of group format, which encourages the members to determine the direction of the group for themselves, is called *unstructured group therapy* (Page & Berkow, 1994; see also, Barrett-Lennard, 1998; Schmid, 1996). Unstructured groups can be viewed as having stages that promote the growth of the members (Page & Berkow, 1994; see also Beck, 1974; Rogers, 1970). These stages occur naturally as the members emphasize certain themes that often emerge from the group process, such as dealing with anger or developing trusting relationships. Such themes are related to the kinds of interpersonal learning experiences within the group that can be internalized and eventually generalized to more caring and responsible relationships outside the group.

Humanistic group therapy can be effective with people who have serious problems, including clinical populations. The emphasis of these groups is on helping the members to learn to trust themselves and their own abilities to engage in constructive personal and interpersonal growth. These groups often underscore the importance of helping each member to develop an enhanced sense of self. Most clients from clinical populations, ranging from drug addicts to people suffering from depression, need to develop both a healthier sense of self and more rewarding interpersonal relationships. Thus, the emphases of humanistic therapy groups are appropriate for clinical populations. The following sections examine research conducted with humanistic therapy groups—a corpus of research that generally supports the utility of using person-centered, Gestalt, and existential groups in clinical settings.

RESEARCH RELATED TO CLINICAL POPULATIONS

In this chapter, we examine research related to applications of humanistic group psychotherapy with actual *clinical* populations. The research that has been conducted is presented in Tables 11.1 through 11.3.

Research on Person-Centered Group Psychotherapy

Table 11.1 summarizes the clinical research that has been conducted on person-centered group therapy over the past 50 years. The original client-centered approach was developed in the early 1940s by Carl Rogers (1942) as a form of individual therapy, yet by the end of that decade, his approach had been extended to group settings as well (see Blocksma & Porter, 1947). Some of the earliest references to research involving *client-centered* or *nondirective* groups emerged in the late 1940s and early 1950s (see, e.g., Gorlow, Hoch, & Telschow, 1952; Hobbs & Pascal, 1946; Peres, 1947).

For the early research that was published between 1946 and 1952, Raskin (1986b) emphasized several noteworthy elements, including (a) emphases on both process and outcome, (b) utilization of verbatim transcripts to replace therapist notes or impressions, (c) supporting evidence for Rogers's therapeutic equation (acceptance of feelings by therapists leading to positive, increasingly sensitive responses by group members), (d) transfer of behavioral changes in a group to changes outside the group, (e) focus on attitudes toward the self and self-concept, and (f) distinctions between successful

TABLE 11.1
Person-Centered Group Research With a Clinical Focus

Author	Population/Focus	Design	Results
Ends and Page (1957)	Hospitalized alcoholic patients, with neo-analytic, client-centered, and learning theory approaches	Pre/post testing with randomization and control	Client-centered group exhibited greatest amount of change
Ends and Page (1959)	Hospitalized alcoholic patients	Pre/post testing with randomization and control	Greater self-acceptance and integration of self and ideal self
Truax and Carkhuff (1967); Truax and Mitchell (1971)	Multiple clinical populations	Multiple	Reviews numerous studies of the relationship between therapist-offered conditions and various outcome measures
Truax (1968)	Hospitalized psychiatric patients	Pre/post testing with randomization and comparison groups	Greater overall self-exploration and improvement with high levels of therapist-offered conditions
Butler (1968)	Self-ideal congruence	Pre/post testing with control	Significant increases in self-ideal correlation on Q sort
Truax, Wittmer, and Wargo (1971)	Hospitalized psychiatric patients	Pre/post testing with randomization and comparison groups	High levels of therapist-offered conditions positively related to therapeutic outcome
Dircks, Grimm, Tausch, and Wittern (1982)	Cancer patients	Pre/post testing with control	Increased social activity, improved family and interpersonal relations, less disease-related anxiety, more positive outlook on life
Westermann, Schwab, and Tausch (1983)	Psychoneurotic counseling center clients	Pre/post/follow-up testing with control	85% improved and 89% expressed satisfaction, with continued positive results 6 months later
Tausch, Langer, and Bergeest (1984)	Couples with relationship difficulties	Pre/post/follow-up testing with control	71%–74% improvement on relational and personal problems; covariation with perception of Rogerian attitudes in partner and therapist
Eckert and Biermann-Ratjen (1985)	Inpatient treatment of neurosis and personality disorders	Comparison of client-centered and psychoanalytic approach; pre/post testing with control	Significant changes in both approaches; however, nature of change different: more intrapsychic in psychoanalytic, more interpersonal in client-centered therapy

Study	Focus	Method	Findings
Beck, Dugo, Eng, and Lewis (1986)	Group phases	Transcript ratings	Delineation of nine developmental phases and four leadership functions
Pomrehn, Tausch, and Tönnies (1986)	Psychoneurotic counseling center clients	Pre/post/follow-up testing with control	72% improved at 1-year follow-up; outcome positively related to perception of therapist attitudes and to process measures such as expression of feelings and confidence in the group
Grimm, Dircks, and Langer (1992)	Unemployed clients	Pre/post/follow-up tests with control; process measures	Clear effects on psychological (e.g., self-esteem), psychosomatic, and psychosocial aspects
Braaten (1990)	Group climate critical incidents and cohesion	Process/Qualitative	Group "listening and empathy" ranked as third highest cohesion category
Schwab (1995)	Lonely clients	Pre/post testing with control	Significant reduction on loneliness scores; less reduction when initial loneliness was high; most successful clients highest scores on many process measures, including their perception of therapist attitudes
Dierick and Lietaer (1990)	Operative therapeutic factors from viewpoints of self, other, and therapist	Qualitative/Thematic Analysis and quantitative Content analysis	Group relational climate was found to be the best barometer for the quality of a session in the group members' experience
Lietaer and Dierick (1996)	80 group therapists of several orientations	Process/Qualitative	Client-centered group therapists' dominant style is one of deepening individual exploration and interpersonal communication

and less-successful clients, particularly with regard to increased numbers of positive affective responses.

While at the University of Chicago during the 1950s, Rogers continued to refine his client-centered theory while gaining recognition in the area of psychotherapy research (Cain, 1987). Although Rogers concentrated most of his research on factors related to individual counseling and psychotherapy, his work stimulated other researchers to examine applications of his theories in both individual and group settings. For example, in the late 1950s, Ends and Page (1957, 1959) studied the effects of Rogerian group therapy on individuals with alcoholism. In their first study of people hospitalized with alcoholism, Ends and Page (1957) compared a CCT group with a learning theory group, a neo-analytic group, and a social discussion control group. The results indicated that the client-centered group manifested the greatest amount of change, both at the end of the 15-week therapy program and at the end of an 18-month follow-up period. A later study (Ends & Page, 1959) examined the effectiveness of Rogerian group therapy as an adjunct to a general alcoholic treatment program. Although the experimental group did not differ significantly from the control group on measures of the Minnesota Multiphasic Personality Inventory, the Rogerian group members did, however, show significantly greater improvement on self-ideal Q-sort measures when compared with the control group following 6 weeks of treatment.

During the 1960s, Charles B. Truax examined Rogers's "necessary and sufficient conditions" hypothesis regarding the effects of therapist empathy, genuineness, and unconditional positive regard with groups (Truax, 1961). Using a variety of group psychotherapy populations ranging from hospitalized psychiatric patients to institutionalized juvenile delinquents, Truax and his colleagues repeatedly examined the relationship between outcome measures and varying process levels of therapist-offered conditions of accurate empathy, nonpossessive warmth, and genuineness (e.g., Truax, Carkhuff, & Kodman, 1965).

In a book titled *Toward Effective Counseling and Psychotherapy*, Truax and Carkhuff (1967) reviewed and summarized the findings of the numerous group therapy studies they and their colleagues conducted regarding the triad of Rogerian core conditions. They concluded: "Research seems consistently to find empathy, warmth, and genuineness characteristic of human encounters that change people—for the better" (p. 141). In the years following the publication of this book, Truax and his associates conducted additional group comparison studies that offered further support regarding the therapeutic importance of accurate empathy, nonpossessive warmth, and genuineness (Truax, 1968; Truax, Wittmer, & Wargo, 1971). Truax and Mitchell (1971) again reviewed the existing research related to the core conditions of the therapeutic relationship and offered similar, highly positive conclusions.

The research of Truax and his colleagues related to therapist-offered conditions was not the only avenue of client-centered group research occurring during the 1960s. A controlled study by Butler (1968) exemplifies a variation of client-centered group research focusing on the Rogerian notion of congruence as one of the keys to psychological health. Butler used a 100-item personality trait Q sort that allowed clients to rank items describing their current self-concept and their ideal self. Using these rankings as pretest–posttest measures, Butler found that client-centered psychotherapy was instrumental in significantly narrowing the gap between client ratings of self and ideal self.

Furthermore, from the 1960s to 1980s, an impressive series of fine-grained studies were undertaken by Beck and colleagues (Beck, Dugo, Eng, & Lewis, 1986; Beck & Keil, 1967). They were able to distinguish empirically, on the basis of transcript ratings of 12 time-limited groups, nine developmental phases in the group process and four types of leadership function (the task leader, the emotional leader, the scapegoat leader, and the defiant leader).

Although research related to CCT flourished while Rogers remained in major university settings, it began to decline once he departed to become affiliated with the Western Behavioral Sciences Institute in La Jolla, California (Raskin, 1986b). Much of the research shifted away from a focus on clinical populations and was, instead, redirected toward examinations of encounter groups associated with the burgeoning human potential movement that peaked in the late 1960s and early 1970s.

Although the 1970s were characterized by a decline in the volume of client-centered research in the United States, numerous investigations related to person-centered group psychotherapy emerged in Europe (Frohburg, Di Pol, Thomas, & Weise, 1986; Raskin, 1986a). Several examples of European research conducted during the past 2 decades can be mentioned here. For example, Dircks, Grimm, Tausch, and Wittern (1982) conducted an 11-week study involving an experimental group of 30 cancer patients who received person-centered group counseling and a control group of 28 cancer patients who received no counseling. Among other findings, the results showed that patients in the experimental group experienced increased levels of social activity and decreased levels of disease-related anxiety while displaying improved family and interpersonal relationships and a more positive outlook on life.

In another European study, Westermann, Schwab, and Tausch (1983) investigated intensive person-centered group psychotherapy involving 16 therapists and 164 patients with psychoneuroses. One of the findings of this study was that at the 4-week follow-up, 85% of the experimental participants had improved (23% clearly improved; 62% improved somewhat), whereas only 18% of the control participants improved (5% clearly improved; 13% improved somewhat). Also, 89% of the experimental participants reported satisfaction with group therapy (63% clearly satisfied; 26% somewhat satisfied).

Tausch, Langer, and Bergeest (1984) investigated 41 couples who had difficulties relating to their partners. All of the participants were psychologically tested 1 month before the group started, at the beginning of the group, right after the last group meeting, and 6 months after the group had ended. The results showed that, after the groups were conducted, the partner-related difficulties had been alleviated significantly more compared with the waiting period alone: In 42% of the cases, there was improvement or considerable improvement (vs. 8% after the waiting period); 32% saw slight improvement (vs. 37%); 20% were unchanged (vs. 41%); and 5% grew worse (vs. 15%). The clients perceived their partners as being significantly more genuine, more empathic, and more caring.

Eckert and Biermann-Ratjen (1985) compared the processes and effects of client-centered and psychoanalytic inpatient group psychotherapy on the basis of data from a total of 209 patients with neurotic problems or personality disorders. The patients were treated for 3 months, participating in approximately 50 group sessions of 90 minutes each. The outcome of therapy was measured by personality questionnaires and standardized interviews; the analysis of the process was based on tape ratings, questionnaires, and a Q sort. Both approaches to group psychotherapy proved to be equally effective, with lasting effects after 2 years and with significant changes not found in a control group.

In a study by Pomrehn, Tausch, and Tönnies (1986), 87 clients with psychoneurotic disturbances participated in 2 days of person-centered group psychotherapy with four subsequent meetings. Prior to the group psychotherapy, as well as at 6 weeks and 1 year after, each client was psychodiagnostically tested. This study yielded numerous results. Six weeks after the group, 26% of the clients had "clearly improved" in their individual disturbances (vs. 2% of wait-list clients), and 44% were "improved" (vs. 27%), 21% "stayed unchanged" (vs. 39%), and 9% worsened (vs. 32%). One year later, 46% of the clients had clearly improved, 26% improved, 23% stayed unchanged, and 5% worsened.

In a study by Grimm, Dircks, and Langer (1992), 57 unemployed clients took part in person-centered group counseling. The effects of these groups were analyzed and compared with a control group of 30 unemployed persons who did not participate in group counseling. The group counseling helped the participants to increase their self-confidence and feelings of self-esteem, stabilize the self-concept that had become weakened as a result of unemployment, better utilize their spare time, improve their social skills and lessen their social withdrawal, avoid a decrease in social activities, overcome aggressiveness, improve unstable psychosomatic conditions, and reduce unemployment-related depression.

Schwab (1995) studied groups for lonely people ($n = 40$) who participated in a 1-day program followed by 12 two-hour evening sessions. He found a significant reduction on the University of California, Los Angeles, Loneliness Scale compared with a wait-list control group ($n = 29$). The group members with the highest loneliness scores at the start had the least positive perceptions of their group experiences.

Two research studies assessed the effects of person-centered groups on clients with psychological problems. One involved a study that compared clients with psychological problems who were involved in client-centered groups and control groups (Bruhn, Schwab, & Tausch, 1980). Results showed that the clients in the client-centered groups perceived their therapists as being empathic, respectful, warm, and congruent compared with the control group members. The levels of self-disclosure, self-exploration, and congruence of the clients in client-centered groups increased compared with the clients in the control groups. Figge (1999) reported the results of a research project that was conducted at a German university with students with psychiatric diagnoses who participated in a person-centered group. He showed that the group members demonstrated significant improvement on 37 variables measured by different personality questionnaires.

Additional studies related to the processes of person-centered group psychotherapy have been conducted by other European researchers, such as Leif Braaten, who has made substantial contributions in the study of interactional variables related to facilitative group climate dimensions (Braaten, 1989b). For example, Braaten (1990) conducted a primarily qualitative process study investigating 958 critical incidents occurring during high- and low-cohesion sessions in person-centered group therapy. Of the 11 factors that constitute a multidimensional model of cohesion, Braaten (1989a) showed that high-cohesion sessions are dominated by critical incidents related to self-disclosure and feedback (24.0%), attraction and bonding (20.2%), and listening and empathy (20.0%).

Dierick and Lietaer (1990) conducted a complicated qualitative study involving a content analysis of the most helpful therapeutic factors operative in group therapy settings. Open-ended responses from 115 participants and 9 therapists clustered into natural category perspectives of self, other, and therapist. The obtained responses were also classifiable into three basic sections: Section A, the relational climate and structural aspects of the group; Section B, specific interventions of the group members or the therapist; and Section C, process aspects in the group member. To differentiate the impact of helpful factors, Dierick and Lietaer obtained group satisfaction evaluations, resulting in a high- and a low-satisfaction subgroup. One of the most interesting results of this study centered around the observation that in Section A (structural/relational climate) there were 15 times more helpful segments mentioned in the high-satisfaction group than in the low-satisfaction group, suggesting that "the relational climate seems thus to be the best barometer for the quality of a session in the group members' experience" (pp. 757–758).

In another group process study, Lietaer and Dierick (1996) examined the intervention styles of 80 therapists from five different theoretical orientations, including client-centered. Using a 45-item intervention-style questionnaire, the researchers developed several dimensions of group intervention styles, clustered under four main classifications: (a) facilitating the experiential process, (b) personal presence, (c) meaning attribution, and (d) executive function. Overall, this process study revealed that client-centered therapists attempt to stimulate the experiential process while being minimally structuring. Likewise, client-centered therapists remain visible and present by explicitly communicating support and concern and by using here-and-now feedback while only occasionally putting forth their own values. Of the many group process dimensions examined in this study, the intervention styles of "deepening individual exploration" and "stimulating interpersonal communication" were almost unanimously endorsed at the highest level, and "thus remains a dominant way of intervening for client-centered therapists" (Lietaer & Dierick, 1996, p. 568).

In summary, person-centered groups have been in existence for more than 50 years, and much of the research on this type of group therapy has focused on outcomes and processes related to the core conditions originally articulated by Rogers. Findings seem to support a strong relationship between therapist-offered and member-offered conditions of empathy, warmth, and genuineness, and positive therapeutic outcomes. Person-centered group approaches have been shown to be effective with clinical populations. The present and future directions of person-centered group psychotherapy seem to point toward ongoing expansions of studies conducted in European countries, as well as an incorporation of more process-oriented, qualitative, and case study research applications.

Research on Gestalt Group Psychotherapy

Table 11.2 summarizes the clinical research that has been conducted on Gestalt therapy groups. In *Gestalt Therapy: Theory, Practice and Research* (1992), O'Leary emphasized the importance of doing research to examine the assumptions, processes, and goals of Gestalt therapy. Although there is a moderate and growing body of research available regarding Gestalt therapy in general (see Gestalt therapy chapter, this volume, chapter 6), such

TABLE 11.2
Gestalt Group Research With a Clinical Focus

Author	Population/Focus	Design	Results
Greenberg and Webster (1982)	Adult clients seeking counseling because of difficulties in making decisions	Combined process–outcome study	Clients classified as "resolvers" experienced significant reductions in indecision and anxiety
Serok and Zemet (1983)	Reality testing with hospitalized schizophrenics using Rorschach	Pre/post testing with randomized matched pairs and control	Significant increase in reality perception scores
Serok, Rabin, and Spitz (1984)	Schizophrenic patients	Pre/post testing with randomized matched pairs and control	Positive impact on reality testing, some improvement in perception of self and others, and significant improvement related to body image
Clarke and Greenberg (1986)	Comparison of Gestalt vs. cognitive–behavioral for resolving decisional conflicts	Pre/post testing with randomization and control	Gestalt intervention proved superior to both cognitive–behavioral intervention and control in reducing indecision
Frew (1988)	Therapist styles	Review and survey	Predominant therapist style was mixed model

research is particularly lacking in regard to Gestalt group therapy. There is an additional difficulty confronting anyone attempting to review the literature related to Gestalt group research. This difficulty relates to the fact that two competing models of Gestalt group therapy exist that cloud the distinction between individual and group therapy: the more traditional, individually oriented "hot seat" workshop approach that was advocated by Fritz Perls and a second, more interactional group process approach (Korb, Gorrell, & Van De Riet, 1989; also see Harman, 1984). Frew (1988) found that the vast majority of 251 Gestalt and Gestalt-oriented therapists that he surveyed used a mixed-model approach to group therapy that integrates both individual and interactional models.

Like Gestalt therapists, Gestalt researchers also appear to share fluid boundaries between individual and interactional approaches; thus, many Gestalt intervention studies do not clearly specify whether the techniques are being used in group (rather than individual) settings. Even when such specifications are made, these studies are typically conducted with nonclinical populations. Although there have been several Gestalt-oriented studies conducted with nonclinical populations, particularly with student volunteers (see, e.g., Foulds & Hannigan, 1976, 1977, 1978), a glance at Table 11.2 reveals a relative dearth of clinical studies in Gestalt group psychotherapy. The most clearly delineated contributions to Gestalt group research with clinical populations have been provided by Leslie S. Greenberg and his associates, and by Shraga Serok. These contributions are now considered in turn.

Greenberg is perhaps the most prolific researcher of Gestalt approaches. His work includes a substantial number of studies related to the popular Gestalt two-chair dialogue intervention, a technique that is used in both individual and group settings by most Gestalt therapists. Greenberg and his associates have studied this particular intervention in both individual (see Greenberg & Clarke, 1979; Greenberg & Dompierre, 1981; Greenberg & Higgins, 1980; Greenberg & Rice, 1981) and group settings (see Clarke & Greenberg, 1986; Greenberg & Webster, 1982).

In regard to group applications of two-chair dialogues in clinical settings, Greenberg and Webster (1982) devised a combined process–outcome study of clients experiencing intrapsychic conflicts related to decision making. Raters were used to classify participants as *resolvers* or *nonresolvers* on the basis of several in-session process indicators observed during two-chair dialogues. Resolvers exhibited three components involved in the process of conflict resolution: (a) expressions of criticism by one part of the personality, (b) expressions of feelings and wants by another part, and (c) an eventual softening of attitude on the part of the "critic." Participants rated as resolvers experienced significant reductions in anxiety and indecision following group treatment, and they also reported greater improvement on target complaints and behavior change when compared with nonresolvers.

A strongly designed study conducted by Clarke and Greenberg (1986) also used the two-chair dialogue technique with clients seeking to resolve decisional conflicts. In this study, 48 adult clients seeking to resolve career-oriented indecision were randomly assigned to a Gestalt group using an affective two-chair intervention, a cognitive–behavioral group using a problem-solving intervention, or a wait-list control group. Although both treatment groups were more effective than the control group in terms of helping clients move through stages of decision making, overall, the Gestalt intervention proved to be the most effective treatment for reducing indecision.

During the 1980s, Serok conducted multiple research applications of Gestalt therapy in clinical settings. Having previously undertaken earlier studies involving patients with psychoses (Serok, 1982b) and hospitalized adolescents (Serok, 1982a), Serok devised two additional studies focused on patients with schizophrenia (Serok, Rabin, & Spitz, 1984; Serok & Zemet, 1983). Both of these studies used a pretest–posttest design with random assignments of matched pairs of participants into control and experimental conditions. Serok and Zemet (1983) used the Rorschach to test the reality perception of the 17 patients with schizophrenia involved in this study. One of these measurements, Neigger's Reality Test (Neigger, 1956), revealed a significant increase in reality perception in the experimental group as opposed to the control group.

Using a similar research design, Serok et al. (1984) also examined the effects of Gestalt group therapy on hospitalized schizophrenic patients' perception of reality. To tap into patients' perceptions of self and others and their ability to correctly integrate elements of reality, this study used such measures as the Bender Gestalt, Goodenough's Human Figure Drawings Test, and the Tennessee Self-Concept Scale. The results showed some improvement in the experimental group members' perception of self and others and significant improvement in the presentation of body image, as measured by the Human Figure Drawing Test.

In summary, despite the relative paucity of research related to applications of Gestalt group psychotherapy in clinical settings, the studies that do exist appear to substantiate the effectiveness of this approach. Gestalt groups using traditional two-chair dialogue techniques have been shown to be effective in reducing anxiety and indecisiveness in clients experiencing conflicts related to decision-making difficulties. These results offer support for the existence of an important affective component in the decision-making process. It has also been shown that Gestalt group psychotherapy facilitates increased reality perception and differentiation among individuals with schizophrenia.

Research on Existential Group Psychotherapy

Table 11.3 presents the clinical research on existential group psychotherapy. One of the central figures associated with existential psychotherapy is Irvin D. Yalom (1980), who suggests that such approaches are not technique- or intervention-driven but are, instead, driven by a focus on *ultimate concerns* related to life and death, freedom and responsibility, isolation and loneliness, and meaning and meaninglessness.

Although an overall emphasis on meaning and meaninglessness is important to existential therapists, this emphasis appears to be important to patients as well. For example, in a study involving rankings of curative factors by 65 acute-care group therapy patients, Lantz (1984) found that a noetic or meaning-related curative factor ("The group helped me find meaning in my life") was chosen most often as the most important curative item by these patients. Beyond emphases on meaning, an even larger portion of the research in the area of existential group psychotherapy focuses on the notion of personal freedom and responsibility. Yalom (1974, 1980, 1995) described research involving successful group therapy patients who were administered a Q sort of 60 items, composing 12 therapeutic (curative) factors. Even though none of the therapists in the study were existentially oriented, the patients ranked one existential item ("Learning that I must take ultimate responsibility for the way I live my life no matter how much guidance and support I get from others") as the fifth most important of the 60 items. Yalom (1980) noted that unpublished replications of this Q sort with two addiction groups resulted in having this same "ultimate responsibility" item being ranked *first* out of 60 items in one group, and *second* in the other.

Yalom's existential interests were also exemplified in his research from the middle of the 1970s to the early 1980s on groups for terminally ill patients (Spiegel et al., 1981; Spiegel & Yalom, 1978; Yalom & Greaves, 1977). These groups assessed the impact of group therapy on patients suffering from metastatic carcinoma. Research by Spiegel et al. (1981) showed that members of a treatment group, when compared with members of a randomly selected control group, had significantly lower mood disturbance scores, fewer phobic reactions, and less death anxiety. A subsequent study on metastatic breast cancer patients was performed by Spiegel, Kraemer, Bloom, and Gottheil (1989). When a 10-year follow-up was conducted, patients from the treatment group were found to have lived almost twice as long (37 months) as the patients in the traditional control group (19 months).

In other clinical settings, some group leaders have attempted to maximize the impact of existential therapeutic factors by opting for less-structured approaches to group psychotherapy, thus shifting responsibility from them-

TABLE 11.3
Existential Group Research With a Clinical Focus

Author	Population/Focus	Design	Results
Yalom (1974)	Curative factors operative in experiences of successful patients	Q sort of a total of 60 items composing 12 curative factors	Existential item related to personal responsibility ranked 5th of 60 items
Spiegel, Bloom, and Yalom (1981)	Women with metastatic breast cancer	One-year randomized control group study	Fewer maladaptive coping responses, less phobic behavior, and less anxiety about death
Page (1982)	Unstructured marathon with male illicit drug users	Process study using Hill Interaction Matrix-G (HIM-G)	Interactions ranked at 79th percentile in time spent in HIM-G Quadrant IV (most therapeutic quadrant)
Page (1983)	Unstructured marathon with female inmate illicit drug users	Posttest only with randomization and control	Evaluated Men, Women, Past, My Real Self more positively on semantic differential
Page and Bridges (1983)	Unstructured marathon with male illicit drug users	Process study using Hill Interaction Matrix-G	Interactions ranked at 99th percentile in time spent in Confrontive Work-Style on HIM-G
Page and Wills (1983)	Unstructured marathon with male illicit drug users	Process study using Hill Interaction Matrix-G	Interactions ranked at 80th percentile in time spent in Relationship Content-Style on HIM-G
Lantz (1984)	Acute-care psychiatric patients and curative factors	Patient rankings of curative factors	Noetic curative factor chosen most often as most important factor
Page (1984)	Unstructured marathon with female inmate illicit drug users	Posttest only with randomization and control	Evaluated Women more positively on semantic differential

continued

TABLE 11.3
Continued

Author	Population/Focus	Design	Results
Page (1986)	Unstructured marathon with male and female inmate illicit drug users	Posttest only with randomization and control	Evaluated Counseling more positively on semantic differential
Page, Richmond, and de la Serna (1987)	Unstructured marathon with male and female inmate illicit drug users	Posttest only with randomization and control	Evaluated My Real Self more positively on semantic differential
Page, Davis, Berkow, and O'Leary (1989)	Unstructured marathon with male illicit drug users	Process study using Hill Interaction Matrix-G	Interactions ranked at 99th percentile in time spent in Confrontive Work-Style on HIM-G
Spiegel, Kraemer, Bloom, and Gottheil (1989)	Women with metastatic breast cancer	One-year randomized control group study	10-year follow-up revealed increased survival rates of treatment group members (37 months vs. 19 months)
L. Campbell and Page (1993)	Unstructured marathon with male illicit drug users	Process study using Hill Interaction Matrix-G	Interactions ranked at 90th percentile in personal-confrontive and relationship-confrontive cells on HIM-G
Page, Campbell, and Wilder (1994)	Unstructured marathon with male illicit drug users	Process study using Hill Interaction Matrix-G	Less active leadership styles yield more therapeutic group interactions
Van der Pompe, Duivenvoorden, Antone, and Visser (1997)	Immune function of female breast cancer patients	Pre/post testing with randomization and control	Improved endocrine and immune function readings

selves to the group members. Such approaches intentionally deemphasize the executive function of the group leader, thus placing the onus of responsibility for interaction and change on group members. A significant amount of research in this area has been carried out by Richard C. Page, whose approach to group psychotherapy can be categorized as *unstructured existential* (see Page & Berkow, 1994).

Although this unstructured-existential group approach has been applied to group work involving clients with disabilities (Page, 1978), the brunt of Page's research has been directed toward studying groups of inmates and illicit drug users. Over the past 20 years, Page and his associates have focused on outcome and process studies related to the use of unstructured marathon groups with male and female illicit drug users. All of the outcome studies used a posttest-only control group design with random selection of participants into control and experimental groups (see D. T. Campbell & Stanley, 1966). In each of these outcome studies, different scales of the semantic differential (Osgood, Suci, & Tannenbaum, 1957) served as the dependent measures. Studies of unstructured marathon groups conducted with female inmate illicit drug users (Page, 1983, 1984) showed that therapy group participants rated the evaluative scales of Women, Men, The Past, and My Real Self more positively compared with their control group counterparts. Similarly, five unstructured marathon groups for both male and female inmate illicit drug users all resulted in more positive ratings on the evaluative scales of Counseling (Page, 1986) and My Real Self (Page, Richmond, & de la Serna, 1987) compared with randomly selected control groups.

In regard to process studies involving unstructured marathon groups of male illicit drug users, Page and his colleagues used the Hill Interaction Matrix (HIM-G; Hill, 1965) to analyze group member interactions. The HIM-G measures two basic dimensions: a *content-style* dimension, focusing on four increasingly therapeutic levels of what group members talk about (topic, group, personal, and relationship), and a *work-style* dimension, focusing on four increasingly invested levels of work in the group (conventional, assertive, speculative, and confrontive). Together, both of these ordinal, four-level dimensions yield a matrix of 16 cells that can be quantified from least therapeutic (topic-conventional) to most therapeutic (relationship-confrontive). Thus, the most therapeutic quadrant of this matrix includes the four cells that combine personal and relationship content styles with speculative and confrontive work styles. One process study by Page (1982) showed that members of the unstructured marathon spent more than 50% of their time in this most therapeutic quadrant, ranking these interactions at the 79th percentile when compared with group norms described by Hill (1965). Subsequent process studies of unstructured marathon groups with male illicit drug users revealed the following: Group members ranked at the 99th percentile in time spent in the most therapeutic (confrontive) work style (Page & Bridges, 1983; Page, Davis, Berkow, & O'Leary, 1989), at the 80th percentile in time spent in the most therapeutic (relationship) content style (Page & Wills, 1983), and at the 90th percentile in the two of the four most therapeutic cells (personal-confrontive and relationship-confrontive; L. Campbell & Page, 1993). Page, Campbell, and Wilder (1994) showed that illicit drug abusers can interact in therapeutic ways without relying on group leaders to direct discussions. When considered together, the outcome and the process studies conducted by Page and his associates strongly suggest that unstructured-existential marathon groups can be used as an effective form of treatment for inmate and illicit drug-using populations.

One final, recent study involving existential group psychotherapy deserves special mention here because it involves a level of physiological research not typically found with the more abstract and philosophical foundations associated with existential approaches. Using an approach called experiential–existential group psychotherapy (EEGP), van der Pompe, Duivenvoorden, Antone, and Visser (1997) conducted a study in the Netherlands focusing on endocrine and immune outcome measures of 50- to 70-year-old women in the early stages of breast cancer. Using a pretest–posttest design with random assignment of participants into experimental and wait-list control conditions (see D. T. Campbell & Stanley, 1966), van der Pompe et al. found that after 13 weeks of EEGP, participants in the experimental group, when compared with those in the wait-list control, had lower levels of plasma cortisol and prolactin, lower percentages of natural killer cells (CD8 cells and CD4 cells), and lower proliferative responses to pokeweed mitogen. In other words, the group ostensibly helped the members to develop more immunity to their cancers. However, these results may be overly optimistic because they only applied to those patients who pretested at relatively high endocrine and immune baseline levels.

In summary, existential approaches to group psychotherapy have been used effectively with terminally ill populations and in facilitating the process and outcome of therapy with inmates and illicit drug-using populations. By focusing heavily on themes and processes related to meaning and personal responsibility, existential approaches address areas that patients rate as some of the most highly valued and therapeutic elements of group work.

FROM RESEARCH TO PRACTICE

The research on humanistic group therapy shows that these groups have been used with various clinical populations. Many of the research designs of studies conducted on client-centered group therapy have used pretest–posttest designs, and these studies have sometimes used the random selection of participants to control and experimental groups. Research designs that used pretest–posttest designs or the random selection of participants into control and experimental groups are particularly strong types of designs, according to D. T. Campbell and Stanley (1966); therefore, much of the group therapy research that has been done on client-centered group therapy has used convincing research designs. Client-centered groups have been used effectively with people with alcoholism, hospitalized psychiatric patients, cancer patients, and counseling center patients. The research on these groups indicates that client-centered groups are often associated with improvements in self/ideal-self congruence and with increased social activity. The relationship of the therapist-offered conditions of accurate empathy, nonpossessive warmth, and genuineness to positive outcomes in group therapy has been well documented.

Less research has been conducted on Gestalt therapy groups than on client-centered groups, yet the research that has been done has generally used pretest–posttest designs and randomly selected participants into control and experimental groups. Gestalt group research has used hospitalized patients with schizophrenia as participants, as well as people who have problems with decision making. These groups have been shown to help people with schizophrenia develop improved perceptions of self and others and of their own body image, and appear to have a positive impact on their level of reality testing. Gestalt therapy groups have also been effective in helping people improve in their decision-making abilities.

The research on existential group therapy has focused on both processes and outcomes and has generally used pretest–posttest designs with the random selection of participants into control and experimental groups. This research has been done with physically disabled, breast cancer, and drug- and alcohol-abusing patients. This research shows that group therapy clients are often concerned with existential issues, such as personal responsibility or death, and that they improve in evaluations of self and counseling after participating in group therapy. All of these outcomes are related to the goals of existential group therapy. The process research on group therapy with illicit drug abusers has also shown that illicit drug abusers can act in therapeutic ways in groups and that they do not need an active or control-oriented leader to benefit from their participation.

This chapter emphasizes the viability of using humanistic group therapy as a form of treatment for a variety of clinical populations. Overall, the research on humanistic group therapy supports the notion that clients with serious problems, such as drug abuse or psychiatric problems, can assume responsibility for helping themselves in groups. Leaders who exhibit the core conditions in group therapy can be reasonably confident that they can help clients develop a stronger sense of self and more caring and satisfying interpersonal relationships. More research with diverse clinical populations is needed on the use of all of these humanistic group therapy approaches.

REFLECTIONS ON TRANSCRIPT

A case study of an actual therapy group that was led by one of the authors and two other therapists is presented next to illustrate how humanistic therapy groups can help therapy clients experience personal growth. This group was conducted with male illicit drug abusers who were members of an inpatient community-based drug treatment center. The members were in a weekly, 2-hour therapy group that had sessions over a 20-week period of time. Membership in this group was voluntary, and material discussed in the group was confidential.

Transcripts of different parts of the ninth session presented below deal primarily with the personal problems discussed by one participant. Several different types of group discussions are offered to illustrate the ways a humanistic therapy group evolves. For instance, the members of a therapy group usually need to establish trust before they feel comfortable discussing personal problems. Once one member is able to self-disclose in a group, it often stimulates other members to do the same. Therapy groups often contain themes that run throughout the life of the group. The theme of discussing abusive family relationships first emerged in the group discussed below when a member named Jim, a former cocaine addict, revealed problems that he was having with his father and sister. The names presented in the transcripts have been changed to maintain the anonymity of the leaders and participants, and some of the facts about the group or members have been changed for the same reason.

The first excerpt presented from the ninth session illustrates the ways that the members of therapy groups are often initially careful about how they present themselves to one another. Certain members of this group, but not the leaders, know that Jim has some serious problems with his father that he has not revealed in the group. These members (Zane, David, Jason, Brian, and Joe) and the two group leaders (Sharon and Bob) are trying to help Jim to be more forthcoming.

> Zane: Well, what is it that you understand about, Jim?
> Jim: Well, I understand that I have, well I am confused about myself, well I know what I will do when I get out of here. But I don't know really now.
> Zane: The question was what is it about you that you understand. You understand something about you. I don't know what.
> Jim: I'm saying that, you know, I couldn't talk to my father, you know, cause I was confused about their relationship, my father and mother.
> Zane: How about your relationship with yourself?
> Sharon: I don't understand what you don't understand.
> Jim: You know, I can accept that there are, you know . . .

Zane: Accept what?

Jim: That, the things that happened. You know. Like my father's and mother's separation. And the other things. You understand. Things I was doing, you know. Selling drugs.

Sharon: You saying things you understand, but you are not saying what you understand about these things.

Jim: Like, uh . . . I'll tell you the reason I started selling drugs and all. What I'm saying is . . .

Zane: You ain't saying nothing yet.

At this point in the group meeting, the members are pressing Jim to discuss a problem that he has with his father and family. Jim is ostensibly unwilling to discuss the problem he has with his father in the group, but he also does not become overly defensive as the members try to get him to disclose what they know is on his mind.

Later in the session,

Jim: You mean about my past like . . .

Sharon: You know what has to surface. I don't.

Zane: How do you feel now? I'm talking about right now. Right now.

Jim: I'm feeling depressed and frustrated. I can't really open up.

Sharon: OK, Jim. What is it that's stopping you from opening up?

Jim: Well, uh . . . I've never talked to anybody except my relatives.

Sharon: OK. I understand that. But what is it that stops you from doing it?

Jim: I can't really say. I guess fear of, a lack of trust I guess. OK, if I tell Zane something, I look at it how he would see it.

The members and one leader again attempt to help Jim to discuss a problem they think he has. The members and Sharon are supportive of Jim, although they confront him when they sense that he avoids discussing his real feelings in the group. Jim still appears not to mind being confronted, although he continues to try to avoid dealing with his personal issues or feelings. This occurs because Jim is afraid of revealing his anger because he lacks confidence in his own ability to handle what he might reveal in the group. Jim is afraid to discuss his family because he feels rage toward his father, who abused his mother and sister. The members know Jim wants to hurt his father when he leaves the treatment center, so they are trying to help him open up in the group so that he can receive help. The confrontations the members are making are done in a respectful manner and are done to help Jim. Jim senses the members are trying to help him, so he does not show much resistance to being confronted. It is important that the personal boundaries of clients are respected when members are confronted; it is also important that participants are not forced to see things in a particular way by the other members. The goal of confrontation is to help clients to grow in personal awareness and not simply to accept what the group says. The members and leader confront Jim to help him become aware of the ways his behavior is being perceived and to help him feel supported enough to disclose his problems in the group.

Later in the session,

Jim: I guess I been trying to wrestle through things, you know. 'Cause I can't really depend on my parents you know.

Bob: You say you still hate your dad.

Jim: I still have some bad feelings for him.

Bob: It sounds like he is pretty confusing too. In some ways you sense that he cares, but in other ways you sense that he . . .

Jim: Yeah. When we talk he tells me all the good things he is going to do for me. I just want him to explain to me someday.

Bob: What things do you want him to explain to you? Like why he beat your mom?

Jim: Right. You know. Just be parents. You know. I'm worried about my baby sister. She is with my mother now. My mother, she just can't take care of my baby sister. I just like for her to get it together. Just do that. You know. I feel bad about telling folks my mother is in Cleveland and my father is in Miami. And I been doing that ever since I been coming up.

Sharon: Do you feel like they betrayed you?

Jim: Yeah, I do. I feel like they just didn't give a damn. I just do what I want to do then. That's mostly what I been doing.

Sharon: So you feel like rebelling against them.

Jim: You know, my mother, I'm disappointed in her. My father, I'm disappointed in him.

Bob: Why are you disappointed with your mother? What's she like?

Jim: She could have kept all of the kids together. You know. Ain't nobody home. We started off in a home together. But before long, we were on our own. Even my baby sister, man. She was out on her own. She was only 12 years old. Out on her own. That's what really hurts me, man.

(Jim cries and then continues talking.)

Jim: That's my baby sister, man. It hurts me, man. She was out on her own at 12 years old, man. They didn't bother to ask where she was at or how she was doing. You know. They didn't try to look for her. She finally come home, you know. They said you left out of here, no sense coming back here, you know. That shows they don't care. There wasn't really nothing I could do about it. I was not doing nothing for myself at that time. Family life has just been messed up, you know. I just disowned my parents. I say I got 'em but when it comes down to it, just ain't so. It's just my baby sister, man. Like she up there in Cleveland out on her own. Supposed to be with my mother, you know. She out on her own. And I haven't talked to her, man, in six years. Haven't seen her or talked to her in six years. Talked with my mother. She doing alright. Give me a number I asked my mother so I can talk to her. I don't know no number or address. She's doing alright. That ain't telling me nothing. I don't know if she still living, not really. (Silence. Crying.)

Jim: I don't know what to say, man. My baby sister . . .

Joe: How old is she?

Jim: She's 16 now. Hell, I don't even know that. You know, I don't even know how old my baby sister is. It's been that long.

This group excerpt shows the manner in which Jim was finally able to discuss the family problems that caused him to experience emotional turmoil. The reason that Jim was able to finally discuss his family situation is because he realized the members, and the leaders, were genuinely concerned about him. Once Jim was able to reveal his feelings about his sister and father, he was then encouraged during later group sessions by the leaders to work through the family problems he was experiencing. If Jim had not been able to self-disclose during this session, it is doubtful that the later progress he made in counseling in resolving his family problems would have occurred at all. When Jim revealed what he was experiencing in his family, other group members also began to reveal family problems they had. The following excerpt shows how the group progressed after Jim discussed what he had experienced in his family:

Brian: I got a baby sister, too.

Bob: How old is she?

Brian: I don't know how old she is. She's pregnant. And I can relate to what he says. All my feelings are directed towards my father. I hate him. By law he is my father. I think I hate him more than anyone or anything in the world. You know. Because my sister's pregnant in the streets. And she has nowhere to go. She has no one to tell her what to do. Without me realizing it, I can't do nothing about it. I need to quit worrying about it because I can't do nothing about it. I feel better because I spoke to her a long time ago. I cried because I share the same feelings. I can see what you're going through. I can't do nothing about it.

Joe: He can do something, man.

(Other members then share family situations and ways of dealing with family problems.)

It is often true that the self-disclosure of one member in a group facilitates self-disclosure from other members because of the positive example it provides. Also, the members can be active in helping one another, and the leaders can assume a less active role when this occurs. Sharon, a leader, was probably too active during this session and may have interfered in some ways with the help the members were trying to provide to Jim.

These transcripts illustrate that the risks one member takes can have synergistic effects within the group. They also illustrate that the members of a humanistic therapy group can be active in helping one another without relying too much on the leader to provide the main initiative for helping participants who experience psychological pain. This is not to say, however, that the leader does not affect what goes on in group therapy. The task of the facilitator of a humanistic therapy group is to create a conducive atmosphere in which the members feel free to explore their perceptions and attitudes and to reveal things about themselves that are not always socially acceptable. The leader should also provide a setting in which it is safe for the members to engage in personal growth. At times the leader may also need to take an active role in helping the members. It is possible to conceptualize the growth process that occurs in a humanistic therapy group as assisting the self-actualization of the members (Page & Berkow, 1994). This self-actualization process occurs as members become more aware of themselves and others in the group, and as they deal with personal and interpersonal issues that limit their self-esteem. This transcript shows how clients, even illicit drug abusers, can engage one another in group therapy in a manner that helps each member deal constructively with problematic personal and interpersonal issues.

CONCLUSION

This chapter has demonstrated that humanistic therapy groups can be used to help clients with a variety of disorders to develop more effective interpersonal relationships and to deal more functionally with their problems. Unfortunately, humanistic group therapy is an underutilized approach in today's managed care environment, where therapists need to demonstrate their effectiveness in concrete and observable ways. The lamentable fact is that humanistic therapy groups have been demonstrated to be effective through research with clinical populations, but many practitioners are unaware of this. Practitioners should consider the advantages of humanistic group therapy as a method of doing therapy when they consider what approaches they want to use with clients. They should also consider doing more process and outcome research on various kinds of humanistic therapy groups to continue to determine the effects these groups have on different types of client populations.

REFERENCES

Barrett-Lennard, G. T. (1998). Group encounter and therapy. In G. T. Barrett-Lennard (Ed.), *Carl Rogers' helping system: Journey and substance* (pp. 145–176). London: Sage.

Beck, A. P. (1974). Phases in the development of structure in therapy and encounter groups. In D. A. Wexler & L. N. Rice (Eds.), *Innovations in client-centered therapy* (pp. 421–463). New York: Wiley.

Beck, A. P., Dugo, J. M., Eng, A. M., & Lewis, C. M. (1986). The search for phases in group development: Designing process analysis measures of group interaction. In L. S. Greenberg & W. M. Pinsof (Eds.), *The psychotherapeutic process: A research handbook* (pp. 615–705). New York: Guilford Press.

Beck, A. P., & Keil, A. V. (1967). *Observations on the development of client-centered, time-limited therapy groups* (Counseling Center Discussion Papers, Vol. 13, No. 5). Chicago: University of Chicago Library.

Blocksma, D. D., & Porter, E. H., Jr. (1947). A short-term training program in client-centered counseling. *Journal of Consulting Psychology, 11,* 55–60.

Braaten, L. J. (1989a). The effects of person-centered group therapy. *Person-Centered Review, 4,* 183–209.

Braaten, L. J. (1989b). Predicting positive goal attainment and symptom reduction from early group climate dimensions. *International Journal of Group Psychotherapy, 39,* 377–387.

Braaten, L. J. (1990). The different patterns of group climate critical incidents in high and low cohesion sessions of group psychotherapy. *International Journal of Group Psychotherapy, 40,* 477–493.

Bruhn, M., Schwab, R., & Tausch, R. (1980). Die Auswirkungen intensiver personenzentrieter Gesprachsgruppen bei klienten mit seelischen Beeintrachtigungen [The consequences of person-centered groups for clients with intense emotional problems]. *Klinische Psychologie, 3,* 266–280.

Butler, J. M. (1968). Self-ideal congruence in psychotherapy. *Psychotherapy: Theory, Research and Practice, 5,* 13–17.

Cain, D. J. (1987). Carl Rogers' life in review. *Person-Centered Review, 2,* 476–506.

Campbell, D. T., & Stanley, J. C. (1966). *Experimental and quasi-experimental designs for research.* Chicago: Rand McNally.

Campbell, L., & Page, R. C. (1993). The therapeutic effects of group process on the behavioral patterns of a drug-addicted group. *Journal of Addictions and Offender Counseling, 13,* 34–45.

Clarke, K. M., & Greenberg, L. S. (1986). Differential effects of the Gestalt two-chair intervention and problem solving in resolving decisional conflict. *Journal of Counseling Psychology, 33,* 11–15.

Dierick, P., & Lietaer, G. (1990). Member and therapist perceptions of therapeutic factors in therapy and growth groups: Comments on a category system. In G. Lietaer, J. Rombauts, & R. Van Balen (Eds.), *Client-centered and experiential psychotherapy in the nineties* (pp. 741–770). Leuven, Belgium: Leuven University Press.

Dircks, P., Grimm, F., Tausch, A. -M., & Wittern, J. -O. (1982). Förderung der seelischen Gesundheit von Krebspatienten durch personenzentrierte Gruppengespräche [Promotion of the mental health of cancer patients through person-centered group counseling]. *Zeitschrift für Klinische Psychologie. Forschung und Praxis, 11*, 241–252.

Eckert, J., & Biermann-Ratjen, E. -M. (1985). *Stationare Gruppenpsychotherapie: Prozesse, Effekte, Vergleiche* [Inpatient group psychotherapy: Processes, effects, comparisons]. Berlin: Springer.

Ends, E. J., & Page, C. W. (1957). A study of three types of group psychotherapy with hospitalized inebriates. *Quarterly Journal of Studies on Alcohol, 18*, 263–277.

Ends, E. J., & Page, C. W. (1959). Group psychotherapy and concomitant psychological change. *Psychological Monographs: General and Applied, 73*(10, Whole No. 480).

Figge, P. (1999). Client-centered psychotherapy in groups: Understanding the influence of the client–therapist relationship on therapy outcome. In C. Lago & M. MacMillan (Eds.), *Experiences in relatedness: Group work and the person-centered approach* (pp. 95–105). Ross-on-Wye, England: PCCS Books.

Foulds, M. L., & Hannigan, P. S. (1976). Gestalt marathon group: Does it increase reported self-actualization? *Psychotherapy: Theory, Research and Practice, 13*, 378–383.

Foulds, M. L., & Hannigan, P. S. (1977). Gestalt workshops and measured changes in self-actualization: Replication and refinement study. *Journal of College Student Personnel, 18*, 200–205.

Foulds, M. L., & Hannigan, P. S. (1978). Gestalt marathon workshop: Changes in a measure of personal and social functioning. *Journal of Humanistic Psychology, 18*, 57–67.

Frew, J. (1988). The practice of Gestalt therapy in groups. *Gestalt Journal, 11*, 77–96.

Frohburg, I., Di Pol, G., Thomas, B., & Weise, K. (Eds.). (1986). *Forschung und Praxis in der Gruppengesprächspsychotherapie* [Research and practice in group psychotherapy]. Berlin: Gesellschaft für Psychologie.

Gorlow, L., Hoch, E. L., & Telschow, E. F. (1952). *The nature of non-directive group therapy*. New York: Columbia University.

Greenberg, L. S., & Clarke, K. M. (1979). Resolving splits: Use of the two-chair technique. *Psychotherapy: Theory, Research and Practice, 16*, 316–324.

Greenberg, L. S., & Dompierre, L. (1981). Special effects of Gestalt two-chair dialogue on intra-psychic conflict in counseling. *Journal of Counseling Psychology, 28*, 288–294.

Greenberg, L. S., & Higgins, H. M. (1980). Effects of two-chair dialogues and focusing on conflict resolution. *Journal of Counseling Psychology, 27*, 221–224.

Greenberg, L. S., & Rice, L. N. (1981). The specific effects of a Gestalt intervention. *Psychotherapy: Theory, Research and Practice, 18*, 31–37.

Greenberg, L. S., & Webster, M. C. (1982). Resolving decisional conflict by Gestalt two-chair dialogue: Relating process to outcome. *Journal of Counseling Psychology, 29*, 468–477.

Grimm, G., Dircks, P., & Langer, I. (1992). Prozesse und Auswirkungen personenzentrierter Gesprächsgruppen bei Arbeitslosen [Processes and consequences of person-centered group counseling with the unemployed]. In M. Behr, U. Esser, F. Petermann, W. M. Pfeiffer, & R. Tausch (Eds.), *Personenzentrierte Psychologie und Psychotherapie. Band 3. Jahrbuch 1992* [Person-centered psychology and psychotherapy] (pp. 116–131). Köln, Germany: GwG-Verlag.

Harman, R. L. (1984). Recent developments in Gestalt group psychotherapy. *International Journal of Group Psychotherapy, 34*, 473–483.

Hill, W. F. (1965). *HIM: Hill Interaction Matrix*. Los Angeles: University of Southern California, Youth Study Center.

Hobbs, N., & Pascal, G. R. (1946). A method for the quantitative analysis of group psychotherapy [In the program for the 54th Annual Convention of the American Psychological Association]. *The American Psychologist, 1*, 297.

Korb, M. P., Gorrell, J., & Van De Riet, V. (1989). *Gestalt therapy: Practice and theory* (2nd ed.). Boston: Allyn & Bacon.

Lantz, J. E. (1984). The noetic curative factor in group therapy. *International Forum for Logotherapy, 7*, 121–123.

Lietaer, G., & Dierick, P. (1996). Client-centered group psychotherapy in dialogue with other orientations: Commonality and specificity. In R. Hutterer, G. Pawlowsky, P. F. Schmid, & R. Stipsits (Eds.), *Client-centered and experiential psychotherapy: A paradigm in motion* (pp. 563–583). Frankfurt: Peter Lang.

Neigger, S. (1956). *Introduction to Rorschach diagnosis: Part II. Specific reactions.* Toronto, Ontario, Canada: Toronto Psychiatric Hospital.

O'Leary, E. (1992). *Gestalt therapy: Theory, practice and research.* London: Chapman & Hall.

Osgood, C. E., Suci, G. T., & Tannenbaum, P. H. (1957). *The measurement of meaning.* Urbana: University of Illinois Press.

Page, R. C. (1978). The social learning processes of severely disabled group counseling participants. *Psychosocial Rehabilitation Journal, 2*, 28–35.

Page, R. C. (1982). Marathon group therapy with users of illicit drugs: Dimensions of social learning. *International Journal of Addictions, 17*, 1107–1115.

Page, R. C. (1983). Marathon group counseling with illicit drug users: A study of the effects of two groups for 1 month. *Journal for Specialists in Group Work, 8*, 114–125.

Page, R. C. (1984). The effects of 16 hour long marathon groups on the ways that female drug users perceive women. *Journal of Offender Counseling, Services, and Rehabilitation, 8*, 13–26.

Page, R. C. (1986). The effects of marathon groups on the ways illicit drug users perceive counseling. *International Journal of Addictions, 20*, 1675–1684.

Page, R. C., & Berkow, D. N. (1994). *Creating contact, choosing relationship: The dynamics of unstructured group psychotherapy.* San Francisco: Jossey-Bass.

Page, R. C., & Bridges, N. (1983). Interpersonal relationship styles in marathon group therapy: A study with illicit drug users. *Small Group Behavior, 14*, 253–259.

Page, R. C., Campbell, L., & Wilder, D. C. (1994). Role of the leader in therapy groups conducted with illicit drug abusers: How directive does the leader have to be? *Journal of Addictions and Offender Counseling, 14*, 57–66.

Page, R. C., Davis, K. C., Berkow, D. N., & O'Leary, E. (1989). Analysis of group process in marathon group therapy with users of illicit drugs. *Small Group Behavior, 20*, 220–227.

Page, R. C., Richmond, B. O., & de la Serna, M. (1987). Marathon group counseling with illicit drug abusers. *Small Group Behavior, 18*, 483–497.

Page, R. C., & Wills, J. (1983). Marathon group counseling with illicit drug users: Analysis of content. *Journal for Specialists in Group Work, 8*, 67–75.

Peres, H. (1947). An investigation of non-directive group therapy. *Journal of Consulting Psychology, 11*, 159–172.

Pomrehn, G., Tausch, R., & Tönnies, S. (1986). Personenzentrierte Gruppenpsychotherapie: Prozesse und Auswirkungen nach 1 Jahr bei 87 Klienten [Person-centered group psychotherapy: Processes and consequences after one year with 87 clients]. *Zeitschrift für personenzentrierte Psychologie und Psychotherapie, 5*, 19–36.

Raskin, N. J. (1986a). Client-centered group psychotherapy: Part I. Development of client-centered groups. *Person-Centered Review, 1*, 272–290.

Raskin, N. J. (1986b). Client-centered group psychotherapy: Part II. Research on client-centered groups. *Person-Centered Review, 1*, 389–408.

Rogers, C. R. (1942). *Counseling and psychotherapy.* Boston: Houghton Mifflin.

Rogers, C. R. (1970). *On encounter groups.* New York: Harper & Row.

Schmid, P. F. (1996). *Personenzentrierte Gruppenpsychotherapie in der Praxis: Band II. Die Kunst der Begegnung* [Person-centered group psychotherapy in practice: Vol II. The art of encounter]. Paderborn, Germany: Junfermann.

Schwab, R. (1995). Zur Prozeßforschung in der gesprächspsychotherapeutischen Gruppentherapie. Überlegungen im Anschluß am empirische Ergebnisse aus Gruppen mit Einsamen [Process research on group therapy: Considerations in relation to empirical outcomes for groups and individuals]. In J. Eckert (Ed.), *Forschung zur Klientenzentrierten Psychotherapie. Aktuelle Ansätze und Ergebnisse* [Research on client-centered psychotherapy: Current approaches and results] (pp. 151–165). Köln, Germany: GwG.

Serok, S. (1982a). Gestalt therapy with hospitalized adolescents. *Journal of Adolescence, 5*, 307–317.

Serok, S. (1982b). Gestalt group therapy with psychotic patients. *Gestalt Journal, 5*, 45–55.

Serok, S., Rabin, C., & Spitz, Y. (1984). Intensive Gestalt group therapy with schizophrenics. *International Journal of Group Psychotherapy, 34*, 431–450.

Serok, S., & Zemet, R. M. (1983). An experiment of Gestalt group therapy with hospitalized schizophrenics. *Psychotherapy: Theory, Research and Practice, 20*, 417–424.

Spiegel, D., Bloom, J. R., & Yalom, I. (1981). Group support for patients with metastatic breast cancer. *Archives of General Psychiatry, 38*, 527–533.

Spiegel, D., Kraemer, H., Bloom, J., & Gottheil, E. (1989). Effects of psychosocial treatments on survival of patients with metastatic breast cancer. *Lancet, 335*, 888–891.

Spiegel, D., & Yalom, I. D. (1978). A support group for dying patients. *International Journal of Group Psychotherapy, 28*, 233–245.

Tausch, C., Langer, L., & Bergeest, H. (1984). Personzentrierte Gruppengespräche bei Paare mit Partnerschwierigkeiten [Person-centered group counseling for couples with marital problems]. *Zeitschrift für personenzentrierte Psychologie und Psychotherapie, 3*, 489–497.

Truax, C. B. (1961). The process of group psychotherapy: Relationships between hypothesized therapeutic conditions and intra-personal exploration. *Psychological Monographs, 75*(14, Whole No. 511).

Truax, C. B. (1968). Therapist interpersonal reinforcement of client self-exploration and therapeutic outcome in group psychotherapy. *Journal of Counseling Psychology, 15*, 225–231.

Truax, C. B., & Carkhuff, R. R. (1967). *Toward effective counseling and psychotherapy: Training and practice*. Chicago: Aldine.

Truax, C. B., Carkhuff, R. R., & Kodman, F. (1965). Relationships between therapist-offered conditions and patient change in group psychotherapy. *Journal of Clinical Psychology, 21*, 327–329.

Truax, C. B., & Mitchell, K. M. (1971). Research on certain therapist interpersonal skills in relation to process and outcome. In A. E. Bergin & S. L. Garfield (Eds.), *Handbook of psychotherapy and behavior change* (pp. 299–344). New York: Wiley.

Truax, C. B., Wittmer, J., & Wargo, D. G. (1971). Effects of the therapeutic conditions of accurate empathy, non-possessive warmth, and genuineness on hospitalized mental patients during group therapy. *Journal of Clinical Psychology, 27*, 137–142.

van der Pompe, G., Duivenvoorden, H. J., Antone, M. H., & Visser, A. (1997). Effectiveness of a short-term group psychotherapy program on endocrine and immune function in breast cancer patients: An exploratory study. *Journal of Psychosomatic Research, 42*, 453–466.

Westermann, B., Schwab, R., & Tausch, R. (1983). Auswirkungen und Prozesse personzentrierter Gruppenpsychotherapie bei 164 Klienten einer Psychotherapeutischen [Outcomes and processes of person-centered group psychotherapy with 164 clients]. *Zeitschrift für Klinische Psychologie. Forschung und Praxis, 12*, 273–292.

Yalom, I. D. (1974). Existential factors in group therapy. *Journal of the National Association of Private Psychiatric Hospitals, 6*, 27–35.

Yalom, I. D. (1980). *Existential psychotherapy*. New York: Basic Books.

Yalom, I. D. (1995). *The theory and practice of group psychotherapy* (4th ed.). New York: Basic Books.

Yalom, I. D., & Greaves, C. (1977). Group therapy with the terminally ill. *American Journal of Psychiatry, 134*, 396–400.

12

HUMANISTIC PLAY THERAPY

SUE CARLTON BRATTON AND DEE RAY

Beginning with the groundbreaking work of Virginia Axline in the early 1940s, humanistic child psychotherapists have used play therapy as the developmentally appropriate treatment modality for helping children. Axline's client-centered view that people possess within themselves the ability to solve their own problems seemed particularly applicable and helpful in her work with children. She found that the major client-centered principles of empathy, unconditional positive regard, and congruence were more readily extended into her work with children through play, the child's natural means of expression. Axline (1950) defined *play therapy* as

> a play experience that is therapeutic because it provides a secure relationship between the child and adult, so that the child has the freedom to and room to state himself in his own terms, exactly as he is at that moment in his own way and in his own time. (p. 68)

Axline's development of client-centered play therapy marked a major development in the field of child psychotherapy.

RATIONALE FOR PLAY THERAPY

Play has long been considered significant in children's lives (Rousseau, 1762/1930). Through play, children learn about themselves, others, and the world around them as they try to organize, make sense of, and communicate their experiences (Landreth, 1991). According to Piaget (1962), children are not capable of formal operational thought processes that allow for abstract thought and verbal expression until approximately the age of 11 years. The child's world is one of concrete realities; thus, children must be afforded a concrete means of expressing their perception of self, others, and the world. Play permits children to bridge the gap between concrete experiences and abstract thought by allowing children to communicate concretely and symbolically through the manipulation of toys (Landreth, 1991).

In play therapy, it is the symbolic function of play that is significant. Toys are viewed as the child's words and play as the child's language. Children can more comfortably, safely, and meaningfully express their inner world through the concrete, symbolic representation of the toys. Through the toys, children are provided with the opportunity to develop mastery and a sense of control over their world as they reenact their experiences directly in the safety of the playroom. In play therapy, regardless of the reason for referral, the therapist has the opportunity to enter into and experience the child's world and actively deal with the issues that brought the child to therapy. Axline (1947) described this process as one in which the child has the opportunity to play out feelings as they emerge, getting them out in the open, and either learning to appropriately control them or abandon them.

DEFINING HUMANISTIC PLAY THERAPY

Humanistic play therapy encompasses several theoretical orientations, including person-centered, existential, and Gestalt, and it is defined by a belief in (a) the phenomenal world of the child; (b) the child's natural striving toward growth, mastery, and maturity; (c) the child's capacity for self-evaluation, self-regulation, self-direction, self-responsibility, and socialization; and (d) the importance of the therapist–child relationship in facilitating the child's growth. Although Axline was the first to apply these principles in play therapy, Clark Moustakas (1959) and, more recently, Louise Guerney (1983) and Garry Landreth (1991) have made significant contributions to the understanding and practice of humanistic play therapy.

Although procedures may vary according to theoretical orientation, all humanistic play therapy approaches view the relationship between the child and the therapist as the vehicle for dynamic growth and healing. In an atmosphere of empathy and genuineness, the child utilizes play to make contact with the therapist in a way that is safe for the child. This process allows the therapist to "experience in a very personal and interactive way the inner dimensions of the child's world" (Landreth & Bratton, 1998, p. 5). Axline (1947) described this process as one in which the play therapist grants the child the freedom to be, without evaluation or pressure to change.

PARENTS AS THERAPEUTIC AGENTS

Parents and other paraprofessionals have also been trained in humanistic principles and procedures to use therapeutically with children. The development of filial therapy by Bernard and Louise Guerney in the early 1960s marked another significant development in the field of humanistic child psychotherapy. Recognizing a shortage of mental health professionals trained to work with children experiencing emotional and behavioral difficulties, the Guerneys were the first to develop a model for training parents in client-centered principles and play therapy procedures to use with their own children. The training was designed to build on and enhance the relationship that already exists between a parent and child by facilitating the development of empathy, genuineness, and acceptance on the part of the parent. In the Guerneys's model, parents attended filial therapy training groups for 12–18 months and conducted weekly play sessions with their children (B. G. Guerney & Stover, 1971).

In response to the time and financial constraints of many families, Landreth (1991) developed a structured 10-week filial therapy training model in which parents receive training and direct supervision in the basic methodology of child-centered play therapy within a small support group format. Parents conduct weekly 30-minute play therapy-type sessions with their child, in which they learn to convey acceptance, empathy, and encouragement, as well as master the skills of effective limit setting (Bratton, 1998).

Gordon (1970) contributed further to the field of humanistic child psychotherapy with the development of his Parent Effectiveness Training (PET) model. Tavormina (1975) described PET as a reflective parent education model that "places a major emphasis on parental awareness, understanding, and acceptance of the child's feelings . . . as a means of affecting the child's behavior and the parent–child interaction" (p. 22). Like the filial therapy models of Guerney and Landreth, Gordon's PET model prepared parents to become therapeutic agents of change by training them to use basic humanistic principles and skills with their own children.

REVIEW OF RESEARCH

Play therapy has been in practice as the developmentally appropriate approach to humanistic child psychotherapy since the early 1940s. However, play therapy, like other humanistic approaches to psychotherapy, typically comes under fire for the perceived lack of research regarding outcome studies. Although it is true that many humanistic play therapists are more dedicated to the practice of play than the research of play, a review of the literature on play therapy research substantiates the effectiveness of humanistic play therapy procedures. The outcome research on the effectiveness of paraprofessionals, primarily parents, trained in client-centered principles and procedures also points to the efficacy of humanistic child psychotherapy applied on a broader scale.

A comprehensive search of humanistic play therapy outcome research, including those studies that used paraprofessionals as therapeutic agents, retrieved hundreds of studies conducted over the last 6 decades. However, on closer inspection, only 75 publications could be included that used an experimental design. It is interesting to note that the research shows a marked difference between decades regarding the number of studies conducted. Humanistic play therapy research clearly hit a peak, as did most humanistic research studies, in the decade of the 1970s. The 1970s also marked an interest in studying the effectiveness of training parents in humanistic principles to use with their own children (Gordon, 1970; B. G. Guerney & Stover, 1971). Surprisingly, and even though research demonstrated the success of play therapy interventions based on humanistic principles, play therapy research has declined in the past 2 decades. On a more positive note, over the past decade there has been an increase in filial therapy research, primarily focusing on Landreth's (1991) child-centered approach to training parents.

The majority of the studies surveyed for this chapter involved the measurement of social maladjustment, with intelligence, maladaptive school behavior, anxiety, and parent–child relationships also topping the list. Early play therapy research tended to focus on intelligence and school achievement. Research in the 1970s and early 1980s, influenced by the humanistic movement, turned to an interest in measuring the effectiveness of play therapy on children's self-concept, social adjustment, and relationships. In the 1990s, research shifted to an interest in societal ills such as domestic violence and child abuse, as well as diagnoses such as attention deficit and conduct disorder. This shift toward examining specific behavioral disorders in children may account for the decline in humanistic play therapy research and a corresponding increase in cognitive–behavioral play therapy research.

Of the studies included, the majority involved a control group compared with at least one experimental group. Experimental interventions ranged from 2 to 100 sessions, with a median number of 12 sessions. Participants ranged from 3 to 13 years old. *Nondirective* and *client-centered* were clearly the terms most used to describe the play therapy intervention used in the experimental groups. *Self-directed, child-centered,* and *relationship-oriented* were also used by authors to describe humanistic play therapy interventions. However, 10 studies did not clearly define the theory and practice of the play therapy used but were included because humanistic principles were used to describe the intervention or results. Another limitation in the majority of the reported research is a lack of description of the training, qualifications, or experience of the therapist. This lack of a clear description of play therapy procedures and therapist's training represents a weakness in the research and tempers the significance of the findings.

Experimental Research in Humanistic Play Therapy

Of the 75 experimental research studies included in this chapter, 48 studies measured the efficacy of humanistic play therapy conducted by trained professionals. Overall, positive outcomes occurred in the areas of (a) self-concept/locus of control, (b) behavioral change, (c) anxiety/fear, (d) cognitive ability, and (e) social skills. However, a few outcomes have not supported the use of play therapy as a viable intervention. They are discussed along with the more successful outcomes.

Self-Concept

The issue of a child's self-concept, although arguably difficult to measure, is one of specific importance to humanistic play therapists, who realize the impact of a child's self-concept on the child's cognitive, social, and behavioral ability. Without a strong self-concept, children are more likely to suffer from additional symptomatic behaviors. Of the 10 studies measuring the effects of humanistic play therapy on self-concept, 8 showed a significant increase. Interestingly, in one of the studies that failed to demonstrate a significant increase in self-concept of treatment participants, the control group's self-esteem dropped at a statistically significant level, whereas the treatment participants' self-esteem remained stable (Post, 1999).

Perez (1987) studied the effect of relationship group play therapy and individual play therapy on the self-concept and sense of mastery of 55 sexually abused children ages 4 to 9 years. Children who received 12 weekly sessions of either intervention scored significantly higher on self-concept and self-mastery when compared with a control group who received no therapeutic services. The control group actually scored lower on self-concept on the posttest than on the pretest, and helplessness increased. At risk for low self-esteem and related difficulties, children living in domestic violence shelters were provided 12 nondirective play therapy sessions in a 2-week period in studies by Kot, Landreth, and Giordano (1998) and Tyndall-Lind (1999). The experimental groups of 11 children in both studies, ages 3 to 10 years, significantly improved their self-concept and demonstrated a significant reduction in total behavior problems, yet there was no change in the matched control group.

House (1970) studied the effect of play therapy on a selected group of 36 second-grade children. The experimental group children, who received 20 child-centered play therapy sessions over 10 weeks, significantly increased self-concept in comparison with children in the control group, who actually decreased slightly. Crow (1989/1990) conducted a study of 22 children retained in the first grade who also scored low on reading or intelligence. The treatment group received 10 weekly nondirective play therapy sessions.

They improved significantly on self-concept and demonstrated improved internal locus of control, whereas the control group showed no improvement. Pelham (1972) studied 52 kindergartners characterized by teachers as being "socially immature." After participating in six to eight sessions of either group or individual nondirective play therapy, both treatment groups scored higher on self-concept and flexibility in relation to the control group.

Gould (1980) researched 84 elementary students identified by teachers as having a low self-image. The children were assigned to three groups: a nondirective activity/play therapy group (12 sessions), discussion group, or control group. Compared with the control group, both treatment groups showed positive change in self-concept, with the strongest change exhibited by the play therapy group. Also, using a school population, Dvarionas (1999) studied the efficacy of child-centered play therapy with 200 Lithuanian primary school children referred for behavioral difficulties and found that the children receiving individual play therapy improved significantly on measures of self-concept while also improving their academic performance. Dorfman (1958) found that maladjusted children, ages 9 to 12 years, who received an average of 19 client-centered play therapy sessions, showed significant improvement on measures of self-adjustment compared with a control group.

Two studies failed to show significant improvement in the self-concept of the experimental group children receiving play therapy. Brandt (1999) researched the effect of humanistic play therapy on 26 preschool and kindergarten children referred for school adjustment difficulties. The 13 children who received 8 to 10 play therapy sessions conducted by master's-level graduate students-in-training did not show a significant change in self-concept; however, both the experimental and control group children's pretest measures of self-esteem were in the average to moderately high range, leaving marginal room for improvement. And, finally, Post (1999) studied the effect of nondirective individual play therapy sessions on the self-concept of 168 at-risk children in the fourth, fifth, and sixth grades. Although the treatment group did not show significant gains in self-esteem at posttesting, Post found that the children participating in a mean of four play therapy sessions over a school year maintained the same level of self-esteem and internal locus of control, whereas the control group dropped at a statistically significant level in both of these areas.

These studies verify the significant impact individual or group play therapy has on the child's self-concept. What seems especially enlightening is that children with no intervention (control groups) often experienced lower self-esteem over time. Following its natural course, the self-esteem of at-risk children appears to be in jeopardy. The efficacy of play therapy and the importance of intervention with children, in terms of self-concept, is emphasized through the findings in these studies.

Behavioral Change

Although play therapists may concentrate on self-esteem, self-concept, and self-responsibility, the typical parent or teacher is more interested in observation of behavioral change. Play therapy has been proven to be effective with specific and general negative behaviors displayed by children. School-related behavior seems especially problematic, considering the number of hours the average child spends in the school environment. Gaulden (1975) studied the impact of nondirective group play therapy on 56 second graders that demonstrated significant behavioral problems in school. A control group and two treatment groups were formed. After both treatment groups participated in 14 sessions over 7 weeks, the play therapy group showed a significant reduction of classroom disturbance when compared with a nontherapeutic play/discussion group or the control group. At an 8-week follow-up, the play therapy group had maintained the behavioral change. Oualline (1975) investigated the use of play therapy with 24 deaf children, ages 4 to 6 years old, exhibiting behavioral problems in school. The children were divided into two groups: an experimental group that received weekly nondirective individual play therapy sessions over 10 weeks and a control group that received 30 minutes of free individual play each week for 10 weeks. Results found that the play therapy group demonstrated a significant increase in mature behavior patterns, although no significant differences were found on other behavioral measures.

Quayle (1991) researched the effects of play therapy on 54 children, ages 5 to 9 years, who were identified by teachers as being at risk for school adjustment. The children were assigned to three groups: 20 sessions of individual child-centered play therapy, 20 sessions of individual tutoring, or control group. Children in both treatment groups improved. However, children receiving play therapy showed more significant improvement, especially in the areas of learning skills, assertive social skills, task orientation, and peer social skills. Also focusing on children with school-adjustment difficulties, McGuire (2000) and Rennie (2000) studied the effects of child-centered play therapy on kindergarten students. McGuire researched the efficacy of 12 sessions of group play therapy with 29 children and found significant improvement in the 15 experimental group children's behavior, as reported by teachers. However, parent reports of the experimental children's behavior did not reflect a significant level of improvement. In a comparison with McGuire's (2000) study, Rennie (2000) conducted a study to determine the effectiveness of 10 to 12 individual play therapy sessions on 27 kindergartners identified with adjustment difficulties. Compared with a control group, the 14 children in the treatment group showed a significant reduction in behavior problems as reported by parents. Teachers reported a similar behavioral improvement in the experimental group children, although not at a statistically significant level. Rennie concluded that individual and group play therapy were equally effective in helping kindergartners with school adjustment difficulties achieve a significant reduction in problematic behaviors. Using a time series design in which the treatment participants served as their own control group, Hannah (1986) observed significant changes in school behavior for 10 children, ages 4 to 6 years old, who received client-centered play therapy. S. Schmidtchen, Hennies, and Acke (1993) compared 14 children, ages 5 to 8 years, who participated in 30 sessions of nondirective play therapy with a matched group of children who received social education. The play therapy group showed a decrease in behavioral disturbance and an increase in person-centered competencies.

Broadening from specific school behaviors to the more general category of oppositional behavior, aggression, and conduct disorder, several researchers have confirmed the positive impact of play therapy on these problematic syndromes. Beers (1985) studied 20 intact families with at least one child, age 4 to 9 years old, diagnosed as oppositionally defiant. Families who participated in a combined child play therapy and parent counseling group condition and those who participated in a videotaped parent–child play condition (therapist reviewed and gave feedback to parents) significantly improved behavior and interpersonal skills compared with the control group. Trostle (1988) studied 48 Puerto Rican children, ages 3 to 6 years old, who were assigned to a treatment group receiving 10 play therapy sessions or a control group. The play therapy group showed greater improvement in self-control and reality play behavior than the control group. In companion studies conducted in shelters, Tyndall-Lind (1999) and Kot et al. (1998) researched the impact of 2 weeks of intensive child-centered play therapy on child witnesses of domestic violence and observed significant changes in reduction of behavior problems for the experimental groups of 11 children in both studies. Tyndall-Lind further concluded that group and individual play therapy were equally effective in reducing behavior problems of children in the experimental group compared with those in a control group.

Dogra and Veeraraghavan (1994) examined the impact of play therapy on 20 children, ages 8 to 12 years old, referred to a clinic for aggressive conduct disorder. The experimental group received two nondirective play therapy sessions per week, as well as parental counseling, for 8 weeks. Compared with a control group, children in the experimental group showed significant positive change on several measures of adjustment, including positive adjustment at home and school. In addition, the experimental group children showed a reduction in aggression, disobedience, temper tantrums, and strong dislike for school. Seeman, Barry, and Ellinwood (1964) also supported this research in their study of aggressive and withdrawn children who responded favorably to nondirective play therapy. Furthermore, Kaczmarek (1983) reported that children identified with behavioral difficulties significantly reduced negative behaviors after participating in individual play therapy or an unstructured play group as compared with participation in a mother–child play condition. Play therapy was most helpful for children who needed to release anger and negative emotions. Unlike Kaczmarek, Brandt (1999) found that individual play therapy was more helpful in reducing internalizing behavior difficulties than externalizing behavior problems, such as aggression. Although positive gains were noted, the experimental group of 13 preschool and kindergarten children referred for school adjustment difficulties did not demonstrate a significant reduction of total behavior problems or externalizing behavior problems, when compared with the 13 control group children. The experimental group children's significant reduction in internalizing behavior problems after 8 to 10 individual play therapy sessions is noteworthy when compared with their scores on externalizing behavior and may, in part, be explained by the use of humanistic principles and procedures, which focus less on changing overt behavior and more on facilitating self-awareness and self-expression.

Two additional studies concentrated on behavioral changes among children who are mentally disabled. Mehlman (1953) investigated 32 mentally disabled residents, ages 7 to 11 years, at a hospital. The children were placed in three groups: group play therapy, a no-intervention group, and a placebo movie group that watched short movies to break the regular routine. The nondirective play therapy group received 29 sessions over 16 weeks and demonstrated higher positive behavioral and personality changes than either control group. Also working with 23 hospitalized mentally disabled children ages 5 to 12 years, Mundy (1957) found that a play therapy treatment group exhibited decreases in temper tantrums and uncooperative behavior while showing an increase in social cooperation and constructive behavior.

Anxiety

Play therapy can also be used for more acute emotional difficulties, such as anxiety or fear. Particularly relevant with hospitalized children, play therapy has been proven to be effective in reducing anxiety. Clatworthy (1981) observed 114 children, ages 5 to 12 years, who were hospitalized for 2 to 4 days. The children were placed in a treatment group receiving play therapy daily and a control group. Children who received play therapy experienced less anxiety than control group children. Rae, Worchel, Upchurch, Sanner, and Daniel (1989) researched 46 children, ages 5 to 10, hospitalized for at least 3 days. The children were placed in four groups: therapeutic play, diversionary play, verbal support, and control group. They were posttested on the third day. Children who participated in the child-centered therapeutic play sessions showed a significantly lower level of fear.

The effects of play therapy on anxiety has also been researched in other settings. Studying a population of diabetic children attending a summer medical camp, Jones (2000) examined the efficacy of 12 sessions of intensive individual play therapy sessions on the anxiety levels and medical compliance of 30 insulin-dependent children, ages 7 to 11 years. Compared with the control group children who attended the same camp, the 15 experimental group children demonstrated significant improvement in medical compliance (giving shots, following diet, etc.), when measured immediately following camp and at a 3-month follow-up. Although a significant reduction of anxiety was not found in the experimental group, interestingly, both the experimental and control group children exhibited normal levels of anxiety at pretesting, allowing marginal room for improvement at posttesting. Tyndall-Lind (1999) found that children in domestic violence shelters demonstrated a significant reduction in anxiety and depression after 12 child-centered sibling group play therapy sessions conducted daily. However, Post (1999) found no significant decrease in the anxiety of at-risk fourth, fifth, and sixth graders who participated in a mean of four sessions of child-centered play therapy.

Cognitive Ability

In addition to desiring substantial changes in behavior, parents and professionals alike are interested in children's ability to increase their intelligence and academic understanding. Although this is not a specific goal of humanistic play therapy, several play therapy studies measuring intelligence and academic improvement have shown promising results, whereas other research has shown humanistic play therapy to have little effect on intelligence.

In Mundy's (1957) study of mentally disabled children, she found that the mean IQ of children in the play therapy treatment group increased 9 points, whereas the control group increased by only 2 points. Sokoloff (1959) reported that of children with cerebral palsy assigned to either group play therapy or individual speech therapy, the children who received group play therapy increased their group's average IQ by approximately 4 points. The children who received speech therapy actually lost over 2 points on IQ. Bouillion (1973/1974) found similar results with 43 language-delayed pre-schoolers who were assigned to five groups: nondirective group play therapy, group speech therapy, individual speech therapy, motor-skill training, or a no-intervention control group. The play therapy participants achieved significantly higher scores than the other treatment groups on fluency and articulation but also showed the least improvement in remediation of receptive language deficits. Axline (1949) observed 37 children, identified as seriously maladjusted readers, in a child-centered classroom environment.

Of the 37 children, 4 children were selected to receive eight play therapy sessions. Twenty-two students improved reading ability over the expected level. The most dramatic increases in IQ were exhibited in 3 of the 4 children who received individual play therapy. Axline (1950) followed up with all available children 5 years later and found 5 were honor roll students and all others were reading at their grade level.

Other studies also reveal an increase in cognitive ability by children participating in play therapy. Siegel (1971) found that children with learning disabilities improved in the dimensions of cognitive, psychomotor, affective, and environment knowledge, as a result of play therapy intervention. Comparatively, the control group decreased in psychomotor and cognitive areas. In addition, Newcomer and Morrison (1974) and Morrison and Newcomer (1975) compared mentally challenged children who were divided into a control group, group play therapy, and individual play therapy condition. They found that both treatment groups increased in gross-motor, fine-motor, language, and social skills as compared with the control group. They further investigated the effectiveness of nondirective versus directive play therapy and found no significant differences between the two modalities. Moulin (1970) studied the effect of client-centered group play therapy on 126 first, second, and third graders identified as underachievers. He found that treatment participants made significant gains in nonlanguage intelligence and meaningful language usage compared with control group participants but found no gains on academic achievement.

Additional studies continue to highlight the efficacy of the play therapy approach with cognitive abilities of children. Bills (1950a) observed 18 third graders labeled as slow learners and emotionally maladjusted who were placed in either a treatment group or control group. The treatment group received six individual play therapy sessions and three group play therapy sessions. By the end of the nine sessions, the treatment group showed significant improvement on reading ability. The treatment group maintained this improvement even 30 days after intervention. Following up on this study, Bills (1950b) studied the effect of nondirective play therapy on eight well-adjusted third graders labeled as slow readers. In contrast to the previous study, Bills found that well-adjusted slow readers failed to make significant gains in reading ability following the play therapy intervention. Additionally, Seeman and Edwards (1954) found that following 67 sessions of child-centered play groups led by a "teacher-therapist," 19 fifth and sixth graders significantly increased their reading ability compared with a matched no-intervention control group.

As mentioned, not all studies have shown play therapy to be effective in increasing intelligence or related cognitive functioning. Elliott and Pumfrey (1972) observed the effect of play therapy on 16 boys, ages 7 to 9 years, who were identified as having poor reading achievement and social maladjustment. The boys were divided into two groups: an experimental group receiving nine weekly 1-hour sessions of nondirective play therapy and a no-intervention control group. The researchers found no differences between the experimental and control groups on reading achievement or social adjustment. Mehlman (1953) found group play therapy to have no effect on the intelligence of 32 mentally challenged children, although the intervention proved effective on behavioral and personality change. Winn (1959) found that even though low-achieving readers receiving 16 sessions of nondirective play therapy showed a significant improvement in personality adjustment, the experimental group did not show significantly greater improvement in reading than the control group. Similarly, Crow (1989/1990) studied the effects of nondirective play therapy on 22 first graders identified as poor readers and found that although the treatment group showed improvement in reading ability, their gain was not statistically significant when compared with the control group's gain.

Although not all research has proved play therapy effective in increasing intelligence or reading ability, the foregoing studies support the use of play therapy for children who are suffering from emotional constraints or emotional maladjustment to help free them from these limitations to express their full cognitive capabilities. The large number of studies indicating the efficacy of humanistic play therapy on cognitive ability assists therapists in broadening their view of the variety of ways that this intervention can assist children in their development.

Social Skills

Just as play therapy offers assistance in the areas of self-concept, behavior, and cognitive ability, children's social skills are also enhanced. Because social skills are highly related to self-concept, behavior, and academic achievement, several of the previously cited research studies address the issue of increased social and communication skills.

In one of the earliest controlled humanistic studies of children, Cox (1953) examined the effects of client-centered play therapy on 52 orphans, ages 5 to 13 years. Following 10 weeks of play therapy and a 13-week follow-up period, treatment participants showed significant gains in social adjustment, as compared with a control group. Because all participants lived together and shared similar influences, play therapy was the only factor to which the gains could be attributed. In addition to finding increases in IQ and advances in behavior, Mundy (1957) found that children with mental retardation who received play therapy increased social cooperation and verbal ability. In a related work, Sokoloff (1959), who studied the effects of play therapy versus speech therapy on children with cerebral palsy, discovered that children who received play therapy showed statistically significant improvement in social maturity. In a study of 50 children, ages 9 to 13, V. S. Schmidtchen and Hobrucker (1978) found that participants who received client-centered play therapy made significant gains in social flexibility, as well as decreased in anxiety and behavior disorders, as compared with two untreated control groups.

Studying the at-risk population, Quayle (1991) found that children who received play therapy not only improved their cognitive skills but also showed gains in assertive social skills and peer social skills. Assessing the impact of humanistic play therapy on "socially immature" children, Pelham (1972) reported that the treatment groups receiving individual or group play therapy made positive gains in social maturity when compared with the control group. Fleming and Snyder (1947) found that maladjusted girls participating in nondirective group play therapy showed significant improvement in personality adjustment compared with the control group, whereas a group of maladjusted boys receiving the same treatment showed no significant change. Thombs and Muro (1973) focused on 36 second graders identified by peers as social isolates according to a sociometric instrument. Three groups of 12 children were formed: relationship play therapy groups, verbal counseling groups, and a control group. Both treatment groups were divided into two groups of six and met 30 minutes each day for 15 days. Children who received either the verbal or play therapy intervention made significant gains in sociometric status as compared with the control group. Furthermore, children who received the group play therapy intervention showed a greater positive change in social position than those who participated in the group verbal counseling sessions.

Other studies have shown less favorable outcomes in this area. Amplo (1980) investigated play therapy versus Adlerian teacher training (in which teachers were taught counseling skills to use with their students) with 78 children, ages 5 to 9 years, identified by teachers as socially immature. Although both treatment groups improved, results indicated that no significant differences were found among the groups on social maturity or school adjustment. However, the play therapy participants showed significantly greater change on a standardized measure of their "willingness to try new tasks." Saucier (1986) examined the effectiveness of nondirective play therapy compared with a directive play therapy condition and a no-intervention control group with 20 abused children, ages 1 to 7 years. After 8 weeks of play therapy, both treatment groups scored significantly higher on personal–social adjustment when compared with the control group. No significant difference was found between the nondirective and directive approach. Yates (1976) studied 53 second graders rated as socially maladjusted who were assigned to a nondirective play therapy condition, a structured-teacher consultation condition, or a control group. No significant differences were found between experimental groups or control group.

Case Studies in Humanistic Play Therapy

Although clinical studies are more often accepted than case studies, case studies lend additional evidence to the effectiveness of an intervention. A literature review of over 100 case studies revealed that the majority of case studies on humanistic play therapy described the play therapy intervention as nondirective or client centered. Perhaps the most notable case study involving play therapy is Axline's (1964) account of Dibs, a 5-year-old child who exhibited selective mutism and catatonic behavior in public while demonstrating violent temper tantrums at home. His teachers and parents suspected him to be mentally challenged. As a result of nondirective play therapy provided by Axline, Dibs became more responsive in the classroom and ceased to have temper tantrums or exhibit odd behavior at home. An IQ test, administered at the conclusion of play therapy, revealed that Dibs was actually quite gifted. The story of Dibs is the most prominent of humanistic play therapy case studies, but there are many more with the same dramatic results. Landreth, Homeyer, Glover, and Sweeney (1996) provided an extensive compilation of summarized case studies that demonstrate the effectiveness of play therapy with a variety of presenting issues.

In such studies, children show the ability to increase positive behavior while decreasing symptomatic behavior following play therapy. Studies have demonstrated the effectiveness of play therapy with enuresis/encopresis (Barlow, Strother, & Landreth, 1986; Warson, Caldwell, Warinner, Kirk, & Jensen, 1954). In these case studies, each child ceased to be enuretic or encopretic, even in as few as 14 sessions. Along the same lines, anxiety-related disorders have also been successfully treated with play therapy. Barlow, Landreth, and Strother (1986) conducted play therapy with a 4-year-old girl diagnosed with trichotillomania (excessive hair-pulling). After eight sessions, the young girl ceased to pull out, and exhibited a regrowth of, her hair. Children with selective mutism, stuttering, and withdrawn behavior have also responded positively following play therapy (Barlow et al., 1986; Carmichael & Lane, 1997). Play therapy has also been successful in the treatment of children referred for acting-out behaviors (Brody, 1992; Carroll, 1995). Allan and Lawton-Speert (1993) conducted play therapy with a severely abused boy diagnosed with schizophrenia. At the end of 18 months of play therapy, the boy ceased to act out sexually, expressed affection appropriately, and was integrated into a regular kindergarten class.

Experimental Research in Filial Therapy

The research findings from 25 experimental studies designed to determine the effectiveness of training paraprofessionals (primarily parents) to conduct client-centered play therapy with children are impressive and support the notion that filial therapy is an effective intervention for children. Of the studies, 21 studies used parents as the therapeutic agents, 3 studies involved training teachers as therapeutic facilitators, and 1 study focused on the effectiveness of high school students trained in child-centered play therapy procedures.

Stover and Guerney (1967) studied mothers who received filial therapy training and found a significant increase in the use of reflective statements, as measured by direct observation. Mothers reported marked improvement in the parent–child relationship and their children's behavior and general emotional adjustment. B. G. Guerney and Stover (1971) supported their earlier 1967 results with a more robust study of 51 mother–child pairs. Results from live observations showed that the mothers demonstrated significant gains in empathic interactions with their children. In addition, all 51 children demonstrated improvement in psychosocial adjustment and symptomatology, with 28 of the children rated significantly improved. Because the above study did not use a control group, Oxman (1972) studied a matched sample of mother–child pairs who received no treatment and found that the filial-trained mothers reported a statistically significant improvement in their children's behavior compared with the matched sample. A longitudinal investigation of B. G. Guerney and Stover's (1971) study was conducted by L. Guerney (1975), with 42 of the original 51 mothers responding. Thirty-two of the respondents reported that their children showed continued improvement 1 to 3 years after treatment.

Using an experimental design in which treatment participants acted as their own control group and following the Guerneys's filial model, Sywulak (1977/1978) trained and supervised 32 parents of children referred for therapy. Results showed a statistically significant improvement in child adjustment as well as in parental acceptance. Interestingly, withdrawn children evidenced faster changes than aggressive children. Sensue (1981) conducted a follow-up of Sywulak's study and found even higher scores 6 months after treatment, with no significant losses 2 to 3 years later. At the time of follow-up, children who had formerly been diagnosed as maladjusted were found to be as well adjusted as a control group of children who had never been diagnosed.

Studies have compared the effectiveness of filial training with other interventions. Payton (1980) conducted a study comparing the effectiveness of parents who received filial therapy training, paraprofessionals who received play therapy training, and a control group. Filial-trained parents reported significant improvement in their children's behaviors when compared with the other groups. In a similar study of 33 children, ages 3 to 9 years, Wall (1979) compared the effectiveness of filial therapy, play therapy, and a group of nontrained parents who played with their children. Of the two parent-facilitated groups, the filial-trained parents made the most gains in empathic interactions with their children. Of the three groups, the children of the filial-trained parents also made the most significant gains in appropriate expression of negative emotions and ability to accurately perceive negative feelings in their families. Wall concluded that parents' acceptance of children's negative feelings may have a more potent effect on children than acceptance of the same feelings by a therapist.

Other studies have used modifications to the traditional filial model. Dematatis (1981) correlated traditional filial training with an integrated filial therapy training program modeled after Kagan's Interpersonal Process Recall training. The results showed significant gains in parental acceptance, affect sensitivity, allowance of self-direction, and involvement for both groups. Boll (1972) studied the effects of filial therapy with 21 mothers of children who were mentally retarded. The study compared a traditional client-centered filial therapy group of 7 mothers, a group of 7 mothers trained in client-centered filial therapy with the inclusion of behavioral reinforcement techniques, and a control group. Results indicated that both filial-trained groups reported improvement in the socially adaptive behavior displayed by their children, with the highest improvement being noted in the traditional filial group. Children who received play therapy sessions with their parents in addition to sessions with a therapist were the focus of a study by Kezur (1980). Findings support the value of training mothers to conduct child-centered play sessions with their children. The most notable results were (a) reciprocal gains in mother–child communication skills, (b) positive correlation between improved mother–child relationship and increases in parent and child self-esteem, and (c) in the most improved mother–child pairs, the mothers reported improvement in other relationships.

Following the Guerneys's model, two additional studies focused on the efficacy of training elementary teachers in client-centered play therapy principles and procedures. B. G. Guerney and Flumen (1970) found that trained teachers were effective therapeutic agents with withdrawn children. The 9 children in the experimental group demonstrated a significant increase in assertive behavior, compared with the 6 control group children. Similarly, Foley (1970) trained 40 undergraduate teacher trainees in the basic methodology of client-centered play therapy. When compared with a control group and a placebo group, the treatment group of 14 student teachers demonstrated significant gains in the acquisition of client-centered attitudes and skills and made significantly fewer negative responses in their interactions with students.

The following 13 research studies measured the effectiveness of the structured 10-week filial therapy training model proposed by Landreth (1991). Collectively, these 13 studies involve over 350 participants from a variety of populations. Each of the studies used a pretest and posttest control group design and obtained statistically significant positive results on the vast majority of all measures. Unless otherwise specified, in each of the studies, parents attended weekly 2-hour filial therapy training sessions for 10 weeks and conducted weekly 30-minute child-centered play therapy sessions with their child.

Landreth and Lobaugh (1998) and Harris and Landreth (1997) investigated the effectiveness of Landreth's filial model with incarcerated parents and found statistically significant positive results on all measures. Landreth and Lobaugh studied the effects of filial training with 32 incarcerated fathers of 4- to 9-year-olds. Compared with the control group, the 16 filial-trained fathers significantly increased their acceptance of their children and reported significant decreases in their children's behavior problems and in their own stress related to parenting. In addition, the children in the experimental group showed a significant increase in self-esteem. Harris and Landreth (1997) studied 12 incarcerated mothers of children 3 to 10 years of age who received 2-hour filial therapy training sessions biweekly for 5 weeks and conducted biweekly 30-minute play sessions with one of their children. Compared with a matched control group, filial-trained mothers significantly increased their empathic interaction with their children and their attitude of acceptance toward their children and reported a significant decrease in their children's behavior problems.

Bratton and Landreth (1995) examined the efficacy of 10 weeks of filial therapy with 43 single-parent families whose children, ages 3 to 7 years, were identified as having behavioral problems or adjustment difficulties. When compared with a control group, the 22 experimental group parents demonstrated a significant increase in empathic interactions with their children when directly observed in play sessions by trained raters. The filial-trained parents also reported significant gains in parental acceptance, while reporting significant decreases in their children's behavior problems and in their own stress related to parenting. Glass (1986/1987) obtained similar results in a controlled study of 27 parents of 5- to 10-year-olds. Parents in the filial group reported statistically significant increases in feelings of unconditional love for their children and understanding of their children, while reporting a significant decrease in perception of expressed conflict in their family. In addition, positive trends were seen in increased self-esteem of both parent and child. Control group parents and children showed no positive change on any measure.

Other studies reveal the effectiveness of Landreth's model with culturally different populations. In independent, yet very similar studies, Chau and Landreth (1997) and Yuen (1997) investigated the use of filial therapy with a total of 69 Chinese parents of children, ages 2 to 10 years, and obtained almost identical results. Compared with the control groups, the 18 filial-trained parents in Chau's study, as well as the 18 filial-trained parents in Yuen's study, demonstrated statistically significant positive changes on all measures. Specifically, the filial-trained parents demonstrated a significant increase in their level of empathic interactions with their children during parent–child play sessions, a significant increase in their attitude of acceptance toward their children, and a significant reduction in their level of stress related to parenting. Glover (1996) used filial therapy training as an intervention for 21 Native American parents and their children, ages 3 to 10 years, residing on the Flathead Reservation in Montana. The 11 children in the experimental group significantly increased their level of desirable play behaviors with their parents when compared with the control group. Although the measures of parental acceptance, parental stress, and children's self-concepts did not show statistically significant change, positive trends were shown on all measures. In light of the findings in similar filial studies with similar measures, this study gives rise to questions regarding the suitability of current self-concept measurements for Native American children and possible cultural differences in the concepts of parental stress and parental acceptance.

Several recent studies examined the effects of the 10-week filial training model with parents of children with specific presenting issues. Tew (1997) investigated the effects of parent-conducted play therapy with 23 parents of chronically ill, hospitalized children. Compared with the control group, the 12 parents who received the filial training reported a significant decrease in stress related to parenting, a significant increase in acceptance of their children, and a significant reduction in their children's behavior problems, including anxious/depressed behaviors. Kale and Landreth (1999) trained 22 parents of elementary school-age children diagnosed with learning difficulties. Compared with the control group, the 11 parents in the filial group significantly increased their acceptance of their children and significantly reduced their level of stress. Examining the effects of filial training with 26 nonoffending parents of sexually abused children, ages 5 to 9 years, Costas and Landreth (1999) found that the 14 parents receiving filial training demonstrated significant gains in their empathic interactions with their children. They also reported a significant increase in acceptance of their children and a significant reduction in parental stress. Although not statistically significant, marked improvement was reported in children's behavior problems, anxiety, emotional adjustment, and self-concept for the children of the filial group. Smith (2000) modified Landreth's (1991) model for use in a domestic violence shelter by collapsing the training into 10 daily sessions over a 2-week period. When compared with a control group, the 11 experimental group parents demonstrated a significant increase in empathic interactions with their children and also reported a significant reduction in their children's behavior problems. In addition, the children in the treatment group showed significant gains in self-esteem. Using the same measurements and control group as two previous studies (Kot et al., 1998; Tyndall-Lind, 1999), Smith also compared the effectiveness of the filial-trained parents in her study with trained, professional play therapists and concluded that they were equally effective in helping children exposed to domestic violence.

Also following Landreth's model, two studies have focused on the efficacy of training nonparent paraprofessionals as therapeutic agents with children. Brown (2000) adapted the model for use with undergraduate student teacher trainees as part of their university preparation. The 18 student teachers in the experimental group who received the filial training and practicum experience demonstrated a significant increase in their empathic interactions with children, in comparison with the 20 teacher trainees who received the standard curriculum. Examining the effects of training high school students to conduct play sessions with at-risk preschool and kindergarten children, Rhine (2000) further adapted the 10-week model to accommodate the developmental needs of adolescents. While following the basic outline proposed by Landreth, (1991), Rhine expanded the 10-week training model to allow for more time to assimilate information and practice new skills. Compared with the 12 control group children, the 14 children in the experimental group, who received an average of 20 individual play sessions conducted by the high school students, showed significant reductions in behavior problems reported by parents. Although not statistically significant, the experimental group children's teachers reported similar improvement in behavior.

The large number of controlled studies indicating the effectiveness of filial therapy verifies that teaching and training parents and other paraprofessionals in humanistic principles and basic child-centered play therapy skills is a highly effective intervention for children exhibiting a variety of emotional and behavioral difficulties. Furthermore, some studies have suggested that play therapy-trained parents are more effective with their own children than a trained professional. These results are particularly enlightening and support the need for humanistic play therapists to consider using filial/family play therapy with the families they encounter.

Experimental Research in Parent Effectiveness Training

PET has been criticized for a lack of outcome research on the effects of PET on children (Medway, 1991). Although it is true that the majority of the considerable research on Gordon's (1970) parent training model has focused on its impact on parental acceptance and parenting attitudes, a few research studies (primarily Teacher Effectiveness Training) have supported the efficacy of this approach in increasing children's self-esteem (Bear, 1983; Nummela & Avila, 1980).

In response to criticism regarding the quality of PET research, as well as the contradiction in findings, Cedar (1986) conducted a meta-analytic study of Gordon's (1970) model, finding 26 studies that met strict criteria for inclusion. The results of the meta-analysis showed that PET had an overall effect size of 0.33, representing a significant difference from the effect size for alternative treatments. Consistent with the criticism regarding a lack of outcome measures on the effects of parent training on children, the majority of the PET studies exclusively reported parent outcomes. Parental attitudes, followed by parenting behavior, showed the greatest measurable effects. Parents and teachers who received training demonstrated a significant gain in knowledge and skills based on client-centered principles. Cedar's results also showed that the benefits of PET are maintained after training is completed. Of the few studies reporting child outcomes, measures of self-esteem showed the greatest effect size (0.38). On measures of child behavior, PET's effect appears to increase over time. Although posttesting measurements immediately following training showed almost no effect on children's behavior, the effect size at follow-up approached statistical significance.

There is an impressive number of controlled studies proving the effectiveness of PET in training parents and teachers in humanistic attitudes, principles, and methodology. Of particular interest is the impact of this training on children's self-esteem and its continued benefits after training has ended. However, as Cedar (1986) concluded, future research should focus on PET's effect on children, specifically the long-term benefits on their self-esteem and behavior.

PLAY THERAPY IN PRACTICE

The following brief excerpts from a play therapy case (Landreth & Bratton, 1998) demonstrate the facilitative dimensions of a humanistic play therapy approach based on child-centered (client-centered) principles. At all times, the client-centered therapist's attitude and actions are guided by a core belief that individuals, regardless of age, have within themselves the innate capacity to direct their own growth and to solve their own problems. Translating person-centered theory into practice may seem more challenging for the child therapist; nevertheless, as illustrated in the following case study, the basic principles are adhered to. However, because children communicate most naturally through play, person-centered principles must be adapted for use with children in play therapy. Axline (1947) was the first to establish principles for facilitating a therapeutic relationship and making contact with the child in play therapy. Landreth (1991) revised and extended these eight basic principles as follows:

1. The therapist is genuinely interested in the child and develops a warm, caring relationship.
2. The therapist experiences unqualified acceptance of the child and does not wish that the child was different in some way.
3. The therapist creates a feeling of safety and permissiveness in the relationship so the child feels free to explore and express self completely.
4. The therapist is always sensitive to the child's feelings and gently reflects those feelings in such a manner that the child develops self-understanding.
5. The therapist believes deeply in the child's capacity to act responsibly, unwaveringly respects the child's ability to solve personal problems, and allows the child to do so.
6. The therapist trusts the child's inner direction, allows the child to lead in all areas of the relationship and resists any urge to direct the child's play or conversation.
7. The therapist appreciates the gradual nature of the therapeutic process and does not attempt to hurry the process.
8. The therapist establishes only those therapeutic limits which help the child accept personal and appropriate relationship responsibility. (pp. 77–78)

Thus, the primary objective of humanistic play therapy is not to solve the child's "problem" but rather on facilitating the child's self-directed growth and healing.

As in all humanistic therapies, the relationship between the therapist and the child is vital. Play is recognized and valued as the child's natural means of expression. Through play, and within the context of the safety of the relationship, the child begins to explore and understand his or her personal world in a meaningful way. Specifically, this case illustrates the child's movement toward self-acceptance, integration, an inner locus of evaluation, self-responsibility, self-direction, and self-control.

Kate, almost 4 years old, was referred to play therapy for temper tantrums, extreme mood swings, and acting-out, impulsive behavior. The initial consultation with Kate's parents revealed their desperation and a sense of helplessness in helping their daughter, who had recently been diagnosed with attention deficit hyperactivity disorder. Kate was under the care of a child psychiatrist and was taking Ritalin and Tegratol. In addition, the psychiatrist had told Kate's parents that he strongly suspected she had the beginnings of bipolar disorder. Kate was described as a sweet, loving child one moment and a "Holy Terror" the next. Her mother had recently quit work after Kate had been "expelled" from three day-care centers for being "out of control." In addition, her pediatrician had expressed concern that Kate might be developmentally delayed because of her disjointed speech. Kate attended a total of 31 play therapy sessions, 45 minutes in length, over an 11-month period. In addition, the play therapist met with Kate's mother weekly for approximately 30 minutes to enlist her help, by encouraging her to make some changes at home. The therapist focused on helping Kate's mother learn how to set limits on Kate's behavior in a less punitive manner and how to respond to Kate in ways that would convey an unconditional acceptance of Kate, even when her behavior was not. During the course of therapy, both parents attended eight parent consultations, which primarily consisted of teaching Kate's parents basic child-centered filial/family play therapy principles and skills to implement at home, and the family (Kate, mom, and dad) participated in four family activity/play sessions. Humanistic principles were used, taught, and modeled in these parent and family sessions to strengthen and enhance family relationships and facilitate the development of parental attitudes and skills necessary for Kate's parents to recognize and respond appropriately to her unique needs.

The goal of play therapy is not to change Kate's problematic behavior, rather the aim is to provide a climate, described by Axline (1947, p. 16) as "good growing ground," in which Kate can fully experience all aspects of self and realize her own potential for growth. As Landreth (1991) pointed out, "When we focus on the problem we lose sight of the child" (p. 78).

Kate's first two play therapy sessions were characterized by an inability to focus on any of the toys long enough to play. She was highly anxious and reluctant to go to the playroom. Kate talked nonstop, but her seemingly disconnected thoughts made it very difficult to understand her. The following excerpts from the second session demonstrate the therapist's (T) acceptance of Kate (K) just as she is. Kate exhibited many of the behaviors that her parents had reported as problematic: impulsivity, disjointed speech, distractibility, and lack of self-control. Unlike most adults in her life, the therapist makes no attempt to "help" Kate by focusing on these behaviors. Even though Kate's verbalization is disjointed and difficult to understand, the therapist is able to respond to the underlying feelings by focusing on Kate's facial expressions and tone of voice rather than trying to rely on her words. Helping Kate feel understood and accepted is crucial in the establishment of the relationship, especially in light of the rejection she has experienced from numerous adults in her life.

> K: My cousin . . . uhh . . . uhh . . . she had a party and we . . . see (Kate leans over toward the therapist, smiles, and points to the lipstick on her lips.)
> T: You wanted me to see that. [This response focuses on the relationship, rather than trying to make sense of Kate's words, and acknowledges Kate's desire to make contact with and involve the therapist.]

K: (Nodding) It's my . . . (Kate is distracted by a hat she sees on the shelf, reaches over to pick it up and quickly puts it on, discovering a whistle on a string that is attached to the hat.) What's this? (Without waiting for an answer, she immediately puts the whistle in her mouth and blows several times.)

T: You decided it was for blowing. [Kate obviously knew what to do with the whistle; this response gives her credit and also conveys to Kate that in this relationship, unlike many adult–child relationships, what is important is what she thinks.]

K: (Blowing the whistle several more times and smiling.) It's like the . . . (Kate uses her hand to demonstrate something). It goes like . . . (uses her hand to demonstrate the same action again, obviously enjoying herself).

T: You really like that. [Even though the therapist didn't have any idea what Kate was doing, it was obvious it was something she enjoyed. This response conveys an understanding of Kate at a feeling/experiencing level.]

In Session 3, Kate began a weekly ritual of painting as a means of expressing her inner world, which often seemed chaotic. Painting was the first activity that she could focus on for more than a few minutes, and became one of Kate's primary avenues of self-exploration, integration, and developing self-control. She would begin most paintings by letting the therapist know that she "couldn't get messy" and that she would not use "too much" paint so it "wouldn't be messy," then proceed to use so much paint that she would pronounce, "it's too messy to take home." This routine seemed to reflect Kate's struggle between perceived external demands and unacceptance of her behavior and her internal need to express all aspects of self. Interestingly, as Kate began to experience the freedom to fully express herself, her play became more focused and sustained, and her speech became more fluid and consistent with her activity.

K: (After the therapist had informed Kate that she had 5 minutes left in the playroom.) Can I use these? (As she touches two paintbrushes and looks at the therapist.)

T: You can if you want to. (Kate looks like she's not sure.) Kate, in here, you can decide what to play with. [Response facilitates an atmosphere of permissiveness and returns responsibility to Kate, conveying that she is free to make the decision to paint, if she wants to paint—just as adult clients are free to decide what they will *talk* about, if they want to talk.]

K: (Immediately begins to paint with two brushes.) I can't get my new clothes dirty.

T: You decided you wanted to paint with both brushes. [Rather than focus on her words (external locus of control), the therapist's response acknowledges Kate's desire and decision to paint (internal locus of control).]

K: (Putting lots of paint on the paper.) It won't be very messy. I'm just going to put some more paint on the bottom, but it won't be very messy (as she puts every color on the paper and mixes them all together—the paint is so thick it begins to run off). I'm just gonna put some more up here. (Kate is obviously enjoying using lots of paint and is unable to stop herself; painting until there isn't any unpainted spot left on the paper.)

T: You like to use *lots* of paint. [Response focuses on Kate's enjoyment of the experience of painting, rather than the external message that it's not OK to be messy.]

K: (Nods) Yeah, I do. It's just gonna be a little messy . . . around the edges.

T: You decided it's okay if it's a little messy. [Response gives Kate the freedom and responsibility to decide how she wants her painting to be and also conveys acceptance of her "messiness."]

T: Kate, we have one minute left in the playroom and then it will be time to go back to the waiting room. [Response provides structure and allows Kate the opportunity to prepare to leave the session under her own direction.]

K: (Begins to hurriedly put more paint on the picture, accidentally getting paint on her hand.)

T: You had something else in mind you wanted to do to your painting before our time was up. [Response touches on the urgency of Kate's actions in response to the 1-minute warning, acknowledges that she had a plan in mind, and gives Kate the responsibility for her actions.]

K: (Impulsively, Kate takes the brush and paints the hand that has paint on it, begins to make hand prints on her painting, and then, as she begins to hum, takes both hands and mixes all the paint together on her painting until the entire painting is brownish-black.)

T: It's fun to mix it all together (no response from Kate; she appears fully absorbed in the sensation of the paint on her hands) . . . you like how that feels. (Kate continues to smear the paint and hum.)

T: Kate, our time together is up for today (therapist slowly rises out of chair). [Response conveys both physically and verbally that the play session has ended. Many children, especially young children, have difficulty leaving the playroom when the time is up. Adherence to the same time limit each week is important in structuring the relationship. Children need consistency, predictability, and security in their relationships.]

K: (Continues to smear paints with hands.) I just need to finish with this part.

T: Kate, I know you'd like to paint some more, but our time is up for today. [Response recognizes Kate's desire to stay and paint but clearly conveys the limit that time is up for this week.] You can paint some more next week. [Response gives Kate the option to finish her painting next week.]

K: I just need to do . . . (Humming to herself, she continues to mix the paint with her hands, obviously caught up in the sensory experience of the paint on her hands. Her nonverbals clearly convey her enjoyment of the freedom to "decide" to be messy.)

T: Sometimes it's just really hard to stop when you're having fun, but *Kate*, our time together in the playroom is over for today. When you come back next week, you can choose to paint some more. [Response acknowledges Kate's difficulty in stopping herself. The limit is firmly set a second time, but the therapist is patient and remains accepting, allowing Kate to struggle with leaving of her own accord.]

K: (Noticing the paint all over her hands, she goes to the sink and tries to turn the water on, but her hands are slippery with paint. Kate looks at the therapist.)

T: It's hard to turn the water on with paint on your hands. (Walking over to the sink.) Looks like you might need some help.

K: Yeah, I do. I don't want paint on my hands. (The therapist helps Kate turn on the water. She works hard to get all the paint off.)

T: It's really important to you to get all the paint off, but it's time for us to leave now. (Kate leaves the water running, runs to the door and opens it, and skips back to her mom.)

Excerpts from the third session illustrate Kate's struggle with self-control and impulsivity demonstrated through her painting and difficulty in leaving the playroom. The therapist's responses convey acceptance of Kate for who she is, whether "messy " or "clean," and convey a belief in Kate's ability to direct her own behavior.

Kate's themes of self-control/out of control and messy/clean continued to be played out over the next 27 sessions. For 22 weeks, Kate started every painting by saying some version of "this painting's not gonna be too messy," and every week she painted until all the colors mixed together to make a brownish-black, leaving no unpainted space on her paper. As the weeks progressed, Kate displayed more planning and less impulsivity in the process of painting, although the final product looked the same. She would often ask the therapist in the middle of her painting, "Do you like it—don't you think it's cute?" The therapist's responses varied from, "You like your painting—you think it's cute" to "Kate, in here what's important is what you think." These responses helped Kate develop an internal locus of evaluation, rather than relying on an external source of validation. An internal locus of evaluation is a prerequisite for internal locus of control, or self-control. Although painting continued as Kate's primary means of expressing her world, in Session 14 Kate began using sand, water, and various animals to depict the theme of "good" versus "bad." Through the sand play, Kate symbolically expressed her struggle to integrate experiences and parts of herself that she had previously denied. Initially, she only allowed the "good" animals to be nurtured and fed and live inside the fence and barn. The "bad" animals were given poison and were not allowed inside with the others. Kate's play provided many opportunities for the therapist to reflect and support her confusion and struggle to understand and accept both the "out-of-control" Kate and the sweet, loving Kate. For example, in Session 20, Kate gives the therapist a dragon and tells the therapist to pretend the "bad" dragon is trying to get in the fence with the cow family and horses.

> T: Show me what you want me to do.
> K: You're a mean dragon (she makes a loud Rrrrrrr noise) and you sneak up to the fence. (Therapist takes dragon, makes the same sound and sneaks ups to the fence.)
> K: Dragon, you can't play with the nice animals. You might hurt them.
> T: (Whispers to Kate:) What should I do next? [Therapist's response allows Kate to direct the play. It is obvious that she has a plan for how she wants the scene to unfold.]
> K: You say, "If you let me play, I'll be nice." (Therapists responds verbatim and Kate stops and thinks before she responds, which is atypical behavior.)
> K: No you won't—you're mean.
> T: You were thinking about if it would be OK to let the dragon in, but you're not sure . . .
> (Kate quickly leaves the sandbox and begins to paint.) [This disruption in play seems to result from Kate's symbolic play becoming too threatening. Although Kate's play seems very meaningful, the therapist does not push her to stay with it or question her more about the "dragon," recognizing that Kate has to move at her own pace.]

This excerpt from Session 20 illustrates Kate's slight movement toward acceptance and integration of both the acceptable and unacceptable parts of herself as Kate considers the possibility of allowing the "bad" dragon to coexist with the "good" animals.

In Session 26, Kate produced her very first painting in which the colors were not mixed together, but she continued to fill every inch of the paper. In Session 27, Kate, again, did not mix the colors on her painting, and for the first time, was able to leave some space on the paper that was unpainted. After finishing it, Kate stepped back and studied it as if she was Van Gogh and announced proudly, "I like it (Kate looks at me with a big grin) . . . it's very cute!" (reflecting her developing inner source of evaluation). Also in Sessions 26 and 27, Kate's play seems to reflect greater integration of both the positive and negative aspects of self. She stopped referring to the animals as "good" or "bad" and allowed them to live and eat together, announcing, "I'm going to make them all good food today!" In Session 28, Kate came into the playroom and announced, "I'm going to paint a rainbow today." She proceeded to paint a rainbow (with lots of paper left unpainted), but then painted over it with black because two of the colors of the rainbow were mixed together. For the first time in 28 sessions, Kate said she was going to paint another picture and proceeded within just a few minutes to paint an identical rainbow, except none of the colors were mixed. She stepped back, looked at her rainbow for several minutes, smiled, and said matter-of-factly, "I'm through," and went over to play in the sandbox. This was the last time Kate painted. In Sessions 29 and 30, Kate no longer needed to paint. She focused primarily on constructive play in which she demonstrated mastery of many things in the playroom. In the final consultation with Kate's parents, it was decided that Kate would enroll in a prekindergarten program in their school district that was designed for 4-year-olds with a variety of special needs. In parting, the parents joked that their daughter, who they had once described as stuck in the "Terrible Two's," was now a "Terrific Four" (at least most of the time!). And, most importantly, they had rediscovered the joy of parenting Kate and were more optimistic about her future.

By using a play therapy approach, humanistic child therapists convey to children their willingness to accept children as they are. The toys and other play media allow children a developmentally appropriate and personal means of expressing their feelings, experiences, thoughts, and wishes in a way that the therapist can understand and respond to. Play is a way of being, a way of relating, and a vehicle of communication between the therapist and child. Through the play therapy relationship, children experience the meaning of self-responsibility, explore alternative behaviors that are more satisfying, and discover new dimensions of themselves that result in revised self-images and new behaviors (Landreth & Bratton, 1998).

CONCLUSION

Although experimental research in humanistic play therapy is not exhaustive by any means, enough hard evidence exists to prove its efficacy as an intervention for children presenting with a variety of concerns. Play therapy, including filial therapy, shows considerable viability when compared with other possible treatments, and certainly, when compared with controlled populations. In the areas of self-concept, behavioral change, cognitive ability, social skills, and anxiety, play therapy is a proven method of treating children with problems. In addition, research findings on the use of parents as therapeutic agents are particularly impressive, suggesting that practitioners might strongly consider using filial/family play therapy training or PET with the families they work with. Furthermore, more research is needed to measure the effectiveness of play therapy delivered by professionals compared with play therapy conducted by parents.

As argued in Lebo (1953) and again, 30 years later, by Phillips (1985), play therapy research lacks credibility in a few areas of what is considered hard research. Some limitations include the use of a small number of participants and lack of comparison with other interventions, such as more traditional behavioral plans or cognitive techniques. Recent play therapy/filial therapy researchers have answered the critics by conducting more experimental research with specific measures and clearly defined treatments. More research is needed to investigate both the immediate and long-term effects of humanistic play therapy. Specifically, as mentioned, there is a need to compare its effectiveness with other child psychotherapeutic techniques. Additionally, studies are needed to investigate the most efficient and effective delivery method of play therapy services to children. Some unanswered questions include the following: Are parents more effective than professionals, or is some combination of the two most helpful? Is increasing the number of sessions over a shorter time span more effective than the traditional once-per-week session format? Is there an optimum number of sessions for children with specific presenting issues? What are the long-term effects of play therapy, filial therapy, and PET? Although many questions remain unanswered, humanistic play therapy certainly not only makes developmental sense but also is proven as an effective intervention with children's problems. Acknowledging that the design of the research may not be without limitations, enough positive outcomes have been found to present humanistic play therapy as an effective treatment option for children in diverse settings with a variety of presenting concerns.

REFERENCES

Allan, J., & Lawton-Speert, S. (1993). Play psychotherapy of a profoundly incest abused boy. *International Journal of Play Therapy, 2*(1), 33–48.

Amplo, J. (1980). Relative effects of group play therapy and Adlerian teacher training upon social maturity and school adjustment of primary grade students (Doctoral dissertation, University of Mississippi, 1980). *Dissertation Abstracts International, 41,* 3001.

Axline, V. M. (1947). *Play therapy.* New York: Ballantine Books.

Axline, V. (1949). Mental deficiency—Symptom or disease? *Journal of Consulting Psychology, 13,* 313–327.

Axline, V. (1950). Play therapy experiences as described by child participants. *Journal of Consulting Psychology, 14,* 53–63.

Axline, V. (1964). *Dibs: In search of self.* New York: Ballantine Books.

Barlow, K., Landreth, G., & Strother, J. (1985). Child-centered play therapy: Nancy from baldness to curls. *School Counselor, 34,* 347–356.

Barlow, K., Strother, J., & Landreth, G. (1986). Sibling group therapy: An effective alternative with an elective mute child. *School Counselor, 3,* 44–50.

Bear, G. C. (1983). Usefulness of Y.E.T. and Kohlberg's approach to guidance. *Elementary School Guidance and Counseling, 17,* 221–225.

Beers, P. (1985). Focused videotape feedback psychotherapy as compared with traditional play therapy in treatment of the oppositional disorder of childhood (Doctoral dissertation, University of Illinois at Urbana-Champaign). *Dissertation Abstracts International, 46,* 1330.

Bills, R. (1950a). Non-directive play therapy with retarded readers. *Journal of Consulting Psychology, 14,* 140–149.

Bills, R. (1950b). Play therapy with well-adjusted retarded readers. *Journal of Consulting Psychology, 14,* 246–249.

Boll, L. (1972). Effects of filial therapy on maternal perceptions of their mentally retarded children's social behavior (Doctoral dissertation, University of Oklahoma). *Dissertation Abstracts International, 33,* 6661A.

Bouillion, K. (1974). The comparative efficacy of non-directive group play therapy with preschool, speech- or language-delayed children (Doctoral dissertation, Texas Tech University, 1973). *Dissertation Abstracts International, 35,* 495.

Brandt, M. (1999). *Investigation of play therapy with young children.* Unpublished doctoral dissertation, University of North Texas.

Bratton, S. (1998). Training parents to facilitate their children's adjustment to divorce using the filial/family play therapy approach. In J. Breismeister & C. Schaefer (Eds.), *Handbook of parent training* (2nd ed., pp. 549–572). New York: Wiley.

Bratton, S., & Landreth, G. (1995). Filial therapy with single parents. *International Journal of Play Therapy, 4*(1), 61–80.

Brody, V. (1992). The dialogue of touch: Developmental play therapy. *International Journal of Play Therapy, 1*(1), 21–30.

Brown, C. (2000). *Filial therapy with undergraduate teacher trainees: Child–teacher relationship training.* Unpublished doctoral dissertation, University of North Texas, Denton.

Carmichael, K., & Lane, K. (1997). Play therapy with children of alcoholics. *Alcoholism Treatment Quarterly, 15,* 43–51.

Carroll, J. (1995). Reaching out to aggressive children. *British Journal of Social Work, 2,* 37–53.

Cedar, R. B. (1986). A meta-analysis of the parent effectiveness training outcome research literature (Doctoral dissertation, Boston University, 1986). *Dissertation Abstracts International, A47/02,* 420.

Chau, I., & Landreth, G. L. (1997). Filial therapy with Chinese parents: Effects on parental empathic interactions, parental acceptance of child and parental stress. *International Journal of Play Therapy, 6*(2), 75–92.

Clatworthy, S. (1981). Therapeutic play: Effects on hospitalized children. *Journal of Association for Care of Children's Health, 9*, 108–113.

Costas, M., & Landreth, G. (1999). Filial therapy with non-offending parents of children who have been sexually abused. *International Journal of Play Therapy, 8*(1), 43–66.

Cox, P. N. (1953). Sociometric status and individual adjustment before and after play therapy. *Journal of Abnormal & Social Psychology, 48*, 354–356.

Crow, J. (1990). Play therapy with low achievers in reading (Doctoral dissertation, University of North Texas, 1989). *Dissertation Abstracts International, 50*, 2789.

Dematatis, C. (1981). A comparison of the traditional filial therapy program to an integrated filial-IPR program (Doctoral dissertation, Michigan State University). *Dissertation Abstracts International, 42*, 4187B.

Dogra, A., & Veeraraghavan, V. (1994). A study of psychological intervention of children with aggressive conduct disorder. *Journal of Clinical Psychology, 21*, 28–32.

Dorfman, E. (1958). Personality outcomes of client-centered child therapy. *Psychological Monographs, 72*(No. 3).

Dvarionas, D. (1999). *Play therapy for behaviorally disruptive children in primary school.* Unpublished doctoral dissertation, Vilniaus Pedagoginis Universitetas, Vilnius, Lithuania.

Elliott, C., & Pumfrey, P. (1972). The effects of non-directive play therapy on some maladjusted boys. *Educational Research, 14*, 157–163.

Fleming, L., & Snyder, W. (1947). Social and personal changes following non-directive group play therapy. *American Journal of Orthopsychiatry, 17*, 101–116.

Foley, J. M. (1970). *Training future teachers as play therapists: An investigation of therapeutic outcome and orientation toward pupils.* East Lansing, MI: National Center for Research on Teacher Learning. (ERIC Document Reproduction Service No. ED 067 794)

Gaulden, G. (1975). Developmental-play group counseling with early primary grade students exhibiting behavioral problems (Doctoral dissertation, North Texas State University, 1975). *Dissertation Abstracts International, 36*, 2628.

Glass, N. M. (1987). Parents as therapeutic agents: A study of the effect of filial therapy (Doctoral dissertation, University of North Texas, 1986). *Dissertation Abstracts International, 47*, A2457.

Glover, G. J. (1996). *Filial therapy with Native Americans on the Flathead Reservation.* Unpublished doctoral dissertation, University of North Texas, Denton.

Gordon, T. (1970). *Parent effectiveness training: The "no-lose" program for raising responsible children.* New York: Peter H. Wyden.

Gould, M. (1980). The effect of short-term intervention play therapy on the self-concept of selected elementary pupils (Doctoral dissertation, Florida Institute of Technology, 1980). *Dissertation Abstracts International, 41*, 1090.

Guerney, B. G., Jr., & Flumen, A. (1970). Teachers as psychotherapeutic agents for withdrawn children. *Journal of School Psychology, 8*(2), 107–113.

Guerney, B. G., Jr., & Stover, L. (1971). *Filial therapy* (Final report on MH 18254-01). Unpublished manuscript, Pennsylvania State University.

Guerney, L. (1983). Client-centered (non-directive) play therapy. In C. E. Schaeffer & K. O'Connor (Eds.), *Handbook of play therapy*. New York: Wiley.

Guerney, L. (1975). *Brief follow-up study on filial therapy*. Paper presented at the meeting of the Eastern Psychological Association, New York City.

Hannah, G. (1986). An investigation of play therapy: Process and outcome using interrupted time-series analysis (Doctoral dissertation, University of Northern Colorado, 1986). *Dissertation Abstracts International, 47*, 2615.

Harris, Z. L., & Landreth, G. (1997). Filial therapy with incarcerated mothers: A five-week model. *International Journal of Play Therapy, 6*(2), 53–73.

House, R. (1970). The effects of non-directive group play therapy upon the sociometric status and self-concept of selected second grade children (Doctoral dissertation, Oregon State University, 1970). *Dissertation Abstracts International, 31*, 2684.

Jones, E. (2000). *The efficacy of intensive individual play therapy for children diagnosed with insulin-dependent diabetes mellitus*. Unpublished doctoral dissertation, University of North Texas, Denton.

Kaczmarek, M. (1983). A comparison of individual play therapy and play technology in modifying targeted inappropriate behavioral excesses of children (Doctoral dissertation, New Mexico State University, 1983). *Dissertation Abstracts International, 44*, 914.

Kale, A., & Landreth, G. (1999). Filial therapy with parents of children experiencing learning disabilities. *International Journal of Play Therapy, 8*(2), 35–36.

Kezur, B. (1980). Mother–child communication patterns based on therapeutic principles (Doctoral dissertation, The Humanistic Psychology Institute). *Dissertation Abstracts International, 41*, 4671B.

Kot, S., Landreth, G. L., & Giordano, M. (1998). Intensive child-centered play therapy with child witnesses of domestic violence. *International Journal of Play Therapy, 7*(2), 17–36.

Landreth, G. L. (1991). *Play therapy: The art of the relationship*. Muncie, IN: Accelerated Development.

Landreth, G., & Bratton, S. (1998). Play therapy. *Counseling and Human Development, 31*(1), 1–12.

Landreth, G. L., Homeyer, L., Glover, G., & Sweeney, D. (1996). *Play therapy interventions with children's problems*. Northvale, NJ: Jason Aronson.

Landreth, G. L., & Lobaugh, A. F. (1998). Filial therapy with incarcerated fathers. *Journal of Counseling and Development, 76*, 157–165.

Lebo, D. (1953). The present status of research on non-directive play therapy. *Journal of Consulting Psychology, 17*, 177–183.

McGuire, M. (2000). *Child-centered group play therapy with children experiencing adjustment difficulties*. Unpublished doctoral dissertation, University of North Texas, Denton.

Medway, F. (1991). Measuring the effectiveness of parent education. In M. J. Fine (Ed.), *The second handbook on parent education* (pp. 237–255). New York: Academic Press.

Mehlman, B. (1953). Group play therapy with mentally retarded children. *Journal of Abnormal and Social Psychology, 48*, 53–60.

Morrison, T., & Newcomer, B. (1975). Effects of directive vs. non-directive play therapy with institutionalized mentally retarded children. *American Journal of Mental Deficiency, 79*, 666–669.

Moustakas, C. E. (1959). *Psychotherapy with children.* New York: Harper.

Moulin, E. (1970). The effects of client-centered group counseling using play media on the intelligence, achievement, and psycholinguistic abilities of underachieving primary school children. *Elementary School Guidance and Counseling, 5*, 85–98.

Mundy, L. (1957). Therapy with physically and mentally handicapped children in a mental deficiency hospital. *Journal of Clinical Psychology, 13*, 3–9.

Newcomer, B., & Morrison, T. (1974). Play therapy with institutionalized mentally retarded children. *American Journal of Mental Deficiency, 78*, 727–733.

Nummela, R., & Avila, D. (1980). Self-concept and teacher effectiveness training. *College Student Journal, 14*, 314–316.

Oualline, V. (1975). *Behavioral outcomes of short-term non-directive play therapy with preschool deaf children.* Unpublished doctoral dissertation, North Texas State University, Denton.

Oxman, L. K. (1972). The effectiveness of filial therapy: A controlled study (Doctoral dissertation, Rutgers University, The State University of New Jersey, 1972). *Dissertation Abstracts International, 32*(11), B6656.

Payton, I. E. (1980). Filial therapy as a potential primary preventive process with children between the ages of four and ten (Doctoral dissertation, University of Northern Colorado). *Dissertation Abstracts International, 41*(07), A2942.

Pelham, L. (1972). Self-directive play therapy with socially immature kindergarten students (Doctoral dissertation, University of Northern Colorado, 1971). *Dissertation Abstracts International, 32*, 3798.

Perez, C. (1987). A comparison of group play therapy and individual play therapy for sexually abused children (Doctoral dissertation, University of Northern Colorado, 1987). *Dissertation Abstracts International, 48*(12-A), 3079.

Phillips, R. (1985). Whistling in the dark?: A review of play therapy research. *Psychotherapy, 22*, 752–760.

Piaget, J. (1962). *Play, dreams, and imitation in childhood.* New York: Routledge.

Post, P. (1999). Impact of child-centered play therapy on the self-esteem, locus of control, and anxiety of at-risk 4th, 5th, and 6th grade students. *International Journal of Play Therapy, 8*(2), 1–18.

Quayle, R. (1991). The primary mental health project as a school-based approach for prevention of adjustment problems: An evaluation. (Doctoral dissertation,

Pennsylvania State University, 1991). *Dissertation Abstracts International,* *52*(4-A), 1268–1269.

Rae, W., Worchel, F., Upchurch, J., Sanner, J., & Daniel, C. (1989). The psychosocial impact of play on hospitalized children. *Journal of Pediatric Psychology,* *14,* 617–627.

Rennie, R. (2000). *A comparison study of the effectiveness of individual and group play therapy in treating kindergarten children with adjustment problems.* Unpublished doctoral dissertation, University of North Texas, Denton.

Rhine, T. (2000). *The effects of a play therapy intervention conducted by trained high school students on the behavior of maladjusted young children.* Unpublished doctoral dissertation, University of North Texas, Denton.

Rousseau, J. (1930). *Emile.* New York: Dent. (Original work published 1762)

Saucier, B. (1986). An intervention: The effects of play therapy on developmental achievement levels of abused children (Doctoral dissertation, Texas Women's University). *Dissertation Abstracts International,* *48,* 1007.

Schmidtchen, S., Hennies, S., & Acke, H. (1993). To kill two birds with one stone? Evaluating the hypothesis of a two-fold effectiveness of client-centered play therapy. *Psychologie in Erziehung und Unterricht,* *40,* 34–42.

Schmidtchen, V. S., & Hobrucker, B. (1978). The efficiency of client-centered play therapy. *Praxis der Kinderpsychologie und Kinderpsychiatrie,* *27,* 117–125.

Seeman, J., Barry, E., & Ellinwood, C. (1964). Interpersonal assessment of play therapy outcome. *Psychotherapy: Theory, Research and Practice,* *1,* 64–66.

Seeman, J., & Edwards, B. (1954). A therapeutic approach to reading difficulties. *Journal of Consulting Psychology,* *18,* 451–453.

Sensue, M. E. (1981). Filial therapy follow-up study: Effects on parental acceptance and child adjustment (Doctoral dissertation, Pennsylvania State University, 1981). *Dissertation Abstracts International,* *42*(01), A148.

Siegel, C. (1971). The effectiveness of play therapy with other modalities in the treatment of children with learning disabilities (Doctoral dissertation, Boston University, 1971). *Dissertation Abstracts International,* *31*(8-A), 3970–3971.

Smith, N. (2000). *A comparative analysis of intensive filial therapy with intensive individual play therapy and intensive sibling group play therapy with child witnesses of domestic violence.* Unpublished doctoral dissertation, University of North Texas.

Sokoloff, M. (1959). A comparison of gains in communicative skills, resulting from group play therapy and individual speech therapy, among a group of non-severely dysarthric, speech handicapped cerebral palsied children (Doctoral dissertation, New York University, 1959). *Dissertation Abstracts International,* *20,* 803.

Stover, L., & Guerney, B. G., Jr. (1967). The efficacy of training procedures for mothers in filial therapy. *Psychotherapy: Theory, Research and Practice,* *4,* 110–115.

Sywulak, A. E. (1978). The effect of filial therapy on parental acceptance and child adjustment (Doctoral dissertation, Pennsylvania State University, 1977). *Dissertation Abstracts International, 38*(12), B6180.

Tavormina, J. B. (1975). Relative effectiveness of behavioral and reflective group counseling with parents of mentally retarded children. *Journal of Consulting and Clinical Psychology, 43*, 22–31.

Tew, K. (1997). *The efficacy of filial therapy with families with chronically ill children.* Unpublished doctoral dissertation, University of North Texas, Denton.

Thombs, M., & Muro, J. (1973). Group counseling and the sociometric status of second grade children. *Elementary School Guidance and Counseling, 7*, 194–197.

Trostle, S. (1988). The effects of child-centered group play sessions on social-emotional growth of three- to six-year-old bilingual Puerto Rican children. *Journal of Research in Childhood Education, 3*, 93–106.

Tyndall-Lind, A. (1999). *A comparative analysis of intensive individual play therapy and intensive sibling group play therapy with child witnesses of domestic violence.* Unpublished dissertation, University of North Texas, Denton.

Wall, L. (1979). Parents as play therapists: A comparison of three interventions into children's play (Doctoral dissertation, University of Northern Colorado, 1979). *Dissertation Abstracts International, 39*, 5597.

Warson, S., Caldwell, M., Warinner, A., Kirk, A., & Jensen, R. (1954). The dynamics of encopresis. *American Journal of Orthopsychiatry, 24*, 402–415.

Winn, E. (1959). The influence of play therapy on personality change and the consequent effect on reading performance (Doctoral dissertation, Michigan State University, 1959). *Dissertation Abstracts International, 22*, 4278.

Yates, L. (1976). The use of sociometry as an identifier of research sample for psychological treatment and quantifier of change among second grade students. *Group Psychotherapy, Psychodrama, and Sociometry, 29*, 102–110.

Yuen, T. (1997). *Filial therapy with immigrant Chinese parents in Canada.* Unpublished doctoral dissertation, University of North Texas, Denton.

13

THE EMPIRICAL VALIDATION OF RELATIONSHIP ENHANCEMENT COUPLE AND FAMILY THERAPY

MICHAEL P. ACCORDINO AND BERNARD G. GUERNEY, JR.

Relationship Enhancement (RE) Couple/Family Therapy is a brief, systemic therapy that is a radical departure from other couple or family therapies. One of the ways it is radical is that it selectively integrates concepts and methods from four major schools of psychotherapy—humanistic, psychodynamic, learning theory (behavioral/cognitive/social), and interpersonal—all of which play essential and synergistic roles. However, it is not eclectic in the usual way; rather, it selects certain concepts and methods from these four models and builds a new, systematic whole (Ford, 1987; Ford & Urban, 1998) that includes some unique therapeutic techniques. An example of the integration of disparate schools is the bridge it has built between the humanistic (specifically the Rogerian) and behavioral schools, an integration which prompted Robert Weiss, when introducing Bernard Guerney, Jr. at a conference, to say, "Guerney has brought soul to behavior therapy" (Weiss, 1992).

The RE therapist strives always to maintain those attitudes and skills that are the hallmarks of the Rogerian approach: unconditional positive regard for the clients, genuineness/congruence, empathy, and a collaborative, equalitarian spirit. Because key Rogerian perspectives and skills also are taught to clients, the Rogerian approach supports and facilitates the contributions of each of the other schools that are part of the RE therapy integration. Two of the major contributions of the Rogerian approach are that it (a) minimizes obstacles to effective therapy by reducing client defensiveness and (b) maximizes the awareness and expression of deep feelings, especially

403

those that previously were outside of a client's awareness. In this manner, the Rogerian school contributes enormously toward successfully harnessing the clients' creative, insightful, and problem-solving strengths. (We briefly discuss key contributions from the other three schools later.)

RE Couple/Family Therapy also is radical in another way: Although there is no practical reason why current standard professional systems cannot be used by an RE therapist for diagnosis, as a guide to medication, or for conceptualizing and reporting one's therapeutic plans and progress with respect to conducting couple/family therapy, RE Couple/Family Therapy follows the Educational Model rather than the Medical Model (B. G. Guerney, 1982, 1985a; B. G. Guerney, Guerney, & Stollak, 1971/1972; B. G. Guerney, Stollak, & Guerney, 1970). Therefore, the therapist not only uses Rogerian and behavioral helping skills but also regards it as a primary responsibility to empower clients by teaching them some of these skills. Then, under the therapist's supervision, first in the office and later at home, clients systematically use those skills to become psychotherapeutic agents (B. G. Guerney, 1969) for each other and for their relationships.

The level of skill and responsibility that couples acquire is attested to by the fact that therapists who convert to RE therapy frequently remark that the RE approach has transformed working with couples from a trial to a true pleasure. The major reason for this difference is that in learning to become effective psychotherapeutic agents, clients are, in fact, also learning to become good clients.

By that, we mean clients learn (a) almost never to interrupt other family members or the therapist; (b) to openly express their deepest thoughts and feelings, positive and negative; (c) yet to do so without belittling or criticizing others' feelings, thoughts, motives, or character; (d) to help their intimates to do likewise; (e) to listen compassionately to each other and intently to the therapist; (f) to actively seek and regularly achieve insight into their intimate's innermost feelings, attitudes, and motives, as well as their own, including many that they have suppressed or repressed in the past; (g) to consistently develop strategies and use procedures for changing their own behavior that will help to overcome problems in their couple/ family relationships; and (h) to do likewise with respect to behavioral changes their intimates wish to make. These client behaviors are mainly established in the early hours of therapy because of the way the therapist structures the interactions and behaviors of the clients, the way the therapist gently but quickly and firmly intervenes to enforce and reinforce those structured behavioral modes, the way the therapist teaches skills, and the readings or audiotapes studied by clients at home and the feedback forms they complete. All of these things work together to empower clients with the motives, understanding, attitudes, habits, and skills of a good client.

THE NATURE OF RE COUPLE AND FAMILY THERAPY

In the remainder of this chapter, in the order given here, we will explain RE Couple/Family Therapy with respect to its: (a) breadth of theoretical foundation and additional factors that underlie its efficacy; (b) major goals; (c) 12 clearly defined methods/procedures and the chief occasions and the circumstances that call for the use of each, with emphasis on those methods which are unique to RE therapy; (d) five types of therapy; (e) brief, briefer, and briefest formats; (f) limitations; and (g) effectiveness as assessed by controlled experimental outcome research with couples and families. We will also refer the reader to empirical studies with people drawn from samples other than couples and families. We will mention additional types of empirical studies and case reports. A meta-analytic study comparing RE to a number of other types of enrichment programs and therapy interventions will be briefly summarized. We will present a transcript of a segment of RE Family Therapy focused on the married couple, and offer some very specific suggestions about when and how to incorporate RE therapy into your clinical practice. In our concluding section, we will again focus on the nature and import of the validation research.

Theoretical Foundations and Other Factors Underlying the Efficacy of RE

Research has shown that RE Couple/Family Therapy brings about positive change in couples and families with exceptional speed and power (e.g., Giblin, Sprenkle, & Sheehan, 1985; B. G. Guerney, Vogelsong, & Coufal, 1983; Ross, Baker, & Guerney, 1985). We believe that the factors contributing to this include the following: (a) the simultaneous, synergistic targeting of affective, cognitive, and behavioral dimensions; (b) harnessing the energy, motivation, and enormous inherent emotional power of family members or other intimates by training them to act as psychotherapeutic agents for one another (B. G. Guerney, 1969); (c) empowering clients by teaching them certain principles and skills they need to develop the attitudes and behaviors that lead to higher levels of psychoemotional health and strength; (d) training clients in the skills necessary to transfer/generalize and practice the new principles and skills at home to resolve problems with their intimates; (e) integrating therapeutic work at various levels—personal, couple, and family; and (f) using audiovisual aids and feedback forms to speedily and efficiently promote all of the above.

RE theory embraces the humanistic, Rogerian tenet that empathy tremendously facilitates openness and healing (B. G. Guerney, 1984, 1985b). It is important to point out here that we do not mean active listening (mirroring) as it usually is taught, which emphasizes possible differences between one's own feelings and perceptions and those of the speaker, as well as cognitive accuracy rather than appreciative, emotional kinship. We call the kind of empathy practiced by therapists and taught to clients in RE therapy *Empathic Responding* or *deep empathy*. An appropriate metaphor for it, in contrast to mirroring, is "X-raying." Such empathy is based on *identification* with the speaker, on the assumption (which can occasionally be proven untrue and dropped in particular areas) of *similarity* between one's own perceptions and feelings and those of the speaker, and on showing not just accurate but *compassionate* understanding. Among intimates, this type of empathy elicits insight, emotional self-expression, and openness not only in the one who receives it but also in the one who provides it. It *changes* the one who gives it as well as the one who receives it.

Interpersonal theory maintains that the key to effective psychotherapy is the ability to change patterns of interpersonal behavior. RE Couple/Family Therapy does that in very direct and powerful ways. It teaches clients (a) that they always have a choice in what interpersonal response they make to others' interpersonal behavior; (b) that each choice they make in an interpersonal interaction determines the nature of the other person's next response in a way that usually is predictable; (c) that by using knowledge and skill about the effects of various interpersonal responses, they can usually assure an outcome of a dialogue or an incident that is more satisfying to self and others than it otherwise would be; (d) that applied to general interaction patterns, especially between intimates, this knowledge and skill would allow them to significantly improve their relationships (and to become aware of those relationships that are impervious to reasonable and skillful modification efforts); (e) that their interpersonal response patterns, more than they probably realize, have always been influencing how others treat them; (f) that while their old, spontaneous patterns of influence and response undoubtedly brought them some satisfaction or relief with significant others in the past, their having come for help shows that they are no longer bringing them what they desire; and, therefore (g) that being flexible enough to learn conscious control of, and more effective types of, interpersonal responses and patterns is highly desirable; (h) that they will learn those things in RE therapy; (i) that if they work at it, what they learn can become their new, spontaneous interpersonal responses and patterns; and then (j) that these new patterns can enable them to function at the very highest levels of the general population in these respects and afford them advantages not only in family relationships but also in other areas, for example, at work and with friends.

Interpersonal responses usually are *reflexive* (see Leary, 1957). The term is used to indicate that because the responses are so deeply ingrained, so habitual, in response to the interpersonal behavior of others and to the person's feelings of the moment, they spring out too fast for an awareness of choice. In RE, when clients are in the first phase of learning the RE skills that will later become their "new spontaneity," the structured interaction and the coaching interventions slow the dialogue down and make the act of choice not only conscious but mandatory. And, of course, the RE therapist intervenes to prevent those cases of interpersonal response that are incompatible with the clients' fundamental couples or family relationship goals and reinforces those that are compatible. Those that are fundamentally compatible are virtually always the core RE Couple/Family Therapy client skills. (RE as used with intrapsychic problems or in organizational development sometimes may call for use of additional parts of a broad spectrum of interpersonal responses.)

Occasionally, one sees in the sessions or reports on behavior at home a pattern of interpersonal response by Person A toward the interpersonal behavior of Person B that is "mysterious." That is, a pattern is observed that runs consistently and strongly counter to the therapist's usual expectations based on clinical experience and interpersonal theory and research, as well as counter to A's own stated desire. And this pattern does not respond to the usual methods of inducing change used in RE. Examples of mysterious patterns follow: Client A does not reciprocate any conciliatory or loving responses from B or consistently fails to respond positively to B's changed behavior at home for which A himself or herself had pushed. In such instances, the therapist hypothesizes that the "unreasonable," counterproductive behavior has roots in traumatic incidents or long-lasting perceived abuse or failure. These may have occurred in the present relationship or previous ones, possibly ones that go back to early childhood. Thinking about those things arouse strong anxiety and from which A protects himself or herself with strong defenses.

Under these circumstances, one of the contributions that psychodynamic theory makes to RE comes into play. We refer to the concept that *abreaction* is sometimes a prerequisite for productive change. Although the way of evoking abreaction in RE is through methods based on the Educational Model and Rogerian principles—rather than, say, through free-association, dream analysis, or hypnosis—abreaction is viewed as the way to help a person to escape the hypothesized steel trap of strong psychological defenses. It is viewed as the painful route that is most likely to take the client to insights; a genuine, strong commitment to change; and the psychological freedom to do so.

But the influence of the psychodynamic school on the theoretical underpinnings of RE is much broader than that. The psychodynamic concept of defense mechanisms, with their power to distort reality and subvert effective interpersonal problem solving, and the need to avoid such subversion, also was the theoretical basis for two of the core skills of RE: Empathic and Expressive. It is true that the skills themselves were devised by Bernard Guerney, Jr. more directly on the basis of aspects of Rogerian theory and practice, interpersonal theory, the Educational Model, and his own personal and clinical experience. Nevertheless, the reason for devising them is easily traced further back to his earlier background in psychodynamic theory and to the concept of defenses (B. G. Guerney, 1990). And, although the concept we accept of precisely how defense mechanisms originate, develop, and take hold is the one derived from learning theory, specifically from Dollard and Miller (1950), it seems to us highly unlikely that learning theorists would have even thought there was a need to explain anything like defense mechanisms until sometime well into this 21st century had it not been for Freud.

As is evident from much of what we have said, the school of psychotherapeutic thought based on learning theory, research, and concepts (behavioral, cognitive, and social) has greatly influenced RE therapy. More specifically, learning theory and the methods based on it underlie several of the nine RE skills, which we discuss below, and have contributed greatly to the manner in which all of the skills are taught and coached.

The Major Goals of RE Therapies

The goals of RE therapies are (a) to eliminate existing psychological symptoms; (b) whenever applicable, to change the dysfunctional or pathogenic family system/"rules"/behaviors into ones that are, instead, therapeutic, harmonious, and supportive; (c) to bring clients to high levels of socioemotional skill; (d) to empower them to prevent future problems or to resolve them more quickly and completely; (e) to have clients transfer and generalize such skills to nonfamily as well as family settings; and (f) to enable clients to maintain gains over time.

The Nature of RE Therapy

The structure and interpersonal atmosphere of RE therapy is designed to accomplish the following for clients: stimulate free, full, and constructive expression of deep emotion; create trust; build hope; develop psychological insight; build motivation for appropriate behavioral changes; and effectively plan, implement, and maintain those changes.

Following the aforementioned Educational Model, clients are taught to employ the nine RE skills in order to create growth-inducing, problem-solving, change-facilitating, therapeutic relationships with their intimates. The nature and rationale for the nine skills may be inferred from their names, with the exception of *Coaching* (also called *Facilitation*). Coaching in RE refers to the skill of encouraging and educating important people in one's life to treat one in ways likely to reduce stress and enhance one's self-concept and mental health. The other eight RE skills are *Expressive, Empathic, Discussion/Negotiation, Problem/Conflict Resolution, Self-Changing, Helping Others Change, Transfer/Generalization,* and *Maintenance.* The specific guidelines of each of these skills have been fully explicated elsewhere (see B. G. Guerney, 1986a, 1994). Many of the same skills learned in RE therapy also are useful for enriching the relationships of individuals, couples, and families, and for helping to prevent intrapsychic and relationship problems. Hence, RE therapies gave rise to parallel psychoeducational programs for the general public (e.g., B. G. Guerney, 1991; L. Guerney, 1987).

It is key to understanding RE that, except for certain clearly defined exceptions, once clients have learned an RE skill, the therapist does not permit them to deviate from using it when speaking to each other within the therapy sessions. So after the first 2 hours or so of therapy, clients know that they are always in one of two incompatible modes of behavior. If they are in the *Expresser* mode, the Expresser Skill Guidelines determine that they can talk only about their own perceptions, thoughts, and feelings and never about objective reality. If they are in the *Empathic Responder* mode, the Empathic Responding Skill Guidelines require them not to talk at all about their own perceptions, thoughts, and feelings but to concentrate only on being empathic with the expresser. How they switch these modes of behavior with with their dialogue partner is determined by the Discussion/Negotiation Skill Guidelines.

Although on paper this may seem rigid or restricting, the whole architecture of RE is designed to provide an unusual degree of emotional freedom—much as we, as citizens of the United States, achieve unusual freedom by adhering strictly to a Bill of Rights. And, once competent in the skills, clients experience in RE therapy this exceptional freedom to deeply know themselves and to be themselves, and to deeply know their partner and, strange as it may sound, to *be* their partner.

In RE Couple/Family Therapy, the therapist uses the following 12 RE methods/procedures (also see B. G. Guerney, 1997; Snyder, 1995, 1996; Snyder & Guerney, 1993).

> 1. *Administering for RE.* These are therapist statements having to do with the details of running an RE session, statements that structure the behaviors of the clients in the ways that make the session an RE therapy session rather than some other type of therapy. Examples include asking clients to hand in a Home Assignment Report Form, discussing possible home assignments, and selecting from a Relationship Questionnaire the most appropriate new issue to discuss in the session or at home (B. G. Guerney, 1986b).

2. *Instructing.* This includes all activities that are in the service of teaching the RE skills to clients (except for those that are so important and distinctive as to deserve categories of their own; e.g., Modeling, Demonstrating, and Reinforcing). Examples of Instructing are explaining the nature of a skill and providing the rationale for using it.

3. *Demonstrating.* This is setting up and implementing role plays with the client in which the therapist shows the client how to use some or all of the guidelines of an RE skill. Demonstration is used often when first teaching a skill used infrequently later on, for example, if the client is having difficulty in using or in transferring/generalizing the skill in a particular type of situation. Demonstration usually is followed by a reversal in the role play, so that the client can practice the skill while the therapist plays the role of the other person involved and, at the same time, supervises the client's skill usage.

4. *Reinforcing.* This is social reinforcement, both verbal and nonverbal (e.g., a thumbs up or a pat on the back or shoulder). Early in therapy, it is the RE therapist's predominant response, and it is used whenever the client does anything at all that is better than they would have done had they not known about the skill. Later, it is used somewhat less frequently, but always when skill usage is particularly good or when there is a situation that is especially challenging emotionally. In addition, self-corrections always are reinforced. And the therapist tries always to find something to reinforce immediately prior to Modeling or Prompting. Reinforcement usually is done in a manner and at the time that best balances the therapist's desire to reinforce promptly with his or her desire not to actually interfere with the flow of the dialogue between the clients. Reinforcing is used for performance in accord with skill guidelines, that is, for process; it is not used to show approval of content, that is, for what clients think, feel, believe, propose to do, or actually do in or out of the session except as these relate to skill usage, such as doing home assignments and following through on the agreements they have made. The clients fully understand that.

5. *Modeling.* In RE therapy, modeling is used in its usual broad sense: behaving toward clients in the same way that the therapist wants the clients to behave. All of an RE therapist's behavior is isomorphic with the manner in which he or she is asking the clients to behave toward one another. However,

that type of modeling follows naturally from simply sticking to the RE therapeutic protocol as a whole and is not coded as Modeling. What is coded as Modeling is a therapist's request that the client rephrase, or add to, something the client has just said to make the statement more skillful. The request is made in a way that makes it very easy for the client to implement it promptly and successfully. That particular way is to give the client a skillful statement that he or she can repeat *without having to change a word* because all the pronouns in the therapist's statement are appropriate for doing that. Also, the request is straightforward, rather than tentative in the form of a suggestion or a question. This is because the therapist does not want to divert attention from the dialogue between the clients toward a dialogue with the therapist. The client is simply told something like, "That was good empathy, now also say to Jack, 'that frustrates you,' or something to that effect."

6. *Preemptive Modeling.* As just implied, one of the teaching and behavior-change strategies of RE is to structure things in such a manner that the client fails as infrequently as possible and succeeds as often as possible. Hence, when the therapist is almost certain that the client will say something unskillfully, he or she does not wait until the client does that. Rather, the therapist models, preemptively, a skillful "ready-to-use" response before the client speaks. For example, saying to an Empathic Responder, who has not yet given a response, "Try something like, 'You're very upset with me about what I said to Andrew.'" Preemptive Modeling can also be used to avoid potential *omissions*. Say, for example, the therapist knows that in general Andrew greatly respects Barbara's performance as a mother because of things that Andrew has said in earlier sessions, and suppose in the current dialogue Andrew is taking issue with one aspect of Barbara's parenting. Immediately prior to one of Andrew's Expresser statements, preferably at the time he is about to first raise this issue, the therapist might say, "Andrew, it would be good to begin your statement here, if true, with an underlying positive statement; something like, 'I think that you are a great mother.'" In another example, the therapist can see that Andrew has been hurt by something Barbara has said but believes that Andrew will not include that failing in what Andrew is about to express. The therapist also believes that Barbara will be more receptive to whatever else Andrew is likely to say if she also

heard about the hurt part of Andrew's feelings. Therefore, the therapist might say, "Andrew, if true, I think it would be good for you to begin with, 'Barbara, what you said really hurt my feelings.'" Should the client reject or modify the Preemptive Modeling, the client's position is not questioned. From the beginning, it is always made clear to clients that in modeling of any kind, the therapist is simply trying to facilitate expression of their true views and feelings, so clients quickly learn to follow their own dictates when it comes to self-expression.

7. *Prompting.* This response is not used at all early in training; it is used only after the client is good at the required skill. In contrast to providing a ready-to-use response as in Modeling, the therapist, being confident that the client immediately will come up with the desired skillful response, prompts the client to do that. For example, the therapist might say to an Empathic Responder: "How does he feel about that?" Or, to an Expresser: "Try to rephrase that so it is subjective rather than stating it as a fact."

8. *Supervising Home Assignments.* Assignments to do at home are negotiated with clients. Some examples are (a) to avoid or skillfully exit from conflicts at home until the clients can use the skills to deal with them productively; (b) reading certain chapters in their *Relationship Enhancement Manual* (B. G. Guerney, 1986a); or (c) listening to an audiotape demonstrating RE skills (B. G. Guerney & Vogelsong, 1981). Those negotiations are classified as *Administering for RE.* However, for virtually every such assignment there is something tangible, for example, a very brief form, or an audiotape of their at-home therapeutic sessions, to be given to the therapist in the following session. This tangible item facilitates getting quickly to the point and is one of the ways the importance of doing work at home is emphasized. Using that material as a starting point, the therapist supervises the home assignments.

9. *Troubleshooting for Client.* One, infrequent occasion for using this response is when the client is unwilling to follow the usual processes of RE therapy. In Troubleshooting for a client's objection, the therapist does not treat the objection as "resistance" due to unreasonable, pathological causes. Rather the therapist deals with it as a legitimate disagreement—a conflict between himself or herself and the client. And, because the therapist believes it is the most effective way to deal

with it, and also because he or she is conscious of wanting to be a model for the clients, the therapist handles this conflict in the same way that he or she would want the clients to handle a conflict with any significant person in their lives: by using the RE skills. The other occasion for Troubleshooting for Client is when the client is so emotional as to be unable to use the skills. Here too, the therapist also uses the RE skills, and only the RE skills, in dealing with a client's emotional breakdown to help the client to relatively quickly achieve catharsis, regain emotional equilibrium and control, and thus be ready to resume skillful dialogue with his or her dialogue partner. When the client has lost emotional control, the therapist waives the requirement that the client speak to him or her skillfully.

10. *Troubleshooting for Self.* In the case of Troubleshooting for Self, it is the emotions, ethics, ideas, or wishes of the therapist, rather than those of the client, that create the need for the therapist to move away from the preferred teaching/ supervisory role into dialogue with the client. The therapist does so because he or she believes that if that shift was not made, problems with the therapeutic process and progress would go unsolved or problems might develop, or a clear opportunity will be missed to improve the motivation, morale, and well-being of the client. As always, the therapist uses RE skills and only RE skills in conducting the dialogue. Generally, clients also use RE skills in a Troubleshooting for Self-dialogue. One situation in which Troubleshooting for Self occurs (usually just once) with a fair percentage of clients arises during the early weeks of therapy. We refer to this as the therapist sharing feelings of frustration (preceded, of course, by sharing the underlying positive feelings of caring, concern, and a strong desire to help) after clients have consistently failed to live up to their voluntary commitments to do home assignments. (This type of Troubleshooting for Self continues until a mutually satisfactory agreement for resolving the problem is reached.) Otherwise, use of Troubleshooting for Self is quite rare. Examples of times it might be used are when: (a) the therapist wants to cut short or prolong a session for some reason; (b) the therapist, troubled by its absence, wants a client to consider adding another problem to the ones already listed on the Relationship Questionnaire; (c) the therapist is concerned that an agreement or decision reached by the clients will have negative effects on others, on

themselves, or on their relationship, effects that were unforeseen by the clients or not weighted strongly enough by them.

10a. There is a subcategory for Troubleshooting for Self that probably would not strike the reader as dealing with trouble. Indeed, responses of this nature are under consideration for a category of their own, perhaps titled "Sharing Positives." They are more commonly used than other types of Troubleshooting for Self types of responses. The reason they have been classified as troubleshooting responses is that they do require that the therapist convey his or her own thoughts and feelings rather than stay in the preferred role of skill-teacher/supervisor. Also, many of these Sharing-Positives responses could be considered as having the long-term general effect of avoiding potential trouble (e.g., avoiding discouragement and loss of confidence or of enthusiasm). Sometimes they resemble Reinforcing responses, but they differ in that they are not being contingently used to strengthen a particular kind of response, but rather stem strictly from feelings and thoughts of the therapist. Examples of the circumstances under which the therapist, using RE skills of course, might share positives are (a) the therapist is feeling admiration over how well the clients have learned or have used the skills during a session or (b) the clients look discouraged at the end of a session because they are still expressing negatives and not seeing much light at the end of the tunnel for the problem they are discussing, whereas the therapist feels encouraged because he or she believes that what they have done represents, in itself, necessary and important steps toward a solution, and the therapist shares that feeling and belief with the clients.

11. *Becoming.* Becoming refers to the therapist assuming the name and identity of the client and speaking for him or her in a therapeutic dialogue with another family member. It is done when the client is unable or unwilling to speak to his or her dialogue partner with sufficient RE skill but is not so out of emotional control as to require Troubleshooting. These circumstances might arise because (a) there has not been enough time for the client to have learned all of the necessary RE skills; (b) one client suffers a temporary or permanent emotional or intellectual disability or disadvantage in relation to a dialogue partner (think of a young adolescent vs. a lawyer parent, or a husband who is not yet very fluent in English vs. a very articulate wife); or (c) the therapist understands

something about the client's internal dynamics or feelings that the therapist believes the client would instantly recognize as valid and, in the last analysis, be pleased or relieved to hear the therapist say for him or her, but would not at that time have the insight, or possibly the courage, to say for himself or herself. The therapist might use Becoming for one sentence or (rarely, of course) for one entire session or more. In Becoming, the clients are given to understand that the therapist's intention is to express accurately the thoughts, wishes, and feelings of the client with whom he or she is identified. That client knows that he or she should interrupt to correct the therapist as soon as something is said that he or she does not see as valid. And the therapist frequently checks, sometimes in midsentence, to confirm that he or she is speaking accurately for the client. Client A, who is being addressed by the therapist, understands that in *Becoming* B, the therapist is not *siding* with B, and A also knows that the therapist stands equally ready to represent A whenever that seems desirable.

12. *Laundering*. Laundering is used when the emotional level of an issue threatens to be too strong for the attained level of skills of both participants to allow them to be sufficiently skillful to deal successfully with the problem. It includes the use of Becoming; however, in Laundering, the therapist assumes each party's identity in turn, in an ongoing dialogue. To gather the necessary information to use Laundering, the therapist allows each client to respond to him or her after having heard the therapist represent the other client. The clients understand that the therapist, when Becoming to facilitate problem/conflict resolution, will feel free to add or subtract things from their statements, so long as the therapist believes that what he or she is saying accurately represents their feelings and desires. Thus, in Laundering, while in the role of, say, Client A, the therapist feels free to make suggestions for problem/conflict resolution that A has not yet thought of but that the therapist believes A will readily validate as matching his or her desires, and that will also be agreeable to B. The clients also know that they can have the therapist modify a representation to better convey their position whenever they wish. To illustrate: At the outset, the therapist gleans the necessary knowledge to represent a client, Amy, by responding empathically to Amy for some time. At the opportune moment, the therapist assumes Amy's

name and identity. As Amy, the therapist speaks to Amy's dialogue partner, Blair. When Blair later speaks to the therapist, Blair will address the therapist by the name Amy. As always when Becoming/Laundering, the therapist represents Amy as if Amy was a thoughtful, sensitive, reasonable, cooperative, and highly RE-skilled individual who is entirely open about her deepest negative and positive feelings. After thus washing Amy's dirty (i.e., possibly unskillful, noncompassionate) statement, the therapist, still as Amy, will now listen to Blair and respond to Blair empathically. Then the same thing is done in reverse: The therapist, assuming Blair's identity, speaks to Amy. This back-and-forth process (i.e., the Laundering) continues until—if clients are skilled enough—the dialogue can be safely returned to them alone, or—if they are not skilled enough—until the problem/conflict is resolved to their genuine, mutual satisfaction.

The Types of RE Therapy

There are five type of RE therapies (B. G. Guerney, 1977, 1986b; L. Guerney & Guerney, 1985):

1. RE Couple Therapy.
2. RE Family Therapy (Ginsberg, 1997).
3. Individual, or Personal, RE Therapy (B. G. Guerney & Snyder, 2000), which is used when the presenting problem is viewed by the client primarily as a personal, individual, intrapsychic problem and there is little reason to think about changing any family member if, indeed, there are any.
4. Unilateral RE Therapy, which involves working with individuals with the objective of changing the behavior not only of that individual but of others with whom the individual has significant relationships, and also changing the "rules" governing the clients' couple or family system.
5. Child RE Therapy, better known as Filial Family Therapy, which is used with young and preadolescent children (see Bratton & Ray, this volume, chapter 12; B. G. Guerney, 2000).

Any of these methods can be applied in a group format.

The Three Time Formats: Brief, Briefer, and Briefest

On the basis of the clients' needs and the time available for treatment, RE Couple/Family Therapy has three delivery modes with varied hours and number of sessions (Cavedo & Guerney, 1999). Note that the times that follow designate *office* hours. As previously indicated, RE therapeutic work is also done by clients themselves at home. Such work at home is encouraged to the extent possible in all three time modes. Thus, total therapeutic time might be as much as four times the number of hours the clients spend in the therapeutic office.

1. In the *Time-Designated Mode*, it is anticipated that successful therapy will be completed in 10 to 20 office hours (and, sometimes longer). In this mode, a designated amount of time needed to successfully complete treatment is estimated by the therapist and then negotiated with the client. Clients are encouraged to do a great deal of work outside the sessions. For example, they listen to audiotapes from an appropriate album of the RE demonstration set (e.g., B. G. Guerney & Vogelsong, 1981), and they read chapters, study RE skill guidelines, and complete forms from their manual (B. G. Guerney, 1986a). In the Time-Designated mode versus the other modes, there is more time (a) for systematic progression in the RE skill training, (b) for clients to have attained a higher level of skill before tackling their tougher problems, and (c) to better train clients through social reinforcement to actually do what they agree to do. These advantages are viewed as enhancing habitual, productive work outside of the therapy hour.

2. In the *Experiential Mode*, the time frame is 5 to 10 office sessions. Instead of waiting until clients have first demonstrated skill competence, fundamental problems are worked on immediately, at the same time that RE skills are initially being taught.

3. The *Crisis Intervention Mode* is designed to resolve one to three of the clients' most critical or fundamental problems in 1 to 5 office hours.

The three modes of RE therapy are flexible; one may start out in one mode and then decide to switch to another. The same RE therapeutic concepts and methods are used in all three modes; however, the briefer the mode, the less skilled the client will be at the time the resolution of fundamental problems is undertaken, hence, the more the therapist makes use of Becoming and Laundering so that, through the therapist, clients can speak to each other as if they already were highly perceptive, sensitive, open, and interpersonally skilled. They, therefore, can avoid many of the behaviors that otherwise would lead to hurt, withdrawal, or escalating anger.

As their representative, the RE therapist is especially mindful of the fact that, for couples who are truly seeking relationship reconciliation, there are strong positive feelings (i.e., caring and love) underlying every single relationship-oriented negative feeling. It is precisely the frustration of unfulfilled caring and love that gives rise to the hurt that gives rise to anger and hate between family members. To borrow W. Somerset Maughm's phrase, "The distance between love and hate is no wider than a razor's edge." As their representative, the therapist must express the ever-present, but presently buried caring and love. Such expression is what allows the clients to pass together over the edge from the hate to the love side of the razor blade without lacerating each other or severing the relationship. The RE skills, including this emphasis on the client's underlying positive feelings while the therapist is engaged in Troubleshooting, Becoming, and Laundering, usually enables the therapist to pilot the clients safely through treacherous passages of deep anger or hate, often with surprising speed. In the Crisis Intervention mode, because it is so brief, a large proportion of the therapy may consist of those three methods.

Limitations of RE Therapy

As judged by case report or uncontrolled preliminary empirical study, some of the kinds of clients that are often regarded as troublesome seem to do better than would be expected in RE Couple/Family Therapy, for example, prisoners (Accordino & Guerney, 1998) or those suffering from borderline personality disorder (Waldo & Harman, 1993), narcissistic personality disorders (Snyder, 1994), or alcohol dependence (Matter, McAllister, & Guerney, 1984; Waldo & Guerney, 1983). However, we have no knowledge of RE Couple/Family Therapy being done with other presumably problematic clients, such as those with mental retardation or those who are actively psychotic.

We do know of one kind of client with whom RE Couple Therapy has had little success in restoring a loving, intimate relationship. Because RE is based on honesty, it is not surprising that this type of client is the habitual liar. Such clients are skillful enough at deception to initially convince their partners and therapists that they wish to save their relationship. Later, it might be learned that what they really wanted was (a) to leave their partner in the hands of a mental health professional when they left them or (b) to gain enough time to rearrange their financial affairs to maximize their financial position at their partner's expense when the divorce occurred. Deep empathy often affects its recipient like a psychological truth serum. It often leads the recipient to be more honest than he or she originally intended to be. So, what RE can sometimes do in these situations is make the deception apparent earlier than it otherwise would have been. The resulting realistic comprehension usually is advantageous to the deceived partner, but at the time it occurs, it is a very upsetting experience to all concerned. And the breakup, although realistic, is not what the deceived partner and the therapist had originally hoped for.

VALIDATION STUDIES: THE EFFECTIVENESS OF RE COUPLE/FAMILY THERAPY

We have included in this review all the studies we know of in which people trained in RE methods have assessed a whole or abbreviated version of RE in terms of outcome. We have not endeavored to include any studies wherein an RE skill may be studied only in isolation or as part of another program. Nor have we reported process studies, or process portions of studies, which included some process variables along with outcome variables.

Although we believed that the intervention would be therapeutic in nature, many of the studies included here were with participants who were not coming for something specifically labeled as "therapy." Rather, they often were responding to public invitation to strengthen and enrich their relationships, troubled or not, and to help them learn how to prevent or resolve their relationship problems and conflicts. For such samples, the average level of relationship distress or adjustment generally fell about halfway between clinic samples and the general population (B. G. Guerney, 1977).

It is important to bear in mind that for couples therapy, it is much more difficult to attain significant treatment results with less-distressed than with more-distressed samples. This was shown clearly when we compared the results of a study with couples coming for therapy with those in a study open to couples with or without problems (see Ross et al., 1985) and in a study with a wide range of distress (e.g., Brock & Joanning, 1983). But most convincing on this point is a meta-analytic study conducted by Giblin et al. (1985), which found a strong, positive relationship between level of initial distress and degree of couples' improvement.

Whenever changes, gains, and improvements are mentioned, it means they were significant at $p < .05$ or lower. We have presented an overview of the RE studies in Table 13.1. Organized alphabetically by author, it presents some types of information (e.g., RE formats and sample sizes) that are not mentioned in the text except when it seemed necessary.

Couples

Collins (1977) found that married couples in an RE group improved more in marital communication and marital adjustment than those in a

TABLE 13.1
Overview of Relationship Enhancement® (RE) Validation Research

Study	Sample	Major Dependent Variables	RE Format/N	Comparison(s)/ N	Follow-up
Avery, Rider, and Haynes-Clements (1981)	Adolescents	Self-disclosure and empathic understanding	Group; 16 hours, 4 weeks/22	NT/21	5 months
Avery, Ridley, Leslie, and Milholland (1980)	Premarital couples	Self-disclosure and empathic skills	Group; 24 hours, 8 weeks/38	Lecture-discussion /36	5 months
Brock (1974)	Married couples	Expressive skills, empathic skills, marital communication, and adjustment	FU of Rappaport (1971)/30	—	14 months
Brock and Joanning (1983)	Married couples	Relationship satisfaction, communication behavior	Group; 20 hours, 10 weeks/52	Couples Communication Program/40 NT/16	3 months
Brooks (1997)	Highly distressed married couples	Trust/intimacy, marital communication, dyadic adjustment, problem solving	Group; 24 hours, 12 weeks/31	Self/10 NT/10	12 weeks
Cavedo (1995)	Married couples	Trust, understanding, fault assessment, problem–conflict resolution, and relationship change	One couple; 2 hours reading-discussion plus 1.5 hours of coaching/72	Self/72	—
Collins (1977)	Married couples	Marital communication and adjustment	Group; 1.5 hours, 24 weeks/48	NT/42	—

continued

TABLE 13.1
Continued

Study	Sample	Major Dependent Variables	RE Format/N	Comparison(s)/ N	Follow-up
Ginsberg (1977)	Father–son	Communication behavior, communication patterns, relationship self-concept	Group; 20 hours, 10 weeks/28	W/30 Self/20	—
Greene (1986)	Married couples	Marital communication and self-esteem	Group; 28/22 (own control) self/22	W/22 Self/22	—
Griffin and Apostal (1993)	Married couples	Quality of relationship; differentiation of self: a) Functional, b) Basic	Group; 15 hours, 6 weeks/40	Self/40	12 months
Guerney, Coufal, and Vogelsong (1981)	Mother–daughter	Empathic skills, expressive skills, communication patterns, relationship	Group; 24–30 hours/38	NT/34 Traditional group Therapy/36	—
Guerney, Vogelsong, and Coufal (1983)	Mother–daughter	Empathic skills, expressive skills, general communication relationship	Group; 24–30 hours/38	NT/34 Traditional group Therapy/36	12 weeks
Haynes and Avery (1979)	Adolescents	Self-disclosure and empathic skills	Group; 16 hours, 4 weeks/25	NT/23	—
Jessee and Guerney (1981)	Married couples	Marital adjustment, communication, trust and harmony, rate of positive change in relationship, relationship satisfaction, and ability to handle problems	Group; 30 hours, 12 weeks/36	Gestalt Relationship Facilitation/36	—

continued

TABLE 13.1
Continued

Study	Sample	Major Dependent Variables	RE Format/N	Comparison(s)/N	Follow-up
Rappaport (1971)	Married couples	Expressive skills, empathic skills, marital adjustment, marital communication, trust/intimacy, relationship improvement, marital satisfaction, problem solving	Group; mini-marathon 24 hours, 8 weeks/40	Self/40	—
Ridley, Avery, Dent, and Harrell (1981)	Premarital couples	Perceived heterosexual competence	Group; 24 hours, 8 weeks/48	Discussion/52 Ridley Problem Solving/48	—
Ridley and Bain (1983)	Married couples	Expressive skills, empathic skills, marital communication, and adjustment	Group; 24 hours, 8 weeks/52	Relationship discussion/58	6 months
Ridley, Jorgensen, Morgan, and Avery (1982)	Premarital couples	Relationship adjustment, trust/ intimacy, empathic skills, warmth and genuineness, and communication	Group; 24 hours, 8 weeks/25	Relationship lecture-discussion/29	—
Ridley and Sladeczek (1992)	Premarital couples	Identifying needs of control, affection, and inclusion	Group; 24 hours, 8 weeks/54	Relationship lecture-discussion/60	—
Ross, Baker, and Guerney (1985)	Highly distressed married couples	Communication, general relationship, and marital adjustment	One couple; 10 weeks/24	Therapists own preferred therapy/24	—
Sams (1983)	Premarital couples	Expressive skills, empathic skills, and problem-solving ability	Group; weekend/36	Engaged Encounter /36	—

continued

TABLE 13.1
Continued

Study	Sample	Major Dependent Variables	RE Format/N	Comparison(s)/N	Follow-up
Schlein (1971/1972); Ginsberg and Vogelsong (1977)	Dating couples	Empathic and expressive skills, communication, warmth-genuineness, relationship	Group/30	W/54	—
Steinweg (1990)	Married couples	Relationship issues-communication (self-report)-marital happiness, cohesion adaptability, real–ideal discrepancies, family goal attainment, communication (behavioral)	One couple; hours not fixed max. 14 weeks/ 9 couples.	Strategic therapy hours not fixed max. 14 weeks/10 couples.	—
Waldo (1988)	Wife abusers	Recidivism	Unilateral group; 24 hours, 12 weeks/30	30/30	Approximately 1 year
Wieman (1973)	Married couples	Marital adjustment, communication, integration, attraction to spouse, client attitudes toward treatment	Group; 16 hours, 8 weeks/20	Reciprocal reinforcement/ 24 NT/24	10 weeks

Note. W = wait-list condition or group; NT = no-treatment condition or group; FU = follow-up. Dashes in the table indicate that follow-up was not studied.

no-treatment group. This greater improvement was found for marital communication and marital adjustment.

Wieman (1973) assigned couples who had responded to newspaper ads for free marital therapy to one of three conditions: (a) RE therapy (then called Conjugal Relationship Modification); (b) Reciprocal Reinforcement therapy, which he patterned after Stuart's (1969) Operant-Interpersonal therapy or; (c) a wait-list group. Participants in the wait-list group showed almost no change, whereas participants in each type of therapy showed significant increases in adjustment, communication, integration, and cooperation between the spouses. The findings were the same at 10-week follow-up.

Rappaport (1971) studied a 2-month RE program for married couples, which consisted of two 8-hour sessions and two 4-hour sessions on alternating Saturdays or Sundays prior to the onset of treatment. They made significantly greater improvements on all of the variables during the RE period than during a previous control period of equal length. Specifically, the couples scored significantly better in the areas of (a) behaviorally measured expressiveness, (b) empathy, (c) marital adjustment, (d) general marital communication, (e) trust–intimacy, (f) relationship improvement, (g) marital satisfaction, and (h) perceived ability to solve relationship problems.

Brock (1974) conducted a 14-month follow-up study of Rappaport's (1971) study. Marital adjustment and general marital communication fell from posttreatment and no longer differed significantly from pretest levels. Empathic skill fell significantly from termination, whereas Expressive skill did not. Both skills remained significantly improved over pretest levels. RE as it existed at the time of this study did not include five of the six RE skills that have since been added to strengthen the effectiveness of RE and to maintain gains over long time periods: Self-Changing, Helping Others Change, Coaching, Transfer/Generalization, and Maintenance.

Brock and Joanning (1983) assigned married couples to no treatment or RE or Couples Communication (CC) programs. CC is one of the best-known couple-enrichment programs and one of the few with substantial scientific evidence of effectiveness in improving couple relationships. Participants in both treatment groups gained more than those not in treatment on all three measures used: marital adjustment, questionnaire-assessed marital communication, and behaviorally assessed marital communication. In all three areas, RE participants gained more than CC participants at the 10-week posttesting. The superiority of RE was maintained at a 3-month follow-up. Additional analyses showed that couples low in marital adjustment prior to training were consistently helped by RE, and they maintained their gains well at follow-up, whereas this was not so consistently the case with CC.

Greene (1986) found that married couples in an RE program improved more than those in a wait-list group. This was true for marital communication and self-esteem within the marital context.

Griffin and Apostal (1993) studied RE's effectiveness in increasing (a) the general quality of married couples' relationships, (b) functional differentiation, and (c) differentiation of self (DOS). DOS is a Bowenian concept widely accepted by family therapists. It refers to the ability to develop one's unique, individual qualities while interacting in close interpersonal relationships. Achieving higher levels of DOS is viewed as vitally important in avoiding or eliminating psychopathology. Couples in an RE group for 2.5 hours per week over 6 weeks had previously served for 6 weeks as their own controls (wait-list group). The couples increased their functional DOS and the quality of their relationships during the treatment period versus the waiting period. At follow-up a year later, these differences were maintained. Bowen saw a change in basic differentiation as first requiring a very long period of improvement in functional DOS. Thus, it is of special interest that such change was found not initially but at follow-up a year later.

After finding positive results in a preliminary study with wife-abusing men in the military (Waldo, 1986), Waldo (1988) randomly selected 30 men from each of three larger groups of civilian men arrested for assault or battery of their wives. Our terms for the three conditions represented by those three groups are RE, Rejected Referral, and Unreferred. It is important to note that the unreferred group was unreferred because many of the staff of the State Attorney's Office were not aware of the program. That is, the failure to refer them did not stem from any judgment about their fitness or lack of fitness for such a program. The RE, conducted by the staff and consultant of a county crisis center for abused women, was a Unilateral RE group program. It was an abbreviated RE program in that it included only the three basic RE skills: Empathic, Expressive, and (by its current name) Discussion/Negotiation. Participants completed the program within 4 months of their referral. Outcome was assessed by checking court records 1 year after initial arrest. The two untreated groups did not differ from each other, and the RE participants differed significantly from both: In each of the untreated groups, 20% had been arrested again for spouse abuse, whereas none in the RE group had been.

Jessee and B. G. Guerney (1981) found that married couples who participated in either Jessee and Guerney's (1981) Therapy-Based Gestalt Relationship Facilitation (GRF) or in an RE program gained on all variables studied: marital adjustment, communication, trust and harmony, rate of positive change in the relationship, relationship satisfaction, and ability to handle problems. RE participants gained more than GRF participants in communication, relationship satisfaction, and ability to handle problems.

Brooks (1997) studied the efficacy of RE therapy in a rural, southern outpatient setting with distressed couples coming for marital therapy. Forty-one participants who had completed the 12-week time-limited RE Couples Group Therapy were compared with 20 participants who initially had not been assigned to therapy for a 12-week period. Significantly more improvement occurred during the treatment than during the waiting period, and this difference was also found at the 12-week follow-up. This was the case for all variables studied: trust–intimacy, marital communication, dyadic adjustment, and problem solving.

Aradi (1985) and Steinweg (1990) investigated RE versus Strategic Marital Therapies with highly distressed couples. This summary is based on the latter report because it covered the ground of the former but contained additional information. With respect to comparative outcome, it was hypothesized that strategic therapies would be superior to RE with respect to improvement on measures that assessed (a) relationship issues (subjectively assessed communication, marital happiness); (b) cohesion–adaptability; (c) male, female, and couple real–ideal discrepancy scores; and (d) family goal attainment. None of these hypotheses were confirmed. It was hypothesized that RE would show more improvement in the quality of couples' communication (behaviorally assessed by coders). This hypothesis was confirmed.

Ross et al. (1985) studied the effects of RE in comparison with the preferred therapies of marital therapists with highly distressed couples coming to a community mental health center for marital therapy. Five marital therapists, averaging 6 years of experience, were given a 3-day training program in RE. Following the training, the couples were randomly assigned to receive either RE or the therapist's own-preferred treatment (TOPT), that is, the approach the therapists had been regularly using. For all five therapists, this was an eclectic therapy wherein they modified their methods depending on the couple and the issues that arose. Within this flexible approach, client-centered, behavior modification, interpersonal, and psychodynamic methods were all well represented. At the 10-week posttesting, participants receiving RE therapy showed more improvement than those who received TOPT on all measures used: communication, general relationship, and marital adjustment.

Cavedo (1995) studied married or cohabiting couples, a third of whom fell in the distressed range. The RE program included only five of the nine RE skills: Expresser, Empathic Responder, Discussion/Negotiation, Problem/Conflict Resolution, and Facilitation/Coaching. Prior to the RE program, participants had completed premeasures, selected their three most serious problems and conflicts on which to work, and had a baseline session in which they attempted to resolve one of the problems. Not more than a week later, they had 2 hours to read about the five included RE skills. This was followed by a session in which they received RE skill coaching as they worked to resolve a second problem or conflict. At that session, posttesting was conducted. In the third phase of the study, almost always within the next week, participants worked without coaching at resolving a third problem or conflict. The third testing, called the *Generalization* testing, took place at this time. At each of these three phases, participants could work for up to 1.5 hours to resolve their problem or conflict.

Hypotheses in this study about coaching methods and four process variables are not pertinent to this chapter. What is pertinent is that the three outcome measures all showed significant change over baseline. This occurred first during the coaching phase for the clients' views of *successful outcome* in resolving the problem or conflict they had worked on, and for positive change in the general *relationship*. For neither variable was there a decline from coached phase to generalization phase. Indeed, by the time of generalization session, the third variable—the clients' greater general *trust* in their partners—had improved enough to also reach significance. Cavedo (1995) viewed as highly impressive the breadth and degree of improvement found in an abbreviated RE skill-training program, which took a maximum of 2.5 hours of a baccalaureate-level coach's time and a maximum of 3.5 hours of a client's time, especially because the positive results carried over to their independent effort to resolve a problem or conflict.

Family

Using a self-control design to supplement an RE versus no-treatment design, Ginsberg (1977) studied fathers and their sons in what was then called Parent–Adolescent Relationship Development, or PARD, an early dyadic form of RE Family Therapy. Space limitations prohibit providing all the details on the many measures. Thus, results are reported in terms of how strongly the data supported each hypotheses of the study, a judgment in which Ginsberg assessed the overall evidence from the multiple measures testing it.

In the RE versus no-treatment design, the hypotheses that participants in RE would improve more in behaviorally assessed empathic and expressive skills was strongly confirmed. The hypothesis that this also would be true when participants were unaware that they were being observed by the investigators was partially confirmed. The hypothesis that RE would yield greater improvement in general patterns of communication at home was strongly supported. The hypotheses that the quality of the general relationship would improve more with RE was confirmed. The above-mentioned conclusions were replicated in the own-control analysis. In addition, improvement in self-concept was found in that study.

B. G. Guerney, Coufal, and Vogelsong (1981) assigned mother–daughter pairs to a no-treatment group, an RE treatment group, or a traditional treatment group. The traditional treatment group was an eclectic, noninterpretive approach aimed at improving the relationships between the pairs through encouraging open communication, stimulated in part by reading assignments about their roles, feelings, and past, present, and desired behaviors toward one another. Participants in the no-treatment group showed virtually zero improvement. Participants in traditional treatment group showed improvement only in the general quality of their relationships. Participants in RE group made greater gains than each of the other two groups in all areas assessed: empathy and expressive skills, general communication patterns, and the general quality of their relationships.

B. G. Guerney et al. (1983) conducted a follow-up to the above study and investigated whether a booster program would contribute to the durability of those effects. Therefore, one half of both the RE and traditional treatment groups took part in a booster program. The measures administered 6 months after the termination of the regular program assessed specific communication skills, the general communication patterns, and the general quality of the relationship. Participants in RE in both the booster and no-booster groups gained more than the traditional treatment and no-treatment groups on all measures: empathy, expressiveness, and general relationship quality. There were no differences between booster and no-booster participants in the traditional treatment group, but RE booster participants gained more than RE participants who were not in the booster program. The fact that the decline so frequently found following posttesting in intervention studies was replaced by significant *gains* on all measures, even among the no-booster participants, is viewed as being just as noteworthy as the fact that participants in the booster program showed even greater posttreatment gains.

Premarital/Adolescent

Schlein (1971/1972; also see Ginsberg & Vogelsong, 1977) studied dating couples. Compared with a no-treatment group, RE couples showed more improvement in empathic acceptance, open expression of feeling in dialogues seeking resolution to their problems and conflicts (although not in two questionnaire measures assessing general communication), their own perceived rate of improvement in resolving problems effectively, their own perceived rate of improvement in empathy–warmth–genuineness (but not so in perception of their partner's), their assessment of current level of satisfaction (but not in their own judgment of *rate* of improvement in satisfaction), and their perceived rate of change in the general quality of their relationship.

Ridley and Sladeczek (1992) compared premarital couples in RE with those in a Relationship Lecture-Discussion Group (RLDG). The RE couples showed significantly greater improvement in being able to identify their needs for control, affection, and inclusion. The researchers also concluded that the effects of the RE training enabled participants to eventually reduce these needs by feeling more secure in their relationships.

Avery, Ridley, Leslie, and Milholland (1980) found that an RE program yielded greater increases in premarital couples both in self-disclosure and empathy than did a RLDG. This finding held true in a 6-month follow-up as well as in the pre–post comparison.

Ridley, Jorgensen, Morgan, and Avery (1982) assessed the effects of RE on premarital couples for these variables: relationship adjustment, trust–intimacy, empathy, warmth–genuineness, and communication. Couples were assigned to either RE or a relationship-discussion group. The RE participants made greater gains on all dependent variables.

Ridley, Avery, Dent, and Harrell (1981) studied self-perceived competence within heterosexual relationships by randomly assigning premarital couples to three programs: (a) RE, (b) the Ridley Problem Solving (PS) group, and (c) RLDG. The PS and RE group did not differ significantly from each other in improvement. RE couples did, however, show significantly greater improvement in their perceived heterosexual competence than couples in the RLDG group, whereas couples in the PS group did not.

Ridley and Bain (1983) found that steady-dating or engaged couples in RE increased significantly more in self-disclosure with their *partners* than did those in a Relationship Discussion group. However, this difference was not maintained at a 6-month follow-up. Greater self-disclosure toward *friends* or *acquaintances* was found neither at posttest nor at follow-up in either group. (The RE program used here did not include the skills designed to produce transfer/generalization or maintenance.)

Sams (1983) compared Premarital Relationship Enhancement (PRE) and Engaged Encounter (EE) programs. Both were sponsored by an archdiocese that had been regularly using the EE program. The programs were led, over a weekend, by trained volunteer couples. Both pre- and posttest, the PRE program produced greater gains than the EE program in behaviorally measured expressive and empathic skills and in ability to problem solve effectively.

Haynes and Avery (1979) found that high school students who received RE training, compared with a control group that continued in its regular curriculum for the same amount of time, demonstrated significantly higher skill levels in self-disclosure and empathic understanding. Avery, Rider, and Haynes-Clements (1981) conducted a 5-month follow-up of this study in which 90% of the original group were assessed. Results showed that RE participants continued to show significantly higher levels than control participants in self-disclosure and in empathic skills.

Other Populations

Space does not permit us to describe or reference seven studies with groups of divorced or separated people, work teams in factories, college students living in dormitories, couples classified according to Fitzpatrick's (1988) marital types, and lay volunteer couple-leaders of a premarital program. All showed very positive outcome results. Those interested may find the references in an Annotated RE Bibliography (see B. G. Guerney, 2000) under these names and dates (listed here alphabetically): Avery and Thiessen (1982); DeLong (1993); Most and Guerney (1983); Rathmell (1991); Thiessen, Avery, and Joanning (1980); and Waldo (1985, 1989).

Preliminary Studies and Case Reports

Aside from the tightly controlled experimental studies reported here, RE has been found to be effective with a wide variety of clinical and other special populations in preliminary empirical studies and case reports. It has been found to be effective in improving relationships and reducing symptoms and problems with psychiatric inpatients, outpatients, and their families; with patients in a community residential rehabilitation center; with alcoholics, codependents, spouse batterers, clients with depression, juvenile delinquents, drug addicts in rehabilitation, and those suffering from narcissistic personality disorder. Because, with rare exceptions, the RE therapist does not intervene except to coach skills, leaving the participants free to resolve their problems or conflicts in accord with their own cultural values, RE has been recommended as particularly suited for African American couples and is the basis for a program designed for cross-cultural couples counseling. Similarly, it has been deemed excellent with respect to gender sensitivity. References to these works may easily be identified by subject area in B. G. Guerney's (2000) Annotated RE Bibliography.

A Meta-Analytic Study

A meta-analytic study by Giblin et al. (1985) analyzed 85 studies with 3,866 couples or families varying widely in age, income, education, and location. It included many couples in therapy as well as in enrichment groups with, as mentioned earlier, the more-distressed couples showing greater change than the less-distressed couples. Outcome comparisons among specific programs were analyzed—16 programs for marital couples and 4 for families. In both categories, RE had by far the highest improvement effect size. Giblin et al. (1985) states that in social, personality, and clinical research, effect sizes typically range from −1 to +1, and the average for psychotherapy research is 0.85. The effect sizes of non-RE couple and family programs ranged from 0.04 (Rational Emotive) to 0.42 and 0.44 (Marriage Encounter and Couples Communication, respectively) to .63 (communications). No comparisons were made for premarital programs. The effect sizes for Marital and Family RE programs each averaged 0.96.

FROM RESEARCH TO PRACTICE

A Transcript From an Experiential RE Family Session

The following transcript is a brief segment from a tape of an experiential family therapy session (B. G. Guerney, 1989). The segment selected from that tape has been slightly edited here for clarity and brevity. The secretary typing the transcript described the emotional tone of the participants' statements (listed here in italics). The transcript is annotated to point out some of the earlier-described 12 therapist responses, which reflect the teachable, replicable, protocol-based nature of RE. It illustrates how these therapist statements fulfill their intended effect of eliciting the fears and desires underlying conflicts to facilitate problem resolution.

In the transcript, the reader will be able to see that family members, once having learned a skill, are always required to use it. The transcript also illustrates that each member of the family learns to stay in one mode, either the Expresser-Skill mode or the Empathic-Skill mode, until a cue occurs that meets the conditions that are part of Discussion/Negotiation skill. At that point, the modes may be exchanged. As is true in the Experiential and Time-Designated modes, except under special circumstances, the therapist's major role is that of an instructor/coach of skills.

The family in this transcript was headed by a working-class couple. The family was seen as part of a workshop at a family therapy institute demonstrating RE Couple/Family Therapy. The parents, a daughter age 13 years, a son age 15 years, and sometimes another daughter age 11 years were seen by Bernard Guerney, Jr., under closed-circuit cable video observation by the workshop participants, for a total of approximately 1.5 hours each morning and 1.5 hours each afternoon for 3 days. During those 9 hours, the family resolved or made substantial progress on what they considered their most important problems.

The parents had reared their children while in a drug- and alcohol-induced haze that had lasted nearly 25 years. With the aid of Alcoholics Anonymous, the parents had been clean for 6 months and had become much more aware of family problems, and they were motivated to do something about them. The workshop sessions were the first therapy sessions for the family.

Not surprisingly, their oldest three children, all males in their late teens and early 20s, were in deep psychological, legal, and substance-abuse troubles, moving in and out of institutions. There had been attempts by one of them to kill another with a knife, resulting in a bloody scene witnessed by the younger children. An attempted suicide by one of them resulted in a similar traumatic situation for the younger children.

The transcript is chosen from an early segment of the therapy. The segment deals with a long-standing conflict between the 13-year-old daughter (D) and her parents as to whether her brother, (P), who was extremely violent, and suicidal, should ever be allowed to set foot in the house again. The daughter did not want him to, and the parents wanted to allow him to visit under certain circumstances. In the beginning, the daughter is in the Expresser mode. Because she looks at her father (F) as she ends her statement, the father and the therapist (T) know by RE guidelines that the father is the family member being asked to be her Empathic Responder.

> D (To F): (*Soft*) Well, I feel good because I know that you care about me. But I'm still very frightened.
> T (Instructing—reminding F to look underneath the spoken words to achieve deeper empathy): (*Suggestive*) I think you probably know something about *why* she's scared. In your (empathic) response to her, you might fill that in.
> F (To D): (*Compassionate*) You're expressing a fear that if he tried to hurt the family or hurt himself, it would upset you greatly.
> D: Yes. [Nonverbal cues indicate that she would like F to become the Expresser now.]
> F: (*Reassuring*) We would only allow P to come back if we were very, very sure that he would be able to handle himself with us. It would be hard for him also to face the family. We would try to supervise the situation to make sure that nothing bad would happen to you or your brothers or sisters. And we would try to use what communication skills we're learning to help each other to see how we feel about each other in the family. (*Warm*) I think it's important that you remember that we also love P very much. The things he did may seem bad, but we love him as a person, and he is trying to make himself better. And so we don't want to shut him out of our family.
> Mother (M) (Asking permission from F to take over the Expresser mode): Can I add something to help reassure her? (F indicates agreement.)
> M (Addressing D): (*Thoughtful*) I visited P twice and talked to him twice on the phone. From my conversations with him, he's working very, very hard to get well. He's made a commitment—a serious one— to himself, to get better, and there's no way in the world we would let him come into the home, even for a visit, unless we felt that it would be safe for him to visit with us—safe not only to us, but to himself. (*Assured*) He told me the last time I talked to him that he had gotten to the root of the problem, to those feelings that made him feel so unworthy and suicidal. (*Understanding*) And he's really sad because of

the effect, the negative effect, that he's had on the family. And he loves us all, too. I feel he realizes and accepts the fact that he will not be allowed to live with us anymore.

T (To M; reinforcing, instructing): (*Helpful*) Okay, that was well put. Ordinarily, one thing that I would have corrected is using "we." (To D; Administering) Okay, you can respond empathically.

D: (*Timid*) So you're saying that you called P and you talked to him, and everything, and he's working real hard to get better. (Ordinarily, the therapist would ask that the "You're saying" be dropped; but in this instance, decided to let it pass.)

T (Reinforcing): Good. (*Comforting*) And add this: "You don't want him back in the house unless you feel as sure as you can be about another person, that he's not going to be dangerous to himself or to other people. You do not want him in the house unless you're completely convinced of that." It's important to reflect that too.

D: (*Meek*) You wouldn't let him in the house unless you were sure it would be safe.

T (To M, prompting M to use Discussion/Negotiation skill to exchange Expresser and Empathic modes with D): Do you want to know how she feels?

M (Using Discussion/Negotiation skill as requested): (*Concerned*) And I'm wondering how you feel. I'm wondering if you feel better, more comfortable now about the situation with P as a result of what I've shared with you.

D: (*Anxious*) You want me to say how I feel. [Note that the Empathic Responder must reflect even requests to become the Expresser.] Ummm, well, I still feel a little uncomfortable.

T (Modeling for Expresser, i.e., giving D a statement to add, if it is true): (*Thoughtful*) "I can't help but still be afraid about this." Is that true?

D: (*Timid*) I can't help but be scared . . .

M: (*Unsure*) You still feel afraid even though I've explained to you what, ummm. (She stops herself because she realizes that the "even though I've explained to you" part of her statement is not good empathy and therefore she now says, to T:) I guess I'm so hung up in what *I* want to say to her that I'm pushing the skills out.

T (To M; responding to M's desire for coaching by Modeling for Empathizer): (*Sympathetic*) Okay, just say, "Because of what happened, you can't help but be somewhat afraid. The fear of what happened is still there and you're scared it might happen again. But you're glad that we're trying to protect you." I think that would be better . . .

M: (*Awkward*) You're glad that we're trying to protect you, but you still have fears. We haven't been able to (*softly*) allay those fears that you have about P's return.

D: Umm hmmm.

M (Taking the Expresser mode following appropriate nonverbal cues): (*Warm*) I'm wondering if you know what you need from us to make those fears go away. I'm wondering if there's anything else that we could do to allay those fears. (D's reply is inaudible.)

T (Becoming D and speaking to M): (*Sensitive*) "I've been just very, very scared and no matter what is said now, if he comes into the picture again, I'm going to be frightened." (To D): Is that what you're saying? (The therapist is asking D a question to better enable himself to become D in speaking as D to M.) Does that mean that what I (as you) really would like is this: "I don't want him ever to come back," or does it mean this: "If he comes back into the house, I will be scared, but it's okay with me for him to come back, even though I expect to be scared"? Which of those is true?

D (She speaks for herself directly to M): (*Vulnerable*) Well, it's okay if he comes back even though I'll still be scared.

T (Becoming D to M): "I'm willing to trust your judgment." (To D): Is that what you're saying?

D (To M): (*Sure*) I'm willing to trust your judgment.

M: (*Warm*) You're saying no matter what we say or do, you're still going to be afraid. But despite the fact that you will be afraid, you are willing to trust us to make decisions related to P and the rest of the family. You feel we'll do the right thing or that we'll do the best that we can in that situation.

D: Umm hmm.

M (Appropriately following nonverbal cues to become the Expresser) (*Optimistic*): It makes me feel good that you trust us. I appreciate that, and I feel that I can try to do the best I can in that situation. And I will try to the best of my ability to protect you and protect that trust.

The father felt likewise, and so a conflict that the family considered one of their most important, conflict-laden, and stressful problems and had earlier been unable to resolve was quickly resolved with good feelings all around because of their skilled exchange.

Using RE Therapy in Your Practice

How might a therapist interested in putting RE into practice proceed? First, it is important to realize that RE therapy is a system rather than a set of techniques. There is no reason to believe that one would obtain the speed or efficacy that research on RE has demonstrated by mechanically pasting this or that RE technique onto another approach. In fact, it is possible that doing this would yield worse results than either RE or the other approach would achieve on its own. However, research has shown that following the RE system as a whole and unmixed with other approaches, even after as little as 3 days of training, is likely to yield experienced couples therapists greater client improvement than does their own previous approach (Ross et al., 1985).

It is extremely difficult for therapists to understand RE from words alone. However, RE therapy as a system is easily learned in, say, a 3-day workshop that emphasizes participant skill practice under supervision, or from a home-study program (e.g., B. G. Guerney, Scuka, & Nordling, 2000) that includes videotapes demonstrating RE techniques and distance supervision of actual practice.

Thus, by far the best way to proceed is to first learn the RE system as such and practice it in its entirety until at least moderate proficiency is reached. That would prepare one to combine it most knowingly, systematically, and effectively with other favored systems or techniques. In such combination, it would be important to maintain appropriate client expectations about how the therapist is going to behave (as instructor-coach in RE as opposed to, for example, problem analyst or advisor in another approach). Therefore, the combination of RE with other approaches should be one in which the two approaches are presented in discreet segments—that is, not as a stew but as identified courses of a meal—preferably in separate sessions. Such distinctiveness also helps a therapist to see which approach works better or which is more useful for what or with whom; moreover, it allows clients to give better feedback about such matters if asked.

What if, despite the above advice, a therapist wants to incorporate something from RE in his or her practice immediately? We believe there is one principle discovered in practicing RE, and alluded to earlier, that could immediately be applied to non-RE approaches. The principle is this: Intimates become motivated to make positive changes when two feelings are in confluence. This confluence consists of simultaneously experiencing the pain that one is causing a partner and the deep satisfaction and sense of security that comes from experiencing that partner's love and appreciation.

To elaborate: Almost by definition, a couples therapist seeks change in the patterns of interactive behavior between the intimates. The first step of this process is the arousal of strong motivation to change. That is often difficult in non-RE couples therapy. Why? Because the negativity of the exchanges occurring prevents this. There is usually much mutual fault finding and criticism and requests for change based on what one party sees as the right or correct or mature thing for the other party to do. In RE, all of that is eliminated by the requirement that the clients use Expressive skill or have it used on their behalf by the therapist. But in approaches wherein that is not the case, it may nevertheless be feasible for the therapist to try to ferret out the positives that both give rise to, and are being hidden by, negative emotions, for example, the hurt stemming from perceived neglect or rejection, these being so intensely felt precisely because of the underlying love felt for the partner, or the fact that the very desire to eliminate the behavior in question and the intensity of the effort to change the partner's behavior arises out of the longing to recapture the deep love that is being threatened or damaged by that behavior.

Once the therapist is able to help, by whatever means, the complaining client (A) to overcome the unwillingness to be vulnerable in this situation and thus be able to bring caring and then love to the surface and then express them, this immediately weakens partner B's needs to be defensive. With a repetition or two, perhaps in even more direct and stronger form, of A's expression of love for B, and the longing of A to experience B's love in return, B's stone wall is fully breached. The hurt of partner A is *experienced* by B. This arouses in B concern for, then with the help of the therapist, B's expression of caring, then of love for A. The exchange of feelings of love almost invariably leads to a strong motivation by one or both parities to change in the ways required by the particular problem. Then the process of successfully implementing the change in the real world can begin. But the hardest part of the problem/conflict solving process already has been accomplished.

CONCLUSION

In summary, there is strong evidence that with both distressed and nondistressed pairs:

1. RE is effective in improving the adjustment level and the general quality of relationships between couples and between parents and their adolescent children, including such variables as trust and intimacy.
2. RE yields even greater improvement with high-distress couples than with low-distress couples.
3. RE improves participants' ability to communicate effectively both as they see it and as assessed by condition-blind expert observers.
4. RE helps clients to transfer the use of their skills to situations outside of the therapy and improves participants' ability, as they see it, to resolve conflicts and problems.
5. RE can enhance personal psychological health not only indirectly through improving family but also in terms of self-esteem and differentiation of self.

The evidence is strong not only because it is based on relatively nondistressed samples, inexperienced leaders, and group rather than dyadic formats, but also because of the variety of samples used and the nature of the studies.

With respect to the nature of the studies, almost all of the RE studies have used control groups and either strict random assignment of participants, or have come as close to random assignment as scheduling and similarly nonobviously biasing factors would allow. Especially noteworthy are the number of studies wherein RE has been shown to be superior not just to a placebo group or to a wait-list group but to alternative therapies that were themselves effective. Also noteworthy is that the same leaders or therapists very often administered both treatments, controlling for personality variables, and that when rated by participants, they were rated as equal in both treatments with respect to all measured traits: confidence, enthusiasm, understanding, acceptance, and genuineness.

When positive results are found under this combination of conditions, one can rule out many of the alternative explanations for positive results that often call the results of therapeutic studies into question. One can have much greater confidence that results based on favorable comparisons with effective alternative treatments are due to specific qualities of the treatment itself. In other words, the controls and other checks found in many of these studies were such as to rule out the conclusion that the results were due to generic factors such as experimenter demand, placebo, suggestion, or Hawthorne effects, or due to the confounding of treatment effects with differences in the personalities, attitudes, or leadership qualities of the therapists. A final source of confidence in the findings summarized here is the meta-analytic comparison (Giblin et al., 1985) with other major enrichment or therapeutic approaches that show that RE has by far the highest effect sizes. Alone among them, RE showed effect sizes comparable with those found in studies of individual psychotherapy and, indeed, they are at the top of the range usually found in psychosocial research in general.

With respect to RE as it currently stands, the evidence indicates that most of the positive effects of RE not only are maintained in follow-ups of approximately a year (Griffin & Apostal, 1993; Waldo, 1986) but can become even stronger over time (Griffin & Apostal, 1993; B. G. Guerney et al., 1983).

REFERENCES

Accordino, M. P., & Guerney, B. G., Jr. (1998). An evaluation of the Relationship Enhancement® program with prisoners and their wives. *International Journal of Offender Therapy and Comparative Criminology, 42*(1), 5–15.

Aradi, N. S. (1985). *The relative effectiveness of the Relationship Enhancement therapy and strategic therapy for the treatment of distressed married couples.* Unpublished doctoral dissertation, Purdue University, Lafayette, IN.

Avery, A. W., Rider, K., & Haynes-Clements, L. A. (1981). Communication skills training for adolescents: A five month follow-up. *Adolescence, 16,* 289–298.

Avery, A. W., Ridley, C. A., Leslie, L. A., & Milholland, T. (1980). Relationship Enhancement with premarital dyads: A six month follow-up. *American Journal of Family Therapy, 8,* 60–66.

Brock, G. W. (1974). *A follow-up study of an intensive conjugal Relationship Enhancement program.* Unpublished master's thesis, Pennsylvania State University, University Park.

Brock, G. W., & Joanning, H. (1983). A comparison of the Relationship Enhancement program and the Minnesota Couple Communication Program. *Journal of Marital and Family Therapy, 9,* 413–421.

Brooks, L. W. (1997). *An investigation of Relationship Enhancement therapy in a group format with rural, southern couples.* Unpublished doctoral dissertation, Florida State University School of Social Work, Tallahassee.

Cavedo, L. C. (1995). Efficacy of an extremely brief Relationship Enhancement intervention format and two coaching styles (Doctoral dissertation, Pennsylvania State University, 1995). *Dissertation Abstracts International, 56,* 9600146.

Cavedo, L. C., & Guerney, B. G., Jr. (1999). Relationship Enhancement® (RE) enrichment/problem-prevention programs: Therapy-derived, powerful, versatile. In R. Berger & M. T. Hannah (Eds.), *Preventive approaches in couples therapy* (pp. 73–105). New York: Brunner/Mazel.

Collins, J. D. (1977). Experimental evaluation of a six-month conjugal therapy and Relationship Enhancement program. In B. G. Guerney, Jr., *Relationship Enhancement: Skill-training programs for therapy, problem prevention and enrichment* (pp. 192–226). San Francisco: Jossey-Bass.

Dollard, J., & Miller, N. E. (1950). *Personality and psychotherapy.* New York: McGraw Hill.

Fitzpatrick, M. (1988). *Between husbands and wives.* Newbury Park, CA: Sage Publications.

Ford, D. H. (1987). *Humans as self-constructing living systems: A developmental perspective on behavior and personality.* (Available from IDEALS, 12500 Blake Road, Silver Spring, MD 20904-2056)

Ford, D. H., & Urban, H. B. (1998). *Contemporary models of psychotherapy: A comparative analysis.* New York: Wiley.

Giblin, P., Sprenkle, D. H., & Sheehan, R. (1985). Enrichment outcome research: A meta-analysis of premarital, marital, and family interventions. *Journal of Marital and Family Therapy, 11,* 257–271.

Ginsberg, B. G. (1977). Parent–adolescent relationship development program. In B. G. Guerney, Jr., *Relationship Enhancement: Skill-training programs for therapy, problem prevention, and enrichment* (pp. 227–267). San Francisco: Jossey-Bass.

Ginsberg, B. G. (1997). *Relationship Enhancement family therapy.* New York: Wiley.

Ginsberg, B. G., & Vogelsong, E. L. (1977). Premarital relationship improvement by maximizing empathy and self-disclosure: The PRIMES Program. In B. G.

Guerney, Jr., *Relationship Enhancement: Skill-training programs for therapy, problem prevention, and enrichment* (pp. 268–288). San Francisco: Jossey-Bass.

Greene, G. J. (1986). The effect of the Relationship Enhancement program on marital communication and self-esteem. *Journal of Applied Social Sciences, 1*(1), 78–94.

Griffin, J. M., Jr., & Apostal, R. A. (1993). The influence of Relationship Enhancement training on differentiation of self. *Journal of Marital and Family Therapy, 19*, 267–272.

Guerney, B. G., Jr. (Ed. & Commentator). (1969). *Psychotherapeutic agents: New roles for nonprofessionals, parents, and teachers.* New York: Holt, Rinehart & Winston.

Guerney, B. G., Jr. (1977). *Relationship Enhancement: Skill-training programs for therapy, problem prevention and enrichment.* San Francisco: Jossey-Bass.

Guerney, B. G., Jr. (1982). The delivery of mental health services: Spiritual vs. Medical vs. Educational models. In T. R. Vallance & R. M. Sabre (Eds.), *Mental health services in transition: A policy sourcebook* (pp. 238–257). New York: Human Sciences Press.

Guerney, B. G., Jr. (1984). Contributions of client-centered therapy to filial, marital, and family Relationship Enhancement therapies. In R. F. Levant & J. M. Shlien (Eds.), *Client-centered therapy and the person-centered approach: New directions in theory, research, and practice* (pp. 261–277). New York: Praeger.

Guerney, B. G., Jr. (1985a). The Medical vs. the Educational Model as a base for family therapy research. In L. F. Andreozzi & R. F. Levant (Eds.), *Integrating research and clinical practice* (pp. 71–79). Rockville, MD: Aspen Systems.

Guerney, B. G., Jr. (1985b, Summer). Person-centered therapy, therapists, and marital and family Relationship Enhancement therapies: Relationships. *Renaissance, 2*(3), 1–3.

Guerney, B. G., Jr. (1986a). *Relationship Enhancement*® manual. (Available from IDEALS, 12500 Blake Road, Silver Spring, MD 20904-2056)

Guerney, B. G., Jr. (1986b). *Relationship Enhancement*®: Marital/family therapists manual. (Available from IDEALS, 12500 Blake Road, Silver Spring, MD 20904-2056)

Guerney, B. G., Jr. (1989). *Relationship Enhancement*® family therapy: The experiential format (P-Family) [Videotapes]. (Available from IDEALS, 12500 Blake Road, Silver Spring, MD 20904-2056)

Guerney, B. G., Jr. (1990). Creating therapeutic and growth-inducing family systems: Personal moorings, landmarks and guiding stars. In F. Kaslow (Ed.), *Voices in family psychology* (pp. 114–138). Beverly Hills, CA: Sage.

Guerney, B. G., Jr. (1991). *Relationship Enhancement*® program manual. (Available from IDEALS, 12500 Blake Road, Silver Spring, MD 20904-2056)

Guerney, B. G., Jr. (1994). *Relationship Enhancement*® audio program [Audiotapes]. (Available from IDEALS, 12500 Blake Road, Silver Spring, MD 20904-2056)

Guerney, B. G., Jr. (1997). *Relationship Enhancement*® PhoneCoach® program [Manual and audiotapes]. (Available from IDEALS, 12500 Blake Road, Silver Spring, MD 20904-2056)

Guerney, B. G., Jr. (2000). *Annotated bibliography: Relationship Enhancement*® therapy, enrichment, and problem prevention programs for individuals, families, and organizations. (Available from IDEALS, P. O. Box 391, State College, PA 16804)

Guerney, B. G., Jr., Coufal, J., & Vogelsong, E. (1981). Relationship Enhancement versus a traditional approach to therapeutic/preventative/enrichment parent adolescent programs. *Journal of Consulting and Clinical Psychology, 49*, 927–939.

Guerney, B. G., Jr., Guerney, L., & Stollak, G. (1971/1972). The potential advantages of changing from a Medical to an Educational Model in practicing psychology. *Interpersonal Development, 2*, 238–245.

Guerney, B. G., Jr., Scuka, R., & Nordling, W. (2000). *Relationship Enhancement*® couple/family therapy: A video training program with distance supervision [Videotapes]. (Available from IDEALS, 12500 Blake Road, Silver Spring, MD 20904-2056)

Guerney, B. G., Jr., & Snyder, M. (2000). *Relationship Enhancement*® individual therapy. Manuscript submitted for publication.

Guerney, B. G., Jr., Stollak, G., & Guerney, L. (1970). A format for a new mode of psychological practice: Or, how to escape a zombie. *Counseling Psychologist, 2*, 97–105.

Guerney, B. G., Jr., & Vogelsong, E. (1981). *Relationship Enhancement*® demonstration tapes [Audiotapes]. (Available from IDEALS, 12500 Blake Road, Silver Spring, MD 20904-2056)

Guerney, B. G., Jr., Vogelsong, E., & Coufal, J. (1983). Relationship Enhancement versus a traditional treatment: Follow-up and booster effects. In D. Olson & B. Miller (Eds.), *Family studies review yearbook* (pp. 738–756). Beverly Hills, CA: Sage.

Guerney, L. (1987). *The parenting skills program: A manual for parent educators.* (Available from IDEALS, 12500 Blake Road, Silver Spring, MD 20904-2056)

Guerney, L., & Guerney, B. G., Jr. (1985). The Relationship Enhancement family of family therapies. In L. L'Abate & M. Milan (Eds.), *Handbook of social skills training and research* (pp. 506–524). New York: Wiley.

Haynes, L. A., & Avery, A. W. (1979). Training adolescents in self-disclosure and empathy skills. *Journal of Counseling Psychology, 26*, 526–530.

Jessee, R. E., & Guerney, B. G., Jr. (1981). A comparison of Gestalt and Relationship Enhancement treatments with married couples. *American Journal of Family Therapy, 9*(3), 31–41.

Leary, T. (1957). *Interpersonal diagnosis of personality.* New York: Ronald Press.

Matter, M., McAllister, W., & Guerney, B. G., Jr. (1984). Relationship Enhancement® for the recovering couple: Working with the intangible. *Focus on Family and Chemical Dependency, 7*(5), 21–23, 40.

Rappaport, A. F. (1971). *The effects of an intensive conjugal relationship modification program.* Unpublished doctoral dissertation, Pennsylvania State University, University Park, PA.

Ridley, C. A., Avery, A. W., Dent, J., & Harrell, J. (1981). Effects of Relationship Enhancement and problem solving programs on perceived heterosexual competence. *Family Therapy, 8,* 60–66.

Ridley, C. A., & Bain, A. B. (1983). The effects of Premarital Relationship Enhancement program on self-disclosure. *Family Therapy, 10,* 13–84.

Ridley, C. A., Jorgensen, S. R., Morgan, A. G., & Avery, A. W. (1982). Relationship Enhancement with premarital couples: An assessment of effects on relationship quality. *American Journal of Family Therapy, 10,* 41–47.

Ridley, C. A., & Sladeczek, I. E. (1992). Premarital Relationship Enhancement: Its effects on needs to relate to others. *Family Relations, 41,* 148–153.

Ross, E. R., Baker, S. B., & Guerney, B. G., Jr. (1985). Effectiveness of Relationship Enhancement therapy versus therapist's preferred therapy. *American Journal of Family Therapy, 13*(1), 11–21.

Sams, W. P. (1983). Marriage preparation: An experimental comparison of the Premarital Relationship Enhancement (PRE) and the Engaged Encounter (EE) programs (Doctoral dissertation, Pennsylvania State University, 1983). *Dissertation Abstracts International, 44,* 3207.

Schlein, S. (1972). Training dating couples in empathic and open communication: An experimental evaluation of a potential preventative mental health program (Doctoral dissertation, Pennsylvania State University, 1971). *Dissertation Abstracts International, 32,* 7213929.

Snyder, M. (1994). Couple therapy with narcissistically vulnerable clients: Using the Relationship Enhancement model. *The Family Journal, 2*(1), 27–35.

Snyder, M. (1995). "Becoming": A method for expanding systemic thinking and deepening empathic accuracy. *Family Process, 34,* 241–253.

Snyder, M. (1996). *Demonstrations of Becoming and Laundering in Relationship Enhancement® couple therapy* [Videotapes]. (Available from IDEALS, 12500 Blake Road, Silver Spring, MD 20904-2056)

Snyder, M., & Guerney, B. G., Jr. (1993). Brief couple/family therapy: The Relationship Enhancement® approach. In R. A. Wells & V. J. Giannette (Eds.), *Casebook of the brief psychotherapies* (pp. 221–234). New York: Plenum Press.

Steinweg, C. K. M. (1990). *A comparison of the effectiveness of Relationship Enhancement and strategic marital therapy using the strength of the therapeutic alliance to predict statistically significant and clinically meaningful outcome.* Unpublished doctoral dissertation, Purdue University, Lafayette, IN.

Stuart, R. B. (1969). Operant-interpersonal treatment for marital discord. *Journal of Consulting and Clinical Psychology, 33,* 675–682.

Waldo, M. (1986). Group counseling for military personnel who battered their wives. *Journal for Specialists in Group Work, 2,* 132–138.

Waldo, M. (1988, January). Relationship Enhancement counseling groups for wife abusers. *Journal of Mental Health Counseling, 10*(1), 37–45.

Waldo, M., & Guerney, B. G., Jr. (1983). Marital Relationship Enhancement therapy in the treatment of alcoholism. *Journal of Marital and Family Therapy, 9*, 321–323.

Waldo, M., & Harman, M. J. (1993). Relationship Enhancement therapy with borderline personality. *Family Journal, 1*(1), 25–30.

Wieman, R. J. (1973). *Conjugal relationship modification and reciprocal reinforcement: A comparison of treatments for marital discord.* Unpublished master's thesis, Pennsylvania State University, University Park.

Weiss, R. (1992, July). Introduction to a presentation by Bernard Guerney, Jr., at the Fourth World Congress on Behavior Therapy, Gold Coast, Australia.

V

THERAPEUTIC ISSUES AND APPLICATIONS

14

RE-VISIONING EMPATHY

JEANNE C. WATSON

Almost 60 years of research have consistently demonstrated that therapist empathy is the most potent predictor of client progress in therapy. Yet many therapists continue to fail to appreciate its power and to understand how it leads to change or how to respond empathically with optimum impact. This chapter presents a view of empathy as an active ingredient of change that facilitates clients' meta-cognitive processes and emotional self-regulation. A review of the research on empathy reveals that it is an essential component of successful therapy in every therapeutic modality (Burns & Nolen-Hoeksma, 1992; Greenberg, Rice, & Elliott, 1993; Linehan, 1997; Luborsky, Crits-Christoph, Mintz, & Auerbach, 1988; Mahoney, 1995; Mearns & Thorne, 1988; Miller, Taylor, & West, 1980; Parloff, Waskow, & Wolfe, 1978; Raue & Goldfried, 1994; Rogers, 1965, 1975; Rounsaville, Weissman, & Prusoff, 1981; Rowe, 1997; Safran & Wallner, 1991; Strupp, Fox, & Lessler, 1969).

Empathy is a basic component of emotional intelligence (Goleman, 1996). It is a multidimensional and complex epistemological process and is a way of knowing that involves both people's affective and cognitive systems (Bohart & Greenberg, 1997; Duan & Hill, 1996; Feschbach, 1997). According to developmental theorists, empathy is a capacity present from birth that develops over time as people's emotional and cognitive systems mature. Titchener (cited in Bozarth, 1997) translated the term *empathy* from the German word *einfuhlung*, as "to feel one's way into." It was originally used in German aesthetics as a means of coming to know a particular work of art. Later, empathy was used by Rogers (1965, 1975) and Kohut (1971, 1977) to describe a way of being toward others to promote healing in psychotherapy.

445

Numerous theorists see empathy as a basic relationship skill (Bohart & Greenberg, 1997; Hogan, 1969; Kohut, 1971; Rogers, 1975; Watson, Goldman, & Vanaerschot, 1998). For interpersonal communication to occur, a certain amount of empathy is required to understand others at even the most basic level (Feschbach, 1997; Hoffman, 1982; Jordan, 1997; Kohut, 1971; Linehan, 1997; Rogers, 1975; Trop & Stolorow, 1997). However, there are different levels of understanding and different types of empathic process. A person can understand another by knowing what he or she means intellectually and by comprehending his or her values, world views, goals, and objectives; but to be truly empathic, this understanding needs to be informed by knowing or understanding how things affect the other person emotionally. People's emotions reveal the significance or meaning of events for them (Goleman, 1996; Greenberg et al., 1993; Orlinsky & Howard, 1986; Rogers, 1965; Taylor, 1990). Thus, to understand and know another person, one must be emotionally responsive to them.

The primary purpose of this chapter is to examine the role and function of empathy in psychotherapy. First, research on empathy from 1940 to the present is examined. This is followed by a discussion of how empathy informs humanistic and experiential therapists' practice. Finally, a theoretical model of empathy's role in promoting change in psychotherapy is presented.

ROGERS'S THREE THERAPIST CONDITIONS

For Carl Rogers, empathy was one of three essential conditions offered by therapists to their clients in psychotherapy. The other two therapist conditions were congruence and unconditional positive regard or a nonjudgmental stance toward the other. The latter attribute was seen as vital to the provision of empathy. Rogers did not think it was possible to empathize fully and completely with others' experiences if one was evaluating them negatively. Moreover, as developmental theorists have observed, it seems highly unlikely that someone could be truly empathic if he or she feels hostility or anger toward the other person (Feschbach, 1997). Thus, for empathy to be therapeutic, it needs to occur in a sympathetic, safe, and nonjudgmental climate, in which clients feel prized. In addition, it is important for therapists to appear congruent if they are to be experienced as empathic.

Rogers (1965) defined *empathy* as the ability to perceive accurately the internal frames of reference of others in terms of their meanings and emotional components. This definition highlights empathy as both an emotional and a cognitive process. Rogers saw empathy as the ability to see the world through others' eyes so as to sense their hurt and pain and to perceive the source of their feelings in the same way as they do. In this regard, he was careful to distinguish identification from empathy. Identification indicates a loss of boundaries as one adopts others' views of reality.

One way Rogers suggested that therapists could demonstrate empathy was through trying to reflect clients' feelings. However, this activity was often misconstrued as merely parroting clients' words or repeating the last thing they said (Rogers, 1975). This view reflects a misunderstanding of empathic responding, which is a sophisticated and highly complex way of being with clients. It is a taxing and demanding exercise to listen empathically, to get at the heart of clients' communications, and to distill the essence and centrality of their messages. Research studies have shown that therapeutic empathy is correlated with therapists' cognitive complexity. Listening attentively to the nuances of clients' narratives is a sophisticated exercise of critical deconstruction in the moment that requires great concentration.

The simplistic way in which empathy came to be understood as a reflection of feelings was problematic and deterred Rogers from discussing it further until his landmark article in 1975. In his 1975 paper, Rogers returned to the subject of empathy and tried to define it more precisely. At that time, Rogers saw empathy as a process, not a state of being. Thus, it is an ongoing attempt to enter the private, subjective world of the other, while at the same time being sensitive to the changes in meaning so that they can be tracked accurately. The process of trying to understand the subjective world of the other is done with careful attention to nuance to sense meanings of which the person may not be fully aware. However, this does not mean uncovering or reporting on feelings and sensations of which the person has no awareness. Moreover, attempts to understand what clients are saying are always done tentatively and are constantly checked with them. Clients remain the final arbiters of whether therapists have understood them correctly or caught a meaning of which they were not fully aware. Rogers (1975) saw empathy as a way to evoke self-directed change and to empower the person. Thus, he took pains not to appear the expert with clients in therapy so that the clients would assume responsibility for their own change processes and behaviors and come to see themselves as the best judge of their own needs and feelings.

RESEARCH ON THE ROLE OF EMPATHY IN PSYCHOTHERAPY

The role of empathy in facilitating change received considerable attention in the research literature after Rogers posited that empathy, unconditional positive regard, and congruence were the necessary and sufficient therapist conditions of psychotherapeutic change. The findings generated considerable debate and heated discussion with respect to the efficacy of these three conditions, with numerous researchers either supporting or discrediting

Rogers's position. After the initial flurry of interest that seemed to reveal conflicting findings, research on empathy and the other two conditions declined (Duan & Hill, 1996; Orlinsky, Grawe, & Parks, 1994; Sexton & Whiston, 1994). The decline in empathy research has been attributed to a number of factors: (a) difficulties defining the construct; (b) poor research tools (Barkham & Shapiro, 1986; Duan & Hill, 1996; Lambert, De Julio, & Stein, 1978; Patterson, 1983; Sexton & Whiston, 1994); and (c) increased interest in the working alliance (Duan & Hill, 1996; Orlinsky et al., 1994). In this section, I discuss how the concept of empathy has been defined and measured and evaluate its role in treatment.

An examination of the research on the role of empathy in psychotherapy reveals that it is an area plagued by methodological difficulties, exposing the tensions in various researchers' paradigmatic assumptions. A thorough review of the area suggests that researchers are, at times, comparing apples and oranges and highlights the inherent difficulty they face in trying to measure a dynamic and interpersonal phenomenon. After Rogers's initial hypothesis, the two most commonly used measures that were developed to measure empathy in the session were the Accurate Empathy Scale (Truax & Carkhuff, 1967) and the Relationship Inventory (Barrett-Lennard, 1962).

Measures of Empathy

The Accurate Empathy Scale (Truax & Carkhuff, 1967) evaluates therapists' responses, on a 10-point scale, in terms of the degree to which they communicate empathy. It is based on independent raters' evaluations of the therapeutic process. According to Duan and Hill (1996), this scale is one of the most common ways of measuring therapist empathy from an observer's perspective. The other way of measuring therapist empathy has been from the clients' perspective, using Barrett-Lennard's Relationship Inventory (Barrett-Lennard, 1962). This is a self-report measure that asks clients to comment on whether they experienced their therapists as genuine, prizing, and empathic. Not surprisingly, from the postmodern perspective, raters and clients provide different views and judgments of empathy. Correlations between external judges' ratings and clients' ratings of empathy are low (Bachrach, Luborsky, & Mechanick, 1974; Beutler, Johnson, Neville, & Workman, 1973; Bozarth & Grace, 1970; Rogers, 1967) or nonexistent (Caracena & Vicory, 1969; Carkhuff & Burstein, 1970; Fish, 1970; Hill, 1974; Kurtz & Grummon, 1972; McWhirter, 1973; Truax, 1966; van der Veen, 1970).

A number of reasons have been posited to account for these anomalous findings. The most cogent is that each measure uses a different criterion for determining empathy. According to this view, it is likely that external raters and clients are attending to different cues on which to base their evaluations of therapeutic empathy. Moreover, most raters are limited to audio recordings and thus are not able to apprise themselves of therapists' nonverbal behaviors as a means of communicating empathy (Duan & Hill, 1996; McWhirter, 1973).

As noted by numerous reviewers, it is ironic that despite Rogers's emphasis on communicated empathy or clients' perceptions of their therapists' empathy as the important determinant of outcome, researchers continue to use external evaluations (Barkham & Shapiro, 1986; Caracena & Vicory, 1969; Duan & Hill, 1996; Gurman, 1973; Orlinsky & Howard, 1986). The questionable validity of using observers' ratings is further underscored by the finding that ratings of therapist empathy can be made independent of client responses (Orlinsky & Howard, 1986). The rationale for not using clients as raters of therapeutic empathy was that they were likely to be unreliable and inclined to distort or incorrectly perceive their therapists' behavior (Gurman, 1977). This conclusion reveals a clash between certain research assumptions based on a positivist research paradigm that undervalues the participation of the research sample and views of pathology that are at odds with the underlying assumptions of client-centered therapy (Bohart & Tallman, 1997; Watson & Rennie, 1994).

The Relationship Between Empathy and Outcome

Numerous studies have been conducted to determine whether empathy is indeed a necessary and sufficient condition along with the other therapeutic conditions of genuineness and unconditional positive regard (Mintz, Luborsky, & Auerbach, 1971; Muller & Abeles, 1971; Truax, Carkhuff, & Kodman, 1965; Truax et al., 1966; Truax, Wittmer, & Wargo, 1971; van der Veen, 1967). Overall, there is a preponderance of evidence to suggest that therapist empathy is indeed a crucial variable in psychotherapy, notwithstanding those studies that have failed to find significant relationships (Bergin, 1966; Gurman, 1977; Luborsky et al., 1988; Orlinsky et al., 1994; Patterson, 1983). In their most recent review of psychotherapy process and outcome research, Orlinsky et al. (1994) noted that, in the period 1972–1989, 54% of studies using either externally rated or client-judged ratings of empathy support the relationship between therapists' communicating empathically with their clients and therapy outcome. Lambert et al. (1978) and Luborsky et al. (1988) reviewed a total of 23 studies looking at the relationship between therapist empathy as rated by an external rater and therapy outcome over an 11-year period from 1962 to 1973. Of this total, 14 studies reported positive significant relationships between therapist empathy and outcome, whereas 9 were not significant.

In their meta-analysis of the studies that they reviewed, Luborsky et al. (1988) reported a mean correlation of .26 between therapist empathy and outcome. Lamb (1981), similarly, reported a weighted mean correlation of .26 in his meta-analysis of research studies, which examined the efficacy of the therapeutic conditions of empathy, genuineness, and positive regard. This is the same as that reported in a meta-analysis of the relationship between the therapeutic alliance and outcome conducted by Horvath and Symonds (1991). Although the overall correlation of .26 is relatively small, it provides considerable support for the relationship between the presence of empathy and outcome, as well as that of the other therapeutic conditions and the quality of the therapeutic relationship.

Stronger evidence to support the hypothesis that therapists' empathy is related to client change in psychotherapy comes from studies that have examined the relationship between client-perceived ratings of therapeutic empathy and outcome (Gladstein, 1977; Gurman, 1977; Orlinsky et al., 1994). Most of these studies have used the Barrett-Lennard (1973) Relationship Inventory to assess clients' experience of the relationship. Gurman (1977) in his review of studies conducted between 1954 and 1974 noted that 17 studies looked at the relationship between empathy and outcome. Of these, 14 reported a positive relationship between empathy and outcome, whereas 3 found no relationship. Gurman (1977) noted that 2 of these 3 studies were analogue studies, and in 1 study, treatment consisted of two sessions only. This is hardly enough time for clients to begin to have an adequate sense of whether their therapists accurately understood them or not. Barrett-Lennard suggested that ratings of empathy be done after the fifth session (Gurman, 1977). Other studies have shown that clients' perceptions of empathy and therapists' understanding of their clients vary over time (Cartwright & Lerner, 1965; Kalfas, 1974, cited in Orlinsky & Howard, 1986; Kurtz & Grummon, 1972; Marangoni, Garcia, Ickes, & Teng, 1995; Patterson, 1983).

A review of studies from 1976 to 1994 (Luborsky et al., 1988; Orlinsky et al., 1994) provides additional support for the relationship between therapists' empathy and outcome, with 8 of 10 studies reporting positive findings and 2 reporting no relationship. Studies that have conducted in-depth interviews with clients to determine the effective elements of treatment have consistently found that an important factor is the opportunity to talk with an understanding, warm, and involved person (Cross, Sheehan, & Khan, 1982; Feiffel & Eels, 1963; Lietaer, 1990; Strupp et al., 1969; Watson & Rennie, 1994). Orlinsky et al. (1994) noted in their review that clients are more discriminating than external raters and therapists with respect to therapist process variables. Moreover, some studies have shown that therapists are not as discriminating of their own behavior and sometimes rate themselves as higher in empathy than do clients or external raters (Gurman, 1977; Kurtz & Grummon, 1972; Lafferty, Beutler, & Crago, 1989).

The weaknesses of the research studies that have been reviewed include (a) the low reliabilities between different raters, including clients, external judges, and therapists, and different outcome measures; (b) the questionable validity between different outcome measures; (c) the restricted range of scores on predictor variables; and (d) the lack of appropriate outcome measures (Patterson, 1983). Other problems that have been identified by reviewers of the studies on the relationship between empathy and outcome include the time of assessment, sampling methods, and the operationalization of empathy (Duan & Hill, 1996; Gurman, 1977; Mitchell, Bozarth, & Krauft, 1977). First, although numerous studies have found that the experience level of the therapist is an important variable in judges' ratings of empathy (Fiedler, 1950a; Fish, 1970; Gonyea, 1963; Luborsky et al., 1988; Parloff, 1961), it is seldom factored into studies that are investigating the relationship between empathy and outcome. Second, numerous studies have found that the time of assessment is an important variable and that judges' and clients' ratings can change depending on when during therapy the assessment is made (Cartwright & Lerner, 1965; Patterson, 1983; Rice, 1965). Cartwright and Lerner (1965) found that therapists' views of clients were more accurate at the end of therapy than at the beginning, but only for clients with good outcome. Other authors have noted that sampling methods may distort findings (Barkham & Shapiro, 1986; Beutler et al., 1973; Gurman, 1977; Kiesler, Klein, & Mathieu, 1965; Lambert et al., 1978). First, brief segments do not provide an adequate sense of the relationship over time. Second, there may be differences in early versus later sessions (Rice, 1965) as well as within sessions (Kiesler et al., 1965).

Another important criticism has to do with the definition and operationalization of empathy. The Accurate Empathy Scale measures how well the therapist reflects clients' feelings. However, the expression of empathy is now recognized as much more than merely reflecting clients' feelings (Bohart & Greenberg, 1997; Bozarth, 1997). Elliott (1986) found that clients' experience of empathy was not related to specific response modes such as empathic reflection. A number of studies suggest that there are a number of behaviors, both verbal and nonverbal, that can contribute to clients' feeling empathically understood. Bachelor (1988) found that clients experienced therapists' cognitive and affective understanding of their problems as well as their self-disclosing and nurturing behaviors as empathic. Moreover, examinations of Rogers's interactions with clients have shown that the majority of his responses focus on clients' actions and cognitions as opposed to their feelings (Brodley, 1990; Tausch, 1988).

To the extent that empathically understanding others means having access not only to their emotional worlds but also to their goals, intentions, and values, it seems important to be able to incorporate these to adequately capture the multifaceted and complex nature of the construct. In their factor analyses of the components of empathy, Lietaer (1974, 1992) and Gurman (1977) found six and five factors, respectively. In addition to affective understanding, other aspects of empathy included respect, unconditional positive regard, transparency, directivity, and congruence. To experience others as empathic, a person must not only feel that the other cognitively understands him or her but also have some sense that the other is involved and receptive to his or her concerns. Empathic understanding evolves as more information becomes available; thus, it is important for therapists to be responsively attuned moment to moment to the clients' narrative and different nuances of meaning.

No study shows a negative relationship between empathy and outcome. To the contrary, the majority of studies indicate a positive relationship between these two variables. A few studies have not found the relationship between empathy and outcome to be significant. Although these are often cited as evidence against it, Patterson (1983) emphasized that lack of significance does not disprove a hypothesis. Rather, given that the studies that have been reviewed are to a greater or lesser extent flawed, the flaws only serve to attenuate the relationship, and their existence speaks more to the actual strength of the findings than against them (Patterson, 1983).

Behavioral Correlates of Empathy

If one is to capture the complexity and interpersonal dynamic of empathy, then it is important to determine the criteria that people use to ascertain whether someone is empathic or not. A number of studies have tried to identify the behavioral correlates of empathy (Barkham & Shapiro, 1986; Barrington, 1961; Bergin & Jasper, 1969; Caracena & Vicory, 1969; D'Augelli, 1974; Gardner, 1971; Heabe & Tepper, 1972; Truax, 1966; Westerman, Tanaka, Frankel, & Khan, 1986). These studies have investigated four different areas associated with the communication of empathy: therapists' nonverbal behaviors, therapists' speech characteristics, therapists' response modes, and therapists' personal characteristics.

Researchers have found a relationship between certain therapists' nonverbal behaviors and perceptions of empathy. Heabe and Tepper (1972) observed that direct eye contact and a concerned expression contributed to therapists being perceived as empathic. In a similar study investigating therapist kinesic and proxemic cues, D'Augelli (1974) found that a forward trunk lean and head nods conveyed an empathic stance.

An examination of therapists' speech characteristics found that similarity between clients and therapists in their rate of speech, that is, the number of words spoken per minute, was positively related to clients' judgments of therapists' empathy (Barrington, 1961). Vocal tone has been found to affect clients' perceptions of empathy. A tone that communicates an expression of interest and as much emotional involvement and intensity as the client is feeling reflects empathy, whereas a tone that is bored and detached does not (Caracena & Vicory, 1969; Heabe & Tepper, 1972). Interruptions by the therapist are also seen as indicating less empathy (Pierce, 1971; Pierce & Mosher, 1967). In fact, Staples and Sloane (1976) found that successful clients spoke more often and had a longer total speech time than less-successful clients and that this was significantly related to therapists' empathy and warmth in the session. Moreover, a decrease in therapist verbosity from first to second interview was positively associated with clients' perceptions of empathy (Barrington, 1961). It has also been observed that there is a significantly shorter pause time by clients following therapist speech. Successful clients respond more quickly to their therapists' comments than less-successful clients (Staples & Sloane, 1976; Westerman et al., 1986). This is a good measure of the degree of synchrony, understanding, and comfort between the participants.

Further support for the importance of vocal quality was provided by a study of therapists' lexical styles conducted by Rice (1965), who found that distorted therapist vocal quality characterized by marked pitch variation and a sing-song quality was related to poor outcome in therapy. Another important dimension of therapist behavior relates to clarity of expression. Disorganized speech can be confusing and may convey incongruence to the receiver. The more clearly a message is communicated, the more understood clients feel (Bohart & Greenberg, 1997; Caracena & Vicory, 1969).

Specific types of therapist response modes are related to clients' perceptions of their therapists' level of empathic understanding. An increase in the percentage of emotional words used by therapists was positively related to clients' perceptions of their therapists' empathy (Barrington, 1961). Similarly, exploratory therapist responses are perceived as empathic. Clients rated reformulated reflections and exploration of their feelings as more empathic than general advice (Barkham & Shapiro, 1986). In contrast, advice and reassurance were negatively correlated to therapist empathy.

More recent studies have sought to examine the therapeutic relationship by looking at specific therapist responses as classified by the Structural Analysis of Social Behavior (SASB; Benjamin, 1974). These studies have found that successful outcome cases across different modalities are characterized by a high proportion of therapist statements that express understanding, attentive listening, and receptive openness to the client's perspective (Henry, Schacht, & Strupp, 1986; Watson, Enright, & Kalogerakos, 1998). In contrast, numerous studies report that critical, hostile, and controlling statements are negatively associated with successful outcome in psychotherapy (Henry et al., 1986; Lorr, 1965; Watson et al., 1998).

A number of studies have sought to look at specific therapist qualities and their relationship to empathy. Tosi (1970) found that dogmatic counselors, as measured by the Rokeach Scale, were seen by their clients to provide a relatively unfavorable therapeutic climate. In a more recent study, Nerdrum (1997) found that therapists who were self-confident in social situations, open, curious, nonjudgmental, and noncategorizing toward others were more empathic after empathy training than those who did not display these qualities. In a study contrasting more- and less-effective therapists, Lafferty et al. (1989) found that less-effective therapists placed more importance on having a stimulating and prosperous life than more-effective therapists, who valued intelligence and reflection. Client–therapist similarity may enhance the experience of empathy (Feshbach & Roe, 1968). Some studies have investigated the relationship between therapists' empathy and their similarity to their clients in terms of race and gender. They found, using both nonparticipant and participant ratings, that more facilitative relationships are established between intraracial dyads than interracial ones (Gardner, 1971; Orlinsky & Howard, 1986; Sattler, 1970) and that female clients experience female therapists as warmer than male therapists (Gurman, 1977).

If one is to facilitate one's understanding of empathic processes in the therapeutic relationship and enhance training, more time needs to be spent researching and identifying the specific behaviors that communicate empathy to others. Currently, I am testing a new measure of empathy based on therapists' nonverbal and verbal behaviors (Watson, 1999). Other than the studies that have looked at therapist and client interactions using SASB, there has been little attention paid recently to refining the operational definitions of empathy, despite numerous reviews indicating its importance (Barkham & Shapiro, 1986; Gurman, 1977; Orlinsky & Howard, 1986).

TRANSLATING RESEARCH INTO PRACTICE

Hogan's (1969) research characterized empathic individuals as imaginative, perceptive, aware of their impact on others, insightful into themselves, and able to evaluate and consider other people's motives. All these characteristics would seem to be important to understand another. Thus, to be empathic, therapists need to be warm, receptive, involved, attentive, concerned, responsively attuned, and exploratory in their communications (Fiedler, 1950a; Luborsky et al., 1988; Rogers, 1965, 1975; Strupp et al., 1969; Waskow, 1963). Therapists can communicate empathy nonverbally by looking concerned, being attentive, leaning forward, looking at their clients directly, and through sensitive vocal quality. Therapists' voices convey empathy and understanding when they are concerned and expressive, with an inquiring, tentative tone. They need to be able to communicate their understanding simply and clearly, using fresh, connotative language, and they need to limit their own verbosity so as not to overwhelm their clients. Most importantly, they need to be responsive to feedback and to alter their perspective or understanding as they acquire more information about their clients. Rice (1965) observed that truly empathic therapists have a high tolerance for ambiguity as they help clients' to unfold their inner worlds. In addition, therapists, like good parents, need to be consistent in the provision of empathy. Kalfas (1974) found that clients who reported more variable ratings of empathy did more poorly than clients who rated their therapists as consistently empathic over the course of therapy.

Truly empathic therapists understand their clients' goals for therapy overall as well as moment to moment in the session as they try to grasp the live edges of clients' narratives. The primary task is to illuminate the nuances and inflections of what people say and reflect them back to them for their consideration. However, because clients express themselves on multiple levels, therapists can choose to focus on their clients' feelings, behaviors, perceptions and construals, values, assumptions, other people, and situations. Therapists need to engage continually in process diagnoses to determine the focus of their empathic responses from one moment to the next. This task is easier if clients are actively exploring their experiences and providing live descriptions because this helps cue therapists to what is relevant. However, the task of listening empathically is more difficult when clients are describing their experiences in deadening ways or are engaged in self-observation and analysis. At these times, therapists can try to use metaphor to evoke clients' experiences, or ask clients to be more concrete and specific about events to evoke their episodic memories to help access their inner subjective experience.

Therapists can assist clients to symbolize their experiences and track their emotional responses by attending to what is not said or what is at the margins or on the peripheries of clients' experiences. For example, when clients are rational and analytical, it may be important for them to try to represent empathically their emotional reactions. Alternatively, when clients are being emotional, it may be important to have them fill in the details of their situation, to make their narratives more concrete and grounded. As Rice (1965) observed, an important function of successful therapy is to help clients get out of repetitive thinking grooves. Next, I discuss the different ways of being empathic.

Empathic Responses

A number of different types of empathic responses have been identified. These include empathic understanding responses, empathic affirmations, empathic evocation, empathic exploration, and empathic conjectures (Greenberg & Elliott, 1997; Greenberg et al., 1993; Watson et al., 1998).

Empathic Understanding Responses

These are simple responses that convey understanding of clients' experiences. For example,

> Client: I have spent the entire day running after job interviews and I am fed up.
> Therapist: It sounds like it has been a frustrating day.
> Client: Oh yes! I feel exhausted and a little despondent that anything will come of it.
> Therapist: So your effort seems wasted right now?

Empathic Affirmations

These are attempts by the therapist to validate the client's perspective. For example,

> Client: He was just so cutting, treating me like a total fool.
> Therapist: Oh, it sounds like you felt he dismissed you, totally scorned your ideas?
> Client: Yes . . . yes exactly . . . it was so humiliating and I had put so much effort into it.
> Therapist: So it left you feeling ashamed and, what, somehow disappointed that your effort wasn't appreciated?

Empathic Evocations

The goal of these responses is to bring the client's experience alive using rich, evocative, concrete, connotative language. For example,

> Client: I am not sure what I feel. I'm so confused . . . I just don't think it is going to get any better and I don't know what to do about it.
> Therapist: Am I right in getting a sense that it is almost as if the lights have gone out and you are just not sure you know where the light switch is to turn them on again.
> Client: That's it . . . I hadn't quite thought of it like that but I do feel as if I am sitting all alone in the dark . . . lost and confused.

Empathic Exploration Responses

These have a probing, tentative quality. They are attempts by the therapist to help clients *unfold* and examine the corners and hidden depths of their experiences. These may focus clients on their feelings, evaluations, or assumptions. For example, a therapist trying to help a client represent her sense of loss and inability to let go after her partner left responded to the client in this way:

> Client: I keep hoping he'll call.
>
> Therapist: Somehow you just can't let go? What, it's almost like you sit there waiting for the phone to ring and even though there is only silence and emptiness, it's just so hard to get up and walk away somehow . . . ?
>
> Client: I keep hoping he will come back. If I stop waiting then it really is over (weeping softly).
>
> Therapist: So somehow staying keeps the door open?
>
> Client: Yes. I guess I have been reluctant to move on . . . but that keeps me sad.

Empathic Conjectures

These are attempts by therapists to get at that which is implicit in clients' narratives. They are similar to interpretations but are not attempts to provide clients with new information. They are grounded in the data even though the information may not be in the foreground. For example, a client, who was having difficulty separating from her mother, was angry when her mother canceled a visit for the weekend.

> Client: My mother left a message on my machine on Friday saying she couldn't make it in on Saturday. Something about my father wanting to fix something on the farm . . . sigh . . . there is always something more important to do . . . I feel so angry with her.
>
> Therapist: I noticed you sighed when you were talking about it . . . am I right in getting a sense that you felt disappointed, what, pushed aside?
>
> Client: Yes! I hadn't been so aware of that till now, but I did feel . . . well . . . jilted almost. I always had to sacrifice what I wanted for the farm and, of course, mother was always trying to keep the peace with dad so he always got his way.

Markers for Empathic Responding

Other cues that therapists can use to alert them for when to be empathic with clients are their own responses, especially their feelings (Vanaerschot, 1990, 1997), images, memories, or resonance to the poignancy of clients' stories. For example, if therapists experience a feeling, either similar to the client's or complementary, like protectiveness or concern for a client's pain, this may be a cue to respond empathically in the moment. In addition, therapists need to attend to clients' statements and behaviors in the session. Some markers for when therapists can be differentially empathic are described below.

Clients' Expression of Live, Immediately Experienced Feelings in the Session

Therapists should respond empathically to moments when clients' feelings are very alive in the session. Such moments are apparent when clients' voices break, when they are crying or expressing anger or fear (Rice, Koke, Greenberg, & Wagstaff, 1979). Other signs that are possible indicators that clients are in touch with their emotions include moments when clients' descriptions are intensely poignant, or when they use vivid, idiosyncratic language. At these times, therapists may have strong inner responses to their clients' narratives. When clients are experiencing their feelings intensely, it is important for therapists to be empathically affirming and validating of their experience. Therapists need to be able to allow clients a safe place to freely and openly experience their feelings without fear of censure or embarrassment and self-consciousness. They need to acknowledge openly their clients' expressions of pain and vulnerability. Often clients do not take the time to sit with painful or difficult feelings, and even as they begin to cry and access them, they have a tendency to rush on with their stories. At these times, it is important for therapists to help clients experience and acknowledge their feelings before resuming exploration. They need to take a little time before asking clients to differentiate their feelings more or to analyze them in more depth. Conversely, this is not a time to challenge the intensity of the clients' feelings. Therapists can deliberately slow down the process by asking clients to slow down. For example, a therapist might say, "Hang on a minute, you seem to be tearful. Can we stay there a minute . . . it hurts when you talk about your Dad? It's just so painful to recall those memories?" This gives clients permission to experience and express their pain and begins to articulate the important task for clients in experiential therapy—that of attending to and processing their emotional experience.

Although research indicates that interruptions are not perceived as empathic, it is important for therapists to be able to gently direct the process and not let clients ramble without direction. One way of making interruptions more empathic is for therapists to provide explanations of their intentions and process suggestions so that clients can agree whether to follow or not. For example, for those clients who speak so quickly that therapists do not have time to interject, a therapist might respond with "Hang on a minute, can I just see whether I have understood you properly. Am I right in getting a sense that you are feeling lonely?" As long as interruptions maintain the focus on the client and are not attempts to hijack the conversation, then they are less likely to be experienced as intrusive and disrespectful.

Analytical Descriptions of Self and Situations

These refer to times when clients are describing themselves as if they were observing a third party. They may appear rational, and their narratives tend to sound rehearsed. There is a tight, seamless quality to what they are saying. Consequently, the therapist feels that there is no way in and no way of seeing other views. At these times, therapists can try to help clients access their feelings and become aware of the impact of events and their significance by using empathic explorations and evocative empathic responses. Using empathic reflections and evocative language, therapists can try to focus on clients' inner experiences. Alternatively, therapists can try to empathically conjecture what their clients are feeling on the basis of what they may feel in a similar situation, or what they imagine their clients may feel given their current knowledge of them.

Reports of Intense Emotions, Reactions, or Repetitions of Some Aspect of Experience

These are usually good clues that clients need to process certain experiences or that certain issues are problematic. After responding with empathic understanding to their clients' feelings, therapists may then attempt to facilitate clients' exploration of their reactions using empathic explorations. For example, if a client found himself flying off the handle, an empathic response by the therapist might be: "It just felt that there was no other way of responding right then, you just felt so enraged. What was happening in the situation?" While this response is empathic in conveying the client's sense of the situation, it also begins to open up the situation for further exploration. Similarly, if clients constantly talk about their emotional reactions while leaving the details hazy, an empathic evocative response might be useful to enable them to give the therapist a clearer sense of their situations. This helps ground clients' reactions in real events so that their patterns of responding become clearer and can be examined more fully.

Expression of Evaluations and Assumptions

When clients are judgmental of themselves or others or make assumptions without considering alternatives, it is often *not* useful to respond with empathic understanding responses. Rather, it is more helpful to slow clients down and empathically explore with them their assumptions or evaluations. For example, one client who was very angry with her husband after he lost his job and was unable to find work said:

> Client: Oh! I am just so frustrated with Fred. He just sits on the sofa all day long and refuses to do something to improve his situation.
> Therapist: You just feel so angry. It is just so hard for you to see him lying there kind of what . . . depressed and hopeless?
> Client: Yes . . . yes . . . I guess seeing him so depressed scares me. I am scared he'll drag us both down or that he'll never get going again.

At these times, therapists are trying to get clients to articulate their perceptions and reactions to the events in their lives so they can reevaluate and reexamine them.

Alternatively, when clients are expressing negative evaluations of themselves, therapists can implement two-chair work (Greenberg et al., 1993). The objective at these times is to elicit clients' affective reactions to their self-criticisms so that alternative responses that are more enhancing and valuing of the self can be accessed. The main purpose of these interventions is to help clients generate new and different reactions to events.

There are times when it is useful to empathically reflect clients' values. This response is likely to be helpful after clients have symbolized their experiences both in terms of what is happening in their worlds and in terms of their inner affective reactions. When clients are carefully scrutinizing their values and assumptions in the light of new and additional information, it is helpful for therapists to facilitate this period of reflection with empathic understanding as clients weigh the utility and relevance of their values and assumptions.

Expressions of Rupture in the Relationship

Therapists need to be alert to possible ruptures in the therapeutic relationship. Signs of possible ruptures include moments when clients refuse to perform or engage in certain activities in therapy, or they suddenly go blank or fall silent. Therapists need to become attuned to the rhythm of a session. Therapists can monitor the latency of clients' responses. If there is a very long delay between their statements and their clients' responses, this might indicate something is wrong in the alliance (Westerman et al., 1986). In the event therapists they feel a certain resistance or lack of responsiveness on the part of their clients, they might wish to self-disclose their perceptions and ask their clients for feedback. At these times, it is very important for therapists to be open and receptive to their clients' feelings. Empathic understanding and affirmation can help clients to openly discuss any difficulties they are having in the therapy. These difficulties can then be explored so that the tasks and goals of therapy can be renegotiated. It is important, at these times, for therapists to disclose their own thoughts, feelings, and experience in a nondefensive way so that clients can become aware of how they are feeling and what is going on for them (Watson & Greenberg, 1998). For example, if a client suddenly goes blank or the session seems to drag, the therapist can inquire: "Did something happen just then?" or "Things seem slow today. Is anything wrong?"

EMPATHY AS AN ACTIVE INGREDIENT OF CHANGE: A PROPOSED THEORY

Research on empathy reveals that it is an essential component of successful therapy across all modalities (Burns & Nolen-Hoeksma, 1992;

Greenberg et al., 1993; Linehan, 1997; Luborsky et al., 1988; Miller et al., 1980; Raue & Goldfried, 1994; Rogers, 1965, 1975; Rounsaville et al., 1981; Rowe, 1997; Safran & Wallner, 1991; Strupp et al., 1969). All therapeutic approaches see empathy as essential to building a positive working relationship with clients. However, the focus and function of empathic understanding are conceptualized differently across orientations. Empathic practices change according to the specific tasks and goals of therapy endorsed by each approach. In cognitive–behavioral approaches, empathy is used in the service of identifying core cognitions and accessing affective reactions (Burns & Nolen-Hoeksma, 1992; Linehan, 1997; Safran & Segal, 1990). In psychodynamic approaches, it is used in the service of facilitating understanding of the transference and clients' interpersonal patterns of behavior (Kohut, 1971; Luborsky et al., 1988; Strupp et al., 1969). In experiential and humanistic approaches, empathy is used to reveal clients' affective reactions and deconstruct their phenomenological world views to promote more satisfying ways of being (Bohart & Tallman, 1997; Keil, 1996; Rice, 1974; Rogers, 1975; Vanaerschot, 1997; Watson & Greenberg, 1998).

Most approaches regard empathy as the essential background condition that facilitates the implementation of the active interventions or the change mechanisms. However, I would like to suggest that empathy has a much more figural and important role in therapy as an active ingredient of change. Linguistic analyses of empathic responses have demonstrated that they function similarly to interpretations, paradoxical interventions, and reformulations (Havens, 1978a, 1978b; Troemel-Ploetz, 1980). But unlike these other interventions, empathic reflections do not violate clients' senses of autonomy but rather foster and maintain more egalitarian relationships than the other types of interventions. As an active ingredient of change, empathy has three important functions in therapy: (a) It promotes a positive working alliance; (b) it deconstructs clients' world views and assumptions; and (c) it promotes and enhances clients' capacities to regulate their affect.

The Interpersonal Function of Empathy

At its most basic level, empathy helps clients to feel safe. Empathic responses help clients to feel heard, understood, and supported. A sense of safety enables clients to focus on their concerns within the therapeutic hour. In addition to creating a safe place, therapists' empathy is important in forming and maintaining the therapeutic alliance. Empathy is vital to negotiating agreement on the tasks and goals of therapy. Empathic therapists are able to monitor their interactions with their clients and modify their responses if their clients are having difficulties in therapy. By being sensitive to the impact of their interventions on clients and to the overall quality of the alliance, empathic therapists are alert for ruptures as well as moment-to-moment shifts in the relationship during a session and over the course of therapy.

The Cognitive Function of Empathy

Empathic responses help to deconstruct clients' world views, constructions, and assumptions about self and others. From this perspective, an empathic therapist is to the client as the translator is to the text. Umberto Eco (1998), recalling the Whorf–Sapir hypothesis (Whorf, 1956, cited in Di Vesta, 1974) in a series of lectures discussing text and translations, argued that there is not a one-to-one correspondence between different languages because of different cultural, historical, and contextual knowledge bases. Thus, for translations to be successful at distilling and rendering the overt and implicit meanings in an original text, sometimes the literal translation must be altered.

This perspective highlights the hermeneutic aspects of empathy (Keil, 1996; Watson & Greenberg, 1998). Therapists are seen as engaged in revealing their clients' meanings and intentions just as translators are charged with revealing the author's intentions in a text. Just as translators and readers may be aware of and reveal additional meanings and references in a text of which the author was not fully aware (Eco, 1998), so too, therapists distill and reflect the various meanings in clients' narratives. These reflections may illuminate aspects of their experience of which clients may be aware only dimly. Empathic responses can assist clients in deconstructing their world views so that they become aware of the subjectivity of their perceptions. An awareness of the subjective nature of their perceptions assists them in being more hypothetical in their formulations of events so as to increase their range of action.

Empathic therapists perform a number of important tasks as they reflect and deconstruct their clients' world views. First, empathic reflections act as microinterpretations of clients' world views as therapists distill the implicit meanings in clients' narratives. As with translations, sometimes the translator is more aware of the complexity of an utterance than is the writer or speaker. Second, empathic responses result in a process of negotiated meaning so that a shared construction of clients' worlds emerges. Third, in the process of building a shared view, clients and therapists are actively engaged in deconstructing clients' phenomenological and subjective world views, as their values, goals, contexts, histories, and the significance of events become revealed and reflexively reconsidered.

The Affective Function of Empathy

Empathy helps clients to regulate their affect and learn to soothe themselves. Affect regulation is an important topic of investigation for social, developmental, and neuropsychologists (Feschbach, 1997; Gross & Muñoz, 1995, Hoffman, 1982; van der Kolk, 1994, 1996). These researchers are recognizing the important role that early attachment experiences have in people's capacities to regulate their emotions and their neurophysiological functioning. Clients who come to therapy are often experiencing acute and chronic conditions related to dysregulation in their affective systems. For example, depression, anxiety, and other disorders like substance abuse and anorexia are often attempts by clients to regulate negative affective states. Empathic responding begins to help clients regulate their emotions both within the session and in the long term.

From this perspective, empathy is to the client as responsive attunement is to the infant. First, there is a tremendous sense of relief and comfort when one feels fully understood in the moment even when experiencing intense and painful emotions. Second, by helping clients to access and process their emotions, therapists are teaching them to contain their emotions by reflexively accessing and symbolizing them in the session. This helps clients become more emotionally resilient by developing more awareness and understanding of their emotional experience and by expressing it more adaptively and functionally (Kennedy-Moore & Watson, 1999). Third, the experience of being listened to empathically helps clients build more positive, nurturing introjects and develop ways of responding to themselves that are more affirming, protective, and soothing. In this way, clients are able to alter their self-concepts and become more accepting and less judgmental of themselves. Developing a more nurturing and affirming repertoire of behaviors toward themselves is especially important for those clients whose attachment experiences have failed to help them develop these attitudes toward themselves as a result of neglect, abuse, or other environmentally stressful experiences (Barrett-Lennard, 1997; Rogers, 1975).

CONCLUSION

In conclusion, to be fully empathic, therapists have to be aware of what is occurring moment to moment in their relationships with their clients and understand their clients' emotional logic. Fiedler (1950a) found that novice therapists understood their clients intellectually but not emotionally. They had difficulty thinking along clients' lines of thought. To understand intellectually is to comprehend the surface meaning of what clients are saying but not the subtext. Full empathy grasps the meaning, feeling, and essence of clients' experiences. It requires the therapist to immerse himself or herself in the experience of the other—to taste it, to smell it, to feel it in order to grasp its edges and implicit aspects. Therapists need to be able to be responsively attuned to their clients and to understand them emotionally as well as cognitively. When empathy is operating at all three levels—interpersonal, cognitive, and affective—it is one of the most powerful tools therapists have at their disposal.

REFERENCES

Bachelor, A. (1988). How clients perceive therapist empathy: A content analysis of perceived empathy. *Psychotherapy, 26,* 372–379.

Bachrach, H., Luborsky, L., & Mechanick, P. (1974). The correspondence between judgements of empathy from brief samples of psychotherapy, supervisor's judgements and sensitivity tests. *British Journal of Medical Psychology, 47,* 337–340.

Barkham, M., & Shapiro, D. A. (1986). Counselor verbal response modes and experienced empathy. *Journal of Counseling Psychology, 33,* 3–10.

Barrett-Lennard, G. T. (1962). Dimensions of therapist response as causal factors in therapeutic change. *Psychological Monographs, 76*(43, Whole No. 562).

Barrett-Lennard, G. T. (1973). *Relationship inventory.* Unpublished manuscript, University of Waterloo, Waterloo, Ontario, Canada.

Barrett-Lennard, G. T. (1997). The recovery of empathy toward self and others. In A. Bohart & L. S. Greenberg (Eds.), *Empathy reconsidered* (pp. 103–121). Washington, DC: American Psychological Association.

Barrington, B. L. (1961). Prediction from counselor behavior of client perception and of case outcome. *Journal of Counseling Psychology, 8,* 37–42.

Benjamin, L. S. (1974). Structural analysis of social behavior. *Psychological Review, 81,* 392–425.

Bergin, A. E. (1966). Some implications of psychotherapy research for therapeutic practice. *Journal of Abnormal Psychology, 77,* 235–246.

Bergin, A. E., & Jasper, L. G. (1969). Correlates of empathy in psychotherapy: A replication. *Journal of Abnormal Psychology, 74,* 477–481.

Beutler, L. E., Johnson, D. T., Neville, C. W., Jr., & Workman, S. N. (1973). Some sources of variance in accurate empathy ratings. *Journal of Consulting and Clinical Psychology, 40,* 167–169.

Bohart, A., & Greenberg, L. S. (1997). *Empathy reconsidered.* Washington, DC: American Psychological Association.

Bohart, A., & Tallman, K. (1997). Empathy and the active client: An integrative cognitive–experiential approach. In A. Bohart & L. S. Greenberg (Eds.), *Empathy reconsidered* (pp. 393–415). Washington, DC: American Psychological Association.

Bozarth, J. D. (1997). Empathy from the framework of client-centered theory and the Rogerian hypothesis. In A. Bohart & L. S. Greenberg (Eds.), *Empathy reconsidered* (pp. 81–102). Washington, DC: American Psychological Association.

Bozarth, J. D., & Grace, D. P. (1970). Objective ratings and client perception of therapeutic conditions with university counseling center clients. *Journal of Clinical Psychology, 26,* 117–118.

Brodley, B. T. (1990). Client-centered and experiential: Two different therapies. In G. Lietaer, J. Rombauts, & R. Van Balen (Eds.), *Client-centered and experiential psychotherapy in the nineties* (pp. 87–108). Leuven, Belgium: Leuven University Press.

Burns, D. D., & Nolen-Hoeksma, S. (1992). Therapeutic empathy and recovery from depression in cognitive–behavioral therapy: A structural equation model. *Journal of Consulting and Clinical Psychology, 60,* 441–449.

Caracena, P. F., & Vicory, J. R. (1969). Correlates of phenomenological and judged empathy. *Journal of Counseling Psychology, 16,* 510–515.

Carkhuff, R. R., & Burstein, J. W. (1970). Objective therapist and client ratings of therapist offered facilitative conditions of moderate to low functioning therapists. *Journal of Clinical Psychology, 26,* 394–395.

Cartwright, R. D., & Lerner, B. (1965). Empathy, need to change, and improvement in psychotherapy. *Journal of Consulting Psychology, 27,* 138–144.

Cross, D. G., Sheehan, P. W., & Khan, J. A. (1982). Short and long term follow-up of clients receiving insight-oriented therapy and behavior therapy. *Journal of Consulting and Clinical Psychology, 50,* 103–112.

D'Augelli, A. R. (1974). Nonverbal behavior of helpers in initial helping interactions. *Journal of Counseling Psychology, 21,* 360–363.

Di Vesta, J. J. (1974). *Language, hearing, and cognitive processes.* Monterey, CA: Brooks/Cole Publishing Company.

Duan, C., & Hill, C. E. (1996). The current state of empathy research. *Journal of Counseling Psychology, 43,* 261–274.

Eco, U. (1998, May). *Text and translation.* Lecture given at the University of Toronto, Toronto, Ontario, Canada.

Elliott, R. (1986). Interpersonal process recall (IPR) as a psychotherapy process research method. In L. S. Greenberg & W. M. Pinsof (Eds.), *The psychotherapeutic process* (pp. 503–528). New York: Guilford Press.

Feiffel, B. S., & Eels, J. (1963). Patients and therapists assess the same psychotherapy. *Journal of Consulting Psychology, 27,* 310–318.

Feschbach, N. (1997). Empathy: The formative years implications for clinical practice. In A. Bohart & L. S. Greenberg (Eds.), *Empathy reconsidered* (pp. 33–59). Washington, DC: American Psychological Association.

Feschbach, N., & Roe, K. (1968). Empathy in six and seven year olds. *Child Development, 39,* 133–145.

Fiedler, F. E. (1950a). A comparison of therapeutic relationships in psychoanalytic, nondirective, and Adlerian therapy. *Journal of Consulting Psychology, 14,* 239–245.

Fiedler, F. E. (1950b). The concept of an ideal therapeutic relationship. *Journal of Consulting Psychology, 14,* 239–245.

Fish, J. M. (1970). Empathy and the reported emotional experiences of beginning psychotherapists. *Journal of Consulting and Clinical Psychology, 35*, 64–69.

Gardner, L. H. (1971). The therapeutic relationship under varying conditions of race. *Psychotherapy: Theory, Research, and Practice, 8*, 78–87.

Gladstein, G. A. (1977). Empathy and counseling outcome: An empirical and conceptual review. *The Professional Forum, 6*, 70–79.

Goleman, D. (1996). *Emotional intelligence.* New York: Bantam Books.

Gonyea, G. G. (1963). The ideal therapeutic relationship and counseling outcome. *Journal of Clinical Psychology, 19*, 481–487.

Greenberg, L. S., & Elliott, R. (1997). Varieties of empathic responding. In A. Bohart & L. S. Greenberg (Eds.), *Empathy reconsidered* (pp. 167–186). Washington, DC: American Psychological Association.

Greenberg, L. S., Rice, L. N., & Elliott, R. (1993). *Facilitating emotional change.* New York: Guilford Press.

Gross, J. J., & Muñoz, R. F. (1995). Emotion regulation and mental health. *Clinical Psychology: Science & Practice, 2*, 151–164.

Gurman, A. S. (1973). Instability of therapeutic conditions in psychotherapy. *Journal of Counseling Psychology, 20*, 16–24.

Gurman, A. S. (1977). The patient's perception of the therapeutic relationship. In A. S. Gurman & A. M. Razin (Eds.), *Effective psychotherapy: A handbook of research.* New York: Pergamon Press.

Havens, L. L. (1978a). Explorations in the uses of language in psychotherapy: Complex empathic statements. *Psychiatry, 42*, 40–48.

Havens, L. L. (1978b). Explorations in the uses of language in psychotherapy: Simple empathic statements. *Psychiatry, 41*, 336–340.

Heabe, R. F., & Tepper, D. T., Jr. (1972). Nonverbal components of empathic communication. *Journal of Counseling Psychology, 19*, 417–424.

Henry, W. P., Schacht, T. E., & Strupp, H. H. (1986). Structural analysis of social behavior: Application to a study of interpersonal process in differential psychotherapeutic outcome. *Journal of Consulting and Clinical Psychology, 54*, 27–31.

Hill, C. E. (1974). A comparison of the perceptions of a therapy session by clients, therapists, and objective judges (Manuscript. No. 564). *JSAS Catalog of Selected Documents in Psychology, 4*, 16.

Hoffman, M. L. (1982). Developmental synthesis of affect and cognition and its implications for altruistic motivation. *Developmental Psychology, 11*, 605–622.

Hogan, R. (1969). Development of an empathy scale. *Journal of Consulting and Clinical Psychology, 33*, 307–316.

Horvath, A. O., & Symonds, B. D. (1991). Relation between working alliance and outcome in psychotherapy: A meta-analysis. *Journal of Counselling Psychology, 38*, 139–149.

Jordan, J. (1997). Relational development with mutual empathy. In A. Bohart & L. S. Greenberg (Eds.), *Empathy reconsidered* (pp. 343–351). Washington, DC: American Psychological Association.

Kalfas, N. S. (1974). Client perceived therapist empathy as a correlate of outcome. *Dissertation Abstracts International, 34*, 5633A.

Keil, W. (1996). Hermeneutic empathy in client-centered therapy. In U. Esser, H. Pabst, & G. Speirer (Eds.), *The power of the person-centered approach: New challenges, perspectives and answers.* Koln, Germany: GwG.

Kennedy-Moore, E., & Watson, J. C. (1999). *Expressing emotional myths, realities, and therapeutic strategies.* New York: Guilford Press.

Kiesler, D. J., Klein, M. H., & Mathieu, P. L. (1965). Sampling from the recorded therapy interview: The problem of segment location. *Journal of Consulting Psychology, 29*, 337–344.

Kohut, H. (1971). *The analysis of self.* New York: International Universities Press.

Kohut, H. (1977). *The restoration of self.* New York: International Universities Press.

Kurtz, R. R., & Grummon, D. L. (1972). Different approaches to the measurement of therapist empathy and their relationship to therapy outcomes. *Journal of Consulting and Clinical Psychology, 39*, 106–115.

Lafferty, P., Beutler, L. E., & Crago, M. (1989). Differences between more and less effective psychotherapists: A study of select therapist variables. *Journal of Consulting and Clinical Psychology, 57*, 76–80.

Lamb, W. K. (1981, June). *A meta-analysis of Rogers' core dimensions: A statistical reappraisal of the therapeutic effectiveness of empathy, warmth and genuineness.* Paper presented to the annual meeting of the Society for Psychotherapy Research, Aspen, CO.

Lambert, M. J., De Julio, S. S., & Stein, D. M. (1978). Therapist interpersonal skills: Process, outcome, methodological considerations, and recommendations for future research. *Psychological Bulletin, 85*, 467–489.

Lietaer, G. (1974, June). *The relationship as experienced by clients and therapist in client-centered and psychoanalytically oriented therapy.* Paper presented at the Fifth Annual Meeting of the Society for Psychotherapy Research, Denver, CO.

Lietaer, G. (1990). The client-centered approach after the Wisconsin Project: A personal view of its evolution. In G. Lietaer, J. Rombauts, & R. Van Balen (Eds.). *Client-centered and experiential therapy in the nineties* (pp. 19–46). Leuven, Belgium: Leuven University Press.

Lietaer, G. (1992). Helpful and hindering processes in client-centered/experiential psychotherapy: A content analysis of client and therapist post therapy perceptions. In S. Toukmanian & D. Rennie (Eds.), *Psychotherapy process research: Paradigmatic and narrative approaches* (pp. 134–162). Newbury Park, CA: Sage.

Linehan, M. M. (1997). Validation and psychotherapy. In A. Bohart & L. S. Greenberg (Eds.), *Empathy reconsidered* (pp. 353–392). Washington, DC: American Psychological Association.

Lorr, M. (1965). Client perceptions of therapists: A study of therapeutic relation. *Journal of Consulting Psychology, 29,* 146–149.

Luborsky, L., Crits-Christoph, P., Mintz, J., & Auerbach, A. (1988). *Who will benefit from psychotherapy? Predicting therapeutic outcomes.* New York: Basic Books.

Mahoney, M. (1995). *Human change process.* New York: Basic Books.

Marangoni, C., Garcia, S., Ickes, W., & Teng, G. (1995). Empathic accuracy in a clinically relevant setting. *Journal of Personality and Social Psychology, 68,* 854–869.

McWhirter, J. J. (1973). Two measures of the facilitative conditions: A correlation study. *Journal of Counseling Psychology, 20,* 317–320.

Mearns, D., & Thorne, B. (1988). *Person-centered counseling in action.* Newbury Park, CA: Sage.

Miller, W., Taylor, C. A., & West, J. (1980). Focused versus broad spectrum behavior therapy for problem drinkers. *Journal of Consulting and Clinical Psychology, 48,* 590–601.

Mintz, J., Luborsky, L., & Auerbach, A. H. (1971). Dimensions of psychotherapy: A factor analytic study of ratings of psychotherapy sessions. *Journal of Consulting and Clinical Psychology, 36,* 106–120.

Mitchell, K., Bozarth, J., & Krauft, C. (1977). A reappraisal of the therapeutic effectiveness of accurate empathy, nonpossessive warmth, and genuineness. In A. Gurman & A. Razin (Eds.), *Effective psychotherapy: A handbook of research* (pp. 482–502). New York: Pergamon Press.

Muller, J., & Abeles, N. (1971). Relationship of liking, empathy and therapists experience to outcome of psychotherapy. *Journal of Counselling Psychology, 18,* 39–43.

Nerdrum, P. (1997). Maintenance of the effect of training in communication skills: A controlled follow-up study of level of communicated empathy. *British Journal of Social Work, 27,* 705–722.

Orlinsky, D., Grawe, K., & Parks, B. K. (1994). Process and outcome in psychotherapy—Noch einmal. In A. Bergin & S. Garfield (Eds.), *Handbook of psychotherapy and behavior change* (pp. 270–376). New York: Wiley.

Orlinsky, D. E., & Howard, K. I. (1986). Process and outcome in in psychotherapy. In S. Garfield & A. Bergin (Eds.), *Handbook of psychotherapy and behavior change* (pp. 283–330). New York: Wiley.

Parloff, M. (1961). Therapist–patient relationships and outcome of psychotherapy. *Journal of Consulting Psychology, 25,* 29–38.

Parloff, M., Waskow, I., & Wolfe, B. (1978). Research on therapist variables in relation to process and outcome. In S. L. Garfield & A. E. Bergin (Eds.), *Handbook of psychotherapy and behavior change* (pp. 233–282). New York: Wiley.

Patterson, C. H. (1983). Empathy, warmth, and genuineness in psychotherapy: A review of reviews. *Psychotherapy, 21,* 431–438.

Pierce, W. D. (1971). Anxiety and the act of communicating and perceived empathy. *Psychotherapy: Theory, Research, and Practice, 8,* 120–123.

Pierce, W. D., & Mosher, D. L. (1967). Perceived empathy, interviewer behavior, and interviewee anxiety. *Journal of Consulting Psychology, 31,* 101–104.

Raue, P. J., & Goldfried, M. R. (1994). The therapeutic alliance in cognitive-behavior therapy. In A. O. Horvath & L. Greenberg (Eds.), *The working alliance: Theory, research, and practice* (pp. 131–152). New York: John Wiley & Sons, Inc.

Rice, L. N. (1965). Therapist's style of participation and case outcome. *Journal of Consulting Psychology, 29,* 155–160.

Rice, L. N. (1974). The evocative function of the therapist. In D. Wexler & L. N. Rice (Eds.), *Innovations in client-centered therapy* (pp. 289–311). New York: Wiley.

Rice, L. N., Koke, C., Greenberg, L. S., & Wagstaff, A. (1979). *Manual for client vocal quality* (Vol. I). Toronto, Ontario, Canada: York University, Counseling and Development Centre.

Rogers, C. R. (1965). *Client-centered therapy: Its current practice, implications, and theory.* Boston: Houghton-Mifflin.

Rogers, C. R. (1967). (Ed.). *The therapeutic relationship and its impact: A study with of psychotherapy with schizophrenics.* Madison: University of Wisconsin Press.

Rogers, C. R. (1975). Empathic: An unappreciated way of being. *The Counseling Psychologist, 5,* 2–10.

Rounsaville, B. J., Weissman, M. M., & Prusoff, B. A. (1981). Psychotherapy with depressed outpatients: Patient and process variables as predictors of outcome. *British Journal of Psychiatry, 138,* 67–74.

Rowe, C. E., Jr. (1997). Expanding attunement: A contribution to the experience near mode of observation. In A. Bohart & L. Greenberg (Eds.), *Empathy reconsidered: New directions in psychotherapy* (pp. 265–278). Washington, DC: American Psychological Association.

Safran, J. D., & Segal, Z. V. (1990). *Interpersonal process in cognitive therapy.* New York: Basic Books.

Safran, J. D., & Wallner, L. K. (1991). The relative predictive validity of two therapeutic alliance measures in cognitive therapy. *Psychological Assessment, 3,* 188–195.

Sattler, J. M. (1970). Racial experimenter effects in experimentation, testing, and psychotherapy. *Psychological Bulletin, 73,* 137–160.

Sexton, T. L., & Whiston, S. C. (1994). The status of the counseling relationship: An empirical review, theoretical implications, and research directions. *The Counseling Psychologist, 22,* 6–78.

Staples, F. R., & Sloane, R. B. (1976). Truax factors, speech characteristics, and therapeutic outcome. *Journal of Nervous and Mental Disease, 163,* 135–140.

Strupp, H. H., Fox, R. E., & Lessler, K. (1969). *Patients view their psychotherapy.* Baltimore: John Hopkins University Press.

Tausch, R. (1988). The relationship between emotions and cognitions: Implications for therapist empathy. *Person-Centered Review, 3,* 277–291.

Taylor, C. (1990). *Human agency and language*. New York: Cambridge University Press.

Tosi, D. J. (1970). Dogmatism within the counselor–client dyad. *Journal of Counseling Psychology, 17*, 284–288.

Troemel-Ploetz, S. (1980). I'd come to you for therapy—Interpretation, redefinition and paradox in Rogerian therapy. *Psychotherapy: Theory, Research, and Practice, 17*, 246–257.

Trop, J. L., & Stolorow, R. D. (1997). Therapeutic empathy: An intersubjective perspective. In A. Bohart & L. S. Greenberg (Eds.), *Empathy reconsidered* (pp. 279–291). Washington, DC: American Psychological Association.

Truax, C. B. (1966). Therapist empathy, warmth, and genuineness and patient personality change in group psychotherapy: A comparison between interaction unit measures, time sample measures, and patient perception measures. *Journal of Consulting and Clinical Psychology, 22*, 225–229.

Truax, C. B., & Carkhuff, R. R. (1967). *Toward effective counseling and psychotherapy*. Chicago: Aldine.

Truax, C. B., Carkhuff, R. R., & Kodman, F., Jr. (1965). Relationships between therapist offered conditions and patient change in group psychotherapy. *Journal of Clinical Psychology, 21*, 327–329.

Truax, C. B., Wargo, D. G., Frank, J. D., Imber, S. D., Battle, C. C., Hoehn-Saric, R., Nash, E. H., & Stone, A. R. (1966). Therapist empathy, genuineness and warmth and patient therapeutic outcome. *Journal of Clinical Psychology, 30*, 395–401.

Truax, C. B., Wittmer, J., & Wargo, D. G. (1971). Effects of the therapeutic conditions of accurate empathy, nonpossessive warmth, and genuineness on hospitalized mental patients during group therapy. *Journal of Clinical Psychology, 27*, 137–142.

van der Kolk, B. A. (1994). The body keeps the score: Memory and the evolving psychobiology of post-traumatic stress. *Harvard Review of Psychiatry, 1*, 253–265.

van der Kolk, B. A. (1996). The complexity of adaptation to trauma: Self-regulation, stimulus discrimination, and characterological development. In B. A. van der Kolk, A. C. McFarlane, & A. C. Weisaeth (Eds.), *Traumatic stress: The effects of overwhelming experience on mind, body and society* (pp. 3–23). New York: Guilford Press.

van der Veen, F. (1967). Basic elements in the process of psychotherapy: Research study. *Journal of Consulting Psychology, 31*, 295–303.

van der Veen, F. (1970). Client perception of therapist conditions as a factor of psychotherapy. In J. T. Hart & T. M. Tomlinson (Eds.), *New directions in client-centered therapy* (pp. 214–222). Boston: Houghton-Mifflin.

Vanaerschot, G. (1990). The process of empathy: Holding and letting go. In G. Lietaer, J. Rombauts, & R. Van Balen (Eds.), *Client-centered and experiential psychotherapy in the nineties* (pp. 269–294). Leuven, Belguim: Leuven University Press.

Vanaerschot, G. (1997). Empathic resonance as a source of experiencing enhancing interventions. In A. Bohart & L. S. Greenberg (Eds.), *Empathy reconsidered* (pp. 141–165). Washington, DC: American Psychological Association.

Waskow, I. (1963). Therapist attitudes and client behavior. *Journal of Consulting Psychology, 27,* 405–412.

Watson, J. C. (1999). *Measure of expressed emotion.* Unpublished manual, Department of Adult Education, Community Development, and Counselling Psychology, University of Toronto, Toronto, Ontario, Canada.

Watson, J. C., Enright, C., & Kalogerakos, F. (1998, June). *The impact of therapist variables in facilitating change.* Paper presented at the annual meeting of the Society for Psychotherapy Research, Snowbird, UT.

Watson, J. C., Goldman, R., & Vanaerschot, G. (1998). Empathic: A post modern way of being. In L. S. Greenberg, J. C. Watson, & G. Lietaer (Eds.), *The handbook of experiential psychotherapy* (pp. 61–81). New York: Guilford Press.

Watson, J. C., & Greenberg, L. S. (1998). The alliance in brief humanistic psychotherapy. In J. Safran & C. Muran (Eds.), *The therapeutic alliance in brief psychotherapy* (pp. 123–146). Washington, DC: American Psychological Association.

Watson, J. C., & Rennie, D. (1994). A qualitative analysis of clients' reports of their subjective experience while exploring problematic reactions in therapy. *Journal of Counseling Psychology, 41,* 500–509.

Westerman, M. A., Tanaka, J. S., Frankel, A. S., & Khan, J. (1986). The coordinating style construct: An approach to conceptualizing patient interpersonal behavior. *Psychotherapy, 23,* 540–547.

15

THE SELF IN PSYCHOTHERAPY

WILLIAM WATSON PURKEY AND PAULA HELEN STANLEY

The self is at the heart of humanistic psychotherapy. Beginning with the early work of Lewin (1935) and Goldstein (1939), continuing with Maslow (1954, 1956), Lecky (1945), Murphy (1947), and culminating with the classic work of Rogers (1947, 1951, 1954, 1958, 1959, 1961, 1965, 1970), the self has been the central ingredient in understanding human existence and the key to professional helping. The purpose of this chapter is to expand and extend early research on the self and psychotherapy by connecting it to recent and innovative work by a host of researchers.

Two caveats are necessary. First, this chapter presents only the tip of the vast iceberg regarding self-theory, self-esteem, self-actualization, self-realization, and many related concepts. Apologies are extended to the hundreds of contemporary researchers of self whose informative work is missing from this article.

Second, the self is a hypothetical construct. It is neither an established fact nor an all-inclusive theory of professional helping. Some individuals who esteem themselves highly do not show commensurate health or achievement, and there is no inevitable relationship between self and success (Robins & John, 1997). To confound things even more, there are issues regarding the culture-specific nature of the self that remain largely unexplained. However, the overwhelming body of contemporary research points insistently to some sort of subtle, pervasive, and profound relationship between the self and human health and happiness, sickness, and despair.

There appears to be a general agreement among psychotherapists that how a person views himself or herself has profound effects socially, psychologically, and even biologically (Dunn, 1985). As reported by Hartman and Blankstein (1986), positive and realistic self-perceptions are pivotal and are in fact a "necessary prerequisite" for psychological well-being. A negative self-view has been associated with a host of physical and psychological problems, including alcohol abuse (Hull & Young, 1983), anorexia nervosa and bulimia (Garner & Garner, 1986; Garner et al., 1992), and extreme shyness (Cheek, Melchior, & Carpentieri, 1986). According to Dunn (1985), "poor self concept is virtually synonymous with psychopathology" (p. 747).

UNDERSTANDING THE SELF

Studying the self has always been a daunting task. As Satir and Baldwin (1987) pointed out, the self is a very personal matter and can never be known in its entirety. Because the self is culturally bound, primarily implicit, and hypothetical, it is difficult to define (Pfuetze, 1958). However, an analysis of various explanations and a review of related research provide a host of relatively compatible avenues to understanding the self. Among these avenues are self-efficacy (Bandura, 1986, 1989, 1997a, 1997b), the "possible self" (Markus & Wurf, 1986, 1987; Nurius, 1986; Stein & Markus, 1994), the "whispering self" (Purkey, 2000), and self as a narrative (Greenberg, 1995; Polkinghorne, 1991; Singer & Salovey, 1993).

As constructed here, the self is defined as the totality of a complex, dynamic, and organized system of learned beliefs that an individual holds to be true about his or her personal existence. It is this self that provides consistency to the human personality and allows the individual to maintain a reference point for antecedents and consequences of perceptions and behaviors.

Markus and associates (Markus, 1977; Markus & Wurf, 1986, 1987) and Goldfried and Robins (1984) have offered a perspective on the self that focuses on individuals' self-schemas and possible selves. Finding traditional views of the self as too "monolithic," Markus (1977) argued that an individual's self-system is composed of self-schemas, which are defined as "cognitive generalizations about the self, derived from past experience, that organize and guide the processing of self-related information contained in the individual's social experiences" (p. 64). Markus proposed that one's self comprises the totality of information available to an individual as the result of past experience but contended that an individual does not make use of this total structure when undergoing day-to-day activities. Instead, people selectively extract from their vast storehouse of self-knowledge the information required to deal with specific events or experiences. The information selected results in the construction of self-schemas that help a person determine the specific stimuli selected for attention, the information to be remembered and incorporated into the self-system, and the inferences and decisions to be made in a particular context. This framework has value for psychotherapists who see self-identity as the heart of human personality. Embedded in the definition of self are five qualities. The self is (a) organized, (b) dynamic, (c) consistent, (d) modifiable, and (e) learned. These qualities can be illustrated by a simple drawing (see Figure 15.1).

Self Is Organized

Most self-theorists agree that the self has a generally stable quality that is characterized by internal orderliness and harmony. It is not simply a hodgepodge of cognitions and feelings. To picture this internal symmetry, consider Figure 15.1 and imagine that the large spiral represents the organized unity of the *global* self. The global self is orchestrated and balanced, centered on the "I", the self-as-subject. This I is the living connection with experience. Humans are aware of past, present, and future selves.

In addition to the I, the self also contains smaller units. These units can be thought of as "subselves" and represent the self-as-object, the various "me's" that are the objects of self-perceptions. Each of the me subselves

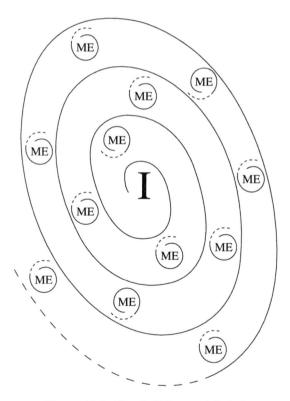

Figure 15.1. The Self-Concept Spiral.

within the global system contains its own balance, and each influences and is influenced by the global self. This idea is consistent with Ashcraft and Fitts's (1964) multifactoral approach to self-concept, which proposed that there are many dimensions of self-concept. Each person's self contains countless me's, but not all are equally significant. Some are highly important and are positioned close to the center of the self, the I. Other me subselves are less central and are located toward the periphery. Subselves closest to the I have the most influence on daily functioning; the individual "hears" these subselves the loudest. By the same token, subselves farthest away from the I have the weakest voices and have diminished influence on perceptions and behavior. For example, defining oneself as a Christian may have vastly greater impact than defining oneself as a golfer, and vice versa. Each subself carries its own plus or minus charge that contributes to the global self. Perceived success and failure tend to generalize throughout the entire self-system. When one me is important and highly valued, a failure in that dimension lowers the self-evaluation in other, seemingly unrelated, abilities. Conversely, success in a highly valued activity tends to raise self-evaluations in other, apparently unconnected, abilities.

Self Is Dynamic

Combs and associates (Combs, 1989; Combs, Avila, & Purkey, 1978; Combs & Gonzales, 1994; Snygg & Combs, 1949) have postulated that the maintenance, protection, and enhancement of the perceived self is the basic motivation behind all human behavior. It is important to note here that the self is not the cause of a person's behavior. For example, in the case of student misbehavior, the student's self does not cause the misbehavior to occur. A better explanation is that the disruptive student has learned to see himself or herself as a troublemaker and behaves accordingly. A person with a negative self-view, according to Swann (1997) and Andrews (1991, 1993), will seek self-verification that is consistent with his or her debilitating self-views. Bandura (1986, 1989), Seligman (1974, 1990), and others have demonstrated that individuals who view themselves as inefficacious in coping with environmental demands and expectations tend to dwell on their perceived deficiencies and view potential challenges and difficulties as far more difficult than they really are.

To understand the dynamic nature of the self, picture the global spiral (see Figure 15.1) as a sort of personal gyrocompass: a continuously active system of beliefs that dependably point to the "true north" of a person's perceived existence. This guidance system serves to direct actions and enables each individual to take a consistent stance in life. Rather than being viewed as the cause of behavior, the self is better understood as the gyrocompass of the human personality, providing cohesion in personality and direction for behavior (Andrews, 1993; Guidano, 1987).

Self Is Consistent

A singular feature of the self is that it requires internal consistency to maintain some degree of homeostatic autonomy (Andrews, 1991, 1993; Lecky, 1945; Swann, 1997). To maintain this consistency, people act in accordance with the ways they have learned to view themselves. From a lifetime of studying their own actions and those of others, people acquire expectations about what things fit and what behaviors are appropriate (Calderhead, 1996; Horney, 1939; Pajares, 1992; Snow, Corno, & Jackson, 1996). All subselves that exist within the global self are expected by the individual to be congruent with all others, no matter how incongruent they may appear from an external viewpoint. Psychotherapists who understand the tendency of the self toward consistency do not expect quick changes in clients (Raimy, 1971). The self is remarkably stable and cannot easily be modified or shaped into something more suitable or desirable. Whether a person's self is healthy or unhealthy, productive or counterproductive, it strives for consistency.

One final thought on the consistency of self is that being validated about one's beliefs about self is rewarding, even if the belief about the self is negative. A client who has lost both his job and his wife might take certain pleasure in stating: "See, just as I thought! Nobody gives a damn whether I live or die!" Being right—even about negative feelings toward oneself—can be self-satisfying. Swann (1997) suggested that therapists can use this tendency to hold a consistent view of self by giving clients accurate feedback that confirms their negative self-views. By confirming their self-view (e.g., "You do have difficulty in appropriately expressing your anger"), clients feel understood by the therapist and feel a sense of mastery and competence in the area of "knowing oneself." This confirmation sets the stage for client self-development.

Self Is Modifiable

In each reasonably healthy person, new perceptions filter into the self throughout life, while old ones fade away. This continuous flow creates flexibility in the self and allows for infinite modifiability (Pahkinen & Cabble, 1990; Raimy, 1948; Svartbert, Seltzer, & Stiles, 1996; Varble & Lanfield, 1969; Williams-Barnard & Lindell, 1992). A likely explanation for the assimilation of new ideas and the expulsion of old ones is the assumption that each person constantly strives to maintain, protect, and enhance the perceived self. This basic assumption is a tremendous "given" for the psychotherapist for it means that the self is predisposed toward development. Under the right conditions, significant positive change in self can be achieved (Andrews, 1993; Mahoney, 1991). Polkinghorne (1991) noted that people often seek therapy when the self-narratives that have provided unity for their personalities are no longer credible and when expectations are incongruent with reality. For example, a person who believes that hard work will always result in success may fail in business, although he or she worked hard at succeeding. The self-narrative that hard work equals success can be reconfigured to reestablish a coherent self-narrative.

According to Combs et al. (1978), Maslow (1954), and others, there is only one kind of human motivation, and this is an internal and continuous incentive that every individual has at all times, in all places, during all activities. It is to maintain, protect, and enhance the self of which one is aware. Viewing human motivation from this perspective means that therapists can best use their time and energies to encourage a cooperative spirit of mutual development, which brings us to a final quality of the self: It is learned.

Self Is Learned

Clients change their perceptions of self, for good or ill, in three general ways. The first way is through an extremely traumatic or ecstatic event as described by Persinger (1993) and Zahniser and Coursey (1995). All of us have witnessed how the tragic loss of a loved one, or the joyous arrival of a baby, can have such impact that the very structure of a person's self undergoes significant change (e.g., "I am now a widow" or "I am now a father!"). The impact of such momentous events, including religious conversion ("I am now saved!"), abruptly interrupts the internal balance of the self and tilts it in a new direction. Erikson (1959, 1968) suggested that such abrupt events force individuals to reevaluate their lives and bring about a renewed struggle with the definition of self.

A second way that people change the self is through a professional helping relationship, such as medical treatment, psychotherapy, or spiritual guidance. An abundance of empirical research has demonstrated that psychotherapy can be beneficial in altering the self (Beck, Rush, Shaw, & Emery, 1979; Carkhuff, 1969; Cartwright, 1957, 1961; Daste, 1985; Ellis & Bernard, 1985; Keilson, Dworkin, & Gelso, 1979; Osborne & Swenson, 1972; Polkinghorne, 1991; Rogers, 1961; Rogers & Dymond, 1954; Stein & Markus, 1994).

The third and most powerful way in which the self is changed is through life-long, everyday experiences. The gradual build-up, or wearing down, of one's self is accomplished through continuous interactions with the world. This process has been described by numerous authors, including Coopersmith (1967), Erikson (1968), McConville (1995), Purkey (2000), and others.

An essential aspect of humanistic psychotherapy is to invite clients to examine their perceived self and explore ways to keep it healthy. A healthy self maintains some congruence with the outer world while retaining some inner strength and efficacy (Benne, 1984). A healthy self is also one that is continuously involved in creating new visions of personal growth and development.

BRIEF HISTORY OF THE SELF AND PSYCHOTHERAPY

At the turn of the 20th century, when American psychology began to take its place among the other academic disciplines, there was a great deal of interest in the self. For example, when William James wrote *Principles of Psychology* (1890), his chapter on the "The Consciousness of Self" was the longest in two volumes. He differentiated between the self as knower (the I) and the self as known (the me). People may raise their self-esteem, James argued, either by succeeding in their endeavors or, in the face of disappointments, by lowering their sights and giving up certain pretensions.

Early 20th Century

During the early 20th century, Charles Horton Cooley (1902) used the metaphor of the looking-glass self to suggest that individuals' self-perceptions are, in part, formed as a result of their perceptions of how other people perceive them. This conception of self brought to the forefront of psychological, sociological, and philosophical thought an emphasis on human interactions and the importance of social comparisons in the development of self. Harry Stack Sullivan (1953), who created the interpersonal school of psychotherapy, proposed that the self did not exist as an individual entity but rather in relationship with others. One's self is embedded within the system of relationships one has and cannot be separated from them.

Thanks to a hectic period of theory building in the early 20th century, followed by strongly held positions on issues, most psychologists rallied around certain systems and organized schools that were characterized by ardent advocacy of their own theory and unrestrained hostility to opposing ones. When the smoke cleared, the radical behaviorism of J. B. Watson (1925) carried the day. Psychology was redirected, attention was turned to observable stimuli and response, and the inner life of the individual was beyond the scope of "scientific" psychology. Self, self-beliefs, self-esteem, and self-perception as psychological constructs were pushed into limbo, along with such internal constructs as mind, consciousness, awareness, and will. From the 1920s through the 1940s, the self received scant attention from the behavior-oriented psychologists who dominated American psychology. However, there were psychologists who continued to define the concept of self. Kurt Lewin (1935) viewed the self as a central and relatively permanent organization that gave consistency to the entire personality. Goldstein (1939) analyzed the process of self-actualization, rather than focusing on psychopathology. His work was a forerunner of Abraham Maslow's (1954) concept of self-actualization.

Coinciding with the zenith of behavioristic influence and the dominance of psychoanalytic thought in traditional psychotherapy circles came what is now referred to as the humanistic revolt in psychology and psychotherapy—the third force. Dissatisfied with the direction that psychology was taking, and apprehensive about what they considered a narrow and passive view of human existence represented by behaviorism and psychoanalytic thought, a group of psychologists and psychotherapists called for renewed attention to the self. In concert with existential and phenomenological movements of the 1950s and 1960s, the humanistic movement was born. As Diggory (1966) noted,

> the fact that the new self psychologists were able to argue substantive matters of learning theory and motivation with the heirs of the behaviorists made the latter pay attention and finally to agree that there might be something to the idea of self after all. (p. 57)

During the 1950s, 1960s, and 1970s, there was an enthusiastic renaissance of interest in the self. The research and writing of Ashcraft and Fitts (1964), Berzon and Solomon (1966), Brookover (1959, 1964), Cartwright (1957, 1961), Coopersmith (1967), Jourard (1971), Mazurkiewicz (1957), Purkey (1970), Raimy (1948), Snygg and Combs (1949), Truax, Carkhuff, Wargo, Kodman, and Moles (1966), Truax, Carkhuff, and Kodman (1965), Truax, Wargo, and Silberg (1966), Truax (1966), and Wylie (1957), among others, provided a deeper understanding of the dynamics of the self and psychotherapy.

The most eloquent and significant voice in this new humanistic movement was that of Carl Rogers (1947, 1951, 1954, 1958, 1959, 1961, 1970). In an influential series of articles, books, and lectures, Rogers presented a system of psychotherapy built around the importance of self in human adjustment. He believed that in every human being there is a drive toward self-actualization and growth so long as this is permitted and nurtured by environmental forces. Rogers's approach went far toward linking earlier notions about the self with solid research to support his observations. In fact, his impact was so powerful and influential that his general approach soon became known as *self theory*.

Late 20th Century

Research concerning the self took a different direction in the late 20th century as there was less direct focus on better understanding the nature of the self and more focus on determining the effect of psychotherapy on self-concept as measured by pencil-and-paper tests. The humanistic movement waned during the 1980s as psychologists shifted their interest to cognitive processes and information processing. This is not to say that interest in the self disappeared completely. In fact, it remained prominent, albeit with a qualitatively different face. In keeping with the "cold cognition" tradition of the cognitive revolution, research on the self maintained a measure of prominence and respectability by adopting a strong quantitative flavor. For a detailed description of the history and rediscovery of the self, see Bergin and Garfield (1994), Garfield and Bergin (1986), and Seeman (1988).

The present emphasis on the self is so pervasive that Graham and Weiner (1996), reviewing the state of knowledge related to theories and principles of motivation for the *Handbook of Educational Psychology*, observed that current research topics such as self-efficacy, learned helplessness, self-worth, and attributions

> reflect what is probably the main new direction in the field of motivation—the study of the self. If we add to this list the constructs of self-concept, self-focus, self-handicapping, self-monitoring, and the remainder of the "self" vocabulary then it is evident that the self is on the verge of dominating the field of motivation. (p. 77)

Next, we review some promising contemporary lines of research on the self.

CONTEMPORARY RESEARCH

With hundreds of entries under the listing of *self* appearing each year, consideration of contemporary research on the self is necessarily limited. The following appear to offer the most promise for applying the self in psychotherapy.

Self-Efficacy and Psychotherapy

The most prominent self-theorist among contemporary voices is that of Albert Bandura (who, like Maslow, is a former behaviorist). Bandura

(1986, 1997a, 1997b) wrote that individuals possess beliefs that enable them to exercise a measure of control over their thoughts, feelings, and actions. According to Bandura, the process of creating and using self-beliefs is simple enough: Individuals engage in behaviors, interpret the outcomes of their actions, and use the interpretations to develop beliefs about their capability to engage in subsequent behaviors in similar domains and act in concert with the beliefs created. This view of self as a mediating construct in human behavior is consistent with the views of humanistically oriented psychotherapists who have long argued that the potent evaluative nature of the self creates a filter through which all new phenomena are interpreted and subsequent behavior mediated. Behavior is not controlled by its consequences (as behaviorists long maintained) or by "unconscious" directives (as proposed by Freudian voices) so much as it is by personal constructions of its meaning or value in relation to the self.

Self-Concept and Psychotherapy

Rogers and Dymond (1954) and their colleagues at the University of Chicago developed a series of studies on the self and psychotherapy and found that positive changes in self resulted from therapy. These changes included "greater self-understanding, increased inner comfort, greater confidence and optimism, increased self direction and self-responsibility, more comfortable relationships with others, and less need for self-concealment" (p. 418). Counselor attitudes of nonpossessive caring were associated with client success in counseling. In a later study, Rogers (1961) reported that a person who successfully completes therapy perceives self as more worthy and becomes more accepting of others. In addition, there is more self-direction; one's beliefs are based on experience rather than relying on external influences. There is also less discrepancy between self and ideal self.

Williams-Barnard and Lindell (1992) found significant increases in self-concept scores of older adults who participated in counseling groups led by a leader who expressed high "prizing" (unconditional positive regard). Older adults who participated in a group where the leader demonstrated low prizing showed no increase in self-concept scores, and almost 50% showed a significant decrease in self-concept scores.

Changes in self and self-ideal have been the focus of much research in the area of self-concept. Brown and Kingsley (1975) reported that adolescents who developed an individual contract to achieve a personal goal in a counseling group showed positive, significant changes in self/self-ideal congruence at the completion of the group. Dombrow (1966) found that there was a significant relationship between therapist-offered empathy and reduction in self/self-ideal discrepancy. In contrast, Satz and Baraff (1962) reported that patients diagnosed as schizophrenic actually reported an increase, rather than decrease, in self/self-ideal discrepancy. In a study of counselor trainees, Stoner and Riese (1971) found no significant changes in "self as counselor" and "the ideal counselor's role" at the end of the academic term (p. 117).

Raimy (1948), a pioneer in studying the self and psychotherapy, reported that clients who experienced successful outcomes in counseling reported more self-approval referents and fewer self-disapproval referents than those who experienced less-successful counseling. More enhanced self-awareness and self-definition can be accomplished by challenging distorted beliefs about self or world (Beck et al., 1979; Ellis & Bernard, 1985).

Increased self-awareness was considered important in improving self-concept in many studies (Coopersmith, 1997; Fryrear, Huell, & Ridley, 1974; Hermans, Diffelaers, de Groot, & Nanta, 1990; Hlongwane & Basson, 1990; Mahoney, 1990; Page & Chandler, 1994; Truax et al., 1965, 1966). Encouraging the client to express deep feelings and identify self-perceptions appears to help clients develop a more real or authentic self (Anderson, 1985–1986; Auerbach, 1985; Coopersmith, 1997; Malon, Paulus, & Hurley, 1994; Miller, 1981; Robertiello, 1985–1986; Rudominer, 1985–1986). Using a case study approach, Hermans et al. (1990) studied a self-confrontation method to determine the "content and organization of the client's self and at the same time . . . to promote the reorganization of the self in the course of time" (p. 156). The case study analysis of one client revealed movement from a "a pattern of uncertainty and lack of direction" to a pattern of less uncertainty and more self-direction (p. 161). In a study of college freshman, Torrance (1954) found that students who have difficulty in college either overevaluate or underevaluate themselves. His research data revealed that overevaluators are likely to seek vocational counseling because of external pressures. Underevaluators initiate vocational counseling because they lack a clear self-definition.

Helping identify a client's strengths to improve self-concept was suggested or implied by a number of researchers (Fryrear et al., 1974; Hermans et al., 1990; Malde, 1988; Page & Chandler, 1994; Schectman, Gilat, Fos, & Flasher, 1996). In a study of disadvantaged urban adolescents, Washington (1977) found that group exercises helped adolescents develop trust in other group members and identify their personal strengths. Group members reported a more positive self-image as a result of the group experience. A photographic self-concept enhancement technique used by Fryrear et al. (1974) was associated with improvement of male juvenile delinquents who had poor body self-concept.

There is evidence that group counseling has positive effects on the self-concept. Guanipaa, Talley, and Rapane (1997) reported that Latin American immigrants who participated in an eclectic counseling group reported significantly higher scores on self-concept measures than those who only participated in a series of information sessions. In a study of Taiwanese students, Peterson, Chang, and Collins (1998) found no significant differences in self-concept between the scores of students who participated in a counseling group and those who participated in a teaching group. However, members of the experimental groups reported higher self-concept scores than the control groups. A study by Pahkinen and Cabble (1990) indicated that 229 Finnish students who participated in psychotherapy reported positive changes in self-concept, whereas the control group did not. The positive effect of psychotherapy on self-concept was still evident at the 5-year follow-up. An interactional group approach used by Schectman et al. (1996) improved self-perceptions of low-achieving elementary school children through activities, which encouraged self-expression and taught listening skills through structured activities, therapeutic games, and bibliotherapy. An activity-oriented self-concept counseling group and a discussion-oriented group were used by Page and Chandler (1994) to assist at-risk ninth graders in improving self-perceptions and behavior. Students in the self-concept group improved their self-concepts significantly when compared with a control group of students who received no treatment.

Analysis of Research on Self and Psychotherapy

Psychotherapy, according to Garfield and Bergin (1986), is not a distinctive profession. Rather, it is an activity performed by members of many different professions. Similarly, addressing the self in psychotherapy is not so much a science or technique as it is a way of being with the client (Holderstock, 1993, 1994; McConville, 1995; Rogers, 1961). This "being with" process reflects those attributes of humanistic psychotherapy listed by Rogers as the characteristics of the helping relationship (Gerber & Purkey, in press; Rogers, 1958, 1961). What we know from examining contemporary research is that the relationship between counselor and client does matter. That therapist-offered conditions of empathy, congruence, and unconditional positive regard provide a therapeutic climate in which clients feel safe to explore the nature of the self. As Rogers (1961) noted, clients begin to listen to themselves more as they experience the attention of the therapist. Clients increase in self-acceptance as they experience unconditional positive regard from the therapist. They also show greater acceptance for others. Self-definition becomes more crystallized, and the discrepancy between self and self-ideal tends to be reduced. Self psychologists, such as Victor (1985–1986), Anderson (1985–1986), and Erskine, Moursund, and Trautmann, (1999), also illuminate the importance of the therapeutic relationship as a consistent, safe environment in which therapist acceptance is key. The content and structure of the self changes as a result of successful therapy. Raimy (1948), Beck et al. (1979), Ellis and Bernard

(1985), and Purkey (2000) provided evidence that self-referents move from predominantly negative to positive with successful therapy. Individuals who over- or underevaluate themselves suffer from feelings of inadequacy and anxiety that may impair performance. Therapy can help individuals develop more realistic self-concepts (Torrance, 1954). Challenging counterproductive self-beliefs, such as overgeneralization or all-or-none thinking, can help create more healthy self-concepts and clearer self-definition (Beck et al., 1979; Ellis & Bernard, 1985). There is evidence that group psychotherapy is valuable in the self-change process. Feedback, acceptance, and support from other group members can facilitate changes in attitudes toward self. Educational groups have been found to be effective in improving self-concepts.

FROM RESEARCH TO PRACTICE

Working with the self in psychotherapy may begin with observations of the client's physical appearance, which can reveal current, and perhaps long-standing, attitudes toward the self. Poor care given to physical appearance may indicate devaluation of self. Interactions with the counselor may elucidate characteristics ways of interacting with others, such as seeking approval from others, seeking reliance on a person who is an authority, or seeking control of the counseling session.

Many researchers have emphasized the importance of helping the client achieve increased clarity of self-definition (Combs, 1989; Mahoney, 1991; Polkinghorne, 1991; Raimy, 1948; Rogers, 1951, 1959, 1961; Singer & Salovey, 1993; Stein & Markus, 1994). The self-concept is a hypothetical construct, which must be inferred from evidence. This is different from self-report, which is what an individual is willing and able to share, or can be induced into sharing, about the self. Because of this feature of the self-concept, psychotherapy of the self is the deepening of self-understanding by focusing, at first, on the client's perceived self. Therapy is, itself, partly a function of the client's own perceived existence.

Helping the client to define self has been accomplished by using the therapist-offered attitudes of empathy, unconditional positive regard, warmth, and respect. These attitudes provide a safe environment in which the client feels increasingly able to reveal self at deeper levels (Carkhuff, 1969; Rogers, 1961). Defenses are loosened, and material that was once considered unacceptable to the client becomes accessible to conscious experiencing and symbolization within the self (Rogers, 1961).

Exploring client self-narratives can be a useful way to develop greater self-understanding and self-definition (Polkinghorne, 1991; Singer & Salovey, 1993). Polkinghorne (1991) proposed that the self is not a substance but rather a "story that seems to configure a person's life into a self and to provide personal identity," which he called the *self-narrative* (p. 145). A goal of therapy is to determine the self-narrative, which provides the organizing themes for the client's life. One determines the story line of hero, martyr, pessimist, warrior, selfless one, or loser, for example. Within stories, one identifies dysfunctional plots, which are incorporations of values and beliefs that may represent the expectations or wishes of others. People often seek psychotherapy when their self-narratives are no longer adequate for dealing with life. For example, women who are battered by their husbands and refuse to leave the relationship express a plot that always ends with self-blame and guilt for not being able to prevent or stop the abuse. In this example, to reconstruct a coherent self-narrative would involve identifying dysfunctional plots (i.e., taking responsibility for others' behavior). The goal is to develop a self-narrative that is consistent with one's own needs, values, and beliefs rather than creating a self-narrative that is a "copy of someone else's story" (Polkinghorne, 1991, p. 150).

Singer and Salovey (1993) framed self-narratives as a collection of self-defining memories of which a person may have little awareness. In therapy, the client explores self by telling his or her life story, which is called the *remembered self*. Current life experiences are viewed and incorporated within the context of the remembered self, which results in a consistency in self-perception between the past, present, and future. In therapy, "one turns to the territory of the remembered self—narrative memories, important goals, and affective responses that link the past and future to the experiences of here and now" (p. 160). Self-defining memories may contain a *nuclear script* that reveal unresolved conflicts that can be identified in life goals, life choices, and relationships with others, including the therapist relationship (p. 172). Use of metaphor to identify nuclear scripts can be helpful because they illuminate the nature of script and underlying unresolved conflicts. The metaphor of a wall may describe the conflict between self and others. The therapist can explore the nature of the wall in terms of its material composition, height, and strength. One can explore how the wall works in therapy. As therapy progresses, one can note changes that might occur in the wall. Is the wall getting weaker? Is it lower or higher?

In addition to self-narratives, the self-concept can be assessed in terms of schemes and levels of self-understanding (Schorin & Hart, 1988). One can determine the schemes that are most salient for a client. Is there a greater focus on the physical, active, social, or psychological self-scheme? One's self-concept may seem most invested in one's appearance or athletic ability, for example. In addition, assessment of levels of self-understanding can be determined for continuity ("How do you know you're the same person you were 5 years ago?"), distinctiveness ("What makes you different from others?"), and volition ("How did you get to be the person you are?") (Schorin & Hart, 1988, pp. 172–173). Dunn (1985) proposed that therapeutic strategies be geared toward four self-concept deficits: individuation (lack of self-definition), internalization (lack of consistency between beliefs and actions), integration (lack of consistency in self-valuing in the face of situational factors), and adjustment (erosion of self-concept strength caused by external challenges). For example, to increase the individuation deficit, the therapist can develop a strong bond with client from which the client experiences emotional independence. To increase internalization of self, a focus on values clarification would be helpful.

The process of therapy of the self is one that encompasses the assessment of the initial status of self-understanding in the therapeutic process, the development of greater clarity of self based on recollection of past experience and its relationship to the present, and a reevaluation of self, with resulting changes in behavior. Reevaluation of self includes the content of self, valence of self-referents (positive or negative), and meaning of self. In the end, successful therapy will result in the client developing the ability to value the self as a reliable guide for behavior and worthy of respect from others.

The excerpts below from actual counseling sessions demonstrate use of self in psychotherapy. Each excerpt is accompanied by explanatory comments (italicized in parentheses).

Initial Session

The following excerpt is from a counseling session with a university student, Virginia, who experienced nervousness, nausea, and headaches that led her to the university medical clinic (Gerber & Purkey, in press). The physician referred her to a therapist (T). The name of the client (C) and the situation have been changed here to protect the confidentiality of the client.

> T: Let's begin by having you talk about yourself.
> (*Such a global request from the therapist can provide clues to the essential nature of the self. The therapist can closely observe nonverbal behaviors, posture, and paralanguage characteristics [i.e., rate of speech or tone of voice] to ascertain attitudes toward self.*)
> C: I'm a student at the university. The doctor at the clinic sent me to see you. I'm not sure why . . . I guess I'm supposed to figure out what is making me sick. The medicine he gave me is supposed to make me feel better. I'm afraid maybe I'm wasting your time.
> T: You're a student and experiencing . . . some physical concerns. The doctor sent you to me, you believe, to find out the cause of your symptoms. You don't want to waste my time.

C: Well, yes. I have been sick to my stomach and nervous at times.

(*It may be that real feelings, which have been at a very low level of awareness, are emerging. The dim realization that these feelings are incongruent with life choices may be the source of anxiety, which has resulted in physical symptoms.*)

T: At times . . .

C: Not at particular times during the day. More often just before test days . . . and when my fiancé is upset at me.

T: For example . . .

C: I really am having difficulty being around Tom. I love him, yet it's easier sometimes just to be alone.

T: Be more specific. Tell me of the most recent incident.

C: Well, last Sunday as we were getting out of the car to go get lunch, I noticed that his hair was sticking up. I said, "Tom, you just must do something about that cowlick." I thought I said it with a smile. He just glared at me and was cold and distant for the rest of the day.

T: You are feeling put off by his coldness and you're afraid to let him know how you feel.

C: I'm so mixed up. I like it when he is happy and when he pays attention to me. He is attractive and has a really good personality when we're around other people, but it seems like he is so sensitive around me that I can't be free to be myself. I'm constantly having to be careful, to avoid offending him.

(*This client appears to have difficulty in keeping a consistent positive view of self when she experiences disapproval from others [a lack of integration]. In addition, she adapts her self to significant others to avoid conflict. Her needs to fulfill self seem to be less important than pleasing others.*)

T: A part of you likes him. A part doesn't. A part of you wants to be with him. A part doesn't.

(*The therapist helps clarify the client's ambivalence toward her boyfriend. It appears that a lack of self-definition and self-integration may impair her ability to examine the relationship with her boyfriend in a realistic manner. It may be worth it to her to deny the real self for the security of the relationship. This is a possibility to consider.*)

A Subsequent Session

C: I feel a little better in my stomach and head, but I'm still confused about what to do. I visited with my older sister, and she told me that I should just dump Tom, that he is really a no good, narcissistic bum. She almost had me convinced, but then I went out with Tom, and he was so nice. Of course I didn't say anything to offend him.

T: Your sister seemed to take sides with that part of you that doesn't really like Tom. The other part was strengthened by your pleasant date.

C: Yes. It's almost like I don't have any control over myself. I just get tossed back and forth. I was thinking that I respond to my father that way. He'd be shocked to know I'm seeing a counselor, yet he has told me to be responsible.

(*The client describes herself as being "tossed back and forth," indicating a lack of self-definition and low feelings of self-worth. It appears that she has a history of letting others' behavior control her. Perhaps she has developed a self-narrative that includes an ineffective plot in which her role is to continually deny her real self to obtain the approval of others. The high price she pays for playing this role is becoming more apparent. Perhaps her self has become physically ill to get her attention. Her self-narrative needs some adjustment to include a more assertive and worthy self.*)

T: It's almost like you are reacting to Tom the same way you do to your father.

(*The therapist could have used a metaphor here to help the client develop clarity about the problem [i.e., "Like a leaf being tossed by the wind"]. Because there is a history of conflict avoidance, it is likely that the client has developed a self-confirmatory cycle, which sustains her behavior with others. She may be able to identify situations in which avoiding conflict and seeking approval from others seemed necessary for her survival or to feel safe. Self-schemas that define the self as inadequate or incompetent may be present.*)

C: And to my sister, and to my roommate. Jenny, my roommate, is constantly rearranging the furniture in our apartment. I really like things to be settled down and sort of samish, you know, but she gets really mad when I ask her why she is changing things again.

(*When the client can maintain a consistent view of herself as worthy, she can be more assertive with significant others in her life. Her sense of value will be based on self-knowledge and experience rather than others' evaluations of her. A clear self-definition is essential to setting appropriate boundaries with others.*)

This case example has demonstrated some of the uses of self in psychotherapy. The client revealed a poor self-definition and lack of self-worth, which was manifested in the need to avoid conflict and obtain approval from others. This pattern of behavior has been reinforced by repeated interactions with others in which anxiety was reduced for the price of self-denial. The client has begun the process of self-definition by exploring her feelings in relationship to others. Her physical illness may indicate that she is becoming more aware of her true feelings in that her historical patterns of behavior no longer provide the safety and security she hoped they would. Her emerging self creates ambivalence in her relationships with others. As she develops a clearer sense of who she is, she will have a stronger foundation from which to make choices about people and other aspects of her life.

The following excerpt is from *Client-Centered Therapy*, in which Carl Rogers provided transcripts from actual counseling sessions (Rogers, 1951, pp. 152–153). The client expresses his role of being the peacekeeper and the need to make other people happy by attending to their needs.

C: That's really the idea I've had. I think the whole business of my standards, or my values, is one that I need to think about rather carefully, since I've been doubting for a long time whether I even have any sincere ones.

(This client experiences and can articulate his sense of not knowing who he is and what he stands for. He reports that this feeling of not knowing what he stands for has existed for a long time. It would be helpful to know what "long time" means and what events or experiences may have precipitated this awareness.)

T: M-hm. Not sure whether you really have any deep values which you are sure of.

C: M-hm. M-hm.

T: You've been doubting that for some time.

C: Well, I've experienced that before. Though one thing, when I make decisions I don't have—I don't think—It seems that some people have—have quite steady values that they can weigh things against when they want to make a decision. Well, I don't and I haven't had, and I guess I'm an opportunist (laughing). I do what seems to be the best thing to do at the moment, and let it go at that.

T: You have no certain measuring rods that you can use.

(The therapist uses a metaphor that is consistent with the client's use of the concept of measuring things to make a decision—by weighing them. The therapist also chooses the word "certain" again to identify the client's emphasis on "steady" values.)

C: I was thinking about this business of standards. I somehow developed a sort of knack, I guess, of—well—habit—of trying to make people feel at ease around me, or to make things to along smoothly. I don't know whether that goes back to early childhood, or—I mean, to our family situation where there was a large family, and so many differences of opinion and all that there always had to be some appeaser around (laughing) and seeing into the reasons for disagreeing and being sorta the oil that soothed the waters.

(The client seems to be describing a self-narrative that defines himself as the go-between, the peacemaker, and the appeaser. The therapist can further explore this narrative by examining plots that are dysfunctional. This client excluded self to make sure others were included. Exploring other self-defining memories may help the client develop a clearer understanding of the origin of the self-narrative he describes. Further exploration of his memories as a child may reveal the origins of his need to make others happy and avoid standing up for his convictions. Exploring his remembered self may reveal nuclear scripts. Memories concerning relationships with parents and siblings would be of particular significance in developing an understanding of his behavior. What family dynamic made his role of making other people happy the easiest one "to play"? Has there ever been a time when he has stood up for his convictions? If so, what happened? If not, what does he imagine would happen if he did stand up for his convictions?)

The client in the above situation is aware that he does not know what values are important to him and that he has played the role of the appeaser and peacemaker from childhood. It is not clear what precipitated this awareness or when he first became aware of his lack of self-definition. This case example is one that illustrates the self-narrative that has given meaning to one's existence. In this case, the dysfunctional plot is the exclusion of self in relationship to others, in which meeting others' needs preclude meeting his own needs or even being aware of them. Although this plot may have functioned well for the client as a child, it no longer is adequate for life satisfaction.

CONCLUSION

This chapter has presented the concept that the use of self is an essential element in psychotherapy. Mahoney (1991) posed that "all psychotherapies are psychotherapies of the self" (p. 235). The nature of self, a brief history, contemporary research, and the use of self in psychotherapy were outlined. From the massive number of studies, we draw the following conclusions:

1. The self-concept, a hypothetical construct, can be inferred from evidence, but it is different from self-report, which is what an individual is willing and able to state, or can be induced into stating, about oneself.
2. Central to all perception is the individual's self. Things are not simply perceived, they are perceived in relation to one's own perceived existence.
3. Self-concept is at the very heart of human personality, and it is characterized by internal organization and stability.
4. The individual perceives different aspects of his or her self at different times with varying degrees of clarity. Therefore, *inner focusing* is a valuable tool in psychotherapy.
5. Any experience that is inconsistent with the self may be perceived by the experiencing person as a threat, and the more of these experiences there are, the more rigidly the self is defended. When a person is unable to get rid of perceived inconsistencies, psychological problems arise.
6. Because the self does not appear to be instinctive but is a social product developing through perceived experience, it possesses relatively boundless potential for actualization.
7. Focusing on the client's perceived self is a valuable aspect to psychotherapy.

In sum, the search for self in psychotherapy is a fragile and delicate adventure, in which clients and therapists work together on their voyage to the center of the self. It now seems abundantly clear that the self is the major player in humanistic psychotherapy, for it is the self that makes humans human.

REFERENCES

Anderson, J. (1985–1986). Finding the concealed self in the "selfless" patient. *Psychotherapy Patient, 2,* 59–70.

Andrews, J. D. (1991). Integrative psychology of depression: A self-confirmation approach. *Psychotherapy, 28,* 232–250.

Andrews, J. D. (1993). The active self model: A paradigm for psychotherapy integration. In G. Stricker & J. Gold (Eds.), *Comprehensive handbook of psychotherapy integration* (pp. 165–183). New York: Plenum Press.

Ashcraft, C., & Fitts, W. H. (1964). Self-concept change in psychotherapy. *Psychotherapy: Theory, Research, and Practice, 1,* 115–118.

Auerbach, C. (1985). What is self?: A construct theory. *Psychotherapy, 22,* 743–746.

Bandura, A. (1986). *Social foundations of thought and action: A social cognitive theory.* Englewood Cliffs, NJ: Prentice Hall.

Bandura, A. (1989). Human agency in social cognitive theory. *American Psychologist, 44,* 1175–1184.

Bandura, A. (1997a). *Self-efficacy in changing societies.* New York: Cambridge University Press.

Bandura, A. (1997b). *Self-efficacy: The exercise of control.* New York: Freeman.

Beck, A. T., Rush, A. J., Shaw, B. F., & Emery, G. (1979). *Cognitive therapy of depression.* New York: Guilford Press.

Benne, C. C. (1984). Know thyself. *Professional Psychology: Research and Practice, 15,* 271–283.

Bergin, A. E., & Garfield, S. L., (1994). *Handbook of psychotherapy and behavior change* (3rd ed.). New York: Wiley.

Berzon, B., & Solomon, L. (1966). The self-directed therapeutic group: Three studies. *Journal of Counseling Psychology, 13,* 491–497.

Brookover, W. B. (1959). A social psychological conception of classroom learning. *School and Society, 87,* 84–87.

Brookover, W. B. (1964). Self-concept of ability and school achievement. *Sociology of Education, 37,* 271–278.

Brown, W., & Kingsley, R. (1975). The effect of individual contracting and guided groups interaction upon behavior in disordered youth's self-concept. *Journal of School Health, 45,* 399–401.

Calderhead, J. (1996). Teacher's beliefs and knowledge. In D. C. Berliner & R. C. Calfee (Eds.), *Handbook of educational psychology* (pp. 709–725). New York: Macmillan.

Carkhuff, R. R. (1969). *Helping and human relations* (Vols. 1–2). New York: Holt, Rinehart & Winston.

Cartwright, R. D. (1957). Effects of psychotherapy on self-consistency. *Journal of Counseling Psychology, 4,* 15–22.

Cartwright, R. D. (1961). The effects of psychotherapy on self-consistency: A replication and extension. *Journal of Consulting Psychology, 25,* 376–382.

Cheek, J. M., Melchior, L., & Carpentieri, A. M. (1986). Shyness and self-concept. In L. M. Hartman & K. R. Blankstein (Eds.), *Perception of self in emotional disorder and psychotherapy* (pp. 113–132). New York: Plenum Press.

Combs, A. W. (1989). *A theory of therapy: Guidelines for counseling practice.* Newbury Park, CA: Sage.

Combs, A. W., Avila, D. L., & Purkey, W. W. (1978). *Helping relationships: Basic concepts for the helping professions.* Boston: Allyn & Bacon.

Combs, A. W., & Gonzales, D. M. (1994). *Helping relationships: Basic concepts for the helping professions* (4th ed.) Boston: Allyn & Bacon.

Cooley, C. H. (1902). *Human nature and the social order.* New York: Scribner's.

Coopersmith, S. (1967). *The antecedents of self-esteem.* San Francisco: Freeman.

Coopersmith, S. E. (1997). The search for the authentic self. *Psychoanalytic Review, 84,* 397–416.

Daste, B. M. (1985). The effects of time limitation in a low self concept children's group. *Social Work With Groups, 8,* 139–143.

Diggory, J. C. (1966). *Self-evaluations: Concepts and studies.* New York: Wiley.

Dombrow, R. (1966). A study of the relationship between therapists' empathy for patients and changes in patients' self concepts during therapy. *Dissertation Abstracts, 27*(1-B), 301–302.

Dunn, R. (1985). Issues of self concept deficit in psychotherapy. *Psychotherapy, 22,* 747–751.

Ellis, A., & Bernard, M. E. (Eds.). (1985). *Clinical applications of rational-emotive therapy.* New York: Plenum.

Erikson, E. H. (1959). *Identity and the life cycle.* New York: Norton.

Erikson, E. H. (1968). *Identity: Youth and crisis.* New York: Norton.

Erskine, R., Moursund, J., & Trautmann, R. (1999). *Beyond empathy: A therapy of contact-in-relationship.* Philadelphia: Brunner/Mazel.

Fryrear, J., Huell, L., & Ridley, S. (1974). Photographic self-concept enhancement of male juvenile delinquents. *Journal of Consulting and Clinical Psychology, 42,* 915.

Garfield, S. L., & Bergin, A. E. (1986). *Handbook of psychotherapy and behavior change* (3rd ed.). New York: Wiley.

Garner, D. M., & Garner, M. V. (1986). Self-concept deficiencies in eating disorders. In L. M. Hartman & K. R. Blankstein (Eds.), *Perception of self in emotional disorder and psychotherapy* (pp. 133–156). New York: Plenum Press.

Garner, D. M., Rockert, W., Davis, R., Garner, M. V., Olmstead, M. P., & Eagle, M. (1992). A comparison between cognitive–behavioral and supportive–expressive therapy for bulimia nervosa. *American Journal of Psychiatry, 150*, 37–46.

Gerber, S., & Purkey, W. W. (2001). Responsive therapy: An invitational counseling model. In R. J. Corsini (Ed.), *Handbook of innovative psychotherapies* (2nd ed.). New York: Wiley.

Goldfried, M., & Robins, C. (1984). Self schemas, cognitive bias, and the processing of therapeutic experiences. In P. C. Kendall (Ed.), *Advances in cognitive–behavioral research and therapy* (Vol. 2, pp. 221–247). New York: Academic Press.

Goldstein, K. (1939). *The organism*. New York: American Book.

Graham, S., & Weiner, B. (1996). Theories and principles of motivation. In D. C. Berliner & R. C. Calfee (Eds.), *Handbook of educational psychology* (pp. 63–84). New York: Macmillan.

Greenberg, G. (1995). Is self a narrative: Social constructions in the clinic. *Journal of Narrative and Life History, 5*, 269–283.

Guanipaa, C., Talley, W., & Rapane, S. (1997). Enhancing Latin American women's self concept: A group intervention. *International Journal of Group Psychotherapy, 47*, 355–372.

Guidano, V. F. (1987). *Complexity of the self: A developmental approach to psychopathology and therapy*. New York: Guilford Press.

Hartman, L. M., & Blankstein, K. R. (Eds.). (1986). *Perception of self in emotional disorder and psychotherapy*. New York: Plenum Press

Hermans, H. J., Diffelaers, R., de Groot, R., & Nanta, J. F. (1990). Self-confrontation as a method for assessment and interaction in counseling. *Journal of Counseling and Development, 69*, 156–162.

Hlongwane, M. M., & Basson, C. J. (1990). Self-concept enhancement of Black adolescents using transactional analysis in a group context. *School Psychology International, 11*, 99–108.

Holderstock, T. L. (1993). Can we afford not to revision the person-centered concept of self? In D. Brazier (Ed.), *Beyond Carl Rogers* (pp. 229–252). London: Constable.

Holderstock, T. L. (1994, September). *Implications of cultural concepts of the self for mental health, mental illness, and psychotherapy*. Paper presented at the XVL International Congress for Psychotherapy, Seoul, Korea.

Horney, K. (1939). *New ways in psychoanalysis*. New York: Horton.

Hull, J. G., & Young, R. D. (1983). The self-awareness reducing effects of alcohol: Evidence and implications. In J. Suls & A. Greenwald (Eds.), *Psychological perspectives on the self* (Vol. 2, pp. 159–190). Hillsdale, NJ: Erlbaum.

James, W. (1890). *Principles of psychology* (Vols. 1–2). Magnolia, MA: Peter Smith.

Jourard, S. M. (1971). *The transparent self: Self disclosure and well-being*. New York: Van Nostrand Reinhold.

Keilson, J., Dworkin, F., & Gelso, C. J. (1979). The effectiveness of time-limited psychotherapy in a university counseling center. *Journal of Clinical Psychology, 35*, 631–636.

Lecky, P. (1945). *Self-consistency: A theory of personality*. New York: Island Press.

Lewin, K. (1935). *A dynamic theory of personality*. New York: McGraw Hill.

Mahoney, M. J. (1990). Representations of self in cognitive therapies. *Cognitive Therapy and Research, 14*, 229–240.

Mahoney, M. J. (1991). *Human change processes: The scientific foundations of psychotherapy*. New York: Basic Books.

Malde, S. (1988). Guided autobiography: A counseling tool for older adults. *Journal of Counseling and Development, 66*, 290–293.

Malon, D., Paulus, M., & Hurley, W. (1994). The interacting self: Its development and phenomenological aspects in psychotherapy. *Journal of Contemporary Psychotherapy, 24*, 51–61.

Markus, H. (1977). Self-schemata and processing information about the self. *Journal of Personality and Social Psychology, 35*, 63–78.

Markus, H., & Wurf, E. (1986). Possible selves. *American Psychologist, 41*, 954–969.

Markus, H., & Wurf, E. (1987). The dynamic self-concept: A social–psychological perspective. *Annual Review of Psychology, 48*, 299–337.

Maslow, A. H. (1954). *Motivation and personality*. New York: Harper & Row.

Maslow, A. H. (1956). Personality problems and personality growth. In C. Moustakes (Ed.), *The self: Explorations in personal growth* (pp. 232–246). New York: Harper & Row.

Mazurkiewicz, J. (1957). A comparison of the effect of a reflective and of a leading type of psychotherapy on client concept of self, of ideal, and of therapist. *Dissertation Abstracts, 17*, 1121.

McConville, M. (1995). *Adolescence: Psychotherapy and the emergent self*. San Francisco: Jossey-Bass.

Miller, A. (1981). *Prisoners of childhood: The drama of the gifted child and the search for the true self*. New York: Basic Books.

Murphy, G. (1947). *Personality*. New York: Harper & Row.

Nurius, P. (1986). Reappraisal of the self-concept and implications for counseling. *Journal of Counseling Psychology, 33*, 429–438.

Osborne, D., & Swenson, W. M. (1972). Counseling readiness and changes in self-evaluation during intensive group psychotherapy. *Psychological Reports, 31*, 646.

Page, R. C., & Chandler, J. (1994). Effects of group counseling on 9th grade at-risk students. *Journal of Mental Health Counseling, 16*, 340–351.

Pahkinen, T., & Cabble, A. (1990). A 5 year followup study of psychotherapy: The stability of changes in the self-concept. *Psychotherapy and Psychosomatics, 54*, 193–200.

Pajares, F. (1992). Teachers' beliefs and educational research: Cleaning up a messy construct. *Review of Educational Research, 62*, 307–332.

Persinger, M. A. (1993). Personality changes following brain injury as a grief response to the loss of sense of self: Phenomenological themes as indices of local lability and neurocognitive structuring as psychotherapy. *Psychological Reports, 72*, 1059–1068.

Peterson, A., Chang, C., & Collins, P. (1998). The effects of reality therapy and choice theory training on self-concept among Taiwanese university students. *Journal for the Advancement of Counselling, 20*, 79–83.

Pfuetze, P. (1958). The concept of the self in contemporary psychotherapy. *Pastoral Psychology, 9*, 9–19.

Polkinghorne, D. (1991). Narrative and self-concept. *Journal of Narrative and Life History, 1*, 135–153.

Purkey, W. W. (1970). *Self concept and school achievement.* Englewood Cliffs, NJ: Prentice Hall.

Purkey, W. W. (2000). *What students say to themselves: Internal dialogue and school achievement.* Thousand Oaks, CA: Corwin Press.

Raimy, V. (1948). Self reference in counseling interviews. *Journal of Consulting Psychology, 12*, 153–163.

Raimy, V. (1971). *The self concept as a factor in counseling and personality organization.* Columbus, OH: Ohio State University Library.

Robertiello, R. (1985–1986). The selfless patient. *Psychotherapy Patient, 2*, 11–15.

Robins, R. W., & John, O. P. (1997). The quest for self-insight: Theory and research on accuracy and bias in self-perception. In R. Hogan, J. Johnson, & S. Briggs (Eds.), *Handbook of personality psychology* (pp. 649–680). New York: Academic Press.

Rogers, C. R. (1947). Some observations on the organization of personality. *American Psychologist. 2*, 358–368.

Rogers, C. R. (1951). *Client-centered therapy.* Boston: Houghton-Mifflin.

Rogers, C. R. (1954). An overview of the research and some questions for the future. In C. R. Rogers & R. F. Dymond (Eds.), *Psychotherapy and personality change* (pp. 413–433). Chicago: University of Chicago Press.

Rogers, C. R. (1958). The characteristics of helping relationships. *Personnel and Guidance Journal, 37*, 6–16.

Rogers, C. R. (1959). *Counseling and psychotherapy: Theory and practice.* New York: Harper & Row.

Rogers, C. R. (1961). *On becoming a person.* Boston: Houghton Mifflin.

Rogers, C. R. (1965). *Client-centered therapy: Its current practice, implications, and theory.* Boston: Houghton-Mifflin.

Rogers, C. R. (1970). *Carl Rogers on encounter groups*. New York: Harrow.

Rogers, C. R., & Dymond, R. F. (Eds.). (1954). *Psychotherapy and personality change*. Chicago: University of Chicago Press.

Rudominer, A. (1985–1986). Depersonalization and the self. *Psychotherapy Patient, 2*, 71–74.

Satir, V., & Baldwin, M. (Eds.). (1987). *The use of self in therapy*. New York: Haworth Press.

Satz, P., & Baraff, A. S. (1962). Changes in the relation between self-concepts and idea concepts of psychotics consequent upon therapy. *Journal of General Psychology, 67*, 291–298.

Schectman, Z., Gilat, I., Fos, L., & Flasher, A. (1996). Brief group therapy with low-achieving elementary school children. *Journal of Counseling Psychology, 43*, 376–382.

Schorin, M. Z., & Hart, D. (1988). Psychotherapeutic implications of the development of self-understanding. In S. Shirk (Ed.), *Cognitive development and child psychotherapy* (pp. 161–186). New York: Plenum.

Seeman, J. (1988). The rediscovery of the self in American psychology. *Person-Centered Review, 3*, 145–164.

Seligman, M. E. P. (1974). *Helplessness: On depression, development and death*. San Francisco: Freeman.

Segliman, M. E. P. (1990). *Learned optimism*. New York: Knopf.

Singer, J., & Salovey, P. (1993). *The remembered self: Emotion and memory in personality*. New York: Free Press.

Snow, R. E., Corno, L., & Jackson, D. (1996). Individual differences in affective and cognitive functions. In D. C. Berliner, & R. C. Calfee (Eds.), *Handbook of educational psychology* (pp. 243–310). New York: MacMillan.

Snygg, D., & Combs, A. W. (1949). *Individual behavior*. New York: Harper & Row.

Stein, K. F., & Markus, H. R. (1994). The organization of the self: An alternative focus for psychopathology and behavior change. *Journal of Psychotherapy Integration, 4*, 317–353.

Stoner, W., & Riese, H. (1971). A study of change in perception of self and ideal self. *Counselor Education and Supervision, 11*, 115–118.

Sullivan, H. S. (1953). *The interpersonal theory of psychiatry*. New York: Norton.

Svartberg, M., Seltzer, M., & Stiles, T. (1996). Self-concept improvement during and after short-term anxiety-provoking psychotherapy: A preliminary growth curve study. *Psychotherapy Research, 6*, 43–55.

Swann, W. B., Jr. (1997). The trouble with change: Self-verification and allegiance to the self. *Psychological Science, 8*, 177–180.

Torrance, E. P. (1954). Some practical uses of a knowledge of self-concepts in counseling and guidance. *Educational and Psychological Measurement, 14*, 120–127.

Truax, C. (1966). Therapist empathy, warmth, and genuineness and patient personality change in group psychotherapy: A comparison between interaction unit measures, time sample measures, patient perception measures. *Journal of Clinical Psychology, 22,* 225–229.

Truax, C., Carkhuff, R. R., & Kodman, F. (1965). Relationships between therapist-offered conditions and patient change in group psychotherapy. *Journal of Clinical Psychology, 21,* 327–329.

Truax, C., Carkhuff, R. R., Wargo, D., Kodman, F., Jr., & Moles, E. (1966). Changes in self-concept during group psychotherapy as a function of alternate sessions and vicarious therapy pretraining in institutional mental patients and juvenile delinquents. *Journal of Consulting Psychology, 30,* 309–314.

Truax, C., Wargo, D., & Silberg, L. (1966). Effects of group psychotherapy with high accurate empathy and nonpossessive warmth upon female institutionalized delinquents. *Journal of Abnormal Psychology, 71,* 267–274.

Varble, D., & Landfield, A. (1969). Validity of the self-ideal discrepancy as a criterion measure of success in psychotherapy—A replication. *Journal of Counseling Psychology, 16,* 150–156.

Victor, G. (1985–1986). Symbolic holding in the treatment of lack of self. *Psychotherapy Patient, 2,* 23–28.

Washington, K. (1977). Success counseling: A model workshop approach to self-concept building. *Adolescence, 12,* 405–410.

Watson, J. B. (1925). *Behaviorism.* New York: Norton.

Williams-Barnard, C., & Lindell, A. (1992). Therapeutic use of "prizing" and its effect on self concept of elderly clients in nursing homes and group homes. *Issues in Mental Health Nursing, 13,* 1–17.

Wylie, R. (1957). Some relationships between defensiveness and self-concept discrepancies. *Journal of Personality, 24,* 600–616.

Zahniser, J. H., & Coursey, R. D. (1995). The self-concept group: Development and evaluation for use in psychosocial rehabilitation settings. *Psychosocial Rehabilitation Journal, 19,* 59–64.

16

EMOTION IN HUMANISTIC PSYCHOTHERAPY

LESLIE S. GREENBERG, LORNE M. KORMAN, AND SANDRA C. PAIVIO

Humanistic therapies have often been characterized as proposing that getting in touch with one's feelings is the core element of psychological health and change. Although this characterization is an unwanted oversimplification, it is true that awareness of feelings has been a central feature of humanistic therapy. Rogers (1959), for example, defined *feeling* as an emotionally toned experience with its personal meanings and saw empathic responses to feelings as a central ingredient of therapy. For Rogers, feelings referred to the synthesis of emotion and cognition as they are experienced in the moment, and he proposed early on (Rogers, 1942) that the expression of feelings was therapeutic. He constructed two process measures related to feelings for rating in-session changes: the Feelings and Personal Meanings Scale and the Experiencing Scale. Therapeutic change on these dimensions involved movement from a process that is rigid, static, and unfeeling to one in which feelings are accepted and experienced in an immediate, fluid, and deep fashion (Rogers, 1961). Gendlin (1962, 1974, 1996) viewed feeling as a complex bodily felt sense associated with all meaningful acts. He distinguished between felt experience and "sheer" emotion, viewing emotional expression as clinically less productive than putting a bodily felt sense into words.

Perls (1973) and the Gestalt psychotherapy movement saw emotion as the force that energized all action. Perls, Hefferline, and Goodman (1951) defined *emotion* as people's direct evaluative experience of the field that provides knowledge of the objects appropriate to their needs. Perls et al. saw emotion as the integrative awareness of a relation between people and their environment. In this view, emotion integrates bodily action, the corresponding somatic arousal, and the awareness of the object of the action. Because emotion both informs the organism about what is important to it and energizes appropriate action, individuals' ability to accurately differentiate their own emotional experience was considered integral to healthy functioning. In addition, Perls et al. claimed that the ability to endure unwanted emotions was essential for mental health. Conversely, overcontrol and avoidance of emotions were considered to be major causes of dysfunction, because they both interrupted the adaptive role of emotion in directing action and prevented the differentiation of emotion through practice. Thus, in line with modern emotion theory, the humanistic tradition has tended to see emotion as an organizing force in human functioning.

In this chapter, we review the current status of emotion in humanistic psychotherapy and compare these with modern theories of emotion. We also review empirical research on the role of emotion in therapy and on the effects of emotional expression and inhibition on health. In the second half of this chapter, we look at the practical applications of emotion theory and research to humanistic psychotherapy.

THEORY OF EMOTION

Emotion involves a meaning system that informs people of the significance of events to their well-being (Frijda, 1986). Emotion gives people feedback about what is important and meaningful, about what is good or bad for them. According to a number of emotion theories, an important source of emotion production at the psychological level is the tacit appraisal of a situation in terms of one's concern or need (Frijda, 1986; Oatley & Jenkins, 1992). Dysfunction in the ability to access emotional information disconnects people from one of their most adaptive meaning production systems that helps them make sense of the world (Greenberg & Safran, 1984, 1987, 1989). The emotion system is thus a crucial focus of attention and an important target of therapeutic change. It needs to be attended to for its adaptive information and to be evoked and restructured when maladaptive.

The discrete emotions, such as anger and fear, result in expression and goal-directed action tendencies, such as anger displays or flight. These emotions are innate and organized and depend on the lower brain. Nevertheless, the experience of these emotions involves awareness of them; therefore, they are always to some degree synthesized with other levels of processing. Feeling an emotion involves experiencing body changes in relation to, and integrated with, the evoking object or situation and one's past emotional learning.

Feeling emotion also allows for the formation of emotion networks or schemes, because consciously feeling something involves higher levels of the brain and entails a synthesis of emotion–cognition–motivation and action. Once formed, emotion schemes produce more complex bodily felt feelings. These feelings are generally no longer a result of purely innate responses to specific cues but of acquired responses based on one's lived emotional experience. Thus, for example, over time the innate response of joy at a human facial configuration becomes differentiated into feelings of pleasure with a specific caretaker and contributes to the development of basic trust.

SOURCES OF EMOTION

Recent developments in neuroscience on the analysis of fear suggest that the emotional processing of simple sensory features occurs extremely early in the processing sequence. According to LeDoux (1993), the initial emotional processing of simple sensory features occurs subcortically, as inputs from the thalamus are received in the amygdala. This processing occurs prior to the synthesis of objects and events from simple sensory perceptions. The amygdala also receives inputs from the cortex, but this occurs only after information is first received from the thalamus. This suggests the operation of a second level of emotional processing that involves complex perceptions and concepts received from the cortex, occurring after a more immediate "intuitive" appraisal by the emotional brain from the initial input (LeDoux, 1993). As LeDoux emphasized, the initial "precognitive" emotional processing is highly adaptive because it allows people to respond quickly to important events before complex and time-consuming processing has taken place.

Neuroscientists like Damasio (1994) have argued that the formation of systematic connections between categories of objects and situations, on the one hand, and primitive, preorganized emotions, on the other, leads the maturing human to be capable of a second, higher order type of emotion experience. Much adult emotional experience is of this higher order, generated by learned, idiosyncratic schemes that serve to help the individual to anticipate future outcomes. These memory-based emotion schemes are thought to be located in the prefrontal cortex and, when activated, signal the amygdala and anterior cingulate, which in turn lead to changes in the viscera, skeletal muscles, and endocrine, neuropeptide, and neurotransmitter systems, and possibly other motor areas of the brain. Damasio argued that these changes, together with the often-implicit meaning represented in the prefrontal cortex, generate humans' complex, synthesized, and embodied sense of self in the world.

An example of this second higher-level type emotion would be the pit in one's stomach that one might experience on unexpectedly encountering one's ex-spouse. Regardless of whether or not the experience can subsequently be fully articulated (i.e., exactly what and why one feels the way one does), the experience nonetheless is tacitly generated. Perhaps most importantly, these representations serve as memory-based schemes associated with emotional experiences that guide appraisals and serve as blueprints for physiological arousal and action. The generation of much emotional experience is driven initially by precognitive, tacit processes that produce primary responses following simple perceptual appraisals (Greenberg & Korman, 1993; Scherer, 1984). These more basic processes are followed immediately by more complex activity in which sensory, memorial, and ideational information are integrated, yielding a felt sense of one's self and of the world. This higher level synthesis of a variety of levels of processing has been referred to as an *emotion scheme* and has been identified as a principal target of intervention and therapeutic change (Greenberg & Paivio, 1997; Greenberg, Rice, & Elliott, 1993; Korman & Greenberg, 1996). An emotion scheme is an internal affective–cognitive structure that when activated produces emotional experience.

RESEARCH ON EMOTION

Research on depth of experiencing in therapy has been shown consistently to relate to outcome, especially in client-centered therapy (Klein, Matheiu-Coughlan, & Kiesler, 1986; Orlinsky & Howard, 1978). The Experiencing Scale (Klein, Matieu, Gendlin, & Kiesler, 1969) measures the degree to which clients are fully engaged in their experience; this 7-point scale ranges from a low score of 1, in which individuals narrate their experience in a detached emotionless manner and do not represent themselves as agents in their own narratives, to a score of 3, representing a simple, reactive emotional response to a specific situation, to a score of 4, in which a person focuses on feelings, to 6, in which readily accessible feelings and meanings are synthesized to solve problems, to 7, in which clients are fully engaged in their momentary experience in a free-flowing, open, focused, manner.

Goldman (1997), in a study of clients with depression in process–experiential therapy (Greenberg, Rice, & Elliott, 1993), found that increase across therapy in clients' depth of experiencing on core themes was significantly related to good outcome. Greenberg, Watson, and Goldman (1996) argued that increase in depth of experience in successful brief treatments produces emotional problem solving on core issues, rather than overall change in level of functioning, as initially argued by Rogers (1961). They further argued that previous failures to find a clear linear increase in experiencing over time in successful treatments (see Klein et al., 1986) has been due to the failure of previous studies to rate experiencing on meaningful therapeutic episodes. Taking a perspective that change occurs in key events, they contended that taking experiencing measurements from random samples across therapy is not that meaningful because random sampling will miss important events. They proposed that resolution of key emotional issues is best measured by an increase in depth of experiencing on core themes and it is this that logically should relate to outcome. Goldman (1997) therefore identified segments in which clients were addressing core themes and found that increase across treatment in experiencing on core therapeutic themes predicted outcome. She also found that increase in depth of experiencing, from early to late in therapy, on core theme material, was superior to the working alliance in predicting outcome (Goldman, 1997). Depth of experiencing also has recently been shown to predict reduction of depressive symptoms in cognitive–behavioral therapy (Castonguay, Goldfried, & Hayes, 1996). These findings suggest that processing one's bodily felt experience may well be a core ingredient of change in psychotherapy regardless of type of therapy.

Korman (1998) showed that emotionally focused, process–experiential therapies of depression (Greenberg & Watson, 1998), when successful, led to significant changes in clients' emotional states from the beginning to the end of therapy. This research used the emotion episode (EE) method (Greenberg & Korman, 1993; Korman, 1998) to identify and demarcate episodes from session transcripts in which clients talk about their emotions in therapy. The EE method identifies four "components" in the episode: (a) the situation, (b) the emotion or action tendency, (c) the appraisal, and (d) the concern associated with the emotion. A sample of 24 clients with depression who were undergoing experiential therapy was divided into two groups of 12 clients each based on therapeutic outcomes. All EEs occurring in the first three and the last three sessions of each client's therapy were identified, and the emotions in each episode were classified according to a list of basic emotions modified from Shaver, Schwartz, Kirson, & O'Connor (1987). Clients with better outcomes showed significantly more changes in their emotions from early to late sessions than did clients with poorer outcomes, indicating that the emotional states that the improved group were in, or talked about at the end of therapy, had changed significantly. Moreover, clinical ratings of clients' therapeutic improvement, based on a reading of clients' EE protocols from early and late in therapy, were correlated significantly with the degree of change in clients' emotional states over treatment. Taken together, these findings suggest that therapeutically positive changes in clients' in-session emotional states from the beginning to the end of therapy correlate significantly with good outcome. Thus, clients with good outcomes might change, for example, from being predominantly angry at the beginning of therapy to feeling predominantly sad at the end or vice versa, or from feeling ashamed to angry, or from feeling sad to happy.

Pos (1999), in a study of emotional processing in process–experiential therapy of depression, found that depth of experiencing on second-session EEs was significantly related to outcome, indicating that clients' entry level of emotional processing is important. When, however, the relationship of early- and late-session depth of emotional experiencing of EEs to outcome were compared, it was found that late-session depth of emotional processing was the unique, significant predictor of outcome. This study thus indicated that increase in depth of experiencing on EEs is an important mediator of outcome in the experiential treatment of depression.

Another source of evidence on the role of affective experience in psychotherapy comes from research on catharsis and the expression of emotion. A survey of analogue studies on the effects of catharsis in therapylike situations found some support for the effectiveness of emotional arousal (Nichols & Zax, 1977). Bohart (1977) investigated the therapeutic effects of emotional discharge in a laboratory analogue. He found that those participants in a role-play condition in which they expressed anger to an imagined other and then responded from the position of the other showed greater reduction in anger and hostile behavior than those in either a pure rational analysis or pure anger expression condition. A subsequent study using a similar analogue paradigm found that cathartic hitting of a pillow was less effective in reducing anger than role play or nondirective counseling. Bohart (1980) concluded that discharge works best when combined with a form of cognitive processing, suggesting that therapeutic change is a function of a dual cognitive–affective process. Thus, for example, expressing anger reduces hostile feelings only if it leads to coping with the stimulus, that is, only if it leads to changing the environment or one's perception of it. Warwar and Greenberg (2000) showed that good-outcome clients in the treatment of depression showed both higher emotional arousal and higher levels of depth of experiencing on EEs. This indicated that emotional arousal plus making sense of this arousal distinguished good and poor outcomes, although contrary to expectation it was found that arousal alone was a unique predictor of outcome. Mergenthaler (1996) also found that emotional tone plus the use of more abstract words distinguished good and poor cases of dynamic therapy, again demonstrating that it is both emotion plus reflection on emotion that is important to the change process. Stalikas and Fitzpatrick (1995) showed that in-session change was related to both higher levels or reflection and strength of feeling. Honos-Webb, Surko, Stiles, and Greenberg (1999) recently showed that change in therapy occurred by replacing a dominant maladaptive, emotionally based voice in the personality with a more adaptive emotionally based one. These studies indicate that emotion needs to be both aroused and transformed.

Studies by Beutler and his group (Beutler et al., 1991; Daldrup, Engle, Holiman, & Beutler, 1994) have shown significant effects for a treatment involving the arousal and expression of anger in the treatment of depression and argued for the importance of anger expression in therapy (Mohr, Shoham-Soloman, Engle, & Beutler, 1991). In a small sample study, however, LeCroy (1988) found that clients in an approach that encouraged anger expression through the use of hitting with batakas reported more self-rated aggression than those in a behavioral skill training treatment. Mahrer and colleagues (Mahrer, Dessaulles, Nadler, Gervaize, & Sterner, 1987; Mahrer, Fairweather, Passey, Gingras, & Boulet, 1999) have shown that certain good moments in therapy are characterized by emotional expression. In a recent study attempting to match treatment to patient variables in a combined sample of varying treatments and problems, Beutler, Clarkin, and Bongar (2000) found that session emotional intensity was one of the strongest predictors of outcome. The treatments included experiential, dynamic, cognitive, and systemic treatment of four different populations, including an outpatient center sample, two samples with depression, and an addiction sample. In this study, the effect of high-session arousal on outcome was found to be mediated by the working alliance, indicating that arousal needs always to be viewed in the context of the alliance. Underscoring this point, Iwakabe, Rogan, and Stalikas (2000) recently showed that high arousal predicts good-session outcome only in the context of a good working alliance. Machado, Beutler, and Greenberg (1999) also found that training in emotionally focused methods increases therapists' affect sensitivity.

The disruptive effects of underregulated emotion, however, have been clinically well documented, and it has been suggested that attachment disorders or trauma may well be at the base of much emotional dysfunction (Bowlby, 1969; van der Kolk, McFarlane, & Weisath, 1996). Emotional distress in certain populations, such as parasuicides or addicts, leads to self-destructive behaviors (Linehan, 1993), and the expression of facial contempt and fear in quarrelling couples predicts divorce (Gottman & Levenson, 1992). The therapeutic effectiveness of emotional arousal is therefore highly dependent on with whom it occurs, when, and for what purpose (Greenberg & Bolger, 2001; Paivio & Greenberg, 2001; Wiser & Arnow, 2001).

Emotion has also been found to be important in resolving interpersonal problems. Research on the relationship between emotional arousal and the resolution of unfinished business with a significant other has shown that emotional arousal is significantly related to outcome (Greenberg & Foerster, 1996; Hirscheimer, 1996; Malcolm, 1999; Paivio & Greenberg 1995). Parkes (1980) and Raphael (1997) concluded from reviews of the bereavement outcome literature that controlled studies offer support for the beneficial effects of treatments that promote emotional expression in bereavement. Some studies, however, failed to demonstrate superior outcome for treatment over controls. Grieving, for example, has not been found to be a requirement for positive future functioning (Bonanno, Keluner, Holon, & Horowitz, 1995).

Johnson and Greenberg (1985, 1988) showed that emotionally focused couples therapy (Greenberg & Johnson, 1988) that helps partners access and express underlying attachment-oriented emotions is effective in increasing marital satisfaction (see Johnson, this volume, chapter 10). Couples who showed higher levels of emotional experiencing in therapy accompanying the softening in the blaming partner's stance were found to interact more affiliatively, and ended therapy more satisfied, than couples who showed lower experiencing (Greenberg, Ford, Alden, & Johnson, 1993; Johnson & Greenberg, 1985). A similar effect of the expression of underlying emotion was found in resolving family conflict (Diamond & Liddle, 1996).

A set of three studies Pierce, Nichols, and DuBrin (1983) found some support for the efficacy of the cathartic expression of feeling in therapy. However, this work on cathartic expression revealed that it is necessary to tease out when, and with whom, expressive methods are effective rather than to assume that catharsis is always helpful. Nevertheless, Pierce et al. concluded from their studies that expressing feeling was correlated with change. In a series of three interesting studies on arousal, Hoehn-Saric and colleagues (Hoehn-Saric, Frank, & Gurland, 1968; Hoehn-Saric et al., 1974; Hoehn-Saric et al., 1972) examined the role of chemically induced emotional arousal on attitude change. The results of the three studies indicated that maladaptive neurotic attitudes were quite resistant to change by persuasive communication in therapy under low-arousal conditions. However, these attitudes tended to change under pharmacologically induced emotional arousal. A client's views of himself or herself appear to be more susceptible to a therapist's influence when they are emotionally aroused.

In studies of behavioral treatments for anxiety disorders, clients who profited most from systematic desensitization (Borkovec & Sides, 1979; Lang, Melamed, & Hart, 1970) and flooding exhibited higher levels of physiological arousal during exposure. These and other findings suggest that the actual experience of fear-activated phobic memory structures is important for change. Foa and Kozak (1986) argued that the two conditions necessary for the reduction of pathological fear are the activation of the fear structure and the introduction of new information incompatible with the phobic structure. Foa and Kozak (1985) also reviewed a considerable number of empirical studies pointing to the efficacy of exposure techniques in the treatment of anxiety. For example, exposure techniques have been shown to result in long-term improvement in 75% of people with agoraphobia (Emmelkamp & Kuipers, 1979) and those who are obsessive–compulsive (Foa et al., 1983), whereas relaxation-based treatments of the same disorders (Chambless, Foa, Groves, & Goldstein, 1982; Marks, Hodgson, & Rachman, 1975) produced little improvement. Methods that increased arousal to help treat panic have been found to be effective (Craske & Barlow, 1993).

Similarly, the posttraumatic stress disorder literature emphasizes the critical role of arousal and complete emotional processing in the cognitive–behavioral treatment of trauma. Foa and Jaycox (1998), for example, suggested that complete emotional processing of the trauma is necessary for recovery. Foa, Rothbaum, Riggs, and Murdock (1991) found support for prolonged exposure in the treatment of rape victims. It appears that treatment requires initial arousal on response to the traumatic scene, and the arousal must dissipate over the session and across sessions. Exposure without sufficient time for arousal to dissipate will result in resensitization (Foa & Kozak, 1986; Frueh, Turner, & Beidel, 1995). However, when a new response of decreased arousal is elicited during the session, positive outcome can be expected. Boudewyns and Hyer (1990) suggested that unsystematic reexposure to trauma material without sufficient control could be harmful but that controlled exposure to traumatic imagery, sustained long enough to allow for extinction of arousal, was helpful. Hunt (1998) demonstrated that, in depression, the only way out may be to go through the emotional experience. She found that an emotional processing group, instructed to deal with an experientially induced depressed mood by writing about their feelings, had more mood change than those who were instructed to dispute in writing the feedback that created the mood.

Cognitive–behavioral therapy is beginning to recognize that clients need to move beyond cognitive content. In addition to the work on anxiety, grief work within this tradition is also seen as requiring the acknowledgment of emotion. Recently, Samoilov and Goldfried (2000) argued that cognitive therapists need to view emotion as an ally in the change process and that emotion is important in reorganizing tacit personal meanings (cf. Greenberg & Pascual-Leone, 1995; Guidano, 1993; Mahoney, 1991). Teasdale and Barnard (1993) similarly have argued that emotion is produced by a high-level tacit meaning system.

Jones and Pulos (1993) found that the strategies and evocation of affect, and the bringing of troublesome feelings into awareness, were correlated positively with outcome in both dynamic and cognitive–behavioral therapies. A number of studies also have shown that successful dynamic therapies involve more verbalization of emotion and the use of more emotion-focused words by therapist (Anderson, Bein, Pinnell, & Strupp, 1999; Holzer, Pokorny, Horst, & Luborsky, 1997), greater emotional activation and reflection by the client (Mergenthaler, 1996), and a clear focus on fundamental repetitive and maladaptive emotions structures (frames) that capture the stories that are characteristic of people's emotional experience in therapy (Dahl & Teller, 1994; Holzer & Dahl, 1996).

Thus it appears from the empirical literature on emotion in psychotherapy that

1. Processing information in an experiential manner, as measured by the Experiencing Scale, implies productive client involvement and predicts successful outcome.
2. Therapies targeting clients' emotional experience, when successful, are associated with changes over treatment, in clients' in-session emotional experiences.
3. Emotional arousal and expression in specific circumstances, and with certain types of individuals and problems, are related to constructive change.
4. Exposure to anxiety-evoking stimuli, while maintaining a high level of emotional arousal, can be effective in reducing anxiety and symptoms of posttraumatic stress.
5. Emotional arousal and reflection on aroused emotion are important in reorganizing personal meaning.

EMOTION: EXPRESSION, INHIBITION, AND HEALTH

There is a wealth of empirical findings demonstrating the importance to physical health of attending to and expressing emotional experience, as well as the perils associated with neglecting or suppressing emotions. For example, individuals who tend to avoid emotional disclosure are more likely to suffer from asthma, headache, cancer, coronary disease, and complications due to heart disease (Pennebaker & Traue, 1993).

Research on alexithymia, literally the absence of words for emotion, also supports that emotion awareness is an integral part of emotion regulation and health (Taylor, 1994). Alexithymia has been found to be present to a greater degree in a large number of both medical and psychological conditions than in normal controls (Taylor, Bagby, & Parker, 1991; Taylor, Bagby, Ryan, & Parker, 1990). It has been associated with several specific psychological disorders. These include posttraumatic stress disorder, eating disorders, psychosomatic complaints, panic disorders, substance abuse disorder, anxiety, and depression (Bagby, Taylor, & Atkinson, 1988; Bagby, Taylor, & Ryan, 1986; Haviland, Shaw, MacMurray, & Cummings, 1988; Sifneos, 1988; Taylor, Parker, Bagby, & Acklin, 1992; Wise, Jani, Kass, Sonnenschein, & Mann, 1988).

Within the specific area of trauma, self-reported failures to disclose traumatic events have been associated with increased rates in both self-reported and actual physician visits (Pennebaker, 1997; Pennebaker & Susman, 1988). In a variety of studies, Pennebaker (1997) found that people benefit from the type of disclosure that involves focusing attention on the emotional aspects of their loss or trauma in such a way as to organize the material in a coherent manner, thereby creating new meaning. Once people have developed a narrative that helps them make sense of their emotional experience, they become more able to modulate the intensity of their experience and develop skills for regulating their own affect. Esterling, Antoni, Fletcher, Margulies, and Schneiderman (1994), using a variant of Pennebaker's approach, also found strong support for the positive effects on immune function of revisiting trauma by writing or talking into a tape recorder.

Dafter (1996) argued for a positive role of both positive and negative emotions in mind–body healing. Stress, clinical depression, mood, and bereavement have all been reliably shown to affect the immune system (Cohen & Herbert, 1996; Dafter, 1996). A daily diary study showed that antibody levels were higher on days of reported positive mood states and lower on negative mood stable days (Stone et al., 1994). Knapp et al. (1992) showed that moods induced by recall affected the immune system. Poor marital relations and availability of emotional support have been found to influence health (Cohen & Herbert, 1996; Kiecolt-Glaser et al., 1987). Negative affect was found to predict development of a cold (Cohen & Herbert, 1996) and episodes of oral herpes, but effects of negative affect on progression of HIV infection are inconsistent (Cohen & Herbert, 1996). Some evidence shows that expression rather than repression of negative feelings has been related to better survival rates in breast cancer (Gross, 1989) and that repressors of negative emotion had lower immune responses than more expressive participants (Esterling et al., 1994; Shea, Burton, & Girgis, 1993). Studies by Spiegel (1994) and Fawzy et al. (1993) have shown positive effects of group treatment on life expectancy in cancer patients supporting the mind–body connection. This suggests that focusing on negative emotions and processing them may lead to improvements in health.

In reviewing research on the effects of emotional expression on psychological and physical health, one must keep in mind certain distinctions in interpreting results. The following factors, which often are not accounted for in the studies, influence whether expression is helpful or harmful:

1. Whether the expression occurs in therapy or in life.
2. Whether the expression involves the undoing of the inhibition of previously over-regulated emotion or the repetition of too freely expressed emotion; for example, hitting a pillow in a laboratory immediately after being insulted by an interviewer differs from hitting a pillow in therapy to express previously

unexpressed anger at a violater, and both differ from expressing anger that has been repeatedly expressed outside therapy.

3. Whether the expression involves only undoing inhibition or further processing of the emotion; for example, does expression involve arousal alone, by simply venting, or arousal plus cognitive change in the form of reprocessing or schematic restructuring (Greenberg & Safran, 1987)?

4. Whether the emotion being experienced and expressed is a signal of distress or is a process of resolving distress; for example, crying tears of hopeless despair differs from crying tears of grief (Kennedy-Moore & Watson, 1999).

5. Whether the emotion being expressed is defensive or core, adaptive or maladaptive.

Which type of expression is investigated will affect the outcomes found.

EMOTION IN PRACTICE

Emotion-Generating Schemes in Therapy

An emotionally focused approach to therapy (e.g., Greenberg, Rice, & Elliott, 1993; Greenberg & Paivio, 1997) contends that emotion-generating schemes produce experience. Adaptive emotions are seen as needing to be accessed in therapy as an aid to problem solving, whereas maladaptive emotions need to be accessed in therapy to make them amenable to change. Change in maladaptive emotion is facilitated by accessing new adaptive emotional responses to help transform the old maladaptive ones.

An example of the development of a maladaptive emotion scheme is seen in a child whose initiatives for closeness are met with unpredictable responses of either love or abusive rejection from parents. As a consequence, the child is likely to develop schemes in which intimacy and fear are associated and are connected with beliefs or expectancies that others will harm. Later in life, when the individual develops relationships with others, these schemes may be activated, and patterns of physiological arousal associated with the original abuse, plus associated negative beliefs or expectations formed by experience, will be evoked. The person may feel afraid and physically shrink away from closeness and tacitly appraise intimacy as threatening, even though the individual knows consciously that this reaction may be unfounded in a current relationship. Change in experience of this type is brought about first by activating the maladaptive experience and then by accessing adaptive feelings of sadness at what is missed and the yearning for closeness, and even anger at the abuse. These adaptive emotions are attended to and validated, and are then integrated with the existing negative experience and views. This process of accessing the adaptive and bringing it into contact with the maladaptive helps transform or replace the maladaptive schemes.

In emotionally focused therapy, adaptive emotions are seen as helpful because they organize the person for adaptive responses. Thus, when therapists help clients to attend to and symbolize their most fundamental adaptive experience, the clients can become organized by their feelings of adaptive sadness, anger, or joy to act in the world to solve problems and to create new meaning. For example, once an aggressive man recognizes the primary feeling of hurt or loneliness underlying his anger, he begins to be able to seek the comfort he really needs. Once clients who suffer panic attacks recognize that their momentary fears of being abandoned are the trigger of their phobic chain of experiences, they begin to acknowledge their attachment needs and find new ways of dealing with their fears of abandonment.

In addition to organizing adaptive action, emotions are also involved in reorganizing old static structures and creating new adaptive structures. Thus, therapy needs to evoke traumatic emotional memories so they may be reprocessed and restructured. In addition, maladaptive emotions such as core fears of abandonment or shame at inadequacy must be activated in therapy in order to be reorganized. As we mentioned earlier, in these instances emotional change occurs by activating incompatible, more adaptive experience to replace or transform the old responses. In development, when opposing emotions are coactivated, new higher level schemes may be formed by synthesizing compatible elements from the coactivated schemes. Just as schemes for standing and falling, in a toddler, can be dynamically synthesized into a higher level scheme for walking, by a dialectical process (Greenberg & Pascual-Leone, 1995), so too can schemes of different emotional states be synthesized from new integrations. For example, fear can be transformed by anger to form a more assertive sense of self, or shame and self-soothing can be synthesized into a sense of comfort that results in a more contactful being. Change through emotional processing thus involves both assimilating nonverbal emotional meaning into conscious narrative structures and replacing or integrating old emotional responses with newly activated aspects of experience to produce more adaptive responses.

Accessing Emotional Expression

In practice, clinical distinctions need to be made between different types of in-session emotional experiences and expression. In deciding whether to access, intensify, modify, or bypass clients' emotional expressions, therapists must make *process diagnoses* (Greenberg & Safran, 1989; Rice & Greenberg, 1984) of the particular type of processing in which the client is currently engaged. For the purposes of intervention, four broad categories of different types of emotional expression have been delineated: primary adaptive, primary maladaptive, secondary, and instrumental (Greenberg & Paivio, 1997; Greenberg & Safran, 1987). These are discussed below.

Primary Adaptive Emotion

There are three kinds of primary adaptive emotion. The first are the discrete emotions, such feelings as sadness at loss, anger at violation, and fear at threat. They tell a person what is significant to him or her, move the person toward need satisfaction and goal attainment, and provide specific action tendencies. These all have universal facial expressions and adaptive action tendencies and emerge in response to specific cues. These emotions' adaptive values are clear. In healthy functioning, it generally is not difficult to identify one's fear and see that it makes sense to run from danger, to access anger at violation and be organized by it to protect one's territory from predators, or for sadness to organize one's attempts to reunite with a lost attachment figure.

Second are the more complex feelings, or what Gendlin (1962) referred to as *experiencing*. These are based on bodily felt sensations, provide a more complex bodily felt sense of meaning, and are complex integrations of feeling and perception and cognition. Here a person may not feel the clarity of anger at violation, or sadness at loss. Rather the person may feel a rich complexity of felt meaning filled with implications, a sense of being "all washed up," or feeling "ready to launch oneself" into something new. In our view, there is a difference in degree of clarity and complexity between emotion and experiencing rather than a difference in kind. Emotion and experiencing both involve symbolization of bodily experience, and both provide information related to one's well-being. Discrete emotion, however, is a purer, simpler, clearer, more action-oriented experience, whereas a felt sense is a more subtle and complex form of meaning. Both help orientation and problem resolution, and both organize a person for taking new steps.

The third subcategory of primary adaptive emotion is that of emotional pain. This emotion is a holistic system response providing information that trauma to the whole sense of self has occurred and is characterized by people feeling broken or shattered (Bolger, 1996). Pain and this sense of brokenness needs to be accessed, not for its adaptive information but to be reexperienced, reprocessed, and resolved in therapy.

One thus works with the different types of primary emotional experience differently. Primary adaptive emotions, such as sadness at loss and anger at violation, are evoked to access the adaptive information and action tendency. They are core and irreducible responses and therefore are not explored to unpack their cognitive–affective components but rather are symbolized or expressed. The felt sense, however, is attended to, to access implicit meaning and to create a bodily felt release or change that helps new meanings emerge. Here intervention involves the facilitation of a searching, exploring style to explicate the implicit. Finally, emotional pain that informs one about injury that requires attention needs to be faced and fully processed until it is assimilated into existing meaning structures and the self feels whole again.

It is important to discriminate among productive, primary, adaptive emotional experience, and unproductive emotional experience, what we have called primary maladaptive emotion and secondary bad feelings (Greenberg & Paivio, 1997; Greenberg, Rice, & Elliott, 1993; Greenberg & Safran, 1987). Gendlin's (1962) "sheer emotions" are more akin to the latter unproductive emotions, in which people are stuck, rather than to the emergence of the former, which are new healthy emotions.

Primary Maladaptive Emotions

These are primary emotional responses that have become dysfunctional, such as the fear experienced in different types of phobias or the shame of feeling worthless. These generally are based on learning and are embedded in emotion schemes. Maladaptive primary emotional responses often result from childhood maltreatment and generally are based on pathogenic learning histories of neglect, abuse, or invalidation. The evocation of these schemes results in maladaptive primary responses to situations. These responses were generally initially adaptive, such as learning to fear closeness because it was associated with abuse or disappointment or feeling shame because one's efforts or expressions were humiliated.

Fear and shame generally are the primary maladaptive emotions that occur most often in therapy (Greenberg & Paivio, 1997). These are the emotions that often overwhelm people or in which they become stuck. These emotions need to be accessed in therapy in order for the emotion scheme in which they are embedded to be restructured by new emotional experiences. Core maladaptive self schemes are the shame-based sense of self as worthless or a failure, a "bad me" sense; or the fear-based sense of feeling fundamentally insecure or anxious, the "weak me" sense.

Secondary Emotional Responses

These emotions are reactions to identifiable, more primary, internal, emotional, or cognitive processes, thus they are secondary to prior internal processes. People express secondary anger when feeling primarily hurt, or they cry when primarily angry or feel guilt and shame in response to their self-criticisms. According to this categorization, bad feelings such as hopelessness, helplessness, depression, and anxiety that people bring to therapy are often secondary or reactive emotional experiences that obscure underlying experience. Crying, for example, may not reflect the true grieving that leads to relief but rather the crying of secondary helplessness or frustration that results in feeling worse. Emotions, especially when they are not symbolized in awareness, often rapidly turn into other emotions. Sadness, hurt, shame, or fear often turn into anger, fear into coolness, jealousy into anger, and anger into fear. People also have feelings about their feelings. Individuals are often afraid of their anger, ashamed of their fear, and angry about their sadness. Distinguishing secondary from primary adaptive emotions is important in therapy because intervention involves either bypassing secondary emotions or accessing and unpacking them to arrive at more primary experience. In therapy, focusing on or intensifying secondary reactions would sustain the dysfunctional process and thus is contraindicated.

Instrumental Emotional Responses

These are learned behaviors that are used to influence or manipulate others. Their purpose is to achieve a desired effect. Examples of instrumental emotions include expressing anger to dominate or crying to elicit sympathy. Such expressions of emotion do not inform the individual about the personal significance of events, but instead are directed toward producing an interpersonal or intrapsychic payoff. Because primary emotion does not underlie instrumental emotional expression, the exploration, intensification, and differentiation of these emotions would neither access adaptive information nor foster action. In therapy, instrumental emotions are best bypassed, confronted, or their function understood. Clients need to become aware of the function of their instrumental feelings. In so doing, they may come to abandon these aims if they are deemed dysfunctional, or alternatively, to explore their inner resources so as to discover other means of achieving their goals.

Emotional Dysfunction

For therapeutic purposes, three kinds of emotional dysfunction have been distinguished (Greenberg & Paivio, 1997; Greenberg, Rice, & Elliott, 1993). The first type results from a failure to acknowledge elements of one's immediate affective experience. Here affect, action tendencies, appraisals, and needs are inaccurately or incompletely symbolized in awareness, leaving people disoriented and confused with no access to their primary orientation system. This often results from feelings that were never symbolized in childhood or life. Consequently, people simply have no words to make sense of their experience. The second major type of emotional dysfunction involves the activation of maladaptive schemes (Greenberg, Rice, & Elliott, 1993).

Salient emotional experiences of a profoundly negative nature, often involving trauma, loss, or threat, can result in the development of maladaptive, complex cognitive–affective schemes (Greenberg & Paivio, 1997). These schemes guide people's perception of affectively relevant patterns in the environment and generate their felt sense of themselves and their orientation to the world. The schemes can be activated automatically in subsequent situations by minor cues. The third type of dysfunction involves the inability to own or integrate different aspects of affective experience that have at some time been symbolized but now are disowned. In extreme cases, this involves the dissociation that occurs when painful feelings are felt as a threat to the integrity of the self. At other times, there is a simple disavowal of experience that is incongruous with other aspects of experience and identity. Thus, for example, a man may avoid acknowledging his vulnerable feelings because these are perceived as "unmanly."

General Principles of Emotion-Focused Interventions

To be used effectively, an emotionally focused style of intervention must occur within a particular relational context and must be sensitive to client individual differences and client readiness. To help clients acknowledge, explore, or regulate feelings that are painful or threatening, therapists must first foster a strong therapeutic alliance (Bordin, 1979) in which clients feel safe, accepted, supported, and validated. In addition to a solid therapeutic bond, clients and therapists need to agree about the goals of therapy and about the tasks necessary to achieve these aims (Bordin, 1979; Horvath & Greenberg, 1994). Furthermore, in those clients who interrupt or constrict their emotional experience, emotion is focused on and aroused. Conversely, with clients who cannot regulate their emotions and are overwhelmed by them, a safe working distance is created and the use of emotion regulation skills, such as regular breathing and self-soothing activities, is facilitated.

The following general principles guide the therapist's emotionally focused interventions to help deepen clients' experience and facilitate the generation of new meaning: empathic attunement, directing attention, refocusing attention, present centeredness, nonverbal expression, intensification, memory evocation, symbolization, and expressing intents (Greenberg & Paivio, 1997; Greenberg & Safran, 1987). These principles require, first and foremost, that the therapist be empathically attuned to clients' moment-by-moment experience. Empathic attunement to emotion is the most general and fundamental principle of all emotion-focused intervention. Beyond this, the first specific principle involves directing clients' attention to internal experience. The aims are to access clients' emotions and to symbolize explicitly their tacitly generated emotional experience. This can be accomplished by suggesting directly that clients attend to what they are feeling, by inquiring (e.g., "What happens inside as you say this?") or by directing a response at clients' internal experience (e.g., "I hear some sadness as you say this").

If clients move their attention away from their internal experience, the second principle involves refocusing their attention inward to attend to bodily felt experience. This requires that therapists notice when clients deviate from their focus on their internally felt experience and then quickly redirect them back to this internal track. The third principle involves maintaining a focus in the here and now on what the client is experiencing rather than talking about experience in a manner that is not grounded concretely in the present. To promote clients' awareness of their experience, therapists observe the manner of verbal and nonverbal expression as it occurs, and then direct clients' attention to or provide feedback about this expression (e.g., "So what are you doing with your hands right now?" or "I see you slumped over in your seat"). Therapists can intensify emerging experience by increasing their clients' levels of arousal and encouraging active expression to make their experience more vivid. Memory evocation is another process that helps access emotion by having clients reenter and reexperience problematic or unresolved situations through episodic memory. Another principle involves working with clients to increasingly differentiate their experience and symbolize it in awareness. The final principle involves focusing on the needs and wants underlying clients' experience and collaborating with them in explicitly stating needs/goals or intentions. The last two principles facilitate the creation of new meaning and provide clients with an emotionally based sense of direction (Greenberg, 1993).

Intervention Framework

In an effort to outline a generic framework for working with emotion, Greenberg and Paivio (1997) outlined a three-phase, eight-step framework for working with emotion in psychotherapy. This is based on their study of a large number of emotion focused, process–experiential therapies and on their review of the empirical literature on emotion in psychotherapy. The framework is shown in Table 16.1. The essence of this intervention framework involves attending to, evoking, and exploring emotion in the session to promote change in emotion schemes.

The first phase, *bonding*, involves the empathic attunement to and validation of experience that has been found so important in working with emotion. Development of a collaborative focus is also a crucial aspect of the first phase. The second phase, *evoking and exploring*, involves bringing the difficult emotional experience alive in the session to further differentiate it and access underlying emotions. The third phase, *emotional restructuring*, involves accessing primary emotions underlying the secondary emotion

TABLE 16.1.
The Framework

Phase	Steps
Phase 1: Bonding	1. Attend to, empathize, and validate feelings.
	2. Establish and develop a collaborative focus: Identify the underlying cognitive–affective processes or generating conditions.
Phase 2: Evoking and exploring	3. Evoke and arouse: The bad feeling or painful experience is brought alive in the session or regulated.
	4. Explore/unpack cognitive–affective sequences in the painful experience or that generate the bad feelings.
Phase 3: Emotion restructuring	5. Access core maladaptive emotion scheme and/or primary emotional experience.
	6. Restructure: Facilitating restructuring of core schemes by challenging maladaptive beliefs with primary adaptive emotions and needs/goals and resources.
	7. Support and validate the emergence of a more self-affirming stance.
	8. Create new meaning. Help construct a new narrative to capture emergent meanings.

evoked in Phase 2. If the primary emotion, accessed initially, is adaptive, it provides useful information and action tendencies to guide orientation and problem solving. If, however, the client's primary emotions are traumatic or maladaptive, they need to be reprocessed or restructured. This transformation process occurs by the client accessing adaptive emotions to transform the maladaptive ones. In this process, the dysfunctional beliefs, associated with the maladaptive emotion scheme, are challenged from within by the newly accessed healthy emotions and needs. Change thus occurs by means of a dialectical confrontation between two parts of the self. The more dominant negative voice or narrative is based on maladaptive emotions, often shame or fear based (e.g., "I am worthless or helpless"). It is challenged by a newly accessed less-dominant voice based on primary adaptive emotions, often those of anger, sadness, or pride (e.g., "I feel violated and won't take it any more," "I hurt and need comfort," or "I am lovable and deserve respect"). This confrontation between the two voices leads to a dynamic synthesis of these alternative views and ultimately to the creation of new experience and meaning. Thus, maladaptive responses of shame and fear are transformed or replaced by a greater sense of self-worth and empowerment, and the person's identity narrative changes accordingly.

Case Example: "I Needed to Know You Cared"

In the following episode, a woman in her mid-40s was dealing in therapy with ongoing interpersonal difficulties with her mother. The client felt dominated and controlled by her mother. She was unable to stand up for herself and continued to feel bitterly resentful about a situation that took place when she was a teenager. At that time, the client had become pregnant and her mother had kicked her out of the family home. Subsequently, the client had raised her child on her own, established a successful career, and reestablished a relationship with her mother. This relationship was very important to the client. She longed for closeness with her mother but was continually disappointed and could not let go of how the mother had betrayed her. The mother refused to discuss the past, and the client felt powerless and furious about her mother's unwillingness to hear her side of the story.

In therapy, the client expressed her bitterness about her mother's narrow mindedness and inflexibility. Above all, she wanted her mother to admit that she had been wrong and to apologize for treating her badly. The client's anger at not being listened to was fused with other emotions like hurt over being rejected. One of the foci of therapy was to differentiate these feelings. Broader goals emerged for the client as therapy progressed. These were to feel more powerful within herself so she could let go of the need for her mother's apology and approval, thus facilitating a greater degree of separation from her mother.

In the episode that follows, the client first accesses her previously unresolved anger. Expression of her primary anger also resulted in her accessing her primary sadness. Anger and sadness often come as the opposite sides of the coin of unresolved feelings toward a significant other. In working with unresolved anger, the therapist therefore always needs to be attuned to and responsive to the evolving moment-by-moment process and not focused on anger alone. Expression of anger is encouraged only when it is salient in the moment or is a central client concern.

The following is a transcript of the client (C) expressing to the therapist (T) her primary anger and sadness in a dialogue with her mother from Session 11:

> T: Uh-hmm. That's good. Okay, so see if you can. . . . Can you actually bring mother here or . . . (C: Okay) Say something to her.
> C: I (Sob), I can't, I can't believe what you did to me. (Sighs) [Secondary sadness, access anger] I can't believe that you did that to me. That you put me in that situation. That was worse than, than death.
> T: Tell her, "I'm angry at you." [Reown/agency]
> C: I'm angry at you for that. How could you just behave so despicably? (T: Uh-huh) (Pause) I'm angry at you and I, I have a right to be angry at you.

T: Uh-huh. Good. Can you say that again. I have a right to be angry at you. [Intensify]

C: I have a right to be angry at you. I know it now because I remember, what it was like.

T: That's good. Say some more to her. [Intensify]

C: I was just a . . . sad, lonely sixteen-year old, and where was my mother? Nowhere. You didn't come. You didn't care. You just left me. I was alone and suffering. And because of your lack of . . . action or . . . lack of caring, I suffered all that . . . You just . . . You can't call yourself honorable. How can you live with yourself, having behaved that way?

T: Mm-hmm. Tell her what you want from her. [Establish need]

C: I want you to recognize what you did—I want you to see how much I suffered when I was sixteen. And I want you to say you are sorry.

T: Uh-huh. I want you to recognize what you did.

C: I won't let you forget. I won't ever forget. And I won't let it be diminished. How could you. And I will always think you should say you're sorry for that. [Accessing primary anger]

T: When you use these words, you're sounding sort of astonished, how she could do that or, you really condemn her behavior somehow. You've used the word morally not right, and (C: Mm-hmm, Mm-hmm) So try saying to her—I condemn. [Reown/agency]

C: I condemn that behavior. It doesn't measure up to decent standards, at all. You behaved despicably. . . . Yes, I'm actually furious with you. It just makes me furious that you didn't, that you weren't able to . . . to stand by me when I needed you. And now I don't need you. [Primary anger]

T: Uh-huh, try and stay with that again. I'm furious with you, that you weren't, that you didn't come to me when I needed you. [Refocus, reown/agency]

C: I'm furious with you. Just makes me furious that you . . . you just seem to be . . . lacking in that way. Doesn't loyalty mean anything to you? Soon as I caused you trouble you just pushed me aside.

T: Tell her what you needed when, when you said I was furious when you didn't come to me when I needed you. What did you really need? What would you have liked then for yourself? [Establish intentions/needs]

C: I would have liked her to care. I would have liked you to show that you cared and to show that you were a strong presence behind me ready to support me through this.

T: What could she have done to show that she cared?

C: You could have just, just thrown that pride of yours by the wayside and come, driving up to where I lived and bursting in to see what was going on with your own daughter. I wanted you to show me that you cared. And then to care, you know, to sort of help me along through this and, and relieve me of some of the difficulty of it.

[Facilitate restructuring]

C: (Client enacts mother) (Pause) (Crying) That this thing I wanted to say, that, I'm sorry that I didn't do that . . . I want you to forgive me. . . . Oh, if I could just have it to do over again. I would come there and I would help you through the worst of it and I could have shared and enjoyed you a bit. It was life happening. It was . . . I was doing what I knew best but I was mistaken. I'm sorry. (Cries)

T: What are you feeling now?

C: (Crying) I just feel so sad for me as a young mother. I was so alone and so needed someone to love me. [Primary sadness] But I was not bad, unworthy. Actually I was very courageous, my mother just couldn't cope.

Review of Case

We use the steps outlined in Table 16.1 to describe progress through this session of emotionally focused treatment. In this session, in addition to the use of empathic responding to acknowledge and validate feelings and consistent focusing on internal experience, empty-chair dialogue was used to evoke unresolved emotions. At a point in which the client's unfinished business with her mother emerged, she was encouraged to confront her imagined mother in the empty chair and begin to tell her how angry she was that she had refused to listen to her. According to Step 2 of the framework, this lingering unresolved resentment toward her mother was established as an important determinant of her current distress and as the focus of treatment. In Step 3, the imaginary dialogue rapidly evoked all the secondary bad feelings, the despair, and hopelessness associated with the earlier episode in her life. This strategy of dialoguing with the imagined other encouraged the client to bring alive, in the present, what was felt. This exemplifies the principle of present-centeredness. This promoted Step 4, the exploration and unfolding of her current experience, and also led to her accessing core emotion schemes and memories related to her abandoned sense of self. This evocation of primary emotional experience contrasts with interventions that focus purely on understanding genetic causes of current conflicts. Here the client experienced in her body what was being talked about. As the therapy progressed, the therapist promoted the client's exploration of her currently felt feelings of abandonment as they emerged in the dialogue. She expressed what she had not been able to say to her mother. This helped her symbolize her experience and facilitated her gaining access to her primary maladaptive feelings of lonely abandonment and to her unexpressed primary adaptive anger.

Part of the therapeutic work at this point was to help the client focus internally and speak from her own internal frame of reference (promote agency). Rather than expressing secondary anger by blaming and lecturing, trying to convince her mother that she was wrong to have cast her out, the client was helped in Step 5 to clearly access and express her primary maladaptive fear and hopelessness and then to access her adaptive anger at violation. She expressed her anger at being treated so cruelly and her sadness at her mother's gross neglect. She then remobilized her associated unmet needs for protection and mothering, saying "I was just a child, you were my mother, I needed you to come to me, to bring me home."

While her expression of anger accessed and heightened emotion memories, evocative empathic reflections helped unfold and symbolize her overwhelming fears at the time about being pregnant and on her own, as well as her deep pain at rejection. Although these feelings were adaptive at the time, they remained as memories that generated current feelings of lonely abandonment and unlovableness that were maladaptive. Unfolding the client's experience heightened her awareness of both her negative beliefs that she was alone, unloved, with no one to care for her, and her old and current unmet needs for her mother's acceptance. The powerful role these needs and beliefs played in her identity and in her current relationships were also brought to awareness. Interventions did not entail interpreting her dependency needs but rather tracking and symbolizing her ongoing experience and highlighting, through empathic reflection and conjecture, the role of her beliefs and the intensity of her need.

Expressing and exploring the client's more vulnerable feelings of primary sadness and distress associated with her unfinished business was another critical part of this therapy. Her proud self-protective beliefs, formed in the time of her abandonment, were articulated and were restructured in Step 6. This was done by combating her beliefs about weakness, from her empowered sense of anger at violation and sadness at loss, and from the remobilization of her legitimate need for support. These beliefs centered on her view that anger and sadness were weakness and were best kept under wraps because no one would be there to hear them. In Step 7, she affirmed herself as worthy and, in the session, soothed her hurt 16-year-old self by empathizing with her pain. By the end of session, she had begun to develop a new experientially based narrative of her adolescent crisis. This was a far more self-validating account of herself as deserving of support and love rather than as bad, alone, and undeserving. It is significant that access to her complex network of feelings, meanings, and needs came about through clear experience and expression of primary anger and primary sadness that previously had been undifferentiated and expressed only as fused complaint and lingering resentment.

After this session, the client, having accessed her primary anger and her need for support, further grieved her loss. This led to her articulating a new view of herself and her mother, a view of herself as valuable and her mother as mistaken rather than herself as bad. She ended therapy with significant reductions in her initial symptom and reported being able to interact more genuinely with her mother, with whom she developed a more caring relationship. She also reported that the instrumental anger that she said she had been expressing to her mother in general interactions "in order to punish her for what she had done" had disappeared.

CONCLUSION

Clients generally arrive in therapy complaining of some form of emotional distress. They are concerned about having too much emotion, too little, or the wrong emotion at the wrong time. Their problematic experience of themselves in the world clearly is felt, and most would agree that changing this experience is a principal goal of therapy. During decades of neglect of emotion in mainstream psychotherapy research and practice, humanistic psychotherapies have kept the light burning on the importance of feelings and have continued to develop emotionally focused interventions to bring about clinical change.

Converging evidence in experimental and social psychology, in neurophysiology, and in psychotherapy research suggests that much of the processing involved in the generation of emotional experience occurs independent of and prior to conscious, deliberate, cognitive operations. Therefore, working at the purely cognitive level to effect emotional change may not produce enduring change. Instead, therapeutic interventions are more likely to succeed if they target the schematic processes that automatically generate the emotional experience that underlie clients' felt senses of themselves. Emotion is important in therapy because it provides vital information about clients' needs and appraisals, makes maladaptive schemes accessible so that they can be restructured, and leads to behavioral change. Humanistic therapies' goal of increasing emotional awareness is important because it helps clients access and symbolize the adaptive information provided by their primary adaptive emotional experience. However, in addition to getting in touch with one's feelings, clients and therapists need to discriminate between different types of feelings and learn which to trust and follow as guides, which to explore to get at more primary feelings, and which to restructure because they are maladaptive.

REFERENCES

Anderson, T., Bein, E., Pinnell, B. J., & Strupp, H. H. (1999). Linguistic analysis of affective speech in psychotherapy: A case grammar approach. *Psychotherapy Research, 9*, 88–99.

Bagby, R. M., Taylor, G. J., & Atkinson, L. (1988). Alexithymia: A comparative study of the three self-report measures. *Psychosomatic Research, 32,* 107–116.

Bagby, R. M., Taylor, G. J., & Ryan, D. P. (1986). Toronto Alexithymia Scale: Relationship with personality and psychopathology measures. *Psychotherapy and Psychosomatics, 45,* 207–215.

Beutler, L. E., Clarkin, J. F., & Bongar, B. (2000). *Guidelines for the systematic treatment of the depressed patient.* New York: Oxford University Press.

Beutler, L., Engle, D., Mohr, D., Daldrup, R., Bergan, M., & Merry, W. (1991). Predictors of differential response to cognitive, experiential and self-directed psychotherapeutic procedures. *Journal of Consulting and Clinical Psychology, 59,* 333–340.

Bohart, A. (1977). Role playing and interpersonal conflict reduction. *Journal of Counseling Psychology, 24,* 15–24.

Bohart, A. (1980). Toward a cognitive theory of catharsis. *Psychotherapy: Theory, Research, and Practice, 17,* 192–201.

Bolger, E. A. (1996). *The subjective experience of transformation through pain in ACOAS.* Unpublished doctoral dissertation, York University, Toronto, Ontario, Canada.

Bonanno, C. A., Keluner, D., Holon, A., & Horowitz, M. J. (1995). When avoiding unpleasant emotions might not be such a bad thing: Verbal-autonomic response dissociation and midlife conjugal bereavement. *Journal of Personality and Social Psychology, 69,* 975–989.

Bordin, E. (1979). The generalizability of the psychoanalytic concept of the working alliance. *Psychotherapy: Theory, Research, and Practice, 16,* 252–260.

Borkovec, T. D., & Sides, J. (1979). The contribution of relaxation and expectance to fear reduction via graded imaginal exposure to feared stimuli. *Behaviour Research and Therapy, 17,* 529–540.

Boudewyns, P. A., & Hyer, L. (1990). Physiological response to combat memories and preliminary outcome in Vietnam veteran PTSD patients treated with direct therapeutic exposure. *Behavior Therapy, 21,* 63–87.

Bowlby, J. (1969). *Attachment.* New York: Basic Books.

Castonguay, L. G., Goldfried, M. R., & Hayes, A. M. (1996). Predicting the effect of cognitive therapy for depression: A study of unique and common factors. *Journal of Consulting and Clinical Psychology, 64,* 497–504.

Chambless, D. L., Foa, E. B., Groves, G. A., & Goldstein, A. J. (1982). Exposure and communications training in the treatment of agoraphobia. *Behaviour Research and Therapy, 12,* 360–368.

Cohen, S., & Herbert, T. B. (1996). Health psychology: Psychological factors and physical disease from the perspective of human psychoneuroimmunology. *Annual Review of Psychology, 47,* 113–142.

Craske, M. G., & Barlow, D. H. (1993). Panic disorder and agoraphobia. In D. H. Barlow (Eds.), *Clinical handbook of psychological disorders: A step-by-step treatment manual* (pp. 1–47). New York: Guilford Press.

Dafter, R. E. (1996). Why "negative" emotions can sometimes be positive: The spectrum model of emotions and their role in mind–body healing. *Journal of Mind–Body Health, 12*(2), 6–18.

Dahl, H., & Teller, V. (1994). The characteristics, identification, and applications of frames. *Psychotherapy Research, 4,* 253–276.

Daldrup, R., Engle, D., Holiman, M., & Beutler, L. E. (1994). The intensification and resolution of blocked affect in an experiential psychotherapy. *British Journal of Clinical Psychology, 33,* 129–141.

Damasio, A. (1994). *Descartes' error: Emotion, reason, and the human brain.* New York: Putnam.

Diamond, G., & Liddle, H. (1996). Resolving a therapeutic impact and parent and adolescent in multidimensional family therapy. *Journal of Consulting and Clinical Psychology, 64,* 481–488.

Emmelkamp, P. M. G., & Kuipers, A. C. M. (1979). Agoraphobia: A follow-up study four years after treatment. *British Journal of Psychiatry, 134,* 352–355.

Esterling, B. A., Antoni, M. H., Fletcher, M. A., Margulies, S., & Schneiderman, N. (1994). Emotional disclosure through writing or speaking modulates latent Epstein-Barr virus antibody items. *Journal of Consulting and Clinical Psychology, 62,* 130–140.

Fawzy, F., Fawzy, N., Hyun, C. S., Elashoff, R., et al. (1993). Malignant melanoma: Effects of an early structural psychiatric intervention, coping, and affective state on recurrence and survival six years later. *Archives of General Psychiatry, 50,* 681–689.

Foa, E. B., Grayson, J. B., Steketee, G. S., Doppelt, H. G., Turner, R. M., & Latimer, P. R. (1983). Success and failure in the behavioral treatment of obsessive–compulsives. *Journal of Consulting and Clinical Psychology, 51,* 287–297.

Foa, E. B., & Jaycox, L. H. (1998). Cognitive–behavioral treatment of posttraumatic stress disorder. In J. Spiegel (Ed.), *Psychotherapeutic frontiers: New principles and practices* (pp. 125–154). Washington, DC: American Psychiatric Press.

Foa, E. B., & Kozak, M. J. (1985). Treatment of anxiety disorders. Implications for psychopathology. In A. H. Tuma & J. D. Maser (Eds.), *Anxiety and anxiety disorders* (pp. 451–452). Hillsdale, NJ: Erlbaum.

Foa, E. B., & Kozak, M. J. (1986). Emotional processing of fear: Exposure to corrective information. *Psychological Bulletin, 99,* 20–35.

Foa, E. B., Rothbaum, B. O., Riggs, D. S., & Murdock, T. B. (1991). Treatment of posttraumatic stress disorder in rape victims. A comparison between cognitive–behavioral procedures and counseling. *Journal of Consulting and Clinical Psychology, 59,* 715–723.

Frijda, N. H. (1986). *The emotions.* Cambridge, England: Cambridge University Press.

Frueh, B. C., Turner, S. M., & Beidel, D. C. (1995). Exposure therapy for combat-related PTSD: A critical review. *Clinical Psychology Review, 15,* 799–817.

Gendlin, E. T. (1962). *Experiencing and the creation of meaning.* New York: Free Press.

Gendlin, E. T. (1974). Client-centred and experiential psychotherapy. In D. A. Wexler & L. N. Rice (Eds.), *Innovations in client-centred therapy* (pp. 312–334). New York: Wiley.

Gendlin, E. T. (1996). *Focusing-oriented psychotherapy: A manual of the experiential method.* New York: Guilford Press.

Goldman, R. N. (1997). *Theme-related depth of experiencing and change in experiential psychotherapy with depressed clients.* Unpublished doctoral dissertation, York University, Toronto, Ontario, Canada.

Gottman, J. M., & Levenson, R. W. (1992). Marital processes predictive of later dissolution: Behavior, physiology and health. *Journal of Personality and Social Psychology, 63,* 221–223.

Greenberg, L. S. (1984). A task analysis of intrapersonal conflict resolution. In L. N. Rice & L. S. Greenberg (Eds.), *Patterns of change* (pp. 67–123). New York: Guilford Press.

Greenberg, L. S. (1993). Emotion and change processes in psychotherapy. In M. Lewis & J. M. Haviland (Eds.), *Handbook of emotions* (pp. 499–508). New York: Guilford Press.

Greenberg, L. S., & Bolger, L. (2001). An emotion focus approach to the overregulation of emotion and emotional pain. *In-Session, 57*(2), 197–212.

Greenberg, L., & Foerster, F. (1996). Resolving unfinished business: The process of changes. *Journal of Consulting & Clinical Psychology, 64*(3), 439–446.

Greenberg, L., Ford, C., Alden, L., & Johnson, S. (1993). In-session change processes in emotionally focused therapy for couples. *Journal of Consulting and Clinical Psychology, 61,* 68–84.

Greenberg, L., & Johnson, S. (1988). *Emotionally focused therapy for couples.* New York: Guilford Press.

Greenberg, L. S., & Korman, L. (1993). Assimilating emotion into psychotherapy integration. *Journal of Psychotherapy Integration, 3,* 249–265.

Greenberg, L. S., & Pascual-Leone, J. (1995). A dialectical constructivist approach to experiential change. In R. A. Neimeyer & M. Mahoney (Eds.), *Constructivism in psychotherapy* (pp. 169–194). Washington, DC: American Psychological Association.

Greenberg, L. S., & Paivio, S. C. (1997). *Working with the emotions.* New York: Guilford Press.

Greenberg, L. S., Rice, L. N., & Elliott, R. (1993). *Facilitating emotional change: The moment by moment process.* New York: Guilford Press.

Greenberg, L. S., & Safran, J. D. (1984). Integrating affect and cognition: A perspective on the process of therapeutic change. *Cognitive Therapy and Research, 8,* 559–578.

Greenberg, L. S., & Safran, J. D. (1987). *Emotion in psychotherapy.* New York: Guilford.

Greenberg, L. S., & Safran, J. D. (1989). Emotion in psychotherapy. *American Psychologist, 44*, 19–29.

Greenberg, L., & Watson, J. (1998). Experiential therapy of depression: Differential effects of client-centred relationship conditions and process experiential interventions. *Psychotherapy Research, 8*, 210–224.

Greenberg, L. S., Watson, J., & Goldman, R. (1996). Change processes in experiential therapy. In R. Hutterer & P. Schmid (Eds.), *Client-centered and experiential therapy: Current developments* (pp. 35–46). Vienna: Peter Lang.

Gross, J. (1989). Emotional expression in cancer onset and progression. *Social Science and Medicine, 28*(1), 239–268.

Guidano, V. F. (1993). *The self in process.* New York: Guilford Press.

Haviland, M. G., Shaw, D. G., MacMurray, J. P., & Cummings, M. A. (1988). Validation of the Toronto Alexithymia Scale with substance abusers. *Psychotherapy and Psychosomatics, 50*, 81–87.

Hirscheimer, K. (1996). *Development and verification of a measure of resolution of unfinished business.* Unpublished master's thesis, York University, Toronto, Ontario, Canada.

Hoehn-Saric, R., Frank, J. D., & Gurland, B. J. (1968). Focused attitude change in neurotic patients. *Journal of Nervous and Mental Disease, 147*, 124–133.

Hoehn-Saric, R., Liberman, B., Imber, S. D., Stone, A. R., Frank, J. D., & Ribich, F. D. (1974). Attitude change and attribution of arousal in psychotherapy. *Journal of Nervous and Mental Disease, 159*, 234–244.

Hoehn-Saric, R., Liberman, B., Imber, S. D., Stone, A. R., Pande, S. K., & Frank, J. D. (1972). Arousal and attitude change in neurotic patients. *Archives of General Psychiatry, 26*, 52–56.

Holzer, M., & Dahl, H. (1996). How to find frames. *Psychotherapy Research, 6*, 177–197.

Holzer, M., Pokorny, D., Horst, K., & Luborsky, L. (1997). The verbalization of emotions in the therapeutic dialogue: A correlate to treatment outcome? *Psychotherapy Research, 7*, 261–274.

Honos-Webb, L., Surko, M., Stiles, W. B., & Greenberg, L. (1999). Assimilation of voices in psychotherapy: The case of Jan. *Journal of Counseling Psychology, 46*, 448–460.

Horvath, A. O., & Greenberg, L. S. (1994). *The working alliance.* New York: Wiley InterScience.

Hunt, M. (1998). The only way out is through: Emotional processing and recovery after a depressing life event. *Behavior Research and Therapy, 36*, 361–384.

Iwakabe, S., Rogan, K., & Stalikas, A. (2000). The relationship between client emotional expressions, therapist interventions, and the working alliance: An exploration of eight emotional expression events. *Journal of Psychotherapy Integration, 10*(4), 375–402.

Johnson, S., & Greenberg, L. (1985). Differential effects of experiential and problem solving interventions in resolving marital conflict. *Journal of Consulting and Clinical Psychology, 53,* 175–184.

Johnson, S., & Greenberg, L. (1988). Relating process to outcome in marital therapy. *Journal of Marital & Family Therapy, 14,* 175–183.

Jones, E. E., & Pulos, S. M. (1993). Comparing the process in psychodynamic and cognitive–behavioral therapies. *Journal of Consulting and Clinical Psychology, 61,* 306–316.

Kennedy-Moore, E., & Watson, J. C. (1999). *Expressing emotion: Myths, realities, and therapeutic strategies.* New York: Guilford Press.

Kiecolt-Glaser, J., Fisher, L., Ogrocki, P., Stout, J., Speicher, C., & Glaser, R. (1987). Marital quality, marital disruption, and immune function. *Psychosomatic Medicine, 49,* 13–34.

Klein, M. H., Mathieu, P. L., Gendlin, E. T., & Kiesler, D. J. (1969). *The Experiencing Scale: A research and training manual.* Madison: University of Wisconsin, Bureau of AudioVisual Research.

Klein, M. H., Mathieu-Coughlan, P., & Kiesler, D. J. (1986). The Experiencing Scales. In L. S. Greenberg & W. M. Pinsof (Eds.), *The psychotherapeutic process: A research handbook* (pp. 21–71). New York: Guilford Press.

Knapp, P., Levy, E., Georgi, R., Black, P., Fox, B., & Heeren, T. (1992). Short-term immunological effects of induced emotion. *Psychosomatic Medicine, 54,* 133–148.

Korman, L. M. (1998). *Changes in clients' emotion episodes in therapy.* Unpublished doctoral dissertation, York University, Toronto, Ontario, Canada.

Korman, L. M., & Greenberg, L. S. (1996). Emotion and therapeutic change. In J. Panksepp (Ed.), *Advances in biological psychiatry* (Vol. II, pp. 1–22). Greenwich, CT: JAI Press.

Lang, P. J., Melamed, B. G., & Hart, J. (1970). A psychophysiological analysis of fear modification using an automated desensitization procedure. *Journal of Abnormal Psychology, 76,* 220–234.

LeCroy, C. W. (1988). Anger management or anger expression: which is most effective? *Residential Treatment for Children & Youth, 5*(3), 29–39.

LeDoux, J. E. (1993). Emotional networks in the brain. In M. Lewis & J. M. Haviland (Eds.), *Handbook of emotions* (pp. 109–118). New York: Guilford Press.

Linehan, M. M. (1993). *Cognitive–behavioral treatment of borderline personality disorder.* NewYork: Guilford Press.

Machado, P., Beutler, L. E., & Greenberg, L. (1999). Emotion recognition in psychotherapy. Impact of therapist level of experience and emotional awareness. *Journal of Clinical Psychology, 55*(1), 39–57.

Mahoney, M. (1991). *Human change processes.* New York: Basic Books.

Mahrer, A., Dessaulles, A., Nadler, W. P., Gervaize, P. A., & Sterner, I. (1987). Good and very good moments in psychotherapy: Content, distribution, and facilitation. *Psychotherapy, 24,* 7–14.

Mahrer, A., Fairweather, D., Passey, S., Gingras, N., Boulet, D. (1999). The promotion and use of strong feelings in psychotherapy. *Journal of Humanistic Psychology, 39*(1), 35–53.

Malcolm, W. (1999). *Relating process to outcome in the treatment of unfinished business in process experiential therapy.* Unpublished doctoral dissertation, York University, Toronto, Ontario, Canada.

Marks, I. M., Hodgson, R., & Rachman, S. (1975). Treatment of chronic obsessive–compulsive neurosis by in vivo exposure. *British Journal of Psychiatry, 127,* 349–364.

Mergenthaler, E. (1996). Emotion-abstraction patterns in verbatim protocols: A new way of describing psychotherapeutic processes. *Journal of Consulting and Clinical Psychology, 64,* 1306–1315.

Mohr, D. C., Shoham-Solomon, V., Engle, D., & Beutler, L. E. (1991). The expression of anger in psychotherapy for depression: Its role and measurement. *Psychotherapy Research, 1,* 124–134.

Nichols, M. P., & Zax, M. (1977). *Catharsis in psychotherapy.* New York: Gardener.

Oatley, K., & Jenkins, J. (1992). Human emotions: Function and dysfunction. *Annual Review of Psychology, 43,* 55–85.

Orlinsky, D. E., & Howard, K. I. (1978). The relation of process to outcome in psychotherapy. In S. L. Garfield & A. E. Bergin, (Eds.), *Handbook of psychotherapy and behavior change: An empirical analysis* (2nd ed., pp. 546–610). New York: Wiley.

Paivio, S., & Greenberg, L. (2001). Introduction to special issue on treating emotion regulation problem in psychotherapy. *In-Session, 57*(2), 153–155..

Paivio, S., & Greenberg, L. (1995). Resolving unfinished business: Efficacy of experiential therapy using empty-chair dialogue. *Journal of Consulting and Clinical Psychology, 63,* 419–425.

Parkes, C. M. (1980). Bereavement counselling: Does it work? *British Medical Journal, 281,* 3–10.

Pennebaker, J. W. (1997). *Opening up.* New York. Guilford Press.

Pennebaker, J. W., & Susman, J. (1988). Disclosure of trauma and psychosomatic processes. *Social Science and Medicine, 26,* 327–332.

Pennebaker, J. W., & Traue, H. C. (1993). Inhibition and psychosomatic processes. In J. W. Pennebaker & H. C. Traue (Eds.), *Emotion, inhibition and health* (pp. 146–163). Gottingen, Germany: Hogrefe & Huber.

Perls, F. (1973). *The Gestalt approach and eyewitness to therapy.* Palo Alto, CA: Science and Behavior Books.

Perls, F., Hefferline, R. F., & Goodman, P. (1951). *Gestalt therapy.* New York: Dell.

Pierce, R. A., Nichols, M. P., & DuBrin, J. R. (1983). *Emotional expression in psychotherapy.* New York: Gardner.

Pos, A. E. (1999). *Depth of experiencing during emotion episodes and its relationship to core themes and outcome.* Unpublished master's thesis, York University, Toronto, Ontario, Canada.

Raphael, B. (1997). Preventive intervention with the recently bereaved. *Archives of General Psychiatry, 34,* 1450–1454.

Rice, L. N., & Greenberg, L. S. (1984). The new research paradigm. In L. N. Rice & L. S. Greenberg (Eds.), *Patterns of change* (pp. 7–26). New York: Guilford Press.

Rogers, C. R. (1942). *Counselling and psychotherapy.* Boston: Houghton-Mifflin.

Rogers, C. R. (1959). A theory of therapy, personality and interpersonal relationships, as developed in the client-centered framework. In S. Koch (Ed.), *Psychology: A study of a science* (Vol. 3, pp. 184–256). New York: McGraw Hill.

Rogers, C. R. (1961). *On becoming a person.* Boston: Houghton-Mifflin.

Safran, J. D., & Greenberg, L. S. (1991). *Emotion, psychotherapy and change.* New York: Guilford Press.

Samoilov, A., & Goldfried, M. (2000). Role of emotion in cognitive behavior therapy. *Clinical Psychology: Science & Practice, 7,* 373–385.

Scherer, K. R. (1984). Emotion as a multicomponent process: A model and some cross-cultural data. In P. Shaver (Ed.), *Review of personality and social psychology* (Vol. 5, pp. 37–63). Beverly Hill, CA: Sage.

Shaver, P., Schwartz, J., Kirson, D., O'Connor, C. (1987). Emotion knowledge: Further exploration of a prototype approach. *Journal of Personality and Social Psychology, 52,* 1061–1086.

Shea, J. D. C., Burton, R., & Girgis, A. (1993). Negative affect, absorption, and immunity. *Physiology and Behavior, 53,* 449–457.

Sifneos, P. E. (1988). Alexithymia and its relationship to hemispheric specialization, affect, and creativity. *Psychiatric Clinics of North America, 11,* 287–292.

Spiegel, D. (1994). *Living beyond limits: New hope and help for facing life threatening illness.* New York: Random House.

Stalikas, A., & Fitzpatrick, M. (1995). Client good moments. An intensive analysis of a single session. *Canadian Journal of Counselling, 29,* 160–175.

Stone, A. A., Neale, J. M., Cox, D. X., Napoli, A., Valdimarsdottir, H., & Kennedy-Moore, E. (1994). Daily events are associated with a secretory immune response to an oral antigen in men. *Health Psychology, 13,* 440–446.

Taylor, G. J. (1994). The alexithymia construct: Conceptualization, validation, and relationship with basic dimensions of personality. *New Trends in Experimental and Clinical Psychiatry, 10,* 61–74.

Taylor, G. J., Bagby, R. M., & Parker, J. D. A. (1991). The alexithymia construct: A potential paradigm for psychosomatic medicine. *Psychosomatics, 32,* 153–164.

Taylor, G. J., Bagby, R. M., Ryan, D. P., & Parker, J. D. A. (1990). Validation of the alexithymia construct: A measurement-based approach. *Canadian Journal of Psychiatry, 35,* 290–297.

Taylor, G. J., Parker, J. D. A., Bagby, R. M., & Acklin, M. W. (1992). Alexithymia and somatic complaints in psychiatric out-patients. *Journal of Psychosomatic Research, 36,* 417–424.

Teasdale, J. D., & Barnard, P. J. (1993). *Affect, cognition, and change: Remodeling depressive thought.* Hillsdale, NJ: Erlbaum.

van der Kolk, B. A., McFarlane, A., & Weisath, L. (1996). *Traumatic stress.* New York: Guilford Press.

Warwar, N., & Greenberg, L. (2000, June). *Catharsis is not enough: Changes in emotional processing related to psychotherapy outcome.* Paper presented at the annual meeting of the International Society for Psychotherapy Research, Chicago.

Wise, T. N., Jani, N. N., Kass, E., Sonnenschein, K., & Mann, L. S. (1988). Alexithymia: Relationship to severity of medical illness and depression. *Psychotherapy and Psychosomatics, 50,* 68–71.

Wiser, S., & Arnow, B. (2001). Emotional experiencing: To facilitate or regulate? *In-Session, 57*(2), 157–168.

17

THERAPIST RELATIONAL VARIABLES

TED P. ASAY AND MICHAEL J. LAMBERT

The relationship between therapist and client is of central importance in the humanistic approach to psychotherapy. Therapists' attitudes and interpersonal skills have also been viewed as the cornerstone of effective psychotherapeutic relationships. Beginning with the seminal work of Carl Rogers and his associates (Rogers, 1957; Rogers & Dymond, 1954), client-centered therapists and researchers have emphasized the crucial role of therapist relational skills in effecting personality change. Rogers based his theory of change on the therapist's ability to offer clients specific facilitative qualities that were thought to be germane to the change process. He further asserted that these facilitative conditions were both necessary and sufficient for effective psychotherapy. Rogers's original formulations were followed by research efforts evaluating the role of the facilitative conditions in the change process, the training of individuals in relationship skills, and the validity of the "necessary and sufficient conditions" hypothesis (Carkhuff, 1972; Gurman, 1977; Lambert, DeJulio, & Stein, 1978; Parloff, Waskow, & Wolfe, 1978; Truax, 1971; Truax & Carkhuff, 1967; see also this volume, Cain, chapter 1, and Bozarth, Zimring, and Tausch, chapter 5).

Rogers's client-centered therapy, with emphasis on the facilitative conditions, has been the foundation for the development of several other experiential approaches to psychotherapy, including those of Gendlin (1981), Mahrer (1983), and Greenberg and associates (Greenberg, Rice, & Elliott, 1983; Greenberg & Johnson, 1987). In addition, the facilitative skills have been integrated into much of contemporary psychotherapeutic theory and are viewed by most researchers as central to the change process (Beutler, Machado, & Neufeldt, 1994). They are also a core element of what has been termed the *working alliance* or *therapeutic alliance*, a construct that has recently received a great deal of attention within the framework of research on the therapeutic relationship.

In this chapter, we review the research on therapist relational variables with a particular focus on their relationship to psychotherapy outcome. We include the early work of Rogers and his followers along with more recent developments that illustrate the relevant research in this area. We conclude with a discussion of how these research findings are applicable to everyday clinical practice.

REVIEW OF RESEARCH

Therapist Relationship Skills

In his conceptualization of effective psychotherapy, Rogers (1957) delineated three specific therapist facilitative conditions that he viewed as necessary and sufficient for personality change. These were (a) *empathic understanding*, the degree to which the therapist is successful in communicating his or her awareness and understanding of the client's current experience in language that is attuned to that client; (b) *unconditional positive regard*, the extent to which the therapist communicates nonevaluative caring and positive regard to the client, respecting the client as a person; and (c) *congruence*, the extent to which the therapist is nondefensive, real, and "nonphony" in his or her interactions with the client.

Although Rogers actively researched and evaluated his therapeutic approach, he worked mostly on evaluating the overall effectiveness of client-centered therapy and did not focus specifically on the impact of the three facilitative conditions. However, many of his associates enthusiastically engaged in the empirical evaluation of the relationship between the facilitative conditions and client change. In one study, Halkides (1958) sampled interviews from 20 client–therapist pairs and had three judges rate them for degree of unconditional positive regard, congruence, and empathic understanding. Data from several change measures revealed highly significant associations between treatment success and the relationship variables. However, Truax (1963) later reported that an attempt to replicate that study was unsuccessful.

Summaries of studies of the facilitative conditions and client outcome have been presented by several authors with varying conclusions. Truax and Carkhuff (1967) and Truax and Mitchell (1971) carried out the most complete and comprehensive review of studies at that time and were optimistic in their conclusions about the strong relationship between therapist interpersonal skills and client improvement. Truax (1971) also concluded that warmth, empathy, and genuineness contributed to positive change with a wide variety of clients across a variety of therapy modalities and theories.

Other reviewers have not been as optimistic in their appraisals of the importance of the facilitative conditions. For example, Bergin (1971) suggested that the results of studies by client-centered researchers may not generalize to other modes of therapy. In a comprehensive review of psychotherapy outcome research, Meltzoff and Kornreich (1970) concluded that research results on the facilitative conditions were ambiguous and inconclusive and that the importance of the Rogerian conditions had not been proven. Likewise, Luborsky, Chandler, Auerbach, Cohen, and Bachrach (1971) reviewed 116 controlled outcome studies between 1946 and 1969 and tried to identify certain therapist skills that showed up across studies. The only therapist variables that showed a reliable relationship with outcome were therapist empathy and experience.

In a comprehensive review of research on therapist interpersonal skills, Lambert et al. (1978) reviewed 17 well-designed and executed studies of facilitative conditions and outcome. They concluded that these studies presented "only modest evidence in favor of the hypothesis that such factors as accurate empathy, warmth and genuineness relate to measures of outcome" (p. 472). These researchers indicated further that there were other unaccounted-for variables contributing to client change and that there was little evidence showing a cause–effect relationship between the facilitative conditions and outcome.

The conclusions set forth by Lambert et al. (1978) have been echoed by other reviewers (Gurman, 1977; Mitchell, Bozarth, & Krauft, 1977; Patterson, 1984), who pointed out that, while the client–therapist relationship is seen as critical to successful psychotherapy, the relationship between therapist attitudes and interpersonal skills and outcome is more ambiguous than was once thought. Much of the uncertainty about this stems from how relationship factors are measured. Specifically, research findings have shown that client *perceived* relationship factors, rather than objective raters' perceptions of the relationship, obtain consistently more positive results. Furthermore, the larger correlations with outcome are often between client process ratings and clients' self-report of outcome. One explanation for this may be that clients as a whole perceive the therapeutic relationship as more positive than observers and that they are more accurate in their perceptions of the quality of the therapeutic relationship.

An interesting outgrowth of research on therapist facilitative conditions has been studies on systematic training of professional therapists and paraprofessional counselors in the use of facilitative skills. This work was spearheaded by Carkhuff (1972), who asserted that training in relationship skills had positive effects on trainees' psychological adjustment and in their ability to function effectively in many life tasks. Carkhuff (1969) also proposed several additional facilitative conditions thought to be important to the psychotherapy relationship. These were therapist self-disclosure, concreteness, confrontation, and immediacy. Carkhuff's work has been severely criticized on a number of points (Lambert & DeJulio, 1977), primarily involving methodological flaws in the studies he used to support the efficacy of his training model. In addition, the impact of these training programs on psychotherapy outcome is questionable (Lambert & DeJulio, 1977).

More recent research studies on therapist facilitative conditions have generally included them as one variable among several that might be related to treatment outcome. In this context, the value of therapist relationship skills has been demonstrated in several studies. For instance, Miller, Taylor, and West (1980) investigated the comparative effectiveness of various behavioral approaches aimed at helping problem drinkers control their alcohol consumption. While the focus of the study was on the comparative effects of focused versus broad-spectrum behavioral therapy, Miller et al. also collected data on the contribution of therapist empathy to client outcome. Surprisingly, they found a strong relationship between empathy and patient outcome obtained from the 6- to 8-month follow-up interviews used to assess drinking behavior. Therapists' rank on empathy correlated ($r = .82$) with patient outcome, thus accounting for 67% of the variance in the outcome criteria. These results argue for the importance of the therapist empathic communicative skills even in behavioral interventions.

In another illustrative study, Lafferty, Beutler, and Crago (1991) explored differences between more and less effective trainee psychotherapists, specifically examining which of several therapist variables most consistently distinguished them. Therapist effectiveness was determined by comparing the level of symptomatic distress experienced by clients before and subsequent to treatment using the Symptom Checklist 90–Revised. Therapists whose clients typically manifested more distress after than before treatment were assigned to the less effective group, whereas therapists whose clients experienced relatively less distress following treatment as compared with before were assigned to the more effective group. Of interest here is the finding that the less effective therapists were shown to have low levels of empathic understanding. As Lafferty et al. (1991) stated, their study "supports the significance of therapist empathy in effective psychotherapy. Clients of less effective therapists felt less understood by their therapists than did clients of more effective therapists" (p. 79).

In a similar investigation, Najavits and Strupp (1994) reported on a study in which 16 practicing therapists were identified as more effective or less effective using time-limited dynamic psychotherapy with outpatient cases. Therapist effectiveness was determined by clients' outcome scores and length of stay in treatment. Multiple measures of outcome were used and completed by clients, therapists, independent observers, and therapist supervisors. Results revealed that more effective therapists showed more positive behavior and fewer negative behaviors than less effective therapists. Positive behaviors included warmth, understanding, and affirmation. Negative behaviors included belittling and blaming, ignoring and negating, and attacking or rejecting. Therapists were differentiated almost entirely by nonspecific (relationship) factors rather than specific (technical) factors. On the basis of these findings, Najavits and Strupp (1994) commented: "Thus, basic capacities of human relating—warmth, affirmation, and a minimum of attack and blame—may be at the center of effective psychotherapeutic intervention. Theoretically based technical interventions were not nearly as often significant in this study" (p. 121).

Recent reviews of process–outcome studies have identified specific therapist qualities, skills, and responses that are related to outcome. In their exhaustive review of over 2,000 process–outcome studies since 1950, Orlinsky, Grawe, and Parks (1994) identified several therapist variables that have consistently been shown to have a positive impact on treatment outcome. Therapist credibility, skill, collaborativeness, empathic understanding, and affirmation of the patient, along with the ability to engage with the patient, invest in the treatment process, facilitate a strong therapeutic bond, focus on the patient's problems, and direct attention to the patient's affective experience were highly related to successful treatment. It is interesting that the therapist interventions of paradoxical intentions, experiential confrontation, and interpretation were also positively related to therapeutic outcome.

Using meta-analysis, Greenberg, Elliott, and Lietaer (1994) examined 19 process–outcome studies of client-centered and experiential therapies and reported results in effect sizes. Of these, four concerned the relationship between therapist facilitativeness and outcome. Although the available research was limited, their results revealed a consistent, reasonably strong relationship between therapist facilitativeness and outcome (mean $r = .43$). In the studies reviewed, Greenberg et al. found improvement was positively correlated with therapist warmth, concreteness, and activeness (mean $r = .34$; Stuhr & Meyer, 1991), with facilitative interventions ($r = .25$; Horton & Elliott, 1991), and with at least two of the three client-centered facilitative conditions ($r = .31$; Rudolph, Langer, & Tausch, 1980). The strongest relationship was reported by Grawe, Caspar, and Ambuhl (1990) for the generic model component, therapist self-relatedness (i.e., genuineness; $r = .61$).

The therapeutic effect of specific therapist verbal interventions has also been obtained from client reports of helpful and nonhelpful therapist responses. In a study by Elliott (1985), therapist responses that helped clients gain a new perspective, resolve problems, clarify issues, focus awareness, increase understanding, become more involved, and maintain personal contact were described as helpful. Therapist interventions that distanced therapists from clients' problems, raised unwanted thoughts, focused on unrelated topics, assigned responsibility for feelings to the client, or produced unacceptable interpretations were judged as not helpful.

The impact of therapist facilitative skills was examined in studies on the treatment of depression. Greenberg and Watson (1998) compared the effectiveness of client-centered psychotherapy and process–experiential psychotherapy in the treatment of adults suffering from major depression. Client-centered therapy was defined by therapist implementation of the facilitative conditions of empathy, positive regard, and congruence. Process–experiential treatment provided an empathic relationship as well as three other interventions designed to help clients deal with cognitive–affective problems (e.g., empty-chair dialogues). Results revealed that both approaches were effective in the treatment of depression. Each treatment produced effect sizes equivalent to the effect sizes generally obtained in other studies that use varying therapeutic approaches in the treatment of depression. There was no difference between treatments on ratings of depression at 6-month follow-up; however, the process–experiential treatment effected greater improvement in clients' self-esteem, in interpersonal functioning, and in reducing clients' overall level of distress at termination and produced quicker changes by midtreatment. Consequently, Greenberg and Watson suggested that client-centered therapists could effect more rapid and pervasive changes in clients by applying more active experiential interventions at appropriate times. Among other things, this study demonstrated the effectiveness of therapist relational attitudes in facilitating a change-producing relationship in a group of depressed adults and marks a first step in evaluating the facilitative conditions in the treatment of specific psychological disorders.

In an investigation comparing psychotherapy process of cognitive–behavioral therapy (CBT) and interpersonal psychotherapy (IPT) in the treatment of adults with depression, Ablon and Jones (1999) rated transcripts from the National Institute of Mental Health Treatment of Depression Collaborative Research Program using the Psychotherapy Process Q Sort (Ablon & Jones, 1998). Findings revealed that both IPT and CBT were equally effective and that both included, in practice, important facilitative factors. The IPT therapists were found to frequently clarify, rephrase, or restate the client's communication and encouraged self-reflection about interpersonal relationships. CBT therapists were also found to offer strong support, encouragement, and approval in an effort to control negative affect. Ablon and Jones concluded that IPT represents a kind of "common factor" or Rogerian treatment in which empathy, support, and nonjudgmental acceptance from the therapist are emphasized.

In summary, findings from 4 decades of research have documented the impact of therapist relational variables on client change. Given the current state of knowledge, it would probably be safe to say that researchers and clinicians alike both agree that therapist facilitative skills are essential to the formation of positive therapeutic relationships and contribute significantly to therapeutic outcome.

More specifically, reviews of studies on the three facilitative conditions specified by Rogers have indicated a modestly positive relationship between the facilitative conditions and outcome, although there have been several methodological problems, particularly involving measurement methods, that have contributed to ambiguity and confusion regarding this relationship. Because of methodological difficulties, some authors have argued that there still has not been a clear test of the Rogerian hypothesis (Lambert et al., 1978; Patterson, 1984). Certainly, improvements in measurement and rating techniques and other methodological advances may still shed more light on the role of the facilitative conditions in outcome. Similarly, the debate over the "necessary and sufficient" hypothesis continues, with most investigators viewing the conditions as necessary in the treatment of most client problems but insufficient for therapeutic change in many others. Further debate over this question is likely to be unproductive until more focal studies on the role of therapeutic facilitativeness in the treatment of specific disorders appear.

Although studies looking specifically at the three original therapist facilitative conditions have diminished markedly, therapist facilitativeness has been found to be an important variable in many studies in which varying treatment methods are used with a spectrum of client disorders. One promising line of research has begun to examine the impact of therapist facilitativeness in the treatment of depression among varying schools of therapy. Further research on the efficacy of the facilitative conditions in the treatment of other specific disorders appears to be on the horizon and will contribute significantly to our knowledge of the role of the therapist relational skills in the treatment of an array of psychological problems. (See, for example, Teusch & Böhme's, 1999, work on agoraphobia that raises questions about the need for exposure treatments.)

Therapist empathy continues to resurface as a central element in treatment success. Recent studies that have included therapist facilitative variables have strongly supported the importance of therapist-offered empathy in all forms of treatment with many types of clients. There is also a growing body of research linking therapist empathy with positive treatment outcomes (Bohart & Greenberg, 1997). The study of empathy is complex and difficult, primarily because of confusion generated by the diversity of definitions of this construct (Hill & Nakayama, 2000). Even so, recent developments in psychoanalytic self-psychology and experiential psycho-therapies have generated a renewed enthusiasm for studying this concept among both theoreticians and researchers (Basch, 1983; Bohart, 1988; Kahn, 1985; Kohut, 1977; see also Watson, this volume, chap. 14). Given the existing evidence for the importance of empathy in psychotherapy, the next line of inquiry might focus on how empathy is perceived and experienced by clients, how it can be most accurately measured, and how and when it is most effectively utilized (Greenberg et al., 1994; Lambert et al., 1978). For example, Bachelor (1988) found that what constitutes an empathic therapist response varies from client to client. In this study, some clients (44%) considered a cognitive-type response (e.g., "He said exactly what I had felt") as most helpful, whereas others (30%) indicated that an affective-style response (e.g., "I felt that she felt what I was telling her") was most meaningful. Finally, a lesser number of clients viewed empathic responding as the sharing of personal information or a nurturant-like response. The results seem to imply that therapists are only empathic to the extent to which they understand what is considered to be "empathic" by a particular client.

Therapeutic Alliance

The concept of the therapeutic or working alliance has recently re-ceived considerable research attention and has been increasingly viewed as an important component of successful psychotherapy (Horvath & Luborsky, 1993). Although current measures of the alliance emphasize patient vari-ables, therapist facilitative conditions are also thought to be a fundamental element in the formation of a positive therapeutic alliance (Lambert, 1983). Furthermore, when the facilitative conditions are viewed as qualities of the client as well as the therapist, they are very similar to conceptualizations of the therapeutic alliance (Beutler et al., 1994). Given the close association between the facilitative conditions and the therapeutic alliance, a review of research on the therapeutic alliance is relevant to our current focus on therapist relational variables.

The concept of the therapeutic alliance was discussed by Freud (1912, 1913), who described the importance of the attachment of the patient to the analyst and the analyst's interest in "sympathetic understanding" of the patient in the early treatment relationship. The concept of therapeutic alliance has subsequently been elaborated and revised by many authors (Bowlby, 1988; Fennichel, 1941; Greenson, 1965; Sterba, 1929; Zetzel, 1956). In an attempt to integrate the various constructs and ideas that have been offered to describe the therapeutic alliance, Gaston (1990) suggested that some of the following components of the alliance are measured by some but not all current scales: (a) the client's affective relationship to the therapist, (b) the client's capacity to purposefully work in therapy, (c) the therapist's empathic understanding and involvement, and (d) patient–therapist agreement on the goals and tasks of therapy.

Bordin (1976, 1989) also identified three components of the therapeutic alliance: tasks, goals, and bonds. *Tasks* involve the behaviors and processes within the therapy session that constitute the actual work of therapy. Both therapist and client must view these tasks as important and relevant for a strong therapeutic alliance to exist. The *goals* of therapy are the agreed-upon objectives of the therapy process that both parties must endorse and value. Finally, *bonds* include the positive interpersonal attachment between therapist and client evidenced by mutual trust, confidence, and acceptance.

Most of the empirical work on the therapeutic alliance has been generated by psychodynamic researchers (Gaston, 1990; Horvath & Greenberg, 1994; Horvath & Luborsky, 1993; Horvath & Symonds, 1991; Luborsky, 1994; Luborsky & Auerbach, 1985), although this construct is receiving increasing attention in studies of behavioral therapy (DeRubeis & Feeley, 1991), cognitive therapy (Castonguay, Goldfried, Wiser, Raue, & Hayes, 1996; Krupnick et al., 1996), Gestalt therapy (Horvath & Greenberg, 1989), and client-centered therapy (Grawe et al., 1990). It has been conceptualized and defined in various ways and has been measured by patient ratings, therapist ratings, and judges' ratings (Horvath & Luborsky, 1993). Reviews of the research on therapeutic alliance (Gaston, 1990; Horvath & Greenberg, 1994; Horvath & Luborsky, 1993; Horvath & Symonds, 1991; Lambert, 1992) have generally revealed a positive relationship between alliance and outcome, although there are instances in which the relationship is small or insignificant. For example, Horvath and Symonds (1991) conducted a meta-analysis of 24 studies examining the relationship between alliance and outcome. They found an average effect size that suggests a 26% difference in the rate of therapeutic success attributable to the quality of the alliance.

In an updated meta-analysis of 79 studies relating the therapeutic alliance to outcome, Martin, Gorske, and Davis (2000) found a moderate ($r = .22$) relationship of therapeutic alliance with outcome. Their findings further indicated that the alliance–outcome relation was consistent regardless of the many variables that have been thought to influence this relationship.

In the National Institute of Mental Health Treatment of Depression Collaborative Research Program, Krupnick et al. (1996) investigated the role of the therapeutic alliance in psychotherapeutic and pharmacological treatment of individuals with depression. In the study, 250 clients suffering from major depressive disorder were randomly assigned to one of four treatment modalities: IPT, CBT, imipramine with clinical management, or placebo with clinical management. Therapists were psychiatrists and psychologists who were carefully selected, trained, and monitored in the specific treatment they offered. Therapy was guided by treatment manuals, and depressive symptomatology was assessed by client self-reports (Beck Depression Inventory; Beck, Ward, Mendelsohn, Mock, & Erbaugh, 1961) and ratings by clinical evaluators (Hamilton Rating Scale for Depression; Hamilton, 1960). Therapeutic alliance was measured using a modified version of the Vanderbilt Therapeutic Alliance Scale (Hartley & Strupp, 1983).

Results indicated that therapeutic alliance had a significant impact on outcome for both psychotherapies and for active and placebo pharmacotherapy. Both early and mean ratings of alliance were significantly related to treatment outcome. However, therapist contribution to the therapeutic alliance was not significantly related to outcome on any of the outcome measures. One explanation for this finding is the lack of variability among the therapists. In summarizing the results of this study, Krupnick et al. (1996) concluded, "these results are most consistent with the view that the therapeutic alliance is a common factor across modalities of treatment for depression that is distinguishable from specific technical or pharmacological factors within the treatments" (p. 538).

In yet another study, Castonguay et al. (1996) investigated the therapeutic alliance in cognitive therapy. These researchers compared the impact of the treatment variable unique to cognitive therapy (the therapist's focus on distorted cognition and depressive symptoms) and two variables common with other forms of treatment (therapeutic alliance and client emotional involvement) on treatment outcome. Participants were 30 clients suffering from major depressive disorder who received either cognitive therapy alone or cognitive therapy with medication over a 12-week period. Clients were treated by experienced therapists who conducted cognitive therapy according to the manualized guidelines. Outcome was assessed through client ratings and independent evaluators.

Results revealed that the two common variables, therapeutic alliance and client's emotional experiencing, were both found to be related to improvement. At the same time, the variable deemed to be unique to cognitive therapy, linking distorted thoughts and negative emotion, was positively related to depressive symptoms after therapy. Castonguay et al. (1996) suggested that the latter finding was likely due to the therapists' attempts to repair strains in the therapeutic alliance by increasing their efforts to persuade the client to accept the validity of the cognitive therapy rationale or by treating alliance strains as manifestations of the client's distorted thoughts that needed to be challenged.

In an investigation of the predictive validity of two alliance measures, the Working Alliance Inventory (WAI) and the California Psychotherapy Alliance Scale (CALPAS), Safran and Wallner (1991) studied a sample of 22 outpatients who received time-limited cognitive therapy that focused on aspects of the therapeutic relationship. Outcome was assessed using a variety of client and therapist measures. Results indicated that both alliance measures were predictive of outcome when administered after the third sessions of treatment. These findings underscore the importance of the alliance in cognitive therapy and are consistent with research indicating that therapy outcome can be predicted by ratings of the therapeutic alliance in the early stages of treatment (Horvath & Luborsky, 1993).

As the empirical data accumulate on the importance of the therapeutic alliance in successful psychotherapy, the question of how the alliance develops and what factors are most important in the development of a positive therapeutic alliance becomes an important focus of inquiry. The ability to form a meaningful, collaborative working relationship between client and therapist can be conceptualized as constituting the foundation of an effective therapeutic alliance. This collaboration not only appears to involve the therapist's ability to communicate acceptance, warmth, and empathy but also requires the client and therapist to come to a mutual agreement on the goals of treatment and how those goals will be accomplished (Hatcher & Barends, 1996). Thus, collaboration between therapist and client begins with the client experiencing security in the therapeutic relationship and further develops as the therapist and client exhibit a willingness to negotiate the goals and tasks of therapy.

Several investigators (Bordin, 1989; Safran, Crocker, McMain, & Murray, 1990; Safran, Muran, & Samstag, 1994) have suggested that successful therapy often involves a rupture–repair cycle in the therapeutic alliance that can occur at any time in therapy but is most likely to occur when the therapist begins to address maladaptive client patterns. These ruptures not only are influenced by clients' past dysfunctional beliefs and fears but may also result from antitherapeutic therapist attitudes and behavior, such as criticism, indifference, and dislike of the client. There is evidence to suggest that therapist focus on the client's inner feelings about the therapy and the therapist is crucial in repairing the rupture and strengthening the alliance (Safran et al., 1994). Failure to address therapeutic ruptures is likely to lead to increased client negativity and unsuccessful therapeutic outcomes. It should be noted too that failure to experience ruptures in the alliance may be an indication of a client's unwillingness to engage in the therapeutic process by avoiding important affective content or idealizing the therapist. This pattern also results when the therapist is unwilling to explore important thinking, emotional, or behavioral patterns in the client.

Evidence from the research studies on the therapeutic alliance points to the value of this construct in understanding aspects of the therapist–client relationship that are related to therapeutic progress. The alliance appears to be a relevant concept in many modes of therapy, remains relatively stable through the course of therapy, and is predictive of therapeutic outcomes. Therapist facilitative conditions are thought to be an essential aspect of the therapeutic alliance, and there is some indication that measures of therapist facilitative conditions and therapeutic alliance reflect the same underlying change-promoting process (Beutler et al., 1994). Consequently, therapist facilitative skills are likely to constitute a major part of the therapist's contribution to an effective therapeutic alliance. In addition to providing empathy, warmth, support, and genuineness, the therapist's ability to effectively and tactfully deal with ruptures or strains in the alliance is crucial to the outcome of the treatment process.

Additional Findings

In addition to research on therapist facilitative conditions and the therapeutic alliance, several other studies have illuminated the importance of therapist relational skills in psychotherapy. For example, Lorr (1965) had 523 psychotherapy patients describe their therapists with 65 different statements. A factor analysis identified five factors: understanding, accepting, authoritarian (directive), independence encouraging, and critical–hostile. Scores on these descriptive factors were correlated with improvement ratings; that is, client ratings of understanding and accepting correlated most highly with client- and therapist-rated improvement.

In an attempt to replicate Lorr's (1965) study, Cooley and LaJoy (1980) studied the relationship between therapist self-ratings of relationship and outcome, as well as discrepancies between client and therapist ratings and outcome ratings. In the study, 56 adult community mental health outpatients were treated by any one of eight therapists. Client ratings of therapist understanding and acceptance once again correlated most highly with client-rated outcomes. However, when self-ratings of therapists' attributes were compared with therapist-rated client outcomes, the correlations were insignificant, suggesting that therapists' self-perceptions of personal attributes were not predictive of therapeutic outcome.

Clients frequently attribute their success to the therapists' personal qualities. That these personal qualities bear a striking resemblance to each other across studies and methodologies is evidence that they are highly important in psychotherapy outcome. This notion was emphasized by Lazarus (1971) in an uncontrolled follow-up study of 112 clients he had seen in therapy. Clients were asked to provide information about the effects of their treatment, durability of improvement, and their perceptions of the therapeutic process and characteristics of the therapist. Those adjectives that most often described the therapist were sensitive, gentle, and honest. Clients clearly believed that the personal qualities of the therapist were more important than specific technical factors about which there was little agreement.

Similarly, Strupp, Fox, and Lessler (1969) found that patients who had a positive attitude toward their therapist proved to have more successful outcomes. Commenting on these findings, Strupp et al. (1969) noted that "patients who rated their own therapy as successful described their therapist as warm, attentive, interested, understanding, and respectful" (p. 116).

In another example of retrospective research, Elliott, Clark, and Kemeny (1991) used content analysis to study clients' postsession descriptions of the most helpful events in process–experiential therapy. The most common categories were self-awareness, client self-disclosure, and therapist experiential techniques. However, clients and therapists' ratings of significant events revealed that the highest ratings by both groups were given to feeling understood, followed by self-awareness and either feeling close to the therapist or feeling supported.

This limited sampling of retrospective ratings of the therapeutic process by clients and therapists has also highlighted the important role that therapist interpersonal skills play in treatment success. In many cases, they are viewed, by clients in particular, as the most important part of the treatment process. Even when other components are rated as more helpful, therapist facilitative skills are often deemed as having played a significant role in achieving positive outcomes. Many additional studies and reviews could be cited as providing research support for the theoretical propositions of the person-centered school. For example, Gaston and Ring (1992) showed that effective therapists focused on the internal experiences of clients, encouraged expression of negative feelings toward others, articulated explicit treatment goals, and directed client's attention to the most central treatment issues. Support for additional factors can be found in the exhaustive review of process–outcome research previously noted in Orlinsky et al. (1994), the review of therapist variables and outcome by Beutler et al. (1994), and in the review on process–outcome research by Sachse and Elliott in chapter 3 of this book. These reviews have emphasized relationship variables as central to therapy outcome and as essential to therapeutic improvement.

IMPLICATIONS FOR PRACTICE AND TRAINING

Our review of the empirical research on therapist relational variables in psychotherapy has revealed important findings that are relevant to clinical practice and training in psychotherapy. The challenge to the practitioner is to integrate these findings into day-to-day professional practice. To assist in this process, we offer the following conclusions and recommendations.

There is an abundance of empirical data, spanning five decades, indicating that therapist facilitative skills such as acceptance, warmth, empathy, and genuineness are fundamental in establishing a good therapist–client relationship and are related to positive outcomes (Lambert & Bergin, 1994). Consequently, focusing on these skills or qualities in the therapeutic process is germane to successful treatment. Training in relationship skills is crucial for the beginning therapist because they are the foundation on which all other skills and techniques are built. In training student therapists, one must teach the trainees (in a relatively short period of time) how to be attuned to clients' feelings. However, it is also clear that the trainees often fail to routinely and persistently offer high levels of empathy once they are not monitored. Successful communication of empathic understanding also requires a flexible approach by the therapist that is based on an evolving understanding of what constitutes an empathic response for a particular client (Bachelor, 1988). Thus, a continual focus on the development and proper utilization of relationship skills, particularly empathic communication, is recommended in professional training programs. This could most effectively be accomplished in the direct supervision of trainee cases, preferably with audiotaped or videotaped cases.

The importance of therapist's relational skills is illustrated in the following case example of an 18-year-old year high school senior who is beginning her second session with her therapist. In this instance, the therapist's (T) warmth, empathy, and understanding is used to help the client (C) to be more emotionally expressive and to gain a greater degree of emotional awareness.

C: (quiet and nervous)
T: How are you feeling today?
C: Good. Pretty good. Things have just been real busy.
T: Uh, huh.
C: It seems like there is something going on every minute—always someplace to be or someplace to go or something to do.
T: You seem kind of tired of it all.
C: I guess I am. It's so busy with schoolwork, piano, church stuff, and things at home. I think it just gets to me sometimes.
T: You certainly have a lot going on. I wonder if it's getting a little frustrating.
C: Well, sometimes I think "Why do I have to do all this, what's the point? I don't get it."
T: It just doesn't make sense sometimes.
C: I know it is all good and important, but it isn't always to me.
T: I noticed as you were talking that you seem to be feeling something that you did not say.
C: (becoming tearful) I just get so tired of having to do all these things; these things I am supposed to do.
T: Supposed to do?
C: All the things my parents want me to do. Like getting good grades, being president of the service club, planning the youth activities at church . . . all of it! All of this crap!

T: You try to please your parents by doing all of these things, but you end up feeling very tired and resentful about it.

C: (crying) They expect all of this stuff! They expect me to do it, they expect me to do it all right, they expect perfection!

T: They expect so much from you that maybe it just doesn't seem fair.

C: It's not fair! I do it all! I try real hard and it is never enough. I get an award for having good grades and when I told my dad about it he said, "Yes, but your chemistry grade was too low."

T: You try your hardest but instead of recognizing your achievement your dad criticizes you. That must have really felt bad.

C: It hurt me so much. It made me wonder if I even want to try to do what they want.

T: Sometimes it just doesn't seem worth it.

In this example, the therapist is focusing exclusively on trying to understand the client's emotional experience and to convey that understanding back to the client. There is no effort to get a history of the problem, generate solutions, or make interpretations because these interventions would be premature and distract from the central task of trying to empathize with the client's experience and communicate understanding about it. The above client–therapist dialogue not only helped the client to gain an increased awareness and acceptance of her feelings but was an important step in the development of a strong therapeutic bond or alliance. This direction is depicted in the interaction that took place at the end of the session.

T: You have shared with me today some very strong and important feelings you have about things that are going on in your life. What was this like for you?

C: It has been pretty upsetting, but it feels good to get it all out. I think I have stronger feelings about it than I realized. I have never really talked about this before with anyone.

T: You have been keeping it all inside.

C: Yes. Sometimes I would tell my friends but only in a joking way; not serious. I think I've just needed to talk about it with someone.

T: Maybe we can talk some more about it next time.

C: That would be good.

Reassessing periodically the incorporation and effective use of relationship skills may also be prudent for more seasoned practitioners. In particular, the increasing influence of managed care, with the accompanying emphasis on symptom reduction, may serve to erode the therapist's capacity to understand and empathize with the client's internal experience and, consequently, inhibit his or her affective expression and processing. This may interfere later with the development of a positive therapist–client relationship or alliance, thus undermining therapeutic progress. It also follows that when therapists become overstressed, fatigued, or "burned out," the first skill that suffers is their ability to empathize with the client and to express warmth and understanding. Deterioration in these skills not only reduces therapeutic effectiveness but may also constitute a red flag for the therapist. That is, it may signal the need for clinicians to focus on their personal circumstances and attend to factors that may be impinging on their therapeutic abilities.

Given the important influence of therapist interpersonal skills on the therapeutic relationship and treatment outcome, it would be advisable for training programs to emphasize the development of the therapist as a person along with the acquisition of therapeutic techniques. This might include such things as involvement of trainees in therapy experiences in which they themselves take part in a group process and experience first-hand their personal impact on others and others on them. Participation in individual psychotherapy is an option that could be valuable for several reasons, including experiencing therapy from the client's point of view and gaining an appreciation of the value of therapist relational skills to the therapeutic process. Lastly, improving and unlocking greater capacities for emotional involvement, self-insight, and empathy, as well as developing a greater ability to tolerate anxiety and strong affects, can often be accomplished in personal therapy.

The course and outcome of therapy will be determined to a large extent by the type of therapeutic relationship or alliance that is formed. Therapists make an important contribution to the quality of the alliance, and it is probable that the differences between effective and less effective therapists is their ability to form and maintain a therapeutic alliance with the client, particularly in treating more difficult or challenging clients. Therapists who are able to communicate warmth, understanding, and positive feelings toward the client and can facilitate a reasonable dialogue leading to understanding and agreement about therapeutic goals, techniques, and roles will be more likely to effect a positive treatment relationship. Therapists should avoid types of communication and behavior that have been shown to be disruptive to the therapist–client relationship. Specifically, behaviors that are critical, attacking, rejecting, blaming, or neglectful have been shown to be associated with less effective treatment (Najavits & Strupp, 1994). Therapist passivity, negative confrontations, inappropriate attempts at humor, mechanical responding, and the like also detract from the quality of the therapeutic relationship. Therapist sensitivity to the deleterious effects of this behavior is essential in avoiding pitfalls that would compromise the therapeutic process. This is especially true with clients who are more negative, hostile, and blaming of the therapist and who are more likely to illicit critical, defensive, attacking, or abusive behavior from the therapist.

Despite the therapist's best efforts to facilitate and maintain a positive working alliance, strains and ruptures in the therapeutic relationship naturally occur and are a part of the evolving therapeutic process (Safran et al., 1994). Disruptions in the alliance can occur in the beginning of treatment if there are difficulties in developing a supportive relationship and if satisfying levels of empathy, understanding, collaboration, and consensual endorsement of therapeutic procedures are not achieved.

Consequently, it is important that therapists carefully monitor client reactions for any indications of problems in the therapy relationship. This is especially important because most clients are reluctant to openly communicate dissatisfaction or negative feelings to the therapist, especially in the early stages of treatment (Hill, Nutt-Williams, Heaton, Thompson, & Rhodes, 1996). Therapists can assist in this process by making it known that discussion about the therapy relationship is an important and integral part of therapy and expressions of negative feelings is not only permissible, but valued.

Information about the nature of the therapy relationship can also be obtained through the therapist's awareness of and reflection about his or her own reactions and feelings toward the client. When these reactions are understood and used therapeutically, they become a valuable tool in facilitating the therapeutic process.

When ruptures to the therapeutic relationship do occur, it is crucial for the therapist to be aware of indications that this is happening and to be able to address the client's feelings and attitudes that are associated with the problem. This process is enhanced as the therapist is able to empathize with the client's affective experience and help the client to recognize, clarify, and understand any negative feelings they may be experiencing in regard to the therapy or therapist. This, in turn, opens the door for progress in repairing the alliance rupture.

One common pitfall for therapists involved in this process is to feel threatened by the client's negative or uncooperative feelings and behaviors and to respond by becoming preoccupied with defending themselves and justifying their therapeutic stance. This may take the form of arguing with or criticizing the client or becoming more rigid and authoritarian. If this occurs, the therapist loses objectivity and the ability to relate empathetically and, consequently, to respond in a way that promotes the client's awareness and understanding of what is happening in the therapeutic exchange. It is our view that the most successful therapists are those who are able to maintain an appropriate therapeutic stance even when there is considerable pressure to engage in a pathological interaction. This necessitates the therapist having the awareness, skill, and psychological maturity to focus on empathizing with the client's experience and understanding the therapeutic process rather than getting caught up in it. As therapists are able to do this, the therapist–client relationship is strengthened and therapeutic effectiveness is enhanced.

An example of one type of rupture in the therapeutic relationship and efforts by the therapist to work with the client to repair the rupture is presented in the following clinical vignette. A 32-year-old woman was seeing one of the authors in weekly psychotherapy because of long-standing depression and difficulties maintaining satisfying interpersonal relationships, especially with men. The first few sessions were spent helping the patient cope with intense anxiety and psychic turmoil caused by stressful events at her job. This required a good deal of support and reassurance from the therapist and led to the beginnings of a positive therapeutic alliance. Once the crisis was over, the therapist was able to take a more exploratory approach with her, and they began to examine together some of her problematic interpersonal behaviors as well as her deep-seated anger and resentment about the disappointments, hurts, and losses she had experienced in her life. The following dialogue occurred at this point in her treatment and immediately followed a session that the therapist canceled because of an emergency.

C: (Silence for 2 to 3 minutes.)

T: You look upset today.

C: (sarcastically) Great observation doctor. Hell yes, I'm upset! I am so damn mad about things, I am ready to explode.

T: Tell me about it.

C: I am just sick and tired of the way people treat me. I try to be a good person and treat people right, but what do I get? Shit on, that's what.

T: You try so hard but it always ends up feeling bad.

C: Always.

T: What happened?

C: The same thing that always happens. It is nothing unusual. No one cares about the way I feel. Nobody! Who cares about me and what I need? Not a damn person! Not my mother, not Bill (boyfriend) or any of my so-called friends.

T: Maybe you feel like I don't care either.

C: You don't really care about me! I am just another person to you; just another paying customer. It doesn't really matter to you what happens to me.

T: You feel like I have no real interest or concern for you.

C: You act like you do but you don't really understand me. You are not interested in my feelings. When I walk out the door it is over; you don't even think about me.

T: It must feel very lonely to think that no one, not even your therapist, really cares about you.

C: Yes, I am just pissed about it. I am pissed at you too. It is not worth it.

T: What's not worth it?

C: It just isn't. I am tired of trying with people and feeling bad all the time.

T: Maybe you feel that it is just not worth it with me either.

C: Why would it be? It is too hard, it hurts too much.

T: You are not sure if you want to take the risk to get close to me because you might get hurt again.

C: Something like that. It's just so hard. It feels so bad. I always get hurt and I'm tired of it.

T: I wonder if I hurt your feelings too when I canceled the last appointment.

C: It felt like all the other times. Something happens and I end up getting my feelings stomped on.

T: When I canceled the appointment it felt like I was stomping on your feelings too.

C: It was the same old thing.

T: And that's why you got angry at me.

C: Yes.

T: Your anger seemed to be a way to push me away and maybe even to hurt me like I hurt you.

C: I was just very angry. I don't know. That's probably right. I wanted you to hurt too. I wasn't thinking about that at the time.

T: What went through your mind when I canceled the appointment?

C: It made me mad. It didn't seem fair. It made me feel bad, like my session didn't matter.

T: Like you weren't very important to me.

C: Yea, like you didn't care . . . and you didn't really want to see me.

T: Because?

C: (Pause) Because I'm a pain in the ass! And I'm somebody you would rather not see.

T: You are just too difficult to deal with.

C: That's right and you wouldn't be the first one to think that way.

T: What is it about you that I wouldn't want to deal with?

C: Just me and all my crap.

T: Crap?

C: All my problems.

T: And all your angry feelings.

C: (sobbing) You've got it.

T: It sounds like you are afraid that your feelings, especially your anger, are going to be too intense and too powerful for me to handle, and I will not want to be around you or work with you.

C: I worry that you will find out that I am just a mean, demanding, complaining, bitch that no one would want to be around.

T: Including me.

C: Yes.

T: Well, you have expressed some pretty strong feelings toward me today.

C: I know and it scares me. I'm worried that you will get tired of it.

T: I think you will only know if I am going to hang in here with you if you give it a try and keep expressing your feelings openly. I think you will see too that things will go better for us if we can talk about what is going on between us, particularly if you are having some angry or negative feelings toward me or about your therapy.

C: Yeah, I can see that now. It's just hard to do when it's happening.

T: It is, but I think it's worth working at.

C: I can try.

This short vignette illustrates the importance of the therapist's willingness to tolerate and accept the patient's negative feelings, particularly her anger at him. It seems likely that part of her expectation was that people did not really care about her, including the therapist, and would ultimately disappoint and hurt her in some way. In addition, her verbal accusations and attacks on the therapist were likely an attempt to test the therapist to see if he was going to respond to her in the same fashion that other people had in the past, namely by counterattacking or rejecting her. When this did not occur, and the therapist proceeded to accept and clarify her feelings, she was able to move deeper into her internal experience and talk about her underlying fears about interpersonal closeness and loss. In this case, the alliance strain was repaired and the therapeutic process was enhanced.

In the current managed-care environment in which accountability in health care is emphasized, it is not surprising to see researchers advocate empirically validated psychotherapy (Task Force, 1995) and the use of treatment guidelines and manual-based interventions (Wilson, 1998). Although therapists who intend to offer the highest level of treatment need to make every effort to stay abreast of new developments in the field and emerging empirical findings, it should be kept in mind that there have been serious criticisms of research on empirically validated treatments (Silverman, 1996) and the use of treatment manuals (Strupp & Anderson, 1997). Unfortunately, many of the empirically validated treatments and manual-based approaches focus heavily on technical procedures and adherence to specific treatment guidelines that may interfere with the therapist's ability to develop and maintain an effective therapeutic relationship (Henry, Strupp, Butler, Schacht, & Binder, 1993). We recommend that clinicians keep an open mind and a balanced perspective in considering the use of empirically validated treatments and treatment manuals. Although validated treatments and manuals can be useful in structuring and guiding treatment, psychotherapy is, at a fundamental level, an interpersonal process largely affected by the therapist's ability to facilitate meaningful interpersonal experiences and the client's ability to take advantage of the therapeutic atmosphere as it unfolds.

CONCLUSION

It is clear from our review that therapist facilitative skills, such as empathy, warmth, acceptance, and genuineness, are of critical importance in the formation of a positive therapeutic relationship which, in turn, is basic to many, if not most, psychotherapeutic approaches. It now appears that research on the therapeutic relationship has shifted from a consideration of therapist facilitative conditions per se to a focus on the more collaborative, interactive aspects of the therapeutic relationship characterized in studies of the therapeutic alliance.

Research on the therapeutic alliance has resulted in advances in the conceptualization and operational definition of the therapeutic relationship as well as methods of measuring meaningful variables (Beutler et al., 1994). Thus, research on the therapeutic alliance appears to be a promising avenue in gaining understanding of those qualities of the therapist–client relationship that are most closely associated with therapeutic progress. Research on the alliance has also made it clear that the client's contribution to outcome is even more important than had been previously thought, accounting for more outcome variance than therapist variables.

Another important line of inquiry relates to the impact of the therapist in psychotherapy outcome. The influence of therapist variables on outcome has not been well documented using current research strategies. However, there is mounting evidence indicating that there are wide differences in the effectiveness of therapists and that some therapists appear to be unusually effective (Lambert & Bergin, 1994; Lambert & Okishi, 1997). Why this is the case is not well understood, but in our view it probably has much to do with the therapist's ability to effect a meaningful interpersonal relationship and to use that relationship therapeutically, especially in working with more difficult treatment cases. In any event, we welcome further research efforts in which the therapist's contribution to the therapeutic relationship and to outcomes in general is more specifically and clearly delineated.

REFERENCES

Ablon, J. S. & Jones, E. E. (1998). How expert clinicians prototypes of an ideal treatment correlate with outcome in psychodynamic and cognitive–behavioral therapy. *Psychotherapy Research, 8*, 71–83.

Ablon, J. S., & Jones, E. E. (1999). Psychotherapy process in the NIMH Collaborative Study of Depression. *Journal of Consulting and Clinical Psychology, 67*, 64–75.

Bachelor, A. (1988). How clients perceive therapist empathy: A content analysis of "received" empathy. *Psychotherapy: Therapy, Research and Practice, 25*, 227–240.

Basch, M. (1983). Empathetic understanding: A review of the concept and some theoretical considerations. *Journal of the American Psychoanalytic Association, 31*, 101–126.

Beck, A. T., Ward, C. H., Mendelsohn, M., Mock, J., & Erbaugh, J. (1961). An inventory for measuring depression. *Archives of General Psychiatry, 4*, 561–571.

Bergin, A. E. (1971). The evaluation of therapeutic outcomes. In A. E. Bergin & S. L. Garfield (Eds.), *Handbook of psychotherapy and behavior change* (pp. 217–270). New York: Wiley.

Beutler, L. E., Machado, P. P. P., & Neufeldt, S. A. (1994). Therapist variables. In A. E. Bergin & S. L. Garfield (Eds.), *Handbook of psychotherapy and behavior change* (4th ed., pp. 229–269). New York: Wiley.

Bohart, A. C. (1988). Empathy: Client-centered and psychoanalytic. *American Psychologist, 43*, 667–668.

Bohart, A. C., & Greenberg, L. S. (1997). Empathy and psychotherapy: An introductory review. In A. C. Bohart & L. S. Greenberg (Eds.), *Empathy reconsidered: New directions in psychotherapy* (pp. 3–31). Washington, DC: American Psychological Association.

Bordin, E. S. (1976). The generalizability of the psychoanalytic concept of the working alliance. *Psychotherapy: Theory, Research and Practice, 16*, 252–260.

Bordin, E. S. (1989, April). *Building therapeutic alliances: The base for integration.* Paper presented at the annual meeting of the Society for Exploration of Psychotherapy Integration, Berkeley, CA.

Bowlby, J. (1988). *A secure base: Clinical applications of attachment theory.* London: Routledge & Kegan Paul.

Carkhuff, R. R. (1969). *Helping and human relations: A primer for lay and professional helpers* (2 vols.). New York: Holt, Rinehart & Winston.

Carkhuff, R. R. (1972). The development of systematic human resource development models. *Counseling Psychologist, 3*, 4–16.

Castonguay, L. G., Goldfried, M. R., Wiser, S., Raue, P. J., & Hayes, A. M. (1996). Predicting the effect of cognitive therapy for depression: A study of unique and common factors. *Journal of Consulting and Clinical Psychology, 65*, 497–504.

Cooley, E. F., & LaJoy, R. (1980). Therapeutic relationship and improvement as perceived by clients and therapists. *Journal of Clinical Psychology, 36*, 562–570.

DeRubeis, R. J., & Feeley, M. (1991). Determinants of change in cognitive therapy for depression. *Cognitive Therapy and Research, 14*, 469–482.

Elliott, R. (1985). Helpful and nonhelpful events in brief counseling interviews: An empirical taxonomy. *Journal of Counseling Psychology, 32*, 307–322.

Elliott, R., Clark, C., & Kemeny, V. (1991, July). *Analyzing clients post-session accounts of significant therapy events.* Paper presented at the Society for Psychotherapy Research, Lyon, France.

Fennichel, O. (1941). *Problems of psychoanalytic technique.* Albany, NY: Psychoanalytic Quarterly.

Freud, S. (1912). The dynamics of transference. In J. Strachey (Ed. and Trans.), *The standard edition of the complete psychological works of Sigmund Freud* (pp. 97–108). London: Hogarth Press.

Freud, S. (1913). On beginning the treatment: Further recommendations on the technique of psychoanalysis. In J. Strachey (Ed. and Trans.), *The standard edition of the complete psychological works of Sigmund Freud* (pp. 121–144). London: Hogarth Press.

Gaston, L. (1990). The concept of the alliance and its role in psychotherapy: Theoretical and empirical considerations. *Psychotherapy, 27*, 143–153.

Gaston, L., & Ring, J. M. (1992). Preliminary results on the inventory of therapeutic strategies. *Journal of Psychotherapy Practice and Research, 1*, 1–13.

Gendlin, E. T. (1981). *Focusing* (2nd ed.). New York: Bantam Books.

Grawe, K., Caspar, F., & Ambuehl, H. (1990). Differentielle psychotherapie-forschung: vier therapieforman in Vergleich. *Zeitschrift for Klinische Psychologie, 19*, 287–376.

Greenberg, L. S., Rice, L. N., & Elliott, R. (1993). *Process–experiential therapy: Facilitating emotional change.* New York: Guilford Press.

Greenberg, L. S., Elliott, R., & Lietaer, G. (1994). Research on experiential psychotherapies. In A. E. Bergin & S. L. Garfield (Eds.), *Handbook of psychotherapy and behavior change* (4th ed., 509–539). New York: Wiley.

Greenberg, L. S., & Johnson, S. (1987). *Emotionally focused therapy for couples.* New York: Guilford Press.

Greenberg, L. S., & Watson, J. (1998). Experiential therapy of depression: Differential effects of client-centered relationship conditions and process experiential interventions. *Psychotherapy Research, 8*, 210–224.

Greenson, R. (1965). The working alliance and the transference neurosis. *Psychoanalytic Quarterly, 34*, 155–181.

Gurman, A. S. (1977). The patients perception of the therapeutic relationship. In A. S. Gurman & A. M. Razin (Eds.), *Effective psychotherapy: A handbook of research* (pp. 503–543). New York: Pergamon.

Halkides, G. (1958). *An investigation of therapeutic success as a function of four variables.* Unpublished doctoral dissertation. University of Chicago.

Hamilton, M. A. (1960). A rating scale for depression. *Journal of Neurology and Neurosurgical Psychiatry, 23*, 56–62.

Hartley, D. E., & Strupp, H. H. (1983). The therapeutic alliance: Its relationship to outcome in brief psychotherapy. In J. Masling (Ed.), *Empirical studies of psychoanalytic theories* (Vol. 1). Hillsdale, NJ: Erlbaum.

Hatcher, R. L., & Barends, A. W. (1996). Patients' view of the alliance in psychotherapy: Exploratory factor analysis of three alliance measures. *Journal of Consulting and Clinical Psychology, 64*, 1326–1336.

Henry, W. P., Strupp, H. H., Butler, S. F., Schacht, T. E., & Binder, J. L. (1993). The effects of training in time-limited dynamic psychotherapy: Changes in therapist behavior. *Journal of Consulting and Clinical Psychology, 61*, 434–440.

Hill, C. E., & Nakayama, E. Y. (2000). Client-centered therapy: Where has it been and where is it going? A comment on Hathaway. *Journal of Clinical Psychology*, 56, 861–875.

Hill, C. E., Nutt-Williams, E., Heaton, K., Thompson, B., & Rhodes, R. H. (1996). Therapist retrospective recall of impasses in long term psychotherapy: A qualitative analysis. *Journal of Counseling Psychology*, 43, 207–217.

Horton, C., & Elliott, R. (1991, November). *The experiential session form: Initial data.* Paper presented at the annual meeting for the Society for Psychotherapy Research, Panama City, FL.

Horvath, A. O., & Greenberg, L. S. (1989). Development and validation of the Working Alliance Inventory. *Journal of Counseling Psychology*, 36, 223–233.

Horvath, A. O., & Greenberg, L. S. (Eds.). (1994). *The working alliance: Theory, research, practice.* New York: Wiley.

Horvath, A. O., & Luborsky, L. (1993). The role of the therapeutic alliance in psychotherapy. *Journal of Consulting and Clinical Psychology*, 61, 561–573.

Horvath, A. O., & Symonds, B. D. (1991). Relation between working alliance and outcome in psychotherapy: A meta-analysis. *Journal of Counseling Psychology*, 38, 139–149.

Kahn, E. (1985). Heinz Kohut and Carl Rogers: A timely comparison. *American Psychologist*, 40, 893–904.

Kohut, H. (1977). *The restoration of self.* New York: International Universities Press.

Krupnick, J. L., Stotsky, S. M., Simmons, S., Moyer, J., Elkin, I., Watkins, J., & Pilkonis, P. A. (1996). The role of the therapeutic alliance in psychotherapy and pharmacotherapy outcome: Findings in the National Institute Mental Health Treatment of Depression Collaborative Research Program. *Journal of Consulting and Clinical Psychology*, 64, 532–539.

Lafferty, P., Beutler, L. E., & Crago, M. (1991). Differences between more and less effective psychotherapists: A study of select therapist variables. *Journal of Consulting and Clinical Psychology*, 57, 76–80.

Lambert, M. J. (1983). Introduction to assessment of psychotherapy outcome: Historical perspectives and current issues. In M. J. Lambert, E. R. Christensen, & S. S. Dejulio (Eds.), *The assessment of psychotherapy outcome* (pp. 3–32). New York: Wiley-Interscience.

Lambert, M. J. (1992). Implications of outcome research for psychotherapy integration. In J. C. Norcross & M. R. Goldstein (Eds.), *Handbook of psychotherapy integration* (pp. 94–129). New York: Basic Books.

Lambert, M. J., & Bergin, A. E. (1994). The effectiveness of psychotherapy. In A. E. Bergin & S. L. Garfield (Eds.), *Handbook of psychotherapy and behavior change* (4th ed., pp. 143–189). New York: Wiley.

Lambert, M. J., & DeJulio, S. S. (1977). Outcomes in Carkhuff's human resource development: Where's the donut? *Counseling Psychologist*, 6, 79–86.

Lambert, M. J., DeJulio, S. S., & Stein, D. M. (1978). Therapist interpersonal skills: Process, outcome, methodological considerations and recommendations for future research. *Psychological Bulletin, 85,* 467–489.

Lambert, M. J., & Okishi, J. C. (1997). The effects of the individual psychotherapist and implications for future research. *Clinical Psychology: Science and Practice, 4,* 66–75.

Lazarus, A. A. (1971). *Behavior therapy and beyond.* New York: McGraw-Hill.

Lorr, M. (1965). Client perceptions of therapists. *Journal of Consulting Psychology, 29,* 146–149.

Luborsky, L. B. (1994). Therapeutic alliances as predictors of psychotherapy outcomes: Factors explaining the predictive success. In A. O. Horvath & L. S. Greenberg (Eds.), *The working alliance: Theory, research, and practice* (pp. 38–50). New York: Wiley.

Luborsky, L. B., & Auerbach, A. (1985). The therapeutic relationship in psychodynamic psychotherapy: The research evidence and its meaning for practice. In R. Hales & A. Frances (Eds.), *Psychiatry update annual review* (pp. 550–561). Washington, DC: American Psychiatric Association.

Luborsky, L. B., Chandler, M., Auerbach, A. H., Cohen, J., & Bachrach, H. M. (1971). Factors influencing the outcome of psychotherapy: A review of quantitative research. *Psychological Bulletin, 75,* 145–185.

Mahrer, A. R. (1983). *Experiential psychotherapy: Basic practices.* New York: Brunner/Mazel.

Martin, D. J., Gorske, J. P., & Davis, M. K. (2000). Relation of the therapeutic alliance with outcome and other variables: A meta-analytic review. *Journal of Consulting and Clinical Psychology, 68,* 438–450.

Meltzoff, J., & Kornreich, M. (1970). *Research in psychotherapy.* New York: Atherton.

Miller, W. R., Taylor, C. A., & West, J. C. (1980). Focused versus broad-spectrum behavior therapy for problem drinkers. *Journal of Consulting and Clinical Psychology, 48,* 590–601.

Mitchell, K. M., Bozarth, J. D., & Krauft, C. C. (1977). A reappraisal of the therapeutic effectiveness of accurate empathy, non-possessive warmth, and genuineness. In A. S. Gurman & A. M. Razin (Eds.), *Effective psychotherapy: A handbook of research* (pp. 482–502). New York: Pergamon.

Najavits, L. M., & Strupp, H. H. (1994). Differences in the effectiveness of psychodynamic therapists: A process–outcome study. *Psychotherapy, 31,* 114–123.

Orlinsky, D. E., Grawe, K., & Parks, B. K. (1994). Process and outcome in psychotherapy—noch einmal. In A. E. Bergin & S. L. Garfield (Eds.), *Handbook of psychotherapy and behavior change* (pp. 257–310). New York: Wiley.

Parloff, M., Waskow, I. E., & Wolfe, B. E. (1978). Research on therapist variables in relation to process and outcome. In A. E. Bergin & S. L. Garfield (Eds.), *Handbook of psychotherapy and behavior changes* (2nd ed., pp. 233–282). New York: Wiley.

Patterson, C. H. (1984). Empathy, warmth, and genuineness: A review of reviews. *Psychotherapy, 21*, 431–438.

Rogers, C. R. (1957). The necessary and sufficient conditions of therapeutic personality change. *Journal of Consulting Psychology, 22*, 95–103.

Rogers, C. R., & Dymond, R. F. (1954). *Psychotherapy and personality change*. Chicago: University of Chicago Press.

Rudolph, J., Langer, I., & Tausch, R. (1980). An investigation of the psychological affects and conditions of person-centered individual psychotherapy. *Zeitschrift fur Klinische Psychologie: Forschung und Praxis, 9*, 23–33.

Safran, J. D., Crocker, P., McMain, S., & Murray, P. (1990). The therapeutic alliance rupture as a therapy event for empirical investigation. *Psychotherapy, 27*, 154–165.

Safran, J. D., Muran, J. C., & Samstag, L. W. (1994). Resolving therapeutic alliance ruptures: A task analytic investigation. In A. O. Horvath & L. S. Greenberg (Eds.), *The working alliance: Theory, research, and practice* (pp. 225–255). New York: Wiley.

Safran, J. D., & Wallner, L. K. (1991). The relative predictive validity of two therapeutic alliance measures in cognitive therapy. *Psychological Assessment: A Journal of Consulting and Clinical Psychology, 3*, 188–195.

Silverman, W. H. (1996). Cookbooks, manuals, and paint-by-numbers: Psychotherapy in the 90's. *Psychotherapy, 33*, 207–215.

Sterba, R. F. (1929). The dynamics of the dissolution of the transference resistance. *Psychoanalytic Quarterly, 9*, 363–379.

Strupp, H. H., & Anderson, T. (1997). On the limitations of therapy manuals. *Clinical Psychology: Science and Practice, 4*, 76–82.

Strupp, H. H., Fox, R. E., & Lessler, K. (1969). *Patients view their psychotherapy*. Baltimore: Johns Hopkins University Press.

Stuhr, U., & Meyer, A. E. (1991). Hamberg short-term psychotherapy comparison study. In L. Beutler & M. Crago (Eds.), *Psychotherapy research: An international review of programmatic studies* (pp. 212–218). Washington, DC: American Psychological Association.

Task Force on Promotion and Dissemination of Psychological Procedures. (1995). Training in and dissemination of empirically-validated therapies. *Clinical Psychologist, 49*, 3–23.

Teusch, L., & Böhme, H. (1999). Is the exposure principle really critical in agoraphobia? The influence of client-centered "nonprescriptive" treatment on exposure. *Psychotherapy Research, 9*, 115–123.

Truax, C. B. (1963). Effective ingredients in psychotherapy: An approach to unraveling the patient–therapist interaction. *Journal of Counseling Psychology, 10*, 256–263.

Truax, C. B. (1971). Effectiveness of counselor and counselor aids: A rejoinder. *Journal of Counseling Psychology, 18*, 365–367.

Truax, C. B., & Carkhuff (1967). *Toward effective counseling and psychotherapy: Training and practice.* Chicago: Aldine.

Truax, C. B., & Mitchell, K. M. (1971). Research on certain therapist interpersonal skills in relation to process and outcome. In A. E. Bergin & S. L. Garfield (Eds.), *Handbook of psychotherapy and behavior change: An empirical evaluation* (pp. 299–344). New York: Wiley.

Wilson, G. T. (1998). Manual-based treatment and clinical practice. *Clinical Psychology: Science and Practice, 5,* 363–375.

Zetzel, E. R. (1956). Current concepts of transference. *International Journal of Psychoanalysis, 37,* 369–376.

18

CLIENT VARIABLES AND PSYCHOTHERAPY OUTCOMES

DAVID M. GONZALEZ

> It is the client more than the therapist who implements the change process. . . . Rather than argue over whether or not "therapy works," we could address ourselves to the question of whether or not "the client works!" . . . As therapists have depended more upon the client's resources, more change seems to occur. (Bergin & Garfield, 1994, p. 826)

Bergin and Garfield (1994) came to this conclusion after compiling an extensive review and analysis of the existing research on psychotherapy and outcome covering well over 800 pages. Recognizing the central position of the client to therapeutic success seems essential if one is to grasp a more complete picture of therapeutic success and failure. Some clients seem to inhibit progress or seem unable to use the counseling process at all, whereas others experience and use therapy in meaningful and life-changing ways. Those involved in the training and practice of psychotherapy can recall saying whether someone is likely to benefit from psychotherapy. "Good clients" are those motivated and willing to engage in the process of self-examination and self-discovery and move toward desired change. Therefore, as therapists, we have a "sense" about who is likely to benefit and who is not, but our understanding can be significantly enhanced by considering some of the research done in the area of client variables and psychotherapy outcome.

ROGERS'S NECESSARY AND SUFFICIENT CONDITIONS

When Carl Rogers described the "Necessary and Sufficient Conditions of Therapeutic Personality Change" (1957), his description had an "if–then" quality to it. That is, if the therapist provided and maintained the conditions of therapist empathy, unconditional positive regard, and congruence, then the client would likely benefit from counseling, regardless of who the client was. Rogers hypothesized that no other conditions were necessary for therapeutic personality changes to occur as long as these conditions existed and continued over time. His hypothesis places the onus for success or failure almost entirely in the hands of the therapist's ability to communicate adequate levels of the core conditions to the client. Therapists know from experience that there must be more than an "if–then" relationship between the hypothesized conditions and successful treatment outcomes. Inevitably, even the most skilled therapists encounter clients who do not seem to benefit from the process.

To recognize the importance of client variables, consider that simply from a logical point of view, if one contends that therapist behaviors can help or hinder the process of therapy, it follows that client behaviors can also influence whether one could expect a positive outcome for psychotherapy. After all, there are two people involved in this unique and interactional process called psychotherapy. Each member of the dyad brings certain characteristics to the relationship that will affect how it evolves. (See also Bozarth, Zimring, and Tausch, this volume, chapter 5, for more on client-centered therapy.) In fairness to Rogers, he did recognize that therapy may not be helpful to everyone as indicated by his statement: "it appears that empirical studies can help to discover the factors which make it likely that client-centered therapy, as it exists at the present time, will be effective or ineffective in helping the client to change" (Rogers, 1954, p. 424). So, if one takes the position that Rogers's stated conditions may not be sufficient in and of themselves, one is free to explore what researchers say about client variables that seem related to outcomes.

While this entire volume is devoted to various dimensions of research relevant to humanistic psychotherapies, this chapter will focus in particular on the client characteristics that are related to positive outcomes in psychotherapy. Specifically, the goals of this chapter are (a) to present outcome research on client variables specific to client-centered psychotherapy, (b) to present other outcome research on client variables that seems to have relevance to client-centered therapy and other humanistic psychotherapies, and (c) to provide ideas and examples of how these research findings can be applied in a humanistic fashion when working with clients.

RESEARCH ON CLIENT VARIABLES AND OUTCOMES

Finding research on client variables about which one could make unequivocal statements regarding the association between client variables and outcome has been a somewhat elusive endeavor. In fact, Bergin and Garfield's (1994) review of research on client variables and outcome found little in which to be confident. They noted the difficulty in forming definitive conclusions about client variables because many of the studies defined and measured outcome differently or may have had design and analysis weaknesses that raise caution in interpreting the meaning and generalizability of the results. Also, there have been contradictory findings in the research.

Bohart and Tallman (1999) argued that it is the client who primarily determines the outcome of psychotherapy: "Our thesis . . . is that the client's capacity for self-healing is the most potent common factor in psychotherapy . . . therapy facilitates naturally occurring healing aspects of clients' lives" (p. 91). They noted a surprising "meta-analysis" by Grencavage and Norcross (1990) of different lists of common factors that revealed that the client is seldom mentioned as a common factor in therapy. They also stated that clients are most often not portrayed as the initiators of change, rather, that status is held by the therapists in the literature. Clients are more typically portrayed in terms of their deficits and in terms of being the recipients of the therapists' wisdom and interventions. In actuality, they argued that the clients are highly active in the process. For example, Rennie (1990) met with clients following their therapy sessions to review their videotapes. Clients stopped the tapes whenever they wished to comment about the session. This process revealed that clients were highly active at a covert level in terms of steering the sessions, reinforcing the therapists, and making use of the process. The primary discovery was that clients were anything but passive in terms of what happened in their sessions. Bohart and Tallman (1999) cited many other studies to support their contention that clients are the primary agent of change. For example, more than 60% of clients arriving for their first session reported improvement in the presenting problem since the appointment was made (Lawson, 1994; Weiner-Davis, deShazer, & Gingerich, 1987). Also, many clients reported improvements following a single session of therapy (Rosenbaum, 1994). Clients appeared to make gains without the assistance of the therapist, providing support for the notion that clients have their own capacity for self-healing. In addition, a number of studies have shown that inexperienced therapists are as effective as experienced therapists (Christensen & Jacobson, 1994) and any significant differences have tended to be small, giving further credence to the idea that it is the client more than the therapist who determines the outcome. In addition, Bohart and Tallman noted that self-help treatments (e.g., self-help books) have been shown to be as effective as therapists, as evidenced by two meta-analyses: the first conducted by Scogin, Bynum, Stephens, and Calhoon (1990) and the second by Gould and Clum (1993). Bohart and Tallman contended that therapists may activate the client's potential for self-healing by various interventions, but it is really a matter of the client making use of the interventions that constitutes the actual therapy. They argued that the explanation for the "no difference" finding among the various therapies resides within the client. That is, the client is the primary force that makes therapy effective, although the research has tended to focus on variables other than the client or to minimize the client's impact on the process. Overall, the research cited by Bohart and Tallman supports the notion that clients have a drive and capacity to move toward health, which is consistent with the position of humanistic therapies.

There are in fact many compelling studies to help one understand and appreciate client variables related to psychotherapy outcome, as well as the complexities involved in such research. For example, one complicating factor involved in psychotherapy outcome research is the difficulty inherent in isolating one variable from a relational process in which multiple variables contribute to the therapy outcome. That is, can one piece of a system be factored out for study and still maintain some semblance of validity? Also, a client who does not do well with one therapist may do well with another simply because of the person of the therapist and the person of the client. Despite these and other limitations involved in conducting research on client variables, the attempt to answer the question remains important. What are the client variables that make it more likely that a client will benefit from the therapy process and, more specifically, what are the variables that make it likely that a client may benefit from client-centered or other forms of humanistic psychotherapy?

THE CHICAGO PROJECT

A number of studies conducted at the University of Chicago Counseling Center in the 1950s examined the effects of client-centered therapy. The studies were conceptualized from a client-centered perspective, and the therapists were all trained as client-centered therapists. Rogers (1954) provided a summary of the results. An important variable that received empirical support in these studies was that the type of relationship most associated with positive outcomes in psychotherapy was a relationship in which the client developed a strong liking and respect for the therapist. In essence, a warm relationship containing mutual liking and respect was more likely to lead to success. Another finding consistent with Rogers's hypothesis was that clients entering therapy with the greatest degree of incongruence made the most progress or movement.

Also, during the therapy sessions themselves, the most notable behavior was that the client began an exploration of himself or herself and moved away from talking about external problems. The interviews became less intellectual or cognitive and more an emotional or experiencing process (feeling and being). Rogers observed that "experiencing the complete awareness of his or her total organismic response to a situation is an important concomitant of the process of therapy" (Rogers, 1954, p. 425).

In the Chicago studies, a change in the client's perception of the self appeared to be a central factor in the process of client-centered therapy. Of those clients considered to be successful, new perceptions of the self emerged into awareness. Rogers noted that there was some evidence that the emerging perceptions of the self were based on material previously denied to awareness. The client typically began his or her therapy with an intellectual discussion of the problem and then moved toward an exploration of the self. Additional findings were that clients with at least moderately democratic and accepting attitudes toward others seemed to reap the most benefit from therapy. Conversely, clients who were high in ethnocentrism (with sharp and rigid distinctions between their own and other groups) and those who were generally antidemocratic tended to be unsuccessful in therapy. Lastly, Rogers found no relationship between initial diagnosis of the clients and outcome of therapy and, in fact, found that the deeply disturbed clients progressed equally as well as the mildly disturbed clients.

Haimowitz and Haimowitz (1952) studied client personality characteristics that were associated with different degrees of success in psychotherapy. They found that clients who were in touch with their internal tensions, who were intrapunitive, and who were tolerant of others were likely to have successful psychotherapy outcomes. In contrast, client who were extrapunitive, ethnocentric, and less sensitive to internal tensions were less likely to have successful psychotherapy outcomes.

Kirtner and Cartwright (1958) found that clients who had brief (fewer than 13 sessions) but successful therapy were relatively open to their impulse life and relatively clear about their gender roles. Successful clients in longer term psychotherapy (more than 21 sessions) showed relatively high anxiety and some confusion about their gender identity. Successful therapy clients in both short- and long-session groups showed a greater need for relationships than was the case for less-successful therapy clients.

CLIENT VARIABLES RELATED TO PSYCHOTHERAPY OUTCOMES

Despite the difficulty involved in isolating the client's impact on psychotherapy outcome, several empirical studies have demonstrated a number of client variables that appear to be related to outcome: client participation/ engagement/involvement, therapeutic alliance, client affirmation, collaboration, openness versus defensiveness, experiencing and self-exploration, expressiveness, locus of control, and ethnocentrism. The research on these variables is discussed below.

Client Participation/Engagement/Involvement

Rogers's (1957) sine qua non condition of successful psychotherapy was that there be two people in psychological contact. Without this preemptive condition, the other conditions are meaningless. Within this framework, it could be argued that a client with sufficient reluctance to engage in the therapy process would not actually be in psychological contact with the therapist.

Research supports Rogers's hypothesis. According to Greenberg and Pinsof (1986), the degree of client involvement is a predictor of outcome. They stated that the findings from "alliance-related work show that patient participation, optimism, perceived task relevance, and responsibility are related to change" (p. 13). Along the same lines, Gomes-Schwartz (1978) examined ratings from taped therapy sessions and found that the variable most predictive of outcome was the client's willingness and capacity to actively engage in the therapy process. Active engagement was defined as having a positive attitude toward the therapist and therapy as well as a commitment to working at change. This particular study compared psycho-analytically oriented therapists, experiential therapists, and college professors popular with students but not trained in doing psychotherapy. All three groups had similar outcomes, with the level of client involvement emerging as the best predictor of outcome. Later studies continued to provide support for this finding. For example, O'Malley, Suh, and Strupp (1983) found that client involvement had the highest relationship to outcome, and Kolb, Beutler, Davis, Crago, and Shanfield's (1985) study found similar results.

Similarly, in their review of research on effective psychotherapy, Weissmark and Giacomo (1998) noted that some of the general categories of client involvement (client exploration, client expectancies, depth of experiencing, patient participation, and positive contribution) have yielded the most consistent evidence. They concluded that outcome was optimized when clients actively collaborated in the therapeutic process.

Orlinsky, Grawe, and Parks (1994) summarized 54 findings regarding client role engagement reflecting the personal involvement of participants in the client role. Sixty-five percent of the 54 findings showed a significant positive association with outcome. They also summarized 28 findings on client motivation, defined as the perceived desire for therapeutic involvement by participants in the client role. Half of the findings showed a significant association with outcome. When this variable was looked at strictly from the client's perspective, the percentage rose to 80%.

Therapeutic Alliance

Moras and Strupp (1982) concluded that the level of interpersonal relations prior to beginning therapy predicted clients' level of collaborative, positively toned participation in a therapeutic relationship. Filak, Abeles, and Norquist (1986) investigated whether clients' interpersonal attitudes prior to beginning therapy related to an affiliation–hostility dimension would have a significant impact on therapy outcome. Seventy-two percent of those with an affiliative stance had a highly successful outcome, whereas only 38% of those with a pretherapy hostile interpersonal stance had a successful outcome.

Orlinsky et al. (1994) summarized 55 findings related to the client's contribution to the therapeutic alliance and found significant relationship in 67% of the cases. The client's positive contribution to the therapeutic alliance was associated with good outcome for cases lasting 20 to 40 sessions but not for short-term cases (fewer than 20 sessions).

Orlinsky et al. (1994) reported a positive association between outcome and the client's total affective response (both negative and positive) in 50% of 10 findings (not differentiating between positive and negative affects). When just positive affective responses were considered, all 9 findings in three relevant studies showed significant associations with favorable outcomes. In other words, when clients respond with positive feelings during sessions, it is likely an indication that therapy is proceeding well. (See Asay & Lambert, this volume, chapter 17, for more on therapeutic alliance.)

Client Affirmation

Orlinsky et al. (1994) summarized 59 studies and found that client affirmation has a more consistent association with outcome than does therapist affirmation (69% vs. 56%). They noted, though, that client affirmation may be a result rather than a precipitant of therapeutic progress. Logically, a reciprocal affirmation between client and therapist should follow. In 78% of 32 findings, reciprocal affirmation were significantly positive (data derived primarily from the client's or external raters' process perspectives).

Horowitz, Marmar, Weiss, and Rosenbaum (1984) concluded, after an extensive review of the literature on outcomes, that the most consistent process predictor of improvement was the client's perception of the therapeutic relationship. Similarly, Morgan, Luborsky, Crits-Christoph, Curtis, and Solomon (1982) found that clients who believed that their therapists were helping them and that they were working in a collaborative fashion were more likely to demonstrate improvement from therapy than clients who did not have such perceptions. Also, Beutler, Crago, and Arizmendi (1986) found a positive correlation between outcome and clients' positive perceptions of their therapists' facilitative attitudes (empathy, genuineness, congruence, nonpossessive warmth, and unconditional positive regard).

Collaboration

Orlinsky et al. (1994) reported on 46 process–outcome findings on therapist collaboration with the client as opposed to the therapist proceeding in a directive or permissive fashion. Overall, 43% of the findings indicated a significant association with a collaborative therapeutic style and outcome. This figure rose to 64% when viewed solely from the client's perspective. Twenty-two percent of the findings showed a significant association with outcome with a directive therapist (9% from the client's perspective). Studies found that when therapists and clients worked in a collaborative style, 64% of 42 findings showed outcome to be positively associated with collaboration, whereas none favored either a dependent or controlling style of relating.

Openness Versus Defensiveness

Orlinsky and Howard (1986) described a category called *patient self-relatedness*, which refers to people's way of responding to themselves. In brief, it has to do with the ways that people experience their internal ideations and feelings, become self-aware, evaluate themselves, and how they monitor their ideas and feelings. People can be open-minded and flexible in responding or be guarded and constrained. In the first instance, they are viewed as open and receptive; in the second, they are typically viewed as defensive. The client's capacity to make use of the therapeutic interventions and relationship come into the picture here. Orlinsky and Howard found that a client's openness versus defensiveness in psychotherapy was related to outcome. Better outcomes were significantly associated with the client's openness during therapy. In a review of 45 findings, Orlinsky et al. (1994) noted that 80% of studies showed client openness to be a positive correlate of therapy outcome. They also noted that several of these studies had large effect sizes that can be indicative of a strong and consistent finding. Orlinsky et al. reported that in nearly 50 findings that examined patient cooperation and patient resistance, 69% of the findings showed significant associations of patient cooperation with favorable outcomes and patient resistance with unfavorable outcomes.

Experiencing and Self-Exploration

A client's willingness to self-explore seems essential to successful therapy. However, not every client who wishes to explore will necessarily be good at it. The capacity to experience has emerged as an important variable in determining whether the client is likely to benefit from therapy (Greenberg & Pinsof, 1986). Klein, Mathieu-Coughlan, and Kiesler (1986) developed the Experiencing Scale to assess the quality of the client's involvement based on Gendlin, Beebe, Cassens, Klein, and Oberlander's (1968) and Rogers's client-centered theories. The Experiencing Scale appears to assess productive clients. More specifically, the scale was indicative of self-involvement and participation in therapy. The researchers described extensive efforts at training clients in experiencing, empathy, and communication.

Gendlin (1984) described felt sense as "the client inside us, a kind of self-response process" (p. 83) and regarded the process as something that could be taught to clients through focusing (Gendlin, 1996). His studies on client-centered therapy found that clients high in the ability for working with inner experience appeared to benefit more from psychotherapy. Klein et al. (1986) found support for the association between high levels of client experiencing and therapeutic change (see also Hendricks, this volume, chapter 7). As a result of these findings, Gendlin created his focusing method in hopes of enhancing the experience process for those clients who were not well developed in their ability to do so. These findings are consistent with those discussed earlier in this chapter in the description of the Chicago studies. Specifically, successful clients not only moved to an exploration of the self but also experienced deeply a new level of awareness of the total organismic response. Some clients may need assistance in developing certain capacities so that they can move to a deeper level of self-exploration.

Client self-exploration and outcome were reported to be significantly associated in 30% of 79 findings by Orlinsky et al. (1994). They noted that even though 67% showed no association with outcome, 30% of the findings still constitutes a significant figure.

Expressiveness

In a large review of studies of patient expressiveness, Orlinsky et al. (1994) reported that out of 51 findings, 63% showed a positive association with outcome. Similarly, a study by Beutler et al. (1986) revealed that clients who were open, in touch with their emotions, and able to express their thoughts and feelings in therapy had a positive prognosis (Seligman, 1990, p. 53). Butler, Rice, and Wagstaff (1962) and Rice and Wagstaff (1967) found that psychotherapy outcomes could be predicted as early as the second session by looking at client expressiveness. Expressive clients had more positive outcomes, whereas inexpressive clients (characterized as having dull, lifeless ways of describing self and inner experience) had less favorable outcomes. Noting that inexpressive clients were likely to have a less hopeful outcome, Wexler and Butler (1976) demonstrated that client expressiveness could be improved by the therapist actions, though their study was limited because it only included a single case study of success. They described the inexpressive client as being a problem in client-centered therapy as well as in other therapeutic modalities. In this single case study, the therapist intentionally modified the behavior of an inexpressive client to alter the course of psychotherapy. Specifically, Wexler and Butler advocated for the therapist to purposefully alter his or her behavior by stating the client's experience in as vivid and evocative manner as possible. By doing so, they noted that a therapist can serve as a model to increase client expressiveness, resulting in new behavior and a richer range of experience for the client.

Locus of Control

From a humanistic perspective, having an internal locus of control is central to psychological health. Each person must take responsibility for the self and his or her actions. Evidence suggests that until a client develops an internal locus of control, the benefits of psychotherapy are limited. Giacomo and Weissmark (1992) examined the work of 15 therapists; specifically, each therapist had one successful case and one unsuccessful case. The client change dimensions were internal–external (defined as whether an individual evaluates an action as a means for affecting the environment or as a means for being affected by it), reactive–selective (defined as whether an individual considers himself or herself as capable or not capable of choosing or influencing a course of action), and unconditional–conditional (defined as whether an individual evaluates the course of an action as dependent or independent of the conditions under which the action occurs). An attempt to understand the differences revealed that successful clients became more internal, more selective, and more conditional, whereas the unsuccessful clients remained external, less selective, and less conditional. Giacomo and Weissmark noted that the client's participation in treatment was significantly related to outcome.

Kirtner and Cartwright (1958) reported that clients who entered the therapy process with the belief that they contributed to their problems and felt responsible for their problems tended to remain in therapy for a longer duration. These clients were evaluated by their therapists as making more progress than clients who felt little or no responsibility for their difficulties.

In a study of 84 institutionalized female drug addicts, Kilmann and Howell (1974) found that those with an internal locus of control rated themselves more favorably, showed more effort in being successful, appeared to be more involved in therapy, became more reflective, and showed more attempts to gain self-understanding. A look at the overall findings indicated that those who had an internal locus of control were better therapy risks than those with an external locus of control. This study was conducted in a group therapy setting that assessed internal versus external locus of control as well as directive therapy versus nondirective therapy and a no-treatment control group.

Ethnocentrism

The concept of ethnocentrism is typically relegated to research and writing in the social psychological domains. However, there seems to be important evidence that this characteristic needs to be considered as a predictor of therapy outcome. Tougas (1952) examined the impact of ethnocentrism on psychotherapy outcome. Ethnocentrism was defined as being

> based on a pervasive and rigid in-group–out-group distinction; invoking a stereotyped negative imagery and hostile attitudes regarding out-groups; and stereotyped positive imagery and submissive attitudes regarding in-groups; and a hierarchical, authoritarian view of group interaction in which in-groups are rightly dominant, out-groups subordinate. (Tougas, 1952, pp. 196–197)

Tougas, assessing the effects of Rogerian and Sullivanian treatments, found that clients low on ethnocentrism had more favorable outcomes, whereas those high on ethnocentrism had poorer outcomes.

FROM RESEARCH TO PRACTICE

Taking research and applying it to actual practice can sometimes be challenging, but in many cases there are some clear applications. Following is a discussion of how one might apply the research knowledge to the actual practice of psychotherapy. Examples are given for (a) client involvement/participation/motivation/cooperation, (b) client contribution to the therapeutic alliance, and (c) depth of client experiencing.

Client Involvement/Participation/Motivation/Cooperation

In most cases, clients come in for therapy because they want something better. The fact that they seek the assistance of a therapist can be taken as an indication that they envision such an outcome as a real possibility. The importance of client involvement to successful outcome has been clearly demonstrated in empirical research. Hence, the need for therapists to foster and maintain client involvement in the process is also clear. From the initial contact with clients, the therapist's presentation about how the process works is critical. Unless a client has been in therapy before, he or she cannot be presumed to know how the process actually works. Many clients are likely to see therapists as experts with the answers to their problems. Thus, in their explanation to the clients about their theoretical orientation, for example, therapists need to be mindful about how they present the process. If the description places the therapist in the role of the expert, then the level of client involvement is likely to be affected. Regardless of theoretical orientation, as therapists familiarize clients with the therapeutic process, their description needs to clearly demonstrate a commitment to therapy as a process of collaboration between the client and therapist working together to explore, clarify, and move toward client-desired change. Therapists then need to follow through by maintaining a collaborative process, that is, not providing answers to all the presenting problems but rather working together to understand problems and discover solutions. For example,

> C: I have never been in therapy before. How does the process work?
> T: Therapy is a collaborative process in which we can work together to explore, clarify your concerns and by working together, hopefully, we can find some answers that fit for you.
> C: What should I talk about? Hmmm, I am not sure where to begin. Maybe you could you ask me some questions?
> T: This is your time to talk about whatever feels important to you.
> C: Well, what really seems to be bothering me is . . .

The therapist in this example is making sure not to take the responsibility from and for the client. The client can potentially learn early on that therapy is collaborative and will require a thoughtful investment for the process to work.

Even though a therapist may ascribe to the notion that collaboration is the most useful fashion to proceed in psychotherapy, challenging clients may in subtle ways influence the therapist to assume a less collaborative position. One suggestion for therapists is to become conscious of their own self-talk. For example, if you as the therapist find yourself saying such things as "if I could just get my client to . . ." or "If I could just convince my client of . . ." or "if I could just get my client to see . . . ," or if you find yourself thinking in terms of "persuading," then you have likely moved to controlling and directing, which is not likely to be helpful (Combs & Gonzalez, 1994). The frustration that can come when working with clients who do not seem to be progressing can result in the therapist taking too much control of the process and losing the collaborative component.

In addition, Bohart and Tallman (1999) emphasized that true collaboration goes beyond the client merely participating in the therapist's agenda. They contended that a truly collaborative model involves, among other things, the therapist carefully listening to the client for client-generated solutions and encouraging the client to more fully explain his or her point of view. This implies a belief and respect on the part of the therapist for the client's capacities for self-healing and problem solving. One technique that works from a collaborative model is termed "Ask the Expert" (Welch & Gonzalez, 1999). For example,

C: I wish I could figure out why I don't stand up to my father. Do you have any ideas?

T: It sounds like you need an expert who can answer your question. Fortunately, we have someone with expertise in that area right in this office. I will have that person come in momentarily. What exactly did you want to ask him or her?

(Have the client formulate the question. Then, ask the client to sit in the therapist's chair and switch seats with client. Then the therapist asks the exact question formulated by the client. The therapist can continue the role playing if additional questions arise as the client speaks in the role of the expert. After the exercise is finished, again switch seats and ask the client to reiterate what he or she heard the expert say.)

A less elaborate but still potentially helpful version of "Ask the Expert" is as follows:

C: I don't know why I won't stand up to my father.

T: Let's switch seats. You are the expert. Why does a person not stand up to his or her father?

A similar effect may be achieved by the following example:

C: I wish I understood why I don't stand up to my father. Why do you think I don't?

T: It sounds like you have thought about this question a great deal. What have you come up with so far?

In each of the above examples, the intent is to provide the opportunity for clients to discover their own solutions to whatever problems they are facing. The client is more likely to feel empowered by discovering answers to confusing problems. The collaborative position requires that the therapist truly believe in the client's self-healing capacities. Consequently, client-generated solutions need to be explored, understood, and respected.

Even while there is ample evidence for the importance of collaboration for therapy to be successful, therapists are experiencing significant pressures to use template models of treatment. That is, therapists are told to use predetermined methods and procedures considered to be "empirically validated" with various presenting problems. Such a medical model, which may be attractive to managed care, flies in the face of what the research has shown in terms of the importance of collaboration. Therapists are faced with the challenge of finding ways to assist clients with prescribed methods imposed from without. As noted by Bohart and Tallman (1999), such template models do not respect the nature of how people change. To leave the client out of the equation should be unthinkable. One suggestion to therapists is to modify the template to incorporate the client's frame of reference as a central component of the entire process.

In terms of willingness to engage in the therapy process, therapists must recognize that not all "clients" are willing consumers. They may, for whatever reason, decline to participate at the level necessary to make change. In such cases, thinking in terms of treatment failure may not be accurate. People pressured to seek psychotherapy find themselves in the underdog position and may through their behavior say, "You can make me do it, but you can't make me like it and you can't make me do it right" (P. G. Ossorio, personal communication, Spring, 1984).

Therapeutic Alliance

The research consistently confirms that the strength and quality of the therapeutic relationship is central to successful therapeutic outcomes. If a quality relationship has been created and is present, both client and therapist know it. Conversely, if the relationship does not feel right or is shallow, both client and therapist will, at some level, know that also. Thus, the suggestion is for the therapist to squarely address the problem. Sometimes therapists may be tempted to avoid bringing up the problem with the relationship, hoping that the next week it will just get better. A willingness to address the problem directly with the client provides the opportunity and potential to improve the relationship. For example,

> T: We have been working together for a few sessions now and I am keenly aware of an uncomfortable distance between us. I am wondering how you are feeling about our working relationship.
> C: Well, now that you mention it, it does feel pretty tense.
> T: Maybe by talking about it we can figure out the problem and go from there.

The therapist in this example is addressing the most pressing issue, which is the therapeutic relationship. Not addressing the problem would be akin to having the proverbial elephant sitting in the room with the therapist and client aware of it but not saying anything.

Client Experiencing

Earlier in this chapter, we saw that the depth of the client's experiencing has an impact on outcome. Therapists use a variety of methods in the helping process, some of which can be used to assist clients needing help in this area. Responding with accurate levels of empathy, using self-disclosure, and using metaphor are but a few examples that can assist clients in deepening their experience of the therapy process. Becoming skilled in empathy requires that therapists not only understand a client's experience but also be able to respond to the client in a way that the client feels understood. Doing so requires the therapist to have an adequate affective vocabulary. The therapist should expand his or her affective vocabulary to better capture the nuances of human experiences. Unfortunately, a therapist may sometimes rely on the word *very* as a way to differentiate levels of feelings. An example follows of a therapeutic response that is not helpful:

C: I have been feeling low since she left.
T: You are feeling sad.
C: Yes, quite low.
T: So, you are feeling *very* sad.

While in this case the client may be feeling very sad, such a response does not really deepen the level of experiencing for the client. Consider the possible other words that have to do with deeper levels of sadness. A look at a thesaurus under sad reveals "unhappy," "melancholy," "sorrowful," "downhearted," "rueful," "dispirited," "dejected," and "disappointed." Having a more adequate affective vocabulary enables the therapist to respond in a way that more fully captures a client's experience and can assist the client in experiencing a deeper level of feeling and significance. Here is an example of a more helpful therapist response:

C: I have been feeling low since she left.
T: You are experiencing a difficult time and feeling downhearted and dejected.
C: Yes. The word downhearted really fits. It feels like my heart is way down here (gestures to the floor).

The response in this second example is more likely to capture the client's experience and may lead to a richer, more meaningful description of the client's struggle. Some clients have the ability to describe experiences in rich and vivid ways that allow for a deeper exploration of their presenting problem. The research shows that there are clients who do seek treatment but do not have such capacities. It is in those cases that therapists' efforts are critical in enabling clients to describe and experience their life events in a deeper fashion. There are exercises one can do to increase one's affective vocabulary (Welch & Gonzalez, 1999). For example, doing "word ladders" in which one selects an affective word and then generates two or more words, each depicting more intensity of feeling and two or more words indicative of less intensity. Take the word *mad*, for example. More intense descriptions would be "provoked" and "furious." Less intense descriptions would be "irritated" and "annoyed." In addition to developing a rich affective vocabulary to more adequately capture the nuances of the clients' experiences, the use of metaphor can also serve as a means to assist clients in deepening their experiences. For example,

C: Since losing my spouse I am lost. I have never been alone like this before. I wish I could find the words to describe it.

T: I have an image of you being untethered in outer space; floating away with nothing to grab onto.

C: Yes, it's feels much like that! It's a frightening experience. In fact, . . .

The use of metaphor was common in the work of Carl Rogers, who described it as a way to more fully capture a client's experience. Images can serve when words fail.

Along the same lines, Gendlin's (1996) contention that a client can be trained to make better use of the therapy process merits serious consideration. Client experiencing has been described as one of the most substantiated constructs related to outcome in psychotherapy (Todd & Bohart, 1999). Although the notion of "training" clients to be able to make use of the therapy process may be new and require a revised conception of how to proceed in psychotherapy, it seems to make a good deal of sense for clients who need help in developing the capacity to experience because their progress may be impaired without this skill. Gendlin developed explicit procedures specified in a training manual designed to enhance the client's ability to experience at deeper levels.

Acceptance of Others

In cases of clients with ethnocentric or rigid beliefs, how can therapists increase the likelihood of a successful outcome? The finding that clients who do not easily accept others tend to have less favorable outcomes presents a challenge for therapists. Clients commonly struggle with self-acceptance, and those nonaccepting of others likely represent those with deeper levels of self-rejection. Clients with adequate perceptions of themselves are more likely to be accepting of others. And the experience of being accepted by the therapist has the potential to assist the client in this endeavor. Helping clients progress toward self-acceptance will likely help them become more accepting of others. This premise is supported by the research that shows the relationship between successful outcomes and accepting attitudes of others. So, the therapy process in itself may assist clients in becoming less rejecting of others.

CONCLUSIONS

There are a number of key variables that are associated with positive therapeutic outcomes. The client's willingness and capacity to engage in the process are strong indicators of success. For clients who are not skilled at introspection or in the expression of feelings, therapists can help clients look inward, experience and describe feelings more fully, and perhaps gain a sense of responsibility for their lives. Also, the research has consistently proven that the quality of the therapeutic relationship is an essential component of successful psychotherapy. Attention to the creation and maintenance of a quality relationship cannot be stressed enough.

Just as client variables more predictive of success do not guarantee therapeutic success, client variables associated with limited success do not guarantee that treatment will not be beneficial. Consistent with humanistic thinking, it seems vital to not make assumptions about clients and their capacities. The client variables associated with a poor outcome should be considered as challenges to work with rather than evidence that there is no hope for a positive outcome. Therefore, therapists need to be proactive to increase the likelihood of desired outcomes. Sometimes the humanistic therapies are inaccurately depicted as being passive with vague goals and directions that take an inordinate amount of time to address. Being nondirective does not mean being passive and laissez-faire. One can be proactive in addressing a wide range of client problems and client styles and still function in a fashion consistent with humanistic psychology.

REFERENCES

Bergin, A. E., & Garfield, S. L. (1994). *Handbook of psychotherapy and behavior change* (4th ed.). New York: Wiley.

Beutler, L. E., Crago, M., & Arizmendi, T. G. (1986). Therapist variables in psychotherapy process. In S. L. Garfield & A. E. Bergin (Eds.), *Handbook of psychotherapy and behavior change* (3rd ed., pp. 257–310). New York: Wiley.

Bohart, A. C., & Tallman, K., (1999). *How clients make therapy work: The process of active self-healing*. Washington, DC: American Psychological Association.

Butler, J. M., Rice, L. N., & Wagstaff, A. K. (1962). On the naturalistic definition of variables: An analogue of clinical analysis. In H. Strupp & L. Luborsky (Eds.), *Research in psychotherapy* (Vol. 2, pp. 178–205). Washington, DC: American Psychological Association.

Christensen, A., & Jacobson, N. S. (1994). Who (or what) can do psychotherapy: The status and challenge of nonprofessional therapies. *Psychological Science, 5*, 8–14.

Combs, A. W., & Gonzalez, D. M. (1994). *Helping relationships: Basic concepts for the helping professions* (4th ed., pp. 24–25). Needham Heights, MA: Allyn & Bacon.

Filak, J., Abeles, N., & Norquist, S. (1986). Clients' pretherapy interpersonal attitudes and psychotherapy outcome. *Professional Psychology: Research and Practice, 17*, 217–222.

Gendlin, E. T. (1984). The client's client: The edge of awareness. In R. F. Levant & J. M. Shlien (Eds.), *Client-centered therapy and the person-centered approach: New directions in theory, research, and practice* (pp. 76–107).

Gendlin, E. T. (1996). *Focusing-oriented psychotherapy: A manual of the experiential method.* New York: Guilford Press.

Gendlin, E. T., Beebe, J., Cassens, J., Klein, M., & Oberlander, M. (1968). Focusing ability in psychotherapy, personality and creativity. In J. M. Shlien (Ed.), *Research in psychotherapy* (Vol. 3, pp. 217–238). Washington, DC: American Psychological Association.

Giacomo, D., & Weissmark, M. (1992). Mechanisms of action in psychotherapy. *Journal of Psychotherapy Practice and Research, 1,* 37–48.

Gomes-Schwartz, B. (1978). Effective ingredients in psychotherapy: Predictions of outcome from process variables. *Journal of Consulting and Clinical Psychology, 46,* 1023–1035.

Gould, R. A., & Clum, G. A. (1993). A meta-analysis of self-help treatment approaches. *Clinical Psychology Review, 13,* 169–186.

Greenberg, L. S., & Pinsof, W. M. (1986). *The psychotherapeutic process: A research handbook.* New York: Guilford Press.

Grencavage, L. M., & Norcross, J. C. (1990). Where are the commonalities among the therapeutic common factors? *Professional Psychology: Research and Practice, 21,* 372–378.

Haimowitz, N. R., & Haimowitz, M. L. (1952). Personality changes in client-centered therapy. In W. Wolff & J. A. Precker (Eds.), *Success in psychotherapy: Personality monographs* (Vol. 3, pp. 74–76). New York: Grune & Stratton.

Horowitz, M., Marmar, C., Weiss, D., & Rosenbaum, R. (1984). Brief psychotherapy of bereavement reactions: The relationship of process to outcome. *Archives of General Psychiatry, 41,* 438–448.

Kilmann, P., & Howell, R. (1974). Effects of structure of marathon group therapy and locus of control on therapeutic outcome. *Journal of Consulting and Clinical Psychology, 42,* 912.

Kirtner, W. L., & Cartwright, D. S. (1958). Success and failure in client-centered therapy as a function of initial in-therapy behavior. *Journal of Consulting Psychology, 22,* 329–335.

Klein, M. H., Mathieu-Coughlan, P., & Kiesler, D. J. (1986). The experiencing scales. In L. S. Greenberg & W. M. Pinsof (Eds.), *The psychotherapeutic process* (pp. 21–72). New York: Guilford Press.

Kolb, D. L., Beutler, L. E., Davis, C. S., Crago, M., & Shanfield, S. B. (1985). Patient and therapy process variables relating to dropout and change in psychotherapy. *Psychotherapy, 23,* 702–710.

Lawson, D. (1994). Identifying pretreatment change. *Journal of Counseling and Development, 72,* 244–248.

Moras, K., & Strupp, H. H. (1982). Pretherapy interpersonal relations, patients' alliance, and outcome in brief therapy. *Archives of General Psychiatry, 39,* 405–409.

Morgan, R., Luborsky, L., Crits-Christoph, P., Curtis, H., & Solomon, J. (1982). Predicting the outcomes of psychotherapy by the Penn Helping Alliance Rating Method. *Archives of General Psychiatry, 39,* 397–402.

O'Malley, S. S., Suh, C. S., & Strupp, H. H. (1983). The Vanderbilt Psychotherapy Process Scale: A report of the scale development and a process–outcome study. *Journal of Consulting and Clinical Psychology, 51,* 581–586.

Orlinsky, D. E., & Howard, K. I. (1986). Process and outcomes in psychotherapy. In S. L. Garfield & A. E. Bergin (Eds.), *Handbook of psychotherapy and behavior change* (3rd ed., pp. 311–384). New York: Wiley.

Orlinsky, D. E., Grawe, K., & Parks, B. K. (1994). Process and outcome in psychotherapy—noch einmal. In S. L. Garfield & A. E. Bergin (Eds.), *Handbook of psychotherapy and behavior change* (4th ed., pp. 270–376). New York: Wiley.

Rennie, D. L. (1990). Toward a representation of the client's experience of the psychotherapy hour. In G. Lietaer, J. Rombauts, & R. Van Balen (Eds.), *Client-centered and experiential therapy in the nineties* (pp. 155–172). Leuven, Belgium: Leuven University Press.

Rice, L. N., & Wagstaff, A. K. (1967). Client voice quality and expressive style as indexes of productive psychotherapy. *Journal of Consulting Psychology, 31,* 557–563.

Rogers, C. R. (1954). *Psychotherapy and personality change.* Boston: Houghton Mifflin.

Rogers, C. R. (1957). The necessary and sufficient conditions of therapeutic personality change. *Journal of Consulting Psychology, 21,* 95–103.

Rosenbaum, R. (1994). Single-session therapies: Intrinsic integration? *Journal of Psychotherapy Integration, 4,* 229–252.

Scogin, F., Bynum, J., Stephens, G., & Calhoon, S. (1990). Efficacy of self-administered treatment programs: Meta-analytic review. *Professional Psychology: Research and Practice, 21,* 42–47.

Seligman, L. (1990). *Selecting effective treatments. A comprehensive systematic guide to treating adult mental disorders.* San Francisco: Jossey-Bass.

Todd, J., & Bohart, A. C. (1999). *Foundations of clinical and counseling psychology* (3rd ed.). Reading, MA: Addison-Wesley.

Tougas, R. R. (1952). Ethnocentrism as a limiting factor in verbal therapy. In C. R. Rogers & R. F. Dymond (Eds.), *Psychotherapy and personality change* (pp. 196–214). Chicago: University of Chicago Press.

Weiner-Davis, M., de Shazer, S., & Gingerich, W. (1987). Building on pretreatment change to construct the therapeutic solution: An exploratory study. *Journal of Marital and Family Therapy, 13,* 359–364.

Weissmark, M. S., & Giacomo, D. A. (1998). *Doing psychotherapy effectively.* Chicago: University of Chicago Press.

Welch, I. D., & Gonzalez, D. M. (1999). *The process of counseling and psychotherapy: Matters of skill.* Pacific Grove, CA: Brooks/Cole.

Wexler, D. A., & Butler, J. M. (1976). Therapist modification of client expressiveness in client-centered therapy. *Journal of Consulting and Clinical Psychology, 44,* 261–265.

19

HUMANISTIC PSYCHOTHERAPY FOR PEOPLE WITH SCHIZOPHRENIA

GARRY PROUTY

In 1954, when Maslow (Misiak, 1973) prepared the first general outline of humanistic psychology, he described it as the scientific study of creativity, love, higher values, autonomy, growth, self-actualization, and basic need gratification. Although invaluable and a greatly needed corrective to contemporary psychology, such a zeitgeist was not conducive to the study of individuals with severely reduced functioning, such as retardation, geriatrics, or psychosis. The result has been a perception of humanistic psychotherapy as being for the "existentially distressed" higher functioning person.

In this chapter, I review 50 years of research on humanistic psychotherapy of hospitalized patients with schizophrenia. The purpose is to draw together evidence that humanistic psychotherapy is indeed relevant to more than the "worried well." This chapter presents research findings, critiques, and suggested research directions for the future. In addition, reference is made to case histories in the existential–phenomenological tradition.

THE ROGERIAN HYPOTHESIS

Rogers's approach to psychotherapy can be briefly described as the provision of a set of *core conditions* that help facilitate the self-actualizing tendency of the client (Mearns & Thorne, 1990). These attitudes are delineated as unconditional positive regard, empathy, and congruence. *Unconditional positive regard* is defined by Rogers as "a warm acceptance of each aspect of the client's experience" (Rogers, 1957, p. 98). *Empathy* is defined as "sensing the client's private world *as if* it were your own" (p. 99).

Congruence is defined as "within the relationship, the therapist is freely and deeply himself, with his actual experience being represented by his awareness of himself" (p. 97). Although not formally stated by Rogers, the *nondirective attitude* (Raskin, 1947) is a powerful element in Rogerian therapy. It can be defined as a "surrendered" following of the client's own intent, directionality, and process by the therapist.

The Silent Young Man: The Case of Mr. Vac

The "Silent Young Man" (Rogers, Gendlin, Kiesler, & Truax, 1967) is the classic presentation of Rogers's therapeutic work with individuals with schizophrenia. In the opinion of Rogers and other client-centered therapists (e.g., Bozarth & Brodley, 1991), this vignette presents the crucial use of Rogers's theory in the successful treatment of a client with schizophrenia. The client is a young man in his late 20s. He was part of a research project and had been hospitalized 2½ years at the time of the treatment session. His hospital diagnosis was "schizophrenic reaction, simple type." Blind rating by four psychotherapists of other theoretical orientations saw the case as providing evidence for therapeutic "movement," whereas two did not agree. The following are extractions from the vignette that illustrate empathy, unconditional positive regard, and congruence.

Empathy

The client had been struggling to express suicidal feelings of hopelessness and worthlessness. The client said, "I just want to run away and die," to which Rogers responded a couple of lines later,

> Rogers: I guess, as I let that soak in, I really do sense how, how deep that feeling sounds, that you—I guess the image that comes to my mind is sort of a—a wounded animal that wants to crawl away and die. It sounds as though that is kind of the way you feel—that you just want to get away from here and vanish. Perish, not exist.
> Client: (almost inaudibly) All day yesterday and all morning I wished I were dead. I even prayed last night that I could die. (Rogers et al., 1967, p. 407)

In this example, Rogers gives the client not only a cognitive understanding but also his personal experiencing of the client's message. His empathy is congruent.

Unconditional Positive Regard

In the example below, the client was directly expressing his suicidal hopelessness.

Client: That's why I want to go, [die] 'cause I don't care what happens. Rogers: Mmm. That's why you want to go, because you really don't care about yourself. You just don't care *what* happens. And I guess I'd just like to say—I care about you and I care what happens. (silence of 30 seconds, Jim burst into tears and unintelligible sobs), (therapist: tenderly) And you just weep and weep and weep. (Jim continues to sob, blows his nose, and breathes in great gasps.) (Rogers et al., 1967, p. 409)

In this quotation, Rogers is expressing his personal caring for the client in an empathic way that releases the pent-up feelings in the client.

Congruence

The client said: "I ain't no good to nobody for nothin', so what's the use of living?" A line or so later Rogers said,

I don't know whether this will help or not, but I would like to say that—I think I can understand pretty well—what it's like to feel that you're just *no damn good* to anybody, because there was a time when—I felt that way about *myself*. And I know it can be *really rough*. (Rogers et al., 1967, p. 408)

Here Rogers is sharing himself deeply with the client and doing so with "as if" empathy.

These three illustrations convey the attitudinal conditions that Rogers postulated are necessary and sufficient for therapeutic change. Rogers himself described the vignette as a moment of change. Two years later, the client was released from the hospital and wrote of his newfound life satisfactions, which included attending school, increased socialization with friends, and a "wonderful summer."

Research: The Wisconsin Project

The Wisconsin Project (Rogers et al., 1967) is generally considered the pioneer effort of its time in exploring the impact of client-centered therapy with the people with schizophrenia. Not only concerned with classical independent and dependent variables, the research also explored *process* measures. As Rogers stated concerning the Wisconsin study, "it is an investigation to see whether certain specified attitudinal conditions existing in the therapist or in the therapeutic relationship are an antecedent of or are significantly related to a specific process or therapeutic change in the client" (Rogers et al., 1967, p. 6).

Hypotheses

In the Wisconsin Project (Rogers et al., 1967), Rogers described the basic questions of the research as follows: (a) What therapist behaviors are effective for client change? (b) What behaviors of the client constitute the "process" of change? and (c) What are the outcomes of this process? The therapist "behaviors" necessary for change are the attitudes (unconditional positive regard, empathy, and congruence). The client change processes evaluated referred to the level of experiencing. The outcome measures included various test measures, assessments of psychopathology, and staff evaluations. Rogers refined these concerns into different hypotheses. The first and more global hypothesis was that the greater the degree the core attitudes exist in the relationship, the greater will be the evidence of experiential process movement. A second, derivative hypothesis was that the same variables of process movement would be characteristic of individuals with acute and chronic schizophrenia as well as individuals considered normal and those with neuroses. A third hypothesis was that process movement would occur to a significantly greater degree in the group receiving therapy than in a control group. A fourth hypothesis was that groups or individuals receiving higher amounts of the therapeutic conditions would evidence more positive outcome than groups or individuals receiving lower amounts of the therapeutic conditions. The last hypothesis predicted that the greater the evidence of process movement, the greater degree of constructive outcome.

Design

The basic research population of the Wisconsin Project was composed of three groups (*N* = 48): (a) more chronic, (b) more acute, and (c) normal participants, who were compared with nontherapy controls. The participants were randomly matched for gender, age, socioeducational status, and degree of disturbance (Luborsky Health–Sickness Rating Scale; Luborsky, 1962). The data were sampled at 3-month intervals. The primary therapeutic variables (unconditional positive regard, empathy, and congruence) were measured by Truax's (1967a) Scale of Accurate Empathy, Truax's (1967b) Scale for the Measuring of Unconditional Positive Regard, and Kiesler's (1967) Scale for the Rating of Congruence. Process variables were measured by Gendlin and Tomlinson's (1967) Scale for the Rating of Experiencing, Gendlin's (1967) Scale for the Manner of Relating, and Van der Veen and Tomlinson's (1967) Scale for the Rating Manner of Problem Expression. Outcome measurements included the Rorschach, Minnesota Multiphasic Personality Inventory (MMPI), and Thematic Apperception Test (TAT) instruments. In addition, the Wechsler Adult Intelligence Scale, Q-sorts, and Truax Anxiety Scale (1961) were used, as well as the Whiteborn Psychiatric Scale (Whiteborn & Betz, 1954) for staff assessments. The Barrett-Lennard Relationship Inventory (1962) was used to measure relationship *perceptions* among judges, patients, and therapists.

Results

The results were mixed with negative and positive findings. The first hypothesis, that is, the greater the degree of attitudinal conditions, the greater the degree of process movement, was not confirmed. People with schizophrenia evidenced extremely little process movement. The second hypothesis, that process movement had the same qualities for individuals with psychoses, those who are normal, and those with neuroses, found that individuals with schizophrenia focused more on relationship formation, whereas individuals with neuroses engaged in self-exploratory experiencing. The third hypothesis, that the process of therapy would be greater with the therapy group than controls, was not confirmed. Hospitalized, nonpsychotherapy clients illustrated nearly as much process movement. A corollary hypothesis that the group receiving higher attitudinal conditions would exhibit more process than a group receiving lower amounts of attitudinal conditions was also not confirmed. On a positive note, however, it was found that those individuals exposed to the highest level of attitudinal conditions exhibited the highest level of experiential process among those with schizophrenia, those with neuroses, and normal participants. The last hypothesis—linking outcome with process movement—was partially confirmed. Individuals with schizophrenia receiving the highest degree of empathy showed improvement on the schizophrenic subscale of the MMPI, as well as significant improvement on the TAT. There was also a strong trend toward reduced hospitalization.

Discussion

These results of the Wisconsin Project should be interpreted first within the context of the research design. Rogers et al. (1967) suggested that results may have been more positive if the clients with schizophrenia and the controls had been matched initially in terms of process levels. One detriment was that sample size was too small. Additionally, the clients were not voluntary, which made a motivational difference. Therefore, this made treatment difficult. Rogers et al. also felt that the attitudinal scales did not capture the full complexity of unconditional positive regard, empathy, and congruence. Another limitation of the study was the limited clinical experience of the therapists with a psychotic population. Also, the sample was not "clean" from treatment drugs or other forms of hospital therapy, thereby confounding variables were introduced whose impact were not assessed. Given this retrospective view, Rogers et al. took satisfaction that the effects of attitudinal conditions and process variables were still able to manifest themselves (high levels of attitudinal conditions were associated with highest level of process movement, and high levels of process were partially associated with outcome). There are additional limitations in my opinion. First, the client was arbitrarily defined as chronic at 8 months! *The research hospital was not a chronic institution.* The research hospital was a county referral hospital dealing with more acute cases. Patients who did not respond to treatment were sent to state hospitals. The research population was highly skewed away from the more deteriorated, long-term patients (approximately 5 years or more), which characterize state hospitals. This understanding limits the findings to moderately severe and acute clients.

Further complexity is introduced by Rogers et al.'s (1967) description of clinical improvement associated with high attitudinal conditions. They described such clients as having higher socioeducational levels, combined with higher verbal functioning. This is consistent with many findings that higher socioeconomic clients do better, in general, with psychotherapy. This draws us back to the issue of social contamination in understanding the treatment of schizophrenia.

Ancillary Studies

An earlier study by Van der Veen (1965), drawing on the Wisconsin Project database, examined the joint interactive effect of therapists and schizophrenic clients in therapy. His general hypothesis was that "the therapist and the patient mutually influence each other's therapeutic behavior and that therapeutic behavior of one is positively related to the therapeutic behavior of the other" (p. 21). Both therapist and client contributed significantly to the level of problem expression and experiencing for clients. Also confirmed was the finding that both the therapist and the client influenced the therapist's attitudes of congruence and empathy.

Again, drawing from the same process measures and outcome variables database, Van der Veen (1967) found no correlation between patient process and level of therapist's conditions, patient perception of therapist attitudes, or case outcome. However, empathy levels and congruence were positively correlated with a combined outcome measure. Unconditional positive regard was associated with less hospitalization. Also, the highest and lowest levels of the therapeutic attitudes (empathy and congruence) differentiated highest and lowest levels of successful outcome. Additionally, on a more positive note, higher levels of experiencing process were associated with the highest levels of case outcome. Case outcome was not related to perceived conditions. As with the original data analysis, limited support existed for the therapeutic effect of the attitudes and experiencing.

Also using the database from the Wisconsin study, Truax (1970) examined the pre- and posthospitalization trends of patients and controls. He found no differences in days out of the hospital for patients and controls. However, the high-therapeutic conditions group got out and stayed out of the hospital significantly more (measured by analysis of variance) than the low-therapeutic conditions group. Recovery rates and early recovery also correlated with higher amounts of the therapeutic conditions.

Related Studies

In an interesting study, Pugh (1949) examined the *combined* effects of electric shock and client-centered therapy on a small sample ($N = 6$) of patients with paranoid schizophrenia. Pugh used pre- and posttest measurements of the Stein Sentence Completion Test, the MMPI, and the Rorschach. Results from the Stein Sentence Completion Test showed increased positive themes at the .05 level of significance. MMPI depression scales were reduced at the .05 level of significance. Rorschach scales of depression were reduced at the .10 level of significance. There was no reduction in paranoid–schizophrenic symptomatology. Because it is well known that depression is reduced by electric shock, these combined findings cannot be fully attributed to the effects of client-centered therapy.

A specific body of empirical research has found that therapists can be differentiated on the Strong Vocational Interest Inventory as "A Type" (Seidman, 1971). Therapists who were not as successful with clients with schizophrenia could also be differentiated and labeled as "B Type" (Betz, 1967). In a related study, Seidman (1971) paired A and B therapists with schizoid and neurotic enactments. He found that therapist levels of respect and empathy varied as a function of A or B status and client "diagnosis." Type A therapists had more respect and empathy for schizoid enactments, and Type B therapists had more respect and empathy for neurotic enactments. Beutler, Johnson, Neville, and Workman (1972) found, as predicted, that Type A therapists working with schizophrenic clients and Type B therapists working with neurotic clients showed significantly more empathy than reversed pairings. These studies seem to indicate that Rogers's therapeutic attitudes are interactional and not unidirectional as generally researched.

Teusch, Beyerle, Lange, Schenk, and Stadmuller (1981) reported client-centered research involving patients with acute schizophrenia ($N = 60$). The patients seemed to fall into three descriptive categories: (a) autistic, lacking in self-propelled process and self-disclosure; (b) somewhat fragile, but near complete remission with minimum affective and drive deficiencies; and (c) a bland group with little or no thought disorder and affective or drive deficiencies.

Hospitalization ranged from 2 to 4 months. The primary measuring tool was the Client-Experiencing Questionnaire (Eckert, Schwartz, & Tausch, 1977). A factor analysis of that instrument yields four elements: (a) insecurity and verbal inhibition, (b) interaction, (c) reassuring change optimism, and (d) physical tension and emotional stress. The first measurement obtained was a reverse correlation between the Client-Experiencing Questionnaire experiencing scale and the Frankfurt Complaint Questionnaire (Sullworld, 1977). According to Teusch et al. (1981), this confirmed the Wisconsin Project finding that patients with schizophrenia did not perceive the "attitudes" when objectively present as measured by independent judges. A second finding was that less disturbed patients showed more initial "change optimism." There was also a marked correlation between the patients with schizophrenia and "insecurity and verbal inhibition." There was a positive trend between change optimism and therapy outcome. Teusch (1990) also reported that pre- and posttest differences on the Freiberger Personality Inventory showed significant reductions in depression and physical complaint for the schizophrenic population. Significant gains in self-confidence were also noted. Seventy-five percent of the patients showed improvement on a global clinical scale as a function of therapy. A major criticism of these findings is the evident lack of a control group. The effect of drug treatment was also not accounted for in interpreting the results.

Hinterkopf and Brunswick (1981) taught reflecting and focusing capabilities to patients with acute and chronic schizophrenia. The reflecting and focusing skills were measured by Helper and Talker Rating Scales (Hinterkopf & Brunswick, 1975). Interrater reliability for the scales was .91. Pre- and postmeasurements of the experimental group showed significant gains. Talker (focusing) and Helper (reflecting) scales were measured by a t test of change scores. Hinterkopf and Brunswick demonstrated that patients with schizophrenia improved in attending their own experiencing (focusing) and in "listening" empathically to others. A gain score analysis found that the experimental group scoring was significantly greater than the control group on the Discharge Readiness Inventory (Community Adjustment Potential; Hogarty & Ulrich, 1972).

Overview

Without question, it is difficult to generalize from these individual "photographs" to construct a complete picture of the empirical relationship between client-centered therapy and schizophrenia. It seems more like finding threads of meaning in the weave of information. It appears reasonable to say there is *limited* support for the Rogerian hypothesis. This view seems to receive support from Greenberg, Elliott, and Lietaer (1994), who found smaller effect scores for clients with schizophrenia as compared with other groups of clients receiving client-centered therapy. There does seem to be a trend in the literature to link the therapeutic attitudes with outcome measures (Rogers et al., 1967; Teusch, 1990; Truax, 1970; Van der Veen, 1965). There also seems to be another important result. There is no direct causal relationship between therapist conditions and client progress as traditionally hypothesized, rather an interactive influence of therapist and client

(Beutler et al., 1972; Seidman, 1971; Van der Veen, 1965). An obfuscating variable is the use of antipsychotic medications for hospitalized patients. Without scientific controls, it is impossible to access the direct or proportional effects of client-centered therapy. None of these studies clarified this point, although Karon and VandenBos (1981) did experimentally separate drug treatment from psychoanalytic therapy with positive results. Perhaps another limiting factor is that these studies seemed focused on acute as opposed to chronic patients, providing a picture of only the upper end of the patient continuum and not revealing much about the limited chronic world. This limitation, more than others, is suggestive of expanding Rogers's original work to include concepts and techniques applicable to the more deteriorated and disorganized client.

GESTALT THERAPY

Noting the lack of quantitative study concerning Gestalt psychotherapy and psychosis, Serok and Zemet (1983) tested the effects of Gestalt group therapy on clients with schizophrenia. Operating on the theoretical premise that directive experiential exercises help integrate reality, Serok and Zemet hypothesized that Gestalt therapy would measurably increase the level of reality differentiation and perception. Nine participants were used for the experimental group and 8 for the control group. The experimental group ran for 75 minutes, once a week, over a 2½-month period. The control group received occupational therapy during the same time period. Serok and Zemet wanted to explore the effects of the therapy on differential concrete perception, logical thinking, and reality internalization. Pre- and posttest measurements were taken with the Neigger and Falk reality scales of the Rorschach. The results showed statistically significant increases on the Neigger scale for reality testing and large increases in reality perception on the Falk test. As with the Rogerian studies, this experiment did not develop controls for medication, thereby limiting interpretation of results.

Serok, Rabin, and Spitz (1984) described the treatment of clients with schizophrenia in classical Gestalt terms as the restoration of figure–ground process. Specifically, they assessed whether clients developed an awareness of reality through the use of various reality oriented exercises.

Newly hospitalized patients were matched on gender, age, education, ethnicity, occupation, socioeconomic status, diagnosis, and number of admissions. Nine patients received group therapy 4 days a week for 3 months. The therapy was directed toward the strengthening of reality perception and internalization as well as logical functions. Measurements were taken 1 week before and 1 week after the experimental duration. The Goodenough Human Figure Drawing Test was used to assess perception of self and others

(Brill, 1935). Also in the Goodenough test, the absence of distortion was examined along with body image, proportions, posture, and line quality. For drawings of male and female participants, there were significant improvements in body image. For male participants, there were significantly reduced distortions in the figure drawings. Female participants showed significant gains in proportion, posture, and line quality.

Overall ratings and developmental levels also increased with statistical significance. Patients were also rated on a Self-Concept Scale (Fitts, 1972) of 100 items and showed measurable improvement at significant levels. These included feelings of self-satisfaction and family identity. Also, measures of personality integration significantly increased. Staff behavioral evaluation showed significant increases in communicative clarity and degree of contact with others. A significant drop in physical and verbal aggression was also noted. As with the previous study, these results show an effect of Gestalt therapy but do not clarify the relative weights of psychotherapy or medications. However, the evidence does show the therapeutic impact of Gestalt awareness exercises on the reality, social, and self-integration of the client.

PSYCHOSOCIAL PROGRAMS

Soteria House

Mosher and Menn (1978, 1979) described Soteria House as a "vintage," 12-room house that accommodates 8 to 10 people comfortably in a "transitional" neighborhood in San Francisco. It was staffed with nonprofessionals with a part-time psychiatric consultant. The nonprofessional staff's role in this residential program was to "be with" the clients in a phenomenological way that accepted patient psychotic experiences in a validating nonjudgmental manner. Mosher and Menn described six programmatic ingredients as critical: (a) positive expectations of learning from psychosis; (b) flexibility of roles, relationships, and responses; (c) sufficient time in residence for imitation and identification with staff to occur with acceptance of the psychotic person's experience of himself or herself as valid; (d) staff's primary responsibility to "be with" the disorganized resident and specific acknowledgment that he or she need not do anything; (e) great tolerance for "crazy" behavior without anxiety or a need to control it; and (f) normalization of the experience of psychosis. Psychiatric drugs were used minimally, ranging from 7% to 10% of the time as compared with the 100% regimen characteristic of standard hospital programs.

Mathews, Roper, Mosher, and Menn (1979) compared the postdischarge relapse rates for Soteria House with those of a psychiatric inpatient mental health center. There were 32 experimental participants and 36 control participants who were matched on diagnosis, gender, marital status, education, social class, and number of previous hospitalizations. A life table of statistical analysis was used. The life table method is widely used to study survivorship in various medical conditions. It is also a useful means of displaying longitudinal data for psychiatric patients. Consistently, Soteria House patients demonstrated greater continuation in the program over 24 months when compared with the traditional program. In a comparison of total patients, Soteria House demonstrated 20% lower relapse rates. Soteria *nondrug* participants, compared with traditional *continuously drug-maintained* participants, showed statistically significant lower relapse rates over 6-, 12-, 18-, and 24-month periods as a function of the psychosocial milieu therapy.

Mosher, Vallone, and Menn (1995) compared two Soteria programs with two psychiatric wards from county hospitals. Forty-five patients were in the experimental group (Soteria programs) and 55 in the control group (county psychiatric wards). Patients were matched in terms of 10 demographic, 5 psychopathological, 7 prognostic, and 7 psychosocial variables. Milieu was accessed by the Ward Atmosphere Scale (WAS) and the Community Environment Program Environmental Scale (COPES; Moos, 1975). The data revealed that the two experimental programs (Soteria) were remarkably similar to each other and significantly different from the two control programs (county psychiatric wards).

When the two environments were compared for a 6-week measurement, there were no differences in measured levels of psychopathology or degree of improvement. Also, there were no measured differences in level of symptom reduction. In other words, the two environments produced similar levels of clinical improvement. A very low drug psychosocial program did as well as a standard drug program during the critical period of personal disorganization. Furthermore, the experimental group, matched on 27 variables, was broken into no drug treatment versus drug treatment received. The no-drug patients showed significantly greater improvement on global pathology scales. Although Soteria House was generally equivalent to the standard psychiatric program, the important finding was the significantly greater improvement for no-drug treatment over drugs received.

Soteria Berne

"Soteria Berne" was a psychosocial treatment program located in Berne, Switzerland. The facility consisted of a 12-room house with a garden. The house could accommodate 6 to 8 resident patients. The therapeutic team consisted of a part-time director, five psychiatric nurses, and four paraprofessionals. Treatment was divided into four stages. First is the acute phase, during which a caretaker provides an "intensely supportive" relationship during psychotic experiences. Next comes the activating phase, which is characterized by gradually getting back in touch with reality. The third phase consists of gradual social, vocational, and residential adjustments. The last phase is a 2-year follow-up to prevent relapse of schizophrenic symptoms and rehospitalization.

Ciompi et al. (1992) provided research on Soteria Berne. First, the Moos Ward Atmosphere Scale (1974) positively differentiated the Soteria Berne from four other psychiatric wards in the community. Approximately two thirds of the residents showed "good" to "fairly good" improvements. This was carried out with drug dosages averaging one fifth to one tenth of U.S. standards. Furthermore, within the Soteria Berne group, patients who received lower amounts or no neuroleptic drugs demonstrated significantly better results for treatment. Similar to the original Soteria study in San Francisco, Ciompi also found no outcome differences when compared with other psychiatric facilities on seven variables: psychopathology, housing, jobs, global outcome, autonomy, relapse, and costs. This demonstrates equal improvement between standard psychiatric programs, with possible drug side effects, and a very low-drug or no-drug psychosocial program with reduced neuroleptic risks.

PRETHERAPY

This section of the chapter presents more recent concepts and developments in client-centered/humanistic therapy with individuals with psychoses. These concepts are based on the recognition that normative therapy procedures generally do not work effectively with this population for two reasons: (a) People with psychoses have far more difficulty in forming interpersonal connections and relationships, and (b) people with psychoses have far more difficulty in interpersonal communication than do those without psychoses. Evolutions in person-centered/experiential psychotherapy were needed for clients who have chronic schizophrenia, clients with psychoses or mental disability, and other low-functioning clients (Prouty, 1994; Prouty, Van Werde, & Portner, 1998). These developments are introduced below.

Psychological Contact

Rogers (1959) postulated psychological contact as the first condition of the therapeutic relationship. Prouty (1990) suggested that Rogers gratuitously *assumes* the presence of psychological contact between therapist and client and that he failed to define it theoretically or clinically. This necessitates the further theoretical development of psychological contact. *Pretherapy* is a theory and method that postulates psychological contact as the necessary precondition of a psychotherapeutic relationship for contact-impaired clients, such as clients with mental disability or chronic schizophrenia. Psychological contact is generally described in existential–phenomenological terms as the lived, prereflective conscious experience of the world, self, or other. Psychological contact is manifested therapeutically as the therapist engages the client through the following means: (a) contact reflections, (b) contact functions, and (c) contact behaviors.

Contact Reflections

Contact reflections are "a pointing at the concrete." They are duplicative, literal, and concrete responses to the client's limited level of expression. There are five contact reflections: situational reflection (SR), facial reflection (FR), word-for-word reflection (WWR), bodily reflection (BR), and reiterative reflection (RR).

Situational reflections. Situational reflections are reflections of the client's situation, environment, or milieu. An example is "Johnny is sitting on the floor" or "Mary is looking out the window." They are attempts to facilitate client reality contact.

Facial reflections. Many of these clients with regression and psychoses have impaired affective contact because of psychological isolation, institutionalization, and overmedication. Facial reflections are reflections of the client's preexpressive affect. They are designed to assist affective experiencing. An example is "You look sad" or, more literally, "There are tears in your eyes."

Word-for-word reflections. Many of the chronic clients communicate in a highly disorganized fashion, including echolalia neologisms and word salads. Often their communication is a mixture of comprehensible and incomprehensible expression. For example, a client may say "tree" (incomprehensible word), "horse" (incomprehensible word), "grass." The therapist would reflect (word-for-word) "tree, horse, grass." The therapists also reflect sentence fragments, incomplete sentences, and, occasionally, sounds to assist the development or restoration of communication contact.

Body reflections. Many clients express themselves through bizarre body expression, such as catatonic posturing or echopraxia. There are two types of body reflection. The first is verbal, such as "Your arm is in the air" or "You are standing stiffly." The second is a more concrete and literal type of reflection in which the therapist uses his or her own body to reflect, by assuming the posture of the client. These techniques are used to help the client develop a bodily sense or bodily ego.

Reiterative reflections. Reiterative reflections are not a specific technique, rather they embody the *principle of recontact*. If any of the contact reflections succeed in producing a response from the client, the therapist repeats it. This strengthens the communicative experience between client and therapist. There are immediate and longer term reiterative reflections. The immediate reiteration generally follows close in time to a successful reflection that previously produced a response. For example, "You just smiled when I said tree." A long-term reiteration follows a significant time lapse. An example would be when I stated to a client, "Last time you pointed at your stomach." This led to the eventual uncovering of an abortion.

These reflections, when combined, produce a method of psychological contact that is empathetically responsive to the client's limited *level of communication*. They provide a web of contact for the isolated client.

Practice. This example illustrates the application of contact reflections. It is drawn from Van Werde's (see Prouty et al., 1998) description of an interaction between a client, Harry (H), and the therapist (T) in a Belgian psychiatric hospital.

> Harry is a young man, 23 years old, with chaotic contact. Since he functions on a low level, he is a member of Group I (a small group with an intensive and individual approach). His motivation, cooperation and emotional moods fluctuate continuously. His lack of concentration, attention and endurance make him very difficult to work with and for him to function in a group setting. He likes to have all the attention and his behavior is often childish. That day, Harry arrives late and without his keyboard for his daily musical lesson of fifteen minutes.
>
> H: (*Comes in and puts his head on the piano.*)
> T: Hello Harry. . .
> (*H. stays with his head on the piano*)
> (*H. says something unintelligible, stays with his head on the piano*)
> T: [SR] You said something . . . I couldn't understand . . .
> T: [SR] Your head is on the piano . . .
> (*H. stays a little while in the same posture. Suddenly he starts to cry*)
> T: [FR] You're crying . . .
> (*H. is continuously crying and stays in the same posture*)
> T: [RR, SR] You're crying with your head on the piano . . .
> (*H. lifts his head . . . sighs . . . dries his tears from his face*)
> T: [SR] You're looking at me . . .
> T: [FR] You sigh . . .
> T: [FR] I see tears on your face . . .
> T: [SR] You dry away your tears . . .
> H: Synthesizer . . .
> (*H. is silent, lets his head and shoulders down*)
> T: [WWR] Synthesizer . . .
> T: [RR] Last week you were here everyday at the same time with your synthesizer . . .
> T: [BR] You let your head and shoulders down . . .
> H: I don't feel like playing today . . . I'm too tired . . .
> (*H. looks into the eyes of the therapist and starts shaking with his hands*)
> T: [SR] You're looking at me . . .

T: [BR] You're shaking your hands . . .
H: I didn't practice this weekend.
T: [WWR] Didn't practice . . .
H: I had a quarrel with my father.
(H. *lets his head down, looks sad*)
T: [WWR] You said you had a quarrel with your father . . .
(H. *keeps silent*)
T: [BR] You let your head hang down . . .
(H. *remains silent, no reaction at first sight*)
T: [FR] You're looking sad . . .
H: My father is so severe, each evening I must go to sleep at 9:30, even on weekends . . .

From that moment, Harry starts talking fluently and on a congruent level about himself and the things he's occupied with: the disturbed relationship between father and son and the communication problems they have. In a "normal" conversation, they talk shortly about these things. In this way, the right mood was created to proceed with the activity planned for the session. As a first step, contact was established. Then, interaction and activity became possible. (Prouty et al., 1998, pp. 139–140)

Contact Functions

Perls (1969) described contact as an *ego function*. Pretherapy expands this notion to contact functions, which are described as (a) reality contact, (c) affective contact, and (c) communicative contact. They operate as awareness functions. Developing or restoring the reality, affective, and communicative contact necessary for psychotherapy is the theoretical purpose of pretherapy.

Reality contact. Reality contact is defined as the awareness of people, places, things, and events. People are physical "things" in the world. Location is where things "emerge." Things are literal objects. Events represent the time in which things emerge. Things are a tangible aspect of one's reality *sense*.

Affective contact. Affective contact is defined as one's awareness of moods, feelings, and emotions. These are phenomenologically distinct forms of affect. Moods are subtle and diffuse backgrounds. They are a coloring of events. Feelings are more pronounced, clearer, and more specifically foreground. Emotions are considerably more intense and sharp and tend to be more articulated as an affective experience. Moods, feelings, and emotions are continuous aspects of one's experience.

Communicative contact. Communicative contact is defined as the symbolization of a person's awareness of reality and affect to others. It is more than information. It is the expression of one's perceived world and self to others. It conveys denotative and connotative meanings from one's experiential universe. It reveals to the other. It enables psychological contact with the other. People *live* in language, another infinite characteristic of their experience.

Vignette. The following example obtained by my student illustrates the presence and facilitation of the contact functions.

> "Dorothy" is a sixty-five-year-old woman who is one of the more regressed women on X ward. She was mumbling something [as she usually did]. This time I could hear certain words in her confusion. I reflected only the words I could clearly understand. After about ten minutes, I could hear a complete sentence.
>
> C: Come with me.
> T: [WWR] Come with me.
> (The patient led me to the corner of the day-room. We stood there silently for what seemed to be a very long time. Since I couldn't communicate with her, I watched her body movements and closely reflected these.)
> C: (The patient put her hand on the wall.) Cold.
> T: [WWR-BR] (I put my hand on the wall and repeated the word.) Cold. (She had been holding my hand all along; but when I reflected her, she would tighten her grip. Dorothy would begin to mumble word fragments. I was careful to reflect only the words I could understand. What she was saying began to make sense.)
> C: I don't know what this is anymore. (Touching the wall) [Reality contact] The walls and chairs don't mean anything anymore [Existential autism].
> T: [WW-BR] (Touching the wall.) You don't know what this is anymore. The chairs and walls don't mean anything to you anymore.
> C: (The patient began to cry) [Affective contact]
> C: (After a while she began to talk again. This time she spoke clearly) [Communicative contact] I don't like it here. I'm so tired . . . so tired.
> T: [WWR] (As I gently touched her arm, this time it was I who tightened my grip on her hand. I reflected:) You're tired, so tired.
> C: (The patient smiled and told me to sit in a chair directly in front of her and began to braid my hair.)

This vignette demonstrates pretherapy as a therapeutic theory and philosophy. It illustrates the use of contact reflections to facilitate the contact functions. In this example, the reality, affective, and communicative functions begin to emerge, thus providing more relatedness.

Contact Behaviors

Contact behaviors are the emergent behaviors resulting from the facilitation of contact functions through the use of contact reflections. They provide the "behavioral" material for operationalized measurements. Reality contact (world) is operationalized as the client's verbalization of people, places, things, and events. Affective contact (self) is operationalized as the bodily or facial expression of affect. Affective contact may also be operationalized through the use of "healing words," such as *sad* or *angry*. Communicative contact (other) is operationalized through the use of social words or sentences.

An early pilot study (Hinterkopf, Prouty, & Brunswick, 1979), utilizing the pretherapy method, found significant increases for gain scores in reality and communicative contact for patients with chronic schizophrenia when compared with a control group receiving recreational therapy. The patients in the study had an average hospitalization of 20 years, thereby providing an exploration of the genuinely chronic part of the schizophrenic continuum lacking in previous client-centered research.

A single-case pilot study (Prouty, 1990) measured the effects of the pretherapy method on a dual-diagnosed client with schizophrenia/autism and mental disability with a Stanford-Binet IQ of 17. Large increases of reality, affective, and communicative contact were measured by frequency of client contact behaviors per minute. A supporting clinical evaluation was provided by an independent psychologist who was unaware of the purposes of the study. He reported an improved ability to tolerate frustration and reduced aggressiveness. He also reported internalized self-control mechanism as well as greater emotional and behavioral stability. This study provided a first client-centered exploration of psychosis at the lower end of the intellectual continuum.

Prouty (1994), in another single-case pilot study, measured the construct validity of psychological contact. The client was a young woman who was hospitalized with schizophrenia/mental disability receiving pretherapy. There were two sets of observations: one set for a single day and one set for a 3-month period. The single-day observations consisted of 24 pairs of rater scorings drawn from the beginning, middle, and end of the session (1–20, 40–60, and 80–100 percentiles). A correlation coefficient of 0.9847 was obtained with a p value of .0001. The pairwise t test produced a value of 2.3738 with a p value of 0.0526. These results indicate no difference between scoring at the .01 or .05 levels of significance. The 3-month observations consisted of nine pairs of mean scores from independent raters that yielded a correlation coefficient 0.9966 with a p value of .0001, presenting strong evidence against the null hypothesis. The pairwise t test resulted in a value of 0.0964 with a p value of .3528. These results indicate no difference between scoring.

In yet another pilot study, DeVre (1992), with her colleagues Van Werde and Deleu, further confirmed construct validity and developed evidence of reliability for the pretherapy scale. There were 3 clients. The first 2 were clients with chronic schizophrenia with normal intelligence, and the 3rd client was mentally disabled. The first measure of agreement between raters was $\kappa = 0.39$. With translation improvements (English to Flemish), the same raters, with a second client, obtained $\kappa = 0.76$. Again, with the same raters and a third client, raters obtained $\kappa = 0.87$. The reliability measure was obtained by using independent psychiatric nurses trained in the pretherapy scale. Their first measure produced a low measure, $\kappa = 0.39$. With improved English to Flemish translation, the nurses produced $\kappa = 0.7$ at a .0005 level of significance.

Danacci (1997) produced a video study of clients receiving pretherapy. This pilot study involved a single therapist, 2 experimental clients, and 2 control clients diagnosed with mental disability/schizophrenia and hospitalized for 30 years. The experiment produced strong clinical and quantitative evidence for marked communicative increases in the near-mute clients, using the Evaluation Criterion for the Pre-Therapy Interview (ECPI) scale, which measures verbal coherence and severe levels of disorganization. Reporting a beta coefficient of .77, Danacci found a corresponding confidence level of 97.5% that the differences will fall between 16.195 and 28.257 communicative units. Controlling for first-session differences, pretherapy patients averaged 22.226 units higher communicative scores than the control group. The difference was significant at $p < .02$. This statistical interpretation revealed that the client communications scores fell within the range predicted by a much larger sample and was not the result of extraneous variables.

In sum, pretherapy evolves from Rogers's conception of psychological contact as the first condition of a therapeutic relationship. It describes psychological contact on the level of therapist method (contact reflections), client process (contact functions), and client measurable behaviors (contact behaviors). Pilot studies with clients with severely limited mental abilities provide suggestive evidence for the further empirical exploration.

CONCLUSIONS AND PROPOSED RESEARCH

It is difficult to present a comprehensive picture of client-centered and humanistic research with individuals with schizophrenia. There are, of course, the issues of comparing different theoretical structures with different variables and measuring instruments. It does seem reasonable to say that, across the humanistic spectrum as a whole, there is evidence that humanistic approaches have value in treatment for this population.

It is clear that the client-centered tradition has been the most productive in research quantity. However, this must be tempered with the understanding that the findings, in general, have only been modestly supportive of Rogers's views and limited to the higher end of the psychotic continuum. Of paramount importance is the expansion of research into the more chronic regressed populations of individuals with schizophrenia. This can be done through researching chronic institutions and chronic patients. Closely connected to this issue is the utilization of the pretherapy method, which is designed specifically for these regressed populations. Although the pretherapy method is in its infancy, as far as empirical research is concerned, perhaps its emphasis on low-functioning clients will provide a clinical and practice supplement. Certainly, continued research exploring the validity and reliability of pretherapy scales is suggested. In addition, more measurements of effectiveness are needed.

A second major area of research concerns the issue of drugs. First, drugs are a confounding variable that can, theoretically, obscure the relative effectiveness of psychotherapy in a positive or negative way. However, Karon and VandenBos (1981), Mosher and colleagues (Mosher & Menn, 1978, 1979; Mosher et al., 1995), and Ciompi et al. (1992) pointed toward much less or no neuropleotic usage. Although it presents a medical complication, there needs to be more research comparing drug treatments and non- or minimal drug treatments. Further research is also needed into the effectiveness of drug therapy on symptomatology. Foltz (2000) found limited effectiveness for drug treatments with hallucinatory voices and paranoid distrust. This psychological study should be replicated.

Another major area for research concerns what Mahrer (1992) called *discovery-oriented psychotherapy*, which involves the use of therapy as an exploratory tool for discovery. Prouty's research (Prouty, 1977, 1983, 1986, 1991; Prouty & Pietrzak, 1988) followed in the European existential–phenomenological tradition (Binswanger, 1963; Boss, 1963; Laing, 1969; Minkowski, 1970; Strauss, 1966). The clinical findings were as follows: (a) Hallucinations are capable of experiential processing, (b) hallucinations process to reality content, (c) hallucinations are a fragment of self-structure, and (d) hallucinations are more severely "extrojected" beyond the self or ego boundary than dreams. Finally, another important phenomenological study (Foltz, 2000) explored the psychotic client's "experience of being medicated." All of these findings have importance for approaching psychotic process from a psychological perspective. It is clear, from the findings and suggestions presented in this chapter, that there is ample basis for a continuation in humanistic research with individuals with severe mental illness.

REFERENCES

Barrett-Lennard, G. T. (1962). Dimensions of therapist response as causal factor in therapeutic change. *Psychological Monographs, 76,* 43(562).

Betz, B. J. (1967). Studies of the therapist's role in the treatment of the schizophrenic patient. *American Journal of Psychiatry, 123,* 963–973.

Beutler, L. E., Johnson, D. T., Neville, C. W., Jr., & Workman, S. N. (1972). "Accurate empathy" and the A–B dichotomy. *Journal of Consulting and Clinical Psychology, 38,* 372–375.

Binswanger, L. (1963). Introduction to schizophrenia. In J. Needleman (Ed.), *Being in the world: Selected papers of Ludwig Binswanger* (pp. 249–341). New York: Basic Books.

Boss, M. (1963). A patient who taught the author to see and think differently. In M. Boss (Ed.), *Psychoanalysis and daseinanalysis* (pp. 5–27). New York: Basic Books.

Bozarth, J., & Brodley, B. T. (1991). Actualization: A functional concept in client-centered therapy [Special issue: Handbook of self actualization]. *Journal of Social Behavior and Personality, 6*(5), 45–58.

Brill, M. (1935). The reliability of Goodenough draw a man test and the validity and reliability of an abbreviated scoring method. *Journal of Educational Psychology, 26,* 701–708.

Ciompi, L., Dauwalder, H., Maier, C., Aebi, E., Trutsch, K., & Ruithauser, C. (1992). The pilot project "Soteria Berne": Clinical experiences and results. *British Journal of Psychiatry, 161*(18), 145–153.

Danacci, A. (1997). Ricerca sperimentale sul trattamento psicologico dei pazienti schizofrenic con la Pre-Therapia. Dr. G Prouty [Experimental research and psychological treatment of schizophrenic patients with Dr. G. Prouty's Pre-Therapy]. *Psychologia Della Persona, 2*(4), 7–16.

DeVre, R. (1992). *Prouty's pre-therapy.* Rijksuniversiteit Eindverhandeling Licentiaat Psychologie. Unpublished manuscript.

Eckert, J., Schwartz, H. J., & Tausch, R. (1977). Klienten-erfahrungen und Zusammenhang mit psychischen Andenrungen in personenzentriertrt Gesprachspsychotherapie. *Zeitschrift für klinische Psychologie, 6,* 177–184.

Fitts, W. H. (1972). The self concept and psychopathology. *Monograph IV.* Dede Wallace Center.

Foltz, R. (2000). *Understanding the medicated patient: A phenomenological study of antipsychotic medications in schizophrenia.* Unpublished doctoral dissertation, Illinois School of Professional Study, Rolling Meadows, IL.

Greenberg, L., Elliot, R., & Lietaer, G. (1994). Research on experiential therapies. In A. Bergin & S. Garfield (Eds.), *Handbook of psychotherapy and behavior change* (p. 516). New York: Wiley.

Gendlin, E. (1967). A scale for rating the manner of relating. In C. Rogers (Ed.), *The therapeutic relationship and its impact: A study of psychotherapy with schizophrenics* (pp. 603–611). Madison: University of Wisconsin Press.

Gendlin, E., & Tomlinson, T. (1967). A scale for the rating of experiencing. In C. Rogers (Ed.), *The therapeutic relationship and its impact: A study of psychotherapy with schizophrenics* (pp. 589–597). Madison: University of Wisconsin Press.

Hinterkopf, E., & Brunswick, L. K. (1981). Teaching therapeutic mental patients to use client-centered and experiential therapeutic skills with each other. *Psychotherapy: Theory, Research and Practice, 18,* 394–403.

Hinterkopf, E., & Brunswick, L. K. (1975). Teaching therapeutic skills to mental patients. *Psychotherapy: Theory, Research, and Pratice, 12*, 8–12.

Hinterkopf, E., Prouty, G., & Brunswick, L. (1979). A pilot study of pre-therapy method applied to chronic schizophrenics. *Psychosocial Rehabilitation Journal, 3*(31), 11–19.

Hogarty, G., & Ulrich, R. (1972). The discharge readiness inventory. *Archives of General Psychiatry, 26,* 419–426.

Karon, B., & VandenBos, G. (1981). *Psychotherapy of schizophrenia.* New York: Aronson.

Keisler, D. J. (1967). A tentative scale for the rating of congruence. In C. Rogers (Ed.), *The therapeutic relationship and its impact: A study of psychotherapy with schizophrenics* (pp. 581–588). Madison: University of Wisconsin Press.

Laing, R. D. (1969). *The divided self.* New York: Pantheon Books.

Luborsky, L. (1962). *Luborsky health-sickness rating scale.* Topeka, KS: Menninger Foundation.

Mahrer, A. (1992). Discovery oriented psychotherapy research, rationale, aims and methods In R. B. Miller (Ed.), *The restoration of dialogue: Readings in the philosophy of clinical psychology* (pp. 570–584). Washington, DC: American Psychological Association.

Mathews, M., Roper, M., Mosher, L., & Menn, A. (1979). A non-neuroleptic treatment for schizophrenia: Analysis of the two-year postdischarge risk of relapse. *Schizophrenia Bulletin, 5,* 322–333.

Mearns, D., & Thorne, B. (1990). *Person-centered counselling in action.* London: Routledge & Kegan Paul.

Minkowski, E. (1970). *Lived time.* Evanston, IL: Northwestern University Press.

Misiak, H. (1973). *Phenomenological, existential, and humanistic psychologies: A historical survey.* New York: Grune & Stratton.

Moos, R. (1974). *Evaluating treatment environments: A social ecological approach.* New York: Wiley.

Moos, R. H. (1975). *Evaluating correctional and community settings.* New York: Wiley and Sons.

Mosher, L., & Menn, A. (1978). Community residential treatment for schizophrenia: Two-year follow up. *Hospital and Community Psychiatry, 29,* 715–723.

Mosher, L., & Menn, A. (1979). Soteria: An alternative to hospitalization for schizophrenia. In H. R. Lamb (Ed.), *New directions for mental health services— Alternatives to acute hospitalization* (pp. 73–84). San Francisco: Jossey-Bass.

Mosher, L., Vallone, R., & Menn, A. (1995). The treatment of acute psychosis without neuroleptics: Six-week psychopathology outcome data from the Soteria project. *International Journal of Social Psychiatry, 41,* 157–173.

Perls, F. S. (1969). *Ego, hunger and aggression.* New York: Random House.

Prouty, G. (1977). Protosymbolic method: A phenomenological treatment of schizophrenic hallucinations. *International Journal of Mental Imagery, 1,* 339–342.

Prouty, G. (1983). Hallucinatory contact: A phenomenological treatment of schizo-phrenics. *Journal of Communication Therapy, 2,* 99–103.

Prouty, G. (1986). The pre-symbolic structure and therapeutic transformation of hallucinations. In M. Wolpin, J. Shorr, & L. Kreuger (Eds.), *Imagery* (Vol. 4, pp. 99–106). New York: Plenum Press.

Prouty, G. (1990). Pre-therapy: A theoretical evolution in the person-centered/experiential psychotherapy of schizophrenia and retardation. In G. Lietaer, J. Rombauts, & R. Van Balen (Eds.), *Client-centered and experiential psychother-apy in the nineties* (pp. 645–658). Leuven, Belgium: Leuven University Press.

Prouty, G. (1991). The presymbolic structure and processing of schizophrenic hallu-cinations: The problematic of a non-process structure. In L. Fusek (Ed.), *New directions in client-centered therapy: Practice with difficult client populations* (pp. 1–18). Chicago: Counseling and Psychotherapy Research Center.

Prouty, G. (1994). *Theoretical evolutions in person-centered/experiential psychotherapy: Applications to schizophrenic and retarded psychoses.* Westport, CT: Praeger.

Prouty, G., & Pietrzak, S. (1988). Pre-therapy method applied to persons experienc-ing hallucinatory images. *Person-Centered Review, 3,* 426–441.

Prouty, G., Van Werde, D., & Portner, M. (1998). *Prae-Therapie* [Pre-therapy]. Stuttgart, Germany: Klett-Cotta.

Pugh, R. W. (1949). *An investigation of some psychological processes accompanying concurrent electric convulsive therapy and non-directive psychotherapy with paranoid schizophrenia.* Unpublished doctoral dissertation, University of Chicago.

Raskin, N. J. (1947). *The non-directive attitude.* Unpublished manuscript.

Rogers, C. (1957). The necessary and sufficient conditions of therapeutic personality change. *Journal of Consulting Psychology, 21,* 95–103.

Rogers, C. (1959). A theory of therapy, personality and interpersonal relationships as developed in the client-centered framework. In E. Koch (Ed.), *Psychology: A study of a science* (Vol. III, p. 251). New York: McGraw-Hill.

Rogers, C., Gendlin, E. T., Kiesler, D. J., & Truax, C. B. (1967). The findings in brief. In C. Rogers (Ed.), *The therapeutic relationship and its impact: A study of psychotherapy with schizophrenics* (pp. 73–93). Madison: University of Wiscon-sin Press.

Seidman, E. (1971). A and B subjects: Therapist's responses to videotaped schizoid and intropunitive–neurotic prototypes. *Journal of Consulting and Clinical Psy-chology, 37,* 201–208.

Serok, S., Rabin, C., & Spitz, Y. (1984). Intensive Gestalt group therapy with schizophrenics. *International Journal of Group Psychotherapy, 34,* 431–450.

Serok, S., & Zemet, R. (1983). An experiment of Gestalt group therapy with hospitalized schizophrenics. *Psychotherapy: Theory, Research and Practice, 20,* 417–424.

Strauss, E. (1966). *Phenomenological psychology.* New York: Basic Books.

Sullworld, L. (1977). *Symtome schizophrener erkrankhungen.* Berlin: Springer.

Teusch, L. (1990). Positive effects and limitation of client-centered therapy with schizophrenic patients. In G. Lietaer, J. Rombauts, & R. Van Balen, (Eds.), *Client-centered and experiential therapy in the nineties* (pp. 637–643). Leuven, Belgium: Leuven University Press.

Teusch, L., Beyerle, U., Lange, H., Schenk, K., & Stadmuller, G. (1981). The client-centered approach to schizophrenic patients: First empirical results. *European Conference on Psychotherapy Research, II*, 141–147.

Truax, C. (1961). The process of group psychotherapy: Relationships between hypothesized therapeutic conditions and intrapersonal exploration. *Psychological Monographs, 75*, 7(511).

Truax, C. B. (1967a). A scale for the rating of accurate empathy. In C. Rogers (Ed.), *The therapeutic relationship and its impact: A study of psychotherapy with schizophrenics* (pp. 555–568). Madison: University of Wisconsin Press.

Truax, C. B. (1967b). A tentative scale for rating of unconditional positive regard. In C. Rogers (Ed.), *The therapeutic relationship and its impact: A study of psychotherapy with schizophrenics* (pp. 569–579). Madison: University of Wisconsin Press.

Truax, C. B. (1970). Effects of client-centered psychotherapy with schizophrenic patients: Nine years pre-therapy and nine years post-therapy hospitalization. *Journal of Consulting and Clinical Psychology, 35*, 417–422.

Van der Veen, F. (1965). Effects of the therapist and the patient on each other's therapeutic behavior. *Journal of Consulting Psychology, 29*, 19–26.

Van der Veen, F. (1967). Basic elements in the process of psychotherapy: A research study. *Journal of Consulting Psychology, 31*, 295–303.

Van der Veen, F., & Tomlinson, T. (1967). A scale for rating the manner of problem expression. In C. Rogers (Ed.), *The therapeutic relationship and its impact: A study of psychotherapy with schizophrenics* (pp. 599–601). Madison: University of Wisconsin Press.

Whiteborn, J., & Betz, B. (1954). A study of psychotherapeutic relationship between physicians and schizophrenic patients. *American Journal of Psychiatry, 3*, 321–331.

VI

ANALYSIS AND SYNTHESIS

20

FUTURE DIRECTIONS IN RESEARCH ON HUMANISTIC PSYCHOTHERAPY

WILLIAM B. STILES

I was pleased to be invited to write this brief chapter on future directions in research, but I had a few misgivings. "Future directions" can sound like predictions, for which I have no talent or, worse, prescriptions. I am wary of individuals or panels who presume to set a research agenda for others, and I feel ambivalent—uncomfortable and guilty as well as honored—about assuming that role myself. My discomfort is not so much about such (misconstrued) prescriptions' direct influence on researchers, who will judge for themselves whether a recommendation is worth the enormous effort that any research entails, as about the possible influence on evaluators (e.g., reviewers of grant proposals or submitted manuscripts), who could use conformity to the prescriptions unthinkingly to judge a project's value.

Nevertheless, I do have some observations and opinions about research on humanistic psychotherapy, which I am happy to offer here (and elsewhere, in references I have cited below) for consideration by future researchers. After an initial section, meant as an endorsement of methodological pluralism, I comment on several categories of research on humanistic therapies.

THE FACTS ARE FRIENDLY

When Carl Rogers (1961, p. 25) wrote, "The facts are friendly," he was referring to scientific research. Nevertheless, humanistic theorists and therapists have often considered research as dehumanizing. Perhaps psychological research's frequent focus on mechanical cause and effect and on linear relations among quantified variables seems to constrict the understanding of

I thank Robert Elliott, Larry M. Leitner, and the editors of this volume for comments on drafts of this chapter.

human experience (see discussion by Walsh & McElwain, this volume, chapter 8). A sad consequence is that humanistic therapies have been researched less than they should have been. I believe that this view of research is too narrow, based partly on a mistaken impression that psychological research must imitate research in chemistry or engineering.

Science encompasses any comparison of ideas with observations. Numbers are admittedly remarkable; compared with words, their meaning is relatively stable across time and people, so they allow scientists to say more or less the same thing to everybody. Likewise, experimental designs and statistical analyses are to be admired for their precision and potential generality. However, many of the most interesting phenomena with which humanistic theories and therapies are concerned, such as the unique life experiences of individuals, cannot be well represented as numbers or as variables susceptible to manipulation or control using currently available techniques (Stiles, 1993).

Humanistic researchers need not let their own or others' admiration of precise methods trap them into "looking under the lamppost" (after the story of the inebriated man who dropped his keys in a dark alley but looked for them under a streetlight because the light was better), that is, into using methods that seem elegant but are nevertheless inappropriate for the topic of interest. If a topic cannot be adequately addressed using available experimental designs and linear statistical analyses—and many cannot—then other observational techniques are available. Among these are case studies and other qualitative approaches, such as idiographic studies, ethnography, ethnomethodology, grounded theory, protocol analysis, discourse analysis, conversational analysis, constructivist approaches, phenomenology, or hermeneutic investigation (e.g., see Rennie's chapter 4, this volume). Distinctive characteristics of qualitative research that could make it suitable for addressing humanistic topics may include the following: (a) results that are reported in words rather than only in numbers, (b) use of many descriptors rather than restriction to a few common dimensions or scales, (c) use of investigators' empathic understanding of participants' inner experiences as data, (d) understanding and reporting of events in their unique context, (e) selecting participants or texts or other material to study because they are good examples rather than because they are representative of some larger population, (f) reports that use alternatives to traditional didactic discourse, including narratives or hermeneutic interpretations, (g) accommodating unpredictability due to sensitive dependence on initial conditions (small initial events may have huge consequences), (h) empowering of participants considered as a legitimate purpose of the research (e.g., encouraging them to change their social conditions), and, above all, (i) tentativeness in interpretations (Stiles, 1993, 1999b). Even though the conclusions of qualitative research may be tentative, however, the gain in realism can compensate for losses in generality (see Levins, 1968).

Case studies in particular are underused (Farmer, 1999; Stiles, 1995). Of course, case studies have the usual weaknesses of anecdotal research: selection of data, possible distortions of introspective reports, investigator biases, lack of generality, and so forth. But humanistic therapists are familiar with the need to hold information tentatively in clinical contexts, and they can similarly report case-based investigations without claiming certainty or generality. A multiple case study approach (Rosenwald, 1988) might be particularly well suited to psychotherapy research. Therapists who have treated similar clients might collaborate in assembling multiple cases around a common theme for research reports.

OUTCOME RESEARCH

Randomized clinical trials (RCTs) of humanistic psychotherapies remain politically necessary, and outcome research using other designs (e.g., pre–post single-group comparisons) are also politically valuable. RCTs are a statistical adaptation of the experimental method, which is the closest science has come to a means for demonstrating causality. RCTs may be flawed for many reasons (Haaga & Stiles, 2000), and their value for determining mental health policy is controversial (Bohart, O'Hara, & Leitner, 1998; Elliott, 1998; Henry, 1998; Strauss & Kaechele, 1998). The question "does it work?" is so salient, however, that other questions seem to remain in the background until this one is addressed.

According to the latest update of a continuing meta-analysis (Elliott, 1996; Elliott & Greenberg, this volume, chapter 9; Elliott, Greenberg, & Lietaer, 1994), humanistic therapies have shown mean pre–post effect sizes in the range of 1.1 to 1.3, which are very respectable effects. In addition to Elliott and Greenberg's report for process–experiential therapy, several other chapters in this volume also reported positive effects of specific humanistic treatments; for example, Johnson and Boisvert (this volume, chapter 10) pointed out that outcomes of relational enhancement and emotionally focused therapy for couples compare favorably with those of the best-researched alternative treatment, behavioral marriage therapy. However, these reviews were based on relatively small numbers of studies, which were themselves based on small numbers of clients and (as usual) open to challenge on methodological grounds.

Researchers designing RCTs and other outcome studies need to be cognizant of the limitations and likely results. For reasons that have long been puzzling (see Rozenzweig, 1936), most alternative psychotherapies appear to be equivalently effective (Lipsey & Wilson, 1993; Wampold et al., 1997), despite the demonstrated diversity of theories and techniques (Stiles, Shapiro, & Elliott, 1986). This paradoxical equivalence is robust, and it seems unlikely that future comparisons will show humanistic therapies to be hugely more effective or less effective than other therapies. Even when results favoring one treatment are found, they may be at least partly attributable to the investigators' allegiance (including unintended effects of allegiance on how the compared treatments were implemented) more reliably than to the ostensible treatment approach (Luborsky et al., 1999). Perhaps the technical differences among therapies are overshadowed by the common features (e.g., mutual responsiveness in a helping encounter) or by case-to-case variation in how each treatment is realized.

An important side benefit of RCT designs and other large-scale outcome studies is providing a context for other sorts of psychotherapy research. Data collected in the course of conducting an outcome study, including tape recordings of sessions, can be used to study alternative outcome measures, individual differences, and the psychotherapeutic process. Though politically less salient, these additional areas of research may be scientifically more informative.

OUTCOME MEASUREMENT

The political purposes of outcome research demand (a) broadly accepted outcome measures of (b) criteria that are common across clients that (c) are easy to collect. The lowest common denominator seems to be symptom intensity, assessed through checklists completed by clients, therapists, or external evaluators. Politically more potent, but far more difficult to assess (and much less used), are indices of life changes that have economic implications: job-holding, divorce, hospitalization, or other use of health-related resources.

As noted in many of this volume's chapters, humanistic conceptions of therapy's purpose and effects go beyond reducing symptom intensity. Clients undoubtedly notice and care about changes in style of working or relating and other idiosyncratic changes that may be only tangentially related to the usual criteria used in outcome research. There may be many different outcomes that yield similar levels of symptom relief (Stiles, 1983). Indeed, as Walsh and McElwain (this volume, chapter 8) pointed out, some symptoms, such as existential anxiety, may be productive, and therapists and clients may sometimes consider treatment successful even when it leaves symptom intensity unchanged.

Research to assess humanistic therapy's specific effects—as contrasted with its efficacy or its effectiveness—demands continuing creative ingenuity.

Rating scales designed to assess dimensions beyond symptom intensity or global evaluations can be useful in this respect. Q-sort measures represent a still-underexploited alternative (see Ablon & Jones, 1998). Changes that are unique to individuals can be documented using qualitative approaches.

Of course, anecdotal or other ad hoc measures may not be potent politically in justifying the cost of psychotherapy. Multiple measurement approaches—symptom intensity checklists and humanistically informed qualitative accounts—probably are best used in parallel. In their own thinking and writing, researchers may wish to distinguish between political and conceptual contributions, but they would be foolish, I think, to restrict their measures to only one of these categories.

DIAGNOSIS AND DIFFERENTIAL TREATMENT

Placing people in categories is potentially dehumanizing. On the one hand, diagnoses can oversimplify and distort perceptions of the person to whom they are applied. For therapists, the danger lies in responding to a textbook concept or a stereotype rather than to the client's immediate and unique life experience. Diagnoses may induce a false sense of security, a feeling that one knows more about another person than one actually does.

On the other hand, ignoring diagnosis or psychological assessment can be a form of anti-intellectualism, of which humanistic therapists are sometimes accused. One must use categories to think at all. Whether the categories come from diagnostic manuals, textbooks, supervisors, parents, folklore, or television, there is a risk of reification—confusing the concept with the reality. Stereotypes and other preconceptions can be dehumanizing, oversimplifying, and distorting regardless of where they come from. Insofar as therapists cannot avoid having some sort of preconceptions, the goal must be to hold those preconceptions tentatively.

I suggest that therapists and researchers serve clients best by gathering a rich repertoire of categories, learning about the full range of human experience from whatever sources are available, including research results and diagnoses. In dealing with clients, responsible humanistic therapists apply all knowledge tentatively, always comparing their current understanding with new observations and always ready to withdraw inferences that are contradicted by their client's individual experience. Bracketing—trying to ignore diagnostic information in listening to clients—may help therapists avoid treating people as diseases, but it risks overlooking useful perspectives that diagnoses can add.

Diagnostic categories need not be dehumanizing, so long as therapists use them to understand rather than to substitute for understanding their clients' personal experience. Case studies have suggested that the common clinical manifestations reflected in formal diagnoses may reflect common client experiences (Bohart, 1990; Schneider & Stiles, 1995). People who appear as depressed or as borderline or as schizophrenic may experience the world in distinctive ways that differ from their therapists' experience. Knowledge of a client's diagnosis, and the distinctive experiences it may entail, may thus help a therapist understand what the client is trying to say more quickly or more deeply. The work of Prouty (this volume, chapter 19) takes important steps in this direction by focusing on repertoires of therapeutic techniques useful for working with people with particular diagnoses (e.g., schizophrenia). Such research might be expanded by shifting the focus slightly to describe the experiences of these clients. Explicitly humanistic alternatives to traditional diagnostic systems (e.g., Leitner, 1995; Leitner & Pfenninger, 1994) may offer additional, particularly useful ways for humanistic therapists to understand clients; however, even humanistically inspired categories and dimensions must be applied tentatively.

Reification of diagnostic concepts can be problematic on many levels. For example, it can seem a matter of professional ethics and responsibility to provide the best-researched treatment for each client's problem. If problems are required (e.g., by research protocols or third-party payers) to be defined in terms of diagnoses or similar descriptors (e.g., depression, phobia, or panic), then it may seem that research on treatments must target diagnostic categories to address treatment selection in an ethical and responsible way. Research in which the treatments are understood as addressing the unique needs of individuals can be seen as irrelevant. And delivering treatments that lack diagnosis-specific efficacy data may be viewed by some people as unethical.

PROCESS RESEARCH

Process research recognizes that there is no long-term change without short-term change. It investigates how changes take place within and between sessions.

The most powerful results reviewed in this book, in my opinion, were those dealing with replicated categories of events within sessions—broadly in line with the concept of the *events paradigm* described by Rice and Greenberg (1984). Some examples include (a) research on markers of readiness to engage in experiential tasks by Greenberg and collaborators, reported in several chapters (e.g., Strümpfel & Goldman, chapter 6; Elliott & Greenberg, chapter 9; Johnson & Boisvert, chapter 10) and Watson's (chapter 14) related extension to markers of readiness for types of empathic responses; (b) processing proposals research by Sachse and Elliott (chapter 3); (c)

Rennie's (chapter 4) work on deference and story-telling; (d) identification of ruptures in the therapeutic alliance (Asay & Lambert, chapter 17; similarly, the "disturbances in reflexivity" reported by Rennie, chapter 4); and (e) Prouty's (chapter 19) categories of contact. Stages of group development (Page, Weiss, & Lietaer, chapter 11) also are often signaled by "barometric events," which could similarly be considered as markers of participants' internal states or readiness to engage in particular tasks (Stiles, 1979). The results of these investigations link recognizable markers with readiness for specific types of interventions in clinically useful ways. Moreover, because they describe psychotherapy at a level close to that used in psychotherapeutic theories, these process studies address the theories better than outcome research can. For example, the descriptions of the softening of one voice toward another in a two-chair exercise is not only a clinically important sign but also a theoretical elaboration of the process by which internal conflicts are resolved.

Therapy theories are meant to explain how therapy works. The bald hypothesis that a treatment is effective, which is what outcome research tests, is a relatively undifferentiated consequence of the theory. Even the repeated finding that positive therapeutic relationships (alliances) are associated with positive outcomes glosses over the important intermediate steps. By contrast, events-paradigm research traces sequences within sessions. Typically, the sequence begins with an observable marker, which signals some internal state of the client, which implies some readiness for a therapeutic intervention, whose effect can be gauged by the client's subsequent behavior.

In discussing process research, I should also mention a limitation: What may seem the most obvious strategy for assessing the effect of process components—measuring them and correlating them with measures of outcome—is blocked by the phenomenon of *responsiveness*, the fact that participants' behavior is affected by emerging context (Stiles, Honos-Webb, & Surko, 1998). Therapists normally try to respond to a client's emerging requirements with interventions that are appropriate, given their theoretical approach, the client's personality and background, and the therapeutic context. To the extent that they succeed, clients tend to experience optimum levels of those interventions. Clients who need less tend to receive less, and—insofar as they still got as much as they needed—their outcomes tend to be just as good as those of clients who needed more and got more. As a result, levels of the process components do not predict outcome. Crucially important process components may have null or even negative correlations with outcomes (Stiles, 1988). Conversely, the relative strengths of process variables' correlations with outcome are uninformative. Variables with null correlations may be as important or more important than variables with significant positive correlations. Thus, process–outcome correlations are not to be trusted. For an illustration and debate of this point, see the series of articles by Stiles and Shapiro (1994), Silberschatz (1994), Sechrest (1994), Stiles (1994, 1996), and Hayes, Castonguay, and Goldfried (1996).

Of course, reliable positive correlations generally have interesting explanations. However, these may not be the obvious ones because of responsiveness or because of possible confounding variables.

The responsiveness problem has frequently been overlooked, and a great deal of process research (including mine!) has futilely sought linear process–outcome relations. Alternative research strategies may require reconceptualizing the problem (Stiles et al., 1998). Unfortunately, researchers' and reviewers' focus on correlations with outcomes has often obscured important achievements in process measurement, in precise descriptions of what happens (e.g., of therapists' and clients' verbal and nonverbal behavior), and in comparisons of the process across roles (e.g., therapist and client), treatments (e.g., client-centered, Gestalt, psychoanalytic, and cognitive–behavioral), and settings (Stiles, Honos-Webb, & Knobloch, 1999).

HUMANISTIC CONCEPTS, HEROES, AND VALUES

Psychotherapy is a laboratory as well as a source of ideas for research (Stiles, 1992) and a treatment (Greenberg, 1991; Stiles, 1999a). Psychotherapy offers exceptional opportunities to study fundamental conceptions of humanistic theories. Examples of such topics include the role of interpersonal power (e.g., the therapist's over the client), the psychology of focusing and felt shifts, the softening of negative emotion in two-chair exercises, the assumption that emotion represents information about an experience's value, the effects of directed repetition and exaggeration of nonverbal behaviors, and the nature of the self. Research based in psychotherapy could address issues that divide humanistic therapies. For example, Rogers's (1951, 1959) assumption of an organismic valuing process—that a person's value judgments are fundamentally trustworthy—was an underpinning of his radically nondirective approach. The scope and limits of this assumption are clearly controversial within humanistic therapies, illustrated by the varied discussions of directive interventions in this book. Methodological ingenuity is needed to find ways to investigate the alternative conceptions.

Humanistic therapies have heroes—for example, Carl Rogers and Fritz Perls—whose visions have defined the field. Their deep understanding allowed them to be effective, and we as therapists who follow try to reproduce their understanding, so we can be equally effective. The heroes' vision is not conveyed by a single reading of their words. On each rereading, their words (and their tape-recorded actions) take on new meanings. We seem to understand more of what they meant each time we return. To put it another way, the major humanistic theories are partly implicit and continually emerging.

The deep appeal of the heroes' visions can make them competitors with research as means of quality control on ideas. That is, to assess the quality of our ideas, we may turn to the words of the heroes rather than to observations. Perhaps this is not entirely misguided. Research based on a weak understanding of the vision (e.g., reductionistic operationalizations of humanistic concepts) is dismissed by proponents and hence has little impact on quality control. Comparing a new idea with the writings of the master may, paradoxically, offer a better test of its fit with clinical reality. However, there are obvious long-term dangers in such a closed system, in which ideas are judged only in relation to other ideas. Part of the research task is to articulate the vision in ways that are simultaneously acceptable to proponents and susceptible to observation.

In good research, when the ideas are compared with the observations, the ideas are thereby changed; they are strengthened, weakened, qualified, or elaborated. Thus, good research on humanistic concepts must put those concepts at risk. The risk may be compounded for humanistic researchers, whose concepts may overlap extensively with their values. Research will not tell us what is good, though people can use research results to argue for their own views and values. Research is most productive when researchers have the courage to face potentially unfriendly findings with an underlying confidence that the facts are friendly.

REFERENCES

Ablon, J. S., & Jones, E. E. (1998). How expert clinicians' prototypes of an ideal treatment correlate with outcome in psychodynamic and cognitive–behavioral therapy. *Psychotherapy Research, 8,* 71–83.

Bohart, A. C. (1990). A cognitive client-centered perspective on borderline personality development. In G. Lietaer, J. Rombauts, & R. Van Balen (Eds.), *Client-centered and experiential psychotherapy in the nineties* (pp. 599–622). Leuven, Belgium: Leuven University Press.

Bohart, A. C., O'Hara, M., & Leitner, L. M. (1998). Empirically violated treatments: Disenfranchisement of humanistic and other psychotherapies. *Psychotherapy Research, 8,* 141–157.

Elliott, R. (1996). Are client-centered/experiential therapies effective? A meta-analysis of outcome research. In U. Esser, H. Pabst, & G.-W. Speierer (Eds.), *The power of the person-centered approach: New challenges, perspectives, answers* (pp. 125–138). Köln, Germany: GwG Verlag.

Elliott, R. (1998). Editor's introduction: A guide to the empirically supported treatments controversy. *Psychotherapy Research, 8,* 115–125.

Elliott, R., Greenberg, L., & Lietaer, G. (1994). Research on experiential psychotherapies. In A. E. Bergin & S. L. Garfield (Eds.), *Handbook of psychotherapy and behavior change* (4th ed., pp. 509–539). New York: Wiley.

Farmer, A. (1999). The demise of the published case report: Is resuscitation necessary? *British Journal of Psychiatry, 174,* 93.

Greenberg, L. S. (1991). Research on the process of change. *Psychotherapy Research, 1,* 3–16.

Haaga, D. A. F., & Stiles, W. B. (2000). Randomized clinical trials in psychotherapy research: Methodology, design, and evaluation. In C. R. Snyder & R. E. Ingram (Eds.), *Handbook of psychological change: Psychotherapy processes and practices for the 21st century.* New York: Wiley.

Hayes, A. M., Castonguay, L. G., & Goldfried, M. R. (1996). The study of change in psychotherapy: A re-examination of the process–outcome correlation paradigm. Comment on Stiles and Shapiro (1994). *Journal of Consulting and Clinical Psychology, 64,* 909–914.

Henry, W. P. (1998). Science, politics, and politics of science: The use and misuse of empirically validated treatment research. *Psychotherapy Research, 8,* 126–140.

Leitner, L. M. (1995). Dispositional assessment techniques in experiential personal construct psychotherapy. *Journal of Constructivist Psychology, 8,* 53–74.

Leitner, L. M., & Pfenninger, D. T. (1994). Sociality and optimal functioning. *Journal of Constructivist Psychology, 7,* 119–135.

Levins, R. (1968). *Evolution in changing environments: Some theoretical explorations.* Princeton, NJ: Princeton University Press.

Lipsey, M. W., & Wilson, D. B. (1993). The efficacy of psychological, educational, and behavioral treatment: Confirmation from meta-analysis. *American Psychologist, 48,* 1181–1209.

Luborsky, L., Diguer, L., Seligman, D. A., Rosenthal, R., Krause, E. D., Johnson, S., Halperin, G., Bishop, M., Berman, J. S., & Schweizer, E. (1999). The researcher's own therapy allegiances: A "wild card" in comparisons of treatment efficacy. *Clinical Psychology: Science and Practice, 6,* 95–106.

Rice, L. N., & Greenberg, L. S. (Eds.). (1984). *Patterns of change.* New York: Guilford Press.

Rogers, C. R. (1951). *Client-centered therapy.* Boston: Houghton-Mifflin.

Rogers, C. R. (1959). A theory of therapy, personality, and interpersonal relationships as developed by the client-centered framework. In S. Koch (Ed.), *Psychology: A study of a science: Vol. III. Formulations of a person and the social context* (pp. 184–256). New York: McGraw-Hill.

Rogers, C. R. (1961). *On becoming a person.* Boston: Houghton-Mifflin

Rosenwald, G. C. (1988). A theory of multiple case research. *Journal of Personality, 56,* 239–264.

Rosenzweig, S. (1936). Some implicit common factors in diverse methods of psychotherapy. *American Journal of Orthopsychiatry, 6,* 412–415.

Schneider, C. K., & Stiles, W. B. (1995). A person-centered view of depression: Women's experiences. *Person-Centered Journal, 2,* 67–77.

Sechrest, L. (1994). Recipes for psychotherapy. *Journal of Consulting and Clinical Psychology, 62,* 952–954.

Silberschatz, G. (1994). Abuse and disabuse of the drug metaphor in psychotherapy research: Hold on to the baby as you throw out the bath. *Journal of Consulting and Clinical Psychology, 62,* 949–951.

Stiles, W. B. (1979). Psychotherapy recapitulates ontogeny: The epigenesis of intensive interpersonal relationships. *Psychotherapy: Theory, Research, and Practice, 16,* 391–404.

Stiles, W. B. (1983). Normality, diversity, and psychotherapy. *Psychotherapy: Theory, Research, and Practice, 20,* 183–189.

Stiles, W. B. (1988). Psychotherapy process–outcome correlations may be misleading. *Psychotherapy, 25,* 27–35.

Stiles, W. B. (1992). Producers and consumers of psychotherapy research ideas. *Journal of Psychotherapy Practice and Research, 1,* 305–307.

Stiles, W. B. (1993). Quality control in qualitative research. *Clinical Psychology Review, 13,* 593–618.

Stiles, W. B. (1994). Drugs, recipes, babies, bathwater, and psychotherapy process–outcome relations. *Journal of Consulting and Clinical Psychology, 62,* 955–959.

Stiles, W. B. (1995). Stories, tacit knowledge, and psychotherapy research. *Psychotherapy Research, 5,* 125–127.

Stiles, W. B. (1996). When more of a good thing is better: Reply to Hayes et al. (1996). *Journal of Consulting and Clinical Psychology, 64,* 915–918.

Stiles, W. B. (1999a). Signs and voices in psychotherapy. *Psychotherapy Research, 9,* 1–21.

Stiles, W. B. (1999b). Evaluating qualitative research. *Evidence-Based Mental Health, 2,* 99–101.

Stiles, W. B., Honos-Webb, L., & Knobloch, L. M. (1999). Treatment process research methods. In P. C. Kendall, J. N. Butcher, & G. N. Holmbeck (Eds.), *Handbook of research methods in clinical psychology* (pp. 364–402). New York: Wiley.

Stiles, W. B., Honos-Webb, L., & Surko, M. (1998). Responsiveness in psychotherapy. *Clinical Psychology: Science and Practice, 5,* 439–458.

Stiles, W. B., & Shapiro, D. A. (1994). Disabuse of the drug metaphor: Psychotherapy process–outcome correlations. *Journal of Consulting and Clinical Psychology, 62,* 942–948.

Stiles, W. B., Shapiro, D. A., & Elliott, R. (1986). "Are all psychotherapies equivalent?" *American Psychologist, 41,* 165–180.

Strauss, B. M., & Kaechele, H. (1998). The writing on the wall: Comments on the current discussion about empirically validated treatments in Germany. *Psychotherapy Research, 8*, 158–170.

Wampold, B. E., Mondin, G. W., Moody, M., Stich, F., Benson, K., & Ahn, H. N. (1997). A meta-analysis of outcome studies comparing bona fide psychotherapies: Empirically, "all must have prizes." *Psychological Bulletin, 122*, 203–215.

21

LOOKING BACK, LOOKING AHEAD:
A SYNTHESIS

JULIUS SEEMAN

LOOKING BACK

In this chapter, I step back from the immediacy of the chapters of the previous sections and view the humanistic scene from a broad perspective. In this sense, humanistic thought and humanistic values may be measured in centuries rather than decades. Consequently, the phenomenon of continuity is an integral part of that history and needs a place in this discourse.

However, the application of humanistic principles in the particular form of humanistic psychotherapy is also remarkably recent, considering the longevity of the larger humanist history. What has happened is that these principles have been applied for the first time in the form of a behavioral science, with its attendant discipline, its public nature, and its consequent need for formal validation structures.

How can one understand the underlying continuities that link this psychotherapy to its history? In my view, an overriding theme that connects past and present in humanistic thought is the emphasis on the positive value of helping people to maximize their optimal human potentialities. It is a theme that appears prominently in the humanistic literature. Consequently, it may be useful to review one illustration of these antecedents of humanistic psychotherapy to emphasize their historic continuity.

An extended study of the contributions of Epictetus has been offered by Pierce (1916). Epictetus was a teacher of philosophy in Rome during the first century AD. He proposed that the universe had an underlying order and that the lives of human beings as part of that order were part of a universal law of growth. Inherent in the growth pattern was the fact that human beings had "that of God" within their personhood and thus had the capacity, and indeed the responsibility, of attaining maximal self-realization. For Epictetus, this emphasis constituted one of life's major ethical commitments. It is a theme that recurs repeatedly in the history of humanist thought. In the early development of humanistic thought, there is also a less differentiated blend of secular values on the one hand and religious thought on the other.

As I turn from this brief note of history, I am aware that the chapters in the earlier sections of this book have given us a broad view of humanistic psychotherapy. There are, nevertheless, more compact core principles that provide a unity to the development of humanistic psychotherapy and that deepen one's understanding of this unifying framework. Before I sketch these principles, however, I acknowledge that there are some aspects of humanistic psychology that cannot be neatly summarized because they are generated by the unique phenomenologies of each person. They represent an inner quality that has to do with basic views of humanity. I see this aspect as personal and often private, and so in this domain no one can define for another who is humanistic. Hence, one can expect to find variations in definitions of humanistic psychotherapy spurred by differing personal emphases.

There are also elements that are more material, discernible through the public commitments that humanistically oriented individuals make in areas of scholarship and research. These tangible elements lend themselves to assessment and reveal several characteristics where broad concordance is evident. In this respect, four major themes emerge. I consider each in turn below. I am not suggesting that any of these characteristics are the exclusive province of humanistic psychotherapy, rather that the cluster of characteristics taken as a whole are descriptive of normative humanistic processes.

Four Major Characteristics of Humanistic Psychotherapy

Whole-Person Perspective

The humanistic approach is generally seen by its proponents as expansive and inclusive. The encompassing personhood of the client is the dominant aspect of the therapist's approach. There is thus little tendency to see the person segmented in trait-oriented ways.

An examination of typical book titles in humanistic literature underlines the breadth of this approach. For example, one of Maslow's book titles refers to *The Farther Reaches of Human Nature* (1971). The most popular of Carl Rogers's books deals with the issue of *On Becoming a Person* (1961). One of Jourard's books centers on *The Transparent Self* (1971), and the other on *Disclosing Man to Himself* (1968). Seeman's major theme has been *Personality Integration* (1983). Additionally, one of the most prominent themes in the humanistic literature has involved a considerable emphasis on theory and research related to the *self*.

Strong Emphasis on Optimal Personality and Positive Functioning

In concert with this whole-person emphasis, an attractive theme for many humanistically oriented writers has been the exploration of optimal personality functioning. This interest fits in with a more general interest in human potentialities and with a positive view of human nature. The accent on positive qualities has far overshadowed any emphasis on dysfunction and psychopathology. Maslow's frequent allusions to "peak experiences," Heath's (e.g., 1965, 1977) interest and study of personal maturity, Landsman's (1968) interest in "the beautiful and noble person," Jourard's (1968) interest in "inspiriting," Rogers's (1961) description of "the fully functioning person," and Seeman's (1983, 1989) research on positive health all illustrate the pervasiveness of the accent on optimal functioning.

Accent on Whole-Person Communication and on "Presentness" and "Experiencing" in Therapeutic Practice

The values embedded in the whole-person approach and the accent on positive functioning have been implemented actively in the therapy hour through a concentrated attention by the therapist on the client as he or she is living at the immediate moment in time. In this respect, one of the core aspects of humanistic psychotherapy has been the centrality of the therapeutic relationship, because it is through relationship that the therapist can maintain connection with the whole-person process as it is revealed by the client.

A basic aspect of this relationship centers on the therapist's awareness of whole-person communication; that is, information from the client is relevant at whatever organismic level it occurs. Thus, in a humanistic orientation, the therapist gives considerable attention to bodily processes as part of the client–therapist communication, because verbal communication alone in no way covers whole-person communication. Thus, the whole-person emphasis is lived in the therapy hour through the therapist's attention to the varied modes by which the client communicates self to the therapist.

Examples abound in the humanistic literature. For example, in their work on facilitating emotional change, Greenberg, Rice, and Elliott (1993) placed much importance on inner experiencing. A wide variety of therapist procedures are described as ways to connect with experiences to make them come alive again in the therapy session. Therapist strategies include two-chair dialogue, focusing, enactment, and a general emphasis on precognitive processes.

Much of Gendlin's work (e.g., 1996) has been on bodily processes, with special reliance on focusing and on facilitating body signals that Gendlin referred to as the *felt sense*. Gestalt therapists, with their emphasis on enhancing awareness, have increasingly resorted to bodily processes. An example of this trend may be noted in a Gestalt-oriented book titled *Body Process* (Kepner, 1993).

As I have indicated, a key element of the client–therapist relationship and of whole-person communication lies in the therapist's concentrated attention on the immediacy of the relationship at each moment in time. The broad designation *experiential therapy* is often used to signify this focal attention on the presentness of the therapeutic process. One client has described her own experience of this focal attention by the therapist thus:

> The therapist presented himself before me. He established himself in relationship to me to help me see who I was. He sat before me—looking to see who I was and reflecting, reporting, or clarifying that back to me. How did he do this? The obvious, verbalizing often back to me whatever he was hearing coming from me—but in more subtle ways reflecting me back to myself—his body language somehow had nothing extraneous in it—no other distractions (so, his words, his tone of voice, his body language, what was in his eyes)—everything about his person seemed focused completely on and available to me to reflect me back to myself . . . (personal communication, March, 1994)

The foregoing report depicts ways in which the therapist concentrates total attention on the livingness of the moment. I have found in my own experience that when I stay with that livingness, I have neither the time nor the inclination to divert my attention into any place or activity that distracts my attention away from the lifelike quality of the immediate phenomenal experience of the client, or of my own.

The full significance of the designation *experiential* should not be lost here, for the concept shapes in large measure the whole thrust of the therapeutic process. One way to describe the centrality of experiencing is to view psychotherapy as a task with two major components, *content* and *process*, where content defines the subject matter that is discussed and process refers to mode of interaction. For many of the varieties of humanistic psychotherapy, the decided focus is on the process, on the interaction experience of the moment. Naturally, content is also necessary, but the content comes from whatever the client chooses to talk about at any given time and is primarily the vehicle through which the process is carried. Thus, much of humanistic psychotherapy can be thought of as a process-centered therapy, because it is the process itself that is considered to facilitate the personal development of the client.

The foregoing description requires a caveat because the idea of a process-centered therapy is sometimes misconstrued to mean that process-centered therapists consider the past history of the client as less important or (worse still) as irrelevant. Nothing could be further from the truth. The ideas of presentness and immediacy refer to process and not to content. I cannot recall a single client with whom I have ever worked who failed to bring in her or his past experiences. That is inevitably the area in which pain and dysfunction begin, the areas to which clients return again and again.

The point of presentness is that such past events become relevant as a topic to be discussed at precisely those times when the client brings them into the therapy session. They then have the quality of presentness through the quality that I have referred to as *livingness*—that is, the client has mobilized personal awareness and energy in the moment around some past issue, and it becomes most alive for her or him then. As therapist, I have little need to bring into the therapy hour a topic that is not alive for the client, that is, not part of the client's energy system at that time. To me the most propitious time is the moment when the client is engaging with the topic, when the topic has come alive for him or her. Then the energy and attention are already in place, and I have no need to select, guide, or suggest topics for the client's attention.

Emphasis on Relationship and Connectedness

Although the early emphasis in humanistic theory was tilted toward the development of the self as an entity, an emerging emphasis has been the increasing focus on the intersubjective and relational aspects of psychotherapy. A significant element in this development has been the increasing influence of the women's movement and feminist therapy, with its accent on self-in-relationship. An accompanying influence has been the research on empathy and the growing recognition of its central role in the therapeutic process. These forces have strengthened the view that relationship and interpersonal connection are in themselves core healing processes virtually independent of the role of content in psychotherapy.

Guisinger and Blatt (1994) tracked the centrality of relationship in the context of phylogenetic development in the human species and noted the following:

> It is proposed that evolutionary pressures of natural selection result in two basic developmental lines: interpersonal relatedness and self-definition, which interact in a dialectical fashion. An increasingly mature sense of self is contingent on interpersonal relationships; conversely, the continued development of increasingly mature interpersonal relationships is contingent on mature self-definition. (p. 104)

On the Role of Inquiry in Humanistic Psychotherapy

The same forces that have shaped the contours of psychotherapy theory and practice were the forces that have guided the development of inquiry in humanistic psychology. The whole-person approach has been reflected in the more molar variables often sought out as subjects of inquiry. The emphasis on relationship has revealed itself through the search for modes of inquiry that maintained connectedness with research participants. There has been an accompanying search for egalitarian patterns of interaction with research participants, in contrast to the impersonal, more detached, and inherently more hierarchical relationships maintained in conventional inquiry modes.

These efforts to establish meaningful investigator–participant relationships have revealed themselves in the vocabularies used to describe these relationships. These vocabularies were invariably indexed by connotations of active involvement on the part of the research participants. The term *subjects*, with its connotation of passivity, is used less often, replaced by other terms. For example, Wolter-Gustafson (1990) alluded to "co-investigators" and "learning partners" to describe her inquiry participants. Reason and Heron (1986) put forth the idea of a "core group" whose members serve as consultants to the investigators. Hunt and Seeman (1990), in their study of women's recovery from alcoholism, described the use of such a core group of consultants. The core group consisted of women who had abstained from alcohol use for 5 years or more and who thus had direct experience with the recovery process. Their contributions to the process of research planning enhanced the realistic quality of the study.

There has also been experimentation with more varied models of research. Qualitative research patterns have been increasing, along with increasingly rigorous procedures that attend closely to issues of validity (e.g., Lincoln & Guba, 1985). A variety of alternative research paradigms have been offered (e.g., Hoshmand, 1989). Moustakas (1990) introduced a model of heuristic research as a way of investigating varieties of human experience. There is a widening use of grounded theory to guide the uses of inductive discovery as a basis for conceptualization. Rennie's chapter (this volume, chapter 4) documents this process more fully. There are studied efforts to gather basic data of experience through attention to the phenomenologies of research participants.

The foregoing ventures into new intellective territory have sometimes created complexities and dilemmas that have required attention. The complexities hinged on the fact that there were two major components that drove the research, components that were not always differentiated. On the one hand were the underlying personal–professional values and commitments that guided the research. On the other hand were the responsibilities attendant on research as a public enterprise that made it necessary to pay attention to the validity dimensions of the inquiry.

Some synthesis of this dialectical dilemma was necessary. Researchers have ultimately learned that a useful way to approach synthesis is to widen the lens of possibilities so that the entire dialectical continuum of inquiry modes becomes available for review. What has come into view is the fact that one need not choose between requirements of value authenticity and public responsibility. It has turned out that both directions could be encompassed without compromising either.

LOOKING AHEAD

In this section, I explore possibilities for further development of humanistic psychotherapy. In particular, the concept of the fully functioning person provides a foothold for potentially important directions of development. The concept encompasses both the whole-person idea and the fulfillment of personal potentialities that mark the goals of humanistic psychotherapy.

The direction in which my own thinking has evolved has been in the growing awareness that a human-system model has promise because of its power both to organize complex structures and to account for their underlying unity. It is, furthermore, a design that is itself sufficiently structured to be helpful in generating empirical inquiry. Indeed, the human-system model that I present here was itself fostered by some 25 or more empirical studies that contributed to the validation of the model (Seeman, 1983).

The Human-System Model

Figure 21.1 depicts the human-system model. The figure displays in a molecular–molar sequence the major behavioral subsystems that constitute the human system. Starting at the base with the biochemical subsystem, the model moves upward toward the more molar subsystems, capped by the most molar dimension, the person–environment transaction.

The horizontal and vertical arrows convey vital information about the model. The bidirectional vertical arrows depict the embedded connections among the behavioral subsystems. These connections have a transactional quality; that is, the subsystems are so intimately linked and mutually embedded that their function and their very definitions are interwoven with each other.

To fully understand organismic processes, one must grasp the full meaning of this transactional quality. Bohm (1981), for example, said, "Each part grows in the context of the whole, so that it does not exist independently,

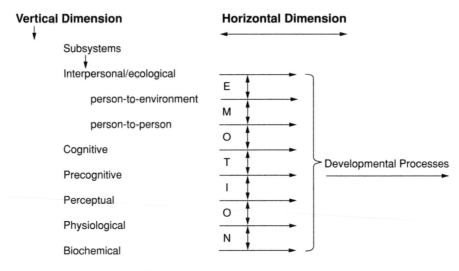

Vertical Dimension

Subsystems

Interpersonal/ecological

person-to-environment

person-to-person

Cognitive

Precognitive

Perceptual

Physiological

Biochemical

Horizontal Dimension

E M O T I O N

Developmental Processes

Figure 21.1. The human-system health structure.

nor can it be said that it merely 'interacts' with the other, without itself being essentially affected in this relationship" (p. 173).

Angyal (1941) used what is probably the most simple and elegant definition of a system when he used the term *unitas multiplex*. In this term, he captured both the existence of multiple subsystems or components of a system and its underlying unity.

Turning again to Figure 21.1, note now the horizontal plane. This plane with its accompanying arrows is where the action takes place across time. The plane depicts the ongoing behavior, history, and development of the person. The bidirectional arrow immediately below the term *Horizontal Dimension* is designed to emphasize the continuity of past, present, and future in a well-functioning human system.

There is one subsystem that requires special description. Although most of the behavioral subsystems listed in Figure 21.1 have descriptive titles that are self-evident, the precognitive subsystem presents at once an important and less well-understood aspect of the human system. By *precognitive*, I refer to those aspects of human behavior that are less fully organized and conceptualized. They occur as fragmentary and ambiguous impressions; they include dreams, affectively toned sensations, "intuitive" fragments, and the like. Their importance in psychotherapy stems from the fact that these precognitive bits of awareness furnish the client and therapist with avenues of access to potential blocks in connectedness and integration. They are less formed but vital emergent sources of information to client and therapist.

To say that these precognitive sources of information are less well understood is in no way to say that they are mysterious or unexplainable. Indeed, the organismic aspects of precognitive functioning have been the object of intensive interest at the biological level in recent years. What is now increasingly understood is the neural circuitry that connects the cortex with the lower levels of brain structure and function and that provides evidence of the connectedness that characterizes a system. On this point, Gray (1981) stated that

> Improvement of methodology of study of fiber tract connections within the brain has led to the interesting finding that there are very extensive fiber connections between the two [the limbic system and the neocortex], and even to the discovery that all impulses entering the cortex or leaving it are routed through the limbic system and other subcortical structures. (p. 303)

Findings from another laboratory were concerned with the avenue through which information was integrated (Foote, 1988). Foote proposed that interactions within the neocortex were facilitated by subcortical structures that provide cortical "activation" or "implementation."

Here I note again that precognitive activity from subcortical regions may be made available for further processing as a consequence of neural linkages from subcortical to cortical regions of the brain. An integral part of the task of psychotherapy is to pay attention to these precognitive signals, for they carry vital information often not fully available to the client. In such instances, the therapist facilitates integration by fostering fuller awareness and symbolization, thus facilitating cognitive mastery of this information by the client.

Another aspect of the model is that the emotion subsystem occupies a special place in the model. Before explaining the rationale for such a placement, I preface my explanation with a broader comment, namely, that I do not consider the human system model that I have presented here as a definitive and finished model. Indeed, I may never regard it as finished. Thus far, the model has gone through at least five iterations, and I still see some open issues with the model. It is in this spirit that the placement that I chose for emotion remains tentative.

My rationale for placing emotion across the subsystem spectrum comes from the broad span with which emotion engages all of the other subsystems. An emotion might begin with a particular perception or with an interpersonal event, transfer rapidly to the biochemical and physiological subsystems, engage then with a cognitive response, and circle back to a revised interpersonal response. Such a broad response spectrum might not be unique, for I have argued that these transactional intersystem responses inhere in the very nature of the human system. What might be different is the breadth of coverage that characterizes the emotion system.

Emotion theory lends some support for this notion of breadth of span. For example, Tomkins (1962) put forth many years ago the notion that emotion in the human system functions as an amplifier of responses, serving to promote added energy to virtually the entire human system. Izard (1993) identified four systems for emotion activation, including both cognitive and noncognitive points of origin. More recently, Smith and Kirby (2000) summarized some of the literature with an equally broad definitional span thus: "The emotional reactions themselves are commonly conceptualized as having multiple response components, including a distinctive subjective feeling state; an organized pattern of skeletomuscular, autonomic, and endocrine activity, and a felt urge to respond to the situation in a particular way" (p. 85). It was the cumulative weight of all of the foregoing comments that prompted for me the vertical placement of the emotion subsystem.

On Communication

Thus far, I have dealt with the central role of connectedness as a defining property of the human system. There is a second and equally important characteristic that defines the human system: communication. Where connectedness defines a critical aspect of human system *structure*, communication is the core of human system *function*. Communication feeds the system, holds the connectedness together, and makes the system work.

Ruesch and Bateson (1951) noted the centrality of communication in their observation that "A person's organism as a whole can be conceived of as an instrument of communication, with sense organs, the receivers; effector organs, the senders; with internal transmitters, the humoral and nervous pathways; and with a center, the brain" (p. 29). Rossi (1987) provided a valuable illustration of the key role that communication plays in holding the system together:

> In the language of communication theory, the hypothalamus functions as a transducer; it converts the neural impulse of "mind" into the humoral "messenger molecules" of the body. . . . Neuropeptides are the hormones or "messenger molecules" that mediate the flow of information through the bloodstream to virtually all the cells of the body; information is typically transmitted via the endocrine and immune systems through this route. (p. 373)

A closer study of hypothalamus function serves to underline another important point with respect to system function as a whole. I have made a distinction between *system structure* and *system function*. It is important to note that this distinction is a matter of cognitive convenience, helping to differentiate activities of the system. But it is equally important to remember the intimate connection between structure and function; the discussion about the hypothalamus underlines this transactional connectedness. For the hypothalamus to act as a transducer, structure and function serve each other. Specifically, the hypothalamus contains cells that have joint properties both of nerve cells and endocrine cells, referred to as *neuroendocrine* cells. Thus, the transducer function is facilitated by the cell structure, for the hypothalamus is the organ that links thought and action (Alberts, 1989).

I have more to say about communication as a system fostering process when I discuss its place in psychotherapy, but for now I underline simply that communication is the underlying process that permits the system to function and develop over time.

Optimal Functioning in the Human System

We come now to a view of behavioral processes that characterize the model's operation and that help us to define what Rogers has called the *fully functioning person* (Rogers, 1961). Here we find grounds for describing what makes the system function well and thus for understanding the place of psychotherapy in enhancing system efficacy. In this description, I revisit the two most fundamental system attributes: connectedness and communication. A basic assertion here is that optimal communication within and between the behavioral subsystems at all levels is what keeps the system integrated and provides the *unitas* segment of Angyal's (1941) system definition.

Weiner (1948, 1954) contributed to human-system theory in his discourse on cybernetics, which he defined as the science of communication and control. A major mechanism is the feedback loop that maintains lawfulness through information circuits. Weiner (1954) emphasized the importance of this process to the well-being of the person in his statement: "To live effectively is to live with adequate information. Thus, communication and control belong to the essence of man's inner life, even as they belong to his life in society" (p. 27).

Miller, Galanter, and Pribram (1960), in their discussion of brain and behavior, proposed a "cybernetic hypothesis, namely, that the fundamental building block of the nervous system is the feedback loop" (pp. 26–27). Brody (1973) and Schwartz (1980) described the properties of healthy human systems. Brody (1973) suggested that for optimal functioning of the system, "Each of the component systems on each hierarchical level must be intact and functioning. All feedback loops must be intact and free from excessive noise or impedance to signal flow" (p. 76).

Schwartz (1980) noted that these feedback loops provide self-regulation through intricate networks of information processing. When adequate information exchange and regulation are in place and working, a state of health exists. Disregulation in the system indexes system dysfunction.

Carl Rogers (1965) had a long-standing interest in what he so elegantly called the fully functioning person and described the fully functioning person in what are essentially human-system terms:

> He is making use of his organic equipment to sense, as accurately as possible, the existential situation within and without. He is using all of the data his nervous system can thus supply. . . . He is a fully functioning organism, and because of the awareness of himself which flows freely in and through his experiences, he is a fully functioning person. (p. 20)

The foregoing position is supported by diverse research studies. The empirical studies carried out by Seeman (1983) and his students led to the following summary:

> Persons who understand and trust their basic organismic self can listen to their own signals. They do not have the need to screen, shut out, or deflect and distort signals in a way that characterizes more vulnerable persons. For the integrated person this ability to receive and process the data of their immediate experience results in the optimal receipt of information. . . . This ability to receive and process the reality data of their world has portentous effects for the integrated person. Reality data serve as nutrition, fully as important to the psychological organism as food is to the biological organism. (p. 233)

What is most consistent in all of the foregoing descriptions is the commanding role of communication in maintaining a healthy organism, and the key role of an open, fluid, and unimpeded communication system in maximizing effective human functioning.

Dysfunction in the Human System

If open access to one's own reality data maximizes the likelihood of effective functioning, then blocked, impeded, and disturbed communication characterizes dysfunction. There are myriad ways of describing dysfunction, as volumes on abnormal psychology indicate. Yet the singular theme that suffuses the many modes of dysfunction refers to impeded access to one's own experiential data; that is, dysfunction in connectedness and communication is a major hallmark of dysfunction and psychopathology.

The views of Reusch and Bateson (1951) are in accord with the foregoing conception of dysfunction as failure in communication: "It is well to remember that almost all phenomena included under the traditional heading of psychopathology are disturbances of communication" (p. 5). Kandel (1983) showed the connection between behavioral dysfunction and the organismic processes that accompany such dysfunction. He described through the study of animal models the interface between the observation of anxiety-related behavior and the biochemical processes associated with anxiety. He indicated that "on the basis of pharmacological and biochemical studies, we have been able to piece together a coherent sequence of biochemical steps that take place in the sensory neurons when the behavior is altered by anxiety" (Kandel, 1983, p. 1285). He went on to describe a regular sequence of biochemically induced neural-circuit impediments that accompany anxiety.

The Human-System Model of Psychotherapy

The foregoing sections on effective functioning and dysfunction have paved the way for a description of psychotherapy according to the human-system model. The model has proposed that dysfunction is indexed by blockage of communication, by signal distortion, and by insensitivity to information from the person–environment matrix, and thus by flawed organismic connectedness and integration. Conversely, effective functioning is indexed by communication that is open, free-flowing, and maximally receptive to information from the person–environment matrix. As a consequence, the fully functioning person is characterized by an optimal level of organismic connectedness and integration.

Following from the foregoing premises, the human-system model of psychotherapy specifies that psychotherapy is a process in which the therapist helps the client to explore his or her modes of communication, enhance communication clarity and effectiveness, and foster maximal organismic connectedness and integration.

The psychotherapist deals necessarily with the issue of connectedness in the first instance because it is only through this work of connectedness that the therapist can make contact with the client's personal system. Little work can begin in the absence of what usually designates as the therapist–client relationship. It is an essential requisite for therapy.

It is precisely at this point—the point of the therapist's connection with the client's personal system—that human-system theory can explain the wide variety of therapy theories and technologies that exist today. Different therapies choose different modes and levels of entry into the client's personal system. The latitude that different therapies have in choosing different entry points flows from the very nature of the system. The transactional connectedness of the different subsystems assures a spread of effect from the therapist's point of entry, whatever that is, to other behavioral subsystems. That is not to say that the character of this spread of effect is an automatic process. Indeed, the efficacy of therapy may very well depend on the therapist's skill in facilitating appropriate connection and integration of the subsystems and in knowing how to make meaningful contact with the client's personal system.

The Human-System Model as a Source of Criterion Measures for Evaluating Therapy Outcomes

One of the characteristics of the human-system model is that it provides potential criterion measures of therapy outcome. Indeed, the initial impetus for the development of the human-system model came from my need to develop such measures. In 1950, the University of Chicago Counseling Center, under the direction of Carl Rogers, had received a research grant to study the process and outcomes of psychotherapy. As coordinator of research for the project, I decided early on that it would be important to spend time in developing theory-based criterion measures to assess therapy outcomes. Ultimately, it became evident that a comprehensive and efficient way to conceptualize these studies would be to use a system-based model of effective human functioning. Such a model could be used in a comprehensive whole-person mode to develop empirically based criterion measures of psychotherapy outcome.

As I have indicated earlier, the basic conceptual grounding for this work was the premise that an effectively functioning human system is characterized by the free and unhampered flow of communication among the behavioral subsystems. Such functioning would enable people to maximize their ability to absorb the reality data of their world, to integrate these data in a meaningful way, and to act on them in ways that could be seen in their observable behavior.

It took many years for the empirical work to set the appropriate grounding for the human-system model. The results indicated that there were indeed consistent patterns of behavior that characterized an effectively functioning human system and that could thus serve in the development of criterion measures for assessing psychotherapy outcome. A detailed report of the studies can be found in Seeman (1983).

Illustrating the Model: Connection and Communication

In this section, I try to make more concrete the earlier account of the human-system model's relevance to psychotherapy by presenting and commenting on verbatim passages from a therapy experience with a client. My purpose here is not to advocate any particular therapy technology but to indicate how the vocabulary and the concepts of the model are pertinent to the actualities of the therapeutic process. The technology in the passage involves an experiential mode because that is my preferred mode of work in psychotherapy and characterizes the working style of many humanistically oriented psychotherapists. It is, however, my premise that connection and communication are relevant to all forms of psychotherapy.

In the following passages, C refers to the client and T refers to the therapist. The passages depicted here were taken from a tape-recorded account of the second interview with a 35-year-old male client who came to therapy because he was at a critical point in a long-term relationship and was contemplating the possibility of ending the relationship.

> 1C: I felt terrific after the last session. The thing that is again a surprise to me is that I feel good about my decision. After we talked last week, I affirmed that I felt good. I found that unbelievable, a situation in which I could feel good, that it would be a positive thing to leave. I felt some excitement that the change was positive. I think I carry a lot of guilt, so some of the surprise was that it was a good surprise.
>
> 1T: What strikes me in your account is the surprise part. I'm tuning in on that now and I want to ask, "What was that like?" I'm not forgetting that you were really pleased—but what was the surprise?
>
> 2C: (long pause) It was a combination: surprise that I did know more of my feelings, that the feeling I was having continued, and I was aware that I did have it and that I had felt it.
>
> 2T: I see; there's such a sense of right-ness about it, and you didn't expect that.
>
> 3C: No. I really expect something to come in on it and say—well, my feeling is that I've been a naughty boy, and that those feelings are not responsible, correct—should not feel that way.
>
> 3T: That is a familiar feeling to you, isn't it? I'm hearing that as a major theme in your life.
>
> 4C: I have an incredible reaction to shoulds. They range from, I cannot hear what anyone is saying when there is a should put in it somewhere.
>
> 4T: Tune out?
>
> 5C: That's all I hear. I react to the should and can't hear any more.
>
> [Here is a classic example of an impasse in which communication appears to be altogether blocked. At this point, the human-system model that I have described offers two leads for me as the therapist: First, I am sensitive to dysfunction in the flow of communication, because the model posits that such a communication disruption is a core issue in human dysfunction. Second, the model suggests that there are multiple avenues in which I can maintain connection with the client. Here I turn to the possibilities of the physiological subsystem.]
>
> 5T: I would like to deal with the issue of shoulds, because it is so central. I want to give you space to get into yourself and even close me out and everything out. Live with that should a bit and find out what it is like in your body. The theme that I'm going to be with you is that your body has wisdom and knowledge, you have wisdom and knowledge in

your body but you have to find ways of reaching it. Give yourself a chance to stay with what that evokes in you. Try to find something in your body that gives you information.

(Pause for a short time)

6C: It feels silly to come to my stomach, but that's the place where I feel I've been kicked.

6T: I see, it must hurt. . . . What does your stomach feel like? What signals are you getting from your stomach?

[Here I feel connected to the client within his physiological subsystem and choose to stay with that avenue of awareness.]

7C: Well, my stomach is pushing up in my chest.

7T: Stay with that pushing up. Let yourself feel that pushing up. Don't worry about the words here.

(Pause)

8C: It feels like it wants to come up to my chest and then it wants to scream . . . I feel squashed and I feel choked. I'm feeling it in my throat now.

8T: Tight grip. Choked.

9C: Very choked . . . I'm not sure this fits, but I feel like I want to throw up.

9T: A revulsion?

10C: That, or there's something caught in there that's really nauseating. But I'm not sure that it's nauseating, because I don't feel sick. I feel . . . UGH! (loud explosive sound) . . . just that I want to cough it, I mean . . .

10T: I get the revulsion rather than sick. Does that fit in?

11C: I want to get rid of . . .

11T: I see, the revul . . . you want to get rid of. . . . What do you want to get rid of?

12C: I have so many things, so I can't tell whether it's exactly right, but I'll try some.

12T: Sure

13C: I want to get rid of what other people have made me eat, what other people have made me swallow.

13T: And you want to get rid of . . .

14C: Yeah, I don't want it . . .

14T: What's been forced down your belly.

15C: And the squashed feeling is that it's there. That's what it is. Somehow, it's being held. I am holding it down there.

[The client's physiological subsystem has led him unerringly to two conclusions: He knows what his organism needs to do about the shoulds, and he knows that he is not yet ready to shed the shoulds—that there is more work to do.]

As the session continues, the client discovers that the obstacle to freedom is his own compliant and submissive aspect of himself. What follows comes from a dialogue that the client was having with himself in which he was expressing his "assertive self" as he addressed his "compliant self" in the empty-chair method.

> 16C: (Yelling) I don't want you anymore! (Loudly, as if clearing his throat) Ugh! Ugh! You taste horrible to me! You're choking me to death and I . . . have . . . had . . . it! (More loud coughing) (Yelling) I want rid of you! (Loud cough, heavy breathing and gasping. Client is yelling here.)
>
> 16T: Sounds like it's hard to dislodge him . . . How does that feel?
>
> 17C: Sometimes it goes away and I can breathe, and then sometimes . . . I feel like I am constantly in the process of trying to get him out (cough). . . . The sensation is a kind of numb swelling of my mouth I know something is going on. I know that I'm not dead, there is something deadening me. I know I'm alive and something is gripping me
>
> 17T: Something is numbing you, but you are alive.
>
> 18C: Makes me feel like I can fight.
>
> 18T: Sounds like there is a lot of relief there. How do you feel?
>
> 19C: I feel grateful, because I think for so long I felt I was the one who was dead. I've never had anyone fight for me before. I feel wonderful that I'm doing it. Because that seems to be the only one who knows. [The client is beginning to give credence to himself as a source of learning and thereby taking a fundamental step toward organismic integration.]
>
> 19T: And that you can do it?
>
> 20C: And that I can do it! That I will fight for myself.
>
> 20T: Sounds like you're saying that up to now you just somehow implicitly looked outside of you. But that's not the way it is now.
>
> 21C: I wanted to scream to my father to save me. He didn't know; he couldn't know. He can do what he wants because I'm here. It's great to know, too that it isn't him, it's me who's holding me in. I don't have to yell at him. I can yell at me now, I can yell at something in me to stop it. That *I* can save me from that. That's what feels so good. That I can do it . . . I like that. I like that a lot.
>
> 21T: You've found some power in you, that you never knew was there.
>
> 22C: And I'm not falling apart. I'm still alive. Getting more so . . .
>
> 22T: OK. It seems like you're saying "I'm feeling stronger."
>
> 23C: (Firmly) Much stronger, much stronger. Much more alive. And that it's me that feels alive. It's because of me that I feel alive.
>
> 23T: I'll tell you how it sounds to me. It's like you're taking your own life back. You're reclaiming your own life.
>
> 24C: Yeah, I am.

The foregoing therapy session illustrates several facets of the human-system model. There are, first, the twin therapist procedures of empathic connection and phenomenological communication, the sine qua non of the human-system therapy model. With respect to the client, his movement in the direction of organismic integration seems palpable. He evolved from immobilizing concern with external signals ("shoulds") to empowerment of self and consequent attention to his own signals. This latter development fits precisely with the definition of organismic integration cited from research reported earlier in this chapter: People who understand and trust their basic organismic self can listen to their own signals.

More on Communication

The centrality of communication to psychotherapy is not in dispute, but there are theorists who have more to say: namely, that communication is not only important but rather the very core of the therapeutic process. For example, Greenhill (1958) suggested,

> It is the nature of the communication itself between the patient and the therapist which is the principal agent in psychotherapy. . . . With these elements we have formulated a theory called the Focal Communication Concept which indicates that focussing upon the immediately charged area . . . in the here and now effects optimal therapeutic relationship and movement. (p. 39)

Finally, it may turn out that the model's twin focus on connection and communication offers at once the ends and means of psychotherapy. The model has already postulated that the fully functioning person is characterized by seamless connectedness and fluid communication. But connection and communication are what the client–therapist process is all about. It may thus be most fitting that the outcome of therapy, the fully functioning person, is the integral endpoint of the therapy process itself.

REFERENCES

Alberts, B. (1989). *Molecular biology of the cell*. New York: Garland.

Angyal, A. (1941). *Foundations for a science of personality*. Cambridge, MA: Harvard University Press.

Bohm, D. (1981). *Wholeness and the implicate order*. London: Routledge & Kegan Paul.

Brody, H. (1973, Autumn). The system view of man: Implications for medicine, science, and ethics. *Perspectives in Biology and Medicine*, 71–92.

Foote, S. L. (1988). The integrative function of the cortex. In P. Rakic & W. Singer (Eds.), *Neurobiology of the neocortex* (pp. 423–445). New York: Wiley.

Gendlin, E. T. (1996). *Focusing-oriented psychotherapy*. New York: Guilford Press.

Gray, W. (1981). System-forming aspects of general system theory. In J. C. Durkin (Ed.), *Living groups* (pp. 297–313). New York: Brunner/Mazel.

Greenberg, L. S., Rice, L. N., & Elliott, R. (1993). *Facilitating emotional change.* New York: Guilford Press.

Greenhill, M. H. (1958). The focal communication concept. *American Journal of Psychotherapy, 12,* 30–41.

Guisinger, S., & Blatt, S. J. (1994). Individuality and relatedness: Evolution of a fundamental dialectic. *American Psychologist, 49,* 104–111.

Heath, D. H. (1965). *Explorations of maturity.* New York: Appleton-Century-Crofts.

Heath, D. H. (1977). *Maturity and competence: A trans-cultural view.* New York: Gardner Press.

Hoshmand, L. L. S. T. (1989). Alternative research paradigms. *Counseling Psychologist, 17,* 3–80.

Hunt, C., & Seeman, J. (1990). A study of women's recovery from alcoholism. *Person-Centered Review, 5,* 233–248.

Izard, C. E., (1993). Four systems for emotion activation: Cognitive and noncognitive processes. *Psychological Review, 100,* 68–90.

Jourard, S. (1968). *Disclosing man to himself.* New York: Van Nostrand.

Jourard, S. (1971). *The transparent self.* New York: Van Nostrand.

Kandel, E. R. (1983). From metapsychology to molecular biology: Concerning anxiety. *American Journal of Psychiatry, 140,* 1277–1292.

Kepner, J. I. (1993). *Body process.* San Francisco: Jossey-Bass.

Landsman, T. (1968). The beautiful person. *Futurist, 3,* 41–42.

Lincoln, Y. S., & Guba, E. G. (1985). *Naturalistic inquiry.* Beverly Hills, CA: Sage.

Maslow, A. H. (1971). *The farther reaches of human nature.* New York: Viking Press.

Miller, G. A., Galanter, E., & Pribram, K. H. (1960). *Plans and structure of behavior.* New York: Holt.

Moustakas, C. (1990). Heuristic research. *Person-Centered Review, 5,* 170–190.

Pierce, U. G. B. (1916). *The creed of Epictetus.* New York: Beacon Press.

Reason, P., & Heron, J. (1986). Research with people: The paradigm of experiential cooperative inquiry. *Person-Centered Review, 4,* 456–476.

Rogers, C. R. (1961). *On becoming a person.* Boston: Houghton-Mifflin.

Rogers, C. R. (1965). The concept of the fully functioning person. *Psychotherapy, 1,* 17–26.

Rossi, E. (1987). The psychobiology of mind–body healing. In J. K. Zeig (Ed.), *The evolution of psychotherapy* (pp. 362–384). New York: Brunner-Mazel.

Ruesch, J., & Bateson, G. (1951). *Communication: The social matrix of psychiatry.* New York: Norton.

Schwartz, G. E. (1980). Behavioral medicine and system theory: A new synthesis. *National Forum, 4,* 25–30.

Seeman, J. (1983). *Personality integration: Studies and reflections.* New York: Human Sciences Press.

Seeman, J. (1989). Toward a model of positive health. *American Psychologist, 44,* 1099–1109.

Smith, C. A., & Kirby, L. D. (2000). Consequences require antecedents. In J. P. Forgas (Ed.), *Feeling and thinking: The role of affect in social cognition* (pp. 83–106). New York: Cambridge University Press.

Tomkins, S. S. (1962). *Affect imagery consciousness.* New York: Springer.

Weiner, N. (1948). *Cybernetics: Control and communication in animal and the machine.* Cambridge, MA: MIT Press.

Weiner, N. (1954). *The human use of human beings.* New York: Avon.

Wolter-Gustafson, C. (1990). How person-centered theory informed my qualitative research on women's lived-experience of wholeness. *Person-Centered Review, 5,* 221–232.

APPENDIX:
RESOURCES IN HUMANISTIC
PSYCHOLOGY AND PSYCHOTHERAPY

Information provided here was accurate at the time this book went to press, June 2001.

UNIVERSITIES WITH HUMANISTIC DEPARTMENTS IN PSYCHOLOGY AND RELATED FIELDS

American School of Professional Psychology
San Francisco Bay Area Campus
1040 Oak Grove Road, Suite 103
Concord, CA 94518
Phone: (510) 215-0277
Website: www.aspp.edu

Antioch University
13274 Fiji Way
Marina del Rey, CA 90202
Phone: (310) 578-1080
Website: www.antiochla.edu

Antioch University Seattle
2326 6th Avenue
Seattle, WA 98121
Phone: (206) 441-5352
Website: www.antioch.sea.edu

California Institute of Integral Studies
1453 Mission Street
San Francisco, CA 94103
Phone: (415) 575-6150
Website: www.ciis.edu

Counseling Centrum
Catholic University, Leuven
B-3000 Leuven
Blijde Inkonatstraat 13
Belgium

Center for Humanistic Studies
40 E. Ferry Avenue
Detroit, MI 48202-3802
Phone: (313) 875-7440
Website: www.petersons.com/sites/o005603si.html

Duquesne University
Department of Psychology
600 Forbes Avenue
Pittsburgh, PA 15282
Phone: (412) 396-5420
Website: www.duq.edu

Goddard College
RR2, Box 235
Plainfield, VT 05667
Phone: (802) 454-8311
Website: www.goddard.edu

Harmony Institute International School for Psychotherapy, Counseling and
  Group Leadership
av Gastello 9
St. Petersburg
196066 Russia
E-mail: group@inschool.spb.su
US Contact: solweean@aol.com

John F. Kennedy University
Graduate School of Professional Psychology
12 Altarinda Road
Orinda, CA 94563-2603
Phone: (925) 254-0200
Website: www.jfku.edu

Lesley College
Graduate School of Arts and Social Sciences
Counseling and Psychology Program
29 Everett Street
Cambridge, MA 02138-2790
Phone: (800) 999-1959; (617) 349-8300
Website: www.lesley.edu

Northern Illinois University
Department of Psychology
DeKalb, IL 60115-2864
Phone: (815) 753-0772
Website: www.niu.edu

Pacifica Graduate Institute
249 Lambert Road
Carpinteria, CA 93013
Phone: (805) 969-3626
Website: www.pacifica.edu

Pepperdine University
400 Corporate Pointe, Suite 400
Culver City, CA 90230
Phone: (310) 568-5600
Website: www.pepperdine.edu

Salve Regina University
100 Ochre Point Avenue
Newport, RI 02840-4192
Phone: (401) 847-6650
Website: www.salve.edu

Saybrook Graduate School & Research Center
450 Pacific, 3rd Floor
San Francisco, CA 94133
Phone: (800) 825-4480
Website: www.saybrook.edu

Sonoma State University
Psychology Department
1801 E. Cotati Avenue
Rohnert Park, CA 94928
Phone: (707) 664-2411; (707) 664-2682
Website: www.sonoma.edu

Temple University
The Graduate School
501 Carnell Hall
1803 North Broad Street
Philadelphia, PA 19122
Phone: (215) 204-1380
Website: www.temple.edu

The Union Institute
Graduate School
440 E. McMillan Street
Cincinnati, OH 45206
Phone: (800) 486-3116; (513) 861-6400
Website: www.tui.edu

Vermont College of
Norwich University
Montpelier, VT 05602
Phone: (800) 336-6794; (802) 828-8500
Website: www.norich.edu/vermontcollege

Walden University
Psychology Division
155 Fifth Avenue South
Minneapolis, MN 55401
Phone: (800) WALDEN-U; (612) 338-7224
Website: www.walden.edu

State University of West Georgia (Formerly West Georgia College)
1600 Maple Street
Carrollton, GA 30118

Department of Psychology Program
Phone: (770) 836-6510

Department of Counseling & Educational Psychology Graduate Program
Phone: (770) 836-6554
Website: www.westga.edu

Universidad Iberoamericana, A.C.
Reforma #880 STA.FE
01210 Mexico City, Mexico
Phone: 52-5-726-9048
Website: www.uia.mx

University of East Anglia
Centre for Counselling Studies
School of Education and Professional Development
Norich, England NR4 7TJ
Phone: +44 1 603 456161

York University
Department of Psychology
4700 Keele Street
North York
Ontario M3J 1P3
Canada
Phone: (416) 736-5115
Website: www.yorku.ca

ORGANIZATIONS

Association for the Development of the Person-Centered Approach
(ADPCA)
P.O. Box 3876
Chicago, IL 60690-3876
E-mail: dmcneal@ripco.com
Website: www.adpca.org

Association for Humanistic Psychology
1516 Oak Street, #320A
Alameda, CA 94501-2947
Phone: (510) 769-6495
E-mail: ahpoffice@aol.com
Website: www.ahpweb.org

Association for Humanistic Psychology in Britain AHP(B)
BM Box 3582
London WC1N 3XX
England
Phone: 0845 7078506
Website: www.ahpb.org.uk

Association for the Person Centered Approach South Africa (APCASA)
P.O. Box 37344
0043 Fairie Glen
South Africa
Phone: +27 12 991 2086
E-mail: bsmit@cis.co.za

British Association for the Person Centred Approach
Bm-BAPCA
London WC1N 3XX
England
Phone: 01 989 770 948
E-mail: info@bapca.org.uk
Website: users.powernet.co.uk/bapca

Center for the Studies of the Person (CSP)
1150 Silverado, Suite 112
La Jolla, CA 92037
Phone: (858) 459-3861
E-mail: stillwell@cari.net
Website: www.centerfortheperson.org

Division of Humanistic Psychology (Division 32)
American Psychological Association
750 First Street, NE
Washington, DC 20002
Phone: (202) 336-5500
Website: www.apa.org

French Association for the Person Centered Approach
F-75 020 Paris
119 Rue des Pyrenees
France
Website: wwwgeocities.com/afcacp

GwG
D-50674 Koln
Richard-Wagner-Str.12
Germany
Phone: +49 221 925908-0

Network of the European Associations for Person Centered
    and Experiential Psychotherapy and Counseling
(NEAPCEPC)
SGGT Office
Schaffelglasse7 CH 8001
Zurich, Switzerland
Phone: +41 1 2516080
E-mail: neapcepc@pce-europe.org
Website: www.pce-europe.org

Person-Centered Association in Austria (PCA)
Institute for Psychology
Wien University
A-1010 Wien, Liebigasse 5
Austria
E-mail: a6213da@awiuni11.edvz.univie.ac.at
Website: www.pfs.kabelnet.at

Pre-Therapy International Network
Phone: 051 6345434
E-mail: pre.therapy@tiscalinet.it
Website: www.pretherapy.com

Portuguese Association for Person Centered Psychotherapy
    and Counseling (APPCPC)
P-1700-173 Lisboa
Av. Estados Unidos da America

Portugal
137 7 Dx
Phone: +35 1 7939381
E-mail: galf@esoterica.pt

Society for Existential Analysis
School of Psychotherapy and Counseling
Regents College
Inner Circle, Regent's Park
London, England NWI 4NS
United Kingdom
Phone: +44 (0) 20 7487 7446
E-mail: spc@regents.ac.uk
Website: www.existential.mcmail.com

Viktor Frankl Institute
Langwiesgasse 6, A-1140 Vienna,
Austria
Phone: (+43-1) 914 2683
E-mail: logos@ap.univie.ac.at
Website: www.logotherapy.univie.ac.at

World Association for Person-Centered and Experiential Psychotherapy
    and Counseling (WAPCEPC)
SGGT Office, Josefatr.798
CH-8005 Zurich, Switzerland
Phone: +41 1 2516080
E-mail: office@pce-world.org
Website: www.pce-world.org

TRAINING PROGRAMS

Emotionally Focused Therapy

Ottawa Couple and Family Institute
#201, 1869 Carling Avenue
Ottawa, Ontario
Canada K2A 1E6.
Phone: (613) 722-5122
E-Mail: sjohnson@eft.ca
Website: www.eft.ca

Existential

Existential-Humanistic Institute
870 Market Street, Suite 463
San Francisco, CA 94102
Phone: (415) 421-3355
E-Mail: drcurtin@humanisticexistentialinstitute.com
Website: www.existentialhumanisticinstitute.com

Experiential

Center for the Study of Experiential Therapy (CSEP)
University Hall 1420
Department of Psychology
University of Toledo
Toledo, OH 43606
Phone: (419) 530-4014
E-Mail: relliott@uoft02.utoledo.edu
Website: www.utoledo.edu/psychology/csep/html

Focusing

The Focusing Institute
34 East Lane, Spring Valley, NY 10977
Phone: (845) 362-5222
E-Mail: send comments to webmaster
Website: www.focusing.org
Note: Contains comprehensive links to other focusing programs and resources

Gestalt

Gestalt Associates Training, Los Angeles
1460 7th Street, Suite 300
Santa Monica, CA 90401
Phone: (310) 395-6844
E-mail: ritaresnick@gatla.org
Website: www.gatla.org

Gestalt Institute of Cleveland
1588 Hazel Drive
Cleveland, OH 44106-1791
Phone: (216) 421-0468
E-mail: gestaltclv@aol.com
Website: www.gestaltcleveland.org

Gestalt Center for Psychotherapy and Training
26 W. 9th Street
New York, NY 10011
Phone: (212) 387-9429
E-mail: info@gestaltnyc.org
Website: www.gestaltnyc.org

Gestalt Training Institute of San Diego
8950 Villa La Jolla
Suite 1242A
La Jolla, CA 92038
Phone: (858) 455-0118
E-mail: sandiego@gestalt.org

The Center for Gestalt Development, Inc.
P.O. Box 990
Highland, NY 12528-0990
Phone: (914) 691-6530
E-mail: tgjournal@gestalt.org
Website: www.gestalt.org

The New York Institute for Gestalt Therapy
P.O. Box 238, Old Chelsea Station
New York, NY 10011
Phone: (212) 864-8277
E-mail: GestalSing@aol.com
Website: www.g-g.org/nyigt

Person-Centered

Association for Rogerian Psychotherapy—Vienna, Austria
Rogergasse 22/32, Postfach 33, A-1090 Wien, Austria
Phone: +43 1 9610533
E-mail: office@vrp.at
Website: www.vrp.at

The Center for Interpersonal Growth
P.O. Box 7275
Albuquerque, NM 87194
Phone: 1-800-699-8206
E-mail: ctr4pg@juno.com
Website: personcenteredtraining.org/index.html

Gordon Training International
531 Stevens Avenue West
Solana Beach, CA 92075-2093
Phone: (800) 628-1197; (858) 481-8121
E-mail: info@gordontraining.com
Website: www.gordontraining.com

IACP
I-00185 Roma
Piazza Vittorio Emanuele II,99
Phone: +39 06 77 200357
E-mail: iacoers@mclink.it
Website: www.iacp.it

Institute for Person-Centered Studies, Austria
  and Academy for Counseling and Psychotherapy, Austria
Disslergasse 5/4
A-1030 Wien / Vienna
Austria
Phone: 0043 1 7137796
E-mail: akademie-ips@gmx.at
Website: www.psychotherapie.org/apg-ips

Person Centered Expressive Therapy Institute (PCETI)
P.O. Box 6518
Santa Rosa, CA 95406
Phone: (707) 584-5526
E-mail: nrogers@nrogers.com
Website: www.nrogers.com

Person Centered Therapy (Scotland)
40 Kelvingrove Street
Glasgow G3 7RZ
Scotland
Phone: +44141 3316888
Website: users.powernet.co.uk/pctmk/training/scotland.htm

Relationship Enhancement

National Institute of Relationship Enhancement®
12500 Blake Road
Silver Spring, MD 20904-2056
Phone: (301) 986-1479
E-mail: niremd@nire.org
Website: www.nire.org

COMPREHENSIVE WEB SITES

Note: The websites listed below provide extensive resources and links to other humanistic websites

Focusing Resources
Website: www.focusingresources.com

Gestalt Associations and Societies, Training Institutes, and Academic
  Programs
Website: www.g-g.org/gestalt_bookmarks/associate.html

Person-Centered Website
Peter F. Schmid
Website: www.pfs-online.at

Person-Centered International (PCI)
Website: www.personcentered.com

PUBLICATIONS

Journals

Australian Gestalt Journal
24 Sundowner Court
Mermaid Waters, Qld. 4218
Australia
Phone: (02) 9876 6018
E-mail: justbruno@bigpond.com
Website: www.users.bigpond.com/justbruno/index.html

British Gestalt Journal
P.O. Box 2994
London N5 1U6
England
Phone: 0171-359-3000
Website: www.britishgestaltjournal.com

Gestalt Journal
The Gestalt Journal Press
P.O. Box 990
Highland, NY 12528-0990
E-mail: tgjournal@gestalt.org
Website: www.gestalt.org

Gestalt Review Journals
The Analytic Press, Inc.
810 E. 10th Street
P.O. Box 1897
Lawrence, KS 66044-8897
Phone: (800) 627-0629
Website: www.analytic press.com/ordering.html

Humanistic Psychologist
Journal of Division 32 (Humanistic Psychology) of the American
 Psychological Association
Editor: Christopher M. Aanstoos
Website: www.apa.org

Japanese Journal of Humanistic Psychology
Psychological Clinic, Faculty of Education
Kyushu University
6-19-1 Hakozaki, Higashi-ku, Fukuoka
812-8581 Japan
Phone: 092-642-3144
Editor: Tsunehisa Abe

Journal of Humanistic Psychology
Sage Publications: 2455 Teller Road
Newbury Park, CA 91320
Editor: Tom Greening
E-mail: www.sagepub.com
Website: www.ahpweb.org/pub/journal/menu.html

Person-Centered and Experiential Psychotherapy
PCCS Books
Editor: Robert Elliott
Phone: +44 1989 770707
E-mail: journal@pce-world.org
Website: www.pce-world.org/idxjournal.htm

Person-Centered Journal
Journal of ADPCA
Editor: Jon Rose
ADPCA
P.O. Box 3876
Chicago, IL 60690-3876
E-mail: dmcneal@ripcvo.com

Person–Centred Practice
Journal of the British Association for the Person–Centred Approach
  (BAPCA)
PCCS Books
Editor: Tony Merry
Phone: +44 1989 770707
E-mail: books@pccs.telme.com
Website: users.powernet.co.uk/bapca/journal.htm

Person–Centered Review (1986–1990)
8590 Indian Ridge Road
San Marcos, CA 92078, USA
Editor: David J. Cain
Phone: (760) 510-9520
E-mail: david4@fda.net

Review of Existential Psychology and Psychiatry
P.O. Box 15680
Seattle, WA 98115
Phone: (206) 367-5764
Editor and Publisher: Keith Hoeller

Self and Society
European Journal of Humanistic Psychology
39 Blenkarne Road
London Sw11 GHZ

LIBRARY RESOURCES

Carl Rogers Archive
The Carl R. Rogers Collection, HPA Mss 32,
Department of Special Collections, Davidson Library,
University of California, Santa Barbara, CA
Phone: (805) 893-3062
Website: www.oac.cdlib.org/cgi-bin/oac/ucsb/rogers

Library of Congress, Washington, DC
Carl Rogers's Material
Website: http://catalog.loc.gov/Comprehensive Bibliography

University of California at Santa Barbara (UCSB) Library Archives
  of Humanistic Psychology
Contact: David Gartrell at gartrell@library.ucsb.edu

AUTHOR INDEX

Numbers in italics refer to listings in reference sections.

Daiuto, A. D., 318, *331*

Daldrup, R., 91, *107*, 198, *213, 218*, 505, *523, 524*

Damasio, A. R., 10, *50, 524*

Danacci, A., 596, *598*

Dandeneau, M., 318, 319, *332*

Daniel, C., 377, *401*

Daste, B. M., 478, *493*

Dattilio, F., *334*

D'Augelli, A. R., 452, *465*

Dauwalder, H., *598*

Davasio, A., *501*

Davidson, B., *246*

Davidson, H. R., 203, *214*

Davis, C. S., 92, *108*, 564, *576*

Davis, K., 57, *77*, 101, *105*, 284, 285, 300, *302*

Davis, K. C., 354, 356, *366*

Davis, K. L., 287, 290, 291, *301*

Davis, M. K., 539, *555*

Davis, R., *332, 494*

de Groot, R., 483, *494*

DeJulio, S. S., 163, *184*, 448, *467*, 531, 534, *554, 555*

DeLancey, A. L. *79,*

de la Serna, M., 354, 355, *365*

Dematatis, C., 384, *398*

Demby, A., 93, *113*

Dent, J., 422, 429, *441*

Denton, W. H., 318, 322, *332*

DeRidder, L. M., 85, 88, *106*

Derogatis, L. R., 323, *332*

DeRubeis, R. J., 539, *552*

deShazer, S., 561, *577*

Dessaulles, A., 76, 193, *217*, 318, 320, *332*, 505, *528*

Deurzen-Smith, E. van, 29, *50*

DeVre, R., 595, *598*

Devriendt, M., 329, *335*

de Vries, M. W., 86, *105, 217*, 266, *273*

Dewitt, D., 91, *107*

Diamond, G., 316, *332*, 506, *524*

Dierick, P., 343, 347, 348, *363365*

Diffelaers, R., 483, *494*

Diggory, J. C., 480, *493*

Diguer, L., 78, *614*

Dijkman, C. I., 86, *105*, 266, *273*

DiLoreto, A., 76, 87, 88, *105*

Di Pol, G., 345, *364*

Dircks, P., 342, 343, 345, 346, *363, 364*

Di Vesta, J. J., 462, *465*

Dogra, A., 376, *397*

Doll, G., 91, *105*, 156, 162, *182*

Dollard, J., 408, *438*

Dolli, G., *113*

Dombrow, R., 482, *493*

Dompierre, L. M., 86, *106*, 196, *215*, 293, *303*, 350, *364*

Donati, R., 67, *78*, 88, *106*

Donovan, J., *334*

Doppelt, H. G., *524*

Dorfman, E., 374, *398*

Dormaar, J. M., 86, *105*, 266, *273*

Dreikurs, R., 80, 150, *187*

Drenth, P. J. D., *110*

Drozf, J. F., 266, *273*

Duan, C., 445, 448, 451, *465*

DuBrin, J. R., 506, *528*

Dugo, J. M., 343, 345, *363*

Duhl, D. S., 3163, *332*

Duhl, F. J., 316, *332*

Duivenvoorden, H. J., 354, 356, *367*

Duncan, B. L., 44, 45, 49, *51*, 150, 168, 179, 180, *182*, 184, *185*

Duncan, M. C., 262, *272*

Dunfee, E. J., 86, *106*

Dunn, R.J., 473, 474, 487, *493*

Dunn, R. L., 319, *332*

du Plock, S., 255, 256, 260, 261, *273*

Dupuy, P., 261, *274*

Durak, G., 233, *246*

Durkin, J. C., *634*

Dvarionas, D., 374, *398*

Dworkin, F., 478, *495*

Dymond, R. F., 19, *52*, 57, *79*, 151, 152, 155, *182*, 186, 478, 482, *496, 497*, 531, *556, 577*

Eagle, M., *332, 494*

Ebrahimi, S., *181*

Eckert, J., 76, 79, 80, 88, 91, *105*, 112, 159, 161, *182*, 342, 346, *364, 366, 598*

Eco, U., 462, *465*

Edwards, B., 379, *401*

Eells, T. D., *214, 302*

Eels, J., 450, *465*

Egan, G., 161, *183*

Egendorf, A., 233, *246*

Ehrendwald, J., 23, *50*

Elashoff, R., *524*

Haaga, D. A. F., 607, *614*
Hagerman, S. M. *79,*
Hahlweg, K., 92, *103,* 317, 318, 319, *333, 336*
Haigh, G. V., 151, *182*
Haimovitz, M. L., *78,* 563, *576*
Haimovitz, N. R., *78,* 563, *576*
Hales, R., *555*
Halkides, G., 85, 87, 88, *106,* 154, *184,* 532, *553*
Hall, S., *216*
Halling, S., *274, 276*
Halperin, G., *78, 614*
Hamilton, M. A., 540, *553*
Handley, N. K., 257, 267, *274*
Hanna, F. J., 261, 266, *274*
Hannah, G., 376, *399*
Hannah, M. T., *331, 438*
Hannigan, P. S., 77, 350, *364*
Harman, M. J., 418, *442*
Harman, R. L., 350, *365*
Harrell, J., 422, 429, *441*
Harris, Z. L., 385, *399*
Hart, D., 486, 487, *497*
Hart, J. T., Jr., 22, *50, 106,* 188, 227, *251,* 470, 506, *527, 576*
Hartley, D. E., 540, *553*
Hartman, L. M., 473, *493, 494*
Hartmann-Kottek, L., 200, *215*
Hatcher, R. L., 541, *553*
Havens, L. L., 22, *51,* 461, *466*
Havik, O. E., 267, *274*
Haviland, J. M., *525, 527*
Haviland, M. G., 508, *526*
Hayes, A. M., 503, *523,* 539, 552, 612, *614*
Haynes, L. A., 421, 429, *440*
Haynes-Clements, L. A., 420, 429, *438*
Hazan, C., 311, 312, *333, 335*
Heabe, R. F., 452, 453, *466*
Heath, D. H., 619, *635*
Heaton, K., 547, *554*
Heeren, T., *527*
Hefferline, R. F., *52,* 190, *218,* 499, *528*
Heine, R. W., 150, 151, *184*
Heinl, H., 201, 202, *216*
Helm, J., 161, *184*
Helms, J. E., *107*
Hemmings, K. A., 287, *305*
Hendel, D. D., 86, *105*
Henderson, J., 235, *248*

Hendricks, M. N., 39, 155, 239, *248,* 567
Hennies, S., 376, *401*
Henningsen, P., *216, 218*
Henry, W. P., 92, *107,* 453, 466, 550, 553, 607, *614*
Henwood, K. L., 118, *141*
Herbert, T. B., 509, *523*
Hermans, H. J., 263, *275,* 483, *494*
Heron, J., 622, *635*
Hersen, M., *273*
Hickey, R. H., *105*
Higgins, H. M., 196, *215,* 233, 235, *247,* 293, *303,* 350, *364*
Hill, C. E., 89, 90, *107,* 117, 126, *141, 143,* 226, *249,* 302, 445, 448, *451,* 465, 466, 537, 547, *554*
Hill, D., 91, *107*
Hill, W. F., 355, *365*
Hinterkopf, E., 233, *248,* 586, 595, 598, *599*
Hirscheimer, K., 290, 295, 296, *303, 304,* 505, *526*
Hitz, L. C., 234, *248*
Hlongwane, M. M., 483, *494*
Hobbs, B. V., 318, *332*
Hobbs, N., 341, *365*
Hobrucker, B., 381, *401*
Hoch, E. L., 341, *364*
Hodgson, R., 507, *528*
Hoehn-Saric, R., *114,* 470, 506, *526*
Hoeller, K., 254, *275*
Hoffman, A. E., 149, *184*
Hoffman, M. L., 446, 463, *466*
Hoffmann, P., *213*
Hogan, R., 446, 454, 466, *496*
Hogarty, G., 586, *599*
Holden, J. M., *78*
Holderstock, T. L., 484, *494*
Holiman, M., 505, *524*
Hollon, S. D., 281, *301*
Holmbeck, G. N., *615*
Holon, A., 506, *523*
Holstein, B., 233, *248*
Holzer, M., 507, 508, *526*
Homeyer, L., 382, *399*
Honos-Webb, L., 504, *526,* 611, 612, *615*
Horne, A. M., *52*
Horney, K., 477, *494*
Horowitz, M. J., 91, *107,* 506, *523,* 565, *576*
Horst, K., 507, *526*

Mahalik, J. R., 89, *107*
Mahoney, J., 445, *468*
Mahoney, M. J., 10, *51*, 262, *275*, *303*,
    478, *483*, *485*, *491*, *495*, *507*,
    525, *527*
Mahrer, A. R., 39, 40, 41, *51*, 193, 194,
    216, *217*, 302, *505*, *528*, 531,
    555, *597*, *599*
Maier, C., *598*
Maier, K., *216*
Main, M., 312, *335*
Maione, P. V., 139, *142*
Malcolm, W., 197, 206, *217*, 296, *304*,
    505, *528*
Malde, S., 483, *495*
Malon, D., 483, *495*
Malone, T. P., 41, *53*
Mancinelli, B., 298, *305*
Manion, I., *81*, 318, 320, *331*, *336*
Mann, F., 91, *104*
Mann, L. S., 508, *530*
Maragkos, M., 199, *213*
Marangoni, C., 450, *468*
Margison, F., *302*
Margulies, S., 509, *524*
Markman, H. J., 317, 319, *333*
Marks, I. M., 507, *528*
Markus, H., 474, *495*
Markus, H. R., 474, 478, 485, *497*
Marmar, C., *107*, 167, *183*, 565, *576*
Marmar, C. R., 91, *106*, *108*
Marris, P., *335*
Martin, D. J., 539, *555*
Maser, J. D., *524*
Masling, J., *553*
Maslove, V. J., 294, *305*
Maslow, A. H., 6, *51*, 263, *275*, 473,
    478, 480, *495*, 618, *635*
Mathews, A. M., *181*
Mathews, M., 588, *599*
Mathieu, P. L., 85, 91, *108*, 131, *142*,
    222, *249*, 320, 334, 448, 451,
    467, 502, *527*
Mathieu-Coughlan, P., 91, *107*, 222, 234,
    246, 248, 298, *304*, 502, *527*,
    566, *576*
Matter, M., 318, *335*, 418, *440*
Maus, C., 91, 95, 96, 97, 101, *111*, *112*,
    232, *250*
Maxson, P., 318, *333*

May, R., 12, 14, 15, 24, 25, 29, *51*, *53*,
    254, 255, 256, 257, 258, 259,
    260, 261, 267, 268, 269, 271,
    275, *276*, *277*
Mazurkiewicz, J., 480, *495*
McAdams, D. P., 263, *276*
McAllister, W., 318, *335*, 418, *440*
McCarthy, D. A., 206, *219*
McClanahan, L. D., 85, 88, *108*
McConville, M., 479, 484, *495*
McCullough, L., 265, *276*, *277*
McCullough Vaillant, L., *301*
McElwain, B., 29, *608*
McFarlane, A. C., 470, *505*, *530*
McGuire, M., 375, *399*
McLeod, J., 118, *142*, 263, *276*
McMain, S., 295, *305*, 541, *556*
McMullin, R. E., 233, 234, *249*
McNally, H. A., 85, 88, *108*
McWhirter, J. J., 448, *468*
Mearns, D., 445, *468*, 579, *599*
Mechanick, P., 448, *464*
Mecheril, P., 194, *216*, *217*
Medway, F., 387, *400*
Mehlman, B., 377, 380, *400*
Melamed. B. G., 506, *527*
Melchior, L., 474, *493*
Melnick, B., 85, 88, *108*
Meltzoff, J., 151, *185*, 533, *555*
Mendelsohn, M., 540, *552*
Mendola, J. J., 86, 87, 88, *108*
Menn, A., 588, 589, *597*, *599*
Meredith, K., *213*
Mergenthaler, E., 504, 507, *528*
Merkel, W. T., 330, *335*
Merry, T., 169, *185*
Merry, W., *213*, *523*
Messer, S., 262, *276*, *304*
Mestel, R., 204, 205, *217*
Meyer, A. E., 58, 79, 90, *108*, 168, *185*,
    535, *556*
Miesler, D. J., 320, *334*
Mikulincer, M., 316, *335*
Milan, M., *440*
Miles, M. B., 192, *216*
Milholland, T., 420, 429, *438*
Miller, A., 483, *495*
Miller, B., *440*
Miller, G. A., 627, *635*
Miller, N. E., 408, *438*

Oatley, K., 500, 528
Oberlander, M., 228, 247, 567, 576
O'Connor, C., 503, 529
O'Grady, K. E., 107
Ogrocki, P., 527
O'Hara, M. M., 49, 58, 76, 267, 272, 607, 613
Ohlsen, M. M., 52
Oishi, E., 264, 276
Okishi, J. C., 551, 555
Okwumabua, T, 336
O'Leary, C. J., 43, 51
O'Leary, E., 348, 354, 356, 365, 366
Olmsted, A. G., 323
Olmsted, M. P., 323, 332, 494
Olsen, L. E., 233, 249
Olson, D., 440
O'Malley, S. S., 91, 92, 109, 564, 577
Omer, H., 262, 276
Orlinsky, D. E., 83, 85, 86, 87, 88, 89, 91, 92, 93, 109, 163, 164, 185, 262, 265, 275, 276, 446, 448, 450, 454, 468, 502, 528, 535, 543, 555, 564, 565, 566, 567, 577
Osborne, D., 478, 495
Osgood, C. E., 355, 365
Ossorio, 572
Oualline, V., 375, 400
Oxman, L. K., 383, 400

Pabst, H., 76, 183, 301, 467, 613
Packer, M., 140, 262, 276
Padawer, W., 265, 274
Page, C. W., 342, 344, 364
Page, R. C., 161, 340, 353, 354, 355, 356, 362, 363, 365, 366, 483, 484, 495, 611
Pahkinen, T., 477, 484, 496
Paivio, S. C., 11, 41, 50, 79, 155, 189, 195, 197, 205, 206, 215, 217, 280, 282, 283, 284, 285, 286, 295, 303, 305, 502, 505, 510, 512, 513, 514, 515, 516, 525, 528
Pajares, F., 477, 496
Pande, S. K., 526
Parikh, B., 162, 185
Parke, L. A., 265, 275
Parker, J. D. A., 508, 529, 530
Parker, M., 262
Parkes, C. M., 335, 505, 528

Parks, B. K., 83, 109, 265, 276, 448, 468, 535, 555, 564, 577
Parloff, M. B., 155, 165, 185, 250, 445, 451, 468, 531, 555
Parsons, B. V., 87, 103, 317, 331
Pascal, G. R., 341, 365
Pascual-Leone, J., 280, 303, 507, 511, 525
Passey, S., 505, 528
Patterson, C. H., 22, 51, 163, 166, 168, 185, 448, 450, 451, 452, 468, 533, 537, 556
Patterson, M. L., 266, 276
Pauls, H., 200, 217
Paulus, M., 483, 495
Pawlik, K., 111
Pawlowsky, G., 41, 51, 76, 185, 187, 365
Payton, I. E., 383, 400
Peak, T. H., 85, 109
Pearson, P. H., 124, 142
Pedersen, R. A., 197, 218, 294, 295, 305
Pelham, L., 400
Pennebaker, J. W., 508, 509, 528
Peres, F. S., 341, 366
Perez, C., 373, 400
Perez, E. L., 323, 331
Perissaki, C., 86, 109
Perlman, D., 311, 331
Perls, F. S., 29, 30, 31, 52, 189, 190, 190–191, 196, 205, 211, 218, 279, 305, 315; 330, 335, 499, 528, 593, 599
Perry, E. S., 107
Persinger, M. A., 478, 496
Perucci, A., 262, 278
Petermann, F., 76, 111
Peterson, A., 484, 496
Petzold, H., 204, 218
Pfeiffer, W. M., 76, 111
Pfenninger, D. T., 610, 614
Pfuetze, P., 474, 496
Phillips, J. R., 118, 119, 120, 142, 143
Phillips, R., 396, 400
Piaget, J., 369, 400
Pidgeon, N. F., 118, 141
Pierce, R. A., 506, 528
Pierce, R. M., 85, 87, 88, 91, 108, 112
Pierce, U. G. B., 617, 635
Pierce, W., D., 453, 468, 469
Piercy, F. P., 319, 335
Pietrzak, S., 597, 600

Simon, R., 317, *336*
Singer, B., 165, *185*
Singer, J., 474, 485, 486, 497
Singer, W., *634*
Singh, M., 194, *219*, 295, *305*
Sinister, S., *246*
Sipiora, M. P., 267, *277*
Siqueland, L., 316, *332*
Sladeczek, I. E., 422, 428, *441*
Slatick, E., 77, 101, *105*, 284, 285, *302*
Sloane, R. B., 87, 88, *113*, 453, 469
Smith, C. A., 626, *636*
Smith, D., 21, *53*, 235, *250*
Smith, D. L., 262, *274*
Smith, E. W. L., 72, 78, 199, *216*
Smith, M. L., 60, 72, 80, 317, *336*
Smith, N., 386, *401*
Snow, R. E., 477, *497*
Snyder, M., 409, 418, *440*, *441*
Snyder, W. U., 149, *187*, 381, *398*
Snygg, D., 476, 480, *497*
Sokol, L., *76*
Sokoloff, M., 378, 380, *401*
Soldz, S., 93, *113*, *301*
Solomon, J., 565, *577*
Solomon, L., 480, *492*
Sonnenschein, K., 508, *530*
Sotsky, S., *109*
Souliere, M. D., 80, 194, *213*
Spanier, G. B., 319, *336*
Speicher, C., *527*
Speierer, G.-W., 76, 80, *183*, *301*, *613*
Speirer, G., *467*
Spence, D. P., 263, *277*
Spiegel, D., 352, 353, 354, *367*, 509, *529*
Spiegel, J., *524*
Spiegel, S. B., *107*
Spiegelberg, H., 7, *53*
Spinelli, E., 8, 29, *53*, 258, 259, 261, 267, 269, *277*
Spitz, Y., 200, *219*, 349, 351, 366, 587, *600*
Sprenkle, D. H., 317, 319, *332*, *335*, 405, *438*
Sreckovic, M., 192, *215*, *217*, *219*
Stadmuller, G., 585, *601*
Stalikas, A., 504, 505, *526*, *529*
Stanley, J. C., 355, 356, 357, *363*
Stanley, P. H., 10, 189
Staples, F. R., 87, *113*, 453, 469
Steer, A. R., 323, *331*

Stein, D. M., 163, *184*, 448, 467, 531, *555*
Stein, K. F., 474, 478, 485, 497
Steinbach, I., 157, 162, 180, *185*, *186*, *187*
Steinbauer, M., *213*
Steinfurth, K., *216*
Steinweg, C. K. M., 423, 426, *441*
Steketee, G. S., *524*
Stephens, G., 561, *577*
Stephenson, W., 151, *187*
Sterba, R. F., 538, *556*
Stermac, L., 287, *306*
Stern, E. M., 49
Sternberg, W.-D., *105*, *113*, *182*
Sterner, I., 193, 194, *213*, *216*, *217*, 505, *528*
Stevenson-Hinde, J. S., *335*
Stich, F., *616*
Stickle, T. R., 318, *331*
Stiles, T., 477, *497*
Stiles, W. B., 62, 77, 88, 106, *113*, 118, *143*, *302*, 504, 526, 606, 607, 608, 610, 611, 612, 614, 615
Stipsits, R., 41, *51*, *76*, *185*, *187*, 365
Stitz, S., 91, *113*
Stock, D., 149, *187*
Stoffer, D. L., 85, 87, *113*
Stoler, N., 87, *114*, 228, *251*
Stollak, G., 404, *440*
Stolorow, R. D., 262, *277*, 446, *470*
Stone, A. A., 509, *529*
Stone, A. R., *114*, *470*, *526*
Stoner, W., 483, *497*
Stotsky, S. M., *554*
Stout, J., *527*
Stover, L., 324, *333*, 371, 372, 383, 399, *401*
Strachy, J., *553*
Strasser, A., 29, *53*, 257, *277*
Strasser, F., 29, *53*, 257, 267, *277*
Strauss, A., 118, 129, *141*, *143*, 163, *183*
Strauss, B. M., 607, *616*
Strauss, E., 597, *600*
Strauss, H., 91, *104*
Strenger, C., 262, *276*
Stricker, G., *492*
Strother, J., 382, *397*
Strümpfel, U., *219*, 610
Strupp, H. H., 92, *107*, *109*, 262, 271, *277*, 445, 450, 453, 454, 461,

Wurf, E., 474, *495*
Wylie, R., 480, *498*

Yakin, P., 234, *251*
Yalom, I. D., 14, 27, 28, *54, 81,* 192,
       200, *216, 219,* 254, 255, 257,
       258, 260, 261, 267, 269, 270,
       271, 272, *276, 278,* 352, 353,
       367, 368
Yates, L., 381, *402*
Yontef, G. M., 30, 31, 32, 33, 36, *54,*
       190, 191, *193, 219*
Yorkson, N. J., 87, *113*
Young, R. D., 474, *494*
Yuba, N., 229, *248*
Yuen, T., 385, *402*

Zahniser, J. H., 478, *498*
Zapotoczky, H.-G., *213*
Zax, M., 504, *528*
Zeig, J. K., *635*
Zeigarnik, B., 190, 196, *219*
Zemet, R. M., 80, 200, *219,* 349, 351,
      366, 587, *600*
Zetzel, E. R., 538, *557*
Zimmerman, E., *81,* 200, *219*
Zimring, F. M., 22, *54, 84,* 225, 247,
      531, *560*
Zinker, J., 34, 36, *54*
Zonker, C. E. 79,
Zoppel, C. L., 88, *107*
Zucker, K., 316, *331*
Zuroff, D. C., 164, *180*

SUBJECT INDEX

Bozarth, Jerold D., x
Braaten, Leif, 347
Bracketing, 8
Bratton, Sue Carlton, ix
Breast cancer
    existential group therapy for, 352,
        356
    and expression of emotion, 509
Brief therapy
    and client variables, 563
    EFT as, 314
    and PE approach, 300
    RE therapy as, 416–418
Buber, Martin, 22, 30, 32, 191, 253
Bugental, James F. T., xxi, 26–27,
        259–260
Bulimia
    in EFFT study, 323
    and negative self-view, 474
"Burn out," and empathy, 545–546

Cain, David J., x
California Psychotherapy Alliance Scale
        (CALPAS), 540–541
Cancer
    and client-centered group therapy,
        357
    existential group therapy for, 352,
        356
    and expression of emotion, 509
Carkhuff scale, 90
Carl Rogers on Encounter Groups, 21
Case studies, 607
    on client-centered therapy
        and client's frame of reference
            (Gerald), 175–177
        and empathic understanding
            (Sylvia), 169–175
    on emotion ("I Needed to Know
        You Cared"), 518–522
    on existential psychotherapy
        (Dawn), 268–269
    on existential psychotherapy (Elva),
        269–271
    in humanistic play therapy, 382
        and nondirective play therapy
            (Dibs), 382
        and therapist-child relationship
            (Kate), 389–395

on schizophrenia ("Silent Young
    man"), 580–581
on self (Virginia), 487–489
on therapist's relational skills,
    544–545
See also Therapy session excerpts
Cathartic expression of feeling, 506
CBT. *See* Cognitive-behavioral therapies
CCT. *See* Client-centered therapy
Change, and existential psychotherapies,
    256, 263, 267
Change event
    in couples therapy, 327–329
    in existential psychotherapies, 263
Chicago project, 562–563
Childbirth, and Gestalt therapy, 203–204
Child-centered play therapy, 372, 374,
    376, 378, 388
Childhood abuse, and PE therapy, 284
Child psychotherapy, humanistic ap-
    proaches to, 28
Children
    and Gestalt therapy, 203
    and Parent Effectiveness Training,
        42–43
    and play therapy, 369 (*see also* Play
        therapy, humanistic)
    and Satir on therapy, 41–42
Child RE therapy, 416
Choice, xix, 12–13
    Boss on, 23
    in process-experiential psychother-
        apy, 283
    and Rank, 13
Clarification of feelings, 18, 95, 96, 97,
    148
Client(s)
    as agent, 124n, 134, 261, 561
    appropriate for process-experiential
        therapy, 299
    as best expert about own life, 147,
        150
    as contributor to therapeutic alli-
        ance, 551
    and explication, 96, 98, 99
    physical appearance of, 485
    as portrayed in literature, 561
    as prime determiner of outcome,
        561, 562
    training of, 574
    varied problems typical of, xxii–xxiii

Client affirmation, 93, 565

Client-centered and experiential therapies (CC/ET), process-outcome research on, 83–84, 102–103

and empathic understanding, 99

Client-centered group therapy, 339
research on, 357

Client-centered play therapy, 372, 382, 388

Client-centered relationship, 150–152, 177

Client-centered therapy (CCT), 16–22
and assessment of client processes, 90
birth of, 3
and Chicago project, 562–563
and depression, 164, 199, 536
and experiential approaches to psychotherapy, 531
in focusing research, 232
intervention style in, 348
and meta-analysis of outcome research, 59, 67, 72
process diagnosis in, 212
vs. process-directive approach, 300
in process-experiential approach, 279
for psychoneurotics, 201
research in, 19, 147–148, 177–180
first period (nondirective therapy), 148–150, 177
second period (client-centered relationship), 150–152, 177
third period (conditions of therapy), 152–167, 178
fourth period (common factors revisited), 167–168, 178
in Germany, 156–160
implications of for practice, 168–177
and Rogers, 17–18, 341, 344 and schizophrenia (research), 585–587, 596
Wisconsin Project, 581–584
Wisconsin Project ancillary studies, 584–585
as widely practiced, 193

Client-Centered Therapy (Rogers), 19, 42, 150, 489

Client-directed therapy, 44–45

Client engagement, study of, 297–298

Client experiencing. *See* Experiencing

Client-Experiencing Questionnaire, 585, 586

Client operations, 132–133

Client processes. *See* Client variables

Client Processing Scale, 234

Clients' agency, 124n. *See also under* Client

Client's frame of reference, 150, 153, 168, 169, 175, 179, 180, 572

Client's Processing: Responding to the Therapist's Challenge (core category), 131

Client's reflexivity, 123, 124, 124n

Client-therapist relationship
case study on (Sylvia), 169–175
in client directed therapy, 44
and creation of collaborative alliance, 324–326
as critical, 5, 533
division of labor in, 96
and EFT effectiveness, 321, 322
and empirically validated treatments or manual-based approaches, 550, 571
for existential psychotherapy, 265, 268–269, 270–271, 272
and felt sense, 238–239, 244–245
grounded-theory research on, 135, 136
and human-system theory, 629
Laing's therapeutic suspension, 26
and listening, 236
in nondirective counseling, 149, 150
outcome from client's perception of, 298
and outcomes research, 168
in play therapy, 370, 389, 395
Rogers' conditions for, 20, 153–154, 164–165, 167, 179, 344, 446, 532, 537, 559–560, 564, 579–580, 581
rupture of, 460, 541, 542, 546–550
and self, 484
and self-talk of therapist, 570
and template models, 571
as therapeutic alliance, 265, 310
in Wisconsin Project on schizophrenics, 584
See also Attitudes of therapist; Client-centered therapy; Client

European research, on person-centered group psychotherapy, 345, 347
Evaluation Criterion for the Pre-Therapy Interview (ECPI) scale, 596
Evaluations, expression of, 459–460
Events paradigm research, 610–611
Every Person's Life Is Worth a Novel (Polster), 35
Eve's Daughters (Polster), 36
Evocations, empathic, 456, 459
Evocative Gestalt interventions, 201
Evocative reflection, 39
Evocative unfolding, of problematic reactions, 291–293
Evoking and exploring, in emotion-focused intervention, 516
Exaggeration techniques, 207
Exercises, in Gestalt therapy, 34
Existence: A New Dimension in Psychology and Psychiatry (May, Angel and Ellenberger), 24
Existential anxiety, 12, 257, 264–265, 272
Existential group psychotherapy, 339, 340, 341
    research on, 352–356, 357
Existential guilt, 257, 264–265
Existential-humanistic therapists, 23–24
Existentialism, and Adler, 16
Existentialists
    and dark aspects of people, 4
    and phenomenology, 7
Existential moments, 194
Existential-phenomenological school, 47, 597
Existential psychotherapies, xix, 22–29, 253–254, 271–272
    and authenticity, 257–258, 265
    and becoming, 256–257, 263–264
    and change, 267–268
    and existential anxiety or guilt, 257, 264–265, 272
    and human freedom, 254–255
    and intersubjectivity, 255–256, 261–262
    and play therapy, 370
    practice of, 267–271
    and psychotherapeutic liberation, 259–260, 261
    research on, 260–267
    and temporality, 256, 262–263

    and therapeutic flexibility, 260, 266–267
    and therapeutic relationship, 258, 265
    and understanding, 258–259, 266
Existential Psychotherapy (Yalom), 27
Existenz, 22
Experience(s)
    affective, 504
    bodily, 38–39
    bodily felt sense, 221–222 (*see also* Felt sense)
    corrective, 266
    description of as goal, 8
    inconsistent with self, 491
    peak, 619
    reports of, 459
    therapists' attention to, 152
    and therapy as constructivist, 310–311
    See also Emotional experience
Experience of psychotherapy, research on, 117, 139–140
    on hour of therapy, 123–126
    implications of for practice, 134–139
    on spontaneous events within therapy session, 127–132
    on therapist-directed tasks, 132–134
    on whole course of therapy, 119–123
Experiencing, 91, 223–225, 512, 620
    as client variable, 566–567, 572–574
    in Chicago project, 562–563
    depth of, 298, 502–503
    enhancing of, 90
    and focusing, 225–226
    and Gestalt therapy, 205, 211
    Mahrer on, 40
    of passage of time, 262–263
    in process-outcome research, 99
    various avenues in, 224
Experiencing level, 222
    research on, 226–231, 234
Experiencing Scale, 222, 225, 226, 499, 502, 508, 566–567
Experiential approach
    and client-centered therapy, 531
    of Mahrer, 40
Experiental-existential group psychotherapy (EEGP), 356
Experiential mode, in RE therapy, 417

Experiential processing, 282
Experiential response modes, 287–291
Experiential teaching, 289, 300
Experiential therapeutic learning, 34
Experiential therapists, xix, 47–48
Experiential therapy(ies), 39–41, 620
    focused experiential therapy, 198
    focusing-oriented/experiential psy-
      chotherapy, 39, 222, 236–246
    See also Client-centered and experi-
      ential therapies; Process-
      experiential (PE) psychotherapy
Experiment
    in Gestalt therapy, 34
    and unique life experiences, 606
Explication process, of clients, 96, 98, 99
Exploration responses, empathic, 288,
    456–457, 459
Exposure techniques, for agoraphobia,
    506–507
Expressiveness, client
    as client variable, 567–568
    in process-outcome research, 93
    See also Emotional expression
Extratherapeutic variables, and outcomes
    research, 168
Eye contact, 452

Facial reflections, 591
Facilitation, 408
Facilitative skills, 533–534, 536, 542,
    543, 551
Family therapy, humanistic, 309, 316–
    317, 329–331
    practice of, 324–329
    recent developments in, 311–312
    relationship enhancement in, 309,
      312–313, 416, 427–428
    research on, 317–324
    and Satir, 41–42
    See also Couples therapy, humanis-
      tic; Filial family therapy
Farther Reaches of Human Nature, The
    (Maslow), 618
Fear
    and felt sense, 239–240
    and play therapy, 377–378
    as primary adaptive emotion, 512
    as primary maladaptive emotion, 513
    reduction of, 506

    replacement of in emotional restruc-
      turing, 517
    in transformation of emotions, 514
    See also Emotion
Fear of living, and Rank, 13
Feedback, and negative self-views, 477
Feelings, 499
    cathartic expression of, 506
    and clients' analytical descriptions,
      458–459
    clients' expression of, 457–458
    and contact in Gestalt therapy, 190
    feelings about, 514
    reflection of, 86
    Rogers on, 18, 499
      and therapist's responses, 148
    See also Emotion
Feelings and Personal Meanings Scale,
    499
Felt sense, 221–222, 223, 223–224, 245,
    567, 620
    client and therapist response to,
      236–238
    vs. emotions, 240
    and focusing questions, 242–245
    Gendlin on, 39
    instead of just thinking or reporting,
      239–240
    therapist failing to respond to cli-
      ent's, 238–239
    unclear or painful, 297
Felt shift, 222, 224–225
Feminism, 330
Feminist therapy, 621
Fenichel, Otto, 29
Field theory, in Gestalt therapy, 33, 190
Figure and ground
    and EFT, 326
    in Gestalt psychology, 30, 190
Filial family therapy, 371, 395, 416
    experimental research in, 382–387
    research on, 372
    as Relationship Enhancement ther-
      apy approach, 312
Flexibility, therapeutic, 260, 266–267
Focal Communication Concept, 634
Focused experiential therapy, 198
Focusing, 222, 223, 245
    clients' failure in, 239
    and emotions vs. felt sense, 240
    and existential psychotherapies, 264

Goodman, Paul, 13, 30, 190
Gordon, Thomas, 41, 42–43
Gottman, John, 311
Graduate students
humanistic approaches abandoned
by, xx
training of, xx–xxi, xxiii–xxiv
Greenberg, Leslie S., xi, 40, 194, 350
Grounded theory method of research,
118–119, 139–140
on hour of therapy, 123–126
implications of for practice, 134–139
on spontaneous events within therapy session, 127–132
on therapist-directed tasks, 132–134
on whole course of therapy,
119–123
*Group-Centered Leadership: A Way of Re-
leasing the Creative Potential of
Groups* (Gordon), 42
Group psychotherapy, humanistic, 339,
362
basic concepts of, 339–341
case study on, 358–362
research on, 341, 356–357
existential group psychotherapy,
352–356, 357
Gestalt group psychotherapy,
348–351, 357
person-centered group psychotherapy, 341–348
and self-concept, 483–484
unstructured, 340
unstructured existential, 355
Growth
as goal of therapy, 310
in process-experiential psychotherapy, 283
as Satir assumption about people, 42
Guerney, Bernard G., Jr., xi, 371, 408
and behavior therapy, 403
and family session transcript, 431
Guerney, Louise, 370, 371
Guilt
Boss on, 23
existential, 257, 264–265
of missed opportunities, 12

Haley, Jay, 42
Hallucinations, 597

Handbook of Educational Psychology
(Berliner and Calfee eds.), 481
*Handbook of Psychotherapy and Behavior
Change* (Garfield & Bergin), 155
Health, drive toward, 4, 17, 562
Health, physical
and emotional expression, 508–510
See also Psychosomatic disorders
Health insurance, xxiii, 57. *See also* Man-
aged care
Heidegger, Martin, 7–8, 23, 253
Heightening technique, 330
Helpful factors research, on process-
experiential therapy, 298–299
Helplessness, as secondary emotional ex-
perience, 513–514
Hendricks, Marion N., xi
Here-and-now
in Gestalt therapy, 33–34
and Rank, 13
in therapy process, 310
focusing on, 516
Hill Interaction Matrix (HIM-G), 355
HIV, 198, 206, 509
Holism, 11–12
and Adler, 15
of Gestalt therapy, 206
in view of person, 5
whole-person perspective, 618–619
Holism and Evolution (Smuts), 29
Holistic diagnosis, 43
Holistic view of person, 5
Home assignments, in RE therapy, 412
Homework, experiential, 289
Hopelessness, as secondary emotional ex-
perience, 513–514
Horney, Karen, 29
"Hot seat" workshop approach, 350
Human growth movement
and "anything goes" era of 1960s, 30
birth of, 480
wane of, 481
Humanistic couples therapy. *See* Couples
therapy, humanistic; Relationship
Enhancement Therapy
Humanistic family therapy. *See* Family
therapy, humanistic
Humanistic group therapy. *See* Group psy-
chotherapy, humanistic
Humanistic play therapy. *See* Play ther-
apy, humanistic

Marker(s)
  conflict split, 293
  for empathic responding, 457–460
  in events-paradigm research,
    610–611
  for meaning-creation work, 296
  micromarkers, 283
  problematic reaction point (PRP),
    291
  of problem state, 291, 292
  task markers, 292, 297
  of unfinished business, 294
Married couples
  Gestalt therapy for, 203
  See also Couples therapy, humanis-
    tic; Family therapy, humanistic
Maslow, Abraham, xxi, 6, 48
  and Adler, 15
  as former behaviorist, 481
  and Goldstein, 480
  on humanistic psychology, 579
  on peak experiences, 619
Matarazzo, Joseph, 19
Maturity, and nondirective therapy,
    149–150
Maughm, W. Somerset, 418
May, Rollo, xxi, 13, 24–25
  and Adler, 15
  on client-therapist relationship, 272
  and Rank, 14
McElwain, Brian, xii
McKeon, Richard, 222
Meaning, xix, 11
  and Adler, 15–16
  and behavior, 482
  and emotional arousal, 508
  and existential psychotherapy, 272
    group psychotherapy, 352
  need to find, 5
Meaning-creation work, 296–297
Meaninglessness, 28
Measures
  of empathy, 448–449, 454
  of outcome, 608–609
  of therapeutic alliance, 540–541
Medical model, xx, xxiii, 571
  vs. Educational Model, 404
Memory evocation, 516
Mental illness
  and Laing, 26
  and Rogers, 20

vs. spiritual distress (Frankl), 25
  See also Depression; Psychoses; Psy-
    chosomatic disorders; Schizo-
    phrenia
Mentally disabled children, and play therapy, 377, 378, 379, 380
Merleau-Ponty, Maurice, 222, 253
Meta-analysis
  on client variables, 561
  of humanistic therapy outcome re-
    search, 58–59, 74
    method in, 59–62, 72–74
    practical implications of, 74–75
    results of, 63–71
  of humanistic therapy pre-post effect
    sizes, 607
  of process-experiential outcome re-
    search, 59, 67, 70, 72, 74,
    283–286
  on randomized clinical trials of EFT,
    319
  on RE therapy, 430–431, 437
  single-group designs, 58
  on therapeutic alliance and out-
    come, 539
Metacommunication, 136–137
  and adolescents, 312
  in exchange during therapy sessions,
    137, 138
Metaphor
  in nuclear scripts, 486
  research on, 194
  in therapy discourse, 128–130
    and client's experiencing, 574
    and therapy sessions, 489, 490
Metaphoric communicative interaction,
    129
Micromarkers, 283
Microprocess research, 48, 93–99,
    193–194
Microtechniques, in Gestalt therapy, 206
Misunderstanding, of client by therapist,
    127–128
Mitwelt, 23
Mixed neuroses
  and effectiveness of humanistic thera-
    pies, 74
  and processing performance, 98
Modeling, in RE therapy, 410–411
Modes of engagement, 282–283
Moral judgments, Adler on, 15

vs. problem (Rogers), 18
uniqueness of, 5, 606, 618
Personal construct theory, 11
Personal disclosure responses, 290
Personality disorders
    Gestalt therapy for, 200–201
    group psychotherapy for, 346
Personality Integration (Seeman), 618
Personal qualities of therapist, 542–543
Personal Questionnaire, 75
Person-centered approach
    and play therapy, 370
    research support for, 543
    and Rogers, 21
    See also Client-centered therapy
Person-centered group therapy, 339, 340,
    341
    research on, 341–348
Person-Centered Review, xx, 21
Perspectives
    diversity of, 6
    in process-outcome research, 84–85
PE therapy. *See* Process-experiential psy-
    chotherapy
Phenomenological reduction, 29
Phenomenology, 7–9, 254
    and Adler, 16
    in Gestalt therapy, 33
    and Jaspers, 22
Philosophy of the Implicit, 222
Phobia, and Gestalt therapy, 199
Phobic memory structures, experience of,
    506
Physical appearance, and attitudes toward
    self, 485
Physical health
    and emotional expression, 508–510
    See also Psychosomatic disorders
Plan of action, 29
Play therapy, humanistic, 369–370,
    395–396
    basic principles of, 388–389
    client-therapist relation in, 370, 389,
    395
    and parents as therapeutic agents,
    371
    in practice, 388–395
    questions on, 396
    research on, 371–381
        case studies, 382
        in filial therapy, 372, 382–387

in Parent Effectiveness Training,
    387–388
Polster, Erving, 14, 35, 193
Polster, Miriam, 14, 35, 35–36, 193
Positive functioning, humanistic psycho-
    therapy's emphasis on, 619
Positive psychology movement, 48
Postmodern epistemology, 330
Posttraumatic stress dissorder
    and absence of emotion awareness,
    508
    and EFT for couples, 322–323
    emotional processing for, 507, 508
    and PE therapy, 284
    therapy excerpt for client with,
    242
Potentials for experiencing, 40
PP (processing proposal), 94–99
    flattening vs. deepening, 96–97
    research on, 234
Precognitive functioning, 624–625
Preemptive modeling, in RE therapy,
    411–412
Premarital couples, RE therapy for, 428
Premarital Relationship Enhancement
    (PRE) program, 429
Presence of therapist, 33, 89, 258,
    289–290
Present-centeredness, 520
Presentness, 619, 620
Pretherapy, for psychotic patients, 590–
    596, 597
Primary adaptive emotion, 512–513
Primary maladaptive emotions, 513
Primary survival triad, 42
Principle of recontact, 591
Principles of Psychology (James), 479
Prison inmates
    in focusing research, 233
    in research on client-centered coun-
    seling, 162
Privacy, patient's right to, 135
Problematic reaction, 132, 291–293
Problematic reaction point (PRP)
    marker, 291
Process, Gendlin's shift to, 222
Process-centered therapy, humanistic psy-
    chotherapy as, 48, 620
Process diagnosis, 212, 511–512
Process direction, in exchange during
    therapy session, 137, 138

Race, and empathy, 454
Randomized clinical trials (RCTs), of humanistic psychotherapies, 607, 608
Randomized designs, need for more studies with, 75
Rank, Otto, 13–15, 222
Rating scales, 609
  of client self-exploration, 90
Ray, Dee, xiii
Reading behavior backwards, Combs on, 37
Reality
  as constructed, 5, 6, 310–311
  postmodern epistemology on, 330
Reality contact, 593
Reciprocal Reinforcement therapy, 424
Recontact, principle of, 591
Recording of psychotherapy, 18, 148. *See also* Therapy session excerpts
Reflection of feelings, 18, 86, 330, 447
  therapists' empathy beyond, 48
Reflexivity
  of client, 123, 124, 124n
  of interpersonal responses, 406–407
Reich, Wilhelm, 29
Reinforcing, in RE therapy, 410
Reiterative reflections, 591–592
Relational emphasis, 6–7, 621
Relational processes, in process-outcome research, 93
Relational variables, therapist. *See* Therapist relational variables
Relationship
  and humanistic theory, 621
  Rank on, 13
  See also Client-therapist relationship
Relationship distress or difficulties, 346
  core elements in, 311
  EFT for, 319
    and individual symptomatology, 322–323
  group therapy for, 346
  See also Interpersonal difficulties
Relationship Enhancement Manual (Guerney), 412
Relationship Enhancement Therapy (RE therapy), 309, 311, 312–313, 329–330, 403–409, 436–437
  limitations of, 418–419
  major goals of, 408
  methods/procedures of, 409–416

in parent format, 323–324
practice of, 431–436
research on, 317–318, 419, 420–423, 437
  for adolescents, 429
  for couples, 419, 424–427
  for families, 427–428
  meta-analytic study, 430–431, 437
  for other populations, 429–430
  preliminary studies and case reports, 430
  for premarital couples, 428–429
skills of, 408–409
theoretical foundations of, 405–408
time formats of, 416–418
types of, 416
Relationship Inventory, 85, 154, 448, 582
Relationship Lecture-Discussion Group (RLDG), 428–429
Relationship oriented play therapy, 372
Relationship therapy, 13
Remembered self, 486
Rennie, David L., xiii
Repetition responses, 206
Representing technique, 207
Research
  grounded theory method of, 118–140
  as lacking for many therapeutic approaches, xxiii
  qualitative, 117–118, 148, 606–607, 622
  quantitative, 57, 117, 148
Researcher theoretical allegiance, and meta-analysis of outcome research, 67–68, 69, 72
Research on humanistic psychotherapies
  in client-centered therapy (CCT), 19, 147–148, 177–180
    first period (nondirective therapy), 148–150, 177
    second period (client-centered relationship), 150–152, 177
    third period (conditions of therapy), 152–167, 178
    fourth period (common factors revisited), 167–168, 178
    in Germany, 156–160
    implications of for practice, 168–177

precision as false goal for, 606
Research reports, 607
Research strategy, discovery-oriented, 41
Resistance potential, 198
Resourcefulness of persons, 4
Respect
    and empathy, 452
    and self, 485
Responses and responding by therapist
    empathic, 406, 447, 455–457, 461,
        538, 544
    influence of, 95–96
Response systems, 169
Responsibility, xix, 4, 12–13, 255, 259,
        261
    and existential group psychotherapy,
        352
    and Rank, 13
Responsiveness, and process research,
        611–612
Restructuring of emotions, in emotion-
        focused intervention, 516–517
Restructuring of interactions, 326–327
    technical restructuring, 121
Retroflection, 192
Rice, Laura N., 39
Riskin, Jules, 42
Rogerian therapy, 148
RLDG (Relationship Lecture-Discussion
        Group), 428–429
Rogers, Carl, xix, 3, 4, 16–22, 45, 47,
        177
    and Adler, 15
    in case study (Sylvia), 170–175
    and Chicago project, 562–563
    on client as agent, 147
    and client-centered approach, 17,
        341, 344
    and client's internal frame of refer-
        ence, 150, 153
    and client's self-actualization, 150
    and client's self-determination, 134
    and conditions for therapy, 20, 153–
        154, 164–165, 167, 179, 344,
        446, 532, 537, 559–560, 564,
        579–580, 581
    on defense mechanisms, 312
    in early tradition, xxi
    on EFT, 330
    on empathy, 445, 447
    on facts as friendly, 49, 605

on feelings, 18, 499
    and therapist's responses, 148
    and focusing-oriented/experiential
        psychotherapy, 222
    on fully functioning person, 627,
        628
    and Gordon, 42
    as hero, 612–613
    on identity, 330
    and metacommunication, 136–137
    on metaphor, 574
    and psychological contact, 590
    on Rank and his followers, 13
    and research, xxiv, 18, 57, 147–148,
        344
    and response patterns, 169
    and schizophrenia, 20, 581
    on self, 225, 480
    on self-actualizing tendency, 224
    and therapeutic relationship, 169,
        222
    and therapist relational skills, 531
    and training of therapists, xxii
    and University of Chicago Counsel-
        ing Center, 19, 630
    on valuing process, 612
    on Wisconsin study, 581
Rogers, Natalie, 21
Role involvement, in process-outcome re-
        search, 92
Rupture in therapeutic relationship. *See*
    Therapeutic rupture

Sachse, Rainer, xiii
Sadness
    in emotion case example, 518, 521
    and unresolved feelings, 518
Safe working environment, 298
Sartre, Jean-Paul, 253
    on choice, 12
Satir, Virginia, xxi, 41–42, 317
Schizophrenia, 579
    case study on, 580–581
    and client-centered therapy (re-
        search), 585–587, 596
        Wisconsin Project, 581–584
        Wisconsin Project ancillary stud-
            ies, 584–585
    Gestalt therapy for, 200, 587–588
    group therapy, 351

Schizophrenia, *continued*
    and play therapy, 382
    possible research directions on,
        596–597
    pretherapy for, 590–596, 597
    psychosocial programs for, 588–590
    and Rogers, 20, 581
    and self/self-ideal discrepancy,
        482–483
    See also Mental illness
Science
    and humanistic approach, 9
    and unique life experiences, 606
Script, nuclear, 486
Secondary emotional responses, 513–514
Seeman, Julius, xiii–xiv. *See also* Human-
    system model
Self, 9–10, 47, 473–479, 491–492
    analytical descriptions of, 458–459
    brief history of, 479–481
    change in perception of, 478–479
    and client-centered therapy (Chi-
        cago project), 563
    and constructivism, 310–311
    and contact cycle, 191
    contemporary research on, 481–485
    as dynamic vs. static, 263
    emphasis on, 619
    in Gestalt therapy, 32, 190–191
        Polster on, 35
    Greenberg and Van Balen on,
        46–47
    and other, 330
    and psychotherapy practice, 485–491
    and reports of emotional pain, 122
    Rogers on, 225
    and subselves, 475–476
    and two-chair technique, 34, 195–
        196 (*see also* Two-chair tech-
        nique)
Self-acceptance, by clients, 574
Self-actualization, 46
    and Goldstein, 480
    and group therapy, 340
    tendency toward, 4, 224
Self-attacking, 241–242
Self-awareness, 4
    and self-concept, 483
Self-concept, 9–10, 491
    assessment of, 486
    Combs on, 37–38

    multifactorial approach to, 476
    and nondirective counseling, 150
    and play therapy, 373–374, 395
    and psychopathology, 474
    and psychotherapy, 482–484, 485
    and self-report, 485, 491
Self-confirmatory cycle, in case study,
    489
Self-deception, 257
Self-definition, 484
    lack of (case studies), 489, 491
Self-determination of clients, 134
Self-diagnosis, 44
Self-directed play therapy, 372
Self-direction
    from psychotherapy, 482
    and Rank, 13
Self-disclosure, therapist, 89, 270–271,
    534
Self-esteem
    James on, 479
    and Parent Effectiveness Training,
        388
Self-exploration
    as client variable, 566–567
    in process-outcome research, 90–91,
        99, 101
Self-focus, 120
Self-help treatments, 561
Self-in-relationship, 621
Self-narrative, 478, 485–486
    in therapy session, 490
Self-reference, and nondirective counsel-
    ing, 150
Self-relatedness, patient, 566
Self-report, 485, 491
Self-report data, 152
Self-talk, of therapist, 570
Self theory, 480–481
Serok, Shraga, 350
Session momentum, 132, 133
Shame
    as primary maladaptive emotion, 513
    replacement of in emotional restruc-
        turing, 517
    in transformation of emotions, 514
Shyness, and negative self-view, 474
Silences, in therapy sessions, 174, 175
"Silent Young Man" (case study),
    580–582
Simkin, Jim, 193

ABOUT THE EDITORS

David J. Cain, PhD, ABPP, received his doctorate in clinical and community psychology from the University of Wyoming. He is director of the Counseling Center at United States International University and adjunct faculty in the Department of Psychology at Chapman University. He is the founder of the Association for the Development of the Person-Centered Approach and was the founder and editor of the *Person-Centered Review*. He is a fellow in clinical psychology of the American Board of Professional Psychology, is a member of the National Register of Certified Group Therapists, and serves on the editorial boards of the *Journal of Humanistic Psychology* and the *Humanistic Psychologist*.

Julius Seeman, PhD, received his degree in counseling in 1948 from the University of Minnesota. His first position was at the University of Chicago Counseling Center, where Carl Rogers was director. He was coordinator of research during the center's first funded study of psychotherapy outcomes. The challenge of deriving theory-based empirical outcome criteria so fascinated him that he devoted most of his subsequent research career at Peabody College to this task. A significant part of his research has focused on developing empirical definitions of the "fully functioning person." Presently he is professor emeritus at Peabody College of Vanderbilt University. He is currently doing consultation and psychotherapy. He is the author of *Personality Integration*.